Second Edition

Appleton & Lange's Review for the

# USMLE STEP 1

APPLETON & LANGE
Stamford, Connecticut

Copyright © 1996, 1993, 1990 by Appleton & Lange
A Simon & Schuster Company
Copyright © 1985 by Fleschner Publishing Co.

97 98 99 00 / 10 9 8 7 6 5 4 3 2
Prentice Hall International (UK) Limited, *London*
Prentice Hall of Australia Pty. Limited, *Sydney*
Prentice Hall Canada, Inc., *Toronto*
Prentice Hall Hispanoamericana, S.A., *Mexico*
Prentice Hall of India Private Limited, *New Delhi*
Prentice Hall of Japan, Inc., *Tokyo*
Simon & Schuster Asia Pte. Ltd., *Singapore*
Editora Prentice Hall do Brasil Ltda., *Rio de Janeiro*
Prentice Hall, *Upper Saddle River, New Jersey*

**Library of Congress**
  **Catalog Card Number:** 96-083674

ISBN 0-8385-0265-2

Acquisitions Editor: Marinita Timban
Editorial Assistant: Amy Schermerhorn
Production: Rainbow Graphics, Inc.

PRINTED IN THE UNITED STATES OF AMERICA

# Table of Contents

# Contributors

**Thomas K. Barton, MD**
Clinical Assistant Professor
Department of Pathology & Laboratory Medicine
University of South Florida
Tampa, Florida
and
Department of Pathology
Palms of Pasadena Hospital
St. Petersburg, Florida

**Andreas Carl, MD, PhD**
Research Assistant Professor
Department of Physiology and Cell Biology
School of Medicine
University of Nevada Reno
Reno, Nevada

**Michael W. King, PhD**
Associate Professor
Department of Biochemistry and Molecular Biology
Indiana University School of Medicine
Terre Haute Center for Medical Education
Terre Haute, Indiana

**Hoyle Leigh, MD, FACP, FAPA**
Professor and Vice-Chairman
Department of Psychiatry
University of California, San Francisco
San Francisco, California
and
Director of Psychiatry
UCSF-Fresno and Fresno VA Medical Center
Fresno, California

**Martin Gwent Lewis, MBBS, MD, FRC (Path)**
Clinical Professor
Department of Pathology & Laboratory Medicine
University of South Florida
Tampa, Florida
and
Department of Pathology
Palms of Pasadena Hospital
St. Petersburg, Florida

**Gregory A. Mihailoff, PhD**
Professor of Anatomy and Neurology
Department of Anatomy
The University of Mississippi Medical Center
Jackson, Mississippi

**Tony Moore, PhD**
Associate Professor of Anatomy
Department of Anatomy
The University of Mississippi Medical Center
Jackson, Mississippi

**John Naftel, PhD**
Assistant Professor of Anatomy
Department of Anatomy
The University of Mississippi Medical Center
Jackson, Mississippi

**Russell K. Yamazaki, PhD**
Associate Professor
Department of Pharmacology
Wayne State University School of Medicine
Detroit, Michigan

**William W. Yotis, PhD**
Professor Emeritus
Department of Microbiology & Immunology
Loyola University of Chicago
Stritch School of Medicine
Maywood, Illinois

# Preface

Success on the USMLE Step 1 requires a thorough understanding of the basic sciences covered in the first and second years of medical education. In order to offer the most complete and accurate review book, we assembled a team of authors and editors from around the country who are engaged in various specialties and involved in both academic and clinical settings.

The author team was asked to research and write test questions using the parameters set forth by the National Board of Medical Examiners. All of the subjects, types of questions, and techniques that will be encountered on the USMLE Step 1 are presented in this book.

*Appleton & Lange's Review for the USMLE Step 1* is designed to provide you with a comprehensive review of the basic sciences as well as a valuable self-assessment tool for exam preparation. A total of 1,200 questions are included in this edition.

**Key Features and Use:**

- Approximately 150 questions are covered in the basic sciences: Anatomy, Physiology, Biochem-istry, Microbiology, Pathology, Pharmacology, and Behavioral Sciences.
- Questions are followed by a section with answers and detailed explanations referenced to the most current and popular resources available.
- A subspecialty list at the end of each chapter helps assess your strengths and weaknesses, thus pinpointing areas for concentration during exam preparation.
- A Practice Test (with more than 300 questions) simulates the USMLE Step 1 and is included at the end of this text.

We believe that you will find the questions, explanations, and format of the text to be of great assistance to you during your review. We wish you luck on the USMLE Step 1.

The Editors and the Publisher

# Review Preparation Guide

If you are planning to prepare for the United States Medical Licensing Examination Step 1, then this book is designed for you. Here, in one package, is a comprehensive review resource with 1200 examination-type basic science multiple-choice questions with referenced, paragraph-length explanations of each answer. In addition, the last section of the book offers an integrated practice test for self-assessment purposes.

This introduction provides specific information on the USMLE Step 1, information on question types, question-answering strategies, and various ways to use this review.

## THE UNITED STATES MEDICAL LICENSING EXAMINATION STEP 1

The USMLE Step 1 is a two-day written examination which tests your knowledge of Anatomy, Physiology, Biochemistry, Microbiology, Pathology, Pharmacology, and Behavioral Sciences. It contains a total of about 720 multiple choice questions which have been proffered by senior academic faculty to test your comprehension of basic science concepts that they feel are relevant to your future successful practice of medicine. In order to correctly answer these test questions you may be required to recall memorized facts, to use deductive reasoning, or both. A minority of the questions will employ graphs, photographs, or line drawings that you will need to interpret.

During each day of the two-day exam you will be asked to answer about 360 questions divided into two sessions of three hours each. The application materials you receive for the USMLE Step 1 will more fully discuss the exam procedure, rules of test administration, types of questions asked, and the scope of material you may be tested on.

## ORGANIZATION OF THIS BOOK

This book is organized to cover sequentially each of the basic science areas specified by the National Board of Medical Examiners (NBME). There are seven sections, one for each of the basic sciences, and an integrated practice test section at the end of the review. The sections are as follows:

1. **Anatomy** (including gross and microscopic anatomy; neuroanatomy; and development and control mechanisms).
2. **Physiology** (including general and cellular functions; major body system physiology; energy balance; and fluid and electrolyte balance).
3. **Biochemistry** (including energy metabolism; major metabolic pathways of small molecules; major tissue and cellular structures, properties, and functions; biochemical aspects of cellular and molecular biology; and special biochemistry of tissues).
4. **Microbiology** (including microbial structure and composition; cellular metabolism, physiology, and regulation; microbial and molecular genetics; immunology; bacterial pathogens; virology; and medical mycology and parasitology).

5. **Pathology** (including general and systemic pathology; and pathology of syndromes and complex reactions).
6. **Pharmacology** (including general principles; major body system agents; vitamins; chemotherapeutic agents; and poisoning and therapy of intoxication).
7. **Behavioral Sciences** (including behavioral biology; individual, interpersonal, and social behavior; and culture and society).
8. **Practice Test** (includes 311 questions from all seven basic sciences, presented in an integrated format).

Each of the eight chapters is organized in the following order:

1. Questions
2. Answers and Explanations
3. References
4. Subspecialty List

These sections and how you might use them are discussed below.

**Question Formats**

The style and presentation of the questions have been fully revised to conform with the United States Medical Licensing Examinations. This will enable you to familiarize yourself with the types of questions to be expected, and provide practice in recalling your knowledge in each format. Following the answer to each question, a reference to a particular and easily available text is provided for further reference and reading.

Each of the seven basic science chapters contains multiple choice questions composed in one of the three allowed query formats:

**Single Best Answer** (example question 1)
**Negatively Phrased Single Best Answer** (example question 2)
**Matching Sets** (example questions 3 through 6)

Questions of the same format type are grouped together and each format group is preceded by directions. Usually, the Single Best Answer format accounts for about 70% of all the questions asked, with the other two formats making up about 15% of the remaining questions each.

*Single Best Answer.* This is the most frequently encountered format in the USMLE Step 1. It generally contains a brief statement, followed by five options of which only ONE is ENTIRELY correct. The answer options on the USMLE are lettered A, B, C, D, and E. Although the format for this question type is straightforward, the questions can be difficult because some of the distractors in the answer list are partially correct. An example of this question format follows.

**DIRECTIONS (Question 1): Each of the numbered items or incomplete statements in this section is followed by answers or by completions of the statement. Select the ONE lettered answer or completion that is BEST in each case.**

1. Liquefaction necrosis is the characteristic result of infarcts in the

   (A) brain
   (B) heart
   (C) kidney
   (D) spleen
   (E) small intestine

The correct answer is A. There are two ways to attack this style of question. If after reading the query an answer immediately comes to mind, then look for it in the answer list. Alternatively, if no answer immediately comes to mind, or if the answer you thought was obvious is not a choice, then you will need to spend time examining all of the answer options to find the correct one. In this case anything you can do to eliminate an answer option will increase your odds of choosing the correct answer. With this in mind, scan all of the possible answers. Eliminate any that are clearly wrong and all that are only partially right. Even if you can eliminate one or two of the answer choices by this method you will have significantly increased your chance of guessing the right answer from the remaining choices. Always answer every question, even if you have to guess among all five answer choices, because there is no penalty for a wrong answer. Your test score is dependent only on the number of correct answers obtained.

---

> **STRATEGIES FOR ANSWERING SINGLE BEST ANSWER QUESTIONS**
>
> 1. Remember that only one choice can be the correct answer.
> 2. Read the question carefully to be sure that you understand what is being asked.
> 3. If you immediately know the answer look for it in the answer choices.
> 4. If no answer is immediately obvious, quickly scan all the five answer choices for familiarity.
> 5. Eliminate any answer that is completely wrong or only partially correct. This increases your odds of picking the correct answer from a lesser number of remaining answer choices.
> 6. If two of the remaining choices are mutually exclusive, the correct answer is probably one of them.
> 7. Fill in the appropriate circle on the answer sheet.
> 8. Always answer every question even if you have to quess.
> 9. Don't spend too much time with any one question. In order to finish each three-hour session you will need to answer a question about every 50 seconds.

*Negatively Phrased Single Best Answer.* These questions always contain a capitalized focus of either LEAST, NOT, or EXCEPT. In order to answer these types of questions you must be able to identify a false or least likely answer choice. An example of this question format follows.

**DIRECTIONS (Question 2): Each of the numbered items or incomplete statements in this section is negatively phrased, as indicated by a capitalized word such as NOT, LEAST, or EXCEPT. Select the ONE lettered answer or completion that is BEST in each case.**

2. All of the following structures drain into the internal jugular vein EXCEPT the

   (A) lingual veins
   (B) facial veins
   (C) superior thyroid veins
   (D) inferior petrosal sinus
   (E) azygos vein

The correct answer is E. This is an unusually vexing format because looking for a false or least likely answer choice runs counter to our normal thought processes which are more adept at finding "right" answers. With this type of format it is usually helpful to reread the negatively phrased question to be certain that you comprehend it. Next, read all the answer choices and mark T or F beside them if they are true or false, respectively. Consider any answer which you feel is only partially correct as a true. Choose your final answer only from those items identified as false. Remember, there is only one best answer which is the LEAST likely, FALSE, or NOT true. Always answer every question even if you have to guess.

> **STRATEGIES FOR ANSWERING NEGATIVELY PHRASED SINGLE BEST ANSWER QUESTIONS**
>
> 1. Remember that only one choice can be the correct answer.
> 2. Read and then reread the question carefully to be certain that you understand what is being asked.
> 3. Scan each answer choice and mark T or F next to it depending on whether it is true or false, respectively.
> 4. Mark all partially true answers as T. This increases your odds of picking the correct answer from a lesser number of remaining F answer choices.
> 5. Pick your answer from among only the remaining F choices.
> 6. Fill in the appropriate circle on the answer sheet.
> 7. Answer every question even if you have to quess.
> 8. Don't spend too much time with any one question. In order to finish each three-hour session you will need to answer a question about every 50 seconds.

*Matching Sets.* This format presents lettered options followed by several items generally related to a common topic. This is a relatively new style of question which in its extended form of up to 26 answer choices has only been employed by the USMLE for the last two years. An example of this question format follows:

**DIRECTIONS (Questions 3 through 6): Each set of matching questions in this section consists of a list of up to twenty-six lettered options followed by several numbered items. For each item select the ONE lettered option that is most closely associated with it.** *Each lettered heading may be selected once, more than once, or not at all.*

   (A) sarcoidosis
   (B) tuberculosis
   (C) histoplasmosis
   (D) coccidiomycosis
   (E) amyloidosis

(F) bacterial pneumonia

(G) mesothelioma

(H) carcinoma

(I) fibrosing alveolitis

(J) silicosis

3. A right lower lobectomy specimen contains a solitary 1.2-cm diameter solid nodule. The center of the nodule is fibrous. The periphery has granulomatous inflammation. With special stains, multiple 2- to 5-µm budding yeasts are evident within the nodule. Acid-fast stains are negative.

4. A left upper lobectomy specimen is received containing a 4.6-cm nodule with central cystic degeneration. Microscopically, the nodule is composed of anaplastic squamous cells. Similar abnormal cells are seen in a concomitant biopsy of a hilar lymph node.

5. After a long history of multiple myeloma, a 67-year-old male is noted to have abundant acellular eosinophilic deposits around the pulmonary microvasculature at autopsy. A Congo red special stain demonstrates apple-green birefringence.

6. A large pleural-based lesion is found on chest x-ray of an asbestos worker. Electron microscopy of the biopsy shows abundant long microvilli.

The correct answers are 3. C, 4. H, 5. E, 6. G. This style of question is challenging because of the time that can be expended examining all potential answer choices and for the uncertainty that is experienced when using an answer choice repeatedly while ignoring others. In attacking questions of this type it is useful to first scan all the lettered answers. Then read one question at a time and try to answer it. In those matching sets with ten or more answer options it may be more efficient to try to generate your own answer to the question and then locate it on the answer list. Remember there is only one best answer. Don't be overly concerned if you reuse certain lettered answers occasionally. Always answer every question even if you have to guess.

---

**STRATEGIES FOR ANSWERING MATCHING SETS QUESTIONS**

1. Read the lettered options through first.
2. Work with one item at a time.
3. Read the item through, then go back to the options and consider each choice individually.
4. As with the other question types, if the choice is partially correct, tentatively consider it to be incorrect.
5. Consider the remaining choices and select the answer.
6. Fill in the appropriate circle on the answer sheet.
7. Remember to make a selection for each item.
8. Again, the test allows for 50 seconds per item.

---

**Answers, Explanations, and References**

In each of the sections of this book, the question sections are followed by a section containing the answers, explanations, and references to the questions. This section (1) tells you the answer to each question; (2) gives you an explanation/review of why the answer is correct, background information on the subject matter, and why the other answers are incorrect; and (3) tells you where you can find more in-depth information on the subject matter in other books and/or journals. We encourage you to use this section as a basis for further study and understanding.

**If you choose the correct answer** to a question, you can then read the explanation (1) for reinforcement and (2) to add to your knowledge about the subject matter (remember that the explanations usually tell not only why the answer is correct, but also why the other choices are incorrect). **If you choose the wrong answer** to a question, you can read the explanation for a learning/reviewing discussion of the material in the question. Furthermore, you can note the reference cited (eg, "Joklik et al, pp 103–114"), look up the full source in the bibliography at the end of the section (eg, "Joklik WK, Willett HP, Amos DB. *Zinsser's Microbiology. 20th ed. Stamford, Conn: Appleton & Lange; 1992.*"), and refer to the pages cited for a more in-depth discussion.

**Subspecialty Lists**

At the end of each section of this book is a subspecialty list for each subject area. These subspecialty lists will help point out your areas of relative weakness and, thus, help you focus your review.

For example, by checking off your incorrect answers on, say, the microbiology list, you may find that a pattern develops in that you are incorrect on most or all of the virology questions. In this case, you could note the references (in the explanation section) for your incorrect answers and read those sources. You might also want to purchase a virology text or review book to do a much more in-depth review. We think that you will find these subspecialty lists very helpful, and we urge you to use them.

### Practice Test

The 311-question practice test at the end of the book consists of approximately 45 questions from each of the seven basic sciences. The questions are grouped according to question type (one best answer–single item, negatively phrased single item, and comparison/matching sets, with the subject areas integrated. This format mimics the actual exam and enables you to test your skill at answering questions in all of the basic sciences under simulated examination conditions.

The practice test section is organized in the same format as the seven earlier sections: questions; answers, explanations, and references; bibliography; and subspecialty lists (which, here, will also list the major subject heading).

### HOW TO USE THIS BOOK

There are two logical ways to get the most value from this book. We will call them Plan A and Plan B.

In Plan A, you go straight to the Practice Test and complete it according to the instructions. Using the subspecialty list, analyze your areas of strength and weakness. This will be a good indicator of your initial knowledge of the subject and will help you identify specific areas for preparation and review. You can now use the first seven chapters of the book to help you improve your relative weak points.

In Plan B, you go through chapters 1 through 7 checking off your answers, and then comparing your choices with the answers and discussions in the book. Once you have completed this process, you can take the Practice Test and see how well prepared you are. If you still have a major weakness, it should be apparent in time for you to take remedial action.

In Plan A, by taking the Practice Test first, you get quick feedback regarding your initial areas of strength and weakness. You may find that you have a good command of the material, indicating that perhaps only a cursory review of the seven chapters is necessary. This, of course, would be good to know early on in your exam preparation. On the other hand, you may find that you have many areas of weakness. In this case, you could then focus on these areas in your review—not just with this book, but also with the cited references and with your current textbooks.

It is, however, unlikely that you will not do some studying prior to taking the USMLE (especially since you have this book). Therefore, it may be more realistic to take the Practice Test after you have reviewed the first seven chapters (as in Plan B). This will probably give you a more realistic type of testing situation since very few of us just sit down to a test without studying. In this case, you will have done some reviewing (from superficial to in-depth), and your Practice Test will reflect this studying time. If, after reviewing the first seven chapters and taking the Practice Test, you still have some weaknesses, you can then go back to the first seven chapters and supplement your review with your texts.

### SPECIFIC INFORMATION ON THE PART I EXAMINATION

The official source of all information with respect to the United States Medical Licensing Examination Step 1 is the National Board of Medical Examiners (NBME), 3930 Chestnut Street, Philadelphia, PA 19104. Established in 1915, the NBME is a voluntary, nonprofit, independent organization whose sole function is the design, implementation, distribution, and processing of a vast bank of question items, certifying examinations, and evaluative services in the professional medical field.

In order to sit for the Step 1 examination, a person must be either an officially enrolled medical student or a graduate of an accredited medical school. It is not necessary to complete any particular year of medical school to be a candidate for Step 1. Neither is it required to take Step 1 before Step 2.

In applying for Step 1, you must use forms supplied by NBME. Remember that registration closes *ten weeks* before the scheduled examination date. Some United States and Canadian medical schools require their students to take Step 1 even if they are noncandidates. Such students can register as noncandidates at the request of their school. A person who takes Step 1 as a noncandidate can later change to candidate status and, after payment of a fee, receive certification credit.

## Scoring

Because there is no deduction for wrong answers, you should **answer every question.** Your test is scored in the following way:

1. The number of questions answered correctly is totaled. This is called the raw score.
2. The raw score is converted statistically to a "standard" score on a scale of 200 to 800, with the mean set at 500. Each 100 points away from 500 is one standard deviation.
3. Your score is compared statistically with the criteria set by the scores of the second-year medical school candidates for certification in the June administration during the prior four years. This is what is meant by the term, "criterion referenced test."
4. A score of 500 places you around the 50th percentile. A score of 380 is the minimum passing score for Step 1; this probably represents about the 12th to 15th percentile. If you answer 50 percent or so of the questions correctly, you will probably receive a passing score.

Remember: You do not have to pass all seven basic science components, although you will re-ceive a standard score in each of them. A score of less than 400 (about the 15th percentile) on any particular area is a real cause for concern as it will certainly drag down your overall score. Likewise, a 600 or better (85th percentile) is an area of great relative strength. (You can use the practice test included in this book to help determine your areas of strength and weakness well in advance of the actual examination.)

## Physical Conditions

The NBME is very concerned that all their exams be administered under uniform conditions in the numerous centers that are used. Except for several No. 2 pencils and an eraser, you are not permitted to bring anything (books, notes, calculators, etc.) into the test room. All examinees receive the same questions at the same session. However, the questions are printed in different sequences in several different booklets, and the booklets are randomly distributed. In addition, examinees are moved to different seats at least once during the test. And, of course, each test is policed by at least one proctor. The object of these maneuvers is to frustrate cheating or even the temptation to cheat.

The number of candidates who fail Step 1 is quite small; however, individual students as well as entire medical school programs benefit when scores are high. No one wants to squeak by with a 380 when a little effort might raise that score to 450. That is why you have made a wise decision to use the self-assessment and review materials available in *Appleton & Lange's Review for the USMLE Step 1.*

# Standard Abbreviations

**ACTH:** adrenocorticotropic hormone
**ADH:** antidiuretic hormone
**ADP:** adenosine diphosphate
**AFP:** $\alpha$-fetoprotein
**AMP:** adenosine monophosphate
**ATP:** adenosine triphosphate
**ATPase:** adenosine triphosphatase
**bid:** 2 times a day
**BP:** blood pressure
**BUN:** blood urea nitrogen
**CT:** computed tomography
**CBC:** complete blood count
**CCU:** coronary care unit
**CNS:** central nervous system
**CPK:** creatine phosphokinase
**CSF:** cerebrospinal fluid
**DNA:** deoxyribonucleic acid
**DNAse:** deoxyribonuclease
**ECG:** electrocardiogram
**EDTA:** ethylenediaminetetraacetate
**EEG:** electroencephalogram
**ER:** emergency room
**FSH:** follicle-stimulating hormone
**GI:** gastrointestinal
**GU:** genitourinary
**Hb:** hemoglobin
**HCG:** human chorionic gonadotropin
**Hct:** hematocrit

**IgA, etc:** immunoglobulin A, etc
**IM:** intramuscular(ly)
**IQ:** intelligence quotient
**IU:** international unit
**IV:** intravenous(ly)
**KUB:** kidney, ureter, and bladder
**LDH:** lactic dehydrogenase
**LH:** luteinizing hormone
**LSD:** lysergic acid diethylamide
**mRNA:** messenger RNA
**PO:** oral(ly)
**prn:** as needed
**RBC:** red blood cell
**RNA:** ribonucleic acid
**RNAse:** ribonuclease
**rRNA:** ribosomal RNA
**SC:** subcutaneous(ly)
**SGOT:** serum glutamic oxaloacetic transaminase
**SGPT:** serum glutamic pyruvic transaminase
**TB:** tuberculosis
**tRNA:** transfer RNA
**TSH:** thyroid-stimulating hormone
**WBC:** white blood cell

# CHAPTER 1

# Anatomy
## Questions

*Greg Mihailoff, PhD, Anthony Moore, PhD, and John Naftel, PhD*

**DIRECTIONS (Questions 1 through 91): Each of the numbered items or incomplete statements in this section is followed by answers or by completions of the statement. Select the ONE lettered answer or completion that is BEST in each case.**

1. A patient in the emergency room has been stabbed in the back of the neck and complains that he is unable to lift his shoulder. Which of the following nerves has likely been damaged?

    (A) suprascapular nerve
    (B) dorsal scapular nerve
    (C) accessory nerve
    (D) thoracodorsal nerve
    (E) lateral thoracic nerve

2. The structure most likely to be damaged in a fracture of the surgical neck of the humerus is the

    (A) radial nerve
    (B) axillary nerve
    (C) scapular circumflex artery
    (D) profunda brachii artery
    (E) brachial artery

3. A penetrating wound to the axilla which severs the posterior cord of the brachial plexus would denervate the

    (A) serratus anterior
    (B) pronator teres
    (C) deltoid
    (D) biceps brachii
    (E) infraspinatus

4. Which of the following is least likely to be involved in a collateral anastomosis which bypasses an obstruction of the first part of the axillary artery?

    (A) suprascapular artery
    (B) subscapular artery
    (C) dorsal scapular artery
    (D) scapular circumflex artery
    (E) posterior humeral circumflex artery

5. The forcible separation of the head of the radius from the capitulum of the humerus is mainly prevented by the

    (A) articular capsule
    (B) annular ligament
    (C) quadrate ligament
    (D) radial collateral ligament
    (E) proximal radioulnar joint

6. The cutaneous innervation to the palmar surface of the middle finger is usually from the

    (A) axillary nerve
    (B) musculocutaneous nerve
    (C) radial nerve
    (D) median nerve
    (E) ulnar nerve

7. The cell bodies of general visceral (GVA) neurons are located in the

    (A) ventral horn
    (B) intermediolateral cell column (IMLCC)
    (C) dorsal root ganglion
    (D) paravertebral ganglion
    (E) prevertebral ganglion

8. The cutaneous innervation over the medial aspect of the elbow is represented by which dermatome?

   (A) C5
   (B) C6
   (C) C7
   (D) C8
   (E) T1

9. A tumor in the posterior mediastinum would most likely involve the

   (A) recurrent laryngeal nerves
   (B) tracheal bifurcation
   (C) thoracic duct
   (D) phrenic nerves
   (E) left atrium

10. Damaged heart muscle resulting from occlusion of the circumflex branch of the left coronary artery would most likely be found in the

    (A) left atrium and left ventricle
    (B) right atrium and right ventricle
    (C) apex
    (D) right and left ventricles
    (E) right ventricle and interventricular septum

11. A radiograph of the patient's abdomen indicates a blockage in an artery running from the epigastric region to the left hypochondriac region. The vessel most likely involved is the

    (A) superior epigastric artery
    (B) superior mesenteric artery
    (C) inferior mesenteric artery
    (D) renal artery
    (E) splenic artery

12. Which of the following organs receives direct innervation from preganglionic sympathetic fibers?

    (A) kidney
    (B) suprarenal gland
    (C) spleen
    (D) liver
    (E) stomach

13. A surgeon's finger placed into the epiploic foramen (of Winslow) will be related superiorly to the

    (A) first part of the duodenum
    (B) caudate lobe of the liver
    (C) head of the pancreas
    (D) common bile duct
    (E) hepatic veins

14. Your patient is unable to dorsiflex and evert his right foot. The nerve most likely damaged is the

    (A) common peroneal
    (B) superficial peroneal
    (C) deep peroneal
    (D) tibial
    (E) obturator

15. Cancer of the testis would most likely metastasize first to which set of nodes?

    (A) superficial inguinal
    (B) deep inguinal
    (C) aortic
    (D) internal iliac
    (E) perianal

16. The nerve most likely to be injured by a fracture of the neck of the fibula is the

    (A) sural cutaneous nerve
    (B) tibial nerve
    (C) common peroneal nerve
    (D) deep peroneal nerve
    (E) femoral nerve

17. The chief ligament preventing forward sliding of the femur on the tibia is the

    (A) tibial collateral ligament
    (B) fibular collateral ligament
    (C) oblique popliteal ligament
    (D) anterior cruciate ligament
    (E) posterior cruciate ligament

18. Derivatives of the hindgut are typically supplied by the

    (A) celiac artery
    (B) superior mesenteric artery
    (C) inferior mesenteric artery
    (D) internal iliac artery
    (E) umbilical artery

19. An incomplete obliteration of the lumen of the allantois may result in

    (A) leakage of urine from the umbilicus
    (B) leakage of feces from the umbilicus
    (C) an omphalocele
    (D) gastroschisis
    (E) an umbilical hernia

20. A failure of the aorticopulmonary septum to follow a spiral course results in

    (A) mitral atresia
    (B) tetralogy of Fallot
    (C) transposition of the great vessels
    (D) tricuspid atresia
    (E) common atrium

21. The horizontal fissure and the inferior part of the oblique fissure form the boundaries of which of the following?

    (A) apex of the left lung
    (B) lingula of the left lung
    (C) middle lobe of the right lung
    (D) superior lobe of the right lung
    (E) inferior lobe of the left lung

22. The bulbourethral glands of the male are embedded in the fibers of which of the following muscles?

    (A) sphincter urethrae
    (B) ischiocavernosus
    (C) superficial transverse perineus
    (D) bulbospongiosus
    (E) corpora cavernosus

23. The digastric muscle is a two-bellied muscle that attaches by an intermediate tendon to which of the following structures?

    (A) sixth cervical vertebra
    (B) mandible
    (C) mastoid process
    (D) cricoid cartilage
    (E) hyoid bone

24. Which of the following veins crosses perpendicularly the superficial surface of the sternocleidomastoid surface directly beneath the platysma muscle?

    (A) retromandibular
    (B) anterior jugular
    (C) posterior auricular
    (D) external jugular
    (E) internal jugular

25. Which of the following structures is located within the prevertebral layer of cervical fascia?

    (A) vagus nerve
    (B) common carotid artery
    (C) internal jugular vein
    (D) esophagus
    (E) middle scalene muscle

26. The superior thyroid artery is usually the first branch of which of the following arteries?

    (A) thyrocervical
    (B) internal carotid
    (C) external carotid
    (D) facial
    (E) costocervical

27. The isthmus of the thyroid gland is located at which of the following structures?

    (A) cricoid cartilage
    (B) tracheal rings two, three, and four
    (C) jugular notch
    (D) thyroid cartilage
    (E) sixth cervical vertebra

28. The superior thyroid veins drain into which of the following veins?

    (A) internal jugular
    (B) facial
    (C) thyrocervical
    (D) subclavian
    (E) brachiocephalic

29. Which of the following laryngeal muscles abduct the vocal folds?

    (A) cricothyroid
    (B) posterior cricoarytenoid
    (C) thyroarytenoid
    (D) transverse arytenoid
    (E) oblique arytenoid

30. Taste from the posterior one-third of the tongue is provided by which of the following nerves?

    (A) trigeminal
    (B) facial
    (C) vagus
    (D) hypoglossal
    (E) glossopharyngeal

31. Which of the following nerves is the principal cutaneous nerve of the cheek?

    (A) auriculotemporal
    (B) mental
    (C) buccal branch of the mandibular
    (D) zygomaticofacial
    (E) zygomaticotemporal

32. Which of the following arteries commonly pass between the two roots of the auriculotemporal nerve?

    (A) inferior alveolar
    (B) middle meningeal
    (C) anterior tympanic
    (D) masseteric
    (E) sphenopalatine

33. The long head of the biceps arises from which of the following structures?

    (A) coracoid process
    (B) radial tuberosity
    (C) supraglenoid tubercle
    (D) bicipital aponeurosis
    (E) head of the humerus

34. Approximately 70% of carpal fractures involve which of the following bones?

    (A) scaphoid
    (B) pisiform
    (C) hamate
    (D) capitate
    (E) lunate

35. Lesions of which of the following nerves may produce a "wristdrop"?

    (A) axillary
    (B) musculocutaneous
    (C) radial
    (D) median
    (E) ulnar

36. A "claw hand" is usually associated with injury to which of the following nerves?

    (A) median
    (B) radial
    (C) ulnar
    (D) axillary
    (E) musculocutaneous

37. Intervertebral disks may protrude or rupture in any direction, but most commonly occur

    (A) anteriorly
    (B) posteriorly
    (C) anterolaterally
    (D) posterolaterally
    (E) laterally

38. Which of the following is commonly associated with a lateral curvature of the vertebral column?

    (A) kyphosis
    (B) ruptured disk
    (C) scoliosis
    (D) lordosis
    (E) "gorilla" rib

39. Which of the following structures is located within epidural space?

    (A) external vertebral venous plexus
    (B) internal vertebral venous plexus
    (C) anterior spinal artery
    (D) posterior spinal arteries
    (E) middle cerebral artery

40. The caudal end of the spinal cord is anchored to the coccyx by which of the following structures?

    (A) denticulate ligament
    (B) filum terminale
    (C) cauda equina
    (D) conus medullaris
    (E) anterior longitudinal ligament

41. Which of the following structures crosses the posterior surfaces of the obturator internus and gemelli and the quadratus femoris?

    (A) femoral artery
    (B) common iliac veins
    (C) obturator nerve
    (D) sciatic nerve
    (E) superior gluteal nerve and artery

42. The femoral canal contains the

    (A) femoral artery
    (B) femoral vein
    (C) femoral branch of the genitofemoral nerve
    (D) connective tissue and lymph nodes
    (E) great saphenous vein

43. Which of the following do not pass under the flexor retinaculum of the foot?

    (A) tendon of the peroneus longus
    (B) tendon of the tibialis posterior
    (C) tendon of the flexor digitorum longus
    (D) tibial nerve
    (E) tendon of the flexor hallucis longus

44. The outflow tract leading into the pulmonary trunk through the pulmonary orifice is known as the

    (A) crista terminalis
    (B) infundibulum
    (C) crista supraventricularis
    (D) limbus fossa ovalis
    (E) ostium of the coronary sinus

45. Which of the following structures is located in the posterior interventricular sulcus?

    (A) oblique vein of the left atrium
    (B) great cardiac vein
    (C) coronary sinus
    (D) middle cardiac vein
    (E) small cardiac vein

46. In quiet breathing, and in the supine position, where is the apex beat of the heart located?

    (A) to the left of the sternal angle at the level of the second rib
    (B) in the left fifth intercostal space in the midclavicular line
    (C) in the right midaxillary line
    (D) at the xiphisternal junction
    (E) in the second intercostal space to the left of the sternum

47. The foramen secundum is formed by the breakdown of an area in the

    (A) septum primum
    (B) septum secundum
    (C) pars muscularis
    (D) pars membranacea of the interventricular septum
    (E) endocardial cushions

48. Which of the following structures is located within the middle mediastinum?

    (A) esophagus
    (B) aorta
    (C) thoracic duct
    (D) heart
    (E) trachea

49. The median umbilical ligament is the remnant of the

    (A) umbilical arteries
    (B) urachus
    (C) umbilical vein
    (D) ductus arteriosus
    (E) septum primum

50. The fossa navicularis is located within the

    (A) glans penis
    (B) corpus spongiosum
    (C) bulb of the penis
    (D) urogenital diaphragm
    (E) prostatic urethra

51. Which of the following structures enters the deep inguinal ring?

    (A) round ligament of the uterus
    (B) uterine tubes
    (C) suspensory ligament of the ovary
    (D) mesosalpinx
    (E) mesovarium

52. Which of the following structures is associated with the small intestine?

    (A) teniae coli
    (B) mesentery
    (C) sacculations
    (D) epiploic appendages
    (E) haustra coli

53. The beginning of the thoracic duct is known as the

    (A) intestinal lymph trunk
    (B) bronchomediastinal lymph trunk
    (C) jugular lymph trunk
    (D) subclavian lymph trunk
    (E) cisterna chyli

54. Which of the following nerves innervates the gluteus maximus muscle?

    (A) pudendal
    (B) sciatic
    (C) femoral
    (D) inferior gluteal
    (E) obturator

55. The saphenous nerve is the terminal branch of which of the following nerves?

    (A) peroneal
    (B) tibial
    (C) femoral
    (D) obturator
    (E) pudendal

56. Microscopic examination of the brain of an aborted fetus revealed the presence of mitotic figures (condensed chromosomes visible during prophase of mitosis). During early histogenesis in the normal, developing cerebral hemisphere, you would expect all of the cells exhibiting mitotic figures to be located

    (A) in the ventricular zone
    (B) in the mantle layer
    (C) in the alar plate
    (D) at the pial surface
    (E) evenly distributed throughout the thickness of the cortical mantle

57. The neurotransmitter released from cerebellar corticonuclear and corticovestibular fibers is

    (A) glutamate
    (B) gamma-aminobutyric acid
    (C) acetylcholine
    (D) serotonin
    (E) glycine

58. Which statement concerning the inverse myotatic reflex is correct?

    (A) type Ia sensory fibers synapse with interneurons that lead to inhibition of the muscle in which the sensory fibers originated

    (B) golgi tendon organ sensory fibers synapse with interneurons that lead to inhibition of the muscle related to that tendon organ

    (C) type Ib sensory fibers do not play a role in this reflex

    (D) a painful stimulus (ie, pinprick) to the skin overlying a Golgi tendon organ is the typical mode of stimulation that will elicit the reflex

    (E) type II sensory fibers are most active in this reflex and their input excites inhibitory interneurons that synapse with gamma motor neurons

59. Which layer of the cerebral cortex contains most of the neurons that give rise to subcortical projections such as the corticospinal fibers?

    (A) external granular
    (B) external pyramidal
    (C) internal granular
    (D) internal pyramidal
    (E) molecular

60. An occlusion of which of the following vessels would simultaneously damage corticospinal fibers in the medullary pyramid *and* exiting fibers of the hypoglossal nerve?

    (A) paramedian branches of basilar artery
    (B) anterior cerebral, A$_2$
    (C) anterior spinal artery
    (D) posterior spinal artery
    (E) anterior inferior cerebellar artery

61. A patient with a meningioma in the posterior fossa is likely to compress a portion of the cerebellar cortex. Beginning with the pial surface, what is the sequence of cerebellar cortical layers that would be compressed by this tumor?

    (A) pia, molecular, Purkinje, granular
    (B) pia, Purkinje, molecular, granular
    (C) pia, granular, Purkinje, molecular
    (D) pia, molecular, granular, Purkinje
    (E) none of the above

62. Which of the following structures in the medulla originates from the basal plate?

    (A) hypoglossal nucleus
    (B) solitary nucleus
    (C) cochlear nuclei
    (D) spinal trigeminal nucleus
    (E) vestibular nuclei

63. Occlusion of which of the following vessels would affect the entire dorsolateral part of the rostral medulla (level of the restiform body) and the choroid plexus of the fourth ventricle?

    (A) posterior spinal artery
    (B) anterior inferior cerebellar artery
    (C) anterior spinal artery
    (D) posterior inferior cerebellar artery
    (E) superior cerebellar artery

64. Pain and temperature signals arising from receptors on the *left* side of the face would pass through which of the following structures?

    (A) left spinal trigeminal nucleus
    (B) right ventral posterior lateral nucleus of the thalamus
    (C) left principal sensory trigeminal nucleus
    (D) left mesencephalic trigeminal nucleus
    (E) left posterior limb of the internal capsule

65. Which statement concerning the lateral medullary syndrome is most correct?

    (A) patients usually exhibit a loss of pain and temperature on the side of the face contralateral to the lesion

    (B) due to involvement of fibers in the restiform body, patients exhibit spastic paralysis involving the upper extremity

    (C) patients typically exhibit loss of pain and temperature sensibility over the upper and lower extremities ipsilateral to the lesion

    (D) an infarct involving the anterior inferior cerebellar artery is typically the cause of this syndrome

    (E) pain and temperature sensibility is lost over the ipsilateral face and the contralateral trunk and extremities

66. In addition to contralateral hemiplegia, which of the following would you expect to see in a patient with occlusion of paramedian branches of the basilar bifurcation on the right (Weber's syndrome)?

    (A) paralysis of most movements of the left eye

    (B) deviation of the tongue to the right

    (C) inability to voluntarily abduct the right eye

    (D) dilation of the pupil on the right

    (E) complete paralysis of facial expression musculature on the left side

67. Which of the following statements concerning Parkinson's disease is correct?

    (A) it involves neuronal degeneration of the substantia nigra *pars reticulata*

    (B) there is a reduction in the release of norepinephrine by nigrostriatal axon terminals

    (C) tachykinesia (an increase in the speed of movement) is a characteristic of the disease

    (D) carbidopa, an inhibitor of aromatic amino acid decarboxylase, is given because it can cross the blood–brain barrier

    (E) it is characterized by a resting or "pill-rolling" type of tremor involving the fingers and hands

68. You observe the following during a neurological examination of your patient: Both eyes can look to the left without difficulty; on attempted horizontal gaze to the right, the right eye abducts (looks laterally), but the left eye does not adduct (does not move much beyond the vertical meridian of the eye). Based on this information, which of the following is the likely location of the lesion?

    (A) trochlear nerve on the left

    (B) abducens nerve on the left

    (C) medial longitudinal fasciculus on the left

    (D) abducens nerve on the right

    (E) medial longitudinal fasciculus on the right

69. In addition to a loss of proprioception and vibratory sensation on the right side of the body, which of the following motor deficits would be seen in a medial medullary syndrome that involves branches of the left anterior spinal artery?

    (A) deviation of the tongue to the left, hemiplegia of arm and leg on left

    (B) deviation of the tongue to the right, hemiplegia of arm and leg on right

    (C) deviation of the tongue to the left, hemiplegia of the arm and leg on right

    (D) only hemiplegia on the right

    (E) only deviation of the tongue to the left

70. A large vascular infarct involves much of the left frontal lobe beginning at the dorsal convexity near the midline and extending ventrally to include the frontal opercular region. Such a patient would exhibit an aphasic syndrome in combination with motor dysfunction in the hand. Which of the following combinations is correct?

    (A) Wernicke's aphasia—right hand

    (B) Broca's aphasia—right hand

    (C) conduction aphasia—right hand

(D) Wernicke's aphasia—left hand

(E) Broca's aphasia—left hand

71. You are asked to evaluate a patient in the neurology clinic. Your neurological examination reveals the following symptoms: (1) loss of pain and temperature sensation over the left side of the face; (2) loss of pain and temperature sensation in the right arm and leg; and (3) normal tactile and vibratory sensations on the face, body, and extremities. Where is the lesion?

(A) mesencephalon at the level of the inferior colliculus

(B) spinal cord at the cervical enlargement

(C) dorsolateral medulla

(D) posterior limb of the internal capsule

(E) diencephalon at the level of the massa intermedia

72. When the stereocilia of an auditory hair cell are deflected in the appropriate direction, potassium channels open in the apical membrane of the cell and

(A) potassium ions flow out of the cell, hyperpolarizing the cell

(B) potassium ions flow out of the cell, depolarizing the cell

(C) potassium ions flow into the cell, hyperpolarizing the cell

(D) potassium ions flow into the cell, depolarizing the cell

(E) there is no *net* movement of potassium ions

73. A patient comes to you in the ear, nose, and throat (ENT) clinic complaining of dizziness. You have a vestibular caloric test done with the following results. Warm caloric irrigation of the left ear produced left beating horizontal nystagmus. Warm caloric irrigation of the right ear produced no response. You conclude which of the following?

(A) receptors in the left ear have been damaged

(B) only the lateral vestibulospinal tract has been destroyed on the right side

(C) the right labyrinth or VIII nerve has been affected either through trauma or possibly an acoustic neuroma

(D) the left labyrinth or VIII nerve has been affected either through trauma or possibly an acoustic neuroma

(E) there is no lesion in the vestibular system

74. A woman has a menstrual cycle of 28 days' duration. At day 8 of her cycle, the dominant ovarian follicle contains

(A) an oogonium

(B) a primary oocyte, but no polar body

(C) both a primary oocyte and a polar body

(D) a secondary oocyte, but no polar body

(E) both a secondary oocyte and a polar body

75. Which normal cell type will most likely be affected by chemotherapy using an antimitotic drug such as vinblastine?

(A) intestinal epithelium

(B) epithelial cells of the lens

(C) neurons in dorsal root ganglia

(D) neurons of the cerebral cortex

(E) cardiac muscle cells

76. Which structure most effectively blocks passage of material between adjacent epithelial cells?

(A) gap junction

(B) tight junction

(C) desmosome

(D) hemidesmosome

(E) terminal bar

77. Examination of a histological section of normal small intestine reveals that the epithelium contains cells with small cytoplasmic granules adjacent to the basal lamina. Such cells are small, pyramidal, and located most frequently deep in the intestinal glands (glands of Lieberkühn). These cells are most likely

    (A) Paneth cells
    (B) goblet cells
    (C) M (microfold) cells
    (D) enteroendocrine cells
    (E) enterocytes (absorptive cells)

78. In contrast to bone, cartilage

    (A) undergoes interstitial growth
    (B) undergoes appositional growth
    (C) contains cells in lacunae located within the matrix
    (D) contains collagen in the extracellular matrix
    (E) is generally bordered by a dense connective tissue sheath

79. Fenestrated capillaries are characteristic of

    (A) the cerebral cortex
    (B) skeletal muscle
    (C) the renal glomerulus
    (D) the splenic red pulp
    (E) the epidermis

80. The nasal cavities, nasopharynx, trachea, and bronchi are lined by an epithelium which has

    (A) no junctional complexes
    (B) mainly squamous or cuboidal cells
    (C) a thin, incomplete basement membrane
    (D) few mucus-secreting cells
    (E) a pseudostratified appearance in histological sections

81. Secretion of pulmonary surfactant is a function of

    (A) alveolar dust cells
    (B) endothelial cells of capillaries in the alveolar septum

    (C) small granule cells
    (D) type I pneumocytes (squamous alveolar cells)
    (E) type II pneumocytes (greater alveolar cells)

**Questions 82 and 83**

A 19-year-old black female was brought to the emergency room complaining of severe abdominal pain that began immediately after eating dinner. The physical examination revealed extreme tenderness in the lower right abdominal quadrant, but no abdominal masses were noted. Her temperature was 100°F. Among other tests, a complete blood count was ordered with the following findings:

| | |
|---|---|
| Hematocrit | 39% |
| Hemoglobin | 14.9 g/dL |
| Total leukocyte count | 24,000/mm³ |

| Differential leukocyte count: | |
|---|---|
| Segmented neutrophils | 71% |
| Band form neutrophils | 16% |
| Eosinophils | 4% |
| Basophils | 0.2% |
| Lymphocytes | 3% |
| Monocytes | 6% |

82. For which leukocytes is there an elevation above the normal range in absolute numbers per microliter of blood?

    (A) only neutrophils
    (B) only neutrophils and eosinophils
    (C) only neutrophils, eosinophils, and monocytes
    (D) only monocytes and lymphocytes
    (E) only band form neutrophils

83. Which of the following conditions is most consistent with the laboratory findings?

    (A) parasitic worm infection
    (B) acute inflammation in response to bacterial infection
    (C) severe allergic condition
    (D) acute lymphocytic leukemia
    (E) sickle cell disease

84. Propagation of an action potential into the interior of a skeletal muscle fiber is a function of

   (A) Z lines
   (B) transverse (T) tubules
   (C) muscle spindles
   (D) the sarcoplasmic reticulum
   (E) the endomysium

85. The space of Disse in the liver

   (A) is delimited entirely by hepatocytes
   (B) contains formed elements of blood
   (C) is bordered partly by microvilli of hepatocytes
   (D) constitutes the initial channel for the flow of bile
   (E) is a constituent of the portal triad

86. The macula densa, a component of the juxtaglomerular apparatus, is a specialization of

   (A) mesangial cells
   (B) the afferent arteriole
   (C) Bowman's capsule
   (D) the proximal tubule
   (E) the distal tubule

87. Production of primary granules occurs during which stage of granulocyte development?

   (A) granulocyte colony-forming unit
   (B) myeloblast
   (C) promyelocyte
   (D) myelocyte
   (E) metamyelocyte

88. The acidophilic staining of the cytoplasm of oxyntic (parietal) cells most likely results from a high content of

   (A) hydrochloric acid
   (B) secretory granules containing intrinsic factor
   (C) secretory granules containing pepsinogen
   (D) rough endoplasmic reticulum
   (E) mitochondria

89. In the placenta, maternal blood comes in direct contact with

   (A) the syncytiotrophoblast
   (B) the cytotrophoblast
   (C) endothelial cells of fetal capillaries
   (D) connective tissue cells of secondary villi
   (E) no fetally derived cells

90. Nuclei in the pars nervosa of the hypophysis predominantly belong to

   (A) neurosecretory neurons
   (B) basophils
   (C) chromophobes
   (D) pituicytes
   (E) Schwann cells

91. Antidiuretic hormone (vasopressin) is released from

   (A) basophils in the pars distalis
   (B) acidophils in the pars distalis
   (C) pituicytes in the pars nervosa
   (D) nerve terminals in the pars nervosa
   (E) nerve terminals in the hypothalamus

**DIRECTIONS (Questions 92–126): Each of the numbered items or incomplete statements in this section is negatively phrased, as indicated by a capitalized word such as NOT, LEAST, or EXCEPT. Select the ONE lettered answer or completion that is BEST in each case.**

92. The urethra does NOT traverse the

   (A) prostate
   (B) clitoris
   (C) urogenital diaphragm
   (D) corpus spongiosum
   (E) glans penis

93. Damage to the coracobrachialis muscle and to the nerve passing through it could reasonably be expected to produce all of the following EXCEPT

    (A) weakened flexion at the elbow
    (B) weakened flexion at the shoulder
    (C) weakened supination of the forearm
    (D) diminished cutaneous sensation over the lateral forearm
    (E) diminished cutaneous sensation over the lateral palm

94. A computed tomography (CT) scan through the transpyloric plane would typically demonstrate all of the following structures EXCEPT the

    (A) pancreas
    (B) right kidney
    (C) celiac trunk
    (D) duodenum
    (E) spleen

95. Which of the following would be LEAST likely to be affected by an ulcer on the posterior aspect of the first part of the duodenum?

    (A) splenic artery
    (B) gastroduodenal artery
    (C) posterior superior pancreaticoduodenal artery
    (D) common bile duct
    (E) portal vein

96. Parasympathetic fibers which influence erection of the penis are found in all of the following EXCEPT

    (A) nervi erigentes
    (B) inferior hypogastric plexus
    (C) sacral plexus
    (D) vesical plexus
    (E) cavernous nerves

97. The wall of the vagina has a direct relationship to all of the following EXCEPT

    (A) urethra
    (B) bladder
    (C) vesicouterine pouch
    (D) rectouterine pouch
    (E) rectum

98. The broad ligament encloses all of the following structures EXCEPT the

    (A) uterine tubes
    (B) ovarian ligaments
    (C) part of the round ligament
    (D) the uterine artery
    (E) the greater vestibular glands

99. All of the following nerves are formed from ventral primary rami EXCEPT the

    (A) greater occipital
    (B) greater auricular
    (C) lateral supraclavicular
    (D) lesser occipital
    (E) transverse cervical

100. All of the following muscles are innervated by the cervical plexus EXCEPT the

    (A) sternohyoid
    (B) sternothyroid
    (C) omohyoid
    (D) thyrohyoid
    (E) mylohyoid

101. All of the following functional components are associated with the vagus nerve EXCEPT the

    (A) general somatic afferent
    (B) general somatic efferent
    (C) general visceral efferent
    (D) general visceral afferent
    (E) special visceral afferent

102. All of the following muscles are considered to be muscles of inspiration EXCEPT the

    (A) pectoralis major
    (B) anterior scalene
    (C) diaphragm
    (D) intercostals
    (E) sternocleidomastoid

103. The inferior laryngeal nerve innervates all of the following muscles EXCEPT the

    (A) cricothyroid
    (B) lateral cricoarytenoid
    (C) posterior cricoarytenoid
    (D) transverse arytenoid
    (E) thyroarytenoid

104. All of the muscles of the pharynx are innervated by the vagus EXCEPT the

    (A) palatopharyngeus
    (B) salpingopharyngeus
    (C) superior constrictor
    (D) stylopharyngeus
    (E) inferior constrictor

105. All of the following nerves are cutaneous branches of the ophthalmic division of the trigeminal nerve EXCEPT the

    (A) supratrochlear
    (B) infraorbital
    (C) external nasal branches
    (D) lacrimal
    (E) supraorbital

106. All of the following muscles are innervated by the mandibular division of the trigeminal nerve EXCEPT the

    (A) lateral pterygoid
    (B) masseter
    (C) buccinator
    (D) anterior belly of the digastric
    (E) temporalis

107. The facial nerve provides the parasympathetic innervation for all of the following glands EXCEPT the

    (A) lacrimal
    (B) submandibular
    (C) parotid
    (D) nasal
    (E) palatine

108. All of the following cortical areas contribute fibers to the corticospinal tract EXCEPT the

    (A) primary motor cortex (precentral gyrus)
    (B) premotor cortex
    (C) supplementary motor cortex
    (D) primary somatosensory cortex (postcentral gyrus)
    (E) inferior temporal cortex

109. All of the following statements can be correctly applied to the basal ganglia and Parkinson's disease EXCEPT

    (A) in Parkinson's disease, the loss of or reduction in nigrostriatal dopamine projections has an influence on both the *direct* and the *indirect* pathways
    (B) typically, activation of the *indirect* pathway leads to a reduction in the output of thalamocortical neuron activity
    (C) typically, activation of the *direct* pathway leads to an increase in motor activity
    (D) loss of function in the *indirect* pathway can lead to the production of involuntary movements called choreiform movements
    (E) the tremor of Parkinson's disease becomes more pronounced (worse) with attempted movement

110. All of the following statements can be correctly applied to the regulation of the autonomic nervous system by the hypothalamus and the amygdala EXCEPT

    (A) the hypothalamus regulates autonomic function on a moment-to-moment (reflexive) basis
    (B) the amygdaloid complex, in general, regulates autonomic function on a long-term basis based upon learning and past experience
    (C) the hypothalamus contains the upper motor neurons controlling autonomic function
    (D) the amygdala contains the lower motor neurons controlling autonomic function
    (E) autonomic nuclei of the brain stem are influenced from both the hypothalamus and the amygdala

111. All of the following are symptoms of cerebellar disease EXCEPT

   (A) resting tremor
   (B) wide-based stance or staggering gait
   (C) hypometria
   (D) kinetic tremor
   (E) dysdiadochokinesia

112. All of the following symptoms can result from interruption of the oculomotor nerve EXCEPT

   (A) the affected eye looks down and out
   (B) the pupillary light reflex is lost
   (C) lens accommodation is lost
   (D) the affected eye looks up and out
   (E) the affected eyelid droops (ptosis)

113. All of the statements below concerning the primary somatosensory cortex (SI) are correct EXCEPT

   (A) cytoarchitectural subdivisions of SI are numbered anterior to posterior as 3a, 3b, 1, and 2
   (B) there is a complete representation of the body surface in each of the cytoarchitectural subdivisions of SI cortex
   (C) the somatotopic representation of the body surface in SI is arranged in a classic "tail-to-tongue" sequence from ventrolateral to dorsomedial
   (D) areas 3a and 2 receive their major input from muscle spindle afferents and Golgi tendon organs
   (E) areas 3b and 1 receive their major input from receptors in the skin

114. All of the following are associated with vesicular release of neurotransmitter EXCEPT

   (A) activation of voltage-gated $Ca^{++}$ channels which allow calcium to enter the axon terminal
   (B) "docking proteins" are present and attach vesicles to the presynaptic membrane
   (C) fusion of vesicles with the presynaptic membrane allows a quantum of neurotransmitter to be released into the synaptic cleft
   (D) movement of neurotransmitter along actin "bridges" which structurally join the pre- and postsynaptic membranes
   (E) binding of neurotransmitter molecules to receptors on the postsynaptic membrane

115. All of the following statements concerning muscle spindles are correct EXCEPT

   (A) at least two types of intrafusal muscle fibers are present in a muscle spindle
   (B) each intrafusal fiber is innervated by two different gamma motor neurons
   (C) type Ia sensory fibers from a spindle can form direct synaptic contact with alpha motor neurons
   (D) activation of type Ib sensory fibers leads to inhibition of the muscle to which this sensory fiber is linked
   (E) gamma motor neurons synapse directly with intrafusal muscle fibers

116. Characteristic signs and symptoms that indicate damage to the corticospinal system include all of the following EXCEPT

   (A) spasticity
   (B) the Babinski sign
   (C) loss of deep tendon reflexes
   (D) immediate muscle degeneration and atrophy
   (E) hypertonia

117. All of the following are characteristic features of "spastic paralysis" EXCEPT

   (A) usually involves extensors (ie, antigravity muscles) most severely
   (B) affected muscles are hypotonic
   (C) increased resistance to passive movement associated with "clasp-knife" phenomenon
   (D) increased resistance to passive movement is velocity dependent
   (E) affected muscles exhibit increased (more brisk) deep tendon reflexes

118. Basal ganglia lesions can be associated with all of the following EXCEPT

    (A) production of involuntary movements
    (B) muscles that exhibit "cog-wheel" rigidity
    (C) resting tremor
    (D) athetosis
    (E) spastic paralysis

119. Pain transmission can be influenced by several descending pathways. All of the following are involved with the descending influence on nociceptive transmission EXCEPT

    (A) ventral lateral thalamic nucleus
    (B) periaqueductal gray
    (C) nucleus raphe magnus
    (D) raphespinal fibers
    (E) serotonin and enkephalins

120. All of the following statements correctly apply to taste receptors EXCEPT

    (A) each receptor responds best to one stimulus quality (ie, sweet, salty, sour, bitter) but also responds less vigorously to other stimulus qualities
    (B) the receptors are arranged in a rostral-caudal pattern on the tongue such that the most anterior respond best to sweet and salty stimuli
    (C) taste receptors have a life span of approximately 7 to 10 days
    (D) taste receptors are stimulated when a food or fluid substance diffuses through the apical pore and depolarizes the cell
    (E) taste receptors are most numerous on the side of the tongue ipsilateral to the dominant hemisphere

121. Which cell does NOT differentiate in bone marrow?

    (A) B lymphocyte
    (B) T lymphocyte
    (C) neutrophil
    (D) basophil
    (E) eosinophil

122. Mucus-secreting cells are LEAST abundant in

    (A) the sublingual gland
    (B) the submandibular gland
    (C) the parotid gland
    (D) esophageal glands
    (E) intestinal glands (of Lieberkühn)

123. Which of the following is NOT a likely site of development of lymphoid follicles following exposure to an infectious agent?

    (A) spleen
    (B) axillary lymph node
    (C) thymus
    (D) Peyer's patch
    (E) pharyngeal tonsil

124. The cytoplasm of a typical steroid hormone-secreting cell does NOT contain

    (A) lipid droplets
    (B) mitochondria with tubular cristae
    (C) abundant smooth endoplasmic reticulum (sER)
    (D) abundant secretory granules at the cell apex
    (E) a Golgi complex

125. Which of the following is NOT found in the superior cervical ganglion (SCG)?

    (A) pseudounipolar neurons
    (B) satellite cells
    (C) synapses
    (D) Schwann cells
    (E) unmyelinated axons

126. Thick skin has each of the following EXCEPT

    (A) sebaceous glands
    (B) sweat glands
    (C) stratum basale
    (D) stratum spinosum
    (E) dermal papillae

DIRECTIONS (Questions 127 through 150): Each set of matching questions in this section consists of a list of lettered options followed by several numbered items. For each numbered item, select the ONE lettered option that is most closely associated with it. Each lettered option may be selected once, more than once, or not at all.

Questions 127 through 131

    (A) pyramidal cell
    (B) Purkinje cell
    (C) Renshaw cell
    (D) granule cell
    (E) hair cell
    (F) mitral cell

For each description, select the correct cell type.

127. The predominant type of neuron found in layers III and V of the cerebral cortex

128. An interneuron in the spinal cord

129. Found in the cochlea

130. Found in the olfactory bulb

131. Principal neurons in the hippocampus whose axons enter the fornix

Questions 132 through 135

    (A) lateral spinothalamic tract
    (B) ansa lenticularis
    (C) spinal trigeminal tract
    (D) dorsal spinocerebellar tract
    (E) anencephaly
    (F) meningomyelocele

For each description, select the correct structure or condition.

132. Axons that originate from neurons in the globus pallidus pars interna

133. Carries pain sensation from the teeth

134. Failure of the anterior neuropore to close

135. Axons that originate from cells in the nucleus dorsalis of Clarke

Questions 136 through 142

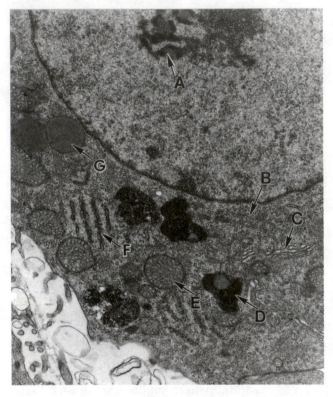

Figure 1.1

For each description, select the corresponding structure in the electron micrograph (Fig. 1.1).

136. Residual body (secondary lysosome) seen as a lipofuscin granule in light microscopy

137. Site of synthesis of ribosomal RNA

138. Contains enzymes of the citric acid cycle

139. Storage site of cholesterol esters and other lipid precursors of steroid hormones

140. Participates with mitochondria in the sequence of enzymatic steps that produce steroid hormones

141. Site of post-translational modification and sorting of proteins destined for membranes, secretory granules, and lysosomes

142. Segregates polypeptides from the cytosol as they are synthesized

**Questions 143 through 146**

    (A) enterocyte

    (B) goblet cell

    (C) enteroendocrine cell

    (D) Paneth cell

    (E) M (microfold) cell

    (F) chief cell

    (G) parietal cell

Select the cell type that can be demonstrated by immunocytochemical staining using each of the following primary antibodies.

143. Anti-lysozyme

144. Anti-pepsinogen

145. Anti-cholecystokinin

146. Anti-intrinsic factor

**Questions 147 through 150**

    (A) migration of primordial germ cells from yolk sac to gonad

    (B) mitotic division of oogonia or spermatogonia

    (C) final S phase preceding meiosis

    (D) first meiotic division (including all its phases)

    (E) second meiotic division (including all its phases)

For each characterization, select the appropriate event in gamete development.

147. In males, this occurs immediately after a type B spermatogonium divides to produce two new primary spermatocytes

148. This lasts about three weeks in spermatogenesis and many years in oogenesis

149. The result of this event is cells containing the haploid (1N) number of chromosomes and 1N of DNA

150. In females, this step is completed only if fertilization occurs

# Anatomy
## Answers and Explanations

1. **(C)** The trapezius muscle has an extensive attachment to the occipital bone, the ligamentum nuchae, the spinous processes, and supraspinous ligaments down to T12, the spine of the scapula, the acromion, and the lateral third of the clavicle. Such a fan-shaped muscle has many actions. The upper and middle fibers, which attach to the clavicle and acromion, lift the point of the shoulder. The trapezius is innervated by the accessory nerve, and the ability to "shrug" the shoulder is often used to test the function of the accessory nerve. *(Hall–Craggs, p 79)*

2. **(B)** The axillary nerve, with the posterior humeral circumflex artery, passes through the quadrangular space and crosses the surgical neck of the humerus, where it is susceptible to injury in fracture and in dislocation of the shoulder joint. *(Hall–Craggs, p 161)*

3. **(C)** The axillary nerve arises from the posterior cord of the brachial plexus and supplies the deltoid and teres minor muscles. The serratus anterior is supplied by the long thoracic nerve which is derived from the roots at C5, C6, and C7. The pronator teres is supplied by the median nerve which is derived from the medial and lateral cords. The musculocutaneous nerve to the biceps brachii arises from the lateral cord, and the suprascapular nerve to the infraspinatus arises from the upper trunk. *(Hall–Craggs, pp 96–98)*

4. **(E)** The suprascapular, dorsal scapular, subscapular, and scapular circumflex arteries participate in a potential collateral anastomosis around the scapula. The suprascapular and dorsal scapular arteries arise, directly or indirectly, from the subclavian artery while the subscapular and scapular circumflex arteries are from the third part of the axillary artery, thus providing a bypass for obstructions of the first or second parts of the axillary artery. *(Hall–Craggs, pp 99–100)*

5. **(B)** The radial notch of the ulna and the annular ligament form a ring in which the head of the radius rotates at its articulation with the capitulum of the humerus. The annular ligament narrows over the neck, cupping the head of the radius and preventing downward dislocation. *(Hall–Craggs, pp 132–133)*

6. **(D)** The cutaneous innervation of the palmar surface of the hand and fingers is provided by the median and ulnar nerves. The separation is a line passing through the midline of the ring finger with the ulnar nerve supplying the medial area and the median nerve the lateral area. *(Hall–Craggs, pp 154–155)*

7. **(C)** Afferent fibers (both somatic and visceral) found in spinal nerves arise from cell bodies located in the dorsal root ganglia. The ventral horn of the spinal cord contains cell bodies of general somatic efferent neurons. The intermediolateral cell column of the lateral horn, the paravertebral ganglia, and the prevertebral ganglia contain the cell bodies of general visceral efferent neurons of the sympathetic nervous system. *(Hollinshead, pp 47, 56–58)*

8. **(E)** The area of skin supplied by a single spinal (segmental) nerve is known as a der-

matome. The medial surface of the upper arm is supplied by the T2 dermatome, and the medial aspect of the lower arm, elbow, and proximal forearm by the T1 dermatome. The T1 and T2 dermatomes frequently receive referred pain from the heart. *(Hall–Craggs, pp 55, 69, 218)*

9. **(C)** The thoracic duct ascends in the posterior mediastinum between the azygous vein and the descending aorta. The phrenic nerves descend through the superior and middle mediastina, and the heart lies completely within the middle mediastinum. The left recurrent laryngeal nerve arises in the superior mediastinum and the right in the root of the neck. *(Hall–Craggs, pp 188–191, 216)*

10. **(A)** The circumflex branch of the left coronary artery circles to the posterior surface of the heart in the coronary sulcus (atrioventricular groove). It gives branches to the left atrium and left ventricle before anastomosing with the posterior interventricular branch of the right coronary artery. *(Hall–Craggs, p 199)*

11. **(E)** The anterior abdominal wall is divided by two transverse and two vertical planes into nine regions used to locate the signs and symptoms of abdominal disease. From superior to inferior, the midline regions are the epigastric, umbilical, and the hypogastric regions, and the lateral regions are the hypochondriac, lateral, and inguinal regions. The epigastric region contains parts of the liver and stomach and the structures of the stomach bed including the pancreas, the celiac trunk, and the splenic artery. The left hypochondrium contains the fundus of the stomach, the tail of the pancreas, the splenic artery, and the spleen. *(Hollinshead, pp 615–618)*

12. **(B)** The abdominal viscera receive sympathetic innervation from preganglionic sympathetic fibers traversing the thoracic and lumbar splanchnic nerves to synapse in prevertebral sympathetic ganglia. Postganglionic fibers are then distributed to the various organs by the periarterial plexuses. The suprarenal gland is unique in that the suprarenal medulla, the cells of which corre-

spond developmentally to postganglionic sympathetic neurons, receives direct supply from preganglionic sympathetic fibers. *(Hall–Craggs, pp 287–288, 295)*

13. **(B)** The greater peritoneal sac communicates with the lesser sac, or omental bursa, through the epiploic foramen (of Winslow). The opening passes behind the free edge of the lesser omentum (the hepatoduodenal ligament). It is bounded posteriorly by the inferior vena cava, superiorly by the caudate lobe of the liver, and inferiorly by the first part of the duodenum. *(Hollinshead, pp 602–603)*

14. **(A)** The muscles that dorsiflex the ankle joint are located in the anterior compartment of the leg and are innervated by the deep peroneal nerve. The evertors of the foot occupy the lateral compartment of the leg and are supplied by the superficial peroneal nerve. Thus, the common peroneal nerve innervates both the dorsiflexors and evertors of the foot. The tibial nerve supplies the muscles of the posterior leg which are plantar flexors and invertors of the foot. *(Hall–Craggs, pp 405–407, 410–414)*

15. **(C)** The lymphatic drainage of an organ is closely related to its blood supply. Lymphatic drainage from the testis travels along the testicular artery to reach lymph nodes along the aorta. *(Hall–Craggs, p 235)*

16. **(C)** The common peroneal nerve leaves the popliteal fossa to wind forward around the lateral surface of the neck of the fibula and is vulnerable at this point. It ends in the lateral compartment of the leg by dividing into the superficial and deep peroneal nerves. *(Hollinshead, p 420)*

17. **(E)** The posterior cruciate ligament prevents forward sliding of the femur on the tibia, and the anterior cruciate prevents backward sliding of the femur on the tibia. Abnormal anteroposterior movement when the knee is flexed is a "drawer" sign. *(Hall–Craggs, p 399)*

18. **(C)** The artery to the hindgut and its derivatives is the inferior mesenteric artery. The

midgut is supplied by the superior mesenteric artery, and the caudal foregut is supplied by the celiac trunk. *(Sadler, pp 253, 268)*

19. **(A)** When the lumen of the allantois remains patent (a urachal fistula), the urinary bladder communicates with the umbilicus, and urine may leak from the umbilicus. Persistence of a patent vitelline duct allows for communication of the terminal ileum with the umbilicus, and feces or mucus may leak from the umbilicus. *(Sadler, pp 263, 285)*

20. **(C)** Transposition of the great vessels occurs when the truncoconal ridges fail to spiral as they divide the outflow tract into two channels. This produces two totally independent circulatory loops with the right ventricle feeding into the aorta and the left ventricle feeding into the pulmonary artery. *(Sadler, p 208)*

21. **(C)** The oblique fissure separates the superior lobe from the inferior lobe. A further subdivision of the superior lobe of the right lung is made by the horizontal fissure. The horizontal fissure and the inferior part of the oblique fissure form the boundaries of the middle lobe of the right lung. *(Woodburne and Burckel, p 404)*

22. **(A)** The bulbospongiosus muscle in the male overlies the bulb of the penis. The ischiocavernosus muscles cover the crura of the penis. The superficial transverse perineus muscles arise on either side from the anterior and medial portions of the ischial tuberosity. The pea-sized bulbourethral glands of the male are embedded in the fibers of the sphincter urethrae muscle. *(Woodburne and Burckel, pp 523–524, 527)*

23. **(E)** The digastric muscle is a two-bellied muscle that attaches by an intermediate tendon to the hyoid bone. With the border of the mandible for a base, the digastric muscle completes the definition of the submandibular triangle, the apex of which is directed inferiorly. *(Woodburne and Burckel, p 213)*

24. **(D)** The external jugular vein crosses perpendicularly the superficial surface of the ster-

nocleidomastoid muscle directly under the platysma muscle. The anterior jugular descends near the median line. The posterior auricular joins the retromandibular to form the external jugular. The internal jugular runs in the carotid sheath deep to the sternocleidomastoid muscle. *(Woodburne and Burckel, pp 188–189)*

25. **(E)** The prevertebral fascia crosses the midline anterior to the prevertebral muscles, continuing laterally to cover the scalene muscles. The esophagus is surrounded by the visceral fascia. The vagus nerve, internal jugular vein, and common carotid artery are surrounded by the carotid sheath. *(Woodburne and Burckel, pp 191–194)*

26. **(C)** The superior thyroid artery is usually the first branch of the external carotid. The internal carotid gives off no major branches in the neck. The inferior thyroid is the largest branch of the thyrocervical trunk. The facial is a branch of the external carotid. The costocervical is a branch of the subclavian. *(Woodburne and Burckel, pp 203, 224)*

27. **(B)** The isthmus of the thyroid gland unites the two lateral lobes across trachea rings two, three, and four. Both the cricoid and thyroid cartilages are superior to the isthmus. The cricoid cartilage is located at the level of the sixth cervical vertebra. *(Woodburne and Burckel, pp 197–198)*

28. **(A)** The superior thyroid veins cross the common carotid artery and empty into the internal jugular veins above the thyroid cartilage. The inferior thyroid veins drain into the brachiocephalic veins. Occasionally, they make a common entry into the jugular with the lingual and facial veins. The two inferior thyroid veins empty into the left and right brachiocephalic veins. The middle thyroid veins empty into the lower end of the internal jugular vein. *(Woodburne and Burckel, pp 200–201)*

29. **(B)** The vocal folds are abducted and the rima glottidis is widened by the posterior cricoarytenoid muscle. The lateral cricoaryte-

noid and the transverse arytenoid muscles are adductors of the vocal folds. The thyroarytenoid muscles may contract for complete glottic closure. Tension of the vocal ligaments is increased by the action of the cricothyroid muscles. (*Woodburne and Burckel, p 233*)

30. **(E)** The glossopharyngeal nerves carries taste from the posterior one-third of the tongue. The lingual nerve proper, a branch of the mandibular division of the trigeminal nerve, is concerned with general sensation from the anterior two-thirds of the tongue and the mucous membrane of the floor of the mouth. The chorda tympani branch of the facial nerve conveys the special sense of taste from the anterior two-thirds of the tongue. The vagus carries tastes from the epiglottic region. The hypoglossal nerve is motor to the tongue. (*Woodburne and Burckel, pp 239–241*)

31. **(C)** The buccal branch of the mandibular nerve is the principal cutaneous nerve of the cheek. The auriculotemporal nerve reaches the subcutaneous tissues from the infratemporal fossa at a point between the condyle of the mandible and the external acoustic meatus. The mental nerve supplies the skin of the chin and mucous membrane of the lower lip. The zygomaticofacial supplies the skin over the prominence of the cheek. The zygomaticotemporal nerve is cutaneous to the anterior temporal region. (*Woodburne and Burckel, p 244*)

32. **(B)** The middle meningeal artery is the principal artery of the cranial dura mater. It passes upward, superficial to the sphenomandibular ligament and between the two roots of the auriculotemporal nerve, and enters the middle cranial fossa via the foramen spinosum. (*Woodburne and Burckel, p 267*)

33. **(C)** The long head of the biceps brachii arises from the supraglenoid tubercle of the scapula. It inserts into the radial tuberosity and the bicipital aponeurosis. The short head of the biceps brachii arises from the tip of the coracoid process. (*Hollinshead, p 200*)

34. **(A)** Approximately 70% of carpal fractures involves the scaphoid only. A fracture through its narrow middle part may deprive the scaphoid of its blood supply, causing the proximal part of the scaphoid to undergo avascular necrosis. (*Hollinshead, p 228*)

35. **(C)** Lesions of the radial nerve in the lower part of the arm may paralyze all of the extensor muscles of the forearm, producing a "wristdrop" (flexion of the hand by gravity when the forearm is horizontal), as well as inability to extend the metacarpophalangeal joints at the digits. (*Hollinshead, p 245*)

36. **(C)** A "claw hand" is usually associated with injury to the ulnar nerve. Injuries to the radial nerve produce a "wristdrop." The median nerve injury interferes with pronation of the forearm and with flexion of the phalanges of digits two and three. The axillary injury involves the deltoid muscle and abduction of the upper limb. The musculocutaneous nerve injury involves the flexors of the forearm and abductors of the arm. (*Hollinshead, pp 210, 245, 280*)

37. **(D)** Intervertebral disks may protrude or rupture in any direction, but most common is a posterolateral direction, just lateral to the strong central portion of the posterior longitudinal ligament. This is usually the weakest part of the disk, since the annulus is thinner here and is not supported by other ligaments. (*Hollinshead, p 297*)

38. **(C)** Abnormal curvatures of the vertebral column are designated as kyphosis (hunchback), lordosis (swayback), and scoliosis (a lateral curvature). Since spinal nerves pass over the posterolateral part of the intervertebral disk, a protruded or ruptured disk frequently causes irritation of one or more nerves. When there is a rib on the first lumbar vertebra, that rib is called a lumbar or "gorilla" rib. (*Hollinshead, pp 286, 297, 301*)

39. **(B)** The spinal cord and its meninges do not fill the vertebral canal. The space between the walls of this canal and the outer menix of the cord, the dura mater, is the epidural space,

which is filled with fat, connective tissue, and a plexus of veins. The venous plexuses in the epidural space are divided into anterior and posterior internal vertebral venous plexuses. The external venous plexuses, anterior to the vertebral bodies and posterior to the vertebral arches, are connected to the internal venous plexus. (*Hollinshead, p 320*)

40. **(B)** The terminal tapered part of the cord is the conus medullaris, and the tough thread continued from the conus is the filum terminale. The conus and filum terminale are surrounded by longitudinally directed roots of the more caudal spinal nerves called the cauda equina. The anterior longitudinal ligament is located on the anterior surface of the vertebral bodies. (*Hollinshead, p 323*)

41. **(D)** The sciatic nerve is the largest nerve in the body and emerges below the piriformis. It runs across the posterior surfaces of the obturatus internus and gemelli and the quadratus femoris. The femoral artery is formed below the inguinal ligament and the common iliac veins form from within the pelvis. (*Hollinshead, pp 368, 386*)

42. **(D)** Within the femoral sheath are three compartments. The lateral compartment contains the femoral artery and the femoral branch of the genitofemoral nerve; the intermediate compartment contains the femoral vein, and the medial compartment is the femoral canal. The femoral canal contains only a slight amount of loose connective tissue and one or two lymphatic vessels and nodes. (*Hollinshead, p 386*)

43. **(A)** The flexor retinaculum of the foot runs between the medial malleolus and the calcaneus. It sends three septa to the tibia and thus contains four compartments that contain tendons of the tibialis posterior, flexor digitorum longus, flexor hallucis longus and the tibial nerve, and posterior tibial vessels. The peroneus longus and brevis pass beneath the superior and inferior peroneal retinacula. (*Hollinshead, pp 416–417*)

44. **(B)** The funnel-shaped infundibulum, or conus arteriosus, leads into the pulmonary trunk through the pulmonary orifice. The crista supraventricularis divides the interior of the right ventricle into two portions, inflow and outflow tracts. The interior of the right atrium is partially divided into two main parts by the crista terminalis. The limbus fossae ovalis forms a prominent margin for the fossa ovalis. Medial to the opening of the inferior vena cava is the ostium of the coronary sinus. (*Hollinshead, pp 527–528*)

45. **(D)** The middle cardiac vein runs in the posterior interventricular sulcus, and the small cardiac vein runs in the coronary sulcus along the right coronary artery. The great cardiac vein lies in the anterior interventricular sulcus. The coronary sinus continues to the right in the coronary sulcus. The oblique vein is usually very small and empties into the coronary sinus. (*Hollinshead, pp 526–537*)

46. **(B)** The apex is the only point of the heart that can be directly identified on the precordium. A cardiac impulse may be visible at the apex, and palpation over it will confirm the presence of the apex beat. The apex is located in the left fifth intercostal space just medial to the midclavicular line. (*Hollinshead, p 542*)

47. **(A)** The foramen secundum is formed by the breakdown of an area in the septum primum. The septum secondum gives rise to the limbus fossa ovalis. The interventricular septum is derived from the endocardial cushions, a muscular portion, the pars muscularis, and a membranous portion, the pars membranacea. (*Hollinshead, pp 546–547*)

48. **(D)** The pericardial sac and its contents comprise the middle mediastinum. The posterior mediastinum is between the vertebral bodies and the pericardial sac. The heart is found in the middle mediastinum. The esophagus, vagi, descending aorta, azygos veins, and thoracic duct are located in the posterior mediastinum. (*Hollinshead, pp 522, 566*)

49. **(B)** The median umbilical ligament, attached to the apex of the bladder, is the remnant of the embryonic urachus. The umbilical arteries, ductus arteriosus, septum primum, and umbilical veins are all embryonic structures associated with fetal circulation. The obliterated umbilical artery remains in the adult as the medial umbilical ligament. *(Hollinshead, pp 548, 767)*

50. **(A)** Within the glans, the urethra dilates to form the fossa navicularis. The posterior expanded end of the corpus spongiosum, the bulb of the penis, is tightly attached to the inferior fascia of the urogenital diaphragm. The prostatic urethra is superior to the urogenital diaphragm. *(Hollinshead, p 801)*

51. **(A)** The round ligament of the uterus runs retroperitoneally from the uterotubal junction to enter the deep inguinal ring. The mesovarium attaches to the ovary and is a reduplication of the posterior lamina of the broad ligament. The ligament of the ovary attaches to the uterus in the inferior angle of the uterotubal junction. The mesosalpinx is located between the uterine tube and the base of the mesovarium. *(Hollinshead, pp 777, 783)*

52. **(B)** Three surface features serve to distinguish isolated loops of the small or large intestine. The large intestine has teniae coli, sacculations or haustra coli, and epiploic appendages. The mesentery is the peritoneal reflection from the body wall to the small intestine. *(Woodburne and Burckel, p 483)*

53. **(E)** The cisterna chyli, or the beginning of the thoracic duct, receives the right and left lumbar trunks. The cisterna lies on the bodies of the upper two lumbar vertebrae between the right crus of the diaphragm and the abdominal aorta and represents a dilated receptacle for the lymph gathered from the lower part of the body. *(Woodburne and Burckel, pp 412, 501)*

54. **(D)** The inferior gluteal nerve, a postaxial branch of the sacral plexus with fibers from L5, S1, and S2, is the sole supply of the gluteus maximus. The pudendal nerve inner-

vates muscles of the perineum. The femoral, sciatic, and obturator nerves innervate muscles of the lower limb. *(Woodburne and Burckel, p 561)*

55. **(C)** The saphenous nerve is the terminal branch of the femoral nerve. Arising from the femoral nerve in the femoral triangle, it enters the adductor canal, where it crosses the femoral vessels anteriorly from their lateral to their medial side. Opposite the knee joint, the nerve becomes cutaneous, emerging between the tendons of the sartorius and gracilis muscles. It descends in the leg in company with the greater saphenous vein. *(Woodburne and Burckel, p 582)*

56. **(A)** During histogenesis in the cerebral hemisphere and elsewhere in the developing brain, germinal or matrix cells undergo cell division in the ventricular zone which is that region that abuts the luminal space (future ventricular space) of the neural tube. At a predetermined time, these cells lose their ability to divide and migrate laterally toward the perimeter of the neural tube where they accumulate as neuroblasts and form the mantle layer. Gradually the sulcus limitans forms as a groove in the wall of the neural tube and cells in the dorsal portion of the mantle layer give rise to the alar plate and become associated with sensory functions. Cells ventral to this groove form the basal plate and eventually give rise to motor neurons. Cells that undergo mitosis are normally not found at the pial surface, nor are they evenly distributed throughout the thickness of the developing neural tube. *(Burt, pp 5–6)*

57. **(B)** Corticonuclear and corticovestibular fibers are axons of Purkinje neurons, and these cells utilize GABA as a neurotransmitter. Glutamate, acetylcholine, serotonin, and glycine are neurotransmitters used by other types of neurons throughout the nervous system. *(Burt, p 362)*

58. **(B)** Fibers (type Ib) that arise from Golgi tendon organs synapse with interneurons which inhibit those motor neurons that innervate the muscle to which the tendon organ is re-

lated. Type Ia and type II sensory fibers originate from muscle spindles and are involved in the myotatic reflex but not the inverse myotatic reflex. An increase in the tension applied to the muscle tendon in which the tendon organ is located is the appropriate stimulus for this reflex. Stimulation of cutaneous pain endings in the region of a Golgi tendon organ is not in itself sufficient to activate the reflex. *(Burt, pp 310–316)*

59. **(D)** The internal pyramidal layer (layer V) is composed of large numbers of pyramidal neurons whose axons make up the bulk of those projections that extend to numerous subcortical locations, and this includes the corticospinal system. The external pyramidal layer (layer III) is also largely composed of pyramidal neurons, but most of their axons distribute intracortically. The axons of cells in the internal and the external granular layers, as well as the molecular layer, also distribute within the cortical gray matter. *(Burt, pp 451–455)*

60. **(C)** The territory supplied by the anterior spinal artery in the caudal medial region of the medulla contains the medial lemniscus, pyramid, and exiting fibers of the hypoglossal nerve. Paramedian branches of the basilar artery supply a similar medial portion of the brain stem at pontine levels, whereas the posterior spinal artery distributes to the dorsal region of the caudal medulla and the spinal cord. The anterior inferior cerebellar artery supplies the dorsolateral pons while the anterior cerebral artery distributes to the medial surface of the cerebral hemisphere. *(Kandel, Schwartz, and Jessell, p 724)*

61. **(A)** A tumor impinging on the surface of the cerebellum would compress the layers of the cerebellar cortex in the following sequence: pia mater, molecular layer, Purkinje layer, and granular layer. *(Burt, p 354)*

62. **(A)** The hypoglossal nucleus contains motor neurons that innervate the musculature of the tongue, and such neurons arise from the basal plate. Sensory neurons such as those found in the solitary, cochlear, spinal trigemi-

nal, and vestibular nuclei arise from the alar plate. *(Burt, pp 15–16)*

63. **(D)** The posterior inferior cerebellar artery supplies the rostral, dorsolateral medulla. The posterior spinal and anterior spinal arteries supply dorsal and ventral portions, respectively, of the caudal medulla. The anterior inferior cerebellar and superior cerebellar arteries supply portions of the pons and mesencephalon. *(Kandel, Schwartz, and Jessell, pp 726–728)*

64. **(A)** Pain and temperature receptors on the left side of the face send afferent signals to the left spinal trigeminal nucleus. Somatosensory information from the left face passes through the right ventral posterior medial nucleus of the thalamus. The left principal sensory and mesencephalic trigeminal nuclei receive proprioceptive and tactile sensory input from the left face but not pain and temperature information. The left posterior limb of the internal capsule carries pain and temperature signals from the right side of the face. *(Burt, pp 209–212)*

65. **(E)** The characteristic feature of the lateral medullary syndrome is that the patient exhibits a loss of pain and temperature sensation that involves the ipsilateral face (the lesion side) and the contralateral side of the body. In addition, due to involvement of the restiform body, the patient may also experience ataxia and hyporeflexia ipsilateral to the lesion. This syndrome is typically the result of a vascular lesion involving the posterior inferior (not anterior inferior) cerebellar artery. *(Kandel, Schwartz, and Jessell, pp 726–728)*

66. **(D)** Patients with Weber's syndrome frequently exhibit involvement of the ipsilateral oculomotor nerve. Interruption of this nerve on the right would eliminate parasympathetic outflow on that side, resulting in a dilated right pupil that does not react to light. Movements of the left eye would not be affected. Involvement of corticobulbar fibers coursing in the right crus cerebri might cause the protruded tongue to deviate to the left and cause paralysis of the facial expression

musculature in the lower left portion of the face. *(Burt, p 334)*

67. **(E)** Parkinson's disease is characterized by a resting tremor that usually involves the fingers and hand. This syndrome results from degeneration of neurons in the substantia nigra pars compacta, cells that normally release dopamine at their synaptic terminals in the neostriatum. Patients with this syndrome also exhibit bradykinesia, a generalized slowing of movement. The syndrome is treated with a variety of compounds that represent an attempt to increase real, or effective, dopamine levels in the striatum, but the utility of most of these substances is decreased because they do not readily cross the blood–brain barrier. *(Burt, p 346; Kandel, Schwartz, and Jessell, pp 654–656)*

68. **(C)** Failure of the left eye to adduct on attempted lateral gaze to the right suggests a lesion involving the left medial longitudinal fasciculus. Interruption of the trochlear nerve would not interfere with conjugate horizontal eye movements. Injury to either abducens nerve would not prevent adduction of either eye, whereas damage to the right medial longitudinal fasciculus would prevent adduction of the right eye on attempted left lateral gaze. *(Kandel, Schwartz, and Jessell, pp 721–722)*

69. **(C)** A lesion of the left anterior spinal artery would involve the left hypoglossal nerve fibers in combination with the left medullary pyramid. Damage to the left hypoglossal nerve would result in deviation of the tongue to the left upon attempted protrusion, whereas damage to the left pyramid might produce spastic hemiplegia involving the right arm and leg. In addition, the tongue would exhibit other signs of lower motor neuron damage, while the hemiparetic right arm and leg would exhibit other signs of upper motor neuron disease. *(Kandel, Schwartz, and Jessell, p 724)*

70. **(B)** Since the left hemisphere is dominant for speech in more than 95% of individuals, large left frontal lobe lesions typically produce a motor or expressive aphasia known as Broca's aphasia. Broca's motor speech area in the left frontal operculum is near the primary motor cortex controlling the right upper extremity and consequently patients with Broca's aphasia frequently exhibit motor deficits involving the right hand. Wernicke's aphasia (sensory or receptive aphasia) and conduction aphasia commonly result from parietal lobe lesions and consequently are not usually seen in association with motor deficits in the hand. *(Burt, pp 468–470)*

71. **(C)** Lesions (usually vascular in nature) that involve the dorsolateral medulla produce the classic signs of the lateral medullary syndrome (Wallenberg's syndrome), which include a loss of pain and temperature sensibility over the *ipsilateral* face and the *contralateral* side of the body. Unilateral lesions that involve somatosensory pathways coursing through either the mesecephalon, diencephalon, or the posterior limb of the internal capsule will give rise to a loss of all or some somatosensation over the contralateral face and the contralateral body surface. Unilateral lesions (hemisections) that interrupt somatosensory pathways in the spinal cord cervical enlargement are likely to produce bilateral somatosensory deficits (mainly ipsilateral tactile and proprioceptive, contralateral pain and temperature) that do not involve the face. *(Kandel, Schwartz, and Jessell, pp 726–728)*

72. **(D)** The opening of potassium channels in the apical membrane of auditory hair cells allows potassium ions to flow into the cell and depolarize the cell. The apical surface of these cells is exposed to endolymph, which contains potassium ions at a much greater concentration than is found inside the cell. A potential difference of 160 mV (outside positive) exists across the apical membrane, and this results in a net movement of potassium ions into the cell when the stereocilia bundle is deflected and ion transduction channels are opened. The membrane potential of the hair cell moves in the positive direction (toward zero) and this results in depolarization of the cell. *(Burt, pp 260–261; Kandel, Schwartz, and Jessell, p 488)*

73. **(C)** The appearance of left-beating horizontal nystagmus with warm caloric stimulation of the left ear, coupled with the absence of nystagmus following warm caloric stimulation of the right ear, suggests that the right (and not the left) labyrinth or the right eighth cranial nerve has been damaged. The absence of right-beating nystagmus under these conditions does not indicate that the right lateral vestibulospinal tract has been affected while the presence of left-beating nystagmus suggests that receptors in the left ear have not been damaged. *(Burt, pp 273–280)*

74. **(B)** When a female individual is born, all germ cells in the ovaries are primary oocytes arrested in prophase of the first meiotic division. Later, after the onset of the menstrual cycle (menarche), normally only one oocyte will resume meiosis during each cycle. This occurs in the dominant follicle following the midcycle luteinizing hormone (LH) surge, a few hours preceding ovulation. At day 8 of the cycle, a dominant follicle has been selected, but its oocyte, although greatly enlarged, is still a primary oocyte. When this cell completes the first meiotic division at about day 14 of the cycle, the products will be a single secondary oocyte and the first polar body. *(Junqueira et al, pp 423–429)*

75. **(A)** Antimitotic drugs disrupt microtubule assembly in the formation of the mitotic spindle. In addition to killing rapidly dividing tumor cells, this can deplete intestinal epithelial cells, blood cells, and other populations of normal cells that have a high rate of replacement. Because neurons, cardiac muscle cells, and lens epithelial cells do not divide, they are not susceptible to spindle poisons. *(Alberts et al, pp 804, 1142–1143, 1154–1155)*

76. **(B)** Membranes of adjacent epithlial cells are fused along narrow anastomosing bands in the tight junction (zonula occludens). This is the apical-most part of the junctional complex typical of epithelia lining tubular and hollow organs. The zonula adherens, macula adherens (desmosome), and hemidesmosome are specializations for adhesion, and the gap junction (nexus) consists of direct channels (connexons) between cells, which are thus electrically and chemically coupled. The terminal bar is not a type of junction, but rather a manifestation of the junctional complex seen with the light microscope. *(Junqueira et al, pp 62–65)*

77. **(D)** Although enteroendocrine (DNES) cells are a heterogeneous population, a common feature of these cells is the orientation of secretory granules toward the base of the cell rather than its apex. All the other cell types listed are also components of the intestinal mucosal epithelium. Paneth cells are concentrated deep in intestinal crypts, but their granules are large and localized apically. Likewise, goblet cells have large, apical granules, and they are more abundant in the epithelium of villi. M cells overlie concentrations of lymphoid tissue (eg, nodules of Peyer's patches) and participate in antigen processing. Enterocytes have no secretory granules. *(Junqueira et al, pp 290–291)*

78. **(A)** With the exception of the ability to undergo interstitial growth, all of the listed properties are shared by bone and cartilage. Interstitial growth can occur in cartilage development due to the distensibility of the tissue. *(Junqueira et al, pp 124, 128, 132)*

79. **(C)** Endothelial cells of the capillaries that form the renal glomerulus have fenestrations which, incidentally, are not bridged by diaphragms. Continuous capillaries are typical of central nervous system tissue, skeletal muscle, and most connective tissue. The epidermis is not penetrated by blood vessels. The predominant capillary in the red pulp of the spleen is the sinusoidal capillary which allows free passage of formed elements between the pulp cord tissue and the vascular compartment. *(Junqueira et al, pp 205–206)*

80. **(E)** Respiratory epithelium is a ciliated pseudostratified columnar epithelium with an unusually thick basement membrane, well-developed junctional complexes, and an abundance of mucous goblet cells. *(Junqueira et al, pp 326–330)*

81. **(E)** All the listed cell types are components of the respiratory system. Type II pneumocytes are the source of pulmonary surfactant. Alveolar dust cells are macrophages. Endothelial cells and type I pneumocytes are components of the blood–air barrier. Small granule cells, which are members of the diffuse neuroendocrine system, function in paracrine and endocrine signaling. (*Junqueira et al, pp 336–341*)

82. **(C)** The laboratory values table can be used to calculate the upper limit of the normal range of absolute counts/mm$^3$ for each leukocyte (maximum normal total leukocyte count times the maximum normal percentage for the cell type). The patient's differential percentages can each be multiplied by 24,000/mm$^3$ to obtain total counts per mm$^3$ for each leukocyte type. The following table shows the results of these calculations. (*Junqueira et al, p 222*)

| Leukocyte | Normal upper limit (per mm³) | Patient's count (per mm³) |
|---|---|---|
| Segmented neutrophils | 6,820 | 17,040 |
| Band form neutrophils | 550 | 3,840 |
| Eosinophils | 330 | 960 |
| Basophils | 82 | 48 |
| Lymphocytes | 3,630 | 720 |
| Monocytes | 770 | 1,440 |

83. **(B)** Although numbers of eosinophils and monocytes are somewhat elevated, the most prominent change in circulating leukocyte numbers is a greatly elevated neutrophil count, with a "shift to the left" (increased numbers of immature forms). This is indicative of a bacterial infection. (*Junqueira et al, pp 241–244*)

84. **(B)** Action potentials (APs) are initiated at the myoneural junction on the surface of a muscle fiber. T tubules are narrow invaginations of the sarcolemma that channel the APs to the vicinity of the sarcoplasmic reticulum organized around myofibrils. The sarcoplasmic reticulum does not conduct APs, rather it responds to APs by releasing calcium. The Z line is a component of the sarcomere that serves as an anchor for actin filaments. Muscle spindles are complex sensory structures that monitor muscle length and changes in muscle length. The endomysium is the thin connective tissue layer surrounding each muscle fiber. (*Junqueira et al, pp 182–184*)

85. **(C)** The space of Disse separates hepatocytes from the endothelial cells that form the hepatic sinusoids, thus it is bordered partly by endothelium on one side and by microvilli of the hepatocytes on the other side. The endothelium of the sinusoids allows free passage of plasma, but not cells, into the space of Disse. The initial channel for flow of bile is the bile canaliculus formed by junctions between adjacent hepatocytes. The portal triad comprises an arteriolar branch of the hepatic artery, a venule conducting blood from the hepatic portal vein, and a bile duct. These are accompanied by one or more lymphatic vessels. (*Junqueira et al, pp 308–313*)

86. **(E)** The macula densa is a modified segment of the distal tubule at its apposition to the afferent arteriole in the vascular pole of the renal corpuscle. The name arises from the close spacing of nuclei of the epithelial cells forming this part of the distal tubule. These cells are thought to sense the chloride content in the passing filtrate and generate signals that regulate caliber of the afferent arteriole. Mesangial cells are incompletely understood cells found in the glomerulus and in the juxtaglomerular apparatus Bowman's capsule encompasses the capillaries of the glomerulus in two layers of epithelium. The inner, closely applied, visceral layer of podocytes is continuous at the vascular pole with the outer, parietal layer of squamous cells. Between the two layers is the urinary space, which is continuous with the lumen of the proximal convoluted tubule. (*Junqueira et al, pp 359, 361, 366*)

87. **(C)** Development of all three types of granulocytes follows a similar sequence of stages: (1) buildup of protein synthesis machinery—myeloblast and promyelocyte, (2) generation of primary granules—promyelocyte, (3) generation of specific granules and condensation of the nucleus—myelocyte, and (4) further condensation and reshaping of the nucleus—metamyelocyte. The granulocyte colony-

forming unit is an undifferentiated progenitor cell of the granulocyte line. *(Junqueira et al, pp 236, 241)*

88. **(E)** The term acidophilic describes the staining behavior of cellular components (eg, proteins with a high content of basic amino acids) that attract acid dyes such as eosin. Concentrations of mitochondria, such as occur in parietal cells, confer cytoplasmic acidophilia. Although parietal cells secrete hydrochloric acid, they do not store it. Chief cells, not parietal cells, synthesize pepsinogen and store it in secretory granules. Parietal cells are the source of intrinsic factor, but they do not contain secretory granules. Rough endoplasmic reticulum, which occurs in only a small degree in parietal cells, is basophilic due to its high RNA content. *(Junqueira et al, pp 2–3, 281–287)*

89. **(A)** The syncytiotrophoblast, a product of division and fusion of cells in the underlying trophoblast, forms the surface layer of the chorionic villi and is bathed by maternal blood flowing through the intervillus space. Fetal capillaries course through the core of connective tissue in villi and thus have no contact with maternal blood when placental structure is intact. *(Junqueira et al, p 436)*

90. **(D)** The pars nervosa is composed largely of axonal processes and terminals of neurons. These have their cell bodies in the hypothalamus (supraoptic and paraventricular nuclei), so their nuclei are not seen in the neurohypophysis. Other constituents are a rich vascular bed of fenestrated capillaries and a large number of glial cells called pituicytes. Thus, most of the cell nuclei seen in the pars nervosa belong to pituicytes. Chromophobes and basophils reside in the adenohypophysis, and Schwann cells are peripheral nerve constituents. *(Junqueira et al, pp 383–384)*

91. **(D)** Vasopressin is synthesized by neurons that have their cell bodies in the supraoptic nucleus of the hypothalamus and project their axons to the pars nervosa where the hormone is secreted. Pituicytes are not hormone-secreting cells, but are glial cells located in the pars nervosa. Basophils of the adenohypophysis secrete corticotropin, thyrotropin, or gonadotropic hormones. Acidophils secrete either growth hormone or prolactin. *(Junqueira et al, pp 282, 284)*

92. **(B)** The clitoris is the homologue of the penis, but it consists of only two erectile bodies (the corpora cavernosa clitoridis), and it is not traversed by the urethra. The male urethra has a prostatic part, membranous portion, and a spongy part. It passes through the prostate, urogenital diaphragm, and the corpus spongiosum of the penis. *(Hollinshead, pp 769, 804)*

93. **(E)** The musculocutaneous nerve passes through the coracobrachialis and continues distally between the biceps brachii and brachialis muscles. It supplies all three muscles. Injury to the nerve will affect flexion at the shoulder (coracobrachialis and biceps brachii), flexion at the elbow (brachialis and biceps brachii), and supination of the forearm (biceps brachii). At the elbow it continues as the lateral cutaneous nerve of the forearm and has no distribution to the hand. *(Hall–Craggs, pp 103, 107)*

94. **(C)** The transpyloric plane is a hypothetic horizontal plane passing through the lower part of the body of the first lumbar vertebra. The pancreas, kidneys, duodenum, and spleen all lie at this level. The celiac trunk, however, arises from the abdominal aorta over the body of the twelfth thoracic vertebra. *(Hall–Craggs, pp 261, 279–281)*

95. **(A)** The gastroduodenal and the posterior superior pancreaticoduodenal arteries descend and the portal vein ascends posterior to the first part of the duodenum. The common bile duct descends behind the first part of the duodenum to join the pancreatic duct before terminating in the second part of the duodenum. The splenic artery is not related to the duodenum as it arises in the bed of the stomach and passes to the left along the superior border of the body and tail of the pancreas. *(Hall–Craggs, pp 259–262, 276)*

96. **(C)** Tumescence of erectile tissue in both sexes is under the influence of parasympathetic outflow in the nervi erigentes (pelvic splanchnic nerves). Nervi erigentes join the inferior hypogastric plexus. Preganglionic parasympathetic fibers synapse on terminal ganglia in this plexus. Parasympathetic postganglionic fibers pass through vesicle and prostatic plexuses (extensions of the inferior hypogastric plexus) and follow the urethra as cavernous nerves to supply the erectile tissue of the penis. The sacral plexus is a somatic plexus and contains no parasympathetic fibers. *(Hollinshead, pp 749, 755)*

97. **(C)** The vagina is related anteriorly to the urethra and the fundus of the bladder and posteriorly to the rectum. Superiorly, the posterior vaginal fornix is related to the peritoneum of the rectouterine pouch (of Douglas). The vesicouterine pouch does not completely separate the bladder and uterus and, thus, is not related to the anterior vaginal wall. *(Hall–Craggs, pp 320–323)*

98. **(E)** The broad ligament encloses the uterine tube, the ovarian ligament, part of the round ligament, the uterine artery and venous plexus, the uterovaginal plexus of nerves, and part of the ureter. The greater vestibular glands are located in the pudendum. *(Woodburne and Burckel, pp 534, 551)*

99. **(A)** The greater occipital nerve is a dorsal ramus of the second cervical nerve. The ventral rami of the first four cervical nerves form the cervical plexus. The cutaneous branches of the plexus are the lesser occipital, great auricular, transverse cervical, and supraclavicular nerves. *(Woodburne and Burckel, pp 189–191)*

100. **(E)** All of the infrahyoid muscles, sternohyoid, omohyoid, sternothyroid, and thyrohyoid muscles are innervated by branches of the cervical plexus. The mylohyoid is innervated by the mandibular division of the trigeminal nerve. *(Woodburne and Burckel, pp 220, 268)*

101. **(B)** The functions of the vagus nerve include special visceral efferent, general visceral efferent, general visceral afferent, special visceral afferent, and general somatic afferent but not general somatic efferent. *(Woodburne and Burckel, p 205)*

102. **(E)** The diaphragm is the principal muscle of inspiration. Muscles which elevate the clavicle, the sternum, or the ribs are accessory muscles of inspiration. The pectoralis major flexes and abducts the arm. *(Woodburne and Burckel, pp 226, 318, 364–365, 499)*

103. **(A)** The long slender external branch of the superior laryngeal nerve descends along the oblique line of the thyroid cartilage to the cricothyroid muscle, which it supplies. All of the other intrinsic muscles of the larynx are innervated by the inferior laryngeal nerve. *(Woodburne and Burckel, p 234)*

104. **(D)** The nerve to the stylopharyngeus muscle arises from the glossopharyngeal nerve. Vagal nerve fibers in the pharyngeal plexus innervate the muscles of the pharynx with the exception of the stylopharyngeus. The inferior pharyngeal constrictor muscle receives an additional supply from the external branch of the superior laryngeal nerve. *(Woodburne and Burckel, p 238)*

105. **(B)** The cutaneous branches of the ophthalmic division of the trigeminal nerve include the supraorbital, supratrochlear, lacrimal, infratrochlear, and external nasal branches. The cutaneous branches of the maxillary division of the trigeminal nerve includes the infraorbital, inferior palpebral, external nasal, zygomaticofacial, and the zygomaticotemporal. *(Woodburne and Burckel, pp 243–244)*

106. **(C)** The buccinator is a muscle of facial expression and is therefore innervated by the facial nerve. The lateral pterygoid, masseter, anterior belly of the digastric, and temporalis are all muscles of mastication and are therefore innervated by the mandibular division of the trigeminal nerve. *(Woodburne and Burckel, pp 253, 265)*

107. **(C)** The facial nerve provides the parasympathetic innervation of the submandibu-

lar, sublingual, lacrimal, nasal, and palatine glands. The glossopharyngeal nerve provides parasympathetic innervation for the parotid gland. *(Woodburne and Burckel, pp 240, 252)*

108. **(E)** The inferior or ventral temporal cortex does not contribute fibers to the corticospinal tract. Each of the other four areas (A through D) does give rise to some corticospinal axons. The largest number arises from the primary motor area followed by the premotor, supplementary motor, and primary somatosensory regions. *(Burt, p 329)*

109. **(E)** The tremor of Parkinson's disease is described as a resting tremor and is most obvious when the affected hand (body part) is at rest. Other deficits associated with Parkinson's disease are due to the loss of dopamine influence over both the direct and the indirect pathways. Normally, activation of the indirect pathway leads to a reduction in the output of thalamocortical neurons, whereas activation of the direct pathway leads to an increase in motor activity produced by excitatory thalamocortical projections. *(Kandel, Schwartz, and Jessell, pp 610–622)*

110. **(D)** The so-called lower motor neurons that control autonomic function are said to be located in certain nuclei of the brain stem reticular formation. The latter nuclei are influenced via projections from the amygdaloid complex and from the hypothalamus, both of which contain the upper motor neurons controlling autonomic function. The hypothalamus regulates autonomic function on a moment-to-moment (reflexive) basis, whereas the amygdaloid complex provides a more long-term regulation that involves learning and past experience. *(Burt, pp 496–497)*

111. **(A)** Basal ganglia dysfunction, and not cerebellar pathology, produces a resting-type tremor. Each of the other symptoms (B through E) can be seen in patients with cerebellar lesions. Postural instability, as manifested by a wide-based stance or staggering gate, is a common feature of cerebellar disease. Hypometria is seen when, for example, a reaching movement falls short of its target.

A kinetic or intention tremor appears when the patient attempts a voluntary movement. The inability to perform rapid alternating movements is termed dysdiadochokinesia. *(Burt, pp 364–365)*

112. **(D)** Interruption of the trochlear nerve causes the affected eye to be directed up and out due to the pull of intact muscles innervated by the third and sixth cranial nerves. If the third cranial nerve is interrupted, the affected eye looks down and out due to the pull of muscles innervated by the fourth and sixth cranial nerves. In addition, third nerve involvement causes the eyelid to droop (ptosis) due to denervation of the levator palpebrae superioris, and the loss of parasympathetic fibers in the third nerve results in the disappearance of pupillary light reflexes and lens accommodation. *(Burt, pp 405–412)*

113. **(C)** The somatotopic representation of the body surface in the primary somatosensory cortex (postcentral gyrus) is not arranged in a "tail-to-tongue" sequence from ventrolateral to dorsomedial. The cytoarchitectural subdivisions of SI are numbered anterior to posterior as 3a, 3b, 1, and 2, and each subdivision contains a complete representation of the body surface. Areas 3a and 2 receive input from muscle spindle afferents and Golgi tendon organs, whereas areas 3b and 1 receive mostly cutaneous inputs. *(Burt, pp 215–217)*

114. **(D)** There are no actin bridges that join the pre- and postsynaptic membranes. Voltage-gated calcium channels open and allow $Ca^{++}$ ions to enter the terminal, and synaptic vesicles to move to the presynaptic membrane where they attach to docking proteins. The synaptic vesicles fuse with the presynaptic membrane, and a quantum of neurotransmitter is released from each vesicle into the synaptic cleft. The transmitter molecules then bind to receptors on the postsynaptic membrane. *(Kandel, Schwartz, and Jessell, pp 203–210)*

115. **(B)** Each intrafusal muscle fiber is innervated only by one gamma motor neuron. However, the axon of this motor neuron bifurcates such that the contractile elements located at either

end of the intrafusal fiber each receive their own branch of the motor axon. The gamma motor neuron axons synapse directly with the intrafusal muscle fibers, whereas type Ia sensory fibers can synapse directly with alpha motor neurons. Type Ib sensory fibers arise from Golgi tendon organs and when such fibers are activated, the muscles to which they are linked are inhibited via a central interneuron. At least two types of intrafusal muscle fibers are typically present in each spindle. *(Burt, pp 308–310)*

116. **(D)** Muscle degeneration and atrophy are not characteristic symptoms of corticospinal tract damage. However, in some instances, with the passage of time, disuse atrophy might appear in such patients. Signs and symptoms of corticospinal tract injury that are nearly always apparent to some degree include spastic paralysis, hypertonia, loss of deep tendon reflexes, and the presence of certain pathological reflexes such as the abdominal and cremasteric reflexes and the Babinski sign. *(Burt, pp 333–334; Brodal, pp 242–245)*

117. **(B)** Muscles that exhibit spastic paralysis are hypertonic, not hypotonic. The muscles typically affected by spasticity are physiological extensors. They are also described as antigravity muscles since their normal action is to oppose the force of gravity and such muscles typically exhibit increased (more brisk) deep tendon reflexes. Spasticity is defined as an increase in the resistance to passive movement, and it is said to be velocity dependent. For example, the faster the examiner tries to move an affected extremity, the greater will be the resistance. This increased resistance is associated with the "clasp-knife" phenomenon, which simply means that when passive movement of the affected limb reaches a certain point, the resistance suddenly collapses. *(Kandel, Schwartz, and Jessell, pp 602–606)*

118. **(E)** Basal ganglia disease does not typically produce spastic paralysis. Signs and symptoms that are characteristic of basal ganglia disorders include cog-wheel rigidity, resting tremor, choreiform movements, athetosis, and other involuntary movements or postures. *(Brodal, pp 257–260)*

119. **(A)** The ventral lateral nucleus of the thalamus is primarily involved with motor function and does not contribute to descending pathways that influence pain transmission. Neurons in the periaqueductal gray project to the nucleus raphe magnus, the cells of which give rise to raphespinal fibers. These axons utilize serotonin as a neurotransmitter, which they release at their terminals on enkephalinergic interneurons in the substantia gelatinosa of the dorsal horn. The latter neurons then form synapses directly with the terminals of incoming primary afferent pain fibers from the dorsal roots. *(Burt, pp 220–221)*

120. **(E)** The distribution and number of taste receptors on the tongue is not lateralized with respect to cerebral dominance. They are arranged in a rostro-caudal pattern such that the most anterior respond best to sweet and salty stimuli, whereas sour and bitter sensations are represented posteriorly. Taste receptors are stimulated when a solid or fluid substance diffuses through its apical pore and depolarizes the cell. Receptors respond best to one stimulus quality but can respond less vigorously to other substances. Taste receptors generally have a life span of 7 to 10 days. *(Burt, pp 283–286)*

121. **(B)** Bone marrow provides the environment for development of precursor cells into erythrocytes, platelets, granulocytes, monocytes, and B lymphocytes. Although it is likely that T lymphocyte progenitor cells also arise in bone marrow, differentiation and programing of new T lymphocytes occurs in the thymus. *(Junqueira et al, pp 234, 244)*

122. **(C)** The parotid gland is the only major salivary gland containing almost exclusively serous secretory cells. The submandibular and sublingual glands are mixed, with differing proportions of serous and mucous cells. Esophageal and intestinal glands are small mucus-secreting glands. *(Junqueira et al, pp 281, 290–291, 301–303)*

123. **(C)** Lymphoid follicles are sites of B-lympho-cyte proliferation in response to antigen stimulation. These occur in lymph nodes, Peyer's patches, tonsils, and the white pulp of the spleen. The thymus provides for development of new T lymphocytes in an environment shielded from foreign antigens. *(Junqueira et al, pp 251–256, 264–267)*

124. **(D)** Cells that secrete steroid hormones have several stereotypical ultrastructural features related to their function. Hormone synthesis is a cooperative activity of the sER and mitochondria with specializations that include tubular rather than shelf-like cristae. Lipid precursor molecules are stored in lipid droplets, but there is no storage of the end product in secretory granules. *(Junqueira et al, pp 84–86).*

125. **(A)** The superior cervical ganglion is sympathetic ganglion. Accordingly, it receives axons from preganglionic neurons that have their cell bodies (somas) in the upper thoracic spinal cord. The preganglionic nerve fibers synapse on dendrites and somas of visceral motor neurons in the ganglion. These postganglionic neurons project unmyelinated axons to effector organs in the head. Schwann cells support both the incoming and outgoing axons of the ganglion. Pseudounipolar neurons are found in sensory ganglia, not autonomic visceral motor ganglia. *(Junqueira et al, pp 153–155, 171–175)*

126. **(A)** Both thin (hairy) and thick (glabrous) skin have sweat glands and dermal papillae. The epidermis of thick skin is generally thicker than that of thin skin, but both have basal, spinous, granular, and corneum layers in the epidermis. Sebaceous glands are associated with hair follicles and accordingly are restricted to thin skin. *(Junqueira et al, pp 346–348, 351)*

127. **(A)** The pyramidal neuron is the predominant type of neuron found in layers III and V of the cerebral cortex. *(Burt, p 450)*

128. **(C)** The Renshaw cell is an inhibitory interneuron found in the spinal cord gray matter. *(Burt, p 90)*

129. **(E)** Hair cells are important sensory transducing elements of the cochlea and vestibular sensory organs. *(Burt, p 258)*

130. **(F)** Mitral cells are projection type neurons found in the olfactory bulb. *(Burt, p 293)*

131. **(A)** Pyramidal neurons form the principal efferent or projection type neuron in the hippocampus. *(Burt, p 488)*

132. **(B)** Some axons that originate from the internal segment of the globus pallidus (pars interna or medial segment) pass through the ansa lenticularis, while others can enter the fasciculus lenticularis. *(Burt, p 344)*

133. **(C)** The spinal trigeminal tract conveys primary sensory afferent fibers that carry pain sensation from the teeth. The lateral spinothalamic tract conveys pain sensation from all spinal levels but not from structures innervated by cranial nerves. *(Burt, pp 207–212)*

134. **(E)** The condition in which the anterior neuropore fails to close is called anencephaly. Meningomyelocele refers to a failure of the spinal canal to fuse, which results in the protrusion or displacement of a portion of the spinal cord and its associated meningeal coverings. *(Burt, p 26)*

135. **(D)** The dorsal spinocerebellar tract is formed by axons that arise from neurons in the nucleus dorsalis of Clarke. *(Burt, p 207)*

136. **(D)** Residual bodies are secondary lysosomes containing material that cannot be broken down by lysosomal acid hydrolases. These are recognized in electron micrographs as membrane-bound vesicles containing heterogeneous electron dense material. In light microscopy, residual bodies are seen as yellowish-brown (lipofuscin) deposits. *(Junqueira et al, pp 36, 46)*

137. **(C)** The nucleolus is a ribosome factory organized around a segment of chromatin containing repetitive tandem copies of DNA encoding ribosomal RNA. Five of the human chromosomes have nucleolus organizer segments, so a diploid somatic cell could have theoretically as many as ten nucleoli. Since nucleoli have a tendency to fuse with each other, usually only one or a few are seen in a given nucleus. The main event in the nucleolus is transcription to produce a 45S RNA segment that will be broken into the RNA fragments that form part of the large and small ribosomal subunits. These RNA pieces are complexed with the many different proteins that contribute to ribosome structure. This assembly of ribonucleoprotein particles occurs in the nucleolus, but synthesis of ribosomal proteins takes place in the cytoplasm where all protein synthesis occurs. *(Alberts et al, pp 377–382)*

138. **(E)** Mitochondria are recognizable by their double membrane and their cristae consisting of distinctive folds or tubules of the inner membrane. These organelles house the enzymes of the citric acid cycle and the electron transport system that generates ATP from ADP and inorganic phosphate. *(Junqueira et al, pp 27–29).*

139. **(G)** Steroid hormone-secreting cells, such as the adrenal cortex cell illustrated here, typically contain lipid droplets that are storage depots of lipid precursors such as cholesterol. These are not secretory granules, and they do not serve to store finished steroid hormones. In electron micrographs, lipid droplets appear as spherical inclusions without a limiting membrane. *(Junqueira et al, pp 45, 84–86, 390)*

140. **(B)** Smooth endoplasmic reticulum (sER) is particularly well developed in steroid hormone-secreting cells. The series of reactions in synthesis of steroid hormones involves cooperation between mitochondria and sER. The obvious distinction between sER and rER is the absence of ribosomes attached to the membrane of the sER. Also, the sER appears as an array of anastomosing tubules

rather than the stacks of flattened cisternae characteristic of rER. *(Junqueira et al, pp 84–85)*

141. **(C)** The Golgi complex is the major site of post-translational modification (eg, glycosylation) and packaging of proteins with different destinations such as the plasmalemma or lysosomes. It appears in electron micrographs as a stack of flattened membrane delimited cisternae. *(Junqueira et al, pp 32–33, 35)*

142. **(F)** The rough endoplasmic reticulum is recognizable as flattened membranous cisternae studded with ribosomes on the cytoplasmic face. Duing translation, the elongating polypeptide is extruded into the cisternal compartment of the rER. *(Junqueira et al, pp 31–32)*

143. **(D)** Lysozyme is an enzyme found in Paneth cells of the small intestine as well as in neutrophils. It hydrolyses glycosides of the cell wall of some gram-positive bacteria, and may be involved in regulation of the intestinal flora. *(Junqueira et al, p 291)*

144. **(F)** Pepsinogen is a proenzyme secreted by chief cells of gastric fundic glands. *(Junqueira et al, p 287)*

145. **(C)** Cholecystokinin is a hormone that promotes gallbladder contraction and enzyme secretion by the pancreas. It is secreted by one type of enteroendocrine cell (type I) in the duodenal mucosa, mainly in response to fat content in the chyme. *(Junqueira et al, pp 293, 305–306, 321)*

146. **(G)** The source of intrinsic factor in humans is parietal cells of gastric glands. Intrinsic factor is required for absorption of vitamin $B_{12}$. *(Junqueira et al, p 285)*

147. **(C)** Prior to the initiation of meiosis, primary spermatocytes in interphases undergo a round of DNA replication. No DNA synthesis occurs during the remaining stages of spermatogenesis. *(Junqueira et al, p 409)*

148. **(D)** The first meiotic division is protracted in both sexes. After completing DNA synthesis, primary spermatocytes enter prophase of the

first meiotic division, but spend most of three weeks in the pachytene stage of prophase before rapidly completing the remaining steps of the first meiotic division to produce secondary spermatocytes. At the time a female is born, all gametes are primary oocytes arrested in prophase of meiosis I. Even the small number of oocytes that resume meiosis will remain arrested for approximately 12 to 50 years before doing so. *(Junqueira et al, pp 409, 423, 429)*

149. **(E)** Secondary spermatocytes and oocytes contain 23 (1N) chromosomes, but the DNA of each chromosome was duplicated before meiosis began, so DNA content is 2n. The duplicated chromatids of each chromosome are separated by the second meiotic division so that the resulting cells have a haploid content of both DNA and chromosomes. *(Junqueira et al, pp 409)*

150. **(E)** A few hours prior to ovulation, the primary oocyte in the mature follicle completes the first meiotic division to produce a primary polar body and a secondary oocyte. The secondary oocyte (ovum) begins the second meiotic division but becomes arrested in metaphase. The division is completed only if fertilization occurs. *(Junqueira et al, p 429)*

## REFERENCES

Alberts B, Bray D, Lewis J, Raff M, Roberts K, Watson JD. *Molecular Biology of the Cell*. 3rd ed. New York: Garland; 1994

Brodal P. *The Central Nervous System, Structure and Function*. New York: Oxford University Press; 1992

Burt AM. *Textbook of Neuroanatomy*. Philadelphia: WB Saunders Co; 1993

Hall–Craggs ECB. *Anatomy as a Basis for Clinical Medicine*. 3rd ed. Baltimore: Williams & Wilkins; 1995

Hollinshead W. *Textbook of Anatomy*. 4th ed. Philadelphia: Harper & Row; 1985

Junqueira LC, Carneiro J, Kelly RO. *Basic Histology*. 8th ed. Norwalk, CT: Appleton & Lange; 1995

Kandel ER, Schwartz JH, Jessell TM. Principles of Neural Science. 3rd ed. Norwalk, CT: Appleton & Lange; 1991

Sadler TW. *Langman's Medical Embryology*. 7th ed. Baltimore: Williams & Wilkins; 1995

Woodburne RT, Burckel WE. *Essentials of Human Anatomy*. 9th ed. New York: Oxford University Press; 1994

# Subspecialty List—Anatomy

1. Central and peripheral nervous systems
2. Musculoskeletal system
3. Central and peripheral nervous systems
4. Cardiovascular system
5. Musculoskeletal system
6. Central and peripheral nervous systems
7. Central and peripheral nervous systems
8. Central and peripheral nervous systems
9. Cardiovascular system
10. Cardiovascular system
11. Cardiovascular system
12. Central and peripheral nervous systems
13. Gastrointestinal system
14. Central and peripheral nervous systems
15. Hematopoietic and lymphoreticular systems
16. Central and peripheral nervous systems
17. Musculoskeletal system
18. Gastrointestinal system
19. General principles—Human development and genetics
20. Cardiovascular system
21. Respiratory system
22. Reproductive system
23. Musculoskeletal system
24. Cardiovascular system
25. Musculoskeletal system
26. Cardiovascular system
27. Endocrine system
28. Cardiovascular system
29. Respiratory system
30. Central and peripheral nervous systems
31. Central and peripheral nervous systems
32. Cardiovascular system
33. Musculoskeletal system
34. Musculoskeletal system
35. Central and peripheral nervous systems
36. Central and peripheral nervous systems
37. Musculoskeletal system
38. Musculoskeletal system
39. Musculoskeletal system
40. Central and peripheral nervous systems
41. Central and peripheral nervous systems
42. Central and peripheral nervous systems
43. Musculoskeletal system
44. Cardiovascular system
45. Cardiovascular system
46. Cardiovascular system
47. Cardiovascular system
48. Cardiovascular system
49. General principles— Human development and genetics
50. Reproductive system
51. Reproductive system
52. Gastrointestinal system
53. Cardiovascular system
54. Central and peripheral nervous systems
55. Central and peripheral nervous systems
56. Central and peripheral nervous systems
57. Central and peripheral nervous systems
58. Central and peripheral nervous systems
59. Central and peripheral nervous systems
60. Central and peripheral nervous systems
61. Central and peripheral nervous systems
62. Central and peripheral nervous systems
63. Central and peripheral nervous systems
64. Central and peripheral nervous systems
65. Central and peripheral nervous systems
66. Central and peripheral nervous systems
67. Central and peripheral nervous systems
68. Central and peripheral nervous systems

69. Central and peripheral nervous systems
70. Central and peripheral nervous systems
71. Central and peripheral nervous systems
72. Central and peripheral nervous systems
73. Central and peripheral nervous systems
74. Reproductive system
75. General principles—Biology of cells
76. General principles—Biology of tissues and their responses to disease
77. Gastrointestinal system
78. Musculoskeletal system
79. Cardiovascular system
80. Respiratory system
81. Respiratory system
82. Hematopoietic and lymphoreticular systems
83. Hematopoietic and lymphoreticular systems
84. General principles—Biology of cells
85. Gastrointestinal system
86. Renal/urinary system
87. Hematopoietic and lymphoreticular systems
88. Gastrointestinal system
89. Reproductive system
90. Endocrine system
91. Endocrine system
92. Reproductive system
93. Musculoskeletal system
94. Gastrointestinal system
95. Gastrointestinal system
96. Central and peripheral nervous systems
97. Reproductive system
98. Reproductive system
99. Central and peripheral nervous systems

100. Central and peripheral nervous systems
101. Central and peripheral nervous systems
102. Respiratory system
103. Respiratory system
104. Central and peripheral nervous systems
105. Central and peripheral nervous systems
106. Central and peripheral nervous systems
107. Central and peripheral nervous systems
108. Central and peripheral nervous systems
109. Central and peripheral nervous systems
110. Central and peripheral nervous systems
111. Central and peripheral nervous systems
112. Central and peripheral nervous systems
113. Central and peripheral nervous systems
114. Central and peripheral nervous systems
115. Central and peripheral nervous systems
116. Central and peripheral nervous systems
117. Central and peripheral nervous systems
118. Central and peripheral nervous systems
119. Central and peripheral nervous systems
120. Central and peripheral nervous systems
121. Hematopoietic and lymphoreticular systems
122. Gastrointestinal system
123. Hematopoietic and lymphoreticular systems

124. Endocrine system
125. Central and peripheral nervous systems
126. Skin and related connective tissue
127. Central and peripheral nervous systems
128. Central and peripheral nervous systems
129. Central and peripheral nervous systems
130. Central and peripheral nervous systems
131. Central and peripheral nervous systems
132. Central and peripheral nervous systems
133. Central and peripheral nervous systems
134. Central and peripheral nervous systems
135. Central and peripheral nervous systems
136. General principles—Biology of cells
137. General principles—Biology of cells
138. General principles—Biology of cells
139. General principles—Biology of cells
140. General principles—Biology of cells
141. General principles—Biology of cells
142. General principles—Biology of cells
143. Gastrointestinal system
144. Gastrointestinal system
145. Gastrointestinal system
146. Gastrointestinal system
147. Reproductive system
148. Reproductive system
149. Reproductive system
150. Reproductive system

# CHAPTER 2

# Physiology
## Questions

*Andreas Carl, MD, PhD*

**DIRECTIONS (Questions 151 through 228): Each of the numbered items or incomplete statements in this section is followed by answers or by completions of the statement. Select the ONE lettered answer or completion that is BEST in each case.**

151. During normal pregnancy, the following physiological changes take place EXCEPT

    (A) decrease in gastrointestinal muscle tone and motility
    (B) decrease in hematocrit
    (C) increase in blood volume
    (D) increase in respiratory tidal volume
    (E) increase in pulmonary functional residual capacity

152. Tremor that is caused by a cerebellar lesion is most readily differentiated from that caused by loss of the dopaminergic nigrostriatal tracts in that

    (A) it is present at rest
    (B) it is decreased during activity
    (C) it only occurs during voluntary movements
    (D) its frequency is very regular
    (E) its amplitude remains constant during voluntary movements

153. Although vasopressin (ADH) significantly contributes to fluid and electrolyte balance, it does not appear to closely regulate blood volume in the long run. Blood volume is maintained at near normal levels in diabetes insipidus (absence of ADH) because

    (A) the peripheral renin–angiotensin system is stimulated
    (B) water intake is appropriately adjusted
    (C) plasma oncotic pressure increases
    (D) sympathetic reflexes decrease glomerular filtration
    (E) renal blood flow decreases

154. All of the following statements about micturition are correct EXCEPT

    (A) patients with damage to the sacral spinal cord lose their micturition reflex (atonic bladder)
    (B) patients with damage to the lumbar spinal cord have an intact micturition reflex but lose almost all voluntary control over micturition (automatic bladder)
    (C) sympathetic fibers originating in L1 and L2 provide continuous tone to the external sphincter, thereby preventing micturition unless "desired"
    (D) higher centers in the brain stem keep the micturition reflex inhibited except when micturition is "desired"
    (E) urination will occur if inhibition of the external sphincter through spinal reflex pathways is stronger than the voluntary constrictor signals to the external sphincter from the brain

## Questions 155 and 156

Figure 2.1 illustrates histological changes in the endometrium during the menstrual cycle.

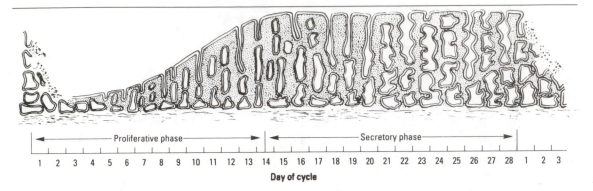

**Figure 2.1.** (*Reprinted with permission from Ganong, WF.* Review of Medical Physiology. 17th ed. *Appleton & Lange, 1995.*)

155. Progesterone levels are highest around

   (A) day 7
   (B) day 12
   (C) day 14
   (D) day 21
   (E) day 28

156. Estrogen levels are highest at around

   (A) day 7
   (B) day 12
   (C) day 14
   (D) day 21
   (E) day 28

157. All of the following statements are correct EXCEPT

   (A) general increase in sympathetic tone during emotional excitement results in pupil dilation
   (B) increase in sympathetic activity in fibers innervating the inner eye muscles during darkness results in pupil dilation
   (C) decrease in parasympathetic activity in fibers innervating the inner eye muscles during darkness results in pupil dilation

   (D) phentolamine causes pupil dilation
   (E) atropine causes pupil dilation

158. The introduction of cold water into one ear may cause giddiness and nausea. The primary cause of this effect of temperature is

   (A) temporary immobilization of otoliths
   (B) decreased movement of ampullar cristae
   (C) increased discharge rate in vestibular afferents
   (D) decreased discharge rate in vestibular afferents
   (E) convection currents in endolymph

159. Which of the following statements about iron metabolism is correct?

   (A) most iron in the body is stored as hemosiderin
   (B) hemosiderin is a product of hemoglobin degradation
   (C) ferritin is a plasma protein that transports iron in the blood
   (D) the gastrointestinal rate of iron absorption is extremely high
   (E) iron is more efficiently absorbed in the ferrous state ($Fe^{2+}$) than in the ferric state ($Fe^{3+}$)

160. Which of the following physiologic responses occurs as the pitch of a sound is increased?

   (A) the frequency of action potentials in auditory nerve fibers increases
   (B) units in the auditory nerve become responsive to a wider range of sound frequencies
   (C) a greater number of hair cells become activated
   (D) the location of maximal basilar membrane displacement moves toward the apex of the cochlea
   (E) the location of maximal basilar membrane displacement moves toward the base of the cochlea

161. All of the following statements about a patient with a history of progressive muscle weakness due to myasthenia gravis are correct EXCEPT

   (A) skeletal muscles will respond normally to direct electrical stimulation
   (B) skeletal muscle response to nerve stimulation will be weakened
   (C) a small dose of physostigmine is likely to improve the symptoms
   (D) a large dose of physostigmine is likely to worsen the symptoms
   (E) the patient should be given α-bungarotoxin to determine the number of acetylcholine binding sites at the post-junctional membrane

162. All of the following statements about blood coagulation are correct EXCEPT

   (A) blood does not coagulate in the absence of $Ca^{2+}$
   (B) patients with hemophilia A have a characteristically prolonged bleeding time
   (C) von Willebrand factor promotes platelet adhesion

   (D) von Willebrand factor is required for blood coagulation
   (E) disseminated intravascular coagulation (DIC) results in depletion of coagulation proteins

163. The stimulation of nerve endings in the Golgi tendon organs leads directly to

   (A) contraction of intrafusal muscle fibers
   (B) contraction of extrafusal muscle fibers
   (C) reflex inhibition of motor neurons
   (D) increased γ-efferent discharge
   (E) increased activity in group II afferent fibers

164. Patients with idiopathic hyperfunction of the juxtaglomerular apparatus (Bartter's syndrome) have all of the following EXCEPT

   (A) high renin levels
   (B) high angiotensin levels
   (C) high aldosterone levels
   (D) increased sensitivity of vascular angiotensin receptors
   (E) normal blood pressure

165. Which of the following statements about patients with total colectomy and ileostomy is correct?

   (A) long-term survival is not possible, since the colon is a vital organ
   (B) long-term survival is possible, but parenteral nutrition is required to maintain fluid and electrolyte balance
   (C) these patients are at increased risk of anemia due to malabsorption of iron
   (D) these patients are at increased risk of anemia due to malabsorption of vitamin $B_{12}$
   (E) following total colectomy and ileostomy, the volume and water content of ileal discharge decreases over time

166. Vagal nerve endings release acetylcholine. The expected effect of stimulating the vagus nerve would be to

   (A) decrease the rate of rhythmicity of the sinoatrial (SA) node by inducing hyperpolarization
   (B) increase conductivity at the atrioventricular (AV) junction by inducing depolarization
   (C) depolarize cells of the SA node by opening potassium channels under the control of the muscarinic acetylcholine receptor
   (D) increase the force of myocardial contractions
   (E) decrease the rate of rhythmicity of the SA node by increasing the upward drift in membrane potential caused by sodium leakage

167. Massage of the carotid sinus results in all of the following EXCEPT

   (A) increased pressure at the carotid sinus baroreceptors
   (B) decreased firing rate of the carotid sinus fibers
   (C) decreased firing rate of cardiac sympathetic fibers
   (D) increased firing rate of the vagus nerve
   (E) decreased heart rate

168. Which of the following circulatory changes normally take place in the newborn within 5 minutes after birth?

   (A) closure of the ductus arteriosus
   (B) closure of the foramen ovale
   (C) increase in pulmonary artery resistance
   (D) all of the above
   (E) none of the above

169. Glucagon is secreted by the alpha cells of the pancreatic islets. Which of the following is most likely to induce glucagon secretion?

   (A) low serum concentrations of amino acids
   (B) low serum concentrations of glucose
   (C) high serum concentrations of glucose

   (D) secretion of somatostatin by the delta cells
   (E) parasympathetic stimulation

170. Vitamin $B_{12}$ is required for a number of metabolic processes. Which of the following lesions would NOT lead to a deficiency of this vitamin?

   (A) chronic gastritis resulting in achlorhydria
   (B) autoimmune destruction of gastric parietal cells
   (C) surgical resection of the jejunum
   (D) surgical resection of the ileum
   (E) total gastrectomy

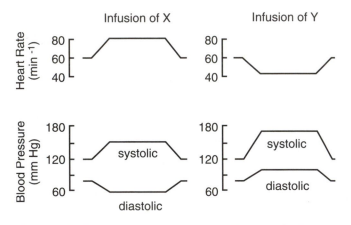

**Figure 2.2.** (*Reprinted with permission from Ganong, WF.* Review of Medical Physiology. 17th ed. *Appleton & Lange; 1995.*)

171. Figure 2.2 shows the effects of infusion of a catecholamine X and a catecholamine Y on heart rate and systolic/diastolic blood pressure. Which of the following statements correctly describes the actions of these drugs?

   (A) the decrease in heart rate following infusion of Y is due to the effect of this drug on cardiac α-adrenergic receptors
   (B) the decrease in heart rate following infusion of Y is due to the effect of this drug on cardiac β-adrenergic receptors
   (C) the decrease in heart rate following infusion of Y is due to the effect of acetylcholine on cardiac muscarinic receptors

(D) the decrease in diastolic blood pressure following infusion of X is due to the effect of this drug on vascular smooth muscle α-adrenergic receptors

(E) catecholamine X is norepinephrine and catecholamine Y is epinephrine

172. When measuring skeletal muscle tension that develops during isometric contractions, it is observed that

(A) total tension is inversely proportional to the length of the fiber

(B) total tension increases monotonically with the length of the fiber

(C) active tension increases monotonically with the length of the fiber

(D) active tension first increases then decreases with the length of the fiber

(E) passive tension first increases then decreases with the length of the fiber

173. A neuronal soma has a resting membrane potential of –60 mV. Opening chloride channels in the neuronal membrane will most likely cause

(A) depolarization to about –30 mV

(B) depolarization to about +30 mV

(C) hyperpolarization to about –70 mV

(D) no change in membrane potential

(E) initiation of an action potential

174. Which of the following is NOT a stimulus for the release of renin from the juxtaglomerular apparatus?

(A) cardiac failure

(B) dehydration

(C) constriction of renal arteries

(D) increased delivery of sodium to the distal tubules

(E) increased sympathetic activity via renal nerves

175. Which of the following statements most accurately describes the response of a cell to a decrease in the conductance of the cell membrane to chloride ions?

(A) the cell will hyperpolarize if its membrane potential is positive with respect to the equilibrium potential for chloride ions

(B) the cell will depolarize if its membrane potential is positive with respect to the equilibrium potential for chloride ions

(C) the cell will hyperpolarize if the external chloride concentration is greater than the internal chloride concentration

(D) the cell will hyperpolarize if the external chloride concentration is less than the internal chloride concentration

(E) no change in membrane potential will occur if the external and internal chloride ion concentrations are equal

176. Which of the following is NOT a stimulus for the release of aldosterone from the adrenal cortex?

(A) hemorrhage

(B) hyponatremia

(C) hyperkalemia

(D) angiotensin II

(E) atrial natriuretic peptide

177. Miniature end-plate potentials that can be recorded from a muscle fiber are believed to represent

(A) the postsynaptic action of a single neurotransmitter molecule released from the presynaptic terminal

(B) the opening of a single receptor-ion channel in the muscle membrane

(C) the opening of multiple ion channels in the muscle membrane because of the spontaneous release of a small amount of transmitter

(D) the spontaneous opening of ion channels in the muscle membrane in the absence of presynaptically released transmitter

(E) the opening of multiple ion channels in the postsynaptic membrane in response to a single presynaptic action potential

178. Which of the following statements correctly describes effects of autonomic nerve activity on the cardiovascular system in a healthy subject?

   (A) stimulation of parasympathetic nerves decreases the strength of cardiac ventricular contractions

   (B) stimulation of sympathetic nerves decreases the strength of cardiac ventricular contractions

   (C) inhibition of parasympathetic nerves increases heart rate

   (D) stimulation of parasympathetic nerves increases total peripheral resistance

   (E) inhibition of parasympathetic nerves increases total peripheral resistance

179. All of the following are true statements about electromechanical coupling EXCEPT

   (A) in smooth muscle, $Ca^{2+}$ ions bind to calmodulin

   (B) smooth muscle contraction is initiated by myosin light chain phosphorylation

   (C) in cardiac muscle, $Ca^{2+}$ ions bind to troponin

   (D) cardiac muscle does not show tetanus

   (E) the major source of $Ca^{2+}$ ions for contraction of skeletal muscle is influx of $Ca^{2+}$ ions from the extracellular space following voltage-dependent opening of L-type $Ca^{2+}$ channels

180. A patient has a total plasma $[Ca^{2+}]$ = 2.5 mM/L and a glomerular filtration rate of 160 L/day. What is the estimated daily filtered load of calcium?

   (A) 20 mM/day
   (B) 40 mM/day
   (C) 64 mM/day
   (D) 240 mM/day
   (E) 400 mM/day

181. If a person suffered a stab injury and air entered the intrapleural space (pneumothorax), the most likely response would be for the

   (A) lung to expand outward and the chest wall to spring inward

   (B) lung to expand outward and the chest wall to spring outward

   (C) lung to collapse inward and the chest wall to collapse inward

   (D) lung to collapse inward and the chest wall to spring outward

   (E) lung volume to be unaffected and chest wall to spring outward

182. Normally, $O_2$ transfer is perfusion limited; that is, the amount of $O_2$ taken up is a function of pulmonary blood flow. All of the following may, however, favor diffusion limitation of transfer of $O_2$ from alveolus to pulmonary capillary blood EXCEPT

   (A) increased extravascular lung water
   (B) breathing hypoxic gas mixture
   (C) interstitial fibrosis
   (D) increased ventilatory rate
   (E) strenuous exercise

183. All of the following statements accurately describe the interaction of respiratory centers in the central nervous system (CNS) and their effect on respiration EXCEPT

   (A) sectioning the brain stem above the pons, near the inferior colliculus of the midbrain, does not alter respiration in animals

   (B) the apneustic and pneumotaxic centers of the pons are not necessary for maintenance of the basic rhythm of respiration

   (C) transection above the apneustic center results in prolonged inspiration and very short expiration

   (D) prolonged inspiration and very short expiration may be exacerbated by transection of the afferent fibers of the vagus and glossopharyngeal nerves

   (E) the medullary rhythmicity center is a discrete group of neurons whose rhythmicity is abolished when the brain is transected above and below this area

**Questions 184 and 185**

Figure 2.3 represents a pair of action potentials.

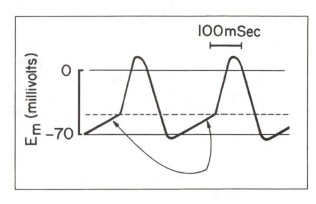

**Figure 2.3**

184. The action potentials shown represent those of

(A) myelinated motor axons
(B) skeletal muscle fibers
(C) vascular smooth muscle cells
(D) cardiac nodal cells
(E) ventricular Purkinje cells

185. The gradual depolarization between action potentials (see arrows) is mainly the result of

(A) a gradual increase in inward $Na^+$ current through fast $Na^+$ channels ($I_{Na}$)
(B) an increase in the "delayed rectifier" current due to outward movement of $K^+$ ($I_K$)
(C) a combination of gradual inactivation of outward $I_K$ along with the presence of an inward "funny" current ($I_f$) due to the opening of channels permeable to both $Na^+$ and $K^+$ ions
(D) changes in permeability of cells to the principal extracellular anions, $Cl^-$ and $HCO_3^-$
(E) a gradual change in the ratio of extracellular to intracellular ion concentrations across the cell membrane

186. All of the following statements are true regarding mechanisms of sweating EXCEPT

(A) stimulation of the preoptic area of the anterior hypothalamus excites sweating
(B) atropine will decrease the rate of sweating by inhibiting the action of postganglionic sympathetic fibers on sweat glands
(C) aldosterone decreases concentration of $Na^+$ in sweat by increasing reabsorption of $Na^+$ in the sweat gland
(D) profuse sweating can seriously affect electrolyte balance
(E) acclimatization to hot weather includes increased sweating with increased concentration of sodium chloride (NaCl)

**Questions 187 and 188**

A middle-aged male with smaller than normal-sized kidneys (by x-ray) and a history of chronic glomerulonephritis has the following laboratory analyses:

| Arterial blood | Urine |
|---|---|
| pH = 7.33 | pH = 6.0 |
| $Pao_2$ = 95 mm Hg | protein = positive |
| $Paco_2$ = 35 mm Hg | glucose = negative |
| $HCO_3^-$ = 18 mEq/L | |

187. This patient most likely has

(A) metabolic acidosis with no respiratory compensation
(B) metabolic acidosis with some respiratory compensation
(C) respiratory acidosis with no renal compensation
(D) respiratory acidosis with some renal compensation
(E) condition of diabetic ketoacidosis

188. The most likely cause of his acid–base imbalance is

    (A) hypoventilation
    (B) hyperventilation
    (C) decreased ability to produce adequate urinary $NH_4^+$ excretion
    (D) excess β-hydroxybutyric and acetoacetic acids in his blood
    (E) decreased catabolism of sulfur-containing amino acids (eg, methionine, cysteine)

189. There is very little protein in the glomerular filtrate. This is because

    (A) all serum proteins are too large to fit through the glomerular pores
    (B) positive charges line the pores, which repel serum proteins
    (C) a combination of pore size and negative charges lining the pores
    (D) active reabsorption of filtered protein by glomerular epithelial cells occurs
    (E) none of the above

190. The extra energy required for a burst of vigorous physical activity lasting between 10 and 100 seconds comes from

    (A) the breakdown of glycogen to lactic acid
    (B) the breakdown of adenosine triphosphate (ATP) in muscle cells
    (C) the breakdown of creatine phosphate
    (D) oxidative reactions
    (E) gluconeogenesis

191. Which of the following is true during far accommodation of the eyes?

    (A) the ciliary muscles are relaxed
    (B) the zonula fibers are relaxed
    (C) the lens is rounded
    (D) the focal length of the lens is short
    (E) the pupils are constricted (accommodation response)

192. Insulin stimulates facilitated diffusion of glucose into cells of all of the following tissues EXCEPT

    (A) fat
    (B) lymphatic
    (C) muscle
    (D) brain
    (E) none of the above

193. A patient presents for elective cholecystectomy. Shortly after induction of anesthesia with halothane, this patient develops circulatory instability, tachypnea, and a sharp rise in body temperature (malignant hyperthermia). What is the cause of fever in this patient?

    (A) increased heat production by skeletal muscle
    (B) increased hypothalamic temperature set point
    (C) decreased convectional heat loss
    (D) decreased sweat production
    (E) increased blood levels of interleukin-1

194. All of the following statements concerning $CO_2$ transport are true EXCEPT

    (A) compared to $O_2$, dissolved $CO_2$ plays a significant role in its transport
    (B) the bulk of $CO_2$ transport involves reversible combination of $CO_2$ with water in red blood cells
    (C) $CO_2$ is rapidly converted to bicarbonate anions in plasma
    (D) chloride ions enter red blood cells in exchange for bicarbonate anions
    (E) $CO_2$ combines with terminal amine groups, and these carbamino compounds are important in $CO_2$ unloading

195. Figure 2.4 shows expiratory and inspiratory flow-volume curves of a healthy person (broken line) and a patient (solid line). Which of the following disease states best explains this finding?

    (A) severe epiglottitis
    (B) panacinar emphysema
    (C) centrilobular emphysema
    (D) chronic obstructive lung disease
    (E) chronic restrictive lung disease

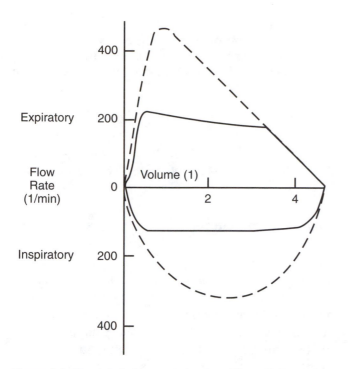

**Figure 2.4.** (*Reprinted with permission from West, JB.* Pulmonary Pathophysiology—The Essentials. *4th ed.* Williams & Wilkins; 1992.)

196. In chronic renal insufficiency (glomerulo-nephritis, pyelonephritis, renal vascular disease), there is a net functional loss of nephrons. If we assume that production of urea and creatinine is constant and that the patient is in a steady state, a 50% decrease in the normal glomerular filtration rate (GFR) will

(A) not affect plasma creatinine

(B) decrease plasma urea concentration

(C) greatly increase plasma $Na^+$

(D) increase the percent of filtered $Na^+$ excreted

(E) significantly decrease plasma $K^+$

197. During REM sleep, all of the following may occur EXCEPT

(A) rapid eye movements

(B) somnambulism

(C) nightmares

(D) penile erection

(E) skeletal muscle relaxation

198. If alveolar ventilation is halved (while breathing room air and if $CO_2$ production remains unchanged), then

(A) alveolar $CO_2$ pressure ($P_A CO_2$) will be halved

(B) arterial $O_2$ pressure ($Pa O_2$) will double

(C) arterial $CO_2$ pressure ($Pa CO_2$) will double

(D) alveolar $O_2$ pressure ($PA O_2$) will double

(E) $Pa O_2$ will not change

199. You see a patient with damage to the left cervical sympathetic chain ganglia as a result of a neck tumor. Which of the following physical signs would be expected?

(A) ptosis (hanging of the upper eye lid) on the left

(B) pupil dilation of the left eye

(C) lateral deviation of the left eye

(D) pale skin on the left side of the face

(E) increased sweat secretion on the left side of the face

200. A patient has a systolic/diastolic blood pressure of 130/70 mm Hg and a cardiac output of 5 L/min. What is his total peripheral resistance?

(A) 18 mm Hg · min/L

(B) 20 mm Hg · min/L

(C) 22 mm Hg · min/L

(D) 0.5 L/min · mm Hg

(E) 20 L/min · mm Hg

201. A patient is admitted to the hospital with a respiratory acidosis. The patient's renal excretion of potassium would be expected to

(A) rise, since acid and potassium excretion are coupled

(B) rise, since acidosis is a stimulus to renin secretion by the juxtaglomerular apparatus

(C) rise, since acidosis increases the affinity of the aldosterone receptor for aldosterone

(D) fall, since the filtered load of potassium to the tubules falls in acidosis

(E) fall, since tubular secretion of potassium is inversely coupled to acid secretion

202. A patient is given 100% $O_2$ to breathe, and arterial blood gases are determined. A $Pao_2$ of 125 mm Hg is associated with

   (A) diffusion abnormality
   (B) ventilation/perfusion inequality
   (C) anatomic right-to-left shunting
   (D) the normal response
   (E) profound hypoventilation

203. All of the following statements concerning the regulation of respiration are true EXCEPT

   (A) the increase in pulmonary ventilation is linearly related to end-tidal $Paco_2$
   (B) the main stimulus to increase ventilation comes from central chemoreceptors
   (C) arterial hypoxemia potentiates the ventilatory drive to elevations in $Paco_2$
   (D) central chemoreceptors respond to increases in local $H^+$ ion concentration or decreases in local $Pao_2$
   (E) an increase in the work of breathing may be associated with a decreased ventilatory response to $CO_2$

204. The slowest conduction rate is found in which of the following cardiac pathways?

   (A) from the sinoatrial (SA) node to the atrioventricular (AV) node
   (B) in the AV node
   (C) in the bundle of His
   (D) in the Purkinje fibers
   (E) in the ventricular muscle

205. Which of the following statements is true for a patient with hyperopia?

   (A) this patient is nearsighted
   (B) the eyeball of this patient is too long
   (C) hyperopia can be corrected with convex glasses
   (D) the lens of this patient has reduced elasticity
   (E) the lens of this patient has unusually large refractive power

206. The anatomic dead space in an individual with a tidal volume of 500 mL is 125 mL when determined by plotting nitrogen concentration vs. expired volume after a single inspiration of 100% $O_2$ (Fowler's method). If the patient's lungs are healthy and the $Paco_2$ is 40 mm Hg, the mixed expired $CO_2$ tension ($Peco_2$) should be about

   (A) 0 mm Hg
   (B) 10 mm Hg
   (C) 20 mm Hg
   (D) 30 mm Hg
   (E) 40 mm Hg

**Questions 207 and 208**

Figure 2.5 represents a continuous record of the relative cell volume of a red blood cell as it is changed from being immersed in a large volume of normal plasma to being in a large volume of a test solution and then returned to the plasma. Changes in cell volume are passive (not due to cell volume regulation).

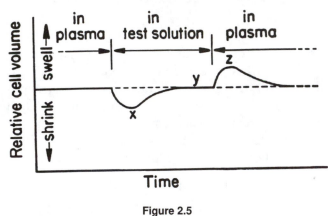

Figure 2.5

207. The change in cell volume that has peaked at point x on the above diagram resulted from

   (A) net exit of water from cell
   (B) net extracellular water entry into cell
   (C) net solute entry into cell
   (D) no net water movement
   (E) increased rate of solute entry into cell

208. The cell volume change that has peaked at point z is a result of

   (A) net exit of water from cell
   (B) no net water movement

(C)  net entry of water into cell caused by prior net entry of solute

(D)  net solute exit that occurred during prior exposure to test solution

(E)  neither net solute nor water movement

209.  In a normal kidney, a large increase in glomerular filtration rate (GFR) would be expected to occur following

(A)  vasoconstriction of glomerular afferent arterioles

(B)  vasoconstriction of glomerular efferent arterioles

(C)  substantial increases in renal blood flow (RBF)

(D)  an increase in mean arterial pressure (MAP) from 90 mm Hg to 140 mm Hg

(E)  strong, acute sympathetic stimulation to kidney

210.  Head injuries can lead to a syndrome in which the hormone vasopressin (ADH) is secreted at abnormally high levels. Patients manifesting the symptoms of the syndrome of inappropriate ADH secretion (SIADH) would be expected to have

(A)  low serum sodium due to the dilutional effect of ADH-induced water retention in the collecting tubules

(B)  low serum sodium due to a direct inhibitory effect of ADH on distal tubular sodium resorption

(C)  no change in serum sodium, since the dilutional effect of ADH-induced water retention is balanced by a direct stimulatory effect of ADH on distal tubular sodium resorption

(D)  high serum sodium due to the direct stimulatory effect of ADH on distal tubular sodium resorption

(E)  high serum sodium due to the concentrating effect of ADH-induced water excretion in the collecting tubules

211.  All of the following statements regarding physiologic adjustments to exercise are true EXCEPT

(A)  alveolar ventilation increases because of an increase in tidal volume and respiratory rate

(B)  cardiac output increases with an increase in heart rate and stroke volume

(C)  body temperature falls because of increased evaporative heat loss

(D)  arteriolar vasodilation occurs in working muscle, with an accompanying vasoconstriction in skin and viscera

(E)  the oxyhemoglobin dissociation curve shifts to the right, enhancing $O_2$ use

212.  If $O_2$ consumption (measured by analysis of mixed expired gas) is 300 mL/min, arterial $O_2$ content is 20 mL/100 mL blood, pulmonary arterial $O_2$ content is 15 mL/100 mL blood, and heart rate is 60/min, what is the cardiac stroke volume?

(A)  1 mL

(B)  10 mL

(C)  60 mL

(D)  100 mL

(E)  200 mL

213.  All of the following statements regarding fetal circulation are true EXCEPT

(A)  a significant portion of inferior vena cava flow is shunted through the foramen ovale to the left

(B)  the major portion of right ventricular output passes through the ductus arteriosus to the aorta

(C)  $Po_2$ of fetal blood leaving the placenta is slightly greater than maternal mixed venous $Po_2$

(D)  the presence of fetal hemoglobin shifts the oxyhemoglobin dissociation to the left

(E)  the liver, heart, and head of the fetus receive the most highly $O_2$-saturated blood

214. The resistance to blood flow in the cerebral circulation of humans will increase when

    (A) $Pa_{O_2}$ decreases to < 50 mm Hg
    (B) an individual inhales a gas mixture enriched with $CO_2$
    (C) an individual's hematocrit is decreased to < 0.30 by isovolemic exchange transfusion
    (D) systemic arterial pressure increases from 100 to 130 mm Hg
    (E) an individual suffers an epileptic seizure

215. Which of the following describes the compliance of the lungs measured under static conditions?

    (A) change in lung volume divided by the corresponding change in distending pressure ($P_{alv} - P_{pl}$)
    (B) change in distending pressure ($P_{alv} - P_{pl}$) divided by change in lung volume
    (C) change in distending pressure ($P_{alv} - P_{pl}$) multiplied by the change in lung volume
    (D) lung volume divided by recoil pressure ($P_{alv} - P_{pl}$)
    (E) change in elastic recoil pressure ($P_{alv} - P_{pl}$)

216. Residual volume

    (A) is part of the expiratory reserve volume
    (B) is part of vital capacity
    (C) cannot be measured directly with a spirometer
    (D) represents the resting volume of the lungs
    (E) is the volume at which the lungs tend to recoil outward

217. An individual has an alveolar ventilation of 6000 mL/min, a tidal volume of 600 mL, and a breathing rate of 12 breaths/min. What is this individual's anatomic dead space?

    (A) 100 mL
    (B) 120 mL
    (C) 150 mL
    (D) 200 mL
    (E) 250 mL

218. A patient's laboratory analysis of arterial plasma showed a pH of 7.56, bicarbonate 21 mEq/L, $P_{O_2}$ = 50 mm Hg and $P_{CO_2}$ = 25 mm Hg. This patient probably

    (A) has severe chronic lung disease
    (B) is a lowlander who has been vacationing at high altitude for two weeks
    (C) is a subject in a clinical research experiment who has been breathing a gas mixture of 10% oxygen and 90% nitrogen for a few minutes
    (D) is an emergency room patient with severely depressed respiration as a result of a heroin overdose
    (E) is an adult psychiatric patient who swallowed an overdose of aspirin

219. All of the following are specific functions of the parasympathetic nerves EXCEPT

    (A) increased gastrointestinal motility
    (B) decreased gastrointestinal sphincter tone
    (C) penile erection
    (D) semen ejaculation
    (E) emptying of urinary bladder and rectum

220. All of the following are associated with an increase in skeletal muscle tone EXCEPT

    (A) activation of $\gamma$-fibers
    (B) upper motor neuron lesions
    (C) lower motor neuron lesions
    (D) Parkinson's disease
    (E) anxiety

221. If the cabin of an airplane is pressurized to an equivalent altitude of 10,000 ft (barometric pressure of 523 mm Hg), the $Pa_{O_2}$ in a healthy person compared with his or her predicted $Pa_{O_2}$ at sea level will

    (A) decrease to < 100 mm Hg because the fraction of inspired air that is $O_2$ ($F_{IO_2}$) will be < 0.2
    (B) not change because $Pa_{CO_2}$ will decrease because of hyperventilation
    (C) not change because the cabin is pressurized

(D) decrease to < 100 mm Hg even though the $F_{IO_2}$ is still around 0.2

(E) remain approximately the same because water vapor pressure is low at high altitude

222. In a normal person, $Pa_{O_2}$ is slightly less than $PA_{O_2}$ primarily because of

(A) shunted blood
(B) significant diffusion gradients
(C) reaction time of $O_2$ with hemoglobin
(D) unloading of $CO_2$
(E) none of the above

223. Which of the following statements about cystic fibrosis is correct?

(A) the gene that is abnormal in cystic fibrosis is located on the X chromosome
(B) the gene that is abnormal in cystic fibrosis encodes a cAMP regulated $Cl^-$ channel
(C) cystic fibrosis is more common in African-Americans than in Caucasians
(D) cystic fibrosis is caused by a defective $Na^+$ transporter across airway epithelial cells, resulting in thick airway mucus
(E) sweat of cystic fibrosis patients has elevated $Na^+$ and low $Cl^-$ content

224. Cutting sympathetic nerve fibers that supply blood vessels in the arms or legs usually results in acute vasodilatation due to

(A) compensatory increase of epinephrine release from the adrenal medulla
(B) parasympathetic fibers dilating blood vessels
(C) loss of sympathetic tone
(D) development of hypersensitivity to circulating catecholamines
(E) all of the above are correct

1 sec.

**Figure 2.6**

225. Figure 2.6 shows an EEG recording of a child with attention deficit disorder. Which of the following events most likely causes the change at the time marked by arrow?

(A) patient's mind "wandering off"
(B) patient falling asleep
(C) petit mal attack
(D) patient closes eyes
(E) patient opens eyes

226. All of the following statements regarding the action of prostaglandins are correct EXCEPT

(A) thromboxane inhibits platelet aggregation
(B) PGF2α contracts bronchial muscle
(C) PGE2 relaxes bronchial smooth muscle
(D) PGF2α and PGE2 contract uterine smooth muscle
(E) PGE2 sensitizes nociceptive nerve endings, causing pain

**Questions 227 and 228**

Illustrated in Figure 2.7 is a left ventricular pressure-volume loop from a normal healthy adult.

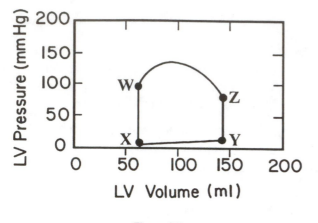

**Figure 2.7**

227. The part of the cardiac cycle described as iso-volumetric relaxation is between points

    (A) W and X
    (B) X and Y
    (C) Y and Z
    (D) Z and W

228. The part of the cardiac cycle that has the highest rate of energy consumption (highest rate of ATP hydrolysis) is between points

    (A) W and X
    (B) X and Y
    (C) Y and Z
    (D) Z and W

**DIRECTIONS (Questions 229 through 277): Each set of matching questions consists of a list of lettered options followed by several numbered items. For each numbered item, select the ONE lettered option that is most closely associated with it. Each lettered option may be selected once, more than once, or not at all.**

**Questions 229 through 233**

For each of the electroencephalographic (EEG) patterns named below, select the phase of sleep most likely to be associated with it.

    (A) alpha waves
    (B) beta waves
    (C) theta waves
    (D) delta waves
    (E) low voltage punctuated by occasional sleep spindles

229. Rapid eye movement (REM) sleep

230. Light sleep (first stage of slow-wave sleep)

231. Deep sleep (stage 4 of slow-wave sleep)

232. Alert wakefulness

233. Quiet wakefulness

**Questions 234 through 236**

For each process listed below, choose the hormone that is most likely to directly stimulate it.

    (A) estradiol
    (B) estriol
    (C) luteinizing hormone (LH)
    (D) follicle-stimulating hormone (FSH)
    (E) inhibin

234. Induction of LH surge

235. Ovulation

236. Stimulates Sertoli cells to convert spermatids to sperm cells

## Questions 237 through 239

Figure 2.8 shows a Davenport diagram plotting arterial plasma bicarbonate against arterial blood pH. Dashed lines are different levels of arterial $P_{CO_2}$ (isobars). On the diagram are nine different points (letters A through I). Match each numbered description below with one of these lettered points.

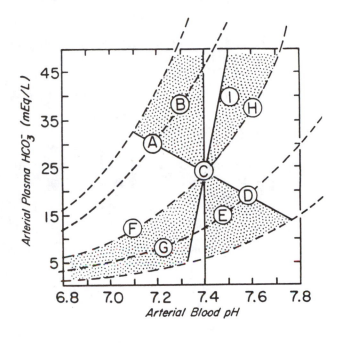

**Figure 2.8**

237. Simple respiratory acidosis with no renal compensation    A

238. Respiratory acidosis with some renal compensation    B

239. Metabolic acidosis with some respiratory compensation    G

## Questions 240 through 242

Figure 2.9 illustrates simultaneous changes in left ventricular (LV) pressure and LV volume over time. There are nine lettered points on the LV pressure curve (points A through I). Match each numbered event named below with one of the lettered points.

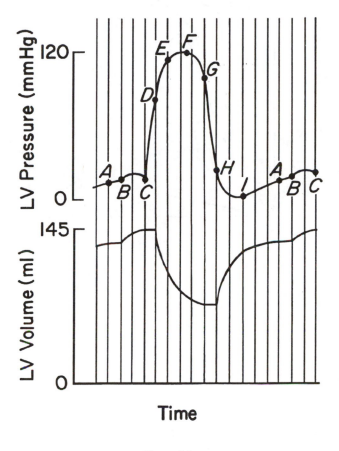

**Time**

**Figure 2.9**

240. LV pressure essentially equal to diastolic aortic blood pressure    G

241. Peak of left atrial V wave    H

242. Peak of T wave of electrocardiogram (ECG)

**Questions 243 through 245**

A series of oxygen binding curves is shown in Figure 2.10. Match these curves with the proper oxygen binding proteins.

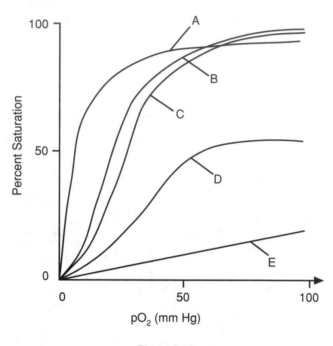

**Figure 2.10**

243.  Adult hemoglobin  C

244.  Fetal hemoglobin  B

245.  Myoglobin  A

**Questions 246 through 248**

Match the following cytokines with their proper description.

    (A)  α-interferon
    (B)  β-interferon
    (C)  γ-interferon
    (D)  interleukin-1
    (E)  interleukin-2

    (F)  interleukin-3
    (G)  interleukin-4
    (H)  interleukin-5
    (I)  interleukin-6
    (K)  interleukin-7
    (L)  tumor necrosis factor

246.  Produced by fibroblasts and has antiviral activity  B

247.  Produced by T cells and induces MHC-II proteins  C

248.  Produced by macrophages and causes fever  D

**Questions 249 through 251**

Match the following gastrointestinal hormones with their proper description.

    (A)  gastrin
    (B)  secretin
    (C)  cholecystokinin (CCK)
    (D)  gastric inhibitory peptide (GIP)
    (E)  vasointestinal inhibitory peptide (VIP)
    (F)  somatostatin

249.  Produced in the duodenum and stimulates the pancreas to produce an enzyme-rich secretion  C

250.  Stimulates insulin secretion in response to glucose entering the duodenum  D

251.  Increases HCl secretion in the stomach  A

## Questions 252 and 253

Illustrated in Figure 2.11 are four different patterns of forced expiratory volume in one second (FEV$_1$) and forced vital capacity (FVC). Match each of the numbered conditions below with one of the lettered patterns (A through D).

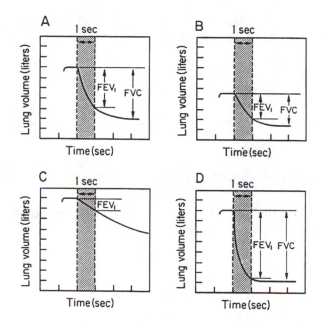

Figure 2.11

252. Patient with asthma    *C*

253. Patient with pulmonary fibrosis    *D*

## Questions 254 through 257

Figure 2.12 illustrates a plot of a blood protein electrophoresis. Match the labeled fractions with the proper description.

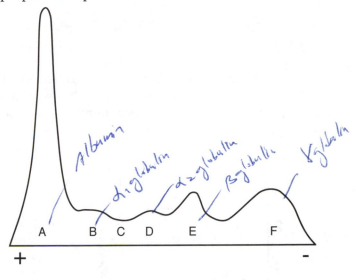

Figure 2.12

254. Proteins in this fraction bind iron    *E*

255. Proteins in this fraction are responsible for humoral immunity    *F*

256. Proteins in this fraction specifically bind thyroid hormones    *C*

257. Proteins in this fraction determine plasma oncotic pressure    *A*

## Questions 258 through 261

Match the following diuretics with their mechanism of action.

(A) ethanol
(B) caffeine
(C) mannitol
(D) carbonic anhydrase inhibitor
(E) thiazide
(F) loop diuretic
(G) potassium-sparing diuretic

258. Suppresses ADH secretion    *A, B*

259. Opposes the action of aldosterone    *G*

**260.** Produces diuresis through an osmotic action ↶

**261.** Inhibits $Na^+$-$K^+$-2 $Cl^-$ cotransport ↶

### Questions 262 and 263

Figure 2.13 is an illustration of changes in body oxygen consumption ($\dot{V}_{O_2}$) and energy requirements (dashed lines) with moderate dynamic exercise. Several different periods are indicated by letters A through E. Below the illustration are numbered descriptions. Match each number with the appropriate letter choice from the illustration.

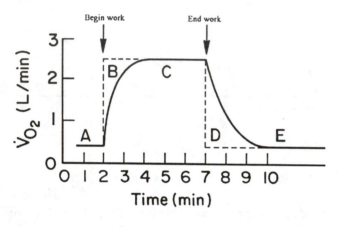

**Figure 2.13**

**262.** Period during which $\dot{V}_{O_2}$ exceeds metabolic needs ↶

**263.** Period during which $O_2$ delivery to exercising muscles is less than that required for aerobic metabolism ↶

### Questions 264 and 265

Below are five different areas of the nephron (letters A through E). Match each number with the appropriate letter.

(A) glomerulus
(B) proximal tubule
(C) juxtaglomerular apparatus
(D) thick ascending limb of Henle's loop
(E) collecting duct

**264.** Primary site for majority of salt and water reabsorption ↶

**265.** Low water permeability under all circumstances ↶

### Questions 266 through 269

Match the following hormones with the proper signal transduction pathway.

(A) activation of tyrosine kinase
(B) increase in cAMP
(C) decrease in cAMP
(D) increase in cGMP
(E) decrease in cGMP
(F) increase in inositol-tris-phosphate
(G) regulation of gene expression

**266.** Estradiol ↶

**267.** Nitric oxide ↶

**268.** Angiotensin II ↶

**269.** Epinephrine acting on $\alpha_1$-receptors ↶

## Questions 270 and 271

The graph below (Fig. 2.14) shows a passive relaxation pressure-volume curve of the lung and the chest wall.

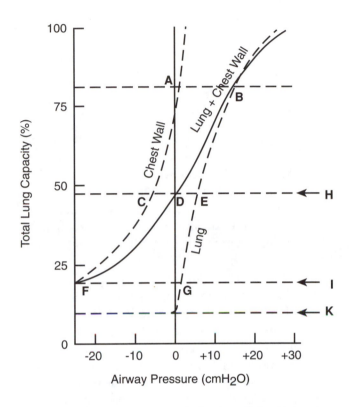

Figure 2.14. (*Reprinted with permission from Rahn, H.* American Journal of Physiology 146.)

270. Indicates the equilibrium position of lung and chest wall    D

271. Indicates the residual volume of the lung    F

## Questions 272 through 277

Match the following ion channels with their proper description.

 (A)  $K^+$ channels
 (B)  $Na^+$ channels
 (C)  L-type $Ca^{2+}$ channels
 (D)  T-type $Ca^{2+}$ channels
 (E)  $Cl^-$ channels
 (F)  non-selective cation channels
 (G)  non-selective anion channels
 (H)  ryanodine receptor
 (I)  $Na^+/K^+$ pump

272. Responsible for the plateau phase of the cardiac action potential    (C)

273. Determine the resting membrane potential of vascular smooth muscle    A

274. Inactivate within milliseconds after membrane depolarization and require repolarization for removal of their inactivation    B

275. Open following depolarization of the sarcolemma (skeletal muscle fibers)    G

276. Cause depolarization of the motor end-plate (skeletal muscle fibers)    F

277. Responsible for the "dark-current" of retinal photoreceptors    B

# Physiology
## Answers and Explanations

151. **(E)** During pregnancy many physiological changes take place in the mother's body. Maternal blood volume increases up to 40% due to elevated aldosterone and estrogen levels. Bone marrow production of erythrocytes also increases but does not keep up with the plasma volume expansion resulting in a decrease in hematocrit ("physiological anemia of pregnancy"). Respiratory minute volume increases by about 50% because of the increased basal metabolic rate and oxygen consumption. This increase is largely due to an increase in tidal volume without increase in respiratory rate. Both residual volume and expiratory reserve volume decrease. Gastrointestinal tone and motility are decreased because of the inhibitory effect of progesterone on these smooth muscles. (*West, 1991, pp 892–896*)

152. **(C)** The cerebellum is generally considered to play an important role in the coordination and smoothing out of voluntary movements. Intention tremor, which may be observed in cerebellar disease, is absent at rest but appears at the onset of voluntary movements. This aspect of the tremors readily differentiates them from those observed with the degeneration of the nigrostriatal dopaminergic tracts in Parkinson's disease, which produces tremors that are present at rest. The amplitude of oscillations caused by cerebellar deficits is not generally constant throughout a voluntary movement. (*Ganong, pp 197, 201*)

153. **(B)** In diabetes insipidus, appropriate water intake from thirst will adequately compensate for the potential excess volume loss.

Only if access to appropriate intake is prevented will tremendous volume loss occur. All of the other changes listed in the question would tend to maintain blood volume, but all are either short-term effects or the result of extreme stimuli, such as hemorrhage or intense sympathetic activity. (*Guyton and Hall, pp 358– 359*)

154. **(C)** As the bladder fills, sensory signals from bladder stretch receptors elicit a micturition reflex via parasympathetic fibers originating in the sacral spinal cord. These transient contractions elicit an urge to urinate, but normally urination does not occur unless the external sphincter relaxes. If the lumbar spinal cord is damaged while the sacral segments are intact, micturition reflexes will occur resulting in spontaneous and uncontrolled bladder emptying (automatic bladder). If the sacral spinal cord is damaged, micturition reflexes are lost and the bladder fills to capacity resulting in "overflow incontinence" (atonic bladder). Urination occurs whenever the bladder pressure exceeds the sphincter tone. The external sphincter is a skeletal muscle innervated by motor neurons from the pudendal nerve, not by sympathetic fibers. (*Guyton and Hall, pp 407–408*)

155. **(D)** Figure 2.1 shows the endometrial changes expected during a "text book" menstrual cycle of 28 days' length. Ovulation occurs on day 14, counting as day 1 the first day of the last menstrual period. Progesterone produced by the corpus luteum reaches its peak around day 21. In the absence of fertilization, the corpus luteum then

degenerates and progesterone levels begin to drop. *(Ganong, pp 401–405)*

156. **(B)** In contrast to progesterone, which is detectable in significant amounts only during the secretory phase, estrogen levels show a biphasic time course. Peak levels are secreted by the growing follicle about 36 hours prior to ovulation, inducing the LH surge. A second but smaller increase of estrogen occurs during the luteal phase of the cycle. *(Ganong, pp 401–405)*

157. **(D)** Pupil diameter is determined by the balance between sympathetic tone to the radial fibers of the iris and parasympathetic tone to the pupillary sphincter muscle. Pupil dilation occurs during increased sympathetic activity (eg, emotional excitement) or decreased parasympathetic activity (darkness), or block of muscarinic receptors (atropine). Phentolamine is a blocker of α-adrenergic receptors and would cause pupil constriction. *(Guyton and Hall, p 661)*

158. **(E)** Water that is either higher or lower than body temperature and that is introduced into the external auditory meatus may set up convection currents within the endolymph of the inner ear. These currents may result in the stimulation of the semicircular canals by causing movements of the ampullar cristae. Conflicting, different information from the right and left sides, in turn, may result in vertigo and nausea. Decreased movement or immobilization of the otoliths or of the ampullar cristae is not caused by such changes in temperature. Furthermore, changes in the discharge rate of vestibular afferents, which must occur with caloric stimulation, are most likely to be caused by the changes in the activity of the receptors rather than being a direct response of the afferents to changes in temperature. *(Ganong, p 166)*

159. **(E)** Seventy percent of the total body iron is used for hemoglobin and myoglobin; the remainder is stored as readily exchangeable ferritin, and some is stored in less easily mobilized hemosiderin. Iron is more efficiently absorbed in the ferrous state ($Fe^{2+}$) than in the ferric state ($Fe^{3+}$), and commercial iron preparations often contain vitamin C to prevent oxidation of $Fe^{2+}$ to $Fe^{3+}$. Still, only 3 to 6% of the daily ingested iron is actually absorbed in the upper gastrointestinal tract. Iron in the plasma is bound to the iron-transporting protein transferrin. Transferrin level (total iron binding capacity) and saturation are clinically important indicators of iron deficiency anemia. *(Guyton and Hall, pp 430–431)*

160. **(E)** The primary change in the cochlea that registers an increase in the frequency of a sound wave is a change in the position of maximal displacement of the basilar membrane. A sound of low pitch produces the greatest displacement toward the apex of the cochlea and produces the greatest activation of hair cells at that location. As the pitch is increased, the position of greatest displacement moves closer to the base of the cochlea. Increases in the number of hair cells that are activated and in the frequency of discharge of units in the auditory nerve fibers, together with an increase in range of frequencies to which such units respond, are all more likely to be observed in response to increases in the intensity of a sound stimulus rather than to increases in pitch. In the auditory cortex, sound frequencies are organized topographically so that a change in pitch may be represented by a change in the location of activated cortical units. *(Ganong, p 162)*

161. **(E)** Myasthenia gravis is an autoimmune disease characterized by progressive muscle weakness due to formation of antibodies against the nicotinic ACh receptor of the motor end-plate. Impairment of neuromuscular transmission results in a weakened response of the muscle to nerve stimulation but a normal response to direct electrical stimulation. Improvement of muscle weakness by small doses of acetylcholine esterase inhibitors physostigmine or edrophonium are diagnostic for this disease. A large dose of physostigmine worsens muscle weakness because of desensitization of the end-plate to persistent ACh. Radiolabeled snake venom α-bungarotoxin is a useful investigative tool to quantify

the number of ACh receptors at the motor end-plate and, naturally, is performed in vitro. (*Harrison's Principles of Internal Medicine, pp 2393–2395*)

162. **(B)** Prolonged bleeding time is characteristic of platelet disorders, eg, thrombocytopenia. Patients with hemophilia A or B (ie, absence of factor XIII or IX, respectively) have a prolonged partial thromboplastin time (PPT) but do not have a prolonged bleeding time. Von Willebrand factor is part of the factor XIII complex and also promotes platelet adherence to the vascular subendothelium. Patients who lack this factor (von Willebrand's disease) have both a prolonged PPT and a prolonged bleeding time. (*Harrison's Principles of Internal Medicine, pp 1800–1808*)

163. **(C)** The stimulation of receptors in the Golgi tendon organs leads to the inverse stretch reflex. This reflex is responsible for the relaxation that is observed when a muscle is subjected to a strong stretch. Impulses from the organs travel in type Ib fibers to the spinal cord, where they activate inhibitory interneurons. These in turn suppress the activity of motor neurons and therefore lead to the relaxation of the extrafusal muscle fibers attached to the tendons. The activity in group II afferent fibers, the γ-efferent discharge rate, and the state of contraction of intrafusal fibers control the stretch reflex, which is distinct from the inverse stretch reflex mediated by the Golgi tendon organs. (*Ganong, pp 116–117*)

164. **(D)** Patients with Bartter's syndrome have primary elevated renin due to idiopathic hyperfunction of the juxtaglomerular apparatus. Consequently, these patients have elevated levels of angiotensin II and aldosterone. Their blood pressures remain normal however, probably because of downregulation of vascular angiotensin II receptors. (*Ganong, p 422*)

165. **(E)** Following total colectomy and ileostomy, the volume and water content of ileal discharge decreases over time, and most patients can lead an essentially normal life. Iron absorption occurs in the upper GI tract and vitamin $B_{12}$-intrinsic factor complex is absorbed in the ileum. As long as the ileum remains intact, deficiency of these factors that are essential for erythropoiesis is not expected. (*Ganong, pp 469–470*)

166. **(A)** Acetylcholine released by the vagal nerve stimulates muscarinic receptors in the cells of the SA node, resulting in the opening of potassium channels and, consequently, in hyperpolarization. It therefore takes longer for sodium leakage to cause the membrane potentials of these cells to reach the threshold required for an action potential. The rate of rhythmicity is thus decreased. A similar hyperpolarization of the fibers at the AV junction decreases conduction of atrial impulses to the ventricle. (*Guyton and Hall, p 126*)

167. **(B)** Increased baroreceptor pressure causes an increase in the firing rate of the carotid sinus nerve (afferent) that inhibits the medullary vasomotor center. Consequently, both a decrease in sympathetic tone and an increase in vagal discharge (efferent) contribute to the fall in heart rate and arterial blood pressure following carotid sinus massage. When performing this maneuver on your patients or peers, be prepared for cardiac sinus arrest and avoid vigorous massage, which might dislodge an embolus and cause permanent neurological damage. (*Ganong, p 551*)

168. **(B)** With the first breath of life, pulmonary arterial resistance drops dramatically. This is due to the oxygenation of the lungs causing vasodilatation of the pulmonary vessels. Clamping of the umbilical cord doubles peripheral resistance and causes an increase in arterial blood pressure. As soon as right atrial pressure drops below left atrial pressure, the foramen ovale will close (valve-like mechanism), establishing the adult-type blood circulation. The rising systemic and falling pulmonary artery pressure causes a flow reversal through the ductus arteriosus from right to left to left to right within minutes of birth. Complete closure of the ductus arteriosus appears to be due to a decline of local prostacyclin levels and usually occurs

within 24 to 48 hours after birth. *(Ganong, pp 573–574)*

169.  **(B)** Hypoglycemia is the most potent stimulus for glucagon secretion. High serum levels of amino acids (especially alanine and arginine) also will induce glucagon release. Somatostatin inhibits glucagon secretion. While parasympathetic stimulation to the pancreas stimulates acinar secretion, it does not stimulate alpha cells to secrete glucagon. *(Guyton and Hall, p 979)*

170.  **(C)** Absorption of vitamin $B_{12}$ requires formation of a complex with intrinsic factor, which is secreted by the parietal cells of the stomach. Destruction of these cells thus results in a vitamin $B_{12}$ deficiency. The vitamin $B_{12}$-intrinsic factor complex is absorbed in the ileum. Thus, surgical resection of the ileum, but not of the jejunum, will also produce a deficiency. *(Guyton and Hall, p 846)*

171.  **(C)** Figure 2.2 shows the effects of epinephrine (X) and norepinephrine (Y) on heart rate and blood pressure. Epinephrine is more potent on β-receptors than α-receptors, while norepinephrine reacts predominantly with α-receptors and $β_1$-receptors. Both catecholamines increase heart rate and cardiac output of the *isolated* heart preparation in identical manner. Because of its β-adrenergic effect, epinephrine dilates blood vessels and lowers overall peripheral resistance, while norepinephrine due to its potent action on α-receptors causes a steep increase in peripheral resistance. This increase in peripheral resistance is reflected in an immediate increase in diastolic and mean arterial blood pressure, causing a reflex bradycardia due to activation of the baroreceptor reflex. Therefore, it is acetylcholine from vagal nerve fibers that is responsible for the decrease in heart rate seen after norepinephrine infusion. *(Ganong, pp 329–331)*

172.  **(D)** The total tension that is developed on stimulating a muscle isometrically is the sum of the passive tension of the unstimulated muscle and the active tension exerted by stimulation. The passive tension increases monotonically with the length of the fiber. Active tension, however, increases up to the resting length of the fiber and then declines as the length is increased further. The total tension therefore also shows first an increase and then a decrease as a fiber is lengthened. *(Ganong, pp 62–63)*

173.  **(C)** Increasing the membrane's conductance to chloride will result in chloride influx and the membrane potential approaching the value dictated by the chloride equilibrium potential (Nernst), which is about −70 mV for neurons. *(Guyton and Hall, p 577)*

174.  **(D)** Conditions of decreased extracellular fluid volume or decreased blood pressure stimulate renin secretion from juxtaglomerular cells located in the media of the afferent arterioles. There are two major mechanisms by which this occurs: (1) Decreased pressure in the afferent arterioles will increase renin secretion, and (2) decreased delivery of $Na^+$ and $Cl^{-1}$ to the distal tubules at the level of macula densa cells will increase renin secretion. Furthermore, renin secretion is modulated by angiotensin II (inhibitory) and by sympathetic activity via renal nerves (stimulatory). *(Ganong, pp 420–421)*

175.  **(B)** Although electrogenic pumps may contribute to the membrane potential of certain cells, the major determinants of membrane potential are the external and internal concentrations of permeant ions and their relative permeabilities in the membrane. Increasing the conductance for an ion causes the membrane potential to approach the equilibrium potential for that ion. Conversely, decreasing the conductance causes the membrane potential to move away from the equilibrium potential for that ion. Thus, a decrease in the conductance of a membrane to chloride ions causes the cells to depolarize— that is, become more positive—if the membrane potential is positive with respect to the chloride equilibrium potential. *(Kandel, Schwartz and Jessel, pp 82–84, 88)*

176.  **(E)** Principal stimuli for aldosterone release are circulating ACTH from the pituitary

gland, angiotensin II, and high plasma K+ levels. In addition, low plasma Na+ may also have a direct stimulatory effect on the adrenal cortex. Volume depletion, eg, hemorrhage, increases aldosterone release through activation of the renin–angiotensin–angiotensin II system. Atrial natriuretic peptide is secreted from atrial myocytes under conditions of expanded extracellular volume and acts on renal mesangial cells and ductal epithelium to decrease Na+ reabsorption. (*Ganong, pp 346–347, 423–425*)

177. **(C)** Acetylcholine, the transmitter at the muscle end-plate, may be released spontaneously in small packets or quanta, without the presynaptic terminal's being invaded by an action potential. These quanta are believed to represent the contents of single transmitter vesicles. Release of acetylcholine activates multiple ion channels in the muscle to produce a miniature end-plate potential. (*Ganong, pp 101–102*)

178. **(C)** Heart rate will increase whenever sympathetic firing rate increases or parasympathetic firing rate decreases since the cardiac atria receive tonic input from both sympathetic and parasympathetic nerves. In humans, the ventricles are not innervated by parasympathetic nerves, and therefore the strength of contraction is determined by the Frank–Starling mechanism and by sympathetic firing rate. With few exceptions, blood vessels are not innervated by parasympathetic nerves, and there is little effect of changes in parasympathetic tone on total peripheral resistance. (*Guyton and Hall, pp 116–117, 774–776*)

179. **(E)** The three types of muscle cells (smooth muscle, cardiac muscle, skeletal muscle) utilize different mechanisms by which membrane depolarization results in muscle contraction, ie, electromechanical coupling. In smooth muscle, Ca²⁺ ions entering through opening of voltage-gated Ca²⁺ channels or following release from the SR, bind to calmodulin. The Ca²⁺-calmodulin complex activates myosin light chain kinase, and phosphorylation of myosin light chain initiates smooth muscle contraction. This is in contrast to cardiac and skeletal muscle, where contraction is triggered by a conformational change induced by Ca²⁺ binding to troponin. Cardiac and skeletal muscle differ in their Ca²⁺ handling. In cardiac muscle, opening of voltage-gated Ca²⁺ channels results in Ca²⁺ influx, which triggers release of Ca²⁺ from the SR via Ca²⁺ induced release of Ca²⁺. In skeletal muscle, depolarization of the T tubule triggers release of Ca²⁺ from the SR. In contrast to cardiac muscle, skeletal muscle contractions can summate during repeated stimulation, resulting in an increase in force with incomplete relaxation between stimuli (tetanic contraction). This difference is due to the much shorter action potential duration in skeletal muscle compared to cardiac muscle. (*Ganong, pp 59–62, 70, 72*)

180. **(D)** About 40% of total plasma Ca²⁺ is bound to proteins and not filtered at the glomerular basement membrane. Therefore, the estimated daily filtered load is $1.5 \text{ mM/L} \cdot 160 \text{ L/d} = 240 \text{ mM/d}$. The exact amount of free versus total Ca²⁺ depends on blood pH: free Ca²⁺ increases during acidosis and decreases during alkalosis. (*Guyton and Hall, p 380*)

181. **(D)** The response to a stab wound that punctures the lung demonstrates the elasticity of the lung and chest wall. The tendency of the lung to collapse is normally balanced by the tendency of the chest wall to spring out. Thus intrapleural pressures are subatmospheric. Introduction of air in this space allows the lung to collapse and the chest wall to spring outward. (*West, 1991, p 566*)

182. **(D)** Normally, O₂ is transferred from air spaces to blood via a perfusion-limited process. Thus, O₂ moves across the alveolar–capillary membrane by a process of simple diffusion, and the amount of gas taken up depends entirely on the amount of blood flow. Processes that impair diffusion of O₂ transform the normal relationship to a diffusion-limited process. Thus, if the O₂ must move a greater distance because of a thickened barrier, as would occur with increased

extravascular lung water or cell components (interstitial fibrosis), the diffusion process is limited. Furthermore, decreasing the driving force (by lowering inspired $O_2$ concentrations) or decreasing passage time (as occurs with strenuous exercise), may also favor diffusion limitation. Increasing the ventilatory rate will not have this effect and will only serve to maintain a high gradient of $O_2$ from air to blood. (*West, 1991, pp 548–551*)

**183. (E)** The respiratory center of the CNS consists of a diffuse group of neurons whose inherent activity persists even after all known afferent stimuli have been eliminated. Although sectioning the brain and observing respiratory changes are a useful approach to locating important central areas of respiratory regulation, this approach interferes with many complex pathways that may interact. Nonetheless, transectioning of the brain above the pons has little effect. An apneustic center may be located in the pons. Transection above the center results in prolonged inspiration and short expiration. Apparently, a pneumotaxic center in the upper pons modulates this effect along with vagal impulses. The medullary center is capable of initiating and maintaining sequences of respiration. (*Guyton and Hall, pp 525–527*)

**184. (D)** The action potentials illustrated must be those of cardiac nodal cells (SA node or AV node). The durations of the action potentials shown are too long for either motor axons (2 msec) or skeletal muscle fibers (5 msec). Also the configuration is different. They certainly do not represent vascular smooth muscle cells which have no appreciable action potential at all. They cannot be ventricular Purkinje action potentials as these have a more negative diastolic component that does not gradually depolarize, a longer duration (200 msec), and a plateau region. (*Berne and Levy, pp 36, 379*)

**185. (C)** One of the principal distinguishing features of nodal cell action potentials is the gradual diastolic depolarization, the so-called pacemaker potential. When the pacemaker potential reaches threshold (dashed line in illustration), an action potential is generated

and propagated along conducting pathways to other cardiac fibers (the basis of autorhythmicity of cardiac pacemaker cells). During the diastolic period the outward $I_K$ (or delayed rectifier current mainly responsible for repolarization) is slowly deactivated. At the same time there is activation of poorly selective channels (permeable to both $Na^+$ and $K^+$), which gives rise to a slow "funny" inward current due mainly to $Na^+$. (*Aidley, pp 315–316*)

**186. (E)** Sweating is a function of eccrine glands that are innervated with sympathetic postganglionic cholinergic fibers, and thus atropine will depress the rate of sweating. Stimulation of the preoptic area of the anterior hypothalamus will stimulate sweating. Normal sweat is low in $Na^+$ and $Cl^-$ because reabsorptive mechanisms are in part regulated by circulating aldosterone. Serious fluid electrolyte imbalance may occur if sodium chloride (NaCl) is not properly reabsorbed. Acclimatization to hot weather involves increased sweat production with decreased concentration of NaCl, thus allowing appropriate heat balance with electrolyte conservation. (*Guyton and Hall, pp 914–915*)

**187. (B)** With arterial blood pH of 7.33, the patient clearly has an acidosis. The first question you should ask yourself is, "Is it respiratory or non-respiratory (metabolic)?" If it were respiratory, the $Pa_{CO_2}$ would have been above normal. Since it is lower than normal, this indicates the acidosis is metabolic with some respiratory compensation in response to the acidemia. The low arterial bicarbonate confirms the diagnosis of metabolic acidosis. It is unlikely that the metabolic acidosis is due to diabetic ketoacidosis; if this were the case, you would expect higher glucose levels in the blood and urine. (*Guyton and Hall, pp 401–402*)

**188. (C)** In healthy subjects on a normal diet, about 70 mEq of hydrogen ion is produced each day (largely from oxidation of sulfur-containing amino acids). This would produce a progressive metabolic acidosis if the $H^+$ were not excreted in the urine as $NH_4^+$ and

$H_2PO_4^-$. Both are decreased in the later stages of renal failure (eg, from chronic glomerulonephritis). Since $NH_4^+$ excretion plays the major role in disposing of daily $H^+$, a deficiency in ammonium excretion explains the metabolic acidosis (probably simply a reflection of the diminished number of functioning nephrons). *(Guyton and Hall, pp 398–400)*

189.    **(C)** Glomerular pores have a diameter of approximately 8 nm. Albumin, the smallest serum protein (with a molecular weight of 69,000) has a diameter of approximately 6 nm. However, albumin is prevented from passing through the pores by electrostatic repulsion, since the pores are lined by negative charges, and albumin, like most serum proteins, is itself negatively charged. *(Guyton and Hall, pp 320–322)*

190.    **(A)** Energy can be derived from either aerobic or anaerobic sources. Although aerobic oxidative processes can provide a significant amount of energy, these processes are too slow to provide all of the energy required. Although stores of ATP and creatinine phosphate are present in muscle, they provide sufficient energy for only very brief periods of exercise (a few seconds). Deaminated proteins may undergo gluconeogenesis, in which they are converted to glucose or glycogen. This pathway is not normally used for strenuous exercise. The breakdown of glycogen to lactic acid provides sufficient energy rapidly enough to support brief periods of strenuous exercise (many seconds to a few minutes). The depletion of glycogen and production of lactic acid contribute to an energy debt, which is repaid via oxidative metabolism in the period after exercise. *(Guyton and Hall, pp 1060–1061)*

191.    **(A)** In order to focus a distant object onto the retina (far accommodation) the lens has to decrease its refractive power, ie, increase its focal length. This is accomplished through relaxation of the ciliary muscles that oppose the pull of the sclera. This results in a tightening of the zonula fibers and a flattening of the lens. The pupils constrict during near accom-

modation, perhaps to increase depth of field. *(Guyton, pp 627–628)*

192.    **(D)** Insulin action stimulates the activation or membrane insertion of glucose carriers in most of its target tissues. These glucose carriers greatly enhance the permeability of the cell membrane to glucose, thus allowing glucose to flow passively down its concentration gradient into the cytoplasm. Glucose uptake is not stimulated by insulin in most neurons of the brain. *(Guyton and Hall, pp 972–973)*

193.    **(A)** Malignant hyperthermia is due to a genetic variation of the skeletal muscle ryanodine receptors (sarcoplasmic $Ca^{2+}$ release channels). Halothane and several other drugs may trigger excessive $Ca^{2+}$ release, leading to muscle contractures, increased muscle metabolism, and an enormous increase in heat production. This condition is fatal if not treated promptly. *(Ganong, p 232)*

194.    **(C)** The solubility of $CO_2$ in blood is twenty times that of $O_2$, and thus a small but considerable portion of $CO_2$ is dissolved in blood (5%). The bulk of $CO_2$ transport involves its reversible combination with water. This occurs rapidly enough because of the action of carbonic anhydrase, an enzyme located inside RBCs. As bicarbonate ion diffuses out of RBCs, chloride ions diffuse in according to Gibbs–Donnan equilibrium. Combination of $CO_2$ with amine groups, especially those of hemoglobin, also accounts for a significant portion of $CO_2$ transport (5%). *(West, 1991, pp 540–542)*

195.    **(A)** The diagram shows an expiratory and inspiratory flow-volume curve of a patient with an upper airway obstruction, eg, severe epiglottitis or tracheal narrowing due to a compressing tumor. Upper airway obstructions limits the maximal flow rate of both inspiration and expiration. In contrast to COPD, end-expiratory flow rates and lung volumes are unaffected. *(West, 1992, pp 7–12)*

196.    **(D)** Substances like creatinine (almost exclusively excreted by glomerular filtration) and urea (some reabsorption) have no adaptive

mechanisms to regulate plasma levels. Thus, a significant decrease in GFR results in significant increases in plasma creatinine and urea (if production of both substances is constant). This is because the amount excreted ($U_x \cdot \dot{V}$) equals the amount produced. Furthermore, $U_x \cdot \dot{V}$ equals $GFR \cdot P_x$. If GFR decreases, $P_x$ increases. However, both $Na^+$ and $K^+$ need to be closely regulated. Thus, as GFR decreases in disease, the percentage of either $Na^+$ or $K^+$ excreted increases in order to maintain a normal amount of $Na^+$ or $K^+$ excretion. *(Mountcastle, pp 1211–1215)*

**197. (B)** Normal sleep occurs in alternating cycles between slow-wave sleep (non-REM sleep) and rapid eye movement (REM) sleep, the latter characterized by high metabolic brain activity and desynchronization of the EEG. Somnambulism (sleep walking), enuresis (bedwetting) and night terrors occur during slow-wave sleep or arousal from slow-wave sleep. During REM sleep there is hypotonia of all major muscle groups except the ocular muscles, due to a generalized spinal inhibition that prevents acting out of dreams. Dreams, nightmares, and penile erections in the male all occur during REM sleep. *(Ganong, pp 177, 181–182; Guyton and Hall, pp 761–763)*

**198. (C)** The relationship between alveolar ventilation ($\dot{V}_A$) and alveolar $CO_2$ pressure ($P_{ACO_2}$) is represented as

$$\dot{V}_A = (\dot{V}_{CO_2}/P_{ACO_2}) \cdot K$$

where K is a constant such that $P_{ACO_2} = F_{ACO_2} \cdot K$. ($F_{ACO_2}$ is the fraction of alveolar $CO_2$.) Since $\dot{V}_{CO_2}$ is constant if $CO_2$ production remains unchanged, $P_{ACO_2}$ will double if $\dot{V}_A$ is halved. In normal persons, alveolar $CO_2$ pressure ($P_{ACO_2}$) is virtually identical to arterial $CO_2$ pressure ($P_{ACO_2}$). Therefore, $P_{ACO_2}$ will also double if $\dot{V}_A$ is halved. Unless inspired air is enriched with $O_2$, arterial $O_2$ pressure ($P_{AO_2}$) and alveolar $O_2$ pressure ($P_{AO_2}$) will decrease. *(West, 1991, pp 546–547)*

**199. (A)** The patient in question has Horner's syndrome. Unilateral loss of sympathetic innervation of the face results in ptosis, pupil

constriction, vasodilation of the skin vessels and loss of sweating (red and dry skin). Lateral deviation of the eye would suggest damage to the third cranial nerve. *(Berne and Levy, p 252)*

**200. (A)** Flow = pressure difference/resistance. If central venous pressure is negligibly small compared to mean arterial pressure, we can calculate the peripheral resistance from the data given. The key in obtaining a correct answer is being able to determine mean arterial pressure from systolic pressure $P_S$ and diastolic blood pressure $P_D$. Because of the particular shape of the pressure curve, this is not simply the arithmetic mean, but rather

$$P_D + 1/3 \, (P_S - P_D), \text{ ie, } 70 + 20 = 90 \text{ mm Hg}$$

Therefore, resistance = 90 mm Hg/5 L/min = 18 mm Hg $\cdot$ min/L. *(Guyton and Hall, p 176)*

**201. (E)** Secretion of acid and potassium by the renal tubule are inversely related. Thus, increased excretion of protons will result in decreased secretion (or increased retention) of potassium ions, with the result that the body's potassium store rises. *(Davenport, p 81)*

**202. (C)** The choices given, except for normal, are causes of hypoxemia. Breathing 100% $O_2$ will greatly relieve the hypoxemia of all except the patient with an anatomic right-to-left shunt. The $P_{AO_2}$ will greatly increase in the normal individual as well. Breathing 100% $O_2$ increases the $P_{AO_2}$ to about 670 mm Hg. In the normal person the $P_{AO_2}$ will be only slightly less than this. In abnormalities of diffusion (eg, alveolar wall thickening) the $P_{AO_2}$ will be farther below 670 mm Hg, but not as low as 125 mm Hg. In $\dot{V}/\dot{Q}$ abnormalities, $P_{AO_2}$ will be quite high in all communicating air spaces after 100% $O_2$, and both alveolar and arterial $P_{O_2}$ will be quite high. In true right-to-left shunt, breathing 100% $O_2$ will not substantially elevate the $P_{AO_2}$, which could be 125 mm Hg. The small rise over normal $P_{AO_2}$ comes mainly from a small amount of additional dissolved $O_2$ in blood passing through ventilated areas. 100% $O_2$ greatly increases the $PaO_2$ in profound hypoventilation. *(West, 1992, pp 165–166)*

203. **(D)** Hypoxemia is an important stimulus to ventilatory drive but derives all its effects via stimulation of peripheral, not central, chemoreceptors. In humans, the most important regulating factor with respect to ventilation is the $PaCO_2$. Ventilation increases linearly with a rise in $PaCO_2$. Although some of the response to $CO_2$ may be attributed to peripheral chemoreceptors, the largest percentage is the result of stimulation of central chemoreceptors. The effect of $CO_2$ presumably is via increase in $H^+$ in the cerebrospinal fluid (CSF) and cerebral extracellular fluid (ECF). Arterial hypoxemia will potentiate this effect, both by increasing the response to $CO_2$ and by reducing the level at which this response occurs. Increased work of breathing will reduce this ventilatory drive by depressing the effector organs involved. *(West, 1991, pp 583–585)*

204. **(B)** Under normal circumstances, depolarization is initiated in the SA node and then propagates to the AV node. From there, action potentials are propagated through the bundle of His and through the Purkinje system to the ventricular muscle. Conduction in the AV node is slower than conduction either from the SA node to the AV node or from the AV node to ventricular muscle. The AV nodal delay is typically of the order of 100 msec. *(Ganong, p 500)*

205. **(C)** Hyperopia, or farsightedness, is either due to an insufficient refractive power of the lens or too short an eyeball. This condition can be corrected using glasses with convex lenses. Myopia, or nearsightedness, is either due to unusually large refractive power of the lens or too long an eyeball. This condition can be corrected using glasses with concave lenses. Presbyopia is a condition of decreased accommodation range of the lens due to a decline of lens elasticity with age. Like hyperopia, this condition can also be corrected with convex glasses (reading glasses). *(Ganong, pp 139–140)*

206. **(D)** Bohr's equation states that

$$\dot{V}D/\dot{V}T = (P_{A}CO_2 - P_{E}CO_2)/P_{A}CO_2$$

where $P_{E}CO_2$ is mixed expired $CO_2$. In a normal person, $PaCO_2$ is virtually identical to $PaCO_2$. Thus

$$\dot{V}D/\dot{V}T = (PaCO_2 - P_{E}CO_2)/PaCO_2$$

Since by Fowler's method, $\dot{V}d/\dot{V}t = 0.25$ in the patient described in the question, the $(PaCO_2 - P_{E}CO_2)/PaCO_2 = (40 - P_{E}CO_2)/40 = 0.25$. Therefore $P_{E}CO_2 = 30$ mm Hg. If considerable inequality of blood flow and ventilation were present, $P_{E}CO_2$ could be much less than 30 mm Hg, and the patient's physiologic dead space would exceed the anatomic dead space. *(West, 1991, pp 526–527)*

207. **(A)** The test solution was isotonic but hyperosmotic. When the red cell was removed from normal isotonic plasma and placed in such test solution, two things happened: (1) the cell shrank, and (2) it then gradually returned to normal size. This would happen if the test solution had two components: (1) a concentration of impermeant solutes giving the same osmolality as plasma, plus (2) an additional amount of permeant solute capable of gradually penetrating the red cell membrane (at a slower rate than water). Examples of such permeant solutes are urea and glycerol. When the cell was placed in the test solution, it initially shrank (as if the test solution were hypertonic due to its higher osmolality). However, as the permeant solute became equilibrated (with the same concentration inside the cell as outside), the cell volume returned to normal. That is, although the test solution initially acted as if it were hypertonic due to its total solute concentration, this effect was only transient because of the penetration of the permeant particles. *(Berne and Levy, pp 12–13)*

208. **(C)** When the cell, with its accumulated gain of permeant solute (from prior exposure to test solution), was placed back into plasma, it had by then a total solute osmolality higher than plasma, so there was a period of net entry of water into the cell, causing it to swell (reaching a peak at point z). However, as the

accumulated solute diffused out of the cell, the cell eventually lost all of this permeant solute and therefore, ultimately, returned to normal volume. *(Berne and Levy, pp 12–13)*

209. **(C)** An increase in the rate of blood flow through the kidney (RBF) greatly increases the glomerular filtration rate (GFR). The filtrate formed is derived by ultrafiltration of plasma in the glomerular capillaries. The more plasma available (from increased RBF), the more filtrate formed. Vasoconstriction of glomerular afferent arterioles would not increase GFR but decrease it because of both a decrease in RBF and a decrease in capillary ultrafiltration pressure. Vasoconstriction of efferent arterioles could produce a slight increase in GFR but not much because of offsetting effects on RBF (decrease) and glomerular colloid osmotic pressure (increase). Indeed, because of a very substantial decrease in RBF with moderate to severe increases in efferent arteriolar resistance, there is actually a decrease in GFR despite increased capillary pressure. Because of the autoregulatory ability of kidneys, an increase in MAP from 90 mm Hg to 140 mm Hg would not have much of an effect on either RBF or GFR. Autoregulation tends to maintain a constant blood flow and capillary pressure by its influence on afferent arteriolar resistance. A strong, acute stimulation of sympathetic activity to the kidneys results in decreased RBF, decreased GFR, and may produce renal shutdown with zero urinary output. *(Guyton and Hall, pp 324, 326)*

210. **(A)** ADH acts on the collecting tubules of the kidney to induce water retention. Inappropriately high levels of ADH, as are achieved in SIADH, result in the renal retention of free water, which consequently exerts a dilutional effect on serum ion concentrations. Thus, serum sodium can fall dramatically in SIADH. ADH does not exert any direct effect on the renal handling of sodium. *(Guyton and Hall, p 373)*

211. **(C)** Strenuous exercise provides a good example of how various physiologic adjustments operate and are integrated. Although the underlying mechanisms are in large part unknown, it is clear that both alveolar ventilation and cardiac output increase. Regional blood flow is altered so that active muscles have increased blood flow and less active, nonessential areas, such as the skin and viscera, have temporally decreased blood flow. $O_2$ use is enhanced by decreases in tissue $P_{O_2}$ in exercising muscle, as well as a shift to the right of the oxyhemoglobin dissociation curve due to increases in $H^+$, temperature, and $CO_2$. The body temperature rises, although sweating mechanisms are significantly increased. *(Mountcastle, pp 1401–1411)*

212. **(D)** The Fick principle is derived by applying the law of conservation of mass ("what comes in must go out"):

$$\dot{V}_{O_2} = \dot{Q} \cdot (Ca_{O_2} - Cv_{O_2})$$

where $\dot{V}_{O_2}$ equals $O_2$ consumption ("what comes in"), $\dot{Q}$ is cardiac output, and $Ca_{O_2}$ and $Cv_{O_2}$ are arterial and mixed venous $O_2$ content, respectively. First, we calculate cardiac output:

$$300 \text{ mL } O_2/\text{min}$$
$$= \dot{Q} \cdot (20 - 15) \text{ mL } O_2/100 \text{ mL blood}$$
$$300 \text{ mL } O_2/\text{min}$$
$$= \dot{Q} \cdot 5 \text{ mL } O_2/100 \text{ mL blood}$$
$$\dot{Q} = 6000 \text{ mL blood}/\text{min}$$

Next, we calculate stroke volume:

$$\text{cardiac output} = \text{stroke volume} \cdot \text{heart rate.}$$
$$6000 \text{ mL}/\text{min} = 100 \text{ mL} \cdot 60/\text{min}$$

*(Berne and Levy, pp 412–413)*

213. **(C)** The high rate of blood flow at the placenta and the significant resistance of the placenta to diffusion of $O_2$ result in blood in the umbilical vein that has a lower $P_{O_2}$ (30 mm Hg) than maternal mixed venous blood. However, the shift in fetal oxyhemoglobin concentration and the Bohr effect all increase the transport of $O_2$ to fetal tissues. A number of significant differences in circulating patterns are present in the fetus, including shunting of blood across a patent foramen

ovale and ductus arteriosus. The net effect of these shunts in the presence of high fetal pulmonary vascular resistance is very low fetal pulmonary blood flow. At birth, these patterns normally are quickly changed to ex utero patterns with high pulmonary perfusion. Since the liver is supplied by umbilical venous blood and the heart and head receive blood before it has mixed with significant amounts of desaturated blood, these important organs receive blood that is relatively high in saturated oxyhemoglobin. *(Berne and Levy, pp 527–529)*

214. **(D)** Cerebral blood flow will increase when $PaO_2$ is decreased to < 50 mm Hg or when $PaCO_2$ increases above normal. A decrease in viscosity will also increase cerebral blood flow. Cerebral blood flow is closely linked to brain parenchymal metabolism, and intense activity during a seizure will result in large, widespread increases in blood flow. The brain autoregulates, and consequently an increase in blood pressure is offset by an increase in local vascular resistance to maintain constant cerebral blood flow. *(Berne and Levy, pp 523–524)*

215. **(A)** $P_{alv}$ is ambient atmospheric pressure, or zero reference pressure, and $P_{pl}$ is a negative intrapleural pressure that becomes even more negative during inspiration. The lungs will expand to a higher volume during inhalation as a result of an increase in the translung pressure, or distending pressure $(P_{alv} - P_{pl})$. Static compliance is measured under conditions of no airflow (stepwise changes in volume with no airflow during measurement of distending pressure). With each increase in distending pressure there is a corresponding increase in lung volume. Compliance is $\Delta V / \Delta P$. *(Berne and Levy, pp 563–565)*

216. **(C)** The volume of air remaining in the lungs after a maximal effort to exhale all the air possible (ie, after your best effort to "empty" your lungs) is the residual volume. This volume cannot be measured directly by a spirometer, which measures only change in volume. Since you cannot voluntarily change your lung volume below the residual volume, the spirometer cannot measure it. Other methods (eg, body plethysmography, inert gas dilution) must be used to measure residual volume. *(Berne and Levy, pp 557–558)*

217. **(A)** The product of tidal volume (volume moved in or out with each breath) times the frequency or breathing rate (number of breaths/min) is the total ventilation per minute (also called minute ventilation). In this case, the total ventilation is 600 mL times 12 breaths/min = 7200 mL/min. As stated in the problem, the alveolar ventilation (air ventilating the respiratory zone for gas exchange each minute) is 6000 mL/min. The difference is that part of the total ventilation going only to non-exchanging conducting airways = 1200 mL/min, or 100 mL per breath at 12 breaths/min. This 100 mL is the dead space volume. *(West, 1991, pp 524–525, 526–527)*

218. **(C)** Either severe chronic lung disease or an overdose of heroin would have caused respiratory acidosis due to abnormally high arterial $PCO_2$ (not low $PCO_2$ which this subject has). A lowlander at high altitude for two weeks would have had both low $PO_2$ and low $PCO_2$ like this subject, but would have had an abnormally low plasma bicarbonate and a more nearly normal pH due to renal compensation in the form of bicarbonate excretion. Acute aspirin overdose in adults usually presents first with a respiratory alkalosis, which includes a low $PCO_2$, but not a low $PO_2$. Breathing a low oxygen gas mixture is similar to being at high altitude, but if this is only for a few minutes there will be no time for renal compensation. The hypoxia stimulates hyperventilation, which lowers the $PCO_2$. The slightly lowered bicarbonate is due to buffering by nonbicarbonate buffers. Decreased $PCO_2$ results in decreased $H_2CO_3$. Decreased $H_2CO_3$ results in the following reaction being pulled to the right:

$$HCO_3^- + H^+ \rightarrow H_2CO_3 \rightarrow H_2O + CO_2$$

thus lowering the plasma bicarbonate $HCO_3^-$ to slightly below normal. Had there been time for renal compensation, the bicarbonate would have been much lower. (*Rose, pp 629–637*)

**219.** **(D)** While sympathetic activation often occurs as a generalized response (Cannon's "flight and fight"), parasympathetic innervation is organ specific. Functions of the parasympathetic nervous system include an increase in gastrointestinal motility, a decrease in gastrointestinal sphincter tone, and emptying of the rectum and urinary bladder. Sacral parasympathetic nerves cause vasodilation of the penis artery and maintain erection. The ejaculation is triggered by sudden discharge from lumbar sympathetic fibers. This explains why patients with a damaged lumbar but intact sacral spinal cord can have reflex penile erections but lose their ability to ejaculate. (*Ganong, pp 206–209; Guyton and Hall, p 1009*)

**220.** **(C)** Muscle tone is determined by the basal firing rate of the $\alpha$-motor neurons and damage to these, ie, lower motor neuron lesions, will result in flaccid paralysis. In contrast, damage of the corticospinal tract, ie, upper motor neuron lesions, will result in spastic paralysis because of hyperactive stretch reflexes. Activation of $\gamma$-efferent fibers to muscle spindles also increases muscle tone due to reflex activation of the $\alpha$-motor neurons (stretch reflex). Pathologically increased $\gamma$-efferent discharge results in muscle clonus. (*Ganong, pp 116–118*)

**221.** **(D)** Even though the cabin of the airplane described in the question is pressurized, the barometric pressure decreased to 523 mm Hg. Thus, the $FIO_2$ remains the same (0.2) but inspired $PO_2$ decreases, since it is the product of $FIO_2$ and barometric pressure. Water vapor pressure remains at 47 mm Hg as long as body temperature is normal, and thus $PO_2$ of humidified alveolar air must be less than that at sea level. Although a decrease in $PACO_2$ (due to some hyperventilation) may slightly enhance $PAO_2$, this is not sufficient to prevent the decrease in $PAO_2$ due to the drop in barometric pressure. (*West, 1991, pp 588–590*)

**222.** **(A)** Shunted blood is blood that bypasses ventilated parts of the lung and directly enters the arterial circulation. In normal persons, this is largely due to mixing of arterial blood with bronchial venous and some myocardial venous blood, which drains into the left heart. Diffusion limitation, although finite, is usually immeasurably small, as is reaction velocity with hemoglobin. (*West, 1991, pp 553–554*)

**223.** **(B)** Cystic fibrosis (CF) is one of the most common genetic disorders of Caucasians, occurring in 1 of 2000 births. The abnormal gene is located on chromosome 7 and encodes a cAMP regulated $Cl^-$ channel (CFTR). Since $Cl^-$ flux via this channel plays different roles in different epithelia it is not surprising that the symptoms of cystic fibrosis are quite diverse. The volume-absorbing airway epithelium in CF patients shows increased $Na^+$ reabsorption, probably because lack of CFTR increases the transepithelial potential difference. This results in a thick, dehydrated mucus predisposing to airway infections. This is in contrast to sweat glands, where CF patients secrete nearly normal volumes of sweat into the acinus, but are unable to absorb NaCl from sweat as it moves through the sweat duct. Therefore, $Na^+$ and $Cl^-$ content of sweat is elevated in CF patients. Lack of $Cl^-$ and water secretion in gastrointestinal epithelia can lead to severe constipation and obstruction of the small and large bowels. Impairment of the $Cl^-/HCO_3^-$ exchange in pancreatic ductal epithelium results in water and enzyme retention and may eventually destroy the pancreas. (*Harrison's Principles of Internal Medicine, pp 1194–1197*)

**224.** **(C)** With few exceptions, blood vessels are not innervated by parasympathetic nerves, and there is little effect of parasympathetic tone on total peripheral resistance. In contrast, sympathetic nerve activity contributes to the basal vascular smooth muscle tone, and cutting these nerve fibers results in immediate vasodilation of the affected extremity. While hypersensitivity to circulating catecholamines will develop over time, this does not contribute to the vasodilation. (*Guyton and Hall, pp 484–486*)

225. **(E)** The initial segment of this EEG recording shows normal alpha brain wave activity. Alpha waves are indicative of a relaxed state, with eyes closed and the mind wandering freely. At the point marked by the arrow, the EEG becomes desynchronized (beta brain waves). Beta waves are seen when the patient performs specific mental tasks such as calculations or when he observes objects after opening eyes. Falling asleep is associated with increased synchronization of brain waves and petit mal attacks are characterized by a 3-per-second spike and dome pattern. *(Guyton and Hall, pp 763–766)*

226. **(A)** Thromboxane A2 and prostacyclin (PGI2) are both derived from PGH2 but have opposite effects on platelets and blood vessels. Thromboxane A2, released from plate-lets, promotes vasoconstriction and platelet aggregation while PGI2, released from endothelial cells, is a potent vasodilator and inhibits platelet aggregation. Most prosta-glandins have a large range of actions and they may contract or relax smooth muscle cells depending on tissue source and species. An increase in prostaglandin production by fetal membranes is believed to be a major factor for onset of uterine contractions and labor in humans. *(Ganong, pp 281–284; West, 1991, pp 889–890)*

227. **(A)** Isovolumetric relaxation involves a drop in left ventricular pressure with no change in left ventricular volume (hence the term "isovolumetric"). This occurs between points W (point at which the aortic valve closes) and X (point at which the mitral valve opens and ends the isovolumetric period). *(Guyton and Hall, pp 114–115; West, 1991, pp 250–256)*

228. **(C)** The production of pressure is not very energy efficient (compared with movement of blood). Since the period of isovolumetric contraction produces the majority of the pressure increase of ventricular systole, and over a rather short period of time, it has the highest rate of energy consumption (either measured by mL $O_2$ consumed per unit time or by mols ATP hydrolized per unit time). *(Guyton and Hall, pp 114–115; West, 1991, pp 250–256)*

229–233. **(229-B, 230-E, 231-D, 232-B, 233-A)** In the first stage of slow-wave sleep, which is associated with very light sleep, the EEG pattern shows very-low-voltage waves punctuated by occasional bursts of alpha activity, called sleep spindles. As sleep progresses, frequency of the EEG waveform decreases until it is approximately 2 to 3 cycles per second. This pattern, called delta waves, is characteristic of the deep sleep of slow-wave stage 4. Alert wakefulness and REM sleep are both characterized by beta waves, which indicate a high degree of brain activity. Quiet wakefulness is associated with alpha waves. *(Guyton and Hall, p 765)*

234–236. **(234-A, 235-C, 236-D)** Although the early maturation of an ovarian follicle is dependent on the presence of FSH, ovulation is induced by a surge of LH. Although estrogen usually has a negative feedback effect on LH and FSH secretion, the LH surge seems to be a response to elevated estrogen levels. In concert with FSH, LH induces rapid follicular swelling. LH also acts directly on the granulosa cells to cause them to decrease estrogen production as well as to initiate production of small amounts of progesterone. These changes lead to ovulation. FSH is required for Sertoli cells to mediate the development of spermatids into mature sperm cells. *(Guyton and Hall, pp 1018–1021)*

237. **(A)** A normal, healthy individual in acid–base balance is represented by point C (pH 7.4, bicarbonate 24 mEq/L, and $Pa_{CO_2}$ 40 mm Hg). Changes in $Pa_{CO_2}$ cause changes in pH along the line A-C-D, which is a $CO_2$ titration curve. Moving either upward or downward along this titration curve represents these changes in pH with changes in $Pa_{CO_2}$ (to higher or lower $CO_2$ isobars). There are small secondary changes in bicarbonate due to buffer reactions with nonbicarbonate buffers. These are not compensatory changes in bicarbonate concentration. At point A no compensation in the form of increased renal production of bicarbonate has occurred yet. *(Guyton, and Hall, pp 399–402)*

**238. (B)** This is respiratory acidosis (as was the previous question) but with some renal compensation in the form of increased production of bicarbonate. Bicarbonate concentration increases upward along the same higher $CO_2$ isobar of the previous question (going from point A to B). This returns the pH partially back toward normal. *(Guyton and Hall, pp 399– 402)*

**239. (G)** Point F represents a simple uncompensated metabolic acidosis (a rare circumstance). But as the pH falls, alveolar ventilation is stimulated (eg, Kussmaul breathing in ketoacidosis of diabetes), producing a lower $Pa_{CO_2}$. Lowering the $Pa_{CO_2}$ moves the pH back toward normal along a lower $CO_2$ isobar. *(Guyton and Hall, pp 399–402)*

**240. (D)** The aortic blood pressure oscillates between a peak (called the systolic blood pressure) and a nadir (called the diastolic blood pressure). This nadir is reached just after the beginning of systole when the rising left ventricular pressure equals, or just exceeds, the aortic blood pressure and forces the left ventricular blood to be ejected through the aortic valve. At this time (the end of the isovolumetric contraction and the beginning of ejection) the left ventricular pressure essentially equals aortic diastolic blood pressure at point D. *(Berne and Levy, pp 407–408)*

**241. (H)** During ventricular systole the blood returning to the heart from the pulmonary circulation causes a gradual rise in left atrial volume and pressure. When ventricular isovolumetric relaxation ends, blood suddenly exits from the left atrium into the left ventricle (beginning of ventricular rapid filling). It is the opening of the mitral valve that brings an end to the rising left atrial pressure. Thus, the peak of the left atrial V wave and the opening of the mitral valve must be simultaneous at point H in the illustration. *(Berne and Levy, pp 407–408)*

**242. (F)** The T wave of the electrocardiogram represents ventricular repolarization (which leads to relaxation). By the peak of the T wave, enough ventricular muscle has be-

gun to relax so that the ventricular pressure starts to fall. Thus, the peak of the T wave and the peak of the ventricular pressure (point F in the illustration) are simultaneous. *(Berne and Levy, pp 407–408)*

**243–245. (243-C, 244-B, 245-A)** Myoglobins and hemoglobins are oxygen-carrying proteins that differ in their $O_2$ affinity. These differences reflect their functional adaptation. HbA, which accounts for 95% of normal adult hemoglobin, consists of 2 alpha chains and 2 beta chains, each carrying one molecule of heme. Initial binding of oxygen to hemoglobin facilitates further binding of additional oxygen, resulting in a characteristic sigmoidal binding curve (curve C). Fetal hemoglobin HbF consists of 2 alpha chains and 2 gamma chains and differs from HbA in two important respects: (1) It doesn't bind organic phosphates including 2,3-DPG as effectively as HbA, and (2) its oxygen-binding curve is shifted to the left (curve B). Therefore, the oxygen content of umbilical vein blood is higher than that of placental vein blood, even though the $pO_2$ of umbilical blood is slightly lower than that of the placental veins. Myoglobin resembles hemoglobins but binds only 1 molecule $O_2$ rather than 4 molecules $O_2$. Its oxygen-binding curve therefore is not sigmoidal (curve A) but has a higher affinity compared to hemoglobins, resulting in a transfer of oxygen from arterial blood to skeletal muscle fibers. *(West, 1991, pp 377–380)*

**246–248. (246-B, 247-C, 248-D and L)** Despite the tremendous progress in understanding the role of cytokines in normal and pathological processes, the therapeutic and research potential of these substances has just begun to be explored. Interferons, by definition, elicit a nonspecific antiviral activity by inducing specific RNA synthesis and protein expression in neighboring cells. Common interferon inducers are viruses, double-stranded RNA, and microorganisms. The three main human interferons are INF-α, INF-β, and INF-γ derived from leukocytes, fibroblasts, and T cells, respectively. INF-α is currently in clinical use against hairy cell leukemia, Kaposi sarcoma and venereal warts (condyloma acuminata). In addition to the common inducers, INF-β production by fibroblasts is also elicited by TNF and IL-1. In contrast to INF-α, INF-β is strictly species specific. INF-β appears to be useful for treatment of squamous sarcomas, viral encephalitis, and possibly multiple sclerosis. INF-γ is produced mainly by CD4- and CD8-positive T-cells, and to a lesser extent by B cells and natural killer cells. INF-γ has antiviral and antiparasitic activity and is synergistic with INF-α and INF-β, but its main biological activity appears to be immunomodulatory. Among its many functions are activation of macrophages and enhanced expression of MHC-II proteins on macrophages. Macrophages produce Il-1, IL-12, and TNF. The effects of IL-1 and TNF are widespread and include activation of T cells, B cells, fever induction, and many others. (*Ganong, pp 483–484; Ibelgaufts, pp 343–354, 367–373, 709*)

**249–251. (249-C, 250-D, 251-A)** Gastrin is produced by G cells in the stomach antrum following vasovagal reflexes, stomach distention, or chemical stimuli, in particular amino acid and protein rich food. Together with histamine and acetylcholine, gastrin stimulates acid secretion from parietal cells. Secretin is produced by duodenal mucosa glands when highly acidic food enters the small intestine. This hormone stimulates secretion of a bicarbonate rich solution from pancreatic ductal epithelium but does not stimulate pancreatic enzyme secretion. Cholecystokinin, like secretin, reaches the pancreas via the bloodstream but causes secretion of large quantities of digestive enzymes by acinar cells. GIP is produced in the duodenum in response to sugars and fat. This peptide inhibits gastric secretion and motility, but its main effect appears to be stimulation of insulin production in pancreatic beta cells. VIP stimulates water and electrolyte secretion of intestinal mucosa. Somatostatin is produced by pancreatic D cells and similar cells in the gastrointestinal mucosa and inhibits secretion of several gastrointestinal hormones, including gastrin and secretin. (*Guyton and Hall, pp 821–826; Ganong, pp 445–448*)

**252. (C)** What is recorded in all of the examples is the forced expiratory volume in one second ($FEV_1$). The patient is connected to a spirometer and after taking in as much air as possible (maximal inhalation) is asked to expire as forcefully as he/she can to exhale as much air as possible as rapidly as possible. The volume exhaled in the first second (shaded area of examples) is the $FEV_1$. The difference between the beginning total lung capacity (TLC) and the residual volume (RV) is the vital capacity. The forced vital capacity (FVC), shown in all but example C, is not always the same as in a less forced measurement. Pattern A represents a normal, healthy adult. The flow rate is high at first (steep downward slope) near the beginning TLC, but then becomes less and less steep as the lung volume decreases until it plateaus (becomes flat) at residual volume and zero flow. Record C represents a patient with an obstructive disease that makes it difficult to force large volumes of air out at a high rate of flow. Thus, the slope is less steep than normal, and it takes a long time to reach the residual volume (may take 20 or 30 seconds; this is why pattern C doesn't include FVC). Asthma, emphysema, and chronic bronchitis are common obstructive diseases. Both the TLC and the RV are higher than normal in such patients. At the bedside the same kind of information can be obtained by asking the patient to blow out a lighted match. Patients with obstructive disease have difficulty doing so. (*West, 1992, pp 3–7*)

**253. (B)** Record B represents the $FEV_1$ of a patient with restrictive lung disease (lungs are restricted in volume). Pulmonary fibrosis is a chronic condition that can follow pulmonary inflammation (pneumonitis) brought about by a number of conditions. Other examples of restrictive disease include problems with chest wall movement (Pickwickian syndrome, scoliosis, myasthenia gravis, etc.) and loss of lung compliance (eg, lack of surfactant, pulmonary edema, fibrosis, etc.). Although flow rates are quite good at any given volume (comparable to that of a normal subject at that same lung volume), the TLC, VC, and RV are all below normal. *(West, 1992, pp 3–7)*

**254–257.** (254-E, 255-F, 256-C, 257-A) Plasma proteins consist of albumin, globulins, and fibrinogen. These can be separated by their rate of migration in an electrical field (electrophoresis). The fractions shown in the figure are (A) albumin, (B) $\alpha_1$-globulins, (D) $\alpha_2$-globulins, (E) β-globulins, and (F) γ-globulins. The smallest of these proteins (albumins) are also the most numerous and are responsible for much of the oncotic pressure of plasma (about 25 mm Hg). Iron bound to transferrin and β-lipoproteins are transported in the β-globulin fraction, while bilirubin, fatty acids, and many drugs are transported adsorbed to albumin. Antibodies (immunoglobulins) constitute the bulk of γ-globulins. More than 99% of T3 and T4 are bound to albumin and to a specific thyroxin-binding globulin (TBG). While albumin has the larger capacity, TBG has the larger affinity for these hormones. TBG is a globulin with an electrophoretic motility between $\alpha_1$-globulins and $\alpha_2$-globulins. *(Berne and Levy, pp 327–328)*

**258–261.** (258-A, 259-G, 260-C, 261-F) As every beer drinker knows, consumption of alcohol causes diuresis. This is partially due to suppression of pituitary ADH secretion by alcohol (and partially due to the often enormous amount of fluid consumed). Permeability of the collecting ducts for water reabsorption remains low in the absence of ADH, producing a large volume dilute urine. Potassium-sparing diuretics act by either antagonizing the action of aldosterone (spironolactone) or by inhibiting $Na^+$ reabsorption in the distal tubules (amiloride). Mannitol is freely filtered at the glomerulus, but in contrast to glucose is not reabsorbed and produces an osmotic diuresis. Clinically it is used to treat cerebral edema and in prerenal azotemia to convert oliguric acute renal failure to non-oliguric acute renal failure. Thiazides inhibit $Na^+$ and $K^+$ reabsorption in the distal tubule and loop diuretics (furosemide, ethacrynic acid) inhibit the $Na^+$-$K^+$-2 $Cl^-$ cotransporter in the ascending loop of Henle. *(Ganong, p 665)*

**262.** (D) The direct source of energy for muscle contraction comes from ATP hydrolysis. The most efficient means of generating new ATP to replace that utilized is through aerobic metabolism (mainly by the Krebs cycle). Aerobic metabolism depends on the supply of oxygen to muscle and cannot immediately rise to supply ATP as fast as it is utilized (period B of illustration). This period is one of an "oxygen deficit." Time is required for sufficient increase in cardiac output and pulmonary ventilation to increase enough to supply oxygen at the rate needed. Between the onset of exercise (at "begin work" in illustration) and the highest level of oxygen supply and consumption (plateau in illustration), energy is mainly supplied by anaerobic depletion of high energy phosphate stores (ATP and CP) and anaerobic glycolysis. Resynthesis of these stores requires that $Vo_2$ remain above normal for a while after cessation of exercise (after "end work" in illustration). This period of time (period D in illustration) is described as repayment of an "oxygen debt." *(McArdle, Katch, and Katch, pp 127–131)*

**263.** (B) This is the period of oxygen deficit during which part of the energy requirements are being met anaerobically by depletion of high energy phosphates (period B of illustration). *(McArdle, Katch, and Katch, pp 127–131)*

**264.** (B) The proximal tubule reabsorbs the majority (about two-thirds) of filtered salt and water. This is done in an essentially iso-osmotic manner. Both the luminal salt concentration and the luminal osmolality remain constant (and equal to plasma values) along the entire length of the proximal tubule. Water and salt are reabsorbed proportionally because the water is dependent on and coupled with the active reabsorption of $Na^+$. The water permeability of the proximal tubule is high, and therefore a significant transepithelial osmotic gradient is not possible (a minute gradient of as little as one mOsm/L may exist). Sodium is actively transported, mainly by basolateral sodium pumps, into the lateral intercellular spaces; water follows. *(Vander, pp 97–100)*

**265. (D)** The thick ascending limb of the loop of Henle has very low permeability to water. Since there are no regulatory mechanisms to alter its permeability, it remains poorly permeable to water under all circumstances. Sodium and chloride are transported out of the luminal fluid into the surrounding interstitial spaces (they are reabsorbed). Since water must remain behind (it is not reabsorbed), the solute concentration becomes less and less (the luminal fluid becomes more dilute). This is one of the principal mechanisms (along with diminution of ADH secretion) for the production of a dilute, hypo-osmotic urine (water diuresis). (*Vander, pp 101–102*)

**266–269. (266-G, 267-D, 268-F, 269-F)** Much progress has been made in the past 10 years elucidating signal-transduction mechanisms, and this has become a popular topic in the medical board exams. Steroid hormones like estrogen, progesterone, testosterone, and mineralcorticoids bind to cytoplasmic receptors and the hormone-receptor complex then diffuses into the nucleus and binds to DNA to modulate gene expression in a specific way. Endothelial cells produce both vasoconstrictor substances, eg, endothelins, and potent vasodilator substances, eg, EDHF and EDRF (nitric oxide). Nitric oxide relaxes vascular smooth muscle by activating guanylate cyclase and increased production of cGMP, then activates protein kinase G and possibly also protein kinase A. Angiotensin II is a potent vasoconstrictor. This action is mediated by $AT_{1A}$ receptors coupled to phospholipase leading to hydrolysis of $PIP_2$ to $IP_3$ and diacylglycerol (DAG). In addition, angiotensin II increases secretion of aldosterone from the adrenal cortex via $AT_{2A}$ receptors. $\alpha_1$-adrenergic receptors are also coupled to phospholipase C via G proteins, while catecholamine binding to $\alpha_2$ receptors results in a decrease in cAMP. (*Ganong, pp 34–40, 86–87, 420*)

**270–271. (270-D, 271-I)** The relaxation pressure-volume diagram shows the interaction between lung elasticity and chest wall elasticity. Note that the combined pressure-volume curve (solid line) is simply the sum of lung and chest wall pressure curves. At rest, when all respiratory muscles are relaxed, this combined pressure equals 0 (equilibrium point D), and the corresponding lung volume (level H) is the functional reserve capacity (FRC). Below FRC, the combined lung and chest wall will spring outwards when the respiratory muscles are relaxed, thus generating a negative relaxation pressure. Residual volume (level I) is achieved after maximal expiration. The isolated lung would further collapse to its minimal volume (level K). (*West, 1991, pp 566–568*)

**272. (C)** The cardiac myocyte action potential is characterized by a rapid depolarization due to opening of $Na^+$ channels and a more slowly developing plateau phase lasting about 200 msec. The plateau is due to opening of "slow" (or L-type) $Ca^{2+}$ channels. This action potential spreads rapidly across the myocardium since cardiac myocytes are electrically coupled via gap junctions. (*Ganong, pp 498–500*)

**273. (A)** The resting membrane potential of excitable cells is largely due to the selective permeability of the cell membrane to potassium ions. The $Na^+/K^+$ pump generates the ion gradient across the cell membrane, ie, high intracellular $K^+$, high extracellular $Na^+$, but it is the back diffusion of $K^+$ ions through $K^+$ channels that are open at rest which charges the cell membrane. If the cell membrane were a perfect $K^+$ electrode, the membrane potential would equal the equilibrium potential for $K^+$ as predicted by the Nernst equation. In reality, the resting membrane potential is more positive because of the contribution of $Na^+$ channels, $Cl^-$ channels, and nonselective cation channels. (*Aidley, pp 22–29*)

**274. (B)** $Na^+$ channels show rapid inactivation upon cell membrane depolarization. This self-limits the $Na^+$ influx and membrane depolarization caused by opening of $Na^+$ channels. The time required for removal of inactivation following repolarization determines the refractory period of neurons and sets an upper limit to their firing frequency. $K^+$ channels and $Ca^{2+}$ channels also show inactivation, but this occurs more slowly than for $Na^+$

channels. Inactivation is due to a part of the molecule located at the cytoplasmic side of the membrane and can be imagined as an inactivating particle or ball swinging into the pore and blocking it once the activation gate is open. *(Aidley, pp 84–86)*

275. **(H)** Depolarization of skeletal muscle sarcolemma results in opening of $Ca^{2+}$ release channels located on the sarcoplasmic reticulum (SR). These channels are locked into the open state by the plant alkaloid ryanodine and therefore also known as "ryanodine receptors." *(Aidley, pp 297–299)*

276. **(F)** The nicotinic ACh receptor of the motor end-plate consists of five subunits that form a transmembrane channel pore. This channel belongs to the class of ligand-gated nonselective cation channels. Binding of ACh to the α-subunits causes opening of these channels, allowing $Na^+$ to enter and $K^+$ to leave the cell. Since the driving force for $Na^+$ is much larger than that for $K^+$, this results in depolarization of the post-junctional membrane. *(Berne and Levy, pp 59–61)*

277. **(F)** The photoreceptor cell membrane is relatively depolarized in darkness due to $Na^+$ entry through nonselective cation channels. Openings of these channels are maintained by the high intracellular cGMP levels in photoreceptors during darkness and the $Na^+$ inward current through these channels is usually called "dark-current." Illumination by light causes a conformational change in the photosensitive pigment rhodopsin which is linked via a G protein to a cGMP specific phosphodiesterase. Activation of phosphodiesterase lowers cGMP levels and, since cGMP is required to maintain openings of the nonselective cation channels, results in membrane hyperpolarization with light exposure. *(Ganong, pp 142–143)*

## REFERENCES

Aidley DJ. *The Physiology of Excitable Cells.* 3rd ed. Cambridge University Press; 1991

Berne RM, Levy MN, eds. *Physiology.* 3rd ed. St. Louis: Mosby Year Book; 1993

Davenport HW. *The ABC of Acid-Base Chemistry.* 7th ed. Chicago: University of Chicago Press; 1974

Ganong WF. *Review of Medical Physiology.* 17th ed. Los Altos, CA: Appleton & Lange; 1995

Guyton AC, Hall JE. *Textbook of Medical Physiology.* 9th ed. Philadelphia: WB Saunders Co.; 1995

*Harrison's Principles of Internal Medicine,* 13th ed. New York: McGraw-Hill Inc.; 1994

Kandel ER, Schwartz JH, Jessel TM. *Principles of Neural Science.* 3rd ed. New York: Elsevier; 1993

Ibelgaufts H. *Dictionary of Cytokines.* New York: VCH; 1994

McArdle WD, Katch FI, Katch VL. *Exercise Physiology.* 3rd ed. Philadelphia: Lea & Febiger; 1991

Mountcastle VB. *Medical Physiology.* 14th ed. St. Louis: CV Mosby Co.; 1980

Rose DB. *Clinical Physiology of Acid-Base and Electrolyte Disorders.* 4th ed. New York: McGraw-Hill Inc.; 1994

Vander AJ. *Renal Physiology.* 5th ed. New York: McGraw-Hill Inc.; 1995

West JB, ed. *Best and Taylor's Physiological Basis of Medical Practice.* 12th ed. Baltimore: Williams & Wilkins; 1991

West JB. *Pulmonary Pathophysiology—The Essentials.* 4th ed. Baltimore: Williams & Wilkins; 1992

# Subspecialty List—Physiology

151. Pregnancy
152. Nervous system
153. Circulation
154. Urogenital system
155. Endocrinology
156. Endocrinology
157. Nervous system
158. Sensory system
159. Gastrointestinal
160. Sensory system
161. Muscle
162. Blood
163. Muscle
164. Circulation
165. Gastrointestinal
166. Cardiac
167. Circulation
168. Circulation
169. Endocrinology
170. Gastrointestinal
171. Circulation
172. Muscle
173. Cell physiology
174. Renal
175. Cell physiology
176. Endocrinology
177. Muscle
178. Circulation
179. Muscle
180. Renal
181. Respiratory
182. Respiratory
183. Respiratory
184. Cardiac

185. Cardiac
186. Thermoregulation
187. Acid/Base
188. Acid/Base
189. Renal
190. Muscle
191. Sensory system
192. Endocrinology
193. Thermoregulation
194. Blood
195. Respiratory
196. Renal
197. Nervous system
198. Respiratory
199. Nervous system
200. Circulation
201. Acid/Base
202. Respiratory
203. Respiratory
204. Cardiac
205. Sensory system
206. Respiratory
207. Cell physiology
208. Cell physiology
209. Renal
210. Endocrinology
211. Exercise physiology
212. Circulation
213. Circulation
214. Circulation
215. Respiratory
216. Respiratory
217. Respiratory
218. Acid/Base

219. Nervous system
220. Muscle
221. Respiratory
222. Respiratory
223. Cell physiology
224. Circulation
225. Nervous system
226. Endocrinology
227. Cardiac
228. Cardiac
229. Nervous system
230. Nervous system
231. Nervous system
232. Nervous system
233. Nervous system
234. Endocrinology
235. Endocrinology
236. Endocrinology
237. Acid/Base
238. Acid/Base
239. Acid/Base
240. Cardiac
241. Cardiac
242. Cardiac
243. Blood
244. Blood
245. Blood
246. Immunology
247. Immunology
248. Immunology
249. Gastrointestinal
250. Gastrointestinal
251. Gastrointestinal
252. Respiratory

253. Respiratory
254. Blood
255. Blood
256. Blood
257. Blood
258. Renal
259. Renal
260. Renal
261. Renal

262. Exercise physiology
263. Exercise physiology
264. Renal
265. Renal
266. Cell physiology
267. Cell physiology
268. Cell physiology
269. Cell physiology
270. Respiratory

271. Respiratory
272. Cell physiology
273. Cell physiology
274. Cell physiology
275. Cell physiology
276. Cell physiology
277. Cell physiology

# CHAPTER 3

# Biochemistry
## Questions

*Michael W. King, PhD*

**DIRECTIONS (Questions 278 through 328): Each of the numbered items or incomplete statements in this section is followed by answers or by completions of the statement. Select the ONE lettered answer or completion that is BEST in each case.**

278. Free purine and pyrimidine bases and nucleosides can be converted to the corresponding nucleoside 5'-monophosphate via salvage pathways. These pathways are important for conversion of certain antimetabolites that are employed for chemotherapy. Which of the following antimetabolites would require salvage for proper function?

   (A) azaserine
   (B) methotrexate
   (C) 5-fluorouracil
   (D) allopurinol
   (E) none of the above

279. Competitive inhibitors

   (A) increase the apparent $K_m$ of the enzyme
   (B) decrease the apparent $K_m$ of the enzyme
   (C) increase the apparent $V_{max}$ of the reaction
   (D) decrease the apparent $V_{max}$ of the reaction
   (E) do not affect the $K_m$ or the $V_{max}$

280. Lactate that is released into the circulation can be converted back to glucose in

   (A) liver
   (B) heart muscle
   (C) erythrocytes
   (D) adipose tissue
   (E) brain

281. All of the following are involved in movement of $CO_2$ from peripheral tissues to the lungs EXCEPT

   (A) carbamate
   (B) carbonic anhydrase
   (C) $CO_2$ bound to the iron of hemoglobin (Hb)
   (D) bicarbonate
   (E) dissolved $CO_2$

282. A deficiency of vitamin D in adults can lead to

   (A) osteomalacia
   (B) xerophthalmia
   (C) macrocytic anemia
   (D) scurvy
   (E) rickets

283. A deficiency in vitamin $B_{12}$ can result from

   (A) its being trapped in the form of $N^5$-methyltetrahydrofolate
   (B) the lack of intrinsic factor in the intestines
   (C) lipid malabsorptive disorders
   (D) the lack of transcobalamin II in the liver

284. The carbohydrate employed in the biosynthesis of nucleic acids is made in which of the following pathways?

   (A) glycolysis
   (B) gluconeogenesis
   (C) urea cycle
   (D) citric acid cycle
   (E) pentose phosphate pathway

285. Decreased wound healing, osteoporosis, hemorrhaging, and muscle fatigue are all symptoms caused by the lack of vitamin

    (A)  E
    (B)  $B_6$
    (C)  K
    (D)  C
    (E)  D

286. The ATPase activity required for muscle contraction is located in

    (A)  myosin
    (B)  troponin
    (C)  myokinase
    (D)  sarcoplasmic reticulum
    (E)  actin

287. All of the following are allosteric effectors regulating the glycolytic pathway EXCEPT

    (A)  glucose-6-phosphate
    (B)  ATP
    (C)  fructose-6-phosphate
    (D)  citrate
    (E)  AMP

288. The rate-limiting step in glycolysis occurs at the step catalyzed by

    (A)  glyceraldehyde 3-phosphate dehydrogenase
    (B)  phosphofructokinase-1
    (C)  pyruvate kinase
    (D)  phosphoglycerate kinase
    (E)  phosphofructokinase-2

289. The primary positive control of gluconeogenesis is exerted by

    (A)  high acetyl-CoA levels
    (B)  high citrate levels
    (C)  low citrate levels
    (D)  low ATP levels
    (E)  high ATP levels

290. All of the following are involved in the cascade of events leading to glycogenolysis in skeletal muscle EXCEPT

    (A)  adenylate cyclase
    (B)  phosphorylase kinase
    (C)  phosphorylase
    (D)  protein kinase
    (E)  glucagon

291. Fluorouracil is a drug that is used in the chemotherapy of several solid tumors. The mechanism of action of fluorouracil is that it is an inhibitor of

    (A)  ribonucleotide reductase
    (B)  thymidylate synthase
    (C)  thymidine kinase
    (D)  de novo pyrimidine biosynthesis
    (E)  de novo purine biosynthesis

292. The activity of the malate–aspartate shuttle is reduced under conditions of high ATP concentrations primarily because

    (A)  the high ATP levels lead to high NADH levels in the mitochondria, which inhibits conversion of malate to oxaloacetate catalyzed by malate dehydrogenase
    (B)  the high ATP levels lead to high NADH levels in the cytoplasm, which inhibits conversion of malate to oxaloacetate catalyzed by malate dehydrogenase
    (C)  the high ATP levels lead to high NADH levels in the mitochondria, which inhibits conversion of oxaloacetate to malate catalyzed by malate dehydrogenase
    (D)  the high ATP levels lead to high NAD+ levels in the mitochondria which inhibits conversion of malate to oxaloacetate catalyzed by malate dehydrogenase.
    (E)  the high ATP levels lead to high NADH levels in the cytoplasm, which favors conversion of malate to oxaloacetate catalyzed by malate dehydrogenase

293. Which of the following is the single most important force in stabilizing protein tertiary structure?

    (A) peptide bonds
    (B) disulfide bonds
    (C) hydrogen bonds
    (D) polar interactions
    (E) hydrophobic interactions

294. Under conditions of anaerobic glycolysis, the NAD$^+$ required by glyceraldehyde 3-phosphate dehydrogenase is supplied by a reaction catalyzed by

    (A) pyruvate dehydrogenase
    (B) α-ketoglutarate dehydrogenase
    (C) glycerol-3-phosphate dehydrogenase
    (D) malate dehydrogenase
    (E) lactate dehydrogenase

295. Pyruvate dehydrogenase activity is regulated by its state of phosphorylation. The activity of the kinase which catalyzes the phosphorylation of pyruvate dehydrogenase is increased by

    (A) acetyl-CoA
    (B) cAMP
    (C) AMP
    (D) NAD$^+$
    (E) coenzyme-A

296. All of the following statements concerning the activation of free fatty acids prior to β-oxidation are true EXCEPT

    (A) only long-chain fatty acids are activated
    (B) activation occurs within the mitochondrial matrix
    (C) activation occurs outside the mitochondrial matrix
    (D) the carboxyl groups of fatty acids form thioester linkages with CoA
    (E) the activation reaction is made irreversible by the hydrolysis of PPi

297. The key regulatory enzyme of fatty acid synthesis is

    (A) citrate cleavage enzyme
    (B) ATP citrate lyase
    (C) acetyl-CoA carboxylase
    (D) malonyl-CoA decarboxylase
    (E) malonyl transacylase

298. Which of the following is a characteristic physiological consequence of type II diabetes?

    (A) impaired glucagon-dependent inhibition of glycolysis
    (B) elevated insulin secretion
    (C) decreased glucagon secretion
    (D) decreased insulin secretion
    (E) impairment of insulin-dependent glucose uptake

299. The major site of regulation of cholesterol synthesis is

    (A) cyclization of squalene to lanosterol
    (B) 3-hydroxy-3-methylglutaryl-CoA synthase
    (C) 3-hydroxy-3-methylglutaryl-CoA lyase
    (D) 3-hydroxy-3-methylglutaryl-CoA reductase
    (E) synthesis of squalene from isoprenoid isomers

300. Lack of which of the following hepatic enzymes leads to fructose intolerance?

    (A) fructokinase
    (B) fructose-1-phosphate aldose
    (C) phosphoglucomutase
    (D) phosphohexose isomerase
    (E) glucose-6 phosphatase

301. Synthesis of glycogen is inhibited in hepatocytes in response to glucagon stimulation primarily as a result of

    (A) a decrease in the levels of phosphorylated phosphoprotein phosphatase inhibitor-1
    (B) an increase in the level of the dephosphorylated form of glycogen synthase
    (C) a decrease in the level of phosphorylated phosphorylase kinase
    (D) an increase in the level of the phosphorylated form of glycogen synthase
    (E) a decrease in the level of phosphoprotein phosphatase

302. Which of the following occurs in the lipidosis known as Tay–Sachs disease?

    (A) synthesis of a specific ganglioside is excessive
    (B) xanthomas due to cholesterol deposition are observed
    (C) phosphoglycerides accumulate in the brain
    (D) ganglioside $GM_2$ is not catabolized by lysosomal enzymes
    (E) synthesis of a specific ganglioside is decreased

303. In diabetes, the increased production of ketone bodies is primarily a result of

    (A) elevated acetyl-CoA levels in skeletal muscle
    (B) a substantially increased rate of fatty acid oxidation by hepatocytes
    (C) increased gluconeogenesis
    (D) decreased cyclic AMP levels in adipocytes
    (E) an increase in the rate of the citric acid cycle

**Questions 304 through 306**

304. Which of the following represents the primary function of the pentose phosphate pathway in erythrocytes?

    (A) production of NADPH
    (B) production of ribose-5-phosphate

    (C) remodeling of dietary carbon atoms into 2,3-bisphosphoglycerate
    (D) synthesis of ATP
    (E) reduction of $H_2O_2$ to two moles of $H_2O$

305. Which of the following is considered the central molecule of gluconeogenesis?

    (A) lactate
    (B) malate
    (C) phosphoenolpyruvate
    (D) pyruvate
    (E) oxaloacetate

306. Hepatocytes deliver ketone bodies to the circulation primarily because they lack

    (A) the form of the β-ketothiolase necessary to hydrolyze acetoacetyl-CoA
    (B) hydroxymethylglutaryl-CoA-lyase
    (C) hydroxymethylglutaryl-CoA-synthetase
    (D) succinyl-CoA-acetoacetate-CoA-transferase
    (E) β-hydroxybutyrate dehydrogenase

307. An overdose of insulin in diabetic persons leads to

    (A) hypoglycemia
    (B) glucosuria
    (C) ketonuria
    (D) hyperglycemia
    (E) ketonemia

308. Refsum's disease results from a greatly reduced capacity to carry out which of the following processes of lipid metabolism?

    (A) β-oxidation of fatty acids
    (B) activation of acetyl-CoA for cholesterol synthesis
    (C) α-oxidation of fatty acids
    (D) proper regulation of acetyl-CoA carboxylase
    (E) lipoxygenase-catalyzed leukotriene synthesis

**309.** Consumption of raw eggs, which contain the protein avidin, could lead to a deficiency resulting in

(A) an inhibition of decarboxylation reactions

(B) an inability to form acetylcholine

(C) a decrease in CoA formation

(D) an increase in transaminations

(E) an inhibition of carboxylation reactions

**310.** Both glutamate transaminase and alanine transaminase require a prosthetic group derived from

(A) vitamin $B_6$ (pyridoxine)

(B) vitamin $B_1$ (thiamine)

(C) vitamin $B_{12}$ (cobalamin)

(D) vitamin $B_2$ (riboflavin)

(E) biotin

**311.** Each of the following reactions generates a reduced electron carrier capable of supplying sufficient reducing equivalents to the oxidative phosphorylation machinery such that three moles of ATP can be generated EXCEPT

(A) pyruvate dehydrogenase

(B) glycerol-3-phosphate dehydrogenase

(C) malate dehydrogenase

(D) isocitrate dehydrogenase

(E) glyceraldehyde-3-phosphate dehydrogenase

**312.** Which of the following is quantitatively the major contributor to routine clinical measurements of circulating plasma cholesterol concentrations?

(A) chylomicrons

(B) low-density lipoproteins (LDLs)

(C) high-density lipoproteins (HDLs)

(D) intermediate-density lipoproteins (IDLs)

(E) very-low-density lipoproteins (VLDLs)

**313.** Long-term treatment of hypercholesterolemia with the cholesterol synthesis inhibitor Lovastatin (and related drugs) can lead to

toxicity. This is most accurately explained by which of the following statements?

(A) products of the cholesterol pathway are necessary for the synthesis of other compounds

(B) a build-up of Lovastatin in the liver leads to hepatic cell death

(C) Lovastatin is lipid soluble and over long-term treatment enters the brain, leading to neuropathies

(D) the loss of cholesterol biosynthesis leads to decreased bile acid production and a concomitant inability of the liver to excrete bilirubin, leading to jaundice

(E) as cholesterol is required for normal membrane integrity, long-term inhibition of its synthesis ultimately leads to disruptions in normal membrane transport processes and cell death

**314.** The process of activating a free fatty acid such that it can enter the β-oxidation pathway uses the equivalent of how many moles of ATP?

(A) 1

(B) 3

(C) 2

(D) 0

(E) 4

**315.** Activated core oligosaccharides that are transferred to the asparagine of proteins are carried by

(A) guanosine diphosphate (GDP)-mannose

(B) N-acetylglucosamine

(C) dolichol phosphate

(D) N-acetylgalactosamine

(E) UDP-glucose

**316.** All of the following statements concerning fatty acid synthesis are true EXCEPT

(A) a decarboxylation takes place

(B) the reductant is NADPH

(C) most of the intermediates are bonded to CoA

(D) a carboxylation takes place

(E) the reactions occur in the cytosol

317. Which of the following is considered to be rate limiting in detoxification of ethanol in alcoholic individuals?

    (A) the oxidized form of nicotinamide adenine dinucleotide (NAD$^+$)
    (B) the oxidized form of flavin adenine dinucleotide (FAD)
    (C) the oxidized form of nicotinamide adenine dinucleotide phosphate (NADP$^+$)
    (D) alcohol dehydrogenase
    (E) acetaldehyde dehydrogenase

318. Concerning the malate–aspartate shuttle, all of the following statements are correct EXCEPT

    (A) the shuttle is bidirectional with respect to electron transfer between cytosol and mitochondria
    (B) both cytosolic and mitochondrial NADH serve as electron transporters
    (C) two ATP are formed for each pair of electrons transferred from cytosolic NADH to mitochondrial electron transport
    (D) oxaloacetate is an intermediate
    (E) α-ketoglutarate is an intermediate

319. The steps of the pathway for β-oxidation of palmitic acid differ from those of the biosynthetic pathway in all of the following respects EXCEPT

    (A) acyl group carrier
    (B) pyridine nucleotide specificity
    (C) effect of citrate
    (D) β-hydroxyacyl intermediate
    (E) intracellular location

320. Which of the following reactions is the major oxidation reaction of energy metabolism in erythrocytes?

    (A) NADPH ↔ NADP$^+$
    (B) FADH ↔ FAD
    (C) dihydroxyacetone phosphate + NADH glycerol-3-phosphate + NAD$^+$

    (D) pyruvate + NADH ↔ lactate + NAD$^+$
    (E) acetaldehyde + NADH ↔ ethanol + NAD$^+$

321. The affinity of Hb for O$_2$ is increased by

    (A) the formation of salt bridges in Hb
    (B) the cross-linking of the β-chains of Hb
    (C) lowering of pH
    (D) decreases in 2,3-bisphosphoglycerate (BPG)
    (E) increases in the partial pressure of CO$_2$

322. A 42-year-old male presents with hepatomegaly, jaundice, refractory ascites, and renal insufficiency, with peripheral leukocytes exhibiting only 20% of normal glucocerebrosidase activity. Which of the following would explain his symptoms?

    (A) Fabry's disease
    (B) Gaucher's disease
    (C) Niemann–Pick disease
    (D) Tay–Sachs disease
    (E) Krabbe's disease

323. The increased intracellular concentrations of 5-phosphoribosyl-1-pyrophosphate (PRPP) and urate in the genetic hyperuricemia called the Lesch–Nyhan syndrome is most likely a consequence of

    (A) allopurinol inhibition of xanthine formation
    (B) increased purine synthesis
    (C) elevated synthesis of hypoxanthine
    (D) deficiency of hypoxanthine–guanine phosphoribosyltransferase (HGPRT)
    (E) elevated PRPP synthetase activity

324. Which of the following amino acids are strictly ketogenic?

    (A) lysine and leucine
    (B) valine and isoleucine
    (C) leucine and isoleucine
    (D) lysine, leucine, and isoleucine
    (E) tyrosine and tryptophan

325. All of the following are feedback inhibitors of either purine or pyrimidine synthesis EXCEPT

   (A) adenosine monophosphate (AMP)
   (B) thymidine monophosphate (TMP)
   (C) guanosine monophosphate (GMP)
   (D) uridine monophosphate (UMP)
   (E) cytidine triphosphate (CTP)

326. Each of the following represent physiological response to prostaglandin-$E_2$ EXCEPT

   (A) increased platelet aggregation
   (B) induction of smooth muscle contraction in the airways
   (C) increased arteriolar vasodilation
   (D) enhancement of the effects of bradykinin
   (E) induction of uterine contractions

327. During the hydrolysis of which compound is sufficient free energy released such that it can be coupled to the synthesis of ATP from ADP and $P_i$?

   (A) glucose-1-phosphate
   (B) 2,3-bisphosphoglycerate
   (C) glycerol-3-phosphate
   (D) phosphoenolpyruvate
   (E) glucose-6-phosphate

328. Which of the following steps is common to both gluconeogenesis and glycolysis?

   (A) fructose-6-phosphate to glucose-6-phosphate
   (B) pyruvate to oxaloacetate
   (C) glucose-6-phosphate to glucose
   (D) fructose-1,6-diphosphate to fructose-6-phosphate
   (E) oxaloacetate to phosphoenolpyruvate

DIRECTIONS (Questions 329 through 368): Each set of matching questions in this section consists of a list of lettered options followed by several numbered items. For each numbered item, select the ONE lettered option that is most closely associated with it. Each lettered option may be selected once, more than once, or not at all.

**Questions 329 through 331**

Select the correct vitamin required as a precursor to the coenzyme needed for each of the following reaction types.

   (A) decarboxylation
   (B) carboxylation
   (C) oxido-reduction
   (D) transamination
   (E) post-translational modification of amino acids

329. Riboflavin

330. Biotin

331. Thiamine

**Questions 332 through 334**

For each of the citric acid cycle reactions shown, select the statement that applies.

   (A) requires a flavoprotein enzyme
   (B) requires coenzyme-A
   (C) requires ATP
   (D) yields GTP
   (E) yields $CO_2$

332. Isocitrate → α-ketoglutarate

333. Succinyl-CoA → succinate

334. Succinate → fumarate

**Questions 335 through 338**

For each reaction described below, choose the enzyme with which it is associated.

    (A)  glycogen phosphorylase
    (B)  glycogen synthase
    (C)  glucose-6-phosphate dehydrogenase
    (D)  glucokinase
    (E)  glucose-6-phosphatase

335.  Catalyzes a reaction in which inorganic phosphate is a substrate  A

336.  Catalyzes a reaction in which ATP is a substrate  D

337.  Catalyzes a reaction in which UDP-glucose is a substrate  B

338.  Catalyzes a reaction in which glucose is a product  E

**Questions 339 through 342**

For each description below, choose the amino acid with which it is associated.

    (A)  serine
    (B)  glutamine
    (C)  glutamate
    (D)  aspartate
    (E)  asparagine

339.  The common intermediate for the entry of several amino acids into the citric acid cycle  C

340.  A major source of carbon for the one-carbon pool  A

341.  Can be formed by the one-step transamination of an intermediate of the citric acid cycle  D

342.  One-step transamination of it forms a citric acid cycle intermediate  D

**Questions 343 through 345**

For each description below, choose the substance with which it is associated.

    (A)  hydroxyproline
    (B)  O-phosphoserine
    (C)  $\gamma$-carboxyglutamate
    (D)  D-valine
    (E)  cystine

343.  Present in large amounts in keratin  E

344.  Occurs in prothrombin

345.  Can be found in collagen  A

**Questions 346 through 349**

Match the techniques to their corresponding descriptions.

    (A)  Southern blotting
    (B)  restriction fragment length polymorphism (RFLP)
    (C)  allele-specific oligonucleotide (ASO) analysis of disease genes
    (D)  site-directed mutagenesis
    (E)  transgenesis
    (F)  reverse genetics
    (G)  polymerase chain reaction (PCR)
    (H)  Western blotting

346.  Introduction of foreign DNA into the germline of an animal or plant  E

347.  Utilization of antisense RNAs or oligodeoxynucleotides (oligos) to selectively modify the activity of a specific gene in order to determine its function  F

348.  Amplification of DNA from as little as a single cell with the use of nucleotide-specific oligos  G

349.  Determination of the effect of single amino acid substitutions on protein function by in vitro alteration of nucleotides of the corresponding codon  D

## Questions 350 and 351

Match a hormone to the signal transduction mechanism.

    (A) progesterone
    (B) parathyroid hormone
    (C) insulin
    (D) adrenocorticotropic hormone (ACTH)
    (E) epinephrine

350. Binds to transmembrane receptors ultimately leading to the activation of glycogen breakdown

351. Interacts with intracellular receptors, then the complex binds to DNA and regulates the expression of specific target genes

## Questions 352 and 353

Using the descriptions, select the correct disease relating to amino acid metabolism.

    (A) phenylketonuria
    (B) Parkinson's disease
    (C) maple syrup urine disease
    (D) alkaptonuria
    (E) albinism
    (F) homocystinuria
    (G) isovaleric acedemia

352. Deficiency of homogentisate oxidase leading to darkening of the urine upon exposure to air.

353. Deficiency in α-keto acid decarboxylase; symptoms in neonate include vomiting, difficulty feeding, and lethargy

## Questions 354 through 356

Within each of the reaction pathways shown below

    (A) ATP is consumed
    (B) GTP is consumed
    (C) ATP is generated
    (D) ATP is both consumed and generated
    (E) ATP is neither consumed nor generated

354. Glycogen → fructose-6-phosphate

355. Fructose-6-phosphate → glyceraldehyde-3-phosphate

356. Glyceraldehyde-3-phosphate → pyruvate

## Questions 357 through 359

For each description, choose the glycosaminoglycan (GAG) family with which it is associated.

    (A) heparan sulfates
    (B) dermatan sulfates
    (C) keratan sulfates
    (D) chondroitin sulfates
    (E) hyaluronates

357. Primarily located on the surface of vessel endothelial cells

358. Most abundant GAGs in the body

359. Contain no sulfate and are not covalently attached to protein

## Questions 360 through 362

For each statement below, choose the process that applies.

    (A) transcription in eukaryotes
    (B) transcription in prokaryotes
    (C) transcription in both eukaryotes and prokaryotes
    (D) translation in eukaryotes
    (E) translation in prokaryotes

360. Initiated with formyl-methionyl-tRNA (fMet-tRNA)

361. Inhibited by α-amanitin

362. Begins at specific sequences on the DNA template

**Questions 363 through 365**

For each statement below, choose the compound that performs the indicated function.

(A) HDL
(B) bile salts
(C) VLDL
(D) LDL
(E) apoprotein E

363. Carries primarily triacylglycerols ᴄ

364. Transports cholesterol from peripheral tissues to the liver    A

365. Transports cholesterol to peripheral tissues ᴅ

**Questions 366 through 368**

Match the following diseases relating to defective connective tissue protein synthesis or processing with the described symptoms.

(A) Marfan syndrome
(B) osteogenesis imperfecta
(C) Menkes disease
(D) Ehlers–Danlos syndrome (type IV)

366. Multiple fractures, bone deformities, and blue sclerae associated with defects in type I collagen    B

367. Skin and joint hyperextensibility, poor wound healing, arterial and intestinal rupture associated with defects in type III collagen    D

368. Ectopis lentis (lens dislocation), arachnodactyly, joint hyperextensibility, and dilation of ascending aorta resulting from defects in fibrillin synthesis    A

**DIRECTIONS (Questions 369 through 389): Each of the numbered items or incomplete statements in this section is followed by answers or by completions of the statement. Select the ONE lettered answer or completion that is BEST in each case.**

369. The terminal processing of the carbohydrate portion of glycoproteins occurs in the

(A) mitochondria
(B) Golgi complex
(C) plasma membrane
(D) endoplasmic reticulum
(E) lysosomes

370. Vitamin K is required for which of the following amino acid modifications?

(A) proline to hydroxyproline
(B) aspartate to β-carboxyaspartate
(C) lysine to β-methyllysine
(D) lysine to hydroxylysine
(E) glutamate to γ-carboxyglutamate

371. Steroid hormones interact with specific receptors within target cells. The steroid/receptor complexes then regulate the rate of

(A) replication of DNA
(B) post-transcriptional processing of specific mRNAs
(C) transcription of specific genes
(D) translation of specific mRNAs
(E) post-translational processing of specific proteins

372. Which of the following vitamins is required as a cofactor during both the synthesis and degradation of fatty acids?

(A) vitamin $B_5$
(B) vitamin $B_1$
(C) vitamin $B_3$
(D) vitamin $B_2$
(E) vitamin $B_6$

373. Which of the following is an essential amino acid for humans?

(A) cysteine
(B) methionine
(C) serine
(D) glycine
(E) glutamate

374. Deficiencies in the enzyme glucose-6-phosphatase are likely to lead to which of the following?

(A) decreased glucagon production
(B) decreased skeletal muscle glycogen accumulation
(C) hyperglycemia
(D) increased hepatic glycogen accumulation
(E) increased accumulation of unbranched glycogen

375. Which of the following is a primary source of fuel for the brain during periods of prolonged starvation?

(A) fatty acids produced in adipose tissue
(B) glycogen stores of the liver
(C) amino acids from skeletal muscle
(D) glycogen stores of the brain
(E) ketone bodies produced in the liver

376. Acetyl-CoA enhances the rate of gluconeogenesis by acting as an allosteric activator of

(A) pyruvate carboxylase
(B) acetyl CoA carboxylase
(C) pyruvate kinase
(D) phosphoenolpyruvate carboxykinase
(E) pyruvate dehydrogenase

377. A reaction important in oxygen transport is catalyzed by carbonic anhydrase. This reaction is

(A) ionization of carbonic acid
(B) production of $CO_2$ from carbonic acid
(C) protonation of hemoglobin
(D) carbamylation of hemoglobin
(E) transport of chloride ion in exchange bicarbonate ion

378. The lack of which enzyme in skeletal muscle prevents these cells from delivering free glucose to the blood?

(A) phosphorylase kinase
(B) phosphohexose isomerase
(C) phosphoglucomutase
(D) glucose-6-phosphate dehydrogenase
(E) glucose-6-phosphatase

379. The accumulation of an oxygen debt during strenuous physical exercise may be accompanied by

(A) an increase in $NAD^+$ in muscle
(B) an increase in lactate in blood
(C) a decrease in pyruvate in blood
(D) an increase in citrate in muscle
(E) an increase in ATP in muscle

380. Dietary triacylglycerides are transported in the plasma as

(A) VLDLs
(B) HDLs
(C) chylomicrons
(D) LDLs
(E) albumin conjugates

381. Which of the following antibiotics is an inhibitor of transcription?

(A) streptomycin
(B) erythromycin
(C) tetracycline
(D) puromycin
(E) rifamycin

382. Carnitine, a zwitterionic compound derived from lysine, is involved in fatty acid metabolism; it is

(A) required for absorption of long chain fatty acids from the intestine
(B) a component of bile salts
(C) a component of coenzyme-A
(D) required for transport of long-chain fatty acids into mitochondria
(E) required for transport of medium-chain fatty acids into mitochondria

383. All of the following are properties of restriction endonucleases EXCEPT

   (A) they recognize specific palindromic sequences in DNA
   (B) they cleave only supercoiled DNA
   (C) they are produced by bacteria to protect against transformation by foreign DNA
   (D) they cleave both strands of DNA at specific sites
   (E) they do not degrade the host cell's DNA because the recognition site is methylated

38461. The synthesis of all steroid hormones involves all of the following EXCEPT

   (A) mono-oxygenases
   (B) pregnenolone
   (C) vitamin D
   (D) molecular $O_2$
   (E) NADPH

385. All of the following are important in the control of *de novo* purine biosynthesis EXCEPT

   (A) stimulation of the conversion of IMP to AMP by GTP
   (B) stimulation of the conversion of IMP to GMP by ATP
   (C) inhibition of the enzyme xanthine oxidase
   (D) availability of 5-phosphoribosyl-1-pyrophosphate (PRPP)
   (E) inhibition of the enzyme PRPP amidotransferase by GMP

386. Which of the following enzyme abnormalities would be expected to lead to hyperuricemia?

   (A) xanthine oxidase deficiency
   (B) adenosine deaminase deficiency
   (C) hypoxanthine–guanine phosphoribosyltransferase (HGPRT) deficiency (Lesch–Nyhan syndrome)

   (D) purine nucleoside phosphorylase deficiency
   (E) PRPP aminotransferase deficiency

387. Reduced glutathione is known to mediate all the following EXCEPT

   (A) react with hydrogen peroxide to detoxify cells
   (B) maintain the disulfide bonds of proteins in the reduced state
   (C) regenerate from the oxidized form in red blood cells (RBCs) by reacting with electrons donated from NADPH to FAD
   (D) regenerate from the oxidized form in RBCs by reacting with electrons donated from NADH to FAD
   (E) maintain hemoglobin in the ferrous state in RBCs

388. In the presence of arsenate, which of the following may or may not occur during glycolysis?

   (A) 1,3-bisphosphoglycerate is formed
   (B) NADH is formed
   (C) $P_i$ reacts with glyceraldehyde-3-phosphate
   (D) 3-phosphoglycerate is not formed
   (E) pyruvate is not formed

389. Each of the following represents an intermediate in glycolysis starting from glucose EXCEPT

   (A) glucose-6-phosphate
   (B) 2-phosphoglycerate
   (C) phosphoenolpyruvate
   (D) glucose-1-phosphate
   (E) 3-phosphoglycerate

DIRECTIONS (Questions 390 through 397): Each set of matching questions in this section consists of a list of lettered options followed by several numbered items. For each numbered item, select the ONE lettered option that is most closely associated with it. Each lettered heading may be selected once, more than once, or not at all.

**Questions 390 through 393**

Given their principal biological activities, select the correct growth factor or cytokine.

(A) platelet-derived growth factor (PDGF)
(B) basic fibroblast growth factor (bFGF)
(C) epidermal growth factor (EGF)
(D) interleukin-2 (IL-2)
(E) erythropoietin (Epo)
(F) insulin-like growth factor type I (IGF-I)
(G) interleukin-6 (IL-6)
(H) interferon-γ (IFN-γ)

390. Synthesized by the kidney and released in response to hypoxia, stimulates proliferation and differentiation of burst-forming unit–erythroid cells of the bone marrow

391. Induces proliferation of connective tissue, glial cells, and smooth muscle cells.

392. Induces proliferation of activated T cells, natural killer (NK) cells and B cells, and immunoglobulin expression on B cells

393. Responsible for the acute phase response of liver to injury and infection, increases thrombopoiesis, synergistic with IL-1 and tumor necrosis factor-α (TNF-α).

**Questions 394 through 397**

For each reaction below, choose the correct description.

(A) generates GTP
(B) utilizes GTP
(C) stimulated by acetyl-CoA
(D) requires NADPH
(E) generates FADH2

(F) yields ATP even in the absence of oxygen
(G) requires NADP⁺
(H) requires NADH
(I) requires NAD⁺

394. oxaloacetate → phosphoenolpyruvate

395. α-ketoglutarate → succinyl CoA

396. glucose-6-phosphate → 6-phosphoglucono-δ-lactone

397. phosphoenolpyruvate → pyruvate

DIRECTIONS (Questions 398 through 401): Each of the numbered items or incomplete statements in this section is followed by answers or by completions of the statement. Select the ONE lettered answer or completion that is BEST in each case.

398. The liver is the only body organ that is capable of

(A) urea formation
(B) ganglioside synthesis
(C) nucleotide synthesis
(D) medium-chain fatty acid catabolism
(E) glycogen degradation

399. The cofactor not required for conversion of pyruvate to acetyl-CoA is

(A) NAD⁺
(B) FAD
(C) thiamine
(D) biotin
(E) lipoic acid

400. The disease pellagra can be prevented by a dietary sufficiency of

(A) vitamin D
(B) riboflavin
(C) retinoic acid
(D) thiamine
(E) niacin

401. All of the following are components of mammalian plasma membranes EXCEPT

    (A) triaclyglycerides
    (B) cholesterol
    (C) sphingolipids
    (D) glycolipids
    (E) phospholipids

**DIRECTIONS (Questions 402 through 404): Each set of matching questions in this section consists of a list of lettered options followed by several numbered items. For each numbered item, select the ONE lettered option that is most closely associated with it. Each lettered heading may be selected once, more than once, or not at all.**

**Questions 402 through 404**

For each description below, choose the appropriate enzyme or inhibitor.

    (A) fluorodeoxyuridine
    (B) allopurinol
    (C) sulfamethoxazole
    (D) glucose-6-phosphate
    (E) hypoxanthine phosphoribosyltransferase
    (F) adenine phosphoribosyltransferase
    (G) purine nucleoside phosphorylase

402. Deficiency results in hypouricemia    G

403. Deficiency results in Lesch–Nyhan syndrome    E

404. Specific inhibitor of thymidylate biosynthesis    A

# Biochemistry
## Answers and Explanations

**278. (C)** Two distinct pathways for nucleotide biosynthesis exist in most cells. In the de novo pathway, nucleotides are synthesized from smaller precursor molecules, such as amino acids, $CO_2$, and ammonia. Free nucleic acid bases or nucleosides are not produced as intermediates in this pathway. These latter compounds, however, may be used for the synthesis of nucleotides via the salvage pathways. Free bases and nucleosides become available either through nucleic acid breakdown or diet. Thymidylate can be synthesized in two steps from thymine via the salvage pathways. Thymine is first converted to thymidine by the enzyme thymidine phosphorylase and then to thymidylate by the action of thymidine kinase. 5-Fluorodeoxyuridylate is a potent inhibitor of thymidylate synthase, the enzyme responsible for de novo thymidylate biosynthesis. Inhibition of this enzyme will have a major effect on DNA synthesis, since thymidylate is a precursor employed specifically for DNA synthesis. Cells cannot take up charged compounds, such as nucleotides, from the surrounding environment, and, therefore, the base fluorouracil must be administered rather than fluorodeoxyuridylate. In order to inhibit thymidylate synthase, the fluorouracil must be converted to its corresponding nucleotide by the salvage pathway. (*Stryer, pp 751–754*)

**279. (A)** Compounds that can competitively inhibit enzyme catalyzed reactions are usually structurally similar to substrate. However, once bound, the enzyme cannot convert the inhibitor to product. Addition of increasing amounts of substrate leads to the displacement of the inhibitor and conversion of substrate to product. Since the inhibitor and substrate are competing for the substrate binding site, the $K_m$ for substrate exhibits an apparent increase. (*Devlin, pp 157–158*)

**280. (A)** Under anaerobic conditions (eg, intense exercise), the production of pyruvate via glycolysis exceeds its oxidation by the citric acid cycle. This results in the synthesis of lactate by muscle. Lactate diffuses into the bloodstream and is taken up by the liver, where it is oxidized back to pyruvate. The latter is converted to glucose in the liver via gluconeogenesis. (*Stryer, pp 577–578*)

**281. (C)** In the interior of peripheral tissues, the concentration of $CO_2$ is high, and the relative $O_2$ tension is low. As a consequence, $O_2$ is unloaded from Hb, and $CO_2$ is taken up. Although some $CO_2$ is transported as a dissolved gas, most $CO_2$ is transported as bicarbonate. Bicarbonate is formed by the action of carbonic anhydrase within red blood cells.

$$CO_2 + H_2O \leftrightarrow HCO_3^- + H^+$$

In addition, $CO_2$ is carried by Hb as carbamino derivatives. The un-ionized $\alpha$-amino groups of Hb react reversibly with $CO_2$.

$$CO_2 + R - NH_2 \leftrightarrow R - NHCOO^- + H^+$$

The charged carbamates form salt bridges that stabilize the T form of Hb and lower its $O_2$ affinity. Unlike $O_2$, $CO_2$ does not bind to the iron of the heme group. (*Stryer, pp 164–165*)

**282.** **(A)** Calcitriol (1,25-dihydroxyD$_3$) is the hormonally active form of vitamin D. The primary function of calcitriol is to regulate calcium and phosphorous homeostasis in cooperation with parathyroid hormone and calcitonin. Calcitriol activates the expression of a specific calcium-binding protein in intestinal epithelial cells to facilitate absorption and delivery of dietary calcium. On bone, calcitriol functions with parathyroid hormone to stimulate resorption by stimulating osteoblast production and function. Deficiencies in vitamin D in children will lead to poorly mineralized osteoid matrix of the bone due to the severely reduced capacity to absorb calcium from the intestine. This leads to rickets. In adults, lack of vitamin D leads to demineralization of pre-existing bone causing them to become soft. This condition is known as osteomalacia. The distinction between osteomalacia and oseteoporosis is the presence of the osteoid matrix in the former and its absence in the latter. *(Devlin, pp 1121–1124)*

**283.** **(B)** Vitamin B$_{12}$ (cobalamin) is synthesized by microorganisms and stored in the liver of animals. Only two reactions in mammalian cells require cobalamin as a cofactor, these being conversion of homocysteine to methionine catalyzed by methionine synthase and in the conversion of methylmalonyl-CoA to succinyl-CoA catalyzed by methylmalonyl-CoA mutase. The significance of a cobalamin deficiency relates to its indirect effects on thymidine nucleotide biosynthesis. The inability to convert homocysteine to methione leads to entrapment of tetrahydrofolate (required for thymidine nucleotide biosynthesis at the thymidylate synthase catalyzed step) as the N$^5$-methyltetrahydrofolate form. Absorption of vitamin B$_{12}$ from the intestine is mediated by specific receptors that only recognize cobalamin bound to intrinsic factor. Therefore, the lack of intestinal parietal cell-derived intrinsic factor prevents its absorption from intestine. *(Murray et al, pp 581–583)*

**284.** **(E)** The carbohydrate moieties in RNA and DNA are ribose and deoxyribose, respectively. A major product of the pentose phosphate pathway is ribose 5-phosphate. The latter is converted to 5-phosphoribosyl-1-pyrophosphate (PRPP), which serves as the donor of ribose in the biosynthesis of nucleotides. *(Stryer, pp 559–562, 740–746)*

**285.** **(D)** Vitamin C is a reducing agent capable of reducing cytochromes a and c and molecular oxygen as well as other compounds and may act as a general water-soluble antioxidant. Vitamin C is also involved in the synthesis of bile acids and epinephrine and the degradation of tyrosine. Additionally, vitamin C is required as a cofactor for numerous hydroxylation reactions in the body, in particular the hydroxylation of lysine and proline residues in procollagen. In this capacity, the lack of vitamin C leads to the inability of procollagen to cross-link into normal collagen fibrils. The net result is an inability to maintain normal connective tissue and poor wound healing since connective tissue is sythesized first in the healing process. Collagen is a necessary component in the organic portion of bone matrix and of the ground substance of capillary walls. Therefore, lack of properly processed collagen leads to impaired bone mineralization and weakened capillaries resulting in increased hemorrhaging. *(Devlin, pp 1136–1137)*

**286.** **(A)** Myosin contains the ATPase activity that hydrolyzes ATP and allows contraction to proceed. The binding of actin to myosin enhances the ATPase activity of myosin. In fact, actin alternatively binds to myosin and is released from myosin as ATP is hydrolyzed. This reaction requires Mg$^{2+}$ and is the driving force of contraction. Although troponin is not directly involved in the ATPase reaction, it binds calcium released by the sarcoplasmic reticulum and in doing so allows conformational changes in tropomyosin and actin to occur, permitting contraction. Myokinase catalyzes the formation of ATP and AMP from two molecules of ADP. *(Stryer, pp 392–402)*

**287.** **(C)** The allosteric regulatory enzymes of glycolysis are hexokinase, phosphofructokinase, and pyruvate kinase. Of these, phosphofructokinase is the key regulatory enzyme. A high-energy charge or the presence of sufficient citric acid cycle precursors causes the inhibition of phosphofructokinase via accumulation of the negative effectors ATP and citrate. ADP and AMP are positive effectors of phosphofructokinase. Accumulation of glucose-6-phosphate inhibits hexokinase. Pyruvate kinase is inhibited by high ATP levels. Fructose-6-phosphate, the substrate of phosphofructokinase, is not an effector. *(Stryer, pp 493–496)*

288. **(B)** There are three reactions of glycolysis that are thermodynamically irreversible. These are the hexokinase (glucokinase), phosphofructokinase-1 (PFK-1) and pyruvate kinase catalyzed reactions. Reactions that are essentially irreversible in most metabolic pathways are subject to complex regulatory controls and represent rate-limiting steps in the pathway. The primary site of regulation of glycolysis occurs at the level of the PFK-1 catalyzed step. Hence, this reaction is the rate-limiting step in glycolysis. PFK-1 is subject to allosteric control by numerous compounds. Citrate and ATP inhibit the activity of PFK-1 while AMP and fructose-2,6-bisphosphate (F-2,6-BP) activate the enzyme. The principal control of PFK-1 activity is exerted by alterations in the level of F-2,6-BP. This compound is synthesized from fructose-6-phosphate (F-6-P) by the bifunctional enzyme, phosphofructokinase-2 (PFK-2). PFK-2 contains two catalytic domains, one a kinase and the other a phosphatase, the activities of which are affected by the state of phosphorylation. The phosphatase domain is active when the enzyme is phosphorylated and converts F-2,6-BP back to F-6-P thereby reducing the levels of this powerful activator of PFK-1. *(Devlin, pp 312–324)*

289. **(A)** The first step in gluconeogenesis is the formation of oxaloacetate from pyruvate. The enzyme controlling this step is pyruvate carboxylase, an allosteric enzyme that does not function in the absence of its primary effector, acetyl-CoA, or a closely related acyl-CoA. Thus, a high level of acetyl-CoA signals the need for more oxaloacetate. If there is a surplus of ATP, oxaloacetate will be used for gluconeogenesis. Under conditions of low

ATP, oxaloacetate will be consumed in the citric acid cycle. Citrate is the primary negative effector of glycolysis and the primary positive effector of fatty acid synthesis. *(Stryer, p 573)*

290. **(E)** In skeletal muscle, the hormone epinephrine or the neurotransmitter norepinephrine binds to sarcolemma receptors and activates adenylate cyclase. Glucagon, which causes similar effects in the liver, is not specific for muscle. Activated adenylate cyclase forms cyclic AMP from ATP. Cyclic AMP activates protein kinase, which in turn activates phosphorylase kinase. Phosphorylase kinase activates phosphorylase, converting it from the inactive b form to the activated a form. Both the phosphorylase kinase and phosphorylase itself are activated by phosphorylation mechanisms. Activated glycogen phosphorylase hydrolyzes glycogen, sequentially cleaving off glucose units as glucose-1-phosphate. *(Stryer, pp 593–597)*

291. **(B)** Thymidylate (TMP) is synthesized by methylation of deoxyuridylate (dUMP) at the five-carbon in a reaction catalyzed by thymidylate synthase. TMP is the only precursor for DNA synthesis that is produced separately from the major biosynthetic pathways for purine and pyrimidine ribonucleotides. For this reason, reactions required for TMP biosynthesis are specific targets for drugs that will inhibit DNA synthesis. 5-Fluorouracil is a modified uracil that contains a fluorine attached to the five-carbon. It binds to thymidylate synthase because it is a structural analog of dUMP and forms a covalent complex with the enzyme. This results in complete inactivation of thymidylate synthase. Cells that are rapidly proliferating, such as tumor cells, carry out high levels of DNA synthesis. They therefore require larger amounts of TMP than normal cells and, for this reason, are more susceptible to the action of fluorouracil. *(Stryer, pp 752–754)*

292. **(A)** The malate–aspartate shuttle is the major pathway by which electrons are transferred from cytoplasmic NADH to mitochondrial NADH for entry into the oxidative-phospho-

rylation process. When the energy charge of a cell is high (ie, the level of ATP is high relative to that of ADP and AMP), the flux of electrons from the reduced electron carriers NADH and $FADH_2$ through the oxidative phosphorylation pathway is reduced. Therefore, concomitant with a rise in cellular ATP levels will be a rise in NADH levels both in the mitochondria and cytoplasm. Within the cytoplasmic portion of the malate–aspartate shuttle, the electrons of NADH are transferred to oxaloacetate generating malate catalyzed by malate dehydrogenase. The malate is transported into the mitochondria where the electrons are transferred to $NAD^+$ in a reversal of the reaction occurring in the cytoplasm. The mitochondrial reaction requires a steady supply of $NAD^+$, which is supplied as the electrons are transferred to the oxidative-phosphorylation pathway. However, as oxidative-phosphorylation slows down, the level of $NAD^+$ declines, and NADH increases in the mitochondria leading to inhibition of the malate to oxaloacetate conversion. (Devlin, pp 266–267, 304–306)

293. **(E)** Tertiary structure refers to the three-dimensional arrangement of amino acid residues in a protein. Studies of many proteins reveal that the nonpolar (hydrophobic) amino acid residues are buried in the interior of the protein structure, whereas the polar residues are on the outside in contact with the aqueous environment. The protein folds so as to shield its nonpolar groups from interaction with water molecules. These hydrophobic interactions are the driving force of protein folding. The tertiary structure is further stabilized by hydrogen bonding, polar interactions, and the formation of disulfide bonds. Peptide bonds are only involved in formation of the primary structure of a protein. (Mathews and van Holde, pp 185–190)

294. **(E)** When glycolysis is proceeding under anaerobic conditions, the electrons transferred to $NAD^+$ (generating NADH) during the glyceraldehyde-3-phosphate dehydrogenase (G3PDH) catalyzed step cannot be transferred to mitochondrial NADH nor

$FADH_2$, which would regenerate cytoplasmic $NAD^+$ levels. This would lead to a deficiency in the $NAD^+$ required by G3PDH and an eventual cessation of glycolysis. Therefore, under anaerobic conditions, tissues such as skeletal muscle reduce pyruvate (the end product of anaerobic glycolysis) to lactate catalyzed by lactate dehydrogenase (LDH). This reaction requires electrons to be donated from NADH and thereby regenerate $NAD^+$, which can be used by G3PDH. (Devlin, p 304)

295. **(A)** Pyruvate dehydrogenase (PDH) activity is regulated both allosterically and by the state of phosphorylation. When phosphorylated, the activity of PDH is reduced. The PDH kinase is associated with the PDH complex and is itself regulated by allosteric factors. High activity of PDH will be observed under conditions of reduced energy charge in order to supply the TCA cycle with acetyl-CoA. As the level of ATP rises the rate of flux through the TCA cycle will begin to decline, leading to a build-up of acetyl-CoA. The increased acetyl-CoA in turn allosterically activates the PDH kinase leading to an increased level of phosphorylation of PDH and a concomitant decline in its activity. (Devlin, pp 251–252)

296. **(A)** Long-chain ($> 10$ carbon atoms) as well as medium-chain (5 to 10 carbon atoms) and short-chain (2 to 4 carbon atoms) fatty acids must be activated before b oxidation, which uses only fatty acids linked to CoA. Long-chain fatty acids are activated outside the mitochondrial matrix and then transported across the inner membrane of mitochondria as acyl carnitine complexes. In contrast, short- and medium-chain fatty acids diffuse across the inner mitochondrial membrane and are activated in the matrix. Fatty acid thiokinase (acyl-CoA synthetase) catalyzes the activation reaction in which the carboxyl group of the free fatty acid forms a thioester linkage with CoA.

$$R\text{-}COO^- + ATP + HS\text{-}CoA \leftrightarrow R\text{-}CO\text{-}S\text{-}CoA + AMP + PP_i$$

The reaction is made irreversible by the consumption of the equivalent of two high-energy phosphate bonds and the hydrolysis of the resulting $PP_i$ by pyrophosphatase. (*Stryer, pp 606–607*)

297.    (C) The formation of the three-carbon CoA thioester malonyl-CoA from acetyl-CoA is the regulatory step of fatty acid synthesis. Acetyl-CoA carboxylase catalyzes this reaction.

$$\text{Acetyl-CoA} + \text{HCO}_3^- + \text{ATP} \leftrightarrow \text{malonyl-CoA} + \text{ADP} + \text{P}_i$$

Citrate, which serves as the means of transport of acetyl-CoA from the mitochondria to the cytosolic site of fatty acid synthesis, is the key allosteric regulator of acetyl-CoA carboxylase. It shifts the enzyme from an inactive protomer to an active filamentous polymer. The end product of the cytosolic fatty acid synthetase complex, palmitoyl-CoA, inhibits the carboxylase. Although acetyl-CoA carboxylase is the prime regulatory enzyme of fatty acid synthesis, it is not a part of the fatty acid synthetase complex, the site where most of the reactions of fatty acid synthesis take place. (*Stryer, pp 614–615*)

298.    (E) Type II diabetes is the non-insulin–dependent form of diabetes mellitus and thus the disorder does not result from a lack of insulin production and secretion as in type I diabetes. The primary defect in type II diabetes is an impaired ability of cells to respond to insulin. There are several different factors leading to this impairment. Some patients exhibit reduced affinity of insulin receptors for insulin; others have receptors that bind insulin normally but have defects in post-receptor signaling processes. All of these defects lead to reduced insulin-dependent glucose uptake by all cells of afflicted individuals. (*Devlin, pp 597–598, 600*)

299.    (D) Cholesterol is obtained from the diet as well as by de novo synthesis. Although many cells can synthesize cholesterol, the liver is the major site of its production. The rate of cholesterol production is highly responsive to feedback inhibition from both dietary cholesterol and synthesized cholesterol. Feedback regulation is mediated by changes in the activity of 3-hydroxy-3-methylglutaryl-CoA reductase. This enzyme is the first committed step in the production of cholesterol from acetyl-CoA. 3-Hydroxy-3-methylglutaryl-CoA, the substrate of the reductase, also can be synthesized into the ketone body acetoacetate by the action of 3-hydroxy-3-methylglutaryl-CoA lyase. (*Stryer, pp 696–697*)

300.    (B) Fructose is a major carbohydrate of many fruits and vegetables and is used as a sweetener. In non-hepatic cells fructose can enter the glycolytic pathway by being phosphorylated to fructose-6-phosphate by hexokinase. However, hepatic glucokinase is specific for glucose and will not phosphorylate fructose. In the liver, fructose is phosphorylated to fructose-1-phosphate by fructokinase. Fructose-1-phosphate is then hydrolyzed to dihydroxyacetone phosphate and glyceraldehyde by fructose-1-phosphate aldolase. Lack of fructose-1-phosphate aldolase leads to fructose intolerance. The disorder is characterized by an accumulation of fructose-1-phosphate and a depletion of ATP in the liver. The inability of hepatocytes to regenerate the ATP utilized to generate fructose-1-phosphate leads to a reduction in normal cellular processes and ultimately cellular damage. In particular, the lowered activity of ATP-dependent cation pumps leads to osmotic lysis. (*Devlin, p 311*)

301.    (D) Glucagon is released from the pancreas in response to low blood glucose and stimulates hepatocytes to synthesize glucose for delivery to the blood. Therefore, it would be counterproductive for hepatocytes to divert any of the gluconeogenically derived glucose into glycogen. This is accomplished by inhibition of glycogen synthase. Glucagon exerts its effects on the liver through the glucagon receptor. When glucagon binds, the receptor activates adenylate cyclase leading to increased production of cAMP. In turn, cAMP activates cAMP-dependent protein kinase (PKA), which then phosphorylates a number of substrates. One of

the substrates of PKA is glycogen synthase/phosphorylase kinase. This enzyme phosphorylates glycogen phosphorylase and glycogen synthase. The effects of phosphorylation on glycogen synthase activity are inhibitory and on phosphorylase activating. In addition, PKA itself can phosphorylate glycogen synthase. The net effect is an increase in the rate of glucose phosphorolysis from glycogen and a reduced incorporation of glucose into glycogen. *(Devlin, pp 349–350)*

302.    **(D)** In the genetic disorder known as Tay–Sachs disease, ganglioside $GM_2$ is not catabolized. As a consequence, the ganglioside concentration is elevated many times higher than normal. The functionally absent lysosomal enzyme is β-N-acetylhexosaminidase. The elevated $GM_2$ results in irreversible brain damage to infants, who usually die before the age of 3 years. Under normal conditions, this enzyme cleaves N-acetylgalactosamine from the oligosaccharide chain of this complex sphingolipid, allowing further catabolism to occur. The cause of most lipidoses (lipid storage diseases) is similar. That is, a defect in catabolism of gangliosides causes abnormal accumulation. *(Stryer, p 691)*

303.    **(B)** In fasting or diabetes, lipolysis predominates in adipocytes because of the inability of these cells to obtain glucose, which is normally used as a source of glycerol-3-phosphate. Glycerol-3-phosphate is necessary for the esterification of fatty acids into triacylglycerides. Circulating fatty acids become the predominant fuel source, and β-oxidation in the liver becomes substantially elevated. This leads to an increased production of acetyl-CoA. Since glucose use in diabetes is reduced, gluconeogenesis is increased in the liver. This predisposes oxaloacetate and makes the citric acid cycle unavailable for heightened use of acetyl-CoA. As a consequence, acetyl-CoA is diverted to the formation of ketone bodies. *(Stryer, pp 612–613)*

304.    **(A)** Erythrocytes are the specialized oxygen transporting cells of the body. As such, they are continuously exposed to an oxidizing environment. These conditions can have pro-

found effects on membrane lipids as a consequence of their attack by peroxides (particularly $H_2O_2$) prevalent in this environment. During the reduction of $H_2O_2$ catalyzed by glutathione peroxidase, glutathione acts as the donor of the necessary reducing equivalents generating oxidized glutathione. Glutathione (GSH) is a tripeptide of the structure, γ-glutamylcysteinylglycine, where the cysteine sulfhydryl side chains can form a disulfide bond between two molecules (designated as GSSG). In order to again perform the role of cofactor for glutathione peroxidase, the disulfide bond of GSSG must be reduced. This reaction is catalyzed by glutathione reductase, which requires NADPH as a cofactor. Therefore, in order to maintain normal red cell membrane structure, erythrocytes utilize the pentose phosphate pathway for the generation of large amounts of NADPH. *(Devlin, pp 361–365)*

305.    **(E)** The principal substrates of gluconeogenesis are pyruvate, lactate, and amino acids with some glucose being synthesized from the glycerol backbone of triacylglycerides. Lactate is oxidized to pyruvate and therefore feeds into gluconeogenesis in the same manner as that of pyruvate. Pyruvate cannot be freely converted into phosphoenolpyruvate (PEP) by pyruvate kinase, the glycolytic enzyme. Therefore, it undergoes a carboxylation step within the mitochondria, catalyzed by pyruvate carboxylase, to yield oxaloacetate (OAA). Oxaloacetate is then transported from the mitochondria to the cytoplasm in the form of malate or aspartate where it is reconverted to OAA. Cytoplasmic OAA is then converted into PEP in a reaction catalyzed by PEP carboxykinase. The degradation products of most of the amino acids feed into pyruvate or TCA cycle intermediates which ultimately lead to the generation of OAA. Therefore, OAA is considered the central molecule of gluconeogenesis. *(Devlin, pp 324–332)*

306.    **(D)** Ketogenesis occurs in the liver from acetyl-CoA during high rates of fatty acid oxidation and during early starvation. The principal ketone bodies are acetoacetate and

β-hydroxybutyrate, which are reversibly synthesized in a reaction catalyzed by β-hydroxybutyrate dehydrogenase. The liver delivers β-hydroxybutyrate to the circulation where it is taken up by non-heptatic tissue for use as an oxidizable fuel. The brain will derive much of its energy from ketone body oxidation during starvation. Within extrahepatic tissues, β-hydroxybutyrate is converted to acetoacetate by β-hydroxybutyrate dehydrogenase. Acetoacetate is reactivated to acetoacetyl-CoA in a reaction catalyzed by succinyl-CoA-acetoacetate-CoA transferase (also called acetoacetate:succinyl-CoA CoA transferase) which utilizes succinyl-CoA as the source of CoA. The acetoacetyl-CoA is then converted to two moles of acetyl-CoA by the thiolase reaction of fatty acid oxidation. (Devlin, pp 416–417)

307. **(A)** Untreated diabetes leads to high blood glucose levels (hyperglycemia) and glucosuria, as glucose exceeds the kidney threshold and spills into the urine. At the same time that blood glucose levels are high, the lack of insulin leads to a favoring of lipolysis and consequent ketogenesis by the liver. The high level of ketogenesis by the liver produces ketonemia (high blood levels of ketone bodies) and ketonuria (ketone bodies in the urine). Insulin injections help to reduce these symptoms and allow diabetic persons to live relatively normal lives. However, insulin injections when blood glucose levels are low, as well as overdoses of insulin, can cause severe hypoglycemia (low blood levels of glucose). If blood glucose levels fall below 80 mg/100 mL, insulin shock occurs. When blood levels fall below 20 mg/100 mL, convulsions and coma occur because of the deprivation of glucose to the brain. IV glucose injections can reverse insulin shock. (Stryer, pp 779–780)

308. **(C)** Phytanic acid is a methylated fatty acid byproduct of the catabolism of phytol, a constituent of chlorophyll. Phytanic acid is found in the milk and fats of ruminants. The normal pathway of phytanic acid oxidation in humans involves an α-hydroxylation followed by dehydrogenation and decarboxylation and is termed α-oxidation as opposed to

the more common β-oxidation pathway of linear fats. The absence of the α-hydroxylating enzyme leads to the accumulation of large amounts of phytanic acid leading to severe neurological complications. (Devlin, p 413)

309. **(E)** Biotin serves as an intermediate carrier of $CO_2$ during carboxylations catalyzed by acetyl-CoA carboxylase, propionyl carboxylase, and pyruvate carboxylase. This vitamin is present in the prosthetic groups of these enzymes. Biotin is made from intestinal bacteria and is also obtained from a wide variety of foods. Avidin, a protein present in egg whites, tightly binds biotin in the gut, preventing its absorption. In individuals who consume large quantities of raw eggs, this leads to a toxic reaction due to biotin's role in carboxylation reactions. (Stryer, pp 614–615)

310. **(A)** The α-amino group of many amino acids is transferred to α-ketoglutarate to form glutamate, which is then oxidatively deaminated to ammonium ion. A similar transamination reaction yields alanine from pyruvate during degradation of amino acids. The prosthetic group of all transaminases is pyridoxal phosphate (PLP), which is derived from pyridoxine. During transamination, the aldehyde group of PLP forms a Schiff's-base linkage with the α-amino group of amino acids, ultimately transferring the amino group to either an α-ketoglutarate or pyruvate. (Stryer, pp 629–634)

311. **(B)** The majority of the dehydrogenases of the cell couple reduction of nicotinamide or flavin adenine nucleotide cofactors during the course of the oxidation of their substrates. Those oxidation reactions which are coupled to nicotinamide nucleotide cofactor reduction generate NADH. The electrons of NADH feed into the oxidative-phosphorylation pathway at complex I and thus supply sufficient reducing power to fuel the production of approximately 3 moles of ATP. Those oxidation reactions coupled to flavin adenine nucleotide cofactor reduction yield $FADH_2$. The electrons of $FADH_2$ feed into the oxidative-phosphorylation pathway at complex II and supply only sufficient reducing power to

generate approximately 2 moles of ATP. The reaction catalyzed by glycerol-3-phosphate dehydrogenase is of this latter class. (Murray et al, pp 119–122)

312. (B) LDLs are the primary carriers of blood cholesterol. Routine plasma lipid measurements are carried out after a 12-hr fast. In this way, the major endogenous plasma lipoproteins, VLDLs, and the major exogenous plasma lipoproteins (chylomicrons) have been cleared from the blood of normal individuals. LDLs, which are the end products of VLDL delipidation, and HDLs, which are protein rich, are the only lipoproteins circulating after a 12-hour fast. LDLs are rich in cholesterol, being composed of about 45% cholesterol or cholesterol esters. In both dietary and familial hypercholesterolemia, circulating LDL levels are increased. (Murray et al, pp 270–273)

313. (A) Lovastatin is a fungal HMG-CoA reductase inhibitor and is therefroe useful for inhibiting de novo cholesterol biosynthesis. However, along the pathway to cholesterol biosynthesis, following the HMG-CoA reductase catalyzed step, important isoprenoid compounds are produced. These isoprenoid compounds are required not only for cholesterol biosynthesis but also for the synthesis of dolichol (important for the synthesis of N-linked glycoproteins), coenzyme Q, the side chain of heme A and in the prenylation (lipid modification) of certain membrane-associated proteins. Therefore, chronic suppression of de novo cholesterol biosynthesis by use of the fungal-based inhibitors of HMG-CoA reductase such as Lovastatin can lead to toxicity. (Murray et al, pp 276–277)

314. (C) Fatty acids destined for the oxidation pathway are activated by acetylation to coenzyme A. This activation is catalyzed by fatty acyl-CoA ligase (also called thiokinase or acyl-CoA synthetase) which utilizes the energy of ATP hydrolysis (to AMP and $PP_i$) to drive the reaction in the forward direction. The coupling of pyrophosphorylase-catalyzed hydrolysis of $PP_i$ affords sufficient energy to ensure the reaction proceeds. The

equivalent of two moles of ATP are thus required to regenerate ATP from the AMP generated in this reaction. (Murray et al, pp 220–221)

315. (C) Carbohydrates attached to asparagine residues have a common inner-core structure. Such a block of oligosaccharides is built up and carried to the asparagine of proteins on a lipid carrier. That carrier is dolichol phosphate, an aliphatic chain composed of isoprene units. N-acetylglucosamine is the sugar residue directly bonded to dolichol phosphate and then transferred to the asparagine side chain. (Stryer, pp 920–921)

316. (C) Except for the initial formation of malonyl-CoA by the carboxylation of acetyl-CoA, most of the reactions of fatty acid synthesis occur on the cytosolic fatty acid synthetase complex. The intermediates are attached to the complex by the sulfhydryl group of the acyl carrier protein (ACP). When malonyl-ACP is condensed with acyl-ACP, the carbon atom derived from bicarbonate is decarboxylated as $CO_2$. The β-ketoacyl intermediate formed is reduced in the presence of NADPH to a β-hydroxyacyl, which then is dehydrated to form an enoyl. The enoyl is reduced by NADPH to a saturated acyl in the final step of each round of elongation. (Stryer, pp 614–620)

317. (A) During ethanol clearance in any individual, including alcoholic persons, ethanol is first converted to acetaldehyde by the action of alcohol dehydrogenase and then to acetate by the action of acetaldehyde dehydrogenase. Both of these enzymes require the oxidized form of NAD+ to function. During alcohol oxidation, the level of the reduced form of nicotinamide adenine dinucleotide (NADH) increases greatly in the liver, leading to an overload of the shuttle normally used to regenerate NAD+. This causes the level of NAD+ to be the bottleneck in the removal of alcohol from the body. The levels of alcohol dehydrogenase may be somewhat higher than normal in chronically alcoholic persons. Nevertheless, NAD+ is still the rate-limiting factor in the oxidation of ethanol. (Stryer, pp 496–498)

**318.** **(C)** In contrast to the glycerol-3-phosphate shuttle operating in skeletal muscle, in the heart and liver the bidirectional malate–aspartate shuttle transfers the electrons of cytoplasmic and mitochondrial NADH between the two cell compartments reversibly. The pathway is complex, with glutamate, aspartate, malate, and α-ketoglutarate serving as diffusible carriers. Mitochondrial and cytosolic oxaloacetate and NADH also serve as electron transporters. In contrast to the glycerol-3-phosphate shuttle, which yields only two ATP per pair of electrons derived from cytosolic NADH, the malate–aspartate shuttle yields three ATP per cytosolic NADH. This occurs because NADH and not the reduced form of flavin adenine dinucleotide (FADH) is the mitochondrial carrier of electrons. *(Stryer, pp 548–549)*

**319.** **(D)** Except for the fact that the carrier groups for fatty acid synthesis (ACP) and β-oxidation (CoA) are different, the attached intermediates are similar. In each group of reactions, the enzymatic steps result in acyl, enoyl, β-hydroxyacyl, and β-ketoacyl intermediates being formed or degraded. The enzymatic steps differ in that fatty acid synthesis is carried out in the cytosol using NADPH as a reductant. Biosynthesis is stimulated by citrate. β-oxidation occurs in the mitochondrial matrix using flavin adenine dinucleotide (FAD) and $NAD^+$ as pyridine nucleotide acceptors of electrons. Citrate levels are low during fatty acid oxidation. *(Stryer, pp 606–620)*

**320.** **(D)** Glycolysis is the only major source of ATP in erythrocytes, since they lack mitochondria. In order for glycolysis to continue uninterrupted, NADH must constantly be reoxidized to $NAD^+$ so that glyceraldehyde-3-phosphate may be oxidized. Conversion of pyruvate to lactate by lactate dehydrogenase accomplishes this. The excess lactate diffuses into the liver, where it is converted to glucose via gluconeogenesis. *(Stryer, pp 577–578)*

**321.** **(D)** Increases in either hydrogen ion concentration (lowered pH), $CO_2$ partial pressure, or 2,3-BPG all lead to a decreased affinity of Hb for $O_2$. Conversely, decreases in these factors lead to an increased affinity of $O_2$ for Hb. A decrease in pH changes the charge on histidine residues in Hb, favoring the release of $O_2$. Binding of BPG to deoxyhemoglobin causes the cross-linking of the b chains, leading to a stabilization of the deoxygenated form of Hb and a lowered affinity for $O_2$. $CO_2$ binds to the un-ionized α-amino groups on the terminal ends of Hb. This results in charged carbamino derivatives, which form salt bridges. The salt bridges further reduce the affinity of Hb for $O_2$. *(Stryer, pp 159–160)*

**322.** **(B)** Numerous severe disorders are associated with the inability to properly degrade the complex carbohydrate moieties of glycosaminoglycans, proteoglycans, and glycoproteins. These disorders fall into a broad category of disease termed the lysosomal storage diseases. Several of the lysosomal storage diseases result in heptosplenomegaly, renal disfunction, and skeletal defect and therefore these symptoms are not diagnostic in themselves of a particular lysosomal storage disesase but only indicative of such disorders. It is necessary to evaluate enzyme function in skin fibroblasts or white cells of the blood. Gaucher's disease is caused by a defect in glucocerebrosidase activity and hence an assayable decrease in the activity of this enzyme would be diagnostic of this disease. *(Devlin, pp 456–461)*

**323.** **(D)** The biochemical deficiency of the enzyme HGPRT results in mental retardation and compulsive self-destructive behavior. This X-linked recessive disease also results in gout because of elevated levels of urate. However, unlike gout alone, allopurinol treatment of patients with Lesch–Nyhan syndrome does not increase the rate of synthesis of purines because it does not lower the level of PRPP. In genetically normal individuals, HGPRT allows the salvage synthesis of guanosine 5′-monophosphate (GMP) or inosine 5′-monophosphate (IMP) from guanine or hypoxanthine plus PRPP. The relationship between salvage pathways of purine synthesis and de novo pathways is not yet understood. *(Stryer, pp 755–758)*

**324. (A)** Catabolism of the amino acids takes place in order to supply the body with needed energy, particularly in the absence of adequate carbohydrate and lipid intake. The carbon atoms of the amino acid are utilized as fuel either by being diverted into glucose production (glucogenic amino acids) or ketone body production (ketogenic amino acids). Several amino acids are both glucogenic and ketogenic. Leucine and lysine are the two amino acids that are strictly ketogenic being catabolized to acetoacetate and acetyl-CoA (leucine) and acetoacetyl-CoA (lysine). *(Devlin, pp 330, 493–495, 513–514)*

**325. (B)** The nucleotide thymine, unlike all the other nucleotides, is synthesized at the level of a deoxyribonucleoside monophosphate by the methylation of deoxyuridylate (dUMP) to deoxythymidylate (dTMP). The enzyme thymidylate synthetase catalyzes this reaction. Thus, TMP as such is not a product of the pathway of thymine synthesis. In contrast, all other nucleotides are synthesized as ribose phosphates. CTP is derived from uridine triphosphate (UTP) and is a feedback inhibitor of aspartate transcarbamoylase, the enzyme catalyzing the formation of carbamoyl aspartate, the precursor of UMP. In turn, UMP is the feedback inhibitor of the formation of carbamoyl phosphate, the precursor of carbamoyl aspartate. In purine nucleotide biosynthesis, the formation of PRPP from ribose-5-phosphate, as well as the conversion of PRPP to phosphoribosylamine, is inhibited by AMP, GMP, and IMP. The conversion of IMP to adenylosuccinate, the AMP precursor, is inhibited by AMP. The conversion of IMP to xanthylate, the GMP precursor, is inhibited by GMP. *(Stryer, pp 740–747)*

**326. (B)** Prostaglandin-E$_2$ has numerous effects on a variety of cell types. These effects include the ability to induce signs of inflammation and reduce blood pressure as a result of arteriolar vasodilation, increase capillary permeability, enhance the intensity and duration of pain caused by histamine and bradykinin, stimulate uterine contraction leading to parturition, inhibit gastric acid secretion, and promote platelet aggregation.

Eicosanoid effects on the airways (bronchoconstriction or dilation) are mediated principally by the leukotrienes, not the prostaglandins. *(Devlin, pp 461–466)*

**327. (D)** During the process of glycolysis, two reactions are coupled to the phosphorylation of ADP to yield ATP, termed substrate level phosphorylations. These two reactions are catalyzed by phosphoglycerate kinase and pyruvate kinase. The former enzyme phosphorylates ADP in the process of converting 1,3-bisphosphoglycerate to 3-phosphoglycerate and the latter during the conversion of phosphoenolpyruvate (PEP) to pyruvate. Of the compounds listed only the hydrolysis of PEP yields sufficient energy to be coupled to ADP phosphorylation. *(Murray et al, pp 107–108)*

**328. (A)** Glucose phosphate isomerase catalyzes the reversible conversion of fructose-6-phosphate to glucose-6-phosphate in both glycolysis and gluconeogenesis. In fact, most of the steps of glycolysis are simply reversed in gluconeogenesis. However, the three regulatory steps in the conversion of glucose to pyruvate are not reversible. These steps are: (1) Glucose → glucose-6-phosphate, which is catalyzed by hexokinase, (2) fructose-6-phosphate → fructose-1,6-diphosphate, which is catalyzed by phosphofructokinase, and (3) phosphoenolpyruvate → pyruvate, which is catalyzed by pyruvate kinase. The reversal of these steps in gluconeogenesis requires the enzymes glucose-6-phosphatase and fructose diphosphatase for the formation of glucose and fructose-6-phosphate, respectively. The formation of phosphoenolpyruvate from pyruvate is more complicated in that the four following steps are involved: (1) Pyruvate carboxylase catalyzes the conversion of pyruvate to oxaloacetate, (2) oxaloacetate is reduced to malate by mitochondrial malate dehydrogenase, (3) malate is reconverted to oxaloacetate by extramitochondrial malate dehydrogenase, and (4) oxaloacetate is transformed to phosphoenolpyruvate by GTP-dependent phosphoenolpyruvate carboxykinase. *(Stryer, pp 569–572)*

**329–331.** **(329-C, 330-B, 331-A)** Riboflavin (vitamin $B_2$) is the precursor of the flavin nucleotide cofactors FMN and FAD. These two cofactors are required in numerous oxidoreduction reactions; eg, the TCA cycle enzyme succinate dehydrogenase, mitochondrial glycerol-3-phosphate dehydrogenase used in the transport of cytoplasmic-reducing equivalents into the mitochondria, xanthine oxidase required for purine nucleotide metabolism, and acyl-CoA dehydrogenase of fatty acid metabolism. Biotin is required by enzymes that carboxylate their substrates; eg, acetyl-CoA carboxylase required to activate acetyl-CoA for fatty acid synthesis and pyruvate carboxylase required for gluconeogenesis. Thiamine (vitamin $B_1$) is the precursor for thiamine pyrophosphate (TPP). TPP is required for oxidative decarboxylations catalyzed by pyruvate dehydrogenase, and the TCA cycle enzyme $\alpha$-ketoglutarate dehydrogenase as well as in the pentose phosphate pathway for the transketolase catalyzed reactions. *(Murray et al, pp 573–575, 581–582)*

**332–334.** **(332-E, 333-D, 334-A)** The conversion of isocitrate to $\alpha$-ketoglutarate is catalyzed by isocitrate dehydrogenase and is an oxidative decarboxylation reaction similar to that catalyzed by pyruvate dehydrogenase. The succinyl-CoA synthase catalyzed reaction converting succinyl-CoA to succinate is a substrate-level phosphorylation reaction of the TCA cycle. The substrate phosphorylated is GDP yielding GTP. Succinate dehydrogenase converts succinate to fumarate and is a flavin nucleotide-requiring enzyme. The second product of this reaction is $FADH_2$. *(Stryer, pp 513–514)*

**335–338.** **(335-A, 336-D, 337-B, 338-E)** Glycogen phosphorylase catalyzes the sequential release of glucose from glycogen. The glycosidic bond between the two terminal glucose residues is split by inorganic phosphate. The reaction is

$$\text{Glycogen}_{(n)} + P_i \rightarrow \text{glucose-1-phosphate} + \text{glycogen}_{(n-1)}$$

Glucokinase catalyzes the reaction

$$\text{Glucose} + \text{ATP} \rightarrow \text{glucose-6-phosphate} + \text{ADP}$$

This enzyme in liver provides the glucose-6-phosphate necessary for glycogen synthesis. The addition of glucose units to a growing glycogen chain is catalyzed by glycogen synthase in the following reaction:

$$\text{Glycogen}_{(n)} + \text{UDP-glucose} \rightarrow \text{glycogen}_{(n+1)} + \text{UDP}$$

An activated derivative of glucose, UDP-glucose, serves as the glucosyl donor in this reaction. Glucose-6-phosphatase catalyzes the reaction.

$$\text{Glucose-6-phosphate} + H_2O \rightarrow \text{glucose} + P_i$$

The enzyme functions primarily in the liver to release free glucose into the blood for uptake by other tissues, chiefly brain and muscle. Glucose-6-phosphate dehydrogenase catalyzes the conversion of glucose-6-phosphate to 6-phosphoglucono-$\delta$-lactone. It requires $NADP^+$ as a cofactor. *(Stryer, pp 495, 560, 582–583, 584–585, 587)*

**339–342.** **(339-C, 340-A, 341-D, 342-D)** The carbon skeletons of glutamine, proline, arginine, and histidine enter the citric acid cycle at the level of $\alpha$-ketoglutarate. All of these amino acids are converted to the common intermediate glutamate, which is oxidatively deaminated by glutamate dehydrogenase to yield $\alpha$-ketoglutarate. In the formation of glycine from serine, the side chain $\beta$-carbon of serine is transferred to tetrahydrofolate to form methylenetetrahydrofolate. The reaction is catalyzed by serine transhydroxymethylase, which is a pyridoxal phosphate enzyme. This is the major source of one-carbon units for tetrahydrofolate derivatives. Transamination of oxaloacetate by glutamate results in the formation of aspartate from oxaloacetate and $\alpha$-ketoglutarate from the glutamate skeleton. In turn, asparagine is produced by the amidation of aspartate with ammonium ion. During amino acid degradation, asparagine is hydrolyzed by asparaginase to aspartate. Transamination of $\alpha$-ketoglutarate by aspartate forms oxaloacetate and glutamate. *(Stryer, pp 638–640, 717–723)*

**343–345.** **(343-E, 344-C, 345-A)** Keratins contain as much as 14% cystine, the disulfide form of the amino acid cysteine. Hair and nails, as well as the cytoskeletal elements known as intermediate filaments, are composed of fibrous keratin proteins. Functional prothrombin contains γ-carboxylated glutamate, which results from a vitamin K-dependent post-translational modification of nascent prothrombin. Agents that competitively block vitamin K action, such as warfarin and dicumarol, act as anticoagulants. Proline is modified to hydroxyproline by a post-translational mechanism in collagen synthesis. The reducing agent ascorbic acid is needed for the hydroxylation reaction. Scurvy, a disease caused by dietary insufficiency of vitamin C (ascorbate), is characterized by abnormal collagen that cannot properly form fibers because of the lack of hydroxylated proline residues. Phosphorylation and dephosphorylation of serine are control mechanisms for the regulation of enzyme activity via protein kinase and phosphatase reactions that are under the control of hormonal mechanisms. D-Valine is not a biologically active amino acid. Only one amino acid is effective in mammalian systems. *(Stryer, pp 25, 30, 254–256, 454–455)*

**346–349 (346-E, 347-F, 348-G, 349-D)** The process of introducing an exogenous gene (either a foreign gene or an in vitro altered endogenous gene) into the germ line of an organism is termed transgenesis. When making transgenic mice, the gene to be introduced is either injected into the nuclei of a fertilized egg or used to transfect embryonic stem (ES) cells. Following injection of the DNA into a fertilized egg, the egg is introduced into a receptive host. If ES cells are used they are cultured in such a way as to allow selection of a single clonal population of cells all harboring the DNA of interest. These clonal cells are then introduced into the blastocyst of an embryo and the blastocyst is implanted into a receptive host. The offspring are then tested for the germ line transmission of the injected gene. If the injected or transfecting DNA is incorporated into the germ line, it will be inherited by all the offspring in classical Mendelian fashion. Synthetic RNA or DNA composed of nucleotides that correspond to the non-coding strand of a gene are said to be of the antisense orientation. The introduction of antisense RNA or DNA into cells, either transiently or stably, allows duplexes to form between the antisense molecules and the corresponding sense nucleotides of in vivo derived RNAs. These duplexes effectively prevent translation of the endogenous RNA, thereby eliminating the expression of a functional gene product, ie, the protein. This process is termed reverse genetics because the process selectively modifies a gene product to evaluate its function. Classical genetics refers to the observation of altered phenotypes and then isolation of cells harboring random mutations that can then be identified as causing the phenotype. The ability to amplify extremely small quantities of DNA with high specificity and fidelity has significant clinical and legal applicability such as in disease gene identification and cases of paternity, respectively. A technique developed to accomplish just such a goal is given the name polymerase chain reaction (PCR). PCR utilizes specific primers for DNA synthesis and thermostable DNA polymerases. The process consists of a continuous cycle of melting a template at high temperature, annealing the primers and extending the primers through DNA synthesis. The discovery of bacteria growing in high temperatures harboring thermostable enzymes (in particular DNA polymerases) allowed the PCR to be automated. By carrying out the PCR through as few as 20 cycles allows for the amplification of a template more than a million fold allowing visualization of the amplification product. This technique is so sensitive that a target in as little as the amount of DNA from a single cell can be detected. Several in vitro techniques have been developed that allow for the specific alteration of the nucleotide sequences of a gene to be carried out. These techniques are termed site-directed mutagenesis because they involve the controlled alteration of sequences at specific sites, directed by synthetic oligonucleotides, during in vitro DNA replication. Single nucleotides can be altered in order to determine the effects on gene function of single amino acid substitutions. *(Devlin, pp 797–800, 842–844)*

**350–351 (350-E, 351-A)** Epinephrine binds to specific α- or β-adrenergic receptors on hepatocytes or β-type on skeletal muscle cells. Upon binding to either receptor type intracellular changes take place to effect alterations in glycogen metabolism. Activation of β-adrenergic receptors leads to increased accumulation of cAMP which in turn activates PKA leading to changes in the level of phosphorylation of numerous enzyme including those involved in glycogen metabolism. Glycogen breakdown is increased by the PKA-mediated phosphorylation and activation of synthase/phosphorylase kinase. Synthase/phosphorylase kinase then phosphorylates both phosphorylase and glycogen synthase. The phosphorylation of phosphorylase increases its activity such that an increase in glucose phosphorolysis from glycogen occurs. Conversely, phosphorylation of glycogen synthase reduces its activity preventing glucose incorporation into glycogen. Glycogen synthase is also phosphorylated by PKA. Concomitant phosphorylation and activation of protein phosphatase inhibitor-1 leads to an inhibition of protein phosphatase-1, preventing removal of the newly incorporated phosphates, thereby maintaining the altered activity of both enzymes. When α-adrenergic receptors are activated by epinephrine binding an increase in phospholipase C activity occurs. This enzyme hydrolyzes membrane phosphoinositides yielding diacylglycerol (DAG) and inositol trisphosphate (IP$_3$). IP$_3$ interacts with intracellular receptors, leading to the release of intracellular stores of Ca$^{2+}$. The increased Ca$^{2+}$ binds to the calmodulin subunit of phosphorylase kinase and activates it in the absence of phosphorylation. The net result is an increased rate of glycogen breakdown. Progesterone is a steroid hormone and binds to intracellular receptors. Steroid hormone receptors contain two distinct domains. One binds hormone, the other binds to specific nucleotide sequences in DNA termed hormone response elements (HREs). Upon binding progesterone the hormone/receptor complex migrates to the nucleus and interacts with progesterone specific HREs. The interaction of hormone/receptor complexes with HREs results in altered rates of transcription of the associated gene(s). *(Devlin, pp 353–355, 916–920)*

**352–353 (352-D, 353-C)** Alkaptonuria is an inherited disorder resulting from a lack of homogentisate oxidase, which is required for the degradation of tyrosine. In the absence of this enzyme, homogentisate is excreted in the urine. Upon exposure to the air, the homogentisate in the urine is oxidized to a brownish-black pigment. Maple syrup urine disease (also called branched-chain ketonuria) results from an absence or greatly reduced level of α-keto acid decarboxylase required for the degradation of the branched-chain amino acids leucine, valine, and isoleucine (and to a minor extent other branched-chain α-keto acids). The disorder is characterized by the maple syrup or burnt sugar odor of the urine. *(Murray et al, pp 311, 322–323)*

**354–356. (354-E, 355-A, 356-C)** The first three reaction sequences are distinct parts of the glycolytic pathway. The precursor for formation of fructose-6-phosphate can be either glucose or glycogen. In the first instance, 1 mol of ATP is consumed to generate glucose-6-phosphate, which is converted to fructose-6-phosphate. In muscle, however, glycogen can be broken down via a phosphorolysis reaction involving inorganic phosphate and catalyzed by glycogen phosphorylase. The product is glucose-1-phosphate, which is converted to glucose-6-phosphate and metabolized via the glycolytic pathway. Thus, the phosphorylated sugar intermediate is generated from glycogen without expenditure of an ATP. Fructose-6-phosphate is converted to fructose-1,6-biphosphate in a reaction that uses ATP. In the conversion of glyceraldehyde-3-phosphate to pyruvate, 2 mol of ATP are generated. Pyruvate may be used for the synthesis of glucose by gluconeogenesis. Four moles of ATP (and 2 mol of

GTP) are consumed in the conversion of pyruvate to glucose via the gluconeogenic pathway. (*Stryer, pp 483–491, 570–574, 582–585*)

**357–359 (357-A, 358-D, 359-E)** Heparan sulfates are predominantly found associated with the surfaces of the endothelial cells of vessels. In this capacity, heparan sulfates exhibit localized antithrombic activity. In contrast, heparins are predominantly located in granules of mast cells and are released to the circulation upon mast cell activation where the heparins also exhibit antithrombic activity. Chondroitin sulfates are the most prevalent GAGs in the human body. Chondroitin sulfates are often found associated with hyaluronates and in such complexes form the ground substance of cartilage. Chondroitin sulfates are also found in the tendons, ligaments, and aorta. Hyaluronates are unique among the GAGs in that they contain no sulfated sugars and are not associated with proteins to form proteoglycans. The hyaluronates form extremely large polymers that have excellent shock-absorbing and lubricating character. Because of this feature, hyaluronates are found in synovial fluid, vitreous humor, and in the umbilical cord. As indicated above hyaluronates also associate with chondroitin sulfates. (*Murray et al, pp 640–645*)

**360–362.    (360-E, 361-A, 362-C)** Protein biosynthesis (translation) in eukaryotes is always initiated at an AUG codon (at CUG on rare occasions), which codes for methionine. A special initiator, tRNA, which is charged with methionine, recognizes the initiation codon. In prokaryotes, the α-amino group on the methionine is blocked by formylation. This is not the case for eukaryotic initiator tRNA. The enzymes that mediate RNA biosynthesis (transcription) are referred to as RNA polymerases. In eukaryotes, there are three different RNA polymerases that are responsible for the transcription of ribosomal RNA, messenger RNA or transfer and 5S RNA, respectively. By contrast, a single RNA polymerase, is responsible for the transcription of all RNA species in prokaryotes. The enzyme responsible for mRNA synthesis in eukaryotes is RNA polymerase II. This enzyme is specifi-

cally inhibited by α-amanitin. RNA synthesis in all organisms begins at a specific nucleotide position. RNA polymerase binds to the DNA template at a specific sequence called a promoter. In prokaryotes, the promoter consists of two sequence elements that occur at 10 and 35 nucleotides before the transcription start site. Similar sequences comprise eukaryotic promoters but, in general, are found 25 and between 40 and 100 nucleotides upstream of the transcription start site. (*Stryer, pp 842–843, 852–854, 894–895*)

**363–365.    (363-C, 364-A, 365-D)** Triacylglycerols are transported in the blood by chylomicrons and VLDLs. The endproducts of VLDL delipidation are LDLs, which are rich in cholesterol. LDLs are taken up by peripheral tissues via specific LDL receptors. In this manner, LDLs are responsible for delivering cholesterol to peripheral tissues. HDLs are protein-rich lipoproteins that are important in the transport of cholesterol from peripheral tissues to the liver for excretion as bile. Bile salts are polar derivatives of cholesterol and are its major breakdown products. Lipoproteins, such as HDL and LDL, contain a variety of proteins that are referred to as apoproteins, one of which is apoprotein E. It is a constituent of chylomicrons, VLDL, and IDL. (*Murray et al, pp 253–258, 270–275*)

**366–368 (366-B, 367-D, 368-A)** Osteogenesis imperfecta encompasses at least four biochemically and clinically distinct maladies. Each of the disorders are characterized by multiple fractures and bone deformities. The root causes of osteogenesis imperfecta are various mutations in the type I collagen gene resulting in shortened α(I)-type polypeptide chains. Ehlers–Danlos syndrome encompasses at least ten clinically and biochemically distinct disorders, all of which can be characterized a structural weakness of the connective tissue. Type IV Ehlers–Danlos results from defects in the type III collagen gene. Type III collagen is prevalent in the arteries, skin, muscle, and hollow organs. Therefore, defects in type III collagen leads to vessel and intestinal rupture and uterine rupture during pregnancy. Marfan syndrome is characterized by skeletal, eye, and cardiac abnormalities that eventually leads to cardiovascular failure. Marfan syndrome was originally thought to be due to defects in collagen synthesis but has since been shown to be caused by defects in fibrillin synthesis. Fibrillin is a protein that plays an integral role in the structure of the non-collagenous fibrils of the extracellular matrix. *(Devlin, pp 760–761)*

369. **(B)** Carbohydrate modification of proteins occurs by attachment of the carbohydrates to either hydroxyl groups (eg, serine and threonine or hydroxylysines in collagen), termed O-linked glycoproteins, or amino groups (of asparagine), termed N-linked glycoproteins. The processing of both types of glycoproteins begins in the endoplasmic reticulum either while the proteins are being synthesized (O-linked) or following completion of synthesis (N-linked). However, the terminal modifications to the carbohydrates occurs as the proteins progress through the Golgi apparatus to the cell surface. *(Murray et al, pp 625–630)*

370. **(E)** Several enzymes of the blood clotting cascade (eg, factors II, VII, IX, X, and protein C) bind calcium and are thus activated following cleavage of their zymogen forms. The ability of these proteins to bind calcium requires post-translationally modified glutamate residues. The modification is a γ-carboxylation yielding γ-carboxyglutamate (gla) residues. The carboxylation reaction has an absolute requirement for vitamin K as a cofactor. *(Devlin, p 1125)*

371. **(C)** Steroid hormones are lipophilic and hence freely penetrate the plasma membrane of all cells. Within target cells, steroid hormones interact with specific receptors. These receptor proteins are composed of two domains; a hormone-binding domain and a DNA-binding domain. Following hormone-receptor interaction the complex is activated and enters the nucleus. The DNA-binding domain of the receptor interacts with specific nucleotide sequences termed hormone response elements (HREs). The binding of steroid-receptor complexes to HREs results in an altered rate of transcription of the associated gene(s). The effects of steroid-receptor complexes on specific target genes can be either stimulatory or inhibitory with respect to the rate of transcription. *(Devlin, pp 916–920)*

372. **(A)** When fatty acids are destined for oxidation they must first be activated by acetylation to coenzyme A to yield fatty acyl-CoAs. The biosynthesis of coenzyme A requires pantothenic acid (vitamin $B_5$) as a portion of the molecule. Therefore, fat oxidation requires vitamin $B_5$ as a cofactor. The synthesis of fatty acids begins with activated acetate (acetyl-CoA) and thus also requires vitamin $B_5$ as a cofactor. Additionally, fatty acid synthase (the multi-functional enzyme of fatty acid synthesis) contains an acyl carrier domain harboring a 4'-phosphopantetheine moiety derived from vitamin $B_5$. *(Murray et al, p 577)*

373. **(B)** Several amino acids required for human protein synthesis can be produced by normal metabolic pathways, provided sufficient precursors are made available in the diet. However, several amino acids are absolutely required in the diet because humans cannot synthesize them and are hence essential amino acids. Methionine is one of the essential amino acids, in particular large amounts are required to produce cysteine (a non-essential amino acid) if cysteine is not supplied in adequate amounts in the diet. *(Devlin, p 476)*

374. **(D)** Glucose-6-phosphatase is required in the liver in order for this organ to supply the rest of the body with glucose that has been produced by hepatic gluconeogenesis or released from stored hepatic glycogen. A deficiency in glucose-6-phosphatase leads to the most common of the glycogen storage diseases, von Gierke's disease. This glycogen storage disease results from excess hepatic glucose-6-phosphate allosterically activating the β-form of glycogen synthase leading to increased incorporation of glucose into glycogen. *(Devlin, pp 340–341)*

375. **(E)** During starvation, the ability of the liver to supply the brain with needed glucose diminishes. This leads to a shift in hepatic metabolism to that of increased fatty acid oxidation in order to produce large amounts of acetyl-CoA that can be diverted into ketone body production. The ketone bodies are then delivered to the blood and utilized by the brain (and other peripheral tissues) as an energy source. *(Devlin, pp 416–417)*

376. **(A)** The major substrates of gluconeogenesis are pyruvate and lactate. During gluconeogenesis, lactate is in turn oxidized to pyruvate. In order for pyruvate to be converted back to glucose, it must first be carboxylated to oxaloacetate, since a reversal of the pyruvate kinase reaction of glycolysis cannot occur in order to convert the pyruvate to phosphoenolpyruvate. The carboxylation of pyruvate is catalyzed by the mitochondrial enzyme, pyruvate carboxylase. The activity of pyruvate carboxylase is absolutely dependent upon the presence of acetyl-CoA, which allosterically activates the enzyme. *(Devlin, pp 334–337)*

377. **(B)** Carbonic anhydrase catalyzes the following reaction:

$$CO_2 + H_2O \leftrightarrow H_2CO_3$$

This reaction is freely reversible and proceeds in one direction or the other dependent upon the relative partial pressures of $CO_2$ and $O_2$. In the lungs where the partial pressure of $O_2$ is high, the $O_2$ leaves the alveoli and enters erythrocytes of the blood. There it is bound by hemoglobin for transport to the peripheral tissues. When $O_2$ is bound, hydrogen ions dissociate from hemoglobin and are titrated by bicarbonate ions to form carbonic acid: $H_2CO_3$. The increase in carbonic acid results in the carbonic anhydrase reaction proceeding to the left, relative to the equation above. The $CO_2$ thus formed flows out of the erythrocytes due to the relatively low partial pressure of $CO_2$ of the lungs. The $CO_2$ is then expelled from the lungs upon expiration. When erythrocytes enter the relatively high partial pressure of $CO_2$ in the tissues, the reverse process occurs leading to release of the hemoglobin bound $O_2$. *(Devlin, pp 1033–1035)*

378. **(E)** Muscle cells lack glucose-6-phosphatase, thereby preventing any glucose that is released from stored glycogen from leaving the muslce cell and entering the blood. During the normal process of glycogen breakdown, a free molecule of glucose is released each time a limit dextrin is acted upon by the debranching enzyme. However, this free glucose is rapidly phosphorylated by the high activity of skeletal muscle hexokinase and trapped within the cell for oxidation. *(Murray et al, pp 182–183)*

379. **(B)** During strenuous physical exercise, the rate of production of pyruvate via glycolysis exceeds the capacity of the citric acid cycle to utilize it and pyruvate accumulates. NADH also accumulates and glycolysis cannot continue unless NAD$^+$ is regenerated. This is accomplished by the conversion of pyruvate to lactate by lactate dehydrogenase, which uses NADH as a cofactor and produces NAD$^+$. Pyruvate and lactate diffuse out of muscle into blood and are taken up by the liver, where pyruvate is converted to glucose. *(Stryer, pp 577–578)*

380. **(C)** Dietary triaclyglycerides are hydrolyzed in the intestines by pancreatic lipase and pancreatic phospholipase A$_2$. The resultant free fatty acids and monoacylglycerols enter intestinal epithelial cells where the triacylglycerides are reformed. These triacylglycerides are packaged into chylomicrons and delivered to the circulation via the lymphatic system. Chylomicrons are, therefore, the molecules produced by the body to deliver dietary triacylglycerides to the circulation. *(Murray et al, pp 253–256)*

381. **(E)** Rifamycin (rifampicin) is an inhibitor of transcription. It specifically blocks initiation of transcription by interfering with formation of the first phosphodiester bond in the RNA chain. The other antibiotics listed are all inhibitors of protein synthesis. *(Stryer, pp 851–852, 902–903)*

**382.** **(D)** Fatty acids are activated to the coenzyme A derivatives at the outer mitochondrial membrane but are oxidized inside the mitochondria. Long chain fatty acyl-CoA molecules do not cross the mitochondrial membrane. A special transport system involving carnitine is utilized for movement of the activated fatty acids into the mitochondria. The fatty acyl moiety is transferred from the CoA to carnitine in a reaction catalyzed by carnitine acyltransferase I. Acyl carnitine thus formed is shuttled across the inner mitochondrial membrane where the fatty acyl group is transferred back to a coenzyme A molecule within the mitochondrial matrix. The latter reaction is catalyzed by carnitine acyltransferase II. Medium chain fatty acyl CoAs can cross the mitochondrial membrane and do not require the carnitine transport system for entry into the mitochondria. *(Stryer, pp 607–608)*

**383.** **(B)** Restriction endonucleases are enzymes produced by bacteria that recognize a specific nucleotide sequence in DNA and cleave the phosphodiester bonds of both DNA strands. In bacteria, these enzymes serve the protective function of preventing transformation by the uptake of foreign DNA. The recognition sites for the enzymes possess a two-fold axis of rotational symmetry, ie, the sites are palindromes. The DNA in the host cell is protected from digestion because the recognition site is modified by methylation. Restriction enzymes cleave DNA regardless of its higher order structure and do not require that the DNA be supercoiled. These enzymes are widely used in the application of recombinant DNA technology. *(Murray et al, pp 452–453)*

**384.** **(C)** The synthesis of all steroid hormones involves formation of progesterone from cholesterol. An intermediate in this conversion is pregnenolone. These reactions, as well as many of the reactions leading from progesterone to other steroid hormone derivatives, require the action of mono-oxygenases (or mixed-function oxygenases). These enzymes mediate hydroxylation reactions necessary for synthesis of the steroid hormones. These reactions involve the incorporation of oxygen atoms from molecular oxygen, using the reductive potential of NADPH. Vitamin D is a steroid that is formed from cholesterol (more specifically, 7-dehydrocholesterol) by the action of ultraviolet light. It does not play a role in steroid hormone biosynthesis. *(Stryer, pp 703–707)*

**385.** **(C)** The initial step in purine nucleotide biosynthesis is the formation of phosphoribosylamine from PRPP and glutamine. This reaction is catalyzed by PRPP amidotransferase and is the committed step in purine biosynthesis. The reaction is regulated by feedback inhibition by AMP and/or GMP. Since PRPP is a substrate in this reaction, the rate of purine biosynthesis is governed by the availability of PRPP. The initial purine nucleotide product of the de novo pathway is IMP. This compound serves as a branch point in the synthesis of AMP and GMP. In one branch of the pathway, IMP is converted to AMP and requires GTP, whereas in the other branch of the pathway, IMP is converted to GMP in reactions requiring ATP. The reciprocal requirements of one purine nucleotide for the synthesis of the other serves to ensure that relatively balanced amounts of both are produced. Xanthine oxidase is involved in the degradation of purines and plays no role in the biosynthesis. *(Stryer, pp 740–745)*

**386.** **(C)** Any condition that results in elevated levels of purine nucleotides is likely to cause hyperuricemia. HGPRT is a salvage pathway enzyme that catalyzes the condensation of hypoxanthine or guanine with PRPP to yield IMP or GMP. In this way, purine bases, which become available in the diet or by virtue of nucleic acid degradation, can be recycled into the corresponding nucleotides and used for nucleic acid biosynthesis. If this salvage is blocked, the purine bases are degraded further to uric acid. Xanthine oxidase, adenosine deaminase, and purine nucleoside phosphorylase are all purine degradative enzymes. The absence of any of these enzymes would prevent the formation of uric acid. PRPP amidotransferase is the enzyme that catalyzes the committed step in purine biosynthesis. Its absence would result in lower levels of purines and would not result in elevated uric acid levels. *(Stryer, pp 740–743, 755–758)*

387. **(D)** Reduced glutathione is an antioxidant. It is regenerated by the transfer of electrons from NADPH to oxidized glutathione via FAD. This reaction, which transfers the electrons to a disulfide bridge of glutathione, is catalyzed by glutathione reductase. In erythrocytes, the reduced form of glutathione maintains the cysteine residues of Hb and other RBC proteins in a reduced state. It also plays a role in cell detoxification by reacting with organic peroxides and hydrogen peroxides. *(Stryer, pp 567–569)*

388. **(A)** Arsenate replaces the $P_i$ that normally reacts with glyceraldehyde-3-phosphate to form 1,3-BPG. Instead, an unstable intermediate, 1-arseno-3-phosphoglycerate, is produced and immediately hydrolyzes to 3-phosphoglycerate. NADH is formed as usual. Thus glycolysis proceeds in the presence of arsenate, but the ATP usually produced in the conversion of 1,3-BPG to 3-phosphoglycerate is lost. Since glycolysis proceeds, pyruvate is formed. *(Stryer, p 503)*

389. **(D)** Glucose can enter the glycolytic pathway either directly as free glucose or by the release of stored glucose in glycogen. When free glucose enters the glycolytic pathway it is phosphorylated by either hepatic glucokinase or hexokinase of non-hepatic tissue yielding glucose-6-phosphate. Only when glucose is released from stored glycogen does it exist, temporarily, as glucose-1-phosphate. *(Devlin, pp 297–304)*

390–393 **(390-E, 391-A, 392-D, 393-G)** Erythropoietin (Epo) is synthesized by the kidney and released in response to loss of blood or hypoxia. Epo is the primary regulator of erythropoiesis. Epo stimulates the proliferation and growth of erythroid progenitor cells (burst-forming erythroid and colony-forming erythroid units) and the proliferation of immature erythrocytes. Platelet-derived growth factor (PDGF) was first isolated from platelets, hence the derivation of its name. PDGF is composed of two distinct polypeptide chains, A and B, that can form both homo- and heterodimers. PDGF is a growth factor for many mesenchymal cell types including those of connective tissue, glial cells, and smooth muscle cells. PGDF dimers bind to cell surface receptors that contain intrinsic tyrosine kinase activity. Activation of these receptors leads to all of the subsequent effects of PDGF on responsive cells. Interleukin-2 (IL-2) is the major cytokine responsible for clonal proliferation of T cells. IL-2 is produced and secreted by activated T cells thereby forming an autocrine loop of T-cell mediated proliferation. IL-2 also exerts its effects on natural killer (NK) cells, B cells, and macrophages. Interleukin-6 (IL-6) is produced by macrophages, fibroblasts, endothelial cells, and activated T-helper cells. IL-6 synergizes with IL-1 and tumor necrosis factor-$\alpha$ (TNF-$\alpha$) in numerous immune responses. IL-6 is the primary inducer of the acute phase response of the liver which leads to the synthesis of fibrinogen, complement proteins, several clotting factors and $\alpha_2$-macroglobulin. *(Murray et al, 689, 720–721; Devlin, pp 598)*

394–397. **(394-B, 395-I, 396-G, 397-F)** One of the key steps in gluconeogenesis is the conversion of pyruvate to phosphoenolpyruvate. This cannot be accomplished by the simple reversal of the pyruvate kinase reaction of glycolysis. Rather, pyruvate is first converted to oxaloacetate, which in turn is decarboxylated and phosphorylated to phosphoenolpyruvate. The latter reaction is catalyzed by phosphoenolpyruvate carboxykinase and requires GTP. $\alpha$-Ketoglutarate is oxidatively decarboxylated to succinyl CoA during the citric acid cycle in a reaction catalyzed by the $\alpha$-ketoglutarate dehydrogenase complex. The reaction requires NAD$^+$ as a cofactor and generates NADH. The initial step in the pentose phosphate pathway is the conversion of glucose-6-phosphate to 6-phosphoglucono-$\delta$-lactone and is catalyzed by glucose-6-phosphate dehydrogenase. The reaction requires NADP$^+$ and generates NADPH, which is one of the major products of the pathway. The last step of glycolysis is the production of pyruvate from phosphoenolpyruvate in a reaction catalyzed by pyruvate kinase. The reaction proceeds with the production of a mole of ATP and is not dependent on mitochondrial oxidative phosphorylation. Therefore, ATP is produced even in the absence of oxygen. *(Stryer, pp 489, 517–518, 560, 570–571)*

**398.** **(A)** The amino groups of amino acids are converted to urea for excretion via the urea cycle. The liver is the only organ capable of carrying this out. The human liver produces some 20 to 30 g of urea each day. Synthesis of gangliosides, which are components of all mammalian plasma membranes, can be carried out in all cells. Nucleotide biosynthesis is also carried out by most cells, as is utilization of medium-chain fatty acids as an energy source. Glycogen can be degraded not only in the liver but also chiefly in muscle. *(Stryer, pp 634–636)*

**399.** **(D)** Formation of acetyl-CoA from pyruvate is catalyzed by the enzymes of the pyruvate dehydrogenase complex.

$$\text{pyruvate} + \text{CoA} + \text{NAD}^+$$
$$\rightarrow \text{acetyl-CoA} + \text{CO}_2 + \text{NADH}$$

As can be seen from the reaction, the stoichiometric cofactors are CoA and $NAD^+$. In addition, pyruvate dehydrogenase requires thiamine pyrophosphate, dihydrolipoyl transacetylase requires lipoic acid, and dihydrolipoyl dehydrogenase requires FAD. Biotin is not required for these reactions. *(Stryer, pp 514–517)*

**400.** **(E)** Niacin (nicotinic acid) is required for the synthesis of $NAD^+$. Its deficiency results in pellagra, a disease characterized by psychic disturbances, diarrhea, and dermatitis. A diet rich in niacin will prevent the disease. *(Stryer, pp 754–755)*

**401.** **(A)** Mammalian membranes are composed of a lipid bilayer with associated proteins.

The bilayer contains a variety of different lipids, including phospholipids, glycolipids, glycosphingolipids, and cholesterol. Triacylglycerides are found only within circulating lipoprotein particles or fat droplets inside cells. *(Devlin, pp 197–205)*

**402–404.** **(402-G, 403-E, 404-A)** Purine nucleoside phosphorylase catalyzes the conversion of guanosine and inosine to guanine and hypoxanthine, respectively. Guanine is then converted to xanthine, and both xanthine and hypoxanthine are substrates for xanthine oxidase yielding uric acid. A deficiency in purine nucleoside phosphorylase will prevent the production of uric acid and will result in hypouricemia. The major effect of this enzyme deficiency, however, is immunodeficiency. Lack of the salvage pathway enzyme hypoxanthine phosphoribosyl transferase results in Lesch–Nyhan syndrome, which is characterized by severe behavioral disorders. It also results in significantly elevated levels of uric acid production. Thymidylate synthase catalyzes the methylation of deoxyuridylate (dUMP) to thymidylate. Fluorodeoxyuridylate is a substrate analogue of dUMP and specifically inhibits the activity of thymidylate synthase. Allopurinol is an inhibitor of xanthine oxidase. Sulfamethoxazole is an inhibitor of folate biosynthesis in bacteria. Since humans do not possess the capacity to synthesize folate, sulfamethoxazole is employed as an antibiotic. Glucose-6-phosphatase catalyzes the conversion of glucose-6-phosphate to glucose in the liver. A deficiency of this enzyme results in glycogen storage disease. Since glucose-6-phosphate is not converted to glucose, it is employed as a substrate in the pentose phosphate pathway. This results in higher than normal amounts of ribose-5-phosphate which, in turn, drives increased levels of purine biosynthesis. As a result, a deficiency of this enzyme leads to hyperuricemia. Adenine phosphoribosyl transferase is a salvage pathway enzyme that converts adenine to AMP. *(Stryer, pp 744, 751–753, 755–758)*

## REFERENCES

Devlin TM. *Textbook of Biochemistry with Clinical Correlations*. 3rd ed. New York; Wiley–Liss; 1992

Murray RK et al. *Harper's Biochemistry*. 23rd ed. Stamford, CT: Appleton & Lange; 1993

Mathews CK, van Holde KE. *Biochemistry*. 2nd ed. Redwood City, CA: Benjamin/Cummings Publishing Co.; 1990

Stryer L. *Biochemistry*. 4th ed. New York: WH Freeman and Co.; 1995

# Subspecialty List— Biochemistry

278. Nucleotide metabolism
279. Kinetics
280. Integration of metabolism
281. Blood
282. Vitamins and disease
283. Vitamins and disease
284. Integration of metabolism
285. Vitamins and disease
286. Muscle contraction
287. Carbohydrate metabolism
288. Carbohydrate metabolism
289. Carbohydrate metabolism
290. Carbohydrate metabolism
291. Nucleotide metabolism
292. Integration of metabolism
293. Proteins
294. Carbohydrate metabolism
295. Carbohydrate metabolism
296. Lipid metabolism
297. Lipid metabolism
298. Diabetes
299. Cholesterol metabolism
300. Carbohydrate metabolism and disease
301. Carbohydrate metabolism
302. Lipid metabolism and disease
303. Lipid metabolism and disease
304. Carbohydrate metabolism
305. Carbohydrate metabolism
306. Ketogenesis
307. Integration of metabolism

308. Lipid metabolism and disease
309. Vitamins
310. Vitamins
311. Energy metabolism
312. Lipoproteins
313. Cholesterol metabolism
314. Lipid metabolism
315. Glycoproteins
316. Lipid metabolism
317. Carbohydrate metabolism
318. Energy metabolism
319. Lipid metabolism
320. Carbohydrate metabolism
321. Blood and oxygen transport
322. Lipid metabolism and disease
323. Nucleotide metabolism
324. Amino acid metabolism
325. Nucleotide metabolism
326. Lipoproteins
327. Carbohydrate metabolism
328. Carbohydrate metabolism
329. Vitamins
330. Vitamins
331. Vitamins
332. Carbohydrate metabolism
333. Carbohydrate metabolism
334. Carbohydrate metabolism
335. Carbohydrate metabolism
336. Carbohydrate metabolism
337. Carbohydrate metabolism
338. Carbohydrate metabolism

339. Amino acid metabolism
340. Amino acid metabolism
341. Amino acid metabolism
342. Amino acid metabolism
343. Protein
344. Protein
345. Protein
346. Molecular biology
347. Molecular biology
348. Molecular biology
349. Molecular biology
350. Hormones
351. Hormones
352. Amino acids and disease
353. Amino acids and disease
354. Carbohydrate metabolism
355. Carbohydrate metabolism
356. Carbohydrate metabolism
357. Complex carbohydrates
358. Complex carbohydrates
359. Complex carbohydrates
360. Molecular biology
361. Molecular biology
362. Molecular biology
363. Lipoproteins
364. Lipids
365. Lipids
366. Proteins and disease
367. Proteins and disease
368. Proteins and disease
369. Glycoproteins
370. Vitamins
371. Hormones

372. Vitamins
373. Amino acids
374. Carbohydrate metabolism and disease
375. Ketogenesis
376. Carbohydrate metabolism
377. Blood and oxygen transport
378. Carbohydrate metabolism
379. Carbohydrate metabolism
380. Lipoproteins
381. Molecular biology
382. Lipid metabolism
383. Molecular biology
384. Hormones

385. Nucleotide metabolism
386. Nucleotide metabolism and disease
387. Carbohydrate metabolism
388. Carbohydrate metabolism
389. Carbohydrate metabolism
390. Hormones and growth factors
391. Hormones and growth factors
392. Hormones and growth factors
393. Hormones and growth factors

394. Carbohydrate metabolism
395. Carbohydrate metabolism
396. Carbohydrate metabolism
397. Carbohydrate metabolism
398. Integration of metabolism
399. Vitamins
400. Vitamins
401. Lipids
402. Nucleotide metabolism
403. Nucleotide metabolism and disease
404. Nucleotide metabolism

# CHAPTER 4

# Microbiology
## Questions

*William W. Yotis, PhD*

**DIRECTIONS (Questions 405 through 528): Each of the numbered items or incomplete statements in this section is followed by answers or by completions of the statement. Select the ONE lettered answer or completion that is BEST in each case.**

405. The leukocytes from a potential kidney transplant recipient (R) were tested in five separate mixed leukocyte reaction cultures with irradiated leukocytes from five potential donors (1, 2, 3, 4, and 5). The results of the test (counts per minutes of $^3$H-thymidine incorporated into each culture) are summarized below.

| Donor + Recipient | Count per Minutes |
|---|---|
| 1 + R | 16,750 |
| 2 + R | 28,830 |
| 3 + R | 85,000 |
| 4 + R | 2,500 |
| 5 + R | 42,000 |

The best kidney donor would be

(A) donor 1
(B) donor 2
(C) donor 3
(D) donor 4
(E) donor 5

406. The immunoglobulin molecule shown in Figure 4.1 represents

(A) IgA
(B) IgE
(C) IgD
(D) IgM
(E) IgG

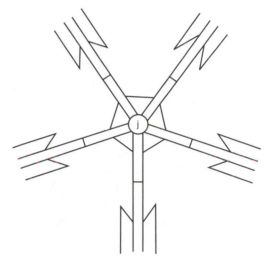

**Figure 4.1**

407. Interferon causes antiviral resistance by inducing formation of antiviral proteins in the cell that

(A) interfere with adsorption of virus to other cells
(B) block transcription of viral nucleic acid
(C) prevent penetration of virus
(D) inhibit viral uncoating
(E) block translation of viral nucleic acid

408. Iodophors are iodine compounds that

(A) are more irritating
(B) release iodine very rapidly
(C) are very active in the presence of organic matter
(D) are excellent antibacterial agents

409. Which of the following statements concerning a bacterial cell that is resistant to bacteriophage infection is true?

(A) it has altered surface receptors that are not recognized by the phage adsorption organs
(B) it produces large amounts of repressor protein that bind to the immunity region of the phage
(C) it produces large amounts of restriction endonucleases
(D) it has an integrated F factor in the chromosome
(E) it usually does not produce lysozyme

410. A 22-year-old man complains to his family physician of fatigue, night sweats, and a dry unproductive cough. For the past several years, the patient resided in Chicago and has recently moved to Detroit. Until the past few months, he had apparently been in good health. A CBC and differential blood count reveal that he is lymphopenic. X-ray examination reveals an interstitial pneumonia. Skin test reactions to a battery of skin test materials are normal. The next step in evaluating this patient's illness should be

(A) identification of the organism that is causing the pneumonia
(B) nitroblue tetrazolium reduction assay
(C) $CH_{50}$ assay
(D) intracellular killing assay
(E) chemotaxis assay

411. Cultures of two streptomycin-sensitive strains of *Escherichia coli* are mixed together. Streptomycin is added, and the mixture is incubated. After 2 hours, the mixture is plated on a medium containing streptomycin. A few streptomycin-resistant colonies develop. This is probably an example of

(A) transduction by bacteriophage
(B) genetic transformation
(C) conjugation via sex pilus bridge
(D) spontaneous chromosomal mutation
(E) genetic complementation

412. A 2-year-old girl with recurrent pulmonary infections has been brought to the hospital by her mother with respiratory difficulties. Gram stain of the sputum reveals numerous polymorphonuclear neutrophils and gram-positive cocci in grape-like clusters. The drug of choice to be employed until the antibiotic sensitivity report is received from the laboratory is

(A) penicillin
(B) methicillin
(C) streptomycin
(D) ampicillin
(E) chloramphenicol

413. Which of the following statements concerning the Ouchterlony diagram (Fig. 4.2) is true?

(A) line 1 will contain Ag ab and Ab b only
(B) line 2 will contain Ag ac and Ab b
(C) the spur will contain Ab a and Ag ab
(D) the spur will contain Ag ac and Ab a
(E) the spur will contain Ag ab and Ab b

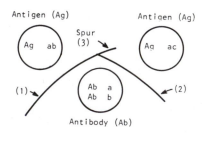

Figure 4.2

414. The base pair substitution that results in the change of a purine for a pyrimidine is a

   (A) transformant
   (B) transition
   (C) transversion
   (D) transposition
   (E) frame shift

415. Transformation of bacteria can be blocked by

   (A) RNAse in the medium
   (B) DNAse in the medium
   (C) antiserum against bacteriophage
   (D) bacteriophage that adsorb to sex pili
   (E) preventing cell-to-cell contact between donor and recipient cultures

416. A lysogenic cell refers to a bacterial cell that

   (A) is susceptible to a virulent phage
   (B) is resistant to lysozyme
   (C) is resistant to lysis
   (D) carries a prophage
   (E) excretes lysozyme

417. A boy is unprovokedly attacked and bitten on the shoulder by a fox and suffers a slight wound. In addition to flushing the wound, cleaning the wound surgically, and giving antitetanus prophylaxis and antibiotics as indicated, the physician should

   (A) order a search for the attacking fox for autopsy
   (B) start rabies vaccine
   (C) start rabies vaccine and give antirabies serum
   (D) observe the boy very carefully
   (E) report the incident to the state epidemiologist

418. Chlamydiae and rickettsiae are correctly described as

   (A) spread by the bite of an infected arthropod
   (B) resistant to the usual broad-spectrum antibiotics

   (C) containing either RNA or DNA, but not both
   (D) obligate parasites of living cells
   (E) dividing solely by binary fission

419. A laboratory worker has been diagnosed as having tuberculosis. He has been ill for 10 months with symptoms that include a productive cough, intermittent fever, night sweats, and a weight loss of 27.3 kg (60 lb). Numerous acid-fast bacilli are seen in a sputum examination, and more than fifty colonies of organisms grow out in culture. In a situation such as this, those contacts who have a positive skin test but no other signs of disease should

   (A) receive prophylactic isoniazid (INH)
   (B) receive a full course of INH and ethambutol
   (C) be checked periodically by x-ray
   (D) be immunized with bacille Calmette–Guérin (BCG) vaccine
   (E) be checked periodically by sputum culture

420. A genetic test of function that depends on the interaction of the products of genes is

   (A) suppression
   (B) post-replication repair
   (C) recombination
   (D) host-induced modification
   (E) complementation

421. Ultraviolet light

   (A) disrupts the bacterial cell membrane
   (B) removes free sulfhydryl groups
   (C) is a common protein denaturant
   (D) causes the formation of pyrimidine dimers
   (E) acts as an alkylating agent

**422.** Genetic elements of defined nucleotide sequence that are able to translocate (ie, move from one relative position in a bacterial chromosome or plasmid to another) and carry genes that specify resistance to antimicrobial agents are referred to as

(A) R plasmids
(B) replicons
(C) insertion sequences
(D) resistance transfer factors (RTFs)
(E) transposons

**423.** Penicillin would be LEAST effective in treating

(A) syphilis
(B) gonorrhea
(C) pneumococcal pneumonia
(D) mycoplasmal pneumonia
(E) streptococcal pharyngitis

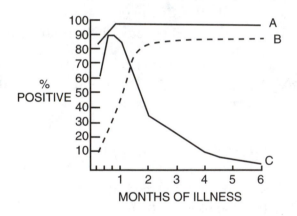

Figure 4.3. (*Reprinted from Huppert:* Mycopathologia 41:107, 1970 *with permission from Kluwer Academic Publishers.*)

**424.** Which of the following statements concerning Figure 4.3 (which shows the frequency of serologic reactivity after exposure to *Coccidioides immitis*) is true?

(A) curve A represents the results of the precipitin assays
(B) curve B shows the results of the complement fixation assays
(C) curve C depicts the data of skin testing
(D) curve B shows the results of either the precipitin or complement fixation assays

**425.** Tetracycline antibiotics specifically inhibit protein synthesis in prokaryotes because they

(A) bind to prokaryotic and not eukaryotic DNA-directed RNA polymerase
(B) are transported by prokaryotes but not eukaryotes
(C) bind to prokaryotic but not eukaryotic membranes
(D) inhibit initiation of protein synthesis, which specifically requires formylmethionyl tRNA
(E) bind to prokaryotic but not eukaryotic ribosomes

**426.** A rising titer of antistreptolysin O indicates a diagnosis of

(A) acute rheumatic fever
(B) glomerulonephritis
(C) a recent streptococcal infection
(D) scarlet fever
(E) erysipelas

**427.** Secretory IgA consists of IgA dimer, secretory component (SC), plus

(A) paraprotein
(B) J chain
(C) SC epitope
(D) γ chain
(E) ε chain

**428.** The antiphagocytosis property of group A streptococci is associated with

(A) M protein
(B) hyaluronidase
(C) streptolysin O
(D) streptolysin S
(E) DNAse

**429.** The mutagen 5-bromouracil (5-BU) preferentially causes

(A) frame shift mutations
(B) transitions
(C) transversions
(D) deletions
(E) recombinations

430. Antigens can best be processed for presentation by

    (A) macrophages
    (B) Kupffer cells
    (C) B cells
    (D) young erythrocytes
    (E) suppressor T cells

431. All of the following substances affect lymphocytes EXCEPT

    (A) migration inhibitory factor (MIF)
    (B) interleukin-1
    (C) transfer factor
    (D) interleukin-2
    (E) blastogenic factor

432. One of the first events that occurs after poliovirus infects a cell is

    (A) hydrolysis of viral DNA
    (B) synthesis of viral DNA
    (C) hydrolysis of viral protein
    (D) hydrolysis of host DNA
    (E) cessation of host cell macromolecular biosynthesis

433. Damage to DNA caused by bifunctional alkylating agents that damage both strands of DNA is repaired by

    (A) photoreactivation
    (B) excision repair
    (C) direct repair
    (D) recombination of post-replication repair
    (E) microinsertion

434. Patients with X-linked infantile agammaglobulinemia are known to

    (A) exhibit profound deficiencies of cell-mediated immunity
    (B) have very low quantities of immunoglobulin in their serum
    (C) have normal numbers of B lymphocytes

    (D) have a depletion of lymphocytes in the paracortical areas of lymph nodes
    (E) be particularly susceptible to viral and fungal infections

435. During a routine pelvic examination, a woman is found to have a tender, open lesion on the vagina. The patient states that she had similar lesions 12 months previously. The causative agent is most likely to be

    (A) echovirus
    (B) coxsackievirus
    (C) rubella virus
    (D) herpes simplex virus
    (E) measles virus

436. Antibodies against acetylcholine neural receptors are thought to be involved in the pathogenesis of

    (A) myasthenia gravis
    (B) multiple sclerosis
    (C) acute idiopathic polyneuritis
    (D) Guillain–Barré syndrome
    (E) postpericardiotomy syndrome

437. A 7-month-old child is hospitalized for a yeast infection that does not respond to therapy. The patient has a history of acute pyogenic infections. Physical examination reveals that the spleen and lymph nodes are not palpable. A differential WBC count shows 95% neutrophils, 1% lymphocytes, and 4% monocytes. A bone marrow specimen contains no plasma cells or lymphocytes. X-ray reveals absence of a thymic shadow. Tonsils are absent. These findings are most compatible with

    (A) multiple myeloma
    (B) severe combined immunodeficiency disease
    (C) X-linked agammaglobulinemia
    (D) Wiskott–Aldrich syndrome
    (E) chronic granulomatous disease

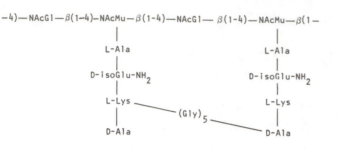

**Figure 4.4**

438. Figure 4.4 represents the

   (A)  O antigen of *Salmonella typhimurium*
   (B)  peptidoglycan of *Staphylococcus aureus*
   (C)  C substance of *Streptococcus pneumoniae*
   (D)  peptidoglycan of *Mycoplasma pneumoniae*
   (E)  H antigen of *S. typhimurium*

439. A stage of competence of recipient cells is necessary for

   (A)  complementation
   (B)  transduction
   (C)  transformation
   (D)  conjugation
   (E)  transposition

440. An acutely ill child is brought to the emergency room. The presence of petechiae and stiff neck suggests meningococcal meningitis. If the diagnosis is correct, examination of cerebrospinal fluid should reveal

   (A)  a decreased number of neutrophils
   (B)  an increased protein content
   (C)  an increased glucose content
   (D)  a decreased opening pressure

441. A rabbit is repeatedly injected with a hapten. Two weeks later, its serum is subjected to a gel diffusion assay with the hapten and a carrier protein. It would be expected that

   (A)  no precipitin line will be present
   (B)  a line of identity between the serum and carrier protein will be detected
   (C)  a line of identity between serum and both the carrier and the hapten will be present

   (D)  a line of partial identity between serum, carrier, and hapten will be detected
   (E)  a line of non-identity between serum, carrier, and hapten will be detected

442. All of the following are components of R plasmids EXCEPT

   (A)  R determinant
   (B)  the pilus
   (C)  RTF component
   (D)  insertion sequences
   (E)  antibiotic resistance genes

443. Oncogenes

   (A)  are genes that may cause cancer
   (B)  have copies in viruses
   (C)  may code for products that are essential for normal cell function
   (D)  may code for cellular surface receptors
   (E)  all of the above

444. The infectiveness of *Chlamydia trachomatis* has been related to its

   (A)  elementary body (EB)
   (B)  capsule
   (C)  cell wall
   (D)  reticulate body (RB)
   (E)  phagosome

445. All of the following viruses have hemagglutinin in their viral envelope EXCEPT

   (A)  rubeola virus
   (B)  influenza B virus
   (C)  parainfluenza virus 3
   (D)  rubella virus
   (E)  human papovavirus

446. Diphtheria toxin mediates

   (A)  dissociation of eukaryotic ribosomal subunits
   (B)  inhibition of peptide bond formation
   (C)  hydrolysis of messenger RNA

(D) adenosine diphosphate ribosylation of eukaryotic elongation factor 2

(E) destruction of the endoplasmic reticulum

447. All of the following are true statements about B-cell antigen-specific receptors EXCEPT

(A) surface immunoglobulin synthesized by a given B-cell clone serves as the antigen receptor for that clone

(B) surface immunoglobulin is dimeric and contains only two heavy chains

(C) it is likely that different receptor iso-types have different functions on the same cell

(D) differentiation of immunoglobulin (Ig) secretion requires further interaction with T cells of T-cell–derived lymphokines

(E) the surface form of the heavy chain of Ig is larger than the secreted form of heavy chains of IgG, IgD, or IgA

448. High-molecular-weight substances that possess both immunogenicity and specificity are termed

(A) simple haptens

(B) determinant groups

(C) adjuvants

(D) antigens

(E) complex haptens

449. A laboratory test used to identify *Staphylococcus aureus* is based on the clotting of plasma. The microbial product that is responsible for this activity is

(A) coagulase-reactive factor

(B) coagulase

(C) prothrombin

(D) thrombin

(E) thromboplastin

450. The Weil–Felix reaction is correctly described as

(A) useful in the diagnosis of rickettsial diseases

(B) based on the agglutination of species of *Salmonella* by the patient's convalescent serum

(C) a test to detect antiviral antibodies

(D) based on scrotal swelling in a male guinea pig infected with the organism

(E) positive for Q fever when *Proteus* OXK is agglutinated

451. The most common cause of meningitis in children in the age range of 6 months to 5 years is

(A) *Haemophilus influenzae* type B

(B) pneumococcus

(C) meningococcus

(D) *Escherichia coli*

(E) *Streptococcus agalactiae*

452. The most common medium used for the cultivation of fungi is

(A) tellurite medium

(B) SS agar

(C) Lowenstein–Jensen medium

(D) selenite F medium

(E) Sabouraud's glucose agar

453. Congenital rubella syndrome is most prominent in an infant when a pregnant woman becomes infected

(A) during the first trimester of pregnancy

(B) one week before a full-term delivery

(C) one month before a full-term delivery

(D) hours before childbirth

(E) during the third trimester of pregnancy

454. The tolerance of facultative anaerobic bacteria to superoxide ($O_{-2}$) and hydrogen peroxide ($H_2O_2$) is due to the

(A) inability to form oxygen

(B) presence of superoxide dismutase and catalase

(C) absence of superoxide dismutase

(D) lack of peroxidase

455. A burn patient developed a would infection, and a bacteriologic culture of the site indicates a gram-negative rod that was oxidase positive and produced a bluish-green pigment. The organism was relatively resistant to antibiotics but susceptible to ticarcillin, gentamicin, and tobramycin. The organism is likely to be identified as

   (A) *Escherichia coli*
   (B) *Klebsiella pneumoniae*
   (C) *Proteus mirabilis*
   (D) *Serratia marcescens*
   (E) *Pseudomonas aeruginosa*

456. Acute glomerulonephritis is a sequela of a previous infection by

   (A) any M type of group A streptococci
   (B) a few M types of group A streptococci
   (C) only lysogenic group A streptococci
   (D) all of the Lancefield groups of streptococci
   (E) only encapsulated strains of *Streptococcus pneumoniae*

457. *Cryptococcus neoformans* differs from other pathogenic fungi in that it

   (A) has a capsule
   (B) is an intracellular parasite
   (C) has septate hyphae
   (D) reproduces by binary fission
   (E) is dematiacious

458. *Diphyllobothrium latum* causes anemia by

   (A) its blood-sucking activities
   (B) the production of a toxin that affects hematopoiesis
   (C) competition with the host for vitamin $B_{12}$
   (D) occlusion of the common bile duct
   (E) inhibition of the absorption of iron

459. Which of the following zoonotic diseases is usually transmitted to humans by the bite of an arthropod vector?

   (A) anthrax
   (B) brucellosis
   (C) salmonellosis
   (D) plague
   (E) leptospirosis

460. The greatest amount of chromosomal DNA can be transferred by

   (A) Hfr X $F^-$ mating
   (B) $F'$ X $F^-$ mating
   (C) plasmid transfer
   (D) transportation of transposable elements
   (E) specialized transduction

461. The specific biochemical reaction that describes the mechanism of action of diptheria toxin is the

   (A) inhibition of acetylcholine release
   (B) glycosylation of mRNA
   (C) inhibition of oxidative phosphorylation
   (D) ADP-ribosylation of elongation factor 2 (EF-2)
   (E) activation of adenylcyclase

462. All of the following are true statements about *S. pneumoniae* EXCEPT

   (A) colonies form readily on blood agar
   (B) colonies are beta hemolytic
   (C) organisms may be isolated in small numbers from normal human throat cultures
   (D) colonies are inhibited by optochin
   (E) organisms are bile soluble

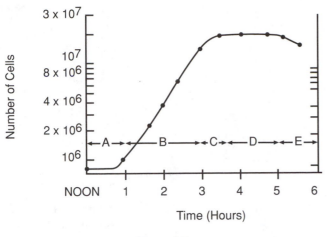

Figure 4.5

**463.** According to Figure 4.5, the rate of growth of the bacterial culture for which it was obtained reaches its maximum rate at growth between

(A) noon and 1:00 PM
(B) 3:00 PM and 4:00 PM
(C) 2:00 PM and 3:00 PM
(D) 4:00 PM and 5:00 PM
(E) 3:00 PM and 5:00 PM

**464.** The best method for assessing the total number of B lymphocytes is

(A) quantitative immunoglobulin levels
(B) Fc receptor assay
(C) E rosette assay
(D) surface immunoglobulin (sIg) assay
(E) phytohemagglutinin A (PHA) mitogenicity

**465.** Functional assessment of T lymphocytes includes

(A) E rosette assay
(B) sIg evaluation
(C) transformation of lymphocytes by PHA
(D) serum immunoglobulin determination
(E) enumeration of y-bearing cells

**466.** Lyme disease

(A) is transmitted by mites
(B) is caused by *Leptospira interrogans*

(C) is a disease in which the serum levels of IgM correlate with disease activity
(D) has not been associated with arthritis
(E) does not respond to tetracycline treatment early in the acute illness

**467.** A gram-negative bacterium is isolated from a patient's cerebrospinal spinal fluid (CSF). It grows on enriched chocolate agar but does not grow on blood agar except adjacent to a streak of staphylococci. The organism most probably is

(A) *Neisseria meningitidis*
(B) *N. gonorrhoeae*
(C) *H. influenzae*
(D) *S. pneumoniae*
(E) *Listeria monocytogenes*

**468.** Which one of the following exotoxins has the lowest 50% lethal dose (LD50)?

(A) *Corynebacterium diphtheriae* exotoxin
(B) *Clostridium perfringens* exotoxin
(C) *Clostridium difficile* exotoxin
(D) *Clostridium botulinum* exotoxin

**469.** The most common cause of bacterial meningitis in newborns is

(A) *S. aureus*
(B) *E. coli*
(C) *S. pyogenes*
(D) *N. meningitidis*
(E) *S. pneumoniae*

**470.** *Helicobacter pylori*

(A) is usually found in the oral cavity
(B) produces an abundant amount of coagulase
(C) appears to be important in the pathogenesis of peptic ulcer
(D) is an obligate intracellular parasite
(E) does not induce specific antibodies in gastritis patients

471. Immunoglobulin class, which passes the placental barrier in human beings, is

    (A) IgM
    (B) IgD
    (C) IgE
    (D) IgA
    (E) IgG

472. Each of the following bacteria can cause diarrhea, EXCEPT

    (A) *Enterococcus faecalis*
    (B) *Clostridium perfringens*
    (C) *Clostridium difficile*
    (D) *Bacillus cereus*

473. A urine sample containing 500 viable *E. coli* bacteria per mL is inoculated into an appropriate medium. Assuming the generation time of *E. coli* cells in this medium is 20 minutes, the number of viable cells per mL after 3 hours' incubation will be

    (A) 8,000
    (B) 32,000
    (C) 16,000
    (D) 64,000
    (E) 256,000

474. Viruses are attractive vectors for gene therapy because

    (A) they infect cells with a much lower efficiency as compared to chemical or physical means of gene transfer
    (B) the genes inserted into viruses may be expressed in a regulated way
    (C) adenovirus vectors cannot be used to target gene transfer into cells of the respiratory tract
    (D) retrovirus vectors can be produced in extremely small quantities from producer cell lines

475. An experiment is performed in which a lawn bacteria is plated onto a nutrient plate and "replica plated" to four media, each containing an antibiotic. Results are shown in Figure 4.6.

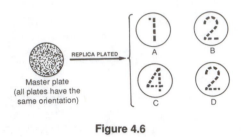

**Figure 4.6**

Which of the following statements is true concerning the interpretation of this experiment?

    (A) plates B and D likely contain the same antibiotics
    (B) Lamarckian theory is supported
    (C) plates B, C, and D all contain different antibiotics
    (D) the replica plate technique is an inappropriate method to answer questions about spontaneous mutation
    (E) mutation is not likely to occur in bacteria

476. Four hours after eating fried rice, a man developed diarrhea, vomiting, and nausea. Which of the following microorganisms is MOST likely involved?

    (A) *Clostridium tetani*
    (B) *Bacillus cereus*
    (C) *Salmonella enteritidis*
    (D) *Clostridium botulinum*
    (E) *Proteus mirabilis*

477. X-linked agammaglobulinemic patients are most likely to present with repeated infections involving

    (A) viruses
    (B) fungi
    (C) intracellular bacteria
    (D) extracellular bacteria
    (E) *Pneumocystis carinii*

**478.** Recent experiments in gene therapy have taken the approach of expressing TNF (tumor necrosis factor) in TIL (tumor-infiltrating lymphocytes). We hope that this approach will

(A) generate high serum levels of endotoxin

(B) allow the TIL to return to the tumor and produce local high levels of TNF

(C) stimulate T-cell proliferation

(D) lyse tumor cells due to retrovirus infection

(E) stimulate natural killer (NK) cell activity

**479.** Each of the following statements concerning exotoxins is correct, EXCEPT

(A) tetanus toxin blocks the release of inhibitory transmitters

(B) botulinum toxin blocks the release of acetylcholine at the myoneural junction

(C) *Clostridium perfringens* produces an enterotoxin that stimulates adenyl cyclase

(D) diphtheria is caused by an exotoxin that inhibits protein synthesis by inactivating an elongation factor

(E) cholera is caused by a toxin that hydrolyzes lecithin

**480.** A college freshman has the typical symptoms of infectious mononucleosis. The most sensitive means of confirming this infection is

(A) antibody to hemagglutinin

(B) antibody to neuraminidase

(C) heterophile antibody that reacts with antigens on sheet erythrocytes

(D) antibody that reacts with Epstein–Barr virus-associated nuclear antigen

(E) nucleic acid hybridization assays for the presence of Epstein–Barr viral nucleic acid

**481.** Prokaryotes differ from eukaryotes in that

(A) peptidoglycan is found only in pokaryotes

(B) prokaryote ribosomes are larger than eukaryote ribosomes

(C) prokaryotes have a single chromosome and a nuclear membrane

(D) prokaryotes usually have sterols in their cell membrane

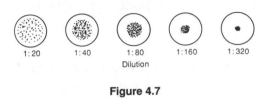

**Figure 4.7**

**482.** A hemagglutination assay was performed with a sample of influenza virus. A fixed number of chicken red blood cells were mixed with increasing dilutions of the influenza virus. The results of the assay are shown in Figure 4.7. The hemagglutination titer of the virus was

(A) 20

(B) 40

(C) 80

(D) 160

(E) 320

**483.** The AIDS virus (HIV) differs from the RNA tumor viruses in that it

(A) does not require $T_4$ receptor protein for adsorption to host cells

(B) contains two copies of single-stranded RNA in its virion

(C) contains the *gag* gene

(D) contains the *pol* gene

(E) lyses the host cells

**484.** Spread of herpesvirus type 1 occurs primarily by

(A) breast milk

(B) blood

(C) frozen plasma

(D) direct personal contact

(E) contaminated syringes

485. A 24-year-old construction worker who had four injections of the DPT (diphtheria, pertussis, and tetanus) vaccine in his first year of life and boosters at ages 5 and 19, received a deep laceration while excavating a building's foundation. The preferred method of treatment would be

(A) an aminoglycoside antibiotic

(B) human tetanus immune globulin, because it will stimulate his anamnestic response

(C) equine tetanus immune globulin, because it will passively immunize him

(D) tetanus toxoid, because it will stimulate his anamnestic response

486. All of the following statements about borreliosis are true EXCEPT

(A) *Borrelia burgdorferi* is the causative organism

(B) there is no vaccine currently available

(C) initial symptoms are flu-like chills, fever, headache, dizziness, fatigue, stiff neck

(D) a good way to prevent Lyme disease (borreliosis) is to inspect your arms and legs for any ticks and then crush any tick between your fingers

(E) the size of a deer tick is about the size of a poppy seed

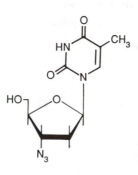

**Figure 4.8**

487. The structure in Figure 4.8 represents

(A) azidothymidine (AZT), which inhibits the AIDS virus reverse transcriptase

(B) dideoxyinosine, which inhibits poliovirus replication

(C) idoxuridine, which inhibits herpesvirus thymidine kinase

(D) acyclovir, which inhibits the herpesvirus-encoded DNA polymerase

(E) enviroxine, which inhibits rhinoviruses

488. All of the following can serve as vectors of rickettsiae EXCEPT

(A) lice

(B) mosquitoes

(C) fleas

(D) ticks

(E) mites

489. The pneumococcal antigen that reacts with a non-antibody serum globulin present in inflammatory states is

(A) capsular polysaccharide

(B) penicillin-binding protein 2

(C) C substance (phosphocholine containing teichoic acid)

(D) pneumolysin

(E) purpura-producing principle

490. A correct characteristic of the members of the genus *Neisseria* is that they are

(A) diplococci

(B) gram-positive cocci

(C) oxidase-negative cocci

(D) acid-fast rods

(E) optochin-sensitive, gram-negative diplococci

491. Humans are the only natural reservoir of the causative agents of all of the following infections EXCEPT

(A) syphilis

(B) typhoid fever

(C) gonorrhea

(D) listeriosis

(E) influenza

492. You are faced with the problem of controlling a virus infection in a community and are told that it has already been determined it is

a togavirus (arbovirus). You know then that your problem most likely is one of

(A) stopping the spread by respiratory droplets and dust of a virus that enters by the respiratory tract
(B) controlling or eliminating biting animals
(C) improving the treatment of sewage, preventing carriers from working as food handlers, and setting up methods for proper treatment of feces and urine from infected persons
(D) stopping spread by reducing the close contact of children in schools
(E) identifying and controlling an insect vector and identifying and controlling an animal reservoir

493. Which of the following statements about the VDRL test is true?

(A) is a widely used non-treponemal test
(B) does not require diphosphatidyl glycerol (cardiolipin) as an antigen
(C) is not useful for screening large numbers of people for syphilis
(D) cannot be used to follow the efficiency of penicillin treatment

494. Jacklyn, a fashion model, had several teeth extracted because she had paradental abscesses. Three months later, she developed a fever of 39.8°C and lower abdominal pain. The liver was slightly enlarged. Blood tests showed an elevated alkaline phosphatase of 425 u/L with a quick subsequent rise to 1100 u/L (normal range 60–270 u/L). A liver biopsy specimen was sent to a microbiology laboratory for aerobic and anaerobic cultures. Aerobic cultures for bacteria, fungi, and viruses were negative. However, anaerobic cultures of the biopsy material showed small spidery colonies in 2 to 3 days. The colonies contained gram-positive, non-acid–fast rods, and branching filaments, while pus from a liver abscess contained yellow granules. Administration of 6 million units of penicillin daily for 2 months brought complete remission of Jacklyn's illness. The most likely causative agent of Jacklyn's disease is

(A) Histoplasma capsulatum
(B) Mycobacterium kansasii
(C) Actinomyces israelii
(D) Mycobacterium tuberculosis
(E) Nocardia asteroides

495. M. pneumoniae (Eaton agent) is an infectious agent that

(A) lacks steroids in its cytoplasmic membrane
(B) contains muramic acid in its cell wall
(C) contains only DNA
(D) causes primary atypical pneumonia
(E) is susceptible to penicillin

496. A gardener pricked his toe while cutting rose bushes. Four days later, a pustule that changed to an ulcer developed on his toe. Then three nodules formed along the local lymphatic drainage. The most likely agent is

(A) Trichophyton rubrum
(B) Aspergillus fumigatus
(C) Candida albicans
(D) Sporothrix schenkii
(E) Cryptococcus neoformans

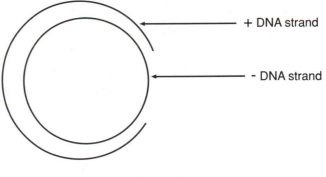

**Figure 4.9**

497. The genome of this virus is a circular molecule of DNA having the structure diagrammed in Figure 4.9.

(A) papillomavirus
(B) hepatitis A virus
(C) Epstein–Barr virus
(D) J.C. virus
(E) hepatitis B virus

**498.** A 19-year-old girl has smooth, annular, scaly, erythematous, vesicular lesions on her leg. Assuming that you suspect tinea corporis, what would be the most suitable laboratory diagnostic approach?

(A) silver staining of tissue scrapping

(B) acid-fast staining on the vesicular fluid

(C) culture of the vesicular fluid on agar

(D) digestion of tissue biopsies with 10 to 20% KOH

(E) serology for *Blastomyces dermatitidis*

**499.** The cause of antigenic drift of influenza viruses is

(A) mixing of the double-stranded DNA genome

(B) reassortment of genome segments during mixed infections

(C) phenotypic mixing

(D) accumulated point mutations in the hemagglutinin gene

(E) phenotypic masking

**500.** A 46-year-old cattle rancher develops a low-grade fever 5 days after his twentieth high school reunion, which included a rabbit hunt. Standard febrile agglutinin titrations reveal low levels of antibodies to the following organisms: *Francisella tularensis*, *Brucella suis*, *Brucella abortus*, *Salmonella typhi*, and *Proteus* OX-19. The differential diagnosis should include

(A) tularemia

(B) brucellosis

(C) typhoid fever

(D) Rocky Mountain spotted fever

(E) tularemia, brucellosis, typhoid fever, and Rocky Mountain spotted fever

**501.** The "virus" responsible may be just infectious protein with no nucleic acid for

(A) subacute sclerosing panencephalitis

(B) distemper

(C) severe multifocal leukoencephalopathy

(D) progressive multifocal leukoencephalopathy

(E) Creutzfeldt–Jacob disease

**502.** Plasmid-encoded genes

(A) specify multiple drug resistance

(B) cannot encode enterotoxins of *E. coli*

(C) have not been associated with bacteriocin production

(D) cannot specify exotoxin production

**503.** The cellular oncogene involved in the chromosomal translocation that is characteristic of many Burkitt's lymphomas is

(A) *V-abl*

(B) *V-ras*

(C) *C-myc*

(D) *V-fms*

(E) *V-src*

**504.** All of the following viral genomes are replicated in the cytoplasm EXCEPT

(A) reoviruses

(B) picornaviruses

(C) poxviruses

(D) paromyxoviruses

(E) herpesviruses

**505.** Congenital syphilis can best be detected by

(A) x-rays

(B) use of Wassermann complement fixation test

(C) dark-field examination

(D) FTA-ABS IgM test

(E) silver nitrate staining of spirochetes

**506.** A positive purified protein derivative (PPD) skin test may indicate that the individual tested has

(A) active tuberculosis

(B) been exposed to *Mycobacterium tuberculosis*

(C) indicates that this individual received BCG vaccine

(D) provides sound information on the health status of the individual that is skin tested

507. Amantadine is often useful in the treatment of infections by

(A) herpes simplex virus

(B) rabies virus

(C) Epstein–Barr virus

(D) influenza virus

(E) rhinovirus

508. Immunologic suppression for transplantation

(A) cannot occur by lymphoid irradiation

(B) can occur by antilymphocyte globulin

(C) cannot be achieved by cyclosporine administration

(D) is not likely to respond to steroid administration

509. The genome of this virus is a linear double-stranded DNA molecule in which the complementary strands are covalently cross-linked at the termini of the genome

(A) herpes simplex virus

(B) varicella–zoster virus

(C) adenovirus

(D) SV40

(E) vaccinia virus

510. Immune complexes

(A) appear to be involved in the pathogenesis of poststreptococcal glomerulonephritis

(B) do not play a role in the Arthus reaction

(C) have not been associated with glomerulonephritis of systemic lupus erythematosus

(D) are not involved in serum sickness

511. Desirable properties of a vector plasmid for use in molecular cloning include

(A) low copy number

(B) selectable phenotype

(C) non-autonomous replication

(D) multiple sites for restriction enzymes

512. *Legionella pneumophila*

(A) cannot survive for months in tap water at 25°C

(B) is not the major cause of legionellosis in humans

(C) is easily demonstrable in Gram stains of clinical specimens

(D) has been found in air-conditioning systems

513. A patient is complaining of a sore throat. Physical examination of the throat indicates a severe redness and an exudate; lymphadenopathy is also evident. This triggers key thoughts of

(A) throat culture

(B) bacitracin discs

(C) blood agar

(D) penicillin

(E) all of the above

514. All of the following statements about viruses are true EXCEPT that they

(A) are obligate intracellular parasites

(B) are filterable agents

(C) are simply organized

(D) are devoid of enzymes

(E) may contain double-stranded DNA

515. All of the following are T-independent antigens EXCEPT

(A) bacterial lipopolysaccharide

(B) polymerized flagellin

(C) pneumococcal polysaccharide

(D) serum albumin

(E) poly-D amino acids

516. All of the following viruses carry molecules of an RNA-dependent RNA polymerase as structural components of the virion EXCEPT

    (A) respiratory syncytial virus
    (B) rabies virus
    (C) influenza viruses
    (D) retroviruses

517. Antigen–antibody interactions are stabilized by

    (A) covalent bonds
    (B) the formation of disulfide bonds at the combining site
    (C) the generation of hydrophilic zones due to a conformational change in the antibody molecule
    (D) non-covalent charge neutralization and hydrogen bonding leading to hydrophobic sites
    (E) complement binding at the $C_H^2$ domain, thereby stabilizing the complex

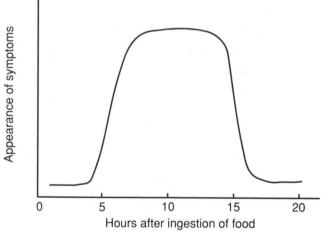

**Figure 4.10**

518. Judging from the graph in Figure 4.10, which microorganism is likely to be the causative agent of food poisoning characterized by diarrhea, abdominal cramps, and severe vomiting?

    (A) *Salmonella typhimurium*
    (B) *Vibrio parahaemolyticus*
    (C) *Yersinia enterocolitica*
    (D) *Campylobacter jejuni*

519. The following are true concerning the hypervariable regions of an immunoglobulin molecule EXCEPT they are

    (A) located at the carboxyl terminal end
    (B) also called the complementarily determined regions
    (C) the antigen-contacting amino acid areas
    (D) defined as the idiotype of the antibody
    (E) located within the $F(ab)_2$ piece of the molecule

520. The following statements concerning a monoclonal antibody are correct EXCEPT

    (A) has antibody-combining sites that are identical
    (B) may belong to the IgM, IgA, IgE, IgD, or IgG classes
    (C) may be present in the serum of patients with multiple myeloma
    (D) can be obtained by the hybridoma technique
    (E) has not been found to have diagnostic or therapeutic use

521. A virus that is not inactivated by mild detergents that solubilize phospholipid membranes is

    (A) poliovirus
    (B) eastern equine encephalitis virus
    (C) variola virus
    (D) vaccinia virus
    (E) cowpox virus

522. A viral genome that does not replicate in the cytoplasm of the infected cell is

    (A) poliovirus
    (B) rabies virus
    (C) mumps virus
    (D) cytomegalovirus
    (E) rubella virus

523. A poliovirus type 2 has been isolated from the stool of a 55-year-old patient who has been clinically diagnosed as having poliomyelitis. There have been no previous cases of polio reported. However, an infant

grandchild was vaccinated about 3 weeks prior to onset of the disease. How can the laboratory determine whether the isolated virus is related to the vaccine strain or a wild-type virus?

(A) inoculate the virus into mice to determine whether it kills mice

(B) inoculate several different kinds of tissue culture to determine the host range

(C) do neutralization studies using the infant's serum

(D) stain the virus with fluorescent antibody

(E) do oligonucleotide mapping of the unknown virus and compare with maps of wild-type and vaccine strains

524. Radial immunodiffusion is used to

(A) establish the heterogeneity of an antigen

(B) demonstrate cross-reactions between antigens

(C) demonstrate the homogeneity (purity) of an antigen

(D) quantitate an antigen

(E) identify the isotype of an antibody

525. The adult stage of the cystode cycle does NOT take place in humans infected with

(A) *Taenia saginata*

(B) *Taenia solium*

(C) *Diphyllobothrium latum*

(D) *Echinococcus granulosus*

526. *Microsporum rubrum*

(A) is not sensitive to griseofulvin

(B) causes nail infections that are difficult to treat

(C) does not produce red pigments

(D) is not an anthropophilic dermatophyte

527. A 25-year-old male patient comes to your office experiencing inability to swallow and speech difficulty. The patient was in perfect health prior to the consumption of home-canned green beans. He also stated that the can was swollen at the ends prior to its opening. Which of the following is the most likely method of treatment?

(A) administration of staphylococcal enterotoxin antiserum

(B) penicillin administration

(C) immunization with *S. aureus* enterotoxin toxoid

(D) administration of trivalent botulinum antitoxin

(E) placement of the patient in a hyperbaric oxygen chamber

528. The biosynthesis of fungal ergosterol is inhibited by

(B) amphotericin B

(B) griseofulvin

(C) flucytosine

(D) nystatin

(E) ketoconazole

DIRECTIONS (Questions 529 through 546): Each set of matching questions consists of a list of lettered options followed by several numbered items. For each numbered item, select the ONE lettered option that is most closely associated with it. Each lettered heading may be selected once, more than once, or not at all.

Questions 529 and 530

For each parasitic organism listed below, choose the mode by which it is usually transmitted to humans.

(A) ingestion of infective egg

(B) ingestion of cyst stage

(C) ingestion of animal tissue that contains the larva

(D) penetration of skin by infective larva

(E) ingestion of adult form

529. *Entamoeba histolytica*

530. *Schistosoma mansoni*

## Questions 531 and 532

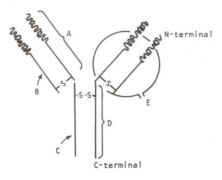

**Figure 4.11**

For each of the components described below, choose the letter on the diagram in Figure 4.11 that represents the portion of the immunoglobulin molecule with which it is associated.

**531.** Fab fragment

**532.** Complement-binding area

## Questions 533 and 534

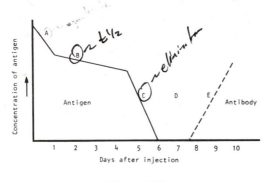

**Figure 4.12**

For each descriptive term below, choose the letter on Figure 4.12 that represents the corresponding phase of antigen clearance in vivo

**533.** Immune elimination

**534.** Metabolic clearance

## Questions 535 and 536

    (A) pili

    (B) endotoxin

    (C) calcium dipicolinate

    (D) heat-stable protein (HPr)

    (E) H antigen

**535.** Participation in bacterial conjugation

**536.** Spore component

## Questions 537 and 538

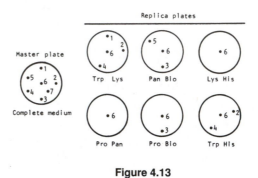

**Figure 4.13**

Two triple auxotrophic strains of *E. coli*, Trp⁻ Lys⁻ His⁻ Pro⁺ Pan⁺ Bio⁺ and Trp⁺ Lys⁺ His⁺ Pro⁻ Pan⁻ Bio⁻, are allowed to conjugate in liquid medium for 30 minutes. After dilution of the broth, the bacteria are plated onto a complete medium. After 24 hours of growth, six replicas are made, each into a plate containing minimal medium and additional nutrient or nutrients as indicated in Figure 4.13. For each of the following genotypes of the colony, choose the mutant strain with which it is associated.

    (A) Trp⁻

    (B) Trp⁻ Lys⁻

    (C) Bio⁻

    (D) Pan⁻ Bio⁻

    (E) Trp⁻ Lys⁻ Bio⁻

**537.** The genotype of colony 1

**538.** The genotype of colony 4

**Questions 539 and 540**

    (A) Graves' disease

    (B) systemic lupus erythematosus (SLE)

    (C) thrombocytopenia

    (D) myasthenia gravis

    (E) rheumatoid arthritis

**539.** Association with antibodies to acetylcholine receptors

**540.** Association with HLA-DR4

**Questions 541 through 543**

    (A) adenovirus

    (B) rhabdovirus

    (C) measles virus

    (D) mumps virus

    (E) J.C. virus

    (F) bunyavirus

    (G) varicella–zoster virus

    (H) cytomegalovirus

    (I) molluscum contagiosum virus

**541.** Etiologic agent or "shingles"

**542.** Transmitted by anthropods

**543.** Bullet-shaped, enveloped virus

**Questions 544 through 546**

For each patient, select the disease from which he or she is most likely to be suffering.

    (A) chronic granulomatous disease

    (B) Chediak–Higashi syndrome

    (C) acquired immunodeficiency syndrome (AIDS)

    (D) X-linked agammaglobulinemia

    (E) DiGeorge syndrome

    (F) systemic lupus erythematosus

    (G) Wiskott–Aldrich syndrome

    (H) severe combined immunodeficiency disorder (SCID)

    (I) selective IgA deficiency

    (J) neutropenia

**544.** A kidney biopsy taken from a young woman complaining of fever, rash, and arthritis shows marked deposits of immunoglobulin, complement (C3), and fibrinogen in the basement membrane; high titers of anti-DNA antibody are also detected in her serum

**545.** A 6-month-old infant has been suffering from repeated pneumonia, otitis, and cutaneous infections. The patient has profound lymphopenia and her lymphocytes do not respond to mitogens. Serum immunoglobulin levels are abnormally diminished. T-cell and B-cell functions are severely impaired

**546.** Neutrophils from this patient, who has been suffering from repeated staphylococcal and *Candida* infections, show normal phagocytotic activity. However, intracellular killing of certain bacteria such as staphylococci is severely impaired and nitroblue tetrazolium reduction test is negative. Myeloperoxidase activity of neutrophils is normal. The patient, however, has no history of streptococcal infection

# Microbiology
## Answers and Explanations

**405.** **(D)** The results of the mixed lymphocyte reaction correlate with the degree of dissimilarity of histocompatibility. Higher counts indicate more stimulation, suggesting immunologic unrelatedness of tissues tested. Human leukocyte–antigen-identical sibs do not stimulate mixed leukocyte reaction, indicating their tissues are mutually transplantable. (Joklik et al, p 269)

**406.** **(D)** The only pentameric immunoglobulin molecule with a molecular weight of approximately 900,000 is immunoglobulin M (IgM). The molecular weights of IgA, IgD, and IgG are in the range of 150,000 to 160,000. IgE has a molecular weight of about 200,000. (Joklik et al, pp 226–227)

**407.** **(E)** Interferon activates cellular genes that code for antiviral proteins. The main target is the translational step in viral replication, which is blocked by two mechanisms—a protein kinase that is activated by double-stranded RAN (dsRNA) and inactivates initiation factor EF-2 by phosphorylation, and a nuclease, also activated by dsRNA, which destroys mRNA. (Joklik et al, pp 863–864)

**408.** **(D)** Iodophors are complexes of iodine with surface-active agents such as detergents. This provides a reservoir of bound $I_2$ in equilibrium with free $I_2$ at a concentration that is less irritating than that found in tincture of iodine. The detergents act as carriers and release iodine slowly to bind irreversibly with protein. The iodophors are excellent fast-acting bactericidal and sporicidal agents that are especially useful for disinfection of the skin. The major drawback of their use is their sensitivity to the presence of organic matter. (Joklik et al, p 193)

**409.** **(A)** The first step in infection of a bacterial cell by a bacteriophage is the adsorption of the bacteriophage to the bacterial cell. Adsorption of the phage involves a specific interaction between the adsorption organelle of the phage (tail) and the receptors of the bacterial cell. Mutations in the bacterial cell that lead to changes in the host cell receptors will allow the host bacterial cell to be *resistant* to bacteriophage. Thus, the bacteriophage will no longer react with the host cell receptors and will not be able to infect the bacterial cell. A bacterial cell that is immune to bacteriophage infection has already been infected and carries a prophage. The lysogenic bacterium produces a repressor protein that binds to the immunity region of the infecting phage. When the repressor protein binds, the infecting DNA cyclizes but is not replicated and the circular DNA survives for several generations as an abortive prophage and is transmitted unilinearly like genes involved in abortive transduction. The key point to understand is the difference between *resistance* and *immunity* to bacteriophage infection. Resistance prevents adsorption and injection of phage DNA; in immunity, the phage adsorbs to the immune cell and injects its DNA, but the DNA does not multiply and does not cause cell lysis. (Joklik et al, pp 906–928)

**410.** **(A)** The patient described in the question probably has AIDS. Such individuals will be lymphopenic and have greatly reduced immune function. **B** through **E** in the question involve innate immunity, either complement activity or phagocytic cell functions, and would not be of much diagnostic assistance. The most important evaluative procedure for the patient described is determining the cause of the pneumonia so that the problem can be corrected. Identifying the infecting organism may assist in the overall diagnosis. AIDS victims commonly develop *Pneumocytis carinii* pneumonia. (*Joklik et al, pp 1051–1054*)

411. **(D)** The key feature in the problem described in the question is that *two* streptomycin sensitive *E. coli* were mixed together and a *few* streptomycin-resistant colonies developed after exposure to streptomycin. This result indicates that no genetic exchange involving streptomycin resistance occurred between the two *E. coli* strains to streptomycin-sensitive bacteria. In transformation, naked or soluble DNA from a streptomycin-resistant culture is used to transform a streptomycin-sensitive culture to streptomycin resistance. In conjugation, a piece of chromosome is mobilized by an F factor and antibiotic resistance is transferred from a streptomycin-resistant donor to a streptomycin-sensitive recipient. The net result is recombination and development of streptomycin-resistant colonies. Complementation is a genetic test of gene function of gene products and involves introducing two mutations together to see if the wild-type phenotype is produced. Complementation does not involve recombination but depends on the interaction of the products of genes. (*Joklik et al, pp 125–151*)

412. **(B)** The child described in the question appears to be suffering from meningitis due to *S. aureus,* which should always be assumed to be a β-lactamase–producing organism until the laboratory reports its antibiotic sensitivity. Methicillin is a lactamase-resistant penicillin that would be the drug of choice among those listed in the question. Other antibiotics that might be used include the cephalosporins, gentamicin, or vancomycin, which may be injected intrathecally. (*Joklik et al, pp 154–175*)

413. **(E)** In the Ouchterlony diagram that accompanies the question, each antibody will react with its homologous determinant group on the antigen molecule. Thus, both antibodies a and b will react with antigen ab, but only antibody a will react with antigen ac. Antibody b will diffuse through the line of precipitate formed by antibody a and antigen ac to precipitate with antigen ab, forming the spur at position 3. Line 1 will contain both antibodies. The spur (3) will contain antibody b, not antibody a. Line 2 will contain antigen ac and antibody a only. (*Joklik et al, p 785*)

414. **(C)** A transformant is a recipient cell that is transformed by naked DNA and gains new properties in the process of transformation. A transition refers to a base pair substitution that results in the substitution of a purine for a purine or a pyrimidine for a pyrimidine. A transversion is a base pair substitution that results in the substitution of pyrimidines for purine and vice versa (AT → CG). Transposition is the process in which a transposon is translocated from one position to another in a replicon or is transferred to a different replicon. A frame shift mutation generates shifts in the reading frame of the transcribed DNA by insertion or deletion of a single nucleotide. On translation of the transcribed DNA (containing the insertion of deletion), the reading frame is shifted, and a nonfunctional protein is produced. (*Joklik et al, pp 126–127*)

415. **(B)** Transformation is the transfer of genetic information from one bacterial cell to another by the introduction of naked DNA into a bacterial cell. Transformation is not affected by RNAse in the medium, since DNA is resistant to RNAse. However, DNAse in the medium destroys the transforming material (DNA), and hence transformation of bacteria can be blocked by DNAse. Antiserum against bacteriophage is not effective in blocking transformation, because bacteriophage are not involved in transformation. Antiserum to bacteriophage will block transfer of genetic information by transduction. In contrast to transformation, transfer of genetic information by conjugation requires effective pair

formation or cell-to-cell contact. In some bacteria, the sex pili are involved in cell-to-cell contact, and bacteriophage that bind to the tips of the pili block effective pair formation. Therefore, bacteriophage that adsorb to sex pili block conjugation but do not affect transformation. As already stated, transformation does not require cell-to-cell contact, and prevention of cell-to-cell contact between donor and recipient cultures does not hinder transformation. *(Joklik et al, pp 136–138)*

416. **(D)** When a temperate bacteriophage infects a susceptible bacterium, the phage may enter either the lytic cycle or the lysogenic cycle of replication. If the phage enters the lytic cycle, the phage replicates, the cell is lysed, and viable progeny phage are released. With the lysogenic cycle, the bacteriophage DNA integrates into the host chromosome, where it is maintained until the lytic cycle is induced. The integrated viral DNA is referred to as a prophage, and the bacterial cell carrying the prophage is referred to as a lysogenic bacterium, or a lysogen. *(Joklik et al, pp 923–928)*

417. **(C)** If exposure to rabies virus appears definite, as in the case described in the question, treatment with human diploid cell live-derived vaccine and with hyperimmune antirabies γ-globulin should be started immediately. Serum antibodies provide an immediate barrier to the growth of virus; meanwhile, antibodies are elicited by the vaccine. If the level of exposure is minimal (eg, no skin puncture) and the animal probably is not rabid, vaccine is not recommended. *(Joklik et al, pp 1028–1030)*

418. **(D)** Chlamydiae and rickettsiae are the largest of the obligate intracellular parasites. They are bacteria-like in that they have a cell wall, contain both DNA and RNA, and are susceptible to certain antibiotics (eg, tetracyclines and chloramphenicol). Most rickettsiae are spread by arthropod vectors; chlamydiae are spread by direct contact or by the respiratory route. In addition, chlamydiae divide by binary fission and by an unequal divisional process involving elementary and reticulate body formation. *(Joklik et al, pp 701–713, 719–729)*

419. **(A)** Exposure to the TB bacillus does not *assure* disease, but a positive skin test makes the diagnosis more likely. Chemoprophylaxis with isoniazid (INH) would be the treatment of choice for contacts of actively infected persons. Ethambutol is very effective against most mycobacteria but would be used in the therapy of TB, not in prophylaxis. The skin test is the most sensitive index of infection, and, for individuals who have already shown a positive response, x-ray would not add much information. Sequential x-rays months apart might indicate if the lesion were increasing in size, but that is most certainly not a high-priority procedure for the persons described in the question. Immunization with the live attenuated TB strain bacillus Calmette–Guérin (BCG) would be pointless, as the contacts have already experienced an infection with *M. tuberculosis*. Individuals receiving INH should periodically be checked by sputum culture and x-ray to assure that the therapy is effective. *(Joklik et al, pp 509–510)*

420. **(E)** Genetic complementation is a genetic tool that is employed to determine whether two mutants lacking the same functions have mutations in the same location on the genes. If the genetic information from one of the mutants is introduced into the other mutant and the resulting diploid organism regains the ability to synthesize the proper end product, one may conclude that the two mutations are located in regions of distinct genetic function. The two types of genetic complementation are intragenic (within the same gene) and intergenic (within different genes) complementation. Intragenic complementation requires an end product that is an oligomeric polypeptide with two or more identical subunits. For example, one mutant may have a mutation that causes a conformational change in the subunit that makes the enzyme inactive. On association with another mutationally altered subunit due to a mutation in the same gene at a different location, the restraints may cancel out to produce an active enzyme. In this case, the peptide subunits coded for by two genes from two mutants can complement each other and produce an active protein. With intergenic

complementation, two non-identical gene products from two mutants complement each other. For example, introduction of a P⁻ Lys⁺ phage (unable to replicate) into a bacterium containing a P⁺ Lys⁻ phage (unable to produce lysozyme) will result in release of viable progeny from the bacterium. Suppression is a method in which a second mutation corrects the damage done by the first mutation. The remainder of the choices listed in the question are not genetic tests of function. (Brooks et al, p 386)

421. **(D)** The germane mode of action of ultraviolet light on microorganisms is related to its absorption by the DNA. This absorption leads to the formation of covalent bonds between adjacent pyrimidine bases. These pyrimidine diamers alter the form of the DNA and thus interfere with normal base pairing during the synthesis of DNA. Disruption of the bacterial cell membrane, removal of free sulfhydryl groups, protein denaturation, and addition of alkyl groups to cellular components are induced by detergents, heavy metals, heat or alcoholic compounds, and ethylene oxide or formaldehyde, respectively. (Joklik et al, pp 190–197)

422. **(E)** Transposons and R determinants are composed of resistance genes bordered by long terminal repeat sequences or insertion sequences (IS elements). The IS elements allow the transposons and R determinants to transpose from one genetic element to another. The R determinant is one component of the R plasmid, and the IS elements allow it to dissociate and reassociate with the second component of the R plasmid, or the resistance transfer factor (RTF). R plasmids are unable to transpose, but the R determinant component of the R plasmid is able to translocate and does contain antibiotic-resistant genes. The term "replicon" is used to denote a unit of replication such as a plasmid or the chromosome. Replicons may contain antibiotic resistance markers but are unable to move from one genetic element to another. IS elements are small (700 to 1400 base pairs long) DNA sequences that compose another class of transposable elements. They do not confer resistance to antibiotics, and their presence in genetic elements is noted by inactivation of the gene in which they are inserted. (Joklik et al, pp 141, 182–183)

423. **(D)** *Mycoplasma* organisms do not have a cell wall and are therefore resistant to penicillin. Other forms of bacteria that lack a cell wall are spheroplasts and protoplasts, which are formed from gram-negative and gram-positive bacteria, respectively, through the action of penicillin or by other procedures that remove the cell wall or interfere with its formation. The remaining organisms listed in the question are all susceptible to the action of penicillin, although certain strains of the gonococcus have acquired a β-lactamase–producing plasmid. Tetracyclines, erythromycin, and the aminoglycosides are effective antibiotics for the treatment of mycoplasmal infections. (Joklik et al, pp 735–736)

424. **(B)** Curves A, B, and C depict the frequency of serologic reactivity following exposure to *Coccidioides immitis* determined by the skin test, complement fixation, and precipitin tests, respectively. The skin test is performed by the intracutaneous injection of either coccidioidin, which is a crude toluene extract of a mycelial culture filtrate, or spherulin prepared from cultured spherules of *C. immitis*. An induration of more than 5 mm in diameter produced within 24 to 48 hours following injection is considered a positive delayed hypersensitivity reaction. The skin test becomes positive approximately 2 weeks after the onset of coccidioidomycosis, precedes the appearance of precipitating or complement fixation antibodies, and tends to remain positive indefinitely. A negative skin test can be used to exclude coccidioidomycosis, except in patients with severe disseminated coccidioidomycosis who may have become nonresponsive to *C. immitis* antigens. A positive skin test indicates past or present infection by *C. immitis*. Detection of IgG complement-fixing antibodies indicates either active coccidioidomycosis or recovery from this illness. The titer of CF antibodies correlates well with the severity of the disease. IgM precipitin antibodies are produced early in the infection

and assist in the diagnosis of primary coccidioidomycosis. These precipitin antibodies can be detected in 90% of patients about 2 weeks after the appearance of the symptoms and disappear in approximately 4 to 5 months. Thus, a positive precipitin test suggests active primary, or reactivation, coccidioidomycosis. *(Joklik et al, pp 1095–1097)*

425.  **(B)** Although the tetracyclines inhibit protein synthesis in both eukaryotic and prokaryotic cells, they are much more effective in prokaryotic cells. The specificity of the drug is attributable to an energy-dependent transport system present in prokaryotes, but not in eukaryotic cells. This transport system results in accumulation of the drug inside the bacterial cell, where it binds to the ribosome and interferes with binding of aminoacyl-tRNA to the acceptor site. *(Joklik et al, pp 173–174)*

426.  **(C)** All of the conditions listed in the question are of streptococcal etiology; therefore, a rise in antistreptolysin O would occur in all of these. The only valid diagnostic conclusion regarding patients with a rising antistreptolysin O titer is that a recent streptococcal infection has occurred. Two of the diseases listed, scarlet fever and erysipelas, are distinguished on the basis of clinical signs. The former is a generalized, febrile disease with an associated sore throat and scarlatinal rash, whereas the latter is a local cellulitis that occurs in the subcutaneous tissues and may radiate locally, involving draining lymphatics. Rheumatic fever and glomerulonephritis are postinfection sequelae of group A streptococcal infections. The organisms cannot be isolated from the patient at the time the disease is developing. As the diseases involve different organs, the symptoms will be correspondingly diverse. *(Joklik et al, p 422)*

427.  **(B)** Polymeric forms of IgM and IgA are held together by a 15,000-dalton polypeptide chain called the J chain. It does not share antigenic determinants or amino acid sequences with H or L chains. The J chain is S-S bonded to the heavy chains in the polymeric forms of these immunoglobulins. *(Joklik et al, pp 224–227)*

428.  **(A)** Group A streptococci produce two antiphagocytic surface components—hyaluronic acid and M protein—which interfere with ingestion. The streptolysins and DNAse are able to kill phagocytic cells by membrane disruption (streptolysin O) or by leukotoxicity exhibited only after phagocytosis. Other streptococcal extracellular products that may have a deleterious effect on leukocytes include DNAse, proteinase, and RNAse. Hyaluronidase and streptokinase are virulence factors that may play a role in the organism's spread through the body. *(Joklik et al, pp 421–423)*

429.  **(B)** The base analog 5-BU causes transitions or subtransitions of AT for GC (or vice versa) to occur in the DNA of cells or viruses. 5-BU is a thymine analog, and on DNA replication, the 5-BU can be incorporated into the new DNA in place of the normal thymine base. Once incorporated, the 5-BU may undergo transient internal rearrangement (tautomerization) from the keto state to the enol state, in which it pairs with guanine instead of adenine. In subsequent replications, the cytosine will be paired with the guanine and the AT will be replaced by a GC. Transversions, which are caused by mutagens, such as the alkylating agent ethylethane sulfonate, result in the substitution of a pyrimidine for a purine and vice versa (AT → GC). Frame shift mutations are induced by acridine derivatives. The acridines shift the reading frame by intercalating between successive base pairs of DNA. The shift of the reading frame produces a nonfunctional protein. Deletions in DNA are induced by agents such as nitrous acid, bifunctional alkylating agents, and irradiation. These agents cause cross-links between complementary DNA strands, and on DNA replication the DNA around the cross-links is not replicated, while the segments on each side replicate and join together. Finally, recombinations are not considered a type of mutation. *(Joklik et al, p 130)*

**430.** **(A)** There is evidence that antigens must be metabolically processed by macrophages before they can be recognized by the T-helper cells. For example, T-helper cells from $F_1$ hybrids between two inbred strains ($P_1 \times P_2$) that have been sensitized on antigen-pulsed macrophages from one parent ($P_1$) will proliferate in response to a second challenge of the antigen only if $F_1$ macrophages or macrophages from $P_1$ are present. Kupffer cells, young erythrocytes, or suppressor T cells from $P_1$ are not considered as inducers of T-helper cell proliferation. B cells may be involved in antigen processing but are not the best antigen processors. (*Levinson and Jawetz, pp 278–279*)

**431.** **(A)** Mediators affecting lymphocytes include the following: interleukin-1 (IL-1), which potentiates mitogenic responses of T cells and thymocytes; interleukin-2 (IL-2), which promotes and maintains the proliferation of T lymphocytes; transfer factor, which prepares nonsensitive lymphocytes to respond to specific antigens and to the transfer of delayed hypersensitivity; and the blastogenic factor, which is involved in lymphocyte proliferation. The MIF does not affect lymphocytes, but it inhibits the migration of macrophages from an antigen reaction site. (*Brooks et al, p 117*)

**432.** **(E)** One of the early steps in viral infections is the cessation of host cell synthesis of macromolecules. Cellular nucleic acids are not degraded, but chromosomal breaks may occur. Polyribosomes are disaggregated, favoring a shift to viral synthetic processes. The virus first directs the synthesis of new proteins (which may require a brief burst of mRNA synthesis), then viral nucleic acids are synthesized, and assembly and release occur. In poliovirus, the viral nucleic acid is composed of a single strand of positive-sense RNA, which thus serves as its own messenger. (*Joklik et al, p 851*)

**433.** **(B)** Excision repair follows damage by bifunctional alkylating agents or ultraviolet (UV) irradiation. With excision repair, a specific endonuclease makes a nick adjacent to the damaged base or dimers. Next, the altered bases are excised from the DNA, DNA polymerase I fills the gap, and the two strands are ligated. Bifunctional alkylating agents (eg, mechlorethamine [nitrogen mustard] and mitomycin) cause cross-links between the complementary strands of DNA. These cross-links are removed by two steps. First, the altered base on one strand is removed, and then the altered base on the opposite strand is removed. Photoreactivation is a method of repairing DNA that has been damaged by UV light. Exposure of bacterial cells to UV light results in the formation of pyrimidine dimers in the DNA. Subsequent exposure to light in the visible region of the spectrum induces an enzyme that cleaves the dimers and restores the original pyrimidine bases. Direct repair is synonymous for photoreactivation. Post-replication repair or recombination repair may occur in bacteria that are incapable of excision repair or photoreactivation. In this type of repair, replication of the DNA occurs, and the new strands contain gaps corresponding to areas of pyrimidine dimers. Multiple crossovers between the daughter strands restore the intact molecule. Since bifunctional alkylating agents cross-link DNA, DNA damaged by this method cannot replicate. Therefore, this is not an acceptable method for repair. (*Joklik et al, pp 130–133*)

**434.** **(B)** Bruton's hypogammaglobulinemia is a B-cell immunodeficiency disorder. Affected patients are deficient in B cells in the peripheral blood and in B-dependent areas of lymph nodes and spleen. Most of the serum immunoglobulins are absent, and the IgG level is < 200 mg/L. Recurrent pyogenic infections usually begin to occur at 5 to 6 months of age, when maternal IgG has been depleted. (*Joklik et al, pp 329–330*)

**435.** **(D)** Recurrent vesiculating lesions in the genital region suggest herpesvirus type II, although type I is seen in some cases. The remaining organisms listed in the question either are not recurring or do not produce vesicular lesions. Rubella and measles are not closely associated with vesiculating genital lesions. Coxsackievirus and echovirus produce a wide variety of diseases, including meningitis, encephalitis, upper respiratory tract infections, and enteritis. A macular rash may accompany some of these conditions, but its presence has no particular diagnostic significance. (Joklik et al, pp 956–957)

436.  (A)  Antiacetylcholine receptor antibodies are found in more than 90% of myasthenia gravis patients. If the clinical symptoms are suggestive of myasthenia gravis, this finding alone is often considered diagnostic. Multiple sclerosis patients tend to have high levels of measles virus antibodies in their spinal fluid. However, the role of this agent in the disease is undetermined. Guillain–Barré syndrome (also called acute idiopathic polyneuritis) is a demyelinating disease of peripheral nerves. It commonly occurs after a viral infection or an injection, such as influenza immunization. The disease seems to be caused by a T-cell response to nervous tissue. (Joklik et al, pp 321–997)

437.  (B)  The patient described in the question has a profound deficiency of both the B-cell and T-cell components of the immune response (ie, severe combined immunodeficiency disease). The dramatic absence of lymphocytes and lymphoid tissue would not be found in any of the other conditions listed. Patients with AIDS may have a similar immune function deficit (absence of effective B- and T-cell responses); however, they will have adequate lymphoid tissues. The cells are present, perhaps in diminished numbers, but are not mature and functional. (Joklik et al, pp 333–338)

438.  (B)  The figure that accompanies the question represents the peptidoglycan of S. aureus. Although the general features of this structure are essentially the same in all bacteria possessing a cell wall (the mycoplasmas lack a cell wall), species-specific variations are present. Variations in the cell walls of other species may occur in the amino acids of the tetrapeptide attached to N-acetylmuramic acid or in the cross-linking peptide bridge. Both the C substance from S. pneumoniae and the O antigen from S. typhimurium are carbohydrates and do not contain peptides. The H antigen of S. typhimurium is composed of a small basic protein of approximately 20,000 daltons. (Joklik et al, pp 77–85)

439.  (C)  Competent cells are necessary for the uptake of naked DNA. Therefore, recipient cells need to be in a state of competency for transformation to occur. A protein called competence factor is produced by bacterial cultures during a brief period of the growth cycle. This protein increases competency of noncompetent bacterial cells when added to the cell culture. Additionally, one can artificially induce competence in a cell culture by making the cell envelope more permeable to DNA by exposure to calcium chloride. Transduction, conjugation, and transposition do not require competent cells for exchange of genetic information from a donor (F$^+$, Hfr) to a recipient cell (F$^-$). Transduction requires infection of a cell by a phage that is carrying chromosomal genes. Transposition is the translocation of genetic information from a plasmid to a chromosome (or vice versa) by a transposon. Complementation involves the interation of gene products (proteins) and does not require competent cells. (Joklik et al, pp 136–137)

440.  (B)  Glucose content in cerebrospinal fluid is decreased due to its utilization by Neisseria meningitis which also tends to increase the protein content of the cerebrospinal fluid as well as the number of neutrophils. Bacterial meningitis also causes an increase in opening pressure on lumbar puncture. If lymphocytes predominate, the diagnostic possibilities shift to viral and perhaps fungal causes of the illness. (Joklik et al, pp 445–449)

441.  (A)  By definition, a hapten is a substance of low molecular weight that by itself does not elicit the formation of antibodies. However, when attached to a carrier protein, antibody production becomes feasible. The hapten-carrier approach has been employed to produce antibodies against penicillin, steroids, nucleotides, lipids, and even 2,4-dinitrophenol. Since the rabbits have been repeatedly injected with the hapten only, their serum

cannot be expected to have antibodies against the hapten. Thus, when the rabbit serum is subjected to the gel diffusion assay with the hapten and a carrier protein that was not used to complex the hapten during immunization, no antigen–antibody precipitin lines of either identity, partial identity, or non-identity can be expected. *(Joklik et al, pp 207, 213, 219, 223, 237)*

442. **(B)** R plasmids are large plasmids composed of two functionally distinct parts: (1) the RTF, and (2) the resistance determinant (R determinant). The RTF constitutes the major part of the R plasmid and contains the genes for autonomous replication and conjugation. The R determinant contains the genes for antibiotic resistance. The RTF and R determinant usually exist together in the cell as one unit. However, the IS elements at the boundaries of these two parts promote crossover and allow the R determinant and the RTF to dissociate. When the R determinant and the RTF are in the same cell, they may associate and dissociate, and the R determinant may be exchanged with a different RTF. The pilus is not a component of the R plasmid but is an appendage of the bacterial cell. *(Joklik et al, pp 147–182)*

443. **(E)** Although we know that oncogenes are normal cellular genes, their discovery came from studies involving a virus that caused tumors in chicken. This virus is a retrovirus, or RNA tumor virus. The oncogenes have copies in viruses (V-onc), and cells (C-onc, or proto-oncogenes). These oncogenes are involved with the production of molecules which are essential to normal cell development and function. For example, they may code for proteins which can be tyrosine kinases, such as the src gene of the Rous sarcoma virus, or the obl gene of the Abelson leukemia virus. They may code for guanine nucleotide binding proteins, that is, the H-ras gene of the Harvey sarcoma virus. They may code for chromatin binding proteins, such as the myc gene of the MC29 myclocytomactosis virus, or the fos gene of FBJ osteosarcoma virus. Finally, the oncogenes may code for cellular surface receptors, that is, the epidermal growth factor receptor. The oncogenes are switched off, or down regulated, in normal cells. *(Joklik et al, pp 887–893)*

444. **(A)** *C. trachomatis* can be found in two forms—a small spherical body 0.2 to 0.4 μm, the EB, which is the infective form, and a large 0.6 to 1.0 μm circular-oval structure, the RB. The EB is responsible for binding and entrance of *C. trachomatis* to the host cells. The EB has a cell wall, but no known capsule, that allows it to survive for brief periods in the extracellular environment. *(Joklik et al, pp 719–727)*

445. **(E)** The viral envelopes of rubeola, influenza B, parainfluenza, and rubella viruses all possess hemagglutinins on their viral envelopes. The human papovavirus is not known to have hemagglutinins. Hemagglutinins are glycoproteins occurring as spikes on viral envelopes and serve as points of attachment to host cells. Five major hemagglutinin types for influenza virus have been identified: H swine, H, H1, H2, and H3. Influenza virus mutates its hemagglutinin types (antigenic drift), and this accounts for the loss of immunity to influenza virus that has led to influenza virus epidemics. *(Joklik et al, pp 766–767)*

446. **(D)** Diphtheria toxin is an exotoxin produced by toxigenic strains of *Corynebacterium diphtheriae*. The toxin consists of two subunits, A and B. Subunit A is a toxigenic moiety that enzymatically adenosine diphosphate-ribosylates the elongation factor 2 (EF-2) of the eukaryotic cell. The modification of EF-2 results in the inhibition of protein synthesis and eventual death of the host cell. Subunit B is a receptor-binding component of the toxin. Mg deficiency causes dissociation of ribosomal subunits. Certain antibiotics such as chloramphenicol and puromycin inhibit peptide bond formation. *(Joklik et al, pp 488–495)*

447. **(B)** Surface immunoglobulins, which are the characteristic marker of cells of the B-lymphocyte lineage, act as the cell-surface antigen receptors. The surface immunoglobulin of the immature B cell has surface IgM,

and the mature (adult) B cell has other classes of immunoglobulin (IgD in most B cells). The surface immunoglobulins are not dimeric. They also contain, in addition to two heavy chains, a kappa or a lambda light chain, but not both. *(Joklik et al, pp 250–252)*

448.  **(D)** Antigens have the ability to induce an immune response (immunogenicity) and also react specifically with the products of that response, either humoral antibodies or specifically sensitized lymphocytes. Determinant groups are the portions of the antigen molecule that determine its specificity. Haptens are partial, or incomplete, antigens. They have specific reactivity but are not immunogenic by themselves. Adjuvants are substances that have the ability to enhance the immune response to antigens without necessarily being antigenic themselves. For example, *Bordetella pertussis* will cause the host to produce large amounts of IgE antibodies to antigens that normally would not induce the production of this antibody at all. Similarly, presence of mycobacterial cells in a vaccine will encourage the development of cell-mediated immunity to other antigens in the vaccine. *(Joklik et al, p 207)*

449.  **(B)** In a laboratory test used to identify *S. aureus,* coagulase reacts with a prothrombin-like compound in plasma to produce an active enzyme (a complex of thrombin and coagulase) that converts fibrinogen to fibrin. This activity of *S. aureus* has a very high correlation with the organism's virulence, although coagulase-negative organisms may also cause disease, which are usually less severe. The necessity for a relatively accurate test to predict virulence stems from the presence of non-pathogenic staphylococci as indigenous flora of many areas of the human body. Another test that is used to identify a pathogenic isolate is the production of DNAse. This assay is somewhat more easily performed than is the coagulase test. Consequently, many laboratories have switched to the DNAse agar plate test. *(Joklik et al, p 407)*

450.  **(A)** The Weil–Felix reaction, which is based on the agglutination of differing strains of *Proteus vulgaris* by serum from patients with rickettsial diseases, is a useful diagnostic test. Another test, rarely used in diagnosis of rickettsial diseases today, is the Neill–Mooser reaction, in which viable murine typhus organisms are injected into laboratory animals. Scrotal swelling is the end point of this test. Q fever does not induce the production of *Proteus* agglutinins. OXK agglutination suggests a diagnosis of scrub typhus. *(Joklik et al, pp 703–704)*

451.  **(A)** *H. influenzae* type B is responsible for 70% of the bacterial meningitides in children between the ages of 2 months and 5 years. The pneumococcus causes meningitis in debilitated adults. Meningococcal meningitis occurs sporadically in all age groups and takes on epidemic proportions in military populations. *E. coli* and *S. agalactiae* cause meningitis in neonates, who acquire the infection during passage through the birth canal. *(Brooks et al, p 238)*

452.  **(E)** Cultivation of fungi requires a medium that is adjusted to the optimal pH of growth for fungi, that is, a pH of 4.0 to 5.0 Such a medium is the one developed by Sabouraud. The SS medium is a medium used to isolate bacterial species belonging to the genus *Salmonella* or *Shigella*. Selenite medium is employed to enrich the number of *Salmonella* species that may be present in small numbers in fecal or other clinical specimens. Tellurite medium is used for the selective isolation of *Corynebacterium diphtheriae*, which is not as sensitive to the concentration of tellurite incorporated into the medium as the other bacteria that may be encountered in specimens submitted for the microbiologic diagnosis of diphtheria. Lowenstein–Jensen medium is used for the cultivation of *Mycobacterium tuberculosis* and other mycobacteria. *(Brooks et al, pp 220, 272, 310)*

453.  **(A)** The route of infection of rubella virus is the respiratory tract, with spread to lymphatic tissue and then to the blood (viremia). Maternal viremia is followed by infection of the placenta, which leads to congenital rubella. Many organs of the fetus support the

multiplication of the virus, which does not seem to destroy the cells but reduces the rate of growth of the infected cells. This leads to fewer than normal numbers of cells in the organs at birth. Therefore, the earlier in pregnancy infection occurs, the greater the chance for the development of abnormalities in the infected fetus. A vast percentage of maternal infections that occur during the first trimester of pregnancy result in such fetal defects as pulmonary stenosis, ventricular septal defect, cataracts, glaucoma, deafness, mental retardation, and other maladies. *(Joklik et al, pp 1016–1017)*

454. **(B)** Superoxide, which is bactericidal, is generated during electron transport and in the autoxidation of hydroquinones, leukoflavins, ferredoxins and flavoproteins. Superoxide dismutase, however, forms oxygen and hydrogen peroxide from superoxide radicals. When catalase is present, it destroys the bactericidal hydrogen peroxide, because catalase hydrolyzes $H_2O_2$ to $H_2O$ and $O_2$. Thus, the presence of both enzymes allows aerobes, facultative anaerobes, and aerotolerant microbes to survive when they grow in the presence of $O_2$. Obligate anaerobic bacteria generally lack superoxide dismutase or catalase or both and thus cannot grow in the presence of oxygen. *(Joklik et al, p 46)*

455. **(E)** *P. aeruginosa* is a gram-negative, oxidase-positive, aerobic rod that produces a green-blue pigment called pyocyanin. This microorganism has been associated frequently with wound infections in burn patients, and it is considered as the second leading cause of burn infections after *S. aureus*. *P. aeruginosa* tends to develop resistance to various antibiotics. However, it may respond to ticarcillin, gentamicin, tobramycin, piperacillin, or azlocillin. *E. coli, K. pneumoniae, P. mirabilis,* and *S. marcescens* may cause urinary or pulmonary tract infections but are not considered leading causes of burn infections. Furthermore, these bacteria are oxidase negative and do not produce blue-green pigments. *(Brooks et al, pp 225–226)*

456. **(B)** There are two nonsuppurative sequelae of group A streptococcal disease, rheumatic fever and acute glomerulonephritis. Although rheumatic fever can follow pharyngeal infection with practically any group A streptococcal organism, the majority of nephritogenic strains belong to only six or seven M types. Types 1, 4, 12, 25, and 49 are the most commonly associated with acute glomerulonephritis. The preceding streptococcal infection need not be restricted to the upper respiratory tract to trigger this condition, and streptococcal erysipelas is a frequent cause. *(Joklik et al, pp 425–426)*

457. **(A)** *C. neoformans* is the only encapsulated yeast that is pathogenic for humans. Visualization of a capsule around yeast cells in an India ink preparation of spinal fluid is diagnostic for cryptococcal disease, although soluble capsular antigen could also be detected by countercurrent immunoelectrophoresis or latex agglutination. This organism is considered to be an opportunistic pathogen, as over 80% of the individuals who become clinically ill are immunosuppressed in some way or have compromised respiratory functions. The organism is abundant in pigeon excreta-contaminated soil, which is most probably the source of human infections. *(Joklik et al, pp 1144–1147)*

458. **(C)** *D. latum,* also known as the fish or broad tapeworm, is the biggest worm and can reach 10 m in size. Humans acquire the infection by eating raw fish containing the larvae of the tapeworm. The worm attaches to the small intestine and causes abdominal discomfort. Nausea, diarrhea, weight loss, and pernicious anemia can result. The anemia is induced by the tapeworm's tendency to compete with humans for vitamin $B_{12}$, which it easily accumulates from the intestinal contents. *(Joklik et al, pp 1206–1207)*

459. **(D)** Plague, a zoonotic disease caused by the bacillus *Yersinia pestis,* is transmitted to humans from its animal reservoir (rats in urban plague, squirrels and other wild animals in sylvatic plague) by fleas (eg, *Xenopsylla cheopis,* the rat flea). Anthrax is an industrial

disease, usually acquired by wool and leather workers. The spores contaminate the hides and raw wool and are inhaled by the workers during processing. Brucellosis and salmonellosis are acquired by ingestion of contaminated foods. Humans may develop leptospirosis if they come in contact with groundwater that has been contaminated with the urine from rodents who are harboring the agent in their normal flora or in a subclinical infection. This disease occurs usually in campers and hunters. Veterinarians are particularly prone to develop zoonotic infections because of their constant contact with infected animals. *(Joklik et al, pp 586–590)*

460.  **(A)** Hfr X F⁻ mating results in the transfer of the greatest amount of chromosomal DNA as compared to F′ X F⁻ mating, specialized transduction, or transposition. Incorporation of the F plasmid into the chromosome produces an Hfr or high frequency of recombination bacterium. When the Hfr bacterium encounters an F⁻ recipient bacterium, the donor bacterial chromosome is mobilized and is transferred to the F⁻ cell. Theoretically, given enough time, the entire donor bacterial chromosome and the F factor can be transferred to the F⁻ recipient. Hfr cells can revert to F⁺ cells by excision of the F plasmid from the bacterial chromosome. Occasionally, the excision is imprecise, and the F plasmid carries a segment of chromosomal DNA adjacent to the integration site of the F plasmid. The resulting F′ hybrid plasmid can then introduce the chromosomal DNA into F⁻ cells with high efficiency. The amount of chromosomal DNA that is transferred by this procedure can vary but is usually not as much as that transferred by Hfr X F⁻ mating. Specialized transduction is the transfer of chromosomal DNA adjacent to the site of integration of a temperate phage in the bacterial chromosome. A very limited amount of DNA is transferred by specialized transduction because of the limited size of the phage capsid. Plasmid transfer is not a common method of transfer of chromosomal DNA, since plas-

mids other than the F factor rarely integrate into the bacterial chromosome. Plasmid transfer of chromosomal markers occurs only if a transposon transfers chromosomal DNA to the plasmid. Transposons can transfer chromosomal DNA, but the amount of chromosomal DNA transferred is limited to the DNA adjacent to IS elements of the transposon. *(Joklik et al, pp 139–141)*

461.  **(D)** There are two portions of the diphtheria toxin molecule; the B fragment is responsible for bringing the molecule into proximity of a mammalian cell, whereas the A fragment is the proenzyme that, when activated by mild proteolysis, will catalyze the ADP-ribosylation of EF-2, thus blocking protein synthesis. Certain strains of pseudomonads also have a toxin with similar biologic activity. Botulinum toxin inhibits acetylcholine release in the peripheral nervous system. Choleragen and the enterotoxin from certain strains of *E. coli* activate adenylcyclase. *(Joklik et al, pp 488–491)*

462.  **(B)** *S. pneumoniae* is a gram-positive, lancet-shaped diplococcus that may be present in small numbers in the human throat. This microorganism is lysed by 10% bile salts, such as desoxycholate at pH 7.0, and it is inhibited by optochin (ethyl hydrocuprein hydrochloride). When it is grown on blood agar, it converts the hemoglobin of the red blood cells to methemoglobin, so that there is a green coloration around the colonies of *S. pneumoniae*, which is called alpha hemolysis. Beta hemolysis refers to the complete breakdown of the hemoglobin of the red blood cells around the colonies of *S. pyogenes* but not of *S. pneumoniae*. *(Joklik et al, pp 432–435)*

463.  **(C)** By definition, the rate of growth of bacteria represents the change in the bacterial cell numbers over the change in time. From the choices given, the maximum rate of growth occurs between 2 PM and 3 PM, where within one hour the number of bacteria has increased approximately three-fold. Between

noon and 1 PM, 3 to 4 PM, 3 to 5 PM, and no increase in the number of cells between 4 and
5 PM where the rate of growth is zero.

$$\frac{2 \times 10^7 - 2 \times 10^7}{5 - 4} = 0$$

*(Joklik et al, pp 63–66)*

**464.** **(D)** Quantitative immunoglobulin levels reflect the secretory activity of B lymphocytes
and could be misleading as to the actual
number of such cells; for example, in multiple myeloma or other B-cell malignancies,
one would expect to find a marked hypergammaglobulinemia. B cells are not the only
cells that have receptors for the Fc fragment
of immunoglobulin. Phagocytic cells also
have such receptors and thus could be included in an Fc receptor assay. E rosetting is
a property of T lymphocytes, as is PHA mitogenic response; hence neither of these assays
would be appropriate for the enumeration of
B lymphocytes. *(Joklik et al, pp 244–245)*

**465.** **(C)** The E rosette assay measures the number
of T lymphocytes and does not indicate their
functional status. Enumeration of Y-bearing
cells also would not give any information of
their functional status. Both sIg and serum
immunoglobulin determinations would measure B-cell functions. PHA induces mitosis in
thymus-derived lymphocytes (T cells). The
mitosis is detected in the assay by measuring
the amount of radioactive thymidine that is
incorporated into the T cells during a 24-hour
period of incubation with this nucleotide.
*(Joklik et al, p 245)*

**466.** **(C)** Lyme disease is a recently discovered illness caused by *Borrelia burgdorferi*, which is
transmitted to humans by tick bites. The disease produces a unique annular skin lesion
called erythema chromicum migrans (ECM).
Certain patients develop neurologic and cardiovascular symptoms and arthritis. Diagnosis of the disease may be assisted by correlat-
ing the serum levels of IgM with Lyme
disease activity, because these patients develop IgM antibodies to *B. burgdorferi* 3 to 6
weeks after infection. *(Levinson and Jawetz, p 285)*

**467.** **(C)** The organisms of the genus *Haemophilus*
are small, gram-negative, non-motile, non-
spore–forming bacilli with complex growth
requirements. *H. influenzae* requires a heat-
stable factor found in blood (X factor), which
can be replaced by hematin, and nicotinamide adenine dinucleotide (V factor), which
can be added to the medium as a supplement
or can be supplied by other microorganisms,
such as staphylococci (satellite phenomenon).
*(Brooks et al, pp 237–238)*

**468.** **(D)** By definition, $LD_{50}$ is the dose of a toxin
that will kill 50% of the animals or individu-
als to whom it is administered. *Clostridium
botulinum* produces one of the most powerful
known bacterial toxins. It has been stated
that the $LD_{50}$ of *C. botulinum* exotoxin for
humans is approximately 1 microgram. The
$LD_{50}$ of the purified exotoxin of *Corybacterium
diphtheriae* is about six times larger than that
of *C. botulinum*. *C. difficile* produces an enterotoxin and a cytoxin, and the lethality of
these toxins, if any, has not as yet been established. *C. perfringens* produces alpha toxin,
which is a lecithinase. Its lethal action is pro-
portionate to the rate at which splits lecithin.
The $LD_{50}$ of this lecithinase has not been established. However, it is larger than that of
*C. difficile*. *(Joklik et al, pp 391, 488–491, 637, 652)*

**469.** **(B)** *E. coli* is the most frequent cause of
meningitis in neonates, who acquire the organism during birth. Group B streptococci
also are an important cause of this disease in
this age group. The remaining organisms
listed in the question cause meningitis in all
age groups on a relatively sporadic basis,
with the exception of *N. meningitidis*, which
can become epidemic in closed populations
such as army training camps. *(Joklik et al,
pp 544–548)*

**470.** **(C)** *H. pylori* is a newly discovered curved
and spiral-shaped gram-negative bacterium
found in the human gastric mucosal layer.
Evidence now shows that *H. pylori* is associated with the pathogenesis of peptic ulcer. It
is found in almost all patients with duodenal
ulcers and more than 80% with stomach ulcers. *H. pylori* produces an abundant amount

of urease. It does not produce coagulase, which is elaborated by *S. aureus*. It is not an obligate intracellular parasite because it can be cultured on a number of artificial media in 2 to 7 days. Patients infected with *H. pylori* develop IgM, IgG, and IgA, which can be used in the diagnosis of *H. pylori*. (*Brooks et al, pp 234–235*)

471. **(E)** There are five known classes of immunoglobulins: IgG, IgA, IgM, IgD, and IgE. IgG is the major immunoglobulin that is found in human serum and the only one that has been shown to pass the placental barrier in human beings. IgG has a molecular weight of 140,000 to 160,000. IgA is the major immunoglobulin of extracellular secretions. It has a molecular weight of 160,000 to 440,000, has modest agglutinating capacity, and its carbohydrate content is 2 to 3 times higher (7.5%) than that of IgG. IgM possesses higher agglutinating and complement fixing capacity than IgG. IgM has a molecular weight of 900,000. Carbohydrates constitute 7 to 11% of the total weight of IgM. IgD constitutes a minor portion of serum immunoglobulins (1%). It contains higher amounts of carbohydrate (13%) than the other immunoglobulins, but it is an important B-cell receptor. No other biological functions have been described for IgD. IgE is the immunoglobulin that has been associated with anaphylactic hypersensitivity. IgE has a molecular weight of 190,000 to 200,000, contains 11 to 12% carbohydrate, and constitutes 0.002% of the total serum immunoglobulin. (*Joklik et al, pp 224–225*)

472. **(A)** *C. perfringens*, *C. difficile*, and *B. cereus* produce enterotoxins which induce diarrhea, vomiting, but no fever, and tend to be associated with food poisoning following infection and production of enterotoxin by *C. perfringens* and *B. cereus*. Fever and no vomiting tend to be present in antibiotic associated colitis caused by *C. difficile*. *E. faecalis* is found in small numbers in the upper respiratory tract and in large numbers (eg, $10^7$ organisms/g of feces) in the large intestine. It does not cause diarrhea. This microorganism has been associated with urinary tract infections, especially in patients with catheters. On occasion, upon entrance into the bloodstream *E. faecalis* may settle on damaged heart valves and produce endocarditis. (*Joklik et al, pp 418, 618–619, 642–645*)

473. **(E)** Bacteria divide by splitting into two equal parts (binary fission). The time required for bacteria to undergo binary fission is called the generation time. The given generation time of *E. coli* is 20 minutes. Thus, within 3 hours (180 minutes), *E. coli* will have undergone nine divisions. Therefore, the number of *E. coli* per mL if we start with 500 bacteria will be as follows: 1000 in 20 minutes, 2000 in 40 minutes, 4000 in 60 minutes, 8000 in 80 minutes 16,000 in 100 minutes, 32,000 in 120 minutes, 64,000 in 140 minutes, 128,000 in 160 minutes, and 256,000 in 180 minutes. (*Joklik et al, pp 62–64*)

474. **(B)** The concept of gene therapy is based on the assumption that definitive treatment for any genetic disease should be possible by directing treatment to the site of the defect itself, the mutant gene, and not to the secondary effects of that mutant gene. Since there are many hereditary diseases that are caused by defects in a single gene, there are many potential applications of this type of therapy to the treatment of human diseases. In addition, gene therapy may be useful for acquired diseases such as cancer or infectious diseases. One of the problems encountered in gene therapy is the need of introducing the desired gene into the host cells. Viruses with weak pathogenic potential, capable of entering into host cells, have been found to be useful gene carriers. They are attractive vectors in gene therapy for the following reasons: They infect cells with a much higher efficiency as compared to chemical or physical means of gene transfer. The genes inserted into viruses may be expressed in a regulated way. Adenovirus vectors may be used to target gene transfer into cells of the respiratory tract. Retrovirus vectors can be produced in large quantities from producer cell lines. (*Brooks et al, pp 95–104*)

475. **(A)** Mutation occurs in bacteria as in all other cells. After the initial observation that

bacterial populations contain mutants (such as a mutant that is resistant to an antibiotic), the question is posed as to whether the mutation is *directed* (induced by the antibiotic) or *random* (spontaneous). This question is most easily answered by the use of the *replica plate technique*. A velveteen pad is used to press over the colonies of the master plate and then pressed to plates A, B, C, and D. When the bacteria are replica plated to plates A, B, C, and D containing a given antibiotic, the resistant colonies always appear in the same places. This is indeed the case in plates B and D, which contain the same antibiotic. This implies that resistant colonies existed before exposure to antibiotic. Hence, mutation is spontaneous. The Lamarckian theory states that acquired characteristics may be transmitted to descendants. *(Davis et al, pp 131–132)*

476. **(B)** The clinical features of food poisoning due to *B. cereus* include an incubation period of 2 to 8 hours during which nausea, vomiting, and diarrhea develop. Usually eating fried rice containing preformed enterotoxin, or *B. cereus*, is the source of food poisoning. *B. cereus* grows in the gastrointestinal tract leading to the production of enterotoxin that causes diarrhea and vomiting. Diplopia, dysphagia, dysphonia, and respiratory distress are the clinical features of food poisoning caused by *C. botulinum*. Gastroenteritis caused by *S. enteritis* has an incubation period of 10 to 48 hours; vomiting is rare, but there is diarrhea and low-grade fever. The organisms grow in the gut, leading to superficial infection with little invasion and no enterotoxin production. The incubation period of tetanus is 4 to 5 days or weeks. The disease is characterized by convulsive tonic contractions of voluntary muscles, leading to lockjaw, and opisthotonos (the spine and extremities are so bent that the body rests on the head and the heels). *P. mirabilis* is a normal inhabitant of the gut, and it may cause occasional urinary tract infections when the bacteria leave the intestinal tract. Diarrhea, vomiting, or nausea are not pathognomonic features of urinary tract infections. *(Brooks et al, pp 134–135)*

477. **(D)** Individuals who have been diagnosed as X-linked agammaglobulinemic lack B lymphocytes and are not able to produce immunoglobulins. They have T cells that are the key players in cell-mediated immunity associated with graft rejection, with intracellular parasites, viruses, and fungi. *P. carinii* is now considered a fungus, causing infections in immunocompromised patients, such as AIDS. The lack of immunoglobulins in X-linked agammaglobulinemia renders individuals susceptible to a succession of infectious diseases caused by extracellular bacteria. These infections may be partially controlled by the injection of specific gamma globulin as a supportive therapy. *(Joklik et al, pp 329–330)*

478. **(B)** Tumor necrosis factor (TNF) is a mediator of endotoxin-induced shock and is involved in inflammation. It is also cytotoxic to certain tumor cells. Recent experiments in gene therapy have taken the approach of expressing TNF in tumor-infiltrating lymphocytes (TIL), with the hope of allowing the TIL to return to the tumor and produce a high concentration of TNF and kill the tumor cells. TNF does not stimulate T-cell proliferation or natural killer (NK) cell activity. NK cells can destroy tumor cells. However, they cannot be stimulated by TNF. *(Joklik et al, p 86)*

479. **(E)** Cholera is not caused by a toxin that hydrolyses lecithin. The main virulence factor contributing to the pathogenesis of cholera is the production of *Vibrio cholerae* enterotoxin, which increases the intracellular levels of the cyclic AMP of the intestinal tract cells and leads to a prolonged hypersecretion of water and electrolytes. Diarrhea occurs with resulting dehydration, shock, acidosis, and death. Cholera is not an invasive infection. *V. cholerae* attaches to microvilli of the intestinal tract. There the bacterial cells multiply and liberate cholera enterotoxin, mucinases, and endotoxin, which contribute to the pathogenesis of cholera. *(Brooks et al, pp 230–232)*

480. **(E)** Infectious mononucleosis is caused by Epstein–Barr virus (EBV), which is a member of the herpesviruses. Nucleic acid hybridization assays for the EBV DNA are the most

sensitive means of diagnosing infectious mononucleosis. Important antigens that also may be used, but which are less sensitive for diagnostic purposes, include the viral capsid protein (VCA), the early proteins (EA), and the Epstein–Barr virus-associated nuclear antigen (EBNA). Infectious mononucleosis patients develop antibody titers exceeding 1:320 and 1:20 against VCA and EA, respectively, during the acute phase of infectious mononucleosis. Antibodies to EBNA develop 1 to 2 months after acute infection. The majority of infectious mononucleosis patients develop what is known as heterophile antibody. That is, antibodies that cross-react with unrelated antigens, such as those found on sheep and horse erythrocytes. Hemagglutinins and neuraminidases are associated with orthomyxoviruses and paramyxoviruses. (*Brooks et al, pp 436–437; Joklik et al, pp 963–964*)

481.   (A) Prokaryotes are distinguished from eukaryotes in that the prokaryotes have naked DNA and lack a nuclear membrane. Peptidoglycan, which is found in most bacterial cell walls, is a polymer unique to the prokaryotes. The prokaryotic ribosome, composed of two subunits of 30S and 50S, is somewhat smaller that the 40S and 60S subunits of eukaryotic ribosomes. Sterols are found in the cell walls of eukaryotic cells such as fungi and RBCs. (*Joklik et al, p 8*)

482.   (C) The ability of certain viruses, such as influenza, mumps, and parainfluenza viruses, to agglutinate red blood cells is used to diagnose these viruses. In general, chicken or human type O red blood cells are employed for the identification of influenza and other viruses. Red blood cells have receptors for the surface component of the influenza virus called hemagglutinin. This hemagglutinin is a glycoprotein. In a hemagglutination assay, a fixed number of red blood cells is mixed with increasing dilutions of the influenza virus. Then, following incubation at 4°C for 2 hours, the tubes containing the red blood cells and the virus are examined for hemagglutination. Unagglutinated cells form a dark

bottom (virus dilutions 1:160; 1:320). Cells agglutinated by the virus form a lattice that covers the entire bottom of the test tube (virus dilutions 1:20; 1:40; 1:80). The hemagglutination titer of the virus is the highest dilution of virus that forms a lattice. In this case, the hemagglutination titer is 1:80. (*Joklik et al, pp 746, 766*)

483.   (E) An important difference between the AIDS (HIV) virus and the tumor RNA viruses is that HIV lyses the host cells while RNA tumor viruses transform the cells, which they invade but lack cytolytic activity. The tropism of the HIV virus for the $T_4$ lymphocytes depends upon the presence of the $T_4$ protein on the surface of the $T_4$ lymphocytes. This protein serves as the receptor for the adsorption of the HIV virus to $T_4$ lymphocytes. HIV virus is a member of the retroviruses. The genomic RNA molecule contains the *gag*, *pol*, and *env* genes. Thus, the HIV viruses cannot be expected to differ from the RNA tumor retroviruses. (*Joklik et al, pp 1048–1063*)

484.   (D) Transmission of herpes simplex virus type 1 occurs primarily by direct contact. Breast milk, blood, frozen plasma, or contaminated syringes have been implicated in the transmission of AIDS virus (HIV) and are not considered the primary vehicles of herpes simplex virus type 1 transmission. (*Joklik et al, pp 955–956*)

485.   (D) Since there are memory lymphocytes primed by a previous tetanus toxoid injection, booster immunization with tetanus toxoid will lead to rapid production of adequate levels of protective antibody. This is the routine procedure followed by physicians for patients with trauma who have been vaccinated against tetanus and received booster immunization for the last 5 to 7 years. The antibody titer to tetanus toxoid remains at protective levels for 5 to 10 years. Aminoglycosides will not be effective against the spores or vegetative cells of *Clostridium tetani*. Tetanus immune globulin is administered to individuals who already exhibit the symptoms of tetanus

in an effort to neutralize tetanus toxin that has not yet been bound to nervous tissue. *(Joklik et al, pp 646–648)*

486. **(D)** Ticks should be carefully removed but they should not be crushed between bare fingers since you may be infected with *Borrelia burgdorferi* harbored by the tick. Removal of the ticks should be accomplished by the use of tweezers. There are no vaccines available for Lyme disease. The tiny tick, which is the size of a poppy seed can be discouraged from attaching to the human skin by the use of insect repellents, and the use of protective clothing over the arms and legs. Initial symptoms of Lyme disease are flu-like chills, fever, headache, dizziness, fatigue and/or stiff neck. Often a "bull-eye" rash or migratory ring-like lesion called erythema chronicum migrans appears days to weeks after a bite. *(Joklik et al, pp 670–671*

487. **(A)** The antiviral drug used currently against the immunodeficiency virus is AZT, or 3-azido-3-deoxythymidine (azidothymidine). Its structure is shown in Figure 4.14. The structures of dideoxyinosine, idoxuridine, acyclovir, and enviroxine, which inhibit poliovirus replication, herpesvirus thymidine kinase, herpesvirus-encoded DNA polymerase, and rhinoviruses, respectively, follow. *(Brooks et al, pp 398–400)*

488. **(B)** The vectors of rickettsiae are arthropods such as lice, fleas, ticks, or mites. Mosquitoes have not yet been shown to serve as vectors for rickettsiae. *(Joklik et al, pp 705–713)*

489. **(C)** C substance, or C polysaccharide, which is a species-specific teichoic acid polymer containing phosphocholine as a major determinant, precipitates with a nonspecific serum beta globulin called C-reactive protein (CRP). Levels of CRP, which is not an antibody are elevated in individuals with a wide variety of acute inflammatory diseases. The high CRP levels may be used as an indication of an individual with an inflammatory disease. The C substance–CRP precipitate activates complement via the classic pathway, and it may function as an opsonin to facilitate the phagocytosis early in pneumococcal infections. *(Joklik et al, pp 433–437)*

490. **(A)** *Neisseria* species are gram-negative cocci usually seen in pairs (diplococci with adjacent flattened sides). All species of *Neisseria* are oxidase-positive diplococci. *S. pneumoniae* is sensitive to optochin. Mycobacteria are acid-fast bacilli. *(Joklik et al, pp 433–434, 444–445, 498)*

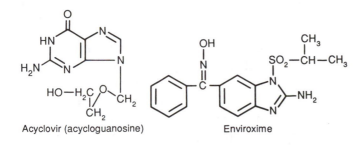

Acyclovir (acycloguanosine)          Enviroxime

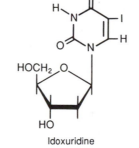

Idoxuridine

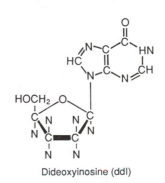

Dideoxyinosine (ddI)

**Figure 4.14**

**491.** **(D)** Listeriosis is caused by *Listeria monocytogenes*, a facultative intracellular gram-positive bacterium. This bacterium can be isolated from a wide range of animals, birds, fish, ticks, and crustacea. There is a high incidence of plant *L. monocytogenes* in soil samples and animal feces. The organism is contracted by humans and animals from many sources. (*Joklik et al, p 283*)

**492.** **(E)** Togaviruses contain viral species that cause encephalitis. They are transmitted via mosquito vectors with birds serving as reservoirs of infection. Western and eastern encephalitis viruses cause infections that have high mortality in children and in aged individuals. These viruses enter the bloodstream from insect inoculation. The virus is removed by the reticuloendothelial cells and multiplies in the spleen and lymph nodes. From these tissues, a secondary viremia is established, spreading the virus to the central nervous system by passage through the blood–brain junction (virus grows through the vascular endothelium or in some way is passively transported across the blood–brain barrier). The brain and spinal cord become edematous and show vascular congestion and small hemorrhages. There are no human vaccines, and control is limited to controlling the insect vectors and identifying and controlling the animal reservoirs of infection. (*Brooks et al, pp 492–495*)

**493.** **(A)** The most widely used nontreponemal test for syphilis is the card rapid plasma reagin (RPR), or the glass slide-flocculation Venereal Disease Research Laboratory (VDRL) tests. In these tests, the antigen employed is an alcoholic extract of beef heart containing cardiolipin (diphosphatidylglycerol), which also happens to be a component of the cytoplasmic membrane of *Treponema pallidum* that causes syphilis. The RPR and the VDRL tests are used to screen large groups of individuals for syphilis. The VDRL titer reflects the activity of the disease. Such titers reach a level of 1:32 or higher in secondary syphilis. A persistent fall in titer following penicillin or other antibiotic treatment, indicates an ad-

equate response to therapy. (*Joklik et al, pp 663–667*)

**494.** **(C)** The detection of yellow granules, or sulfur granules, in pus obtained from the liver abscess suggests hepatic actinomycosis, because the sulfur granules represent colonies of *Actinomyces israelii* or other oral *Actinomyces* species. The *Actinomyces* associated with hepatic actinomycosis, which may follow teeth extractions, especially in patients with paradental abscesses, are usually *A. israelii*, *A. bovis*, or *A. odontolyticus*. All these fail to grow aerobically, but can be cultured anaerobically or brain heart infusion agar where at 37°C *A. israelii* produces small, white, spidery colonies in 2 to 3 days that contain gram-positive rods and filaments. In pus, *A. israelii* is found as sulfur granules which represent colonies of this microorganism. When the sulfur granules are washed, crushed between two glass slides, and Gram stained, they show under the microscope a twisted aggregation of filaments which break up into bacilli, cocci, or small filaments that are gram-positive and non-acid–fast. *Mycobacterium tuberculosis*, *M. kansasii*, and *Nocardia asteroides* are aerobic, acid-fast microorganisms. *A. israelii* and *N. asteroides* are sensitive to penicillin, while *M. tuberculosis*, *M. kansasii*, and the fungus *Histoplasma capsulatum* are resistant to penicillin. (*Joklik et al, pp 528–531*)

**495.** **(D)** *M. pneumoniae* requires sterols for growth, usually in the form of cholesterol that is incorporated in the cell membrane. Similarly and in harmony with other species of the genus, *Mycoplasma* contains both DNA and RNA, is completely resistant to penicillin, and lacks muramic acid because it does not possess a cell wall. *M. pneumoniae* is the causative agent of primary atypical pneumonia, which was initially described by Eaton, giving rise to the eponym Eaton agent. (*Joklik et al, pp 733–736*)

**496.** **(C)** *S. schenckii* is found on thorns, and it is introduced into the skin of extremities through trauma. A regional lesion begins as a pustule, abscess, or ulcer, and then nodules and abscesses are formed along the lymphatics. The history and the symptoms described in this patient are consonant with a diagnosis of sporotrichosis. *T. rubrum* is the cause of dermatophytosis (ringworm) of skin, scalp, and especially nails. The nails thicken and are discolored. *A. fumigatus* and *C. albicans* are associated with deep opportunistic infections in immunocompromised patients such as AIDS patients. Aspergillosis is basically a pulmonary infection. Candidiasis can be associated with pathological conditions of the mucous membranes of the respiratory, genital, and gastrointestinal tract, where it is found as a normal inhabitant. *C. neoformans* is the cause of meningitis. (*Brooks et al, pp 310–327*)

**497.** **(E)** The genome of hepatitis B virus is composed of a circular, double-stranded DNA. It has a negative strand of 3200 nucleotides and another positive, incomplete strand of 1700 to 2600 nucleotides. Hepatitis A virus, the cause of infectious hepatitis, has a linear single-stranded RNA genome, and as such it is a member of the enteroviruses. Papilloma and polyomaviruses belong to the family of *Papoviridae*, which are viruses without envelopes and have a double-stranded, circular DNA genome. Both DNA circular strands are complete and thus differ from the genome of hepatitis B virus that has two incomplete circular DNA strands. J.C. virus is a member of the polyomaviruses. Epstein–Barr virus (EBV) is a member of the herpesviruses and as such has a double-stranded, linear DNA genome. EBV has been associated with infectious mononucleosis, Burkitt's lymphoma, and nasopharyngeal carcinoma. (*Joklik et al, pp 803, 810–811, 874, 877, 975, 980*)

**498.** **(D)** The most appropriate laboratory diagnostic procedure for cases of suspected tinea corporis is digestion of tissue biopsies with 10 to 20% KOH and a search for hyaline, branched septate hyphae on squamous epithelial cells. A 10 to 20% potassium hydroxide solution dissolves the tissue without destroying the fungal cytology, thus allowing easy visualization of the fungal cells. Silver staining is used for the detection of spirochetes. Acid-fast stain is employed for the identification of mycobacteria. Culture of the vesicular fluid on agar does not permit growth of the fungal cells. Fungi are grown on Sabouraud's nutrient agar, which contains peptones, carbohydrates, vitamins, minerals, and water, and it has a pH of 5.3, which is optimal for fungal growth. Serology for *B. dermatitides* is inappropriate, because *T. rubrum* is the causative agent of tinea corporis. Furthermore, serology is of marginal value for the diagnosis of tinea corporis. (*Joklik et al, p 1130*)

**499.** **(D)** The cause of antigenic drift of influenza viruses is accumulated point mutations in the hemagglutinin gene. The genome of the influenza virus is composed of segmented, simple-stranded RNA. Influenza virus has a lipid envelope where the important antigens of influenza virus are localized. The virus-encoded surface glycoproteins hemagglutinin and neuraminidase undergo frequent variation independent of each other. Minor antigenic alterations are called *antigenic drift*, while major antigenic variations are termed *antigenic shift*. Antigenic drifts can be diagnosed by amino acid changes in the hemagglutinin glycoprotein molecule and are the results of the accumulations of point mutations in the hemagglutinin gene. Antigenic shifts are due to reassortment of the eight RNA segments of the viral genome. This occurs when persons are infected with two influenza viruses, ie, a human influenza virus to which the person has partial immunity and an animal influenza virus possessing different hemagglutinins and neuraminidases. Now, the proteins surrounding the RNA influenza virus genome (capsids) may be encoded by the genomes of the human and animal viruses (*phenotypic masking*). This situation can be detected by antigenic analysis. (*Joklik et al, pp 825, 844–846, 993–998*)

**500.** **(E)** The history of the patient described in the question would require careful consideration of all of the diseases listed, and the serology would not serve to rule out any. In the acute phase of the illness, an elevation of antibodies specific for the causative agent might not occur. Usually the rise in antibody levels does not occur until the second or third week of the infection, thus the significance of paired (acute and convalescent) serum samples, which allow the observation of an increase in the antibody specific for the causative agent of the infection. Identifying the cause of most bacterial infections is ideally accomplished by culture of the organism. Serology is used to confirm these identifications and is used also when the agent is slow growing or very expensive to culture, or when the agent cannot be grown at all (as in the case of syphilis). *(Joklik et al, pp 561–562, 596–597, 611–613, 705–707)*

501.  **(E)** Creutzfeldt–Jacob disease is a degenerative central nervous human disease. The etiological agent does not seem to be a conventional virus, but infectivity is related to a proteinaceous macromolecule that appears to be devoid of any nucleic acid. This macromolecule is resistant to formaldehyde. It is inactivated by autoclaving, iodine disinfectants, ether, acetone, 6 M urea, 10% sodium dodecyl sulfate, or 0.5% sodium hypochlorite. Subacute sclerotizing panencephalitis is currently believed to be caused by measles virus, or a defective variant of the measles virus (rubeola virus). Distemper is a canine viral infection. It is caused by an RNA virus that is a member of the paramyxoviridal family. Progressive multifocal leukoencephalopathy has been associated with the J.C. virus, which is a member of the polyomaviruses. These viruses have a double-stranded, circular DNA genome. Dengue fever is caused by an arbovirus. Arboviruses have a RNA genome. Dengue fever is transmitted by a mosquito bite, and it is prevalent in tropical areas. It can be prevented by vaccination. *(Joklik et al, pp 778, 874, 1014–1015, 1019–1025, 1066)*

502.  **(A)** Plasmid-encoded genes specify a variety of functions that include multiple drug resistance, resistance to heavy metals, and sex pilus formation (F plasmids). Bacteriocinogens are a group of plasmids that specify the production of the bactericidal proteins known as bacteriocins. The heat-labile and heat-stable enterotoxins of *E. coli* are plasmid encoded. The gene for exfoliative toxin, an exotoxin responsible for the staphylococcal scalded skin syndrome, is also located on a plasmid. Plasmids also contain genes responsible for the production of proteases (of *Streptococcus lactis*), resistance to phages (*E. coli*), metabolism of sugars and hydrocarbons, exotoxin of *Clostridium botulinum*, and tumorigenesis in plants. *(Joklik et al, pp 145–149, 404–409, 546)*

503.  **(C)** Burkitt's lymphoma is associated with Epstein–Barr virus (EBV), which is a member of the herpesviruses. In this herpetic virus lymphoma, under the influence of EBV, an oncogene called *c-myc*, which is usually located on the 8th chromosome of B lymphocytes, is translocated to chromosome 14 of the B lymphocytes at the region of immunoglobulin heavy-chain genes. This translocation places the *c-myc* gene side by side to an active promoter, and high levels of *c-myc* RNA are formed. The oncogenes, or transforming genes *v-abl* and *v-fms*, have been associated with the Abelson murine leukemia virus. They appear to be involved in the synthesis of proteins p160 and gp180. The *v-ras* oncogene has been linked to Harvey murine sarcoma virus that causes sarcoma and leukemia in rats. The *v-ras* oncogene is involved in the production of a protein known as p21. The *v-src* oncogene has been connected with the Rous sarcoma virus, which is the etiological agent of chicken sarcoma. The product of the *v-src* oncogene appears to be a protein known as pp60. *(Joklik et al, pp 886–891)*

504.  **(E)** In contrast to rheoviruses, picornaviruses, poxviruses, and paramyxoviruses, the genomes of which replicate in the cytoplasm of the host cells, the genome of herpesviruses is replicated in the nucleus of the host cell. The first genes expressed are the alpha genes, which encode for phosphoproteins that act as activators of the next set of genes called beta genes. Expression of the beta 1 and 2 genes results in the synthesis of a DNA-binding protein, a DNA polymerase,

a deoxyprimidine kinase, and a moiety of a ribonucleotide reductase. The formation of these enzymes leads to the synthesis of the viral DNA. Following initiation of the synthesis of viral DNA, another set of genes called gamma genes is activated, giving rise to the formation of more than fifty viral proteins. (*Joklik et al, pp 804–805*)

505. **(D)** The best way to detect congenital syphilis is by the use of florescent treponema antibody-absorption-IgM (FTA-ABA IgM). All newborn infants of mothers with reactive VDRL, or reactive FTA-ABS tests, will themselves have reactive tests, whether or not they have actually acquired syphilis, because of the passive placental transfer of maternal immunoglobulins. However, if IgM anti-syphilitic antibody is present in the infant's serum, it will reflect fetal antibody production in response to intrauterine infection (congenital syphilis) because maternal IgM antibody does not penetrate a healthy placenta. (*Joklik et al, pp 664–665*)

506. **(B)** A positive PPD skin test indicates that the individual has experienced mycobacterial infection at some time. It does not necessarily indicate current disease or give any information on the health status of the individual. Conversion to negative does not occur naturally and, if it occurs, has grave significance. Conversions occur in the terminal stages of tuberculosis and in certain immunodeficiency states (eg, AIDS). (*Joklik et al, pp. 502–508*)

507. **(D)** Amantadine (generic name) or symmetral (trade name) inhibit an early event in the multiplication cycle of influenza virus as well as arenaviruses. It blocks the uncoating process. Mutations in the M protein genes result in the development of drug-resistant mutants. The drug is not used extensively in the United States because it seems impractical to control this type of infectious disease that is not ordinarily fatal. To protect individuals at high risk, and in those when the infection is of potential danger, there is a choice between this drug and the influenza vaccine. In most

cases, the vaccine would seem to be preferred. (*Joklik et al, pp 996–997*)

508. **(B)** The immunologic basis of graft rejection was proved by the classic experiments, which showed that accelerated destruction of second grafts from the original donor could be reproduced by infusion of B and T cells from a graft recipient into a naive animal before transplantation. It is logical, then, to expect that destruction of the effector B and T cells would suppress graft rejection. Irradiation, antilymphocyte globulin, and steroids all have been shown to cause lymphoid cell destruction when they were administered in appropriate doses. Cyclosporine is thought to inhibit interleukin-2, which drives antigen-activated cells into proliferation. (*Joklik et al, pp 282–283*)

509. **(C)** Adenoviruses do not have an envelope. Their linear, double-stranded DNA is enclosed within a capsid with icosahedral symmetry. Spikes project from each of the 12 vertices. The viral DNA contains a virus-encoded protein that is covalently cross-linked to each 5' end of the linear adenovirus genome. Herpesviruses, and varicella–zoster virus, belong to the same family of herpesviridae and have a linear, double-stranded DNA genome, in which the complementary strands are not covalently cross-linked at the termini of the genome. SV40 virus is a member of the polyoma group of viruses, which possesses a circular, double-stranded DNA genome. Finally, the genome of the vaccinia virus is linear, double-stranded DNA with inverted terminal repeats. (*Brooks et al, pp 408, 418, 427, 441, 562*)

510. **(A)** Immune complexes are involved in the pathogenesis of all of the diseases listed in the question. They contribute to tissue damage by activating complement and attracting neutrophils that, through a process of exocytosis, release lysosomal enzymes into the microenvironment. Poststreptococcal nephritis is a nonsuppurative sequela of infection by a few M types of group A streptococci. The Arthus reaction is a laboratory phenomenon

that is usually evoked in the skin of an immune rabbit by the intradermal injection of antigen. Lupus erythematosus is one of the most significant complications of autoimmune disease and occurs as a result of DNA/antiDNA antibody complexes. Serum sickness occurs in humans after the injection of foreign materials. Any foreign substance against which the host can produce antibody can cause this disease, although horse serum historically was the culprit. The immune complexes in serum sickness may localize in the vascular bed, producing vasculitis, or may cause arthritis or glomerulonephritis. (Joklik et al, pp 321–322)

511. **(B)** To be useful as a cloning vector, a plasmid should possess several properties. It should code for one or more selectable markers (such as antibiotic resistance) to allow identification of transformants and to allow maintenance of the plasmid in a bacterial population. Also, it should contain single sites for restriction enzymes in regions of the plasmid that are not essential for replication. Single sites for restriction enzymes allow for insertion of foreign DNA molecules that have been cleaved with the restriction enzymes. Autonomous replication is necessary and allows a high copy number of plasmids to be obtained. With high copy numbers, large amounts of a specific segment of foreign DNA can be obtained readily in pure form. (Brooks et al, pp 95–104)

512. **(D)** Legionellosis, or legionnaire's disease, was first detected in 1976 when an outbreak of deadly pneumonia occurred in over 200 persons attending an American Legion convention. Epidemiologic investigations showed that the disease was caused by a gram-negative rod that was named L. pneumophila. The organism was spread from water reservoirs, contaminated air-conditioning units, nebulizers filled with water, or evaporative condensers. The organism can survive for over a year in tap water at room temperature (23 to 25°C). L. pneumophila is difficult to stain with the Gram stain or other common bacterial stains. It will stain faintly gram-negative when the safranin is left on for an

extended period. The organism can be demonstrated by the direct fluorescent antibody procedure or by the silver impregnation method. (Joklik et al, pp 694–697)

513. **(E)** The physical examination supports a provisional diagnosis of streptococcal pharyngitis. This is a common infection caused by group A, β-hemolytic streptococci, which are usually susceptible to penicillin and bacitracin. Laboratory diagnosis of group A streptococcal pharyngitis is based on blood agar cultures, bacitracin sensitivity tests, and various serologic assays. (Joklik et al, pp 418–424)

514. **(D)** There are many enzymes in animal viruses, although not all viruses have enzymes. Examples of some of the viral enzymes are DNA-dependent RNA polymerase, messenger RNA-capping enzymes, and polyadenylic acid polymerase. (Joklik et al, pp 749–781)

515. **(D)** There are a relatively small group of antigens, the T-independent antigens share some common properties: they are large polymers, have repeating antigenic determinants, and show resistance to rapid degradation. In addition some of them can also, at relatively high concentrations, activate B-cell clones that are not specific for that particular antigen, a process called polyclonal B-cell activation. Serum albumin clearly does not share those properties, ie, it is an animal protein composed of twenty different L-amino acids. Therefore, it is a T-dependent antigen. (Joklik et al, pp 209, 220)

516. **(D)** The negative-stranded, single-stranded RNA viruses (the first three viruses listed in the question) must all carry RNA-dependent RNA polymerase as a structural component because their negative-stranded RNA cannot serve directly as messenger RNA. The retroviruses carry a reverse transcriptase, an RNA-directed DNA polymerase. (Brooks et al, pp 510, 517, 539, 553)

517. **(D)** Antigen–antibody reactions are highly specific. The binding of antigen to antibody

does *not* involve covalent bonds but only relatively weak, short-range forces (eg, hydrogen bonding, electrostatic, van der Waals forces). The strength of antigen–antibody bonds depends on the closeness of tie between the configuration of the antigen determinant site and the combining site of the antibody. Antibodies with the best fit and strongest bindings are said to have high affinity for the antigen. (*Joklik et al, pp 336–337*)

518. **(D)** The short incubation of 4 hours indicates staphylococcal food poisoning. This is a situation arising from the ingestion of preformed staphylococcal enterotoxin which induces—within 1 to 6 hours following consumption of contaminated food—diarrhea, abdominal cramps, and severe vomiting. These symptoms last for 6 to 12 hours, and complete recovery usually occurs in less than one day. The incubation period for *Salmonella typhimurium*, *Vibrio parahaemolyticus*, *Yersinia enterocolitica*, and *Campylobacter jejuni* is 8 to 12, 24 to 96, 24 to 48, and 48 to 168 hours, respectively. These longer incubation periods, when compared to the short incubation period of staphylococcal food intoxication, are due to the need for the above named bacteria to invade the human intestinal tract, and then multiply and form the toxins responsible for the infective form of food poisoning. (*Ryan, pp 771, 772*)

519. **(A)** The hypervariable regions are located on the Fab piece, not on the Fc piece. All other statements are correct. (*Joklik et al, pp 226–230*)

520. **(E)** Conventional antibody responses are polyclonal and include many antibody molecules differing somewhat in their binding affinity. Monoclonal antibody is formed by a single clone of antibody-producing cells. Any given clone may produce any class of immunoglobulin. Characteristically, it has antibody combining sites that are identical. Monoclonal antibodies are produced by the hybridoma technique (fusion of immune competent B cells to a myeloma cell). They are also produced by neoplastic plasma cells (multiple myeloma). Monoclonal antibodies

are widely used in both diagnostic and therapeutic purposes. (*Joklik et al, pp 206, 378, 941, 945*)

521. **(A)** Poliovirus is not enveloped and therefore is not inactivated by mild detergents that solubilize the phospholipid cytoplasmic membranes derived by budding through the host cell. (*Brooks et al, p 468*)

522. **(D)** All of the viral genomes listed in the question, except that of cytomegalovirus, a herpesvirus, replicate in the nucleus. (*Brooks et al, p 375*)

523. **(E)** To determine whether the poliovirus is a wild-type virus or whether it is related to that used for vaccination, it will be necessary to prepare oligonucleotide maps of the isolated virus and compare the oligonucleotide maps of the wild-type and vaccine strains. Many viruses may kill mice; thus, one cannot determine whether poliovirus strains are related or unrelated by mouse lethality studies. Similarly, cytopathology cannot be used for definitive diagnosis of poliovirus strains or other types of viruses. Viral neutralization assays using the grandchild's serum will only indicate whether the grandchild has been exposed to and vaccinated for the polioviruses in question, but will not establish whether the poliovirus isolated from the stool of the 55-year-old grandfather is related to the poliovirus used to vaccinate his grandchild. (*Joklik et al, p 768*)

524. **(D)** Radioimmunoassays are the most sensitive and versatile techniques for the quantitation of antigens or haptene. Radioimmunoassay is particularly applicable to the measurement of serum levels of many hormones, drugs, and other biologic materials. The method is based on competition for specific antibody between the labeled (known) and unlabeled (unknown) concentration of the antigen or haptens. (*Joklik et al, pp 240–241*)

525. **(D)** *E. granulosus* is a dog tapeworm in which sheep are the usual intermediate host. Humans, when closely involved with dogs

and sheep, may accidentally ingest eggs from sheep or dog feces and become intermediate hosts. (Joklik et al, pp 1210–1211)

**526.** **(B)** Dermatophytosis caused by *M. rubrum* is one of the hardest mycotic infections to cure completely. *M. rubrum* is sensitive to griseofulvin, produces red pigments and it is a human pathogenic fungus. (Joklik et al, pp 1125–1132)

**527.** **(D)** The patient described in this question is showing the typical symptoms of botulism, which is commonly caused by types A, B, or E *Clostridium botulinum* toxin. Therefore, early administration of potent botulinum antitoxin containing antibodies to toxins A, B, and E constitutes the most appropriate type of treatment. (Joklik et al, pp 648–653)

**528.** **(E)** Ketoconazole inhibits the biosynthesis of ergosterol by blocking demethylation at the C-14 site of the ergosterol precursor, lanosterol. This results in the accumulation of lanosterol-like sterols in the cell, altered properties of the cell membrane, the leakage of potassium ions and small phosphorus-containing compounds. Amphotericin B and nystatin disturb the permeability of the cell membrane by directly complexing with the membrane sterols. The target of griseofulvin is microtubules. Flucytosine (5'-fluorocytosine) is incorporated into RNA after being deaminated and then phosphorylated. It also interferes with DNA synthesis because it is a noncompetitive inhibitor of thymidylate synthetase. (Joklik et al, pp 165–166, 181)

**529–530.** **(529-B, 530-D)** A few parasitic diseases are acquired by ingestion of the eggs of organisms, such as *Enterobius vermicularis*, *Ascaris lumbricoides*, *Toxocara canis*, and *Trichuris trichiura*. Cysts are the infective form of *Entamoeba*, *Toxoplasma*, and *Giardia*. Ingestion of larvae is the source of *Trichinella* and *Taenia* infestations. Larval penetration of skin is the mode of transmission for hookworms, *Strongyloides* and *Schistosoma*. Larval inoculation by vector insects occurs in onchocercal and wuchereria infections. Although both organisms have an intestinal phase in their life

cycle in humans, major pathology involves tissues other than the gut. In addition to the primary abscesses affecting the large intestine of patients with *E. histolytica* infection, secondary abscess formation may occur in the liver or, rarely, in other organs. *S. mansoni* (and *Schistosoma japonicum*) cause granulomatous reactions in the host to the eggs deposited in intestinal venules or to those trapped in the liver or other organs. (Joklik et al, pp 1164, 1170, 1183, 1189, 1192, 1209)

**531–532.** **(531-E, 532-D)** The antibody molecule is composed of two identical light chains and two identical heavy chains. The light chains are either κ or λ chains and have two domains, a constant domain (represented by the straight line in the figure that accompanies the question) and a variable domain (represented by the wavy line). The heavy chains carry the determinant group responsible for the immunoglobulin class of the molecule and are either α, γ, μ, δ, or ε chains. They have either four or five domains, only one of which is variable (represented by the wavy line). The portion of the molecule marked **A** is called the Fd fragment; this is the heavy-chain portion of the fragment antigen-binding (Fab) fragment, which results from mild proteolysis of the molecule. Another fragment of the pepsin digestion of the molecule is the crystallizable (Fc) fragment, marked by the **D** in the diagram. It is in this area of the molecule where most of the carbohydrate is located. Various biologic properties are controlled by this area as well. For example, complement is bound in this portion, and the ability of IgE molecule to fix to mast cells is controlled here. (Joklik et al, pp 223–230)

**533–534.** **(533-C, 534-B)** When an antigen is injected into an animal, it first undergoes an equilibration in which the concentration in the intravascular compartment is equalized with that outside this compartment (if the material can readily escape through the vascular endothelium), and any aggregated material is rapidly removed by the reticuloendothelial system. The next phase **(B)** is the phase of normal metabolic decay that reflects the molecule's half-life intravascularly. This will vary in slope depending on the half-life of the molecule in question. If the substance is antigenic, the host will respond immunologically to it and a phase of immune elimination, or clearance **(C)**, will ensue. It is during this period of rapid removal of the antigen in the form of antigen–antibody complexes that tissue damage can occur (such as that seen in serum sickness). If the host has been exposed to the antigen before, the metabolic clearance (or decay) phase will be very short, since there either are already circulating antibodies present to opsonize the antigen, or the anamnestic response will occur, in which event new antibodies will be produced very rapidly. *(Joklik et al, pp 247–249)*

**535–536.** **(535-A, 536-C)** Pili are hair-like proteinaceous appendages found on some bacteria. Pili are of two kinds. The thin, abundant, short ones (ordinary pili) are responsible for the adherence of bacteria to host cells. The few long pili, known as sex pili, play a role in the transfer of genetic information from one bacterial cell to the other during the process of bacterial conjugation. The sex pili appear to be responsible for the attachment of DNA donor and recipient cells in bacterial conjugation. Members of the genus *Bacillus* and *Clostridium* produce spores. These are considered resting cells that are resistant to dryness, heat, and chemical agents. When spores are returned to an appropriate growth environment, they germinate to produce a vegetative cell. Part of their heat resistance has been attributed to a unique chemical known as calcium dipicolinate. *(Brooks et al, pp 25–28)*

**537–538.** **(537-B, 538-A)** Conjugation is the contact-dependent transfer of DNA from one bacterial cell to another. Auxotrophic mutants are those that differ from the wild-type organism in having one or more additional nutritional requirements. In the case presented in the question, one organism requires exogenous tryptophan, lysine, and histidine (Try⁻ Lys⁻ His⁻) and is able to synthesize its own proline, pantothenic acid, and biotin (Pro⁺ Pan⁺ Bio⁺). The second organism in the pair has the opposite genetic capabilities (ie, it is Try⁺ Lys⁺ His⁺ Pro⁻ Pan⁻ Bio⁻). Conjuga-

tion that resulted in complete restitution of biosynthetic capabilities would produce an organism (Try⁺ Lys⁺ His⁺ Pro⁺ Pan⁺ Bio⁺) that could grow on minimal medium devoid of any of these nutrients. Colony 6 in the question is such an organism. Colony 1 still needs tryptophan and lysine for growth, as it was only able to grow on a plate supplemented with these two amino acids; its genotype then is Try⁻ Lys⁻. Colonies 2 and 4 both need tryptophan only; they are Try⁻. Colony 3 is Bio⁻, 5 is Pan⁻ Bio⁻, and colony 7 needs something in the complete medium that has not been added to the plates used in this experiment. *(Joklik et al, pp 139–141)*

**539.** **(D)** Autoantibody reactions can develop in individuals who have formed antibodies to their own modified cellular components that the immunological system, due to modification of cell molecules, can no longer recognize as part of itself. Thus, autoantibody to acetylcholine receptors of neuromuscular junctions is now considered the basis of myasthenia gravis. Certain individuals with Graves' disease develop autoantibodies to thyroid stimulating hormone (TSH) receptors. When these autoantibodies bind to TSH receptors, they resemble biologically active TSH and induce the thyroid gland to synthesize thyroxine. Thrombocytopenia has been attributed to the development of autoantibodies to the cell surface receptors of the thrombocytes and the subsequent destruction of thrombocytes. The presence of autoantibodies to DNA has been associated with the development of systemic lupus erythematosus. *(Joklik et al, pp 320–321)*

**540.** **(E)** Rheumatoid arthritis is an autoimmune disease. Autoimmune diseases involve the production of antibodies to an individual's own components. Thus, these antibodies are called autoantibodies. Normally, an individual does not produce antibodies to his own components. However, when his antigenic components become altered to the point that the immunological system can no longer recognize a component as being part of itself, it responds with the development of autoantibodies that can cause damage to this individual. Rheumatoid arthritis has been associated with the production of autoantibodies to immunoglobulin G (rheumatoid factor). It has been reported that there are over 100 diseases that have associated with a given human lymphocyte antigen (HLA) allele. For example, rheumatoid arthritis has been connected with possession of the HLA-DR4 allele, while Graves' disease, myasthenia gravis, and systemic lupus erythematosus have all been associated with the HLA-DR3 allele. *(Joklik et al, pp 281, 320–321)*

**541–543. (541-G, 542-F, 543-B)** "Shingles" or herpes zoster is a recurrence of chickenpox caused by the varicella–zoster virus, which is a medium-sized, square-like, enveloped virus containing double-stranded DNA genome. The disease is characterized by inflammation of the dorsal root ganglion, neuralgic pain, and crops of clustered vesicles located along the affected nerves. Adenoviruses cause such diseases as pharyngitis, conjunctivitis, pneumonia, hemorrhagic cystitis, and gastroenteritis. Adenovirus is a nonenveloped, cubical virus with a double-stranded genome. Rhabdovirus is a bullet-shaped, enveloped virus, which contains a single-stranded genome. An example of a rhabdovirus is the rabies virus. Measles, or rubeola virus, is an enveloped, round, single-stranded RNA virus. Measles is characterized by the development of maculopapules that coalesce to form blotches, becoming brownish in 5 to 10 days. There is also sneezing, coughing, Koplik spot formation, and lymphopenia. Mumps virus, like the measles virus, is a member of the paramyxoviridae family, which is composed mostly of spherical, enveloped viruses that are single stranded, linear, nonsegmented RNA genomes. Mumps is characterized by swelling of the parotid glands. Significant complications include orchitis and aseptic meningitis. J.C. virus is a member of the polyomaviruses that has been implicated in progressive multifocal leukoencephalopathy. It is a spherical, nonenveloped virus that belongs to the family of papoviridae, the members of which possess a double-stranded, circular DNA

genome. Bunyavirus is a spherical, enveloped virus. It is transmitted by arthropods, and can cause encephalitis. Cytomegalovirus and molluscum contagiosum viruses are brick-shaped, enveloped viruses. Cytomegalovirus has been associated with microcephaly, seizures, deafness, jaundice, and purpura in 20% of infants infected during pregnancy. Molluscum contagiosum virus causes small, pink, wartlike, benign skin tumors. *(Levinson and Jawetz, pp 158, 160, 163, 164, 168–170, 173, 187)*

**544. (F)** Systemic lupus erythematosus (SLE) is an autoimmune disease (type III hypersensitivity or immune-complex disease). All other diseases listed in the question are not autoimmune diseases. SLE patients produce antinuclear, anti-DNA antibodies. Immune complexes are detected by immunofluorescent staining of kidney sections, and antinuclear antibodies have been detected in serum by indirect immunofluorescence. *(Joklik et al, pp. 221–222; Roitt et al, pp 21.1–21.9)*

**545. (H)** Severe combined immunodeficiency disorder (SCID) is characterized by the absence of all adaptive immune function from birth. Infants with SCID have profound lymphopenia; an absence of lymphocytes' proliferative response to mitogens, antigens, and allogenic cells in vitro; and delayed cutaneous anergy. Serum immunoglobulin concentrations are diminished to absent, and no antibody formation occurs after immunization. Unless immunologic reconstitution can be achieved through immunocompetent tissue transplants or enzyme replacement therapy or germ-free isolation can be carried out, the patient will not survive beyond his or her first birthday. *(Joklik et al, pp 333–334)*

**546. (A)** Chronic granulomatous disease of children is characterized by chronic suppurative infections, draining adenopathy, pneumonia, hepatomegaly with liver abscesses, osteomyelitis, splenomegaly, hypergammaglobulinemia, and dermatitis, with onset of symptoms usually before 1 year of age. The cause of these problems is the genetic defect in

NADPH-oxidase. Neutrophils contain myeloperoxidase, which utilizes hydrogen peroxide and halide ions to produce hypohalite ions such as hypochlorite, which is highly microbicidal. Because of the defective NADPH-oxidase, the patient's phagocytes cannot generate sufficient hydrogen peroxide, thus the myeloperoxidase-hydrogen peroxide and halide system cannot function normally. Neutrophils from these patients can phagocytose bacteria and fungi normally, but phagocytosed agents cannot be killed efficiently because of the defective myeloperoxidase-$H_2O_2$-halide system. Streptococcal infections in chronic granulomatous disease patients are rare because the defective myeloperoxide-$H_2O_2$-halide system can utilize hydrogen peroxide accumulated by phagocytosed streptococci (streptococci are catalase-negative). *(Joklik et al, pp 340–341, 350–351)*

## REFERENCES

Brooks GF, Butel JS, Ornston LN, Jawetz E, Melnick JL, Adelberg EA, *Medical Microbiology*. 19th ed. Norwalk, CT; Appleton & Lange; 1991

Davis BD, Dulbecco R, Eisen HN, Ginsberg HS. *Microbiology*. 3rd ed. New York: Harper & Row; 1980

Joklik WK, Willett HP, Amos BD, Wilfert CM. *Zinsser Microbiology*. 20th ed. Norwalk, CT: Appleton & Lange; 1992

Levinson WE, Jawetz E. *Medical Microbiology and Immunology*. 2nd ed. Norwalk, CT: Appleton & Lange; 1992

Roitt I, Brostoff J, Maele DK. *Immunology*. 2nd ed. London and New York: Gower Medical Publishing; 1989

Ryan KJ. *Sherris Medical Microbiology*. 3rd ed. Norwalk, CT: Appleton & Lange; 1994

# Subspecialty List—Microbiology

405. Cellular immunology
406. Antibody structure
407. Virology
408. Microbial physiology
409. Virology
410. Virology
411. Microbial genetics
412. Pathogenic bacteriology
413. Antigen–antibody reaction
414. Microbial genetics
415. Microbial genetics
416. Virology
417. Virology
418. Pathogenic bacteriology
419. Pathogenic bacteriology
420. Microbial genetics
421. Microbial physiology
422. Microbial genetics
423. Pathogenic bacteriology
424. Mycology
425. Microbial physiology
426. Pathogenic bacteriology
427. Antibody structure
428. Pathogenic bacteriology
429. Microbial genetics
430. Cellular immunology
431. Cellular immunology
432. Virology
433. Microbial genetics
434. Immune deficiency disease
435. Virology
436. Autoimmune disease
437. Immune deficiency disease
438. Microbial physiology

439. Microbial genetics
440. Pathogenic bacteriology
441. Antigen–antibody reaction
442. Microbial genetics
443. Virology
444. Pathogenic bacteriology
445. Virology
446. Pathogenic bacteriology
447. Cellular immunology
448. Antigenicity
449. Pathogenic bacteriology
450. Serology
451. Pathogenic bacteriology
452. Mycology
453. Virology
454. Bacterial physiology
455. Pathogenic bacteriology
456. Pathogenic bacteriology
457. Mycology
458. Parasitology
459. Pathogenic bacteriology
460. Microbial genetics
461. Pathogenic bacteriology
462. Pathogenic bacteriology
463. Bacterial physiology
464. Cellular immunology
465. Cellular immunology
466. Pathogenic bacteriology
467. Pathogenic bacteriology
468. Pathogenic bacteriology
469. Pathogenic bacteriology
470. Pathogenic bacteriology
471. Immunology
472. Pathogenic bacteriology

473. Microbial physiology
474. Virology
475. Microbial genetics
476. Pathogenic bacteriology
477. Immunology
478. Immunology
479. Bacterial physiology
480. Serology
481. Bacterial physiology
482. Virology
483. Virology
484. Microbial physiology
485. Pathogenic bacteriology
486. Pathogenic bacteriology
487. Virology
488. Pathogenic bacteriology
489. Pathogenic bacteriology
490. Pathogenic bacteriology
491. Pathogenic bacteriology
492. Virology
493. Pathogenic bacteriology
494. Pathogenic bacteriology
495. Pathogenic bacteriology
496. Mycology
497. Virology
498. Mycology
499. Virology
500. Pathogenic bacteriology
501. Virology
502. Microbial genetics
503. Virology
504. Virology
505. Pathogenic bacteriology
506. Pathogenic bacteriology

507. Virology
508. Cellular immunology
509. Virology
510. Allergy
511. Microbial genetics
512. Pathogenic bacteriology
513. Pathogenic bacteriology
514. Virology
515. Cellular immunology
516. Virology
517. Antigen–antibody reaction
518. Pathogenic bacteriology
519. Antibody structure
520. Antibodies
521. Virology
522. Virology
523. Virology
524. Antigen–anitbody reactions
525. Parasitology
526. Mycology
527. Pathogenic bacteriology
528. Mycology
529. Parasitology
530. Parasitology
531. Antibody structure
532. Antibody structure
533. Antigens
534. Antigens
535. Microbial physiology
536. Microbial physiology
537. Microbial genetics
538. Microbial genetics
539. Autoimmunity
540. Autoimmunity
541. Virology
542. Virology
543. Virology
544. Autoimmunity
545. Immunodeficiency
546. Host defense

# CHAPTER 5

# Pathology
## Questions

*Thomas K. Barton, MD and Martin Gwent Lewis, MBBS, MD, FRCP*

**DIRECTIONS (Questions 547 through 585): Each of the numbered items or incomplete statements in this section is followed by answers or by completions of the statement. Select the ONE lettered answer or completion that is BEST in each case.**

547. Which of the following chronic pulmonary conditions is associated with $\alpha_1$-antitrypsin deficiency?

   (A)  Goodpasture's syndrome
   (B)  panlobular emphysema
   (C)  bronchiectasis
   (D)  Hamman–Rich syndrome
   (E)  bronchitis

548. A middle-aged woman suffers from weakness of her ocular and facial muscles, which worsens with repeated use. She has antibodies to acetylcholine receptors in her serum. The likely diagnosis is

   (A)  lymphangioma
   (B)  Parkinson's disease
   (C)  osteoid osteoma
   (D)  myasthenia gravis
   (E)  polymyositis

549. A chronic demyelinating neurologic disorder of young adults that is characterized by plaques within the central nervous system and cerebrospinal fluid oligoclonal immunoglobulins is

   (A)  multiple sclerosis
   (B)  Huntington disease
   (C)  pemphigus vulgaris

   (D)  amyotrophic lateral sclerosis
   (E)  spinocerebellar degeneration

550. The photomicrograph (Fig. 5.1) depicts a diseased fallopian tube. What is the most likely diagnosis?

   (A)  chronic salpingitis
   (B)  endometriosis
   (C)  endosalpingiosis
   (D)  ectopic tubal pregnancy
   (E)  serous papillary carcinoma

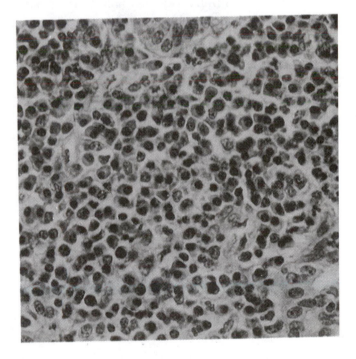

**Figure 5.1**

551. Extreme generalized edema with marked expansion of the extracellular fluid space within the subcutaneous tissues, visceral organs, and body cavities is called

(A) anasarca
(B) apoptosis
(C) angioedema
(D) hemochromatosis
(E) hyperthecosis

552. A patient who is allergic to penicillin is inadvertently given an injection of penicillin and immediately develops anaphylactic shock. This is an example of

(A) type I hypersensitivity
(B) type II hypersensitivity
(C) type III hypersensitivity
(D) type IV hypersensitivity
(E) type V hypersensitivity

553. An aspirate of joint fluid from a painful and inflamed metatarsophalangeal joint of the great toe reveals abundant needle-shaped, negatively birefringent crystals within neutrophils. The most likely diagnosis is

(A) acute bacterial pyarthrosis
(B) ochronosis
(C) gout
(D) calcium pyrophosphate deposition disease
(E) ganglion cyst

554. Metaplasia is defined as

(A) an increase in the size of cells
(B) an increase in the number of cells
(C) irregular, atypical proliferative changes in epithelial or mesenchymal cells
(D) replacement of one type of adult cell by another type of adult cell
(E) loss of cell substance producing shrinkage of cell size

555. Niacin deficiency is associated with

(A) night blindness
(B) a bleeding diathesis
(C) altered formation of connective tissues
(D) neuromuscular and cardiac problems and edema
(E) dermatitis, diarrhea, and dementia

556. An adult with an untreated growth hormone-secreting microadenoma of the pituitary gland is likely to develop

(A) dwarfism
(B) Addison's disease
(C) hyperparathyroidism
(D) Cushing's disease
(E) acromegaly

557. A deficiency state caused by a lack of dietary vitamin C is termed

(A) beriberi
(B) scurvy
(C) pernicious anemia
(D) rickets
(E) marasmus

558. An individual with chronic hepatitis C viral infection has a chemistry profile performed. Which serum analyte is most likely to be decreased?

(A) gamma globulin
(B) alanine aminotransferase
(C) albumin
(D) lactate dehydrogenase
(E) asparate aminotransferase

559. A young adult has been complaining of intermittent diarrhea, fever, and abdominal pain for several months. A radiograph of the small bowel reveals several separate areas of luminal narrowing. A photomicrograph of this patient's ileal biopsy is displayed in Figure 5.2. What is the diagnosis?

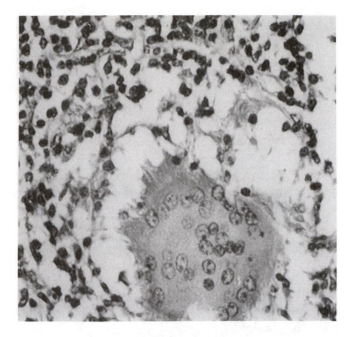

**Figure 5.2**

(A) abetalipoproteinemia

(B) Crohn's disease

(C) ulcerative colitis

(D) carcinoid tumor

(E) adenocarcinoma

560. Patients with Sjögren's syndrome show an increased risk for the development of

(A) pleomorphic adenoma

(B) melanoma

(C) lymphoma

(D) esophageal carcinoma

(E) leukemia

561. The human embryo or fetus is most susceptible to malformation caused by environmental factors during

(A) days 1 to 15

(B) days 15 to 60

(C) the second trimester

(D) the third trimester

(E) delivery

562. The Philadelphia chromosome is most often associated with which disease?

(A) follicular lymphoma

(B) Burkitt's lymphoma

(C) Down syndrome

(D) acute lymphoblastic leukemia

(E) chronic myelogenous leukemia

563. DiGeorge's syndrome may be defined as

(A) a deficiency of T lymphocytes due to thymic hypoplasia

(B) a deficiency of B lymphocytes due to toxins

(C) an abnormal proliferation of atypical monocytes

(D) a deficiency of dietary fatty acids

(E) multiple mucosal neurofibromatous tumors

564. Diverticulosis occurs most frequently in the

(A) cecum

(B) ascending colon

(C) transverse colon

(D) descending colon

(E) sigmoid colon

565. Which of the following disease states characteristically produces the nephrotic syndrome?

(A) interstitial nephritis

(B) membranous glomerulonephritis

(C) unilateral hydronephrosis

(D) acute crescentic glomerulonephritis

(E) polycystic disease of the kidneys

566. An elevation of the MB isoenzyme of creatine phosphokinase is usually seen with

(A) cadmium poisoning

(B) protein C deficiency

(C) aspergillosis

(D) acute myocardial infarction

(E) prostatic nodular hyperplasia

**567.** The most common cause of a pulmonary abscess is

(A) irritant gases
(B) alveolar proteinosis
(C) aspiration
(D) vasculitis
(E) cigarette smoking

**568.** What is the most likely diagnosis for the lesion pictured in the photograph in Figure 5.3?

(A) peptic ulceration
(B) adenocarcinoma
(C) adenomatous polyp
(D) Brunner gland adenoma
(E) leiomyoma

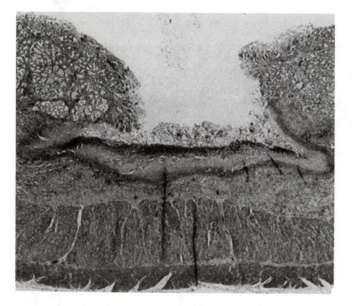

**Figure 5.3**

**569.** Auer rods are usually evident in the cytoplasm of

(A) silicotic pneumocytes
(B) neurons infected with rabies virus
(C) diabetic islet cells
(D) transformed urothelial cells
(E) myeloblasts

**570.** Which of the following tumors occurs mainly during adulthood?

(A) neuroblastoma
(B) retinoblastoma
(C) medulloblastoma
(D) nephroblastoma
(E) meningioma

**571.** A young black female has noticed a slowly growing firm nodule near the site of a recent earpiercing. Excision and microscopic examination of the nodule reveals it to be composed of densely collagenized fibrous tissue. The most probable diagnosis is

(A) teratoma
(B) hamartoma
(C) keloid
(D) dermoid cyst
(E) Brenner tumor

**572.** Which of the following neoplasms is benign?

(A) adenocarcinoma
(B) cystadenoma
(C) fibrosarcoma
(D) lymphocytic leukemia
(E) melanoma

**573.** The development of which of the following tumors is associated with the ingestion of aflatoxin?

(A) hepatocellular carcinoma
(B) pulmonary sarcomas
(C) chordomas of the lower spine
(D) uterine leiomyomas
(E) sebaceous carcinoma of the eyelid

**574.** An elderly male with congestive heart failure undergoes a thoracentesis, which yields about 200 mL of straw-colored watery fluid. A laboratory study of the fluid reveals:

| | |
|---|---|
| Specific gravity | 1.010 |
| Total protein | 0.4 g/dL |
| Cell count | Very rare mesothelial cell present |
| Fat stain | Negative |

These pleural fluid findings are indicative of a(n)

(A) exudate

(B) empyema

(C) hemothorax

(D) transudate

(E) chylothorax

575. The characteristic inflammatory cell seen in the tissues in response to infection by *Salmonella typhi* is the

(A) polymorphonuclear leukocyte

(B) eosinophil leukocyte

(C) monocyte

(D) multinucleate giant cell

(E) plasma cell

576. What is the term used to describe an abnormal toxic yellow pigmentation found in the brains of neonates exposed to excessive unconjugated hyperbilirubinemia?

(A) kernicterus

(B) mucoviscidosis

(C) zellballen

(D) cholestasis

(E) sequestrum

577. A microscopic examination of a 20-hour-old myocardial infarct would be expected to demonstrate

(A) fibrosis and collagen deposition

(B) coagulative necrosis without many neutrophils

(C) abundant neutrophils and monocytes

(D) monocytes and neovascularization

(E) plasma cells and caseous necrosis

578. Which of the following statements is true regarding breast cancer?

(A) incidence is higher in Japan than in the United States

(B) there is a decreased incidence with early menarche or late menopause

(C) there is a decreased incidence with a high-fat diet

(D) there is a decreased incidence with atypical ductal or lobular hyperplasia

(E) there is an increased incidence with a family history of breast cancer

579. A rectal biopsy is the usual approach to the morphologic documentation of Hirschsprung's disease. Which of the following findings is considered diagnostic of Hirschsprung's disease on histologic examination of the rectal biopsy specimen?

(A) hypertrophy of the muscle coat of the wall of the rectum

(B) atrophy of the mucosal lining of the wall of the rectum

(C) absence of the nerve fibers that innervate the wall of the rectum

(D) absence of parasympathetic ganglion cells in the submucosal and myenteric plexus

(E) presence of multiple small polyps along the mucosal surface of the rectal wall

580. The most common cause of neonatal cholestasis is

(A) intrahepatic biliary atresia

(B) extrahepatic biliary atresia (EBA)

(C) choledochal cyst

(D) primary biliary cirrhosis

(E) Budd–Chiari syndrome

581. With the TNM cancer staging system, the T component is defined as

(A) the time between diagnosis and definitive treatment

(B) the size or extent of the primary tumor

(C) the type of cells identified

(D) the treatment plan

(E) the presence of nodal metastases

582. Red hepatization is a pathologic term characterizing

    (A) fibroblast proliferation
    (B) WBCs, RBCs, and fibrin filling the alveolar spaces
    (C) hyaline membrane formation
    (D) congestion of the hepatic sinusoids
    (E) hemorrhage and abscess formation

583. Calcium salt deposition is most likely to occur in association with

    (A) fat necrosis
    (B) hyaline change
    (C) lipofuscin pigmentation
    (D) liquefaction necrosis
    (E) granulation tissue

584. A genetic autosomal recessive disorder of copper metabolism characterized by hepatolenticular degeneration is

    (A) Wilson's disease
    (B) Reye's syndrome
    (C) primary sclerosing cholangitis
    (D) congenital hepatic fibrosis
    (E) peliosis hepatis

585. The vegetation characteristically seen in acute rheumatic carditis most commonly occurs in

    (A) the aortic sinuses of Valsalva
    (B) the line of closure (free margins) of mitral valve
    (C) the insertion of the chordae tendinae
    (D) the mitral valve annulus
    (E) just lateral to the coronary artery ostia

**DIRECTIONS (Questions 586 through 610): Each of the numbered items or incomplete statements in this section is negatively phrased, as indicated by a capitalized word such as NOT, LEAST, or EXCEPT. Select the ONE lettered answer or completion that is BEST in each case.**

586. Edema is caused by all of the following mechanisms EXCEPT

    (A) increased vascular permeability
    (B) obstruction to lymphatic flow

    (C) sodium retention
    (D) increased plasma proteins
    (E) increased capillary blood pressure

587. All of the following statements are true about radiation-induced carcinogenesis EXCEPT

    (A) the amount of damage is related to the dose of radiation
    (B) RNA is the major cell target for radiation injury
    (C) cells can repair radiation-induced cell damage
    (D) past history of therapeutic radiation has been implicated in carcinogenesis
    (E) occupational exposure to radiation is a well-documented cause of cancer

588. The teratogenic effect of high-dose radiation to the fetus in utero may produce all of the following abnormalities EXCEPT

    (A) microcephaly
    (B) mental retardation
    (C) skeletal malformation
    (D) mutation in fetal germ cells
    (E) masculinization of the female fetus

589. All of the following statements concerning skin melanocytes and the response of skin melanocytes to ultraviolet (UV) light are true EXCEPT

    (A) in whites, an increase in the size and functional activity of melanocytes can be seen after a single exposure to UV light
    (B) in whites, repeated UV light exposure produces an increase in the concentration of melanocytes
    (C) melanocytes may undergo mitosis when exposed repeatedly to UV light
    (D) blacks have a higher concentration of melanocytes for any given area of skin than do whites
    (E) the skin of blacks has larger melanocytes with more dendritic processes than does the skin of whites

590. All of the following statements concerning Duchenne muscular dystrophy are true EXCEPT

(A) pseudohypertrophy of the calf is the result of regeneration of the muscle
(B) it is the most common type of muscular dystrophy
(C) it occurs as symmetrical involvement of the pelvic girdle muscles
(D) Becker's muscular dystrophy is a more benign form of the disease
(E) elevated serum creatine phosphokinase (CPK) levels may be helpful in detecting the carrier state

591. True statements about infectious sialoadenitis include all of the following EXCEPT

(A) it may be associated with an obstruction of the duct
(B) most bacterial infections are unilateral
(C) minor salivary glands are more frequently involved than major glands
(D) mumps is the most common viral etiology
(E) suppurative inflammation may accompany bacterial infections

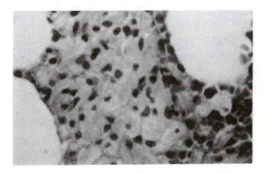

Figure 5.4

592. The depicted bone marrow biopsy (Fig. 5.4) was obtained from an infant with mental retardation and hepatosplenomegaly. What is NOT true about this disorder?

(A) glucocerebrosidase activity is lacking
(B) the prevalence is high in Ashkenazi Jews
(C) the lysosomes are full of glucocerebroside

(D) the enzymatic defect usually self corrects during adulthood
(E) similar abnormal cells can be found in the liver and spleen

593. True statements about human immunodeficiency virus infection include all of the following EXCEPT

(A) there is an increased incidence in homosexual males
(B) a major target for cytopathic effects is T8 suppressor lymphocytes
(C) there is a decreased incidence with celibacy
(D) the infective agent is a retrovirus
(E) there is an increased prevalence in Central Africa

594. Which of the following statements concerning carcinoma of the uterine cervix is NOT true?

(A) adenocarcinomas are the most frequent cell type
(B) the five-year survival of adequately treated stage I disease is about 90%
(C) there is often a recognizable preinvasive stage
(D) prior infection with human papillomavirus may predispose to subsequent carcinomatous development
(E) multiple sexual partners is a risk factor

595. Which of the following statements concerning *Schistosoma mansoni* infestation is FALSE?

(A) the eggs are usually shed in the feces
(B) liver fibrosis may be a long-term complication
(C) one of the phases in the life cycle includes the fresh water snail
(D) the initial phase of infection in humans is from water contact with the skin
(E) it is a frequent cause of hematuria

596. All of the following statements are true concerning polyarteritis nodosa EXCEPT

(A) the disease is a systemic vasculitity

(B) medium- and small-sized arteries are preferentially affected

(C) inflammation and fibrinoid necrosis of arterial walls are the usual histologic findings in the acute phase

(D) parenchymal infarcts may result from obliteration of arterial lumens

(E) the antineutrophil cytoplasm antibody (ANCA) test is usually negative

597. Malignant neoplasms differ from benign neoplasms by showing all of the following features EXCEPT

(A) metastases to distant viscera

(B) encapsulation

(C) blood vessel invasion

(D) rapid, erratic growth

(E) disorganized cell architecture

598. All of the following are frequently seen with chronic alcoholism EXCEPT

(A) cirrhosis

(B) pancreatitis

(C) pyelonephritis

(D) steatosis

(E) toxic hepatitis

599. All of the following disorders are inherited mucopolysaccharidoses EXCEPT

(A) Hurler's syndrome

(B) Morquio's syndrome

(C) Hunter's syndrome

(D) Sanfilippo's syndrome

(E) McArdle's disease

600. An elderly male expires with a clinical diagnosis of adult respiratory distress syndrome. At autopsy a pathologic diagnosis of diffuse alveolar damage is rendered. All of the following would support these diagnoses EXCEPT

(A) heavy, wet, meaty lungs on gross examination

(B) a clinical history of relative unresponsiveness to oxygen therapy

(C) intra-alveolar hyaline membrane formation

(D) sloughing and loss of type I pneumocytes

(E) saddle-type embolus in the main pulmonary artery

601. Which is LEAST likely to produce an intravascular thrombus?

(A) damage to endothelium

(B) hypercoagulable states

(C) warfarin therapy

(D) stasis of blood

(E) hyperviscosity syndromes

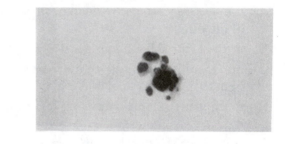

Figure 5.5

602. A young adult has self-limited episodes of cutaneous vesicle formation around the lips. A diagnostic Tzanck smear of vesicle fluid is displayed in Figure 5.5. Which of the following is NOT correct regarding this disease?

(A) both epidermal and neuronal cells are infected

(B) latency typifies this infection in immunocompetent individuals

(C) the etiologic agent is an RNA virus

(D) encephalitis is rarely a complication of this infection

(E) treatment with acyclovir may reduce the frequency and severity of recurrences

603. Which of the following is NOT an example of a paraneoplastic syndrome?

(A) hypercalcemia

(B) cerebral metastases

(C) acanthosis nigricans

(D) syndrome of inappropriate antidiuretic hormone secretion

(E) hypoglycemia

604. All of the following are known adverse factors that increase the risk of coronary artery disease EXCEPT

(A) obesity and physiologic inactivity

(B) high levels of high-density lipoprotein (HDL) cholesterol

(C) diabetes mellitus

(D) hypertension

(E) cigarette smoking

605. Passive splenic congestion could display all of the following features EXCEPT

(A) sinusoids filled with erythrocytes

(B) increase in splenic weight

(C) hemosiderin deposition

(D) cyanotic discoloration

(E) shrunken capsule

606. Irreversible morphologic changes associated with cell death include all of the following EXCEPT

(A) karyorrhexis

(B) hydropic swelling

(C) pyknosis

(D) apoptosis

(E) rupture of the nuclear membrane

607. Colon carcinoma is LEAST likely to occur in individuals with

(A) diets that are high in fiber and cruciferous vegetables

(B) Crohn's colitis

(C) diets that are high in animal fats

(D) ulcerative colitis

(E) hereditary polyposis

608. All of the following statements characterize chronic lymphocytic leukemia (CLL) EXCEPT

(A) it is a malignancy of elderly persons

(B) patients may be asymptomatic at diagnosis

(C) patients may exhibit hepato-splenomegaly

(D) hypergammaglobulinemia is usually present

(E) the peripheral blood smear alone may be diagnostic

609. Which of the following is NOT a chronic myeloproliferative syndrome?

(A) chronic myelogenous leukemia

(B) polycythemia vera

(C) hairy cell leukemia

(D) idiopathic thrombocythemia

(E) agnogenic myeloid metaplasia

610. Tetralogy of Fallot includes all of the following EXCEPT

(A) atretic right ventricle

(B) pulmonary stenosis

(C) ventricular septal defect

(D) dextroposition of the aorta

(E) right ventricular hypertrophy

DIRECTIONS (Questions 611 through 673): Each set of matching questions in this section consists of a list of lettered options followed by several numbered items. For each numbered item, select the ONE lettered option that is most closely associated with it. Each lettered heading may be selected once, more than once, or not at all.

Questions 611 through 613

For each description below, choose the compound with which it is usually associated.

(A) histamine

(B) bradykinin

(C) $\overline{C567}$

(D) prostaglandin E

(E) neutral proteases

611. Vasodilatory product of Hageman factor with no chemotactic action

612. Important in early increases in vascular permeability

**613.** Lysosomal product important in extracellular degradation

**Questions 614 through 616**

(A) synaptophysin
(B) chromogranin
(C) cytokeratin
(D) desmin
(E) glial fibrillary acid protein

**614.** Intermediate filament most likely to be found in malignant epithelial tumors

**615.** Intermediate filament most likely to be found in smooth muscle tumors

**616.** Intermediate filament most likely to be found in glial cell tumors

**Questions 617 through 619**

(A) tularemia
(B) lymphogranuloma venereum
(C) pertussis
(D) plague
(E) Rocky Mountain spotted fever

**617.** *Rickettsia rickettsi*

**618.** *Chlamydia trachomatis*

**619.** *Yersinia pestis*

**Questions 620 through 622**

(A) pseudomembraneous colitis
(B) gastic ulceration
(C) bacillary dysentery
(D) esophageal diverticulum
(E) anorectal hemorrhoids

**620.** *Helicobacter pylori*

**621.** *Clostridium difficile*

**622.** *Shigella* species

**Questions 623 through 625**

(A) Addison's disease
(B) Hashimoto's disease
(C) Cushing's syndrome
(D) de Quervain's thyroiditis
(E) Cori's disease

**623.** Autoimmune thyroid disorder

**624.** Chronic adrenocortical insufficiency

**625.** Hereditary disorder of glycogen metabolism

**Questions 626 through 628**

(A) squamous cell carcinoma of the uterine cervix
(B) adenocarcinoma of the endometrium
(C) malignant teratoma of the ovary
(D) sarcomas of the fallopian tube
(E) clear cell carcinoma and adenosis of the vagina

**626.** In utero exposure to diethylstilbestrol

**627.** Tumor of prepubertal adolescents and young adults containing immature neuroepithelium

**628.** Highest incidence associated with nulliparity, diabetes, and obesity

**Questions 629 through 631**

(A) ventricular septal defect
(B) tricuspid atresia
(C) atrial septal defect
(D) patent ductus arteriosus
(E) truncus arteriosus

**629.** Failure to close intrauterine vascular channel between pulmonary artery and aorta

**630.** Most common congenital heart anomaly

**631.** Developmental failure of aorta and pulmonary artery to separate

## Questions 632 through 634

  (A)  beryllium granulomatosis

  (B)  stannosis

  (C)  byssinosis

  (D)  silicosis

  (E)  asbestosis

**632.**  Asthma-like disorder caused by inhaled cotton fibers

**633.**  Increased risk of malignant mesothelioma

**634.**  Associated with tin oxide inhalation

## Questions 635 through 637

  (A)  Goodpasture's syndrome

  (B)  Chagas' disease

  (C)  Dubin–Johnson syndrome

  (D)  Peutz–Jeghers syndrome

  (E)  Kawasaki's disease

**635.**  Myocarditis caused by protozoan organism

**636.**  Familial disease with intermittent jaundice and black pigmentation of the liver

**637.**  Diffuse pulmonary hemorrhages and rapidly progressive glomerulonephritis

## Questions 638 through 640

  (A)  autosomal dominant inheritance

  (B)  autosomal recessive inheritance

  (C)  X-linked recessive inheritance

  (D)  X-linked dominant inheritance

  (E)  non-hereditary disorder

**638.**  Hemophilia A

**639.**  Achondroplasia

**640.**  Alkaptonuria (ochronosis)

## Questions 641 through 643

  (A)  *Necator americanus*

  (B)  *Ascaris lumbricoides*

  (C)  *Entamoeba histolytica*

  (D)  *Plasmodium falciparum*

  (E)  *Entamoeba coli*

**641.**  Etiologic agent of amebic dysentery

**642.**  Etiologic agent of malaria

**643.**  Etiologic agent of hookworm disease

## Questions 644 through 646

  (A)  Sipple syndrome

  (B)  Stein–Leventhal syndrome

  (C)  Wermer syndrome

  (D)  Zollinger–Ellison syndrome

  (E)  MEN I

**644.**  Peptic ulcer disease, gastric hypersecretion, and ectopic gastin production

**645.**  Medullary thyroid carcinoma, parathyroid neoplasms, and pheochromocytoma

**646.**  Polycystic ovaries, obesity, oligomenorrhea, and hirsutism

## Questions 647 through 649

  (A)  pemphigus

  (B)  mycosis fungoides

  (C)  actinic keratosis

  (D)  ichthyoses

  (E)  dermatitis herpetiformis

**647.**  Cutaneous T-cell lymphoma

**648.**  Immunologically mediated dysadhesion between keratinocytes

**649.**  Hereditary disorder with marked hypertrophy of stratum corneum

**Questions 650 through 652**

(A) thalassemia

(B) myelophthisic anemia

(C) sideroblastic anemia

(D) hereditary elliptocytosis

(E) pernicious anemia

650. Pancytopenia due to cobalamin deficiency

651. Usually seen with carcinomatous metastases to the bone

652. Hereditary disease of discordant globin chain synthesis

**Questions 653 through 655**

(A) acetaminophen overdose

(B) methyl alcohol poisoning

(C) carbon monoxide poisoning

(D) chronic lead posioning

(E) cocaine overdose

653. Toxic metabolite causes massive hepatic necrosis

654. Systemic asphyxiant

655. Toxic metabolites formaldehyde and formic acid can cause blindness and neuronal damage

**Questions 656 through 658**

(A) hypertrophy

(B) hyperplasia

(C) atrophy

(D) metaplasia

(E) dysplasia

656. The size of individual cells is increased but the number of cells present remains unchanged

657. Shrinkage in cell size by loss of substance

658. Atypical cellular development that may be precancerous

**Questions 659 through 664**

(A) Down syndrome

(B) Edwards' syndrome

(C) Patau's syndrome

(D) cat-cry syndrome

(E) Klinefelter's syndrome

(F) Turner's syndrome

(G) double Y males

(H) normal male karyotype

(I) normal female karyotype

(J) multi-X female

659. On physical examination, a 17-year-old male is noted to have only minimal secondary sexual development, gynecomastia, and an eunuchoid, tall habitus. His chromosome analysis is reported as 47,XXY

660. An amniocentesis is performed on a 16-week fetus because of advanced maternal age. The chromosome analysis is reported as 46,XX

661. A mentally retarded female adolescent with a history of congenital cardiac disease has a chromosome analysis reported as 47,XX,+21

662. An autopsy is done on a 53-year-old woman who was killed in an accident. She had been in apparent good health. The chromosome analysis is reported as 47,XXX

663. A 17-year-old short-statured girl is found to have streak gonads. Her karyotype is reported as 45,X

664. An infant dies shortly after birth. At autopsy the occiput is prominent, there are multiple renal and intestinal defects, and there is micrognathia. A chromosome analysis is reported as 47,XX,+18

## Questions 665 through 668

(A) sarcoidosis

(B) tuberculosis

(C) histoplasmosis

(D) coccidiomycosis

(E) amyloidosis

(F) bacterial pneumonia

(G) mesothelioma

(H) carcinoma

(I) fibrosing alveolitis

(J) silicosis

665. A right lower lobectomy specimen contains a solitary 1.2 cm diameter solid nodule. The center of the nodule is fibrous. The periphery has granulomatous inflammation. With special stains, multiple 2 to 5 μm budding yeasts are evident within the nodule. Acid-fast stains are negative

666. A left upper lobectomy specimen is received containing a 4.6 cm nodule with central cystic degeneration. Microscopically, the nodule is composed of anaplastic squamous cells. Similar abnormal cells are seen in a concomitant biopsy of a hilar lymph node

667. After a long history of multiple myeloma, a 67-year-old male is noted to have abundant acellular eosinophilic deposits around the pulmonary microvasculature at autopsy. A congo red special stain demonstrates apple green birefringence

668. A large, pleural-based lesion is found on chest x-ray of an asbestos worker. Electron microscopy of the biopsy shows abundant long microvilli

## Questions 669 through 673

(A) renal cell carcinoma

(B) diabetic kidney

(C) renal papillary necrosis

(D) glomerulonephritis

(E) endometriosis

(F) transitional cell carcinoma

(G) seminoma

(H) teratoma

(I) prostatic carcinoma

(J) condyloma acuminatum

669. A sexually active 24-year-old male has recently developed multiple 0.2 to 0.6 cm normally pigmented papillary tumors at his penile meatus. Histologic examination reveals perinuclear vacuoles, papillomatosis, and positive immunoperoxidase stains for human papilloma virus

670. The left kidney is surgically removed and found to contain a 6.3 cm diameter solitary solid nodule with a variegated red, white, and yellow hue. The nodule grows into the renal vein. Histologically, the nodule is composed of anaplastic cells with clear cytoplasm and focal abortive gland formation

671. A 34-year-old female is found to have intermittent hematuria. A bladder biopsy demonstrates a focus of benign endometrial glands and stroma with associated hemorrhage

672. A 77-year-old male has bone pain and a markedly elevated prostatic specific antigen. A prostate biopsy demonstrates anaplastic glands in a fibrous stroma and in perineural spaces

673. A 7-year-old female suddenly experiences hematuria and hypertension two weeks after a streptococcal throat infection

# Pathology
## Answers and Explanations

**547.** **(B)** Panlobular emphysema is a diffuse loss of alveolar septa throughout the lung, extending from the hilum to the periphery. In 1963, an association was shown between patients with a hereditary deficiency of $\alpha_1$-antitrypsin and patients with severe panlobular emphysema. These patients have bilateral emphysema, primarily basilar, which occurs in both sexes and at an earlier age than do other forms of chronic obstructive pulmonary diseases. This disease has an autosomal recessive inheritance pattern. Heterozygous individuals with the $\alpha_1$-antitrypsin deficiency gene also may show an increased risk of developing emphysematous changes in their lungs, especially with environmental and smoking insults. Homozygous patients with $\alpha_1$-antitrypsin deficiency accounts for fewer than 10% of all patients with emphysema. (*Cotran, Kumar, and Robbins, pp 683–688*)

**548.** **(D)** Myasthenia gravis in an autoimmune disease caused by the production of antibodies against acetylcholine receptors. The ocular and facial muscles are usually weakened. The weakness worsens with repeated contractions of the muscles. Treatment with anticholinesterase agents can improve the weakness and fatigability by increasing the quantity of acetylcholine available at the motor endplate. (*Chandrasoma and Taylor, pp 944– 945*)

**549.** **(A)** Multiple sclerosis is a chronic demyelinating neurologic disease of young adults. Plaque formation within the brain and spinal cord is typical of the disorder. Oligoclonal immunoglobulins are frequently found in the cerebrospinal fluid. (*Rubin and Farber, pp 1423– 1425*)

**550.** **(A)** The photomicrograph depicts a stromal infiltrate of plasma cells and a few mature lymphocytes, which constitute the diagnostic criteria for chronic salpingitis. Other features that may occur with chronic salpingitis include fibrosis, luminal adhesions, and hydrosalpinx formation. (*Chandrasoma and Taylor, p 767*)

**551.** **(A)** Anasarca is the pathologic term used to describe an extensive systemic transudative fluid accumulation that affects the subcutaneous tissues, visceral organs, and body cavities. A marked reduction in the serum oncotic pressure is the usual etiology. Clinically, anasarca is seen with cirrhosis and the nephrotic syndrome. (*Rubin and Farber, p 275*)

**552.** **(A)** Type I hypersensitivity, or anaphylaxis, is an IgE-mediated immediate reaction to a previously sensitizing antigen. Mast cells and basophils orchestrate this process through the release of preformed substances such as histamine, heparin, neutrophil chemotactic factor, and eosinophil chemotactic factor. (*Rubin and Farber, pp 105–107*)

**553.** **(C)** Gout is a disease caused by elevated uric acid levels. It may be idiopathic or secondary to enzyme defects causing overproduction of uric acid. Patients with secondary gout may also have hyperuricemia due to increased production from cell breakdown or decreased excretion. The uric acid tends to build up in joint fluids and precipitate out.

Initially, affected patients suffer transient attacks of acute arthritis because of an acute inflammatory reaction to the precipitated urate crystals. One or two joints are typically affected, most commonly the great toe and ankle joints. The precipitated urate crystals are taken up by macrophages and neutrophils in phagosomes. These crystals then damage the lysosomal membranes, causing release of the inflammatory mediators, enzymes, and cell debris, which stimulate the arthritis. The tophus is the characteristic lesion of gout and is caused by the inflammatory reaction. It is a urate deposit composed of chronic inflammatory cells, macrophages, and foreign body giant cells. These tophi are found in the external ear, around the knee joints, in connective tissue, and in the medullary pyramids of the kidney. Treatment is directed toward lowering the concentration of serum uric acid and inhibiting its synthesis. *(Cotran, Kumar, and Robbins, pp 1255–1258)*

554. **(D)** A number of cell alterations can be produced or identified as a response to a variety of changes or stresses in the cell's environment. Hypertrophy refers to an increase in the size of cells—for example, myocardial fiber hypertrophy in response to increased demands in the setting of hypertension. Hyperplasia refers to an increase in the number of cells—for example, the increase in breast glandular epithelium in females at the time of puberty. Dysplasia refers to irregular, atypical proliferation changes of epithelial or mesenchymal cells in response to chronic inflammation or irritations—as is often seen, for example, in the uterine cervix. Atrophy is the loss of cell substance, producing a shrinkage in cell size—striated muscle response to disuse is an example. Metaplasia refers to the replacement of one type of adult cell, epithelial or mesenchymal, by another type of adult cell. The replacement of the normal type of adult ciliated columnar epithelium of the bronchial mucosa by the adult type of squamous epithelium in response to chronic irritation due to cigarette smoking is such an example. *(Chandrasoma and Taylor, pp 245–254)*

555. **(E)** A wide variety of afflictions may be caused by vitamin deficiencies. Niacin deficiency, also known as pellagra, is associated with dermatitis, diarrhea, and dementia. Night blindness (nyctalopia), with or without keratomalacia, and papular dermatitis suggest vitamin A deficiency. Vitamin K deficiency may manifest itself as a bleeding diathesis due to the role of vitamin K in the formation of prothrombin and clotting factors VII, IX, and X. Scurvy, or vitamin C deficiency, results in the altered formation of connective tissues, such as collagen, osteoid, dentin, and intercellular cement substance. Vitamin B deficiency, or beriberi, occurs in three ways that generally overlap to some extent in any given patient. Neuromuscular signs and symptoms alone are known as "dry beriberi" but in association with edema are known as "wet beriberi." Heart failure, generally high-output failure, accounts for so-called cardiac beriberi. *(Chandrasoma and Taylor, p 155)*

556. **(E)** Acromegaly commonly occurs in individuals with growth hormone-secreting adenomas of the pituitary gland. The clinical features of acromegaly include thick facial bones with prognathism, enlarged hands and feet, diabetes, arthritis, and hypertension. Transsphenoidal surgical removal of the tumor is the treatment of choice. *(Rubin and Farber, pp 1105–1106)*

557. **(B)** Vitamin C, ascorbic acid, is a water-soluble vitamin widely distributed in nature. Citrus fruits and fresh vegetables are particularly rich sources of the vitamin. Vitamin C plays a pivotal role in collagen synthesis through hydroxylation of proline and lysine residues. Hypovitaminosis C leads not only to a bleeding diathesis but also to poor wound healing, loose teeth, and in children, abnormalities of bone development. Subperiosteal hemorrhage and joint hemorrhage are particularly characteristic in scorbutic infants. *(Chandrasoma and Taylor, pp 153–154)*

558. **(C)** Hepatocytes synthesize a diverse population of proteins, including albumin, blood clotting factors, and enzymes (lactate dehy-

drogenase, aminotransferases, glutamate dehydrogenase, ornithine carbamyl transferase, and isocitrate dehydrogenase). In chronic liver disease, albumin production is reduced, leading to a drop in serum albumin levels. Elevated albumin levels in chronic liver disease would be truly exceptional. Increased serum levels of hepatic enzymes (alanine aminotransferase, aspartate aminotransferase, and lactate dehydrogenase) are seen with chronic liver disorders as damaged or dying hepatocytes release these enzymes into the serum. Gamma globulin levels are increased in all chronic disease states, particularly in chronic liver diseases. (*Chandrasoma and Taylor, pp 622–626*)

559. **(B)** The photomicrograph displays granulomatous inflammation—the microscopic morphologic hallmark of Crohn's disease. The inflammation is usually transmural. Distinct skip lesions and fissure formation are frequently evident. The accompanying history and radiographic findings are typical of patients with Crohn's disease. (*Cotran, Kumar, and Robbins, pp 800–804*)

560. **(C)** The constellation of dry eyes (keratoconjunctivitis sicca or xerophthalmia), dry mouth (xerostomia), and chronic arthritis constitutes the clinicopathologic entity known as Sjögren's syndrome. In the absence of arthritis, the symptoms are referred to as the sicca syndrome. Sjögren's syndrome primarily affects middle-aged women, either alone or in combination with other connective tissue disorders. About 50% of patients have rheumatoid arthritis. Large numbers of autoantibodies are seen in the serum of patients with Sjögren's syndrome. Symptoms are, in part, the result of the infiltration of salivary and lacrimal glands by lymphocytes, both B- and T-cell types. Over time, atrophy, fibrosis, hyalinization, and fatty change ensue. The lymphoid infiltrate may be heavy with the formation of lymphoid follicles with germinal centers and may mimic lymphoma. Of interest, however, is the finding that patients with Sjögren's syndrome show an increased tendency to develop lymphoma and so-called pseudolymphoma. Involvement of the

respiratory tract, stomach, and kidneys (tubulointerstitial nephritis) also may occur. (*Chandrasoma and Taylor, p 468*)

561. **(B)** The human embryo is most susceptible to malformations caused by environmental factors during days 15 to 60 of gestation. This time period is referred to as the "organogenetic period." Although environmental factors acting during the first 2 weeks (days 1 to 15) after fertilization may interfere with implantation or the development of the early embryo, rarely do they produce congenital malformations. Instead, these very early disturbances usually result in death or abortion of the blastocyst or early embryo. Exposure to teratogenic agents during the described critical period (days 15 to 60) may lead to death or abortion of the same embryo but usually produces major malformation. (*Cotran, Kumar, and Robbins, pp 437–442*)

562. **(E)** Ninety percent of individuals with chronic myelogenous leukemia have an acquired Philadelphia chromosome abnormality. The Philadelphia chromosome usually consists of a translocation of a portion of the long arm of chromosome 22 to chromosome 9. The oncogene, c-abelson (c-abl), is present at the breakpoint of chromosome 9 and is usually reciprocally translocated to chromosome 22. (*Chandrasoma and Taylor, pp 290, 403– 404*)

563. **(A)** DiGeorge's syndrome is a deficiency of T lymphocytes due to thymic hypoplasia. Developmental failure of the third and fourth pharyngeal pouches is responsible for total or partial thymic, parathyroid, thyroid, and ultimobranchial pouch abnormalities. These structural anomalies lead to the absence of the cell-mediated T lymphocyte immune response, tetany, and congenital heart and great vessel abnormalities. B lymphocyte and plasma cell populations tend to be normal, as do serum immunoglobulin levels. The syndrome appears to be the result of an intrauterine insult to the fetus sometime before the eighth week of gestation. (*Cotran, Kumar, and Robbins, pp 265, 654–655*)

**564. (E)** Clinically detectable diverticulosis is seen in about 1 in 8 patients beyond 45 years of age. In autopsy series, this incidence estimate appears to be higher. Diverticulosis occurs in the sigmoid colon in 99% of affected individuals. Other segments of the large bowel become involved by diverticulosis as follows: descending colon, 30%; transverse colon, 4%; entire colon, 16%. The sigmoid is the region of the colon exclusively involved in about 41% of cases. In underdeveloped and tropical countries and Japan, diverticulosis is rare, apparently partially because of the high-residue diets in these regions of the world. The most consistent abnormality seen in diverticulosis is an abnormality of the muscle wall, leading to herniation of the colonic mucosa and submucosa through the muscularis and eventually into the pericolic adipose tissue. Fecal material may become trapped in the diverticulum, leading to ulceration, inflammation, and rarely perforation. (*Rubin and Farber, pp 674–675*)

**565. (B)** The nephrotic syndrome is defined as a syndrome in which there are proteinuria, edema, and to a variable degree, hypercholesterolemia. Whatever the cause, the common factor appears to be leakage of protein through the glomerular basement membranes, and the proteinuria is a characteristic finding. In interstitial nephritis, this is a chronic inflammatory change between the renal tubules, and only in a very late stage of disease does it alter glomerular function. There is no proteinuria. Unilateral hydronephrosis may cause complete disruption of the function of one kidney, but the other functions normally. In acute crescentic glomerulonephritis, which usually occurs after a streptococcal infection, there may be hematuria and a rise in blood pressure or even anuria, but proteinuria and edema, in the absence of these other findings so typical of the nephrotic syndrome, are not seen, particularly in the acute phase. Some forms of acute glomerulonephritis may progress to a chronic form that may have some elements of the nephrotic syndrome. Polycystic disease of the kidneys is associated with hypertension and some hematuria but not with the classic nephrotic syndrome. Membranous glomerulonephritis is the most typical form of glomerular disease associated with the nephrotic syndrome, particularly in adults, and can be recognized by both light microscopy and electron microscopy and immunofluorescence. (*Rubin and Farber, pp 812– 821*)

**566. (D)** The cytoplasm of cardiac muscle cells contains an abundance of the MB isoenzyme fraction of creatine phosphokinase. When these cells are damaged, such as by infarction, this isoenzyme fraction leaks out of the dying cells and may be detected in the blood. Physicians frequently order blood tests for the MB fraction to assist them in the diagnosis of an acute myocardial infarct. (*Cotran, Kumar, and Robbins, p 537*)

**567. (C)** Aspiration is the most common cause of pulmonary abscess formation. Alcoholics, epileptics, drug addicts, and neurologically compromised individuals are likely to aspirate. Cough, chest pain, fever, and the production of a large quantity of fetid sputum are the expected clinical signs of a pulmonary abscess. The complications of an abscess may include empyema, massive hemoptysis, and sepsis. (*Rubin and Farber, pp 574–576*)

**568. (A)** The photo depicts a chronic peptic ulcer. There is loss of mucosal continuity, an ulcer bed with necrotic tissue, and fibrosis of the submucosa. Peptic ulcers are associated with increased gastric acid secretion. Hemorrhage, perforation, and penetration may complicate these ulcers. (*Rubin and Farber, pp 637–643*)

**569. (E)** Auer rods are intensely azurophilic cytoplasmic inclusions frequently seen in leukemic myeloblasts. Most are rod-shaped and represent an aberrant form of granulocytic primary granules. Their presence serves as a useful aid for the morphologic and cytochemical diagnosis of acute myeloid leukemias. (*Rubin and Farber, pp 1058–1062*)

**570. (E)** Meningioma is a neoplasm that arises from the dura or its invaginations. It is a neoplasm that commonly occurs in older adults.

Neuroblastoma, retinoblastoma, medulloblastoma, and nephroblastoma are childhood tumors that arise in the adrenal gland, eye, cerebellum, and kidney, respectively. (*Chandrasoma and Taylor, pp 931–933*)

571. **(C)** The described lesion is a keloid. Keloids are an example of excessive scar formation due to a relative abundance of matrix ground substance (collagen). Not only is the quantity of collagen excessive, but it is laid down in a disorganized, haphazard pattern. Keloids most frequently occur in blacks and may recur after excision. (*Rubin and Farber, pp 91, 1266*)

572. **(B)** Benign tumors are designated by adding the suffix *oma* to their primary cell type. However, some malignant neoplasms have retained the *oma* suffix that was used in previous nomenclature schemes. Examples include hepatoma and melanoma, which are accepted names for hepatocellular carcinoma and melanocarcinoma, respectively. An adenoma is a benign epithelial neoplasm composed of glandular tissue. Cystadenomas form benign cystic masses, whereas papillomas form benign fingerlike projections. Sarcomas are malignant tumors arising from mesenchymal tissue. Carcinomas are malignant neoplasms arising from epithelial cells—either endodermal, ectodermal, or mesodermal. A prefix such as *adeno* or *squamous* may further describe the microscopic growth patterns. Melanomas are malignant tumors derived from melanocytes. Leukemias are malignancies derived from hemapoietic cells, and lymphomas are malignant tumors with a lymphoid tissue origin. Teratomas are benign compound tumors derived from more than one germ layer, and teratocarcinoma is the malignant counterpart. (*Chandrasoma and Taylor, pp 259–263*)

573. **(A)** Aflatoxin is a known potent chemical carcinogen that can produce hepatocellular carcinoma in humans. It is a fungal-derived contaminant of improperly stored foods. An increased incidence of liver cell carcinoma parallels those geographic areas, such as

Africa and the Far East, in which aflatoxin tainted foodstuffs arise. (*Rubin and Farber, p 772*)

574. **(D)** Transudates are an ultrafiltrate of plasma that enter the extracellular space by either increased hydrostatic pressure or decreased colloid oncotic pressure. The chemical composition of a transudate includes a specific gravity near 1.010, a low total protein (less than 1.5 g/dL), no fibrin, and a lack of inflammatory cells. Clinically, transudates are associated with right heart failure, cirrhosis, kwashiorkor, and Meigs' syndrome. (*Chandrasoma and Taylor, pp 37–39*)

575. **(C)** Although most bacteria invoke a polymorphonuclear leukocyte response and produce a characteristic form of inflammation, the organism causing typhoid fever produces a negative chemotaxis toward polymorphs. The cells of first response and those seen most characteristically in either the primary lesions in the Peyer's patches of the intestine or the regional lymph nodes are sheets of monocytes. Eosinophils tend to be attracted toward protozoal and fungal proteins and are not seen particularly in this type of infection. Multinucleated giant cells are characteristically seen in granulomatous disease, and typhoid fever is more in keeping with an acute bacterial infection. Plasma cells have an intermediate function and may be seen in small numbers. (*Chandrasoma and Taylor, pp 594–596*)

576. **(A)** Kernicterus (bilirubin encephalopathy) is the morphologic term that describes toxic yellow discoloration seen in brains of severely jaundiced neonates. The pigment is especially prominent in the basal ganglia, pontine nuclei, and cerebellar dentate nuclei. Premature infants are more susceptible to developing kernicterus at lower levels of hyperbilirubinemia than are term infants. Surviving infants all experience some degree of neurologic impairment. (*Rubin and Farber, p 257*)

**577. (B)** A twenty-hour-old ischemic infarct of myocardium should demonstrate coagulative necrosis without much of an inflammatory response. Over the next day or two, neutrophils, hemorrhage, and edema appear. The neutrophilic infiltrate is replaced by monocytic phagocytes during days three to five. After day five there is neovascularization and early new collagen deposition. Over the next four weeks, the inflammatory cells subside and the collagen matures into a fibrous scar. *(Rubin and Farber, pp 526–527)*

**578. (E)** About 1 in 11 women in the United States will have breast cancer in her lifetime. Many western nations (USA, Canada, Australia, western Europe, and New Zealand) have similar, high rates of carcinoma of the breast. Most Asian nations, including Japan, have a much lower incidence of mammary cancer. In one or two generations, Japanese women who emigrate to the United States develop the high rate of breast cancer of native-born American women. Factors other than geography that are associated with an increased rate of breast cancer include menarche at an early age, late age of menopause, a diet high in fat and calories, a family history of breast cancer, and atypical hyperplastic lesions of the breast. *(Chandrasoma and Taylor, p 812)*

**579. (D)** Hirschsprung's disease (idiopathic megacolon) usually appears soon after birth, with abdominal distention, failure to pass stool, and occasionally, acute intestinal obstruction. The pathogenesis involves abnormal functioning and coordination of the propulsive forces in the distal segment of the large bowel. This motility disorder occurs because of an absence of parasympathetic ganglion cells in the submucosal and myenteric plexus, the diagnostic histologic feature of Hirschsprung's disease. Hypertrophied, disorganized nonmyelinated nerve fibers are often identified in place of ganglion cells. The length of large bowel involved varies. Proximal to the involved segment, however, the colon may be dilated and hypertrophied. The mucosa often appears normal or inflamed. A full-thickness rectal biopsy is the standard procedure employed in diagnosis. Mucosal polyps are not associated with Hirschsprung's disease. *(Cotran, Kumar, and Robbins, pp 786–787)*

**580. (B)** Neonatal cholestasis in most cases results from bile duct obstruction, the most common cause (more than 90% of cases) of which is EBA. Clinically, EBA may mimic neonatal hepatitis, which is an abnormality of unknown cause and requires a diagnosis by exclusion. $\alpha_1$-Antitrypsin deficiency, metabolic disorders, and infectious processes must be ruled out before a diagnosis of neonatal hepatitis can be made. Histologically, neonatal hepatitis and EBA may appear similar—in particular, both generally contain giant cells. EBA, however, usually can be identified by evidence of large biliary duct obstruction when examined microscopically. The cause of EBA is still undetermined. Originally, it was thought to represent a congenital anomaly. Some investigators consider it to be an acquired disorder secondary to neonatal hepatitis with cholangitis and sclerosis of large bile ducts, either in utero or in early neonatal life. Overall, few cases can be corrected with standard therapy. The natural history is progression to secondary biliary cirrhosis and death in early childhood. Liver transplantation is a viable alternative therapeutic approach in these patients. Neonatal cholestasis may also, but rarely, be caused by intrahepatic biliary atresia, which is characterized by choledochal cysts and the absence of bile duct elements in the liver. Primary biliary cirrhosis is seen in middle-aged persons, typically females. The Budd–Chiari syndrome describes obstruction of the hepatic veins by a number of varied processes. *(Rubin and Farber, p 769)*

**581. (B)** With the TNM international staging system for cancer, the letter T refers to the size or extent of the primary tumor, the letter N to the number and distribution of lymph node metastases, and the letter M to the presence of distant metastases. Values for these letters may be assigned by either pathologic examination of a resected specimen or clinical estimation if no surgical tissue is available. *(Rubin and Farber, pp 157–158)*

582.    **(B)** Red hepatization is the second stage in the course of bacterial lobar pneumonia. It is histologically described as filling and dilatation of the alveolar spaces with neutrophils, WBCs, fibrin strands, RBCs, and bacteria. There is preservation of the pulmonary architecture, but it is obscured by the massive cellular exudate. This stage of bacterial pneumonia is accompanied by a fibrinous pleuritis. It characteristically develops in untreated, debilitated patients and is caused by a strain of pneumococcus in 90% of all cases. *(Cotran, Kumar, and Robbins, pp 694–699)*

583.    **(A)** Fat necrosis often occurs when pancreatic digestive enzymes leak out into the surrounding fat. Free fatty acids are enzymatically released from adipocytes by the action of these pancreatic lipases and readily precipitate as calcific soaps. Microscopically, this reaction is visualized as deeply basophilic debris peripheral to areas of necrotic fat. *(Rubin and Farber, p 14)*

584.    **(A)** Wilson's disease is an autosomal recessive disorder of copper metabolism, probably due to defective biliary excretion of the metal. Cells of the liver and brain are particularly vulnerable to the toxic effects of excessive copper accumulation. Abnormalities of the eyes (Keyser–Fleischer ring), bones (fractures and osteomalacia), and kidney (proteinuria) may also occur. Treatment with copper chelating agents, such as penicillamine or triethylene tetramine, have a dramatic beneficial effect. *(Rubin and Farber, pp 751–752)*

585.    **(B)** All connective tissue, valves, and muscle of the heart are affected to some degree in rheumatic carditis; hence the term "pancarditis." Certain areas are more selectively involved in a higher proportion of cases. In the early acute phase of rheumatic carditis, the pericardium shows fibrinous pericarditis, and the valve rings, particularly the mitral valve, show thickening and swelling of the free margins, with small fibrinous vegetations on the free margins. The characteristic Aschoff nodules and fibrosis may occur throughout the other mentioned aspects of the heart, but the characteristic vegetation seen in the early phase of the disease is usually confined to the free margins of the mitral valve. It has been thought that, in some instances, if there are no further occurrences of rheumatic fever, these may even resolve. Often, however, with or without recurrence, these fine verrucous vegetations are converted into more dense fibrous tissue, leading to narrowing of the mitral valve. *(Cotran, Kumar, and Robbins, pp 547–550)*

586.    **(D)** Edema is increased volume of extracellular extravascular fluid due to interference with the normal flow of fluids between blood, lymphatics, and tissue. The lymphatic circulation takes up a significant portion of fluid from the interstitial tissues, along with extravascular proteins, and returns it to the blood. If the lymphatic circulation is obstructed, the lymphatic drainage is interrupted. Affected areas have large accumulation of fluid and are edematous. The vascular system also aids in maintaining fluid volume. The endothelium is the lining of the vessels and serves as a semipermeable membrane for fluids and components, primarily by keeping proteins intraluminally. If the endothelium is damaged, there is increased permeability to proteins, reducing the intraluminal colloidal pressure and causing fluid leakage and edema. Capillary blood pressure (BP), or hydrostatic pressure, is the force in capillaries that drives fluids from the capillaries into the tissues. By increasing the hydrostatic pressure, fluids tend to be forced out of the capillaries into tissues, causing edema. Sodium and water also aid in maintaining fluid balance. Sodium retention causes water retention, leading to an expansion of the extracellular fluid volume both intravascularly and in the tissues with edema. Increased tissue colloid osmotic pressure can be an important factor in causing edema. The protein concentration of plasma also functions in the maintenance of fluid balance. The major protein involved is albumin. By decreasing the plasma protein concentrations, there is a decreased colloid osmotic pressure in the blood, so there is a decreased counterforce to the hydrostatic BP. Thus, there is increased fluid escaping from the capillaries and decreased re-

sorption of fluid from tissues. Fluid tends to accumulate extravascularly, with generalized edema. *(Chandrasoma and Taylor, pp 20–24)*

587. **(B)** Radiation energy is a well-documented carcinogen. The sources of the radiation include sunlight and occupational and therapeutic exposure. Therapeutic radiation was previously used to treat many benign conditions as well as thyroid disease, and a 10- to 20-year follow-up of patients who received this therapy shows an increased incidence of several types of cancer. People exposed to occupational irradiation also have a marked increase in carcinoma. Classic among these are employees who painted the faces of watches with radioactive paints and miners of radioactive ores. Survivors of atomic bombs show a markedly increased rate in the development of cancers and leukemias. The major biochemical theory of radiation-induced carcinogenesis is linked to damage of the cell's DNA. Radiation injures the DNA, inducing a mutation. The amount of cell damage is related to the dose, rate, quality, and length of total exposure to the radiation energy. Cells also have reparative capabilities for radiation damage, and they may repair or ignore the injured DNA. The exact mechanism of radiation-induced carcinogenesis is still unclear, but the existence of this phenomenon is well documented. *(Chandrasoma and Taylor, pp 164–171)*

588. **(E)** High doses of radiation delivered in utero to the embryo during its susceptible period may be a potent teratogen. Recognized abnormalities associated with high-dose radiation include microcephaly, mental retardation, and skeletal malformation. It is also believed to cause genetic mutations in fetal germ cells. Diagnostic doses of radiation, although not conclusively responsible for malformations, must be cautioned against, since the developing CNS is particularly sensitive to radiation injury. Masculinization of the female fetus is generally associated with maternal use of androgenic agents during pregnancy, not with radiation. *(Cotran, Kumar, and Robbins, pp 319–325)*

589. **(D)** For any given area of skin, there is no significant difference in the number of melanocytes in blacks as compared with whites. Blacks do, however, have larger melanocytes that are reactive (as determined by dopa reactivity) and have more dendritic processes. In whites who are not exposed to UV light, melanocytic dopa activity is quite variable. After a single exposure to UV light, the melanocytes present demonstrate an increase in size and dopa activity. With repeated exposure to UV light, there is also an increase in the concentration of melanocytes. Studies of mice have shown sufficient mitotic activity in skin melanocytes repeatedly exposed to UV light to account for the increase in concentration. *(Rubin and Farber, pp 1178–1181, 1218–1219)*

590. **(A)** Duchenne muscular dystrophy, also known as X-linked muscular dystrophy, is the most common of the muscular dystrophies. It usually occurs in early life, with symmetrical weakness and involvement of the pelvic girdle musculature. Later, the shoulder girdle muscles may be affected. As the disease progresses, pseudohypertrophy of the calves occurs and may be attributed to replacement of muscle by adipose tissue. This disease progresses rapidly and usually results in death by the age of 20 to 30 years. A more benign form of the disease, known as Becker's muscular dystrophy, is considered a separate entity. It has its onset in the second decade of life and progresses slowly. Serum CPK is elevated in the X-linked muscular dystrophies and may be used to help identify the carrier state. *(Rubin and Farber, pp 1352–1355)*

591. **(C)** Infectious sialoadenitis is a disease of the major (parotid, submandibular, and lingual) salivary glands. Infectious sialoadenitis is extremely infrequent in the minor salivary gland tissue. The bacterial organisms that cause infectious sialoadenitis typically affect only one major gland, so that the patient presents clinically with unilateral disease. Bacterial infections may be complicated by stone formation, duct obstruction, loss of parenchyma, and suppuration. The most common

viral etiology of infectious sialoadenitis is mumps. *(Cotran, Kumar, and Robbins, pp 748–749)*

592. **(D)** Gaucher's disease is an autosomal recessive disease caused by a deficiency of glucocerebrosidase, which is the enzyme that breaks down glucocerebroside in reticuloendothelial cells and neurons. A shortage of this enzyme interferes with the breakdown of glycolipids from dead WBCs and RBCs, so these metabolic products build up in phagocytic cells in the body. The reticuloendothelial cells of the spleen, liver, bone marrow, and lymph nodes are primarily affected. They fill up with glucocerebroside, obscuring the normal cell architecture. These distended cells are called Gaucher's cells, and they characteristically are large, with one or more small, dark eccentric nuclei in cytoplasm filled with eosinophilic fibrillar material resembling wrinkled tissue paper. Gaucher's cells grossly cause bone erosions, as well as enlargement of the spleen, liver, and lymph nodes. Gaucher's disease predominantly affects adult Jews of European descent, but juvenile and infantile forms also are described. Affected individuals show signs of splenomegaly and hepatomegaly, with bone pain and pancytopenia. *(Rubin and Farber, pp 234–237)*

593. **(B)** Acquired immunodeficiency syndrome (AIDS) is caused by the human immunodeficiency virus (HIV). The virus is spread parenterally and venereally. There is an increased incidence of the disease in homosexual male populations and throughout central Africa. Celibate populations who are not exposed to contaminated blood and who are not intravenous drug users have a decreased incidence of AIDS. HIV produces an immunodeficiency state through cytopathic killing of T4 helper lymphocytes. *(Rubin and Farber, pp 124–130)*

594. **(A)** The vast majority of carcinomas of the cervix are squamous cell in type. Known risk factors for the development of squamous cell carcinoma of the uterine cervix include multiple sexual partners, prior infection with human papillomavirus, early age at first coitus,

and pre-existing dysplasia. Most squamous carcinomas are preceded by a recognizable preinvasive dysplastic stage. The five-year survival of adequately treated stage I disease is about 90%. *(Rubin and Farber, pp 926–931)*

595. **(E)** All of the statements are true of schistosomiasis in general, but *S. mansoni* primarily affects the gastrointestinal tract and liver, not the bladder. It is *Schistosoma haematobium* that affects the bladder and causes hematuria. *(Cotran, Kumar, and Robbins, pp 371–372)*

596. **(E)** Polyarteritis nodosa is a systemic vasculitity that preferentially affects medium- and small-sized arteries. Histologically, the acute phase of the disease displays fibrinoid necrosis of the artery wall with an associated transmural inflammatory infiltrate. Parenchymal infarcts may result from occluded vessels. The ANCA test is almost always positive. *(Cotran, Kumar, and Robbins, p 494)*

597. **(B)** Neoplasms are tumors that may be either benign or malignant. They are composed of proliferating parenchymal cells (tumor cells) and stromal cells. Malignant tumors have the cell characteristics of anaplasia, with increased nucleus/cytoplasm ratios, hyperchromatic nuclei, and pleomorphic cells. There may also be multiple mitoses. High degrees of anaplasia are diagnostic of malignancy, but malignant tumors may mimic so closely the normal structures and be so well differentiated that they even elaborate the normal products of the cells and can be very difficult to diagnose on the basis of cytologic aspects alone. However, most tumors show some degree of anaplasia, and the architecture of the normal tissue is disorganized and destroyed. Malignant tumors have a rapid, erratic growth pattern, with abnormal mitoses. They tend to grow in an infiltrative pattern, invading local structures directly. They never have structurally well-formed capsules. The most definitive criterion of malignancy is tumor invasion of blood and lymphatic vessels. Benign tumors do not metastasize, they are composed of cells resembling the tissue of origin, and they form structures typical of that organ. They grow slowly and

expand, with few mitoses, and they have a well-formed capsule that completely surrounds the tumor. Cytologically benign tumors show no anaplastic changes, and the cells are innocuous and uniform, without malignant criteria. In rare cases, it is impossible to determine if the tumor is benign or malignant, since some tumors show histologic features of both malignant and benign neoplasms. These are borderline tumors, and their clinical course and treatment are usually intermediate between those of benign and malignant neoplasms. *(Chandrasoma and Taylor, pp 255–258)*

598. **(C)** Common detrimental effects of chronic alcoholism include cirrhosis, toxic (alcoholic) hepatitis, pancreatitis, steatosis (fatty change), Wernicke's syndrome, Korsakoff's syndrome, peripheral neuropathy, testicular atrophy, cardiomyopathy, and rhabdomyolysis. Pyelonephritis does not usually accompany chronic alcoholism. *(Cotran, Kumar, and Robbins, pp 388–390)*

599. **(E)** All of the mucopolysaccharidoses are genetic disorders with autosomal recessive inheritance. Each disease entity lacks a specific degradative enzyme, which results in a toxic cellular accumulation of unmetabolized mucopolysaccharide. The central nervous system, liver, spleen, bone marrow, and heart are variously affected depending on the distinctive enzyme defect. McArdle's disease is a disorder of glycogen metabolism. *(Rubin and Farber, pp 238–240)*

600 **(E)** Diffuse alveolar damage is a nonspecific reaction pattern of the peripheral lung to an acute insult. Grossly, the lungs are heavy, meaty, and wet. They cut with increased consistency and weep only a small amount of bloody fluid. With microscopic examination, fibrin membranes are found adherent to the alveolar walls, the type I pneumocytes are sloughed, and there may be ongoing organization if the insult is old enough. Clinically, there is respiratory insufficiency which is relatively unresponsive to oxygen therapy. *(Rubin and Farber, pp 576–579)*

601. **(C)** Thrombogenesis, the formation of thrombi, is caused by injury to endothelial surfaces, alterations in normal blood flow, and hypercoagulable states. Injury to endothelium may expose vascular wall collagen and initiate clotting via the intrinsic pathway. Alterations in the normal laminar flow of blood in vessels leads to stasis and turbulence, with a concomitant increased risk of thrombosis. Hyperviscosity syndromes (such as polycythemia, cryoglobulinemia, or macroglobulinemia) increase resistance to flow, with resultant stasis. Hypercoagulable states include disseminated intravascular coagulation (DIC) and carcinomatosis. Treatment with warfarin, an anticoagulant, would inhibit clotting, making intravascular thrombogenesis unlikely. *(Cotran, Kumar, and Robbins, pp 105–110)*

602. **(C)** The Tzanck preparation demonstrates a multinucleate epithelial cell diagnostic of an infection by one of the viruses of the family *Herpesviridae.* The clinical history and morphology support the diagnosis of a fever blister caused by herpes simplex, type I. This is a DNA virus that infects both epidermal and neuronal cells. Latency characterizes the disease in immunocompetent individuals. Encephalitis may rarely complicate an infection. The antiviral agent, acyclovir, may reduce the frequency and severity of recurrences. *(Rubin and Farber, pp 346–349)*

603. **(B)** Paraneoplastic syndromes are systemic effects of cancer on the host that are not directly attributable to the local actions of the primary tumor or its metastases. Paraneoplastic syndromes include weight loss, fever, endocrine syndromes, skeletal muscle syndromes, renal syndromes, cutaneous syndromes, hematologic syndromes, neurologic syndromes, and gastrointestinal syndromes. *(Rubin and Farber, pp 188–192)*

604. **(B)** An increased risk of coronary artery disease is associated with elevated LDL cholesterol, elevated LDL/HDL ratio, diabetes, hypertension, sedentary lifestyle, type A personality, cigarette smoking, and male gender.

Elevated HDL cholesterol levels confer a protective benefit against the development of coronary artery disease. (*Cotran, Kumar, and Robbins, pp 473–476*)

**605 (E)** Chronic passive splenic congestion is characterized grossly by an enlarged swollen cyanotic organ with a tense, non-shrunken capsule. On sectioning, the spleen oozes dark red blood and fluid. Microscopically, sinusoidal erythrocytic congestion, hemosiderin deposits, and fibrosis are evident. Right heart failure and cirrhosis are the most common clinical causes of chronic passive congestion of the spleen. (*Rubin and Farber, p 266*)

**606. (B)** Hydropic swelling is a form of reversible cell injury due to the accumulation of fluid within the cisternae of the endoplasmic reticulum. Various reversible insults to the plasma membrane or its active sodium exchange pump may be responsible for these intracellular fluid shifts within organelles, which are perceived microscopically as hydropic swelling. The other listed choices are all examples of irreversible cell injury. (*Rubin and Farber, p 3*)

**607. (A)** Individuals whose diets are high in indigestible fiber and cruciferous vegetables have a reduced risk of developing carcinoma of the colon. Diets rich in selenium and antioxidants may also exhibit a salubrious effect. Conversely, factors that increase the risk of colon carcinoma include diets that are high in animal fats, hereditary polyposis, ulcerative colitis, Crohn's disease, and adenomatous polyps. (*Rubin and Farber, pp 690–692*)

**608. (D)** CLL is common in the elderly population and uncommon in younger individuals. Affected patients may initially experience hepatosplenomegaly, lymphadenopathy, pancytopenia, malaise, and weight loss. Fever does not occur and is uncharacteristic of CLL unless there is a superimposed infectious process. About one-fourth of patients are asymptomatic at the time of diagnosis, with the diagnosis having been made on the basis of an abnormal peripheral CBC. The diagnosis often can be made from the peripheral

blood smear alone without the need for a bone marrow biopsy or aspirate. This tends to be true particularly when > 15,000 mature lymphocytes are seen in the peripheral blood smear. The malignant lymphocytes are usually B cells that demonstrate small amounts of monoclonal surface immunoglobulin, usually IgM. Hypogammaglobulinemia affects at least 50% of patients and, in combination with neutropenia, may eventually render these patients susceptible to infection. Survival in CLL is long, with a median range of between 6 and 9 years. Treatment is noncurative and is reserved for those patients who are symptomatic. Death is usually the result of infection, hemorrhage, or inanition. (*Rubin and Farber, pp 1062–1067*)

**609. (C)** Chronic myeloproliferative syndromes are interrelated neoplastic disorders of myeloid multipotential cells. Presently, four distinct clinical syndromes are recognized: polycythemia vera, chronic myelogenous leukemia, agnogenic myeloid metaplasia, and idiopathic thrombocythemia. Hairy cell leukemia is a lymphoproliferative disorder of B cells. (*Rubin and Farber, pp 1051–1058*)

**610. (A)** Tetralogy of Fallot is the most common cyanotic congenital heart disease. The anomaly includes hypertrophy of the right ventricle, a ventricular septal defect, pulmonary outflow tract stenosis, and an aorta that overrides the right ventricle (dextroposition of the aorta). An atretic right ventricle is not a feature of tetralogy of Fallot. (*Chandrasoma and Taylor, p 337*)

**611–613. (611-B, 612-A, 613-E)** There are many compounds important chemically in mediating the acute inflammatory response. Histamine is an example of the vasoactive amines, which are principally important in the acute phase of increased vascular permeability. It causes vasodilatation and increased venular permeability. It is released from mast cells and platelets. The kinin system produces vasoactive peptides, of which bradykinin is the most potent. It causes vasodilatation, increased vascular permeability, smooth muscle contraction, and pain, but it is not chemotactic. It is derived from the clotting cascade from factor XII, the Hageman factor, through a kallikrein intermediate step. The complement system produces many compounds that help mediate the inflammatory response. These include C3 and C5a, which cause increased vascular permeability, and C5a and $\overline{C567}$, which are chemotactic factors. Prostaglandins are arachidonic acid derivatives that are important in the inflammatory response. Prostaglandin E potentiates the permeability effect of the other chemical mediators and is also important in the production of pain, fever, and vasodilatation. The neutrophils themselves also release into the media lysosomal enzymes that are important chemical mediators. These compounds are released during phagocytosis, reverse endocytosis, or with neutrophil death. They consist of neutral proteases, which degrade such extracellular material as collagen, fibrin, and cartilage, acid proteases, which digest proteins, and cationic proteins. *(Chandrasoma and Taylor, pp 40–41)*

**614–616.   (614-C, 615-D, 616-E)** Intermediate filaments can be used as immunomarkers to identify cell type. In tissue specimens, monoclonal antibodies—coupled with known visual tags (fluorescent or enzymatic)—are reacted with tumors to demonstrate the presence of certain intermediate filaments. The retained intermediate filaments can confirm the lineage of tumors. Epithelial cells, mesenchymal cells, smooth muscle cells, glial cells, and neurons possess the intermediate filaments of cytokeratin, vimentin, desmin, glial fibrillary acidic protein, and neurofilament, respectively. *(Rubin and Farber, pp 150–151)*

**617–619.   (617-E, 618-B, 619-D)** Tularemia, pertussis, and plague are examples of bacterial diseases. Tularemia is caused by *Francisella tularensis,* a small gram-negative pleomorphic coccobacillus. Affected animals and arthropods serve as the vectors, of which wild rabbits and squirrels are the most common in the USA. Pertussis is caused by *Bordetella pertussis,* a gram-negative coccobacillus, and is transmitted via airborne droplets to the respiratory tract. Plague is transmitted through a

number of animal vectors, the major reservoir being squirrels. The causative agent is *Y. pestis,* an encapsulated, gram-negative, pleomorphic bacillus. Rocky Mountain spotted fever is among the rickettsial diseases, caused by obligate intracellular microorganisms smaller than bacteria and larger than viruses. The vector is an infected tick. Lymphogranuloma venereum is a disease attributed to *Chlamydia* microorganisms, specifically *C. trachomatis.* Chlamydiae are also obligate intracellular microorganisms intermediate between bacteria and viruses but are transmitted through sexual contact (a venereal disease). *(Cotran, Kumar, and Robbins, p 309)*

**620–622.   (620-B, 621-A, 622-C)** *Helicobacter pylori* infestations of the stomach are strongly associated with mucosal ulcerations at this site. Most cases of pseudomembraneous colitis result from an overgrowth of *Clostridium difficile* within the intestines secondary to prior antibiotic therapy. This organism produces a potent exotoxin that evokes a severe diarrhea with fibrin membrane formation over the colonic mucosa. *Salmonella* species are a frequent cause of bacillary dysentery, an acute illness characterized by bloody diarrhea. *(Chandrasoma and Taylor, pp 565–568, 593–594, 596)*

**623–625.   (623-B, 624-A, 625-E)** Hashimoto's thyroiditis is an autoimmune disorder characterized by autoantibodies against thyroid stimulating hormone, thyroid microsomal fractions, and thyroglobulin. Chronic adrenocortical insufficiency, usually due to autoimmune destruction, is also termed Addison's disease. Cori's disease is a hereditary disorder of glycogen catabolism in which the debrancher enzyme activity is absent. Excess glucocorticoid production is termed Cushing's syndrome. De Quervain's thyroiditis is a subacute thyroid inflammation that may have a viral etiology. *(Chandrasoma and Taylor, pp 234, 834–835, 853–858)*

**626–628.   (626-E, 627-C, 628-B)** In utero exposure to diethylstilbestrol is associated with an increased incidence of both vaginal adenosis and clear cell carcinoma of the vagina. Malignant teratoma of the ovary is a neoplasm of prepubertal and young adults that contains immature neuroepithelium. Risk factors for the development of endometrial adenocarcinoma include nulliparity, diabetes, preceding hyperplasia, hypertension, breast cancer, late menopause, exogenous estrogens, and obesity. (*Rubin and Farber, pp 920–922, 941, 958–959*)

**629–631.    (629-D, 630-A, 631-E)** The ductus arteriosus is a normal intrauterine vascular channel connecting the pulmonary artery to the aorta. It usually closes shortly after birth. Prolonged patency requires surgical correction or pharmacologic closure. The most common congenital heart anomaly is a ventricular septal defect. It accounts for about 30% of all congenital cardiac malformations. Truncus arteriosus arises from an incomplete separation of the aorta from the pulmonary artery. This anomaly is usually accompanied by other malformations including valvular defects, right aortic arch, and absence of the ductus arteriosus. (*Chandrasoma and Taylor, pp 333–337*)

**632–634.    (632-C, 633-E, 634-B)** A large number of inhaled dust-like substances are able to produce pathologic changes in the respiratory system, which are generally referred to as pneumoconioses. Inhaled cotton fibers may produce an asthma-like disorder termed byssinosis. Inhalation of asbestos fibers is associated with an increased risk of developing malignant mesothelioma. Tin oxide miners may acquire a chronic fibrosing pulmonary disorder called stannosis. Silicosis is a pneumoconiosis caused by inhaled silica particles. Beryllium granulomatosis is seen with chronic beryllium inhalation. (*Cotran, Kumar, and Robbins, pp 707–712*)

**635–637.    (635-B, 636-C, 637-A)** Chagas' disease is caused by *Trypanosoma cruzi*, a protozoan organism. One of the hallmarks of the disease is destructive myocarditis. Dubin–Johnson syndrome is a familial disease characterized by intermittent jaundice and black pigment deposition in the liver. Goodpasture's syndrome is rapidly progressive glomerulonephritis and diffuse pulmonary hemorrhages, usually with autoantibodies to

basement membrane material. Peutz–Jeghers syndrome is an autosomal dominant hereditary disorder consisting of intestinal polyps and mucocutaneous melanin pigmentation. Kawaski's disease (mucocutaneous lymph node syndrome) is an acute vasculitis of infancy and early childhood. (*Rubin and Farber, pp 432–434, 490, 581, 666–667, 712–713*)

**638–640.    (638-C, 639-A, 640-B)** Hemophilia A is an X-linked recessive hereditary disorder due to a deficiency of blood clotting factor VIII. Dwarfism (achondroplasia) is an autosomal dominant disease characterized by early ossification of the epiphyseal plate in the long bones. Normal head and truncal size, with significantly shortened extremities, are hallmarks of the disease. Ochronosis (alkaptonuria) is an autosomal recessive disorder due to a lack of the enzyme homogentisic oxidase. Homogentisic acid accumulates within collagen in connective tissue, tendons, and cartilage, imparting a blue-black discoloration. The articular cartilage is particularly damaged, with resultant severe arthritis. (*Cotran, Kumar, and Robbins, pp 147–148, 622–623, 1218*)

**641–643.    (641-C, 642-D, 643-A)** Amebic dysentery is caused by *Entamoeba histolytica*. Colonic ulcers are typical. Liver abscesses and cutaneous perineal amebiasis may complicate the infection. *Plasmodium falciparum* is an etiologic agent of malaria. Hookworm disease is caused by either *Necator americanus* or *Ancylostoma duodenale*. Hookworm disease may be asymptomatic. Alternatively, individuals may suffer from anemia or pruritis. (*Rubin and Farber, pp 421–424, 426–430, 440*)

**644–646.    (644-D, 645-A, 646-B)** The classic triad of ectopic gastrin production, excess gastric acid secretion, and persistent peptic ulcer disease comprise the Zollinger–Ellison syndrome. The majority of gastrinomas arise from either the pancreas or the duodenum. MEN IIa, also termed Sipple syndrome, is characterized by medullary carcinomas of the thyroid, parathyroid neoplasia, adrenocortical neoplasia or hyperplasia, and pheochromocytomas. The disorder is usually inherited in an autosomal dominant mode with incomplete penetrance. Stein–Leventhal syndrome includes polycystic ovaries, oligomenorrhea, hirsutism, and obesity. The major biochemical abnormality is low levels of follicle-stimulating hormone and androgens. Wedge resection of ovarian tissue is often curative. *(Chandrasoma and Taylor, pp 678–679, 756–757, 862)*

**647–649.    (647-B, 648-A, 649-D)** Mycosis fungoides is a cutaneous T-helper cell lymphoma with epidermal infiltrates of atypical lymphocytes. Late in disease these cells may spill out into the peripheral blood (Sézary syndrome). Pemphigus is characterized by skin blister formation due to diminished cohesiveness of the keratinocytes. Autoantibodies to surface epidermal antigens is the primary etiology of pemphigus. Ichthyoses are hereditary disorders that show marked hypertrophy of the strateum corneum. Both autosomal dominant and X-linked recessive forms exist. *(Rubin and Farber, pp 1084–1085, 1186–1187, 1193–1198)*

**650–652.    (650-E, 651-B, 652-A)** Pernicious anemia is due to a deficiency of vitamin $B_{12}$ (cobalamin). Most instances of pernicious anemia are characterized by autoimmune destruction of gastric parietal cells leading to inadequate production of vitamin $B_{12}$ absorption factor (intrinsic factor). Myelophthisic anemia is seen with bone marrow infiltrative disorders. The peripheral blood demonstrates a leukoerythroblastic pattern. Carcinoma with bony metastases is the most common cause of myelophthisic anemia. Thalassemia is a genetic disorder typified by defects in globin chain synthesis. The anemia is usually microcytic and hypochromic. *(Cotran, Kumar, and Robbins, pp 596–601, 605–608, 615–616)*

**653–655.    (653-A, 654-C, 655-B)** Acetaminophen is present in many over-the-counter analgesic preparations. Overdose causes massive hepatic necrosis via a toxic metabolite. Carbon monoxide poisons as a systemic asphyxiant by binding irreversibly to hemoglobin. Methyl alcohol exerts its prime poisoning effect on the retina and brain through its toxic

metabolites, formaldehyde, and formic acid. *(Cotran, Kumar, and Robbins, pp 14, 385, 397, 1340)*

**656–658.    (656-A, 657-C, 658-E)** Hypertrophy is an increase in the size of individual cells, but the actual number of cells present remains unchanged. Hypertrophy, such as left cardiac ventricular hypertrophy, occurs as an adaptive function in response to trophic signals or increased demand. Atrophy is the shrinkage of the cell size by a loss of substance. Atrophy is commonly seen with aging, ischemia, diminished workload, loss of innervation, or inadequate nutrition. Dysplasia is an atypical proliferative process that may be precancerous. Dysplastic cells typically display nuclear atypia, loss of cellular polarity, and impaired cellular maturation. *(Rubin and Farber, pp 5–10)*

**659–664.    (659-E, 660-I, 661-A, 662-J, 663-F, 664-B)** Klinefelter's syndrome has a 47,XXY karyotype, testicular atrophy, eunuchoid tall habitus, gynecomastia, and a female distribution of hair. The normal female and male karyotypes are 46,XX and 46,XY, respectively. Down syndrome is characterized by trisomy 21, congenital cardiac defects, epicanthic folds, mental retardation, dysplastic ears, and increased risk of developing leukemia. The multi-X female karyotype, particularly in the 47,XXX karyotype, is usually phenotypically normal. Turner's syndrome includes a 45,X karyotype, webbing of the neck, amenorrhea, streak gonads, cardiac defects, short stature, and a broad chest. Edwards' syndrome (trisomy 18) is seen in about 1 of 8000 live births and is characterized by mental retardation, prominent occiput, micrognathia, low-set ears, rocker bottom feet, and hypertonicity. *(Chandrasoma and Taylor, pp 226–229)*

**665–668.    (665-C, 666-H, 667-E, 668-G)** Histoplasmosis is a granulomatous pulmonary disorder caused by the fungal organism, *Histoplasma capsulatum*. Old foci tend to become fibrotic and may be undistinguishable from pulmonary carcinoma by chest x-ray. Surgically removed nodules usually demonstrate small budding yeast forms with methenamine silver stains. Squamous cell carcinoma is associated with smoking and usually presents as a bronchogenic lesion. Metastases are first seen in the draining bronchial and hilar lymph nodes. Later, metastases may be found in the pleura, liver, adrenals, and brain. Secondary amyloidosis can be seen as a complication of myeloma or chronic infections. Histologically, the acellular material has apple green birefringence on polarized light examination after congo red staining. The characteristic electron microscopic feature of mesothelioma is abundant long microvilli. Most mesotheliomas are associated with asbestosis exposure. (*Cotran, Kumar, and Robbins, pp 231–238, 327–328, 720–725, 730–732*)

**669–673.  (669-J,  670-A,  671-E,  672-I,  673-D)** Condyloma accuminatum is a sexually acquired warty growth with a predilection for the penile meatus, perianal skin, and cervix. Human papilloma viruses are the etiologic agent. Renal cell carcinoma is characteristically a variegated tumor of large size. Extension into the renal vein is a common finding. Endometriosis is more commonly found in the ovary or peritoneum, but may be present in the bladder. Endometriosis of the bladder is typified by benign endometrial glands and stroma in a hemorrhagic background. Hematuria is a common clinical complaint. Prostatic adenocarcinoma is a disease of elderly males. Bone metastases are common in the late stages of the disease. Prostate specific antigen is elevated in most patients with bony metastases. Glomerulonephritis following streptococcal infection is most often seen in a pediatric age group. Hematuria, edema, and hypertension are usual concomitant clinical findings. (*Rubin and Farber, pp 828–831, 862–865, 899–905, 956–957*)

## REFERENCES

Chandrasoma P, Taylor CR. *Concise Pathology.* 2nd ed. Norwalk, CT: Appleton & Lange; 1995

Cotran RS, Kumar V, Robbins SL. *Robbins Pathologic Basis of Disease.* 5th ed. Philadelphia: WB Saunders Co.; 1994

Rubin E, Farber JL, eds. *Pathology.* 2nd ed. Philadelphia: JB Lippincott Co.; 1994

# Subspecialty List—Pathology

547. Respiratory system
548. Immunopathology
549. Nervous system
550. Inflammation
551. Miscellaneous
552. Immunopathology
553. Genetic syndromes and metabolic diseases
554. Cell injury and response
555. Nongenetic syndromes
556. Endocrine system
557. Nongenetic syndromes
558. Alimentary system
559. Alimentary system
560. Immunopathology
561. Abnormal growth and development
562. Blood and lymphatic system
563. Immunopathology
564. Alimentary system
565. Kidney and urinary system
566. Cardiovascular system
567. Respiratory system
568. Alimentary system
569. Blood and lymphatic system
570. Processes of neoplasia
571. Abnormal growth and development
572. Processes of neoplasia
573. Processes of neoplasia
574. Inflammation
575. Inflammation
576. Nervous system
577. Cardiovascular system

578. Breast pathology
579. Alimentary system
580. Abnormal growth and development
581. Processes of neoplasia
582. Respiratory system
583. Cell injury and response
584. Genetic syndromes and metabolic disorders
585. Cardiovascular system
586. Circulatory system
587. Processes of neoplasia
588. Abnormal growth and development
589. Cutaneous pathology
590. Muscular system
591. Alimentary system
592. Genetic syndromes and metabolic diseases
593. Infectious diseases
594. Genital system
595. Infectious diseases
596. Cardiovascular system
597. Processes of neoplasia
598. Nongenetic syndromes
599. Genetic syndromes and metabolic disorders
600. Respiratory system
601. Hemostasis and coagulation
602. Infectious diseases
603. Processes of neoplasia
604. Cardiovascular system
605. Miscellaneous
606. Cell injury and response

607. Alimentary system
608. Blood and lymphatic system
609. Blood and lymphatic system
610. Cardiovascular system
611. Inflammation
612. Inflammation
613. Inflammation
614. Processes of neoplasia
615. Processes of neoplasia
616. Processes of neoplasia
617. Infectious diseases
618. Infectious diseases
619. Infectious diseases
620. Infectious diseases
621. Infectious diseases
622. Infectious diseases
623. Endocrine system
624. Endocrine system
625. Genetic syndromes and metabolic disorders
626. Genital system
627. Genital system
628. Genital system
629. Cardiovascular system
630. Cardiovascular system
631. Cardiovascular system
632. Environmental pathology
633. Environmental pathology
634. Environmental pathology
635. Cardiovascular system
636. Genetic syndromes and metabolic disorders
637. Immunopathology
638. Blood and lymphatic system

639. Genetic syndromes and metabolic disorders
640. Genetic syndromes and metabolic disorders
641. Infectious diseases
642. Infectious diseases
643. Infectious diseases
644. Endocrine system
645. Endocrine system
646. Endocrine system
647. Cutaneous pathology
648. Cutaneous pathology
649. Cutaneous pathology
650. Blood and lymphatic system
651. Blood and lymphatic system
652. Blood and lymphatic system
653. Environmental pathology
654. Environmental pathology
655. Environmental pathology
656. Abnormal growth and development
657. Abnormal growth and development
658. Abnormal growth and development
659. Genetic syndromes and metabolic disorders
660. Genetic syndromes and metabolic disorders
661. Genetic syndromes and metabolic disorders
662. Genetic syndromes and metabolic disorders
663. Genetic syndromes and metabolic disorders
664. Genetic syndromes and metabolic disorders
665. Respiratory system
666. Respiratory system
667. Respiratory system
668. Respiratory system
669. Kidney and urinary system
670. Kidney and urinary system
671. Kidney and urinary system
672. Kidney and urinary system
673. Kidney and urinary system

# CHAPTER 6

# Pharmacology
## Questions

*Russell Yamazaki, PhD*

**DIRECTIONS (Questions 674 through 723): Each of the numbered items or incomplete statements in this section is followed by answers or by completions of the statement. Select the ONE lettered answer or completion that is BEST in each case.**

**Questions 674 and 675**

Use the following graph (Fig. 6.1) for Questions 674 and 675.

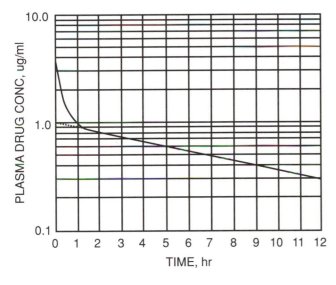

**Figure 6.1**

674. Drug L, when administered as a single-bolus IV dose of 30 mg to a 70-kg (154-lb) patient, yields the above plasma values as a function of time after injection. The apparent volume of distribution is

    (A) 0.25 L
    (B) 4.0 L

    (C) 14 L
    (D) 30 L
    (E) 100 L

675. In the above graph, the elimination half-life for drug L is

    (A) 0.25 hr
    (B) 1.0 hr
    (C) 7.0 hr
    (D) 12.0 hr
    (E) 28.0 hr

676. Assuming the use of equal doses, which of the following routes of drug administration should result in the lowest area-under-curve (AUC) for the plasma concentration-time function for the drug diazepam?

    (A) oral
    (B) intravenous
    (C) subcutaneous injection
    (D) rectal suppository
    (E) sublingual tablet

**Questions 677 through 679**

| Patient | Body Wt | Vd | Half-life | k Elimination |
|---|---|---|---|---|
| Normal | 65 kg | 50 L | 3.5 hr | 0.20/hr |
| Obese | 122 kg | 200 L | 14.0 hr | 0.05/hr |

The above pharmacokinetic data for drug T were determined from analyses of the concentration-time curves for single IV doses of 25 mg in a normal and an obese subject.

677. If the IV loading dose for drug T is 200 mg in the *normal* subject, what is the IV loading dose that should be used in the *obese* subject to achieve the same target plasma concentration?

(A) 25 mg
(B) 50 mg
(C) 200 mg
(D) 800 mg
(E) 4000 mg

678. If the IV maintenance infusion rate for the *normal* patient is 25 µg/hr, what maintenance infusion rate should be used in the *obese* patient to achieve and maintain the same target plasma concentration?

(A) 25 µg/hr
(B) 50 µg/hr
(C) 200 µg/hr
(D) 800 µg/hr
(E) 4000 µg/hr

679. Based on the pharmacokinetic data given above, which description best fits the drug T?

(A) highly polar molecule probably cleared by the kidney
(B) highly polar molecule probably cleared by hepatic metabolism
(C) highly lipophilic molecule probably cleared by the kidney
(D) highly lipophilic molecule probably cleared by hepatic metabolism
(E) negatively charged molecule probably cleared by biliary secretion

680. A patient being continuously infused at 25 µg/min has a plasma steady state level of drug Q (half-life = 6 hr) of 200 µg/mL. Misinterpretation of instructions causes the infusion rate to be increased from 25 µg/min to 50 µg/min. If toxicity usually becomes detectable at a plasma level of 350 µg/mL, how long will it take after the increase in infusion rate for symptoms of toxicity to appear?

(A) 6 hr
(B) 9 hr
(C) 12 hr
(D) 18 hr
(E) 24 hr

681. What is the plasma clearance for a drug that is infused at a rate of 1 mg/min and achieves a steady-state plasma concentration of 4 mg/L?

(A) 50 mL/min
(B) 200 mL/min
(C) 250 mL/min
(D) 500 mL/min
(E) 2000 mL/min

682. The neurotoxic actions of botulinum toxin are associated with

(A) nicotinic receptor depolarization blockade
(B) blockade of somatic nerve transmitter exocytosis
(C) inhibition of smooth muscle myosin light-chain kinase
(D) irreversible inhibition of cholinesterase
(E) reversal by infusion of heroic doses of choline

683. Which of the following is a rational choice for treatment of open-angle glaucoma, a condition requiring chronic miosis?

(A) scopolamine
(B) pilocarpine
(C) tropicamide
(D) atracurium
(E) hexamethonium

**684.** A patient has started taking a medication and now complains about dizziness to the point of almost fainting upon standing up rapidly. This complaint is frequently encountered with therapy using

(A) diazepam

(B) chlorpromazine

(C) meprobamate

(D) fluoxetine

(E) chlordiazepoxide

**685.** Which of the following correctly describes the antiarrhythmic mechanism of action for lidocaine?

(A) blockade of sodium/calcium exchanger

(B) blockade of ATP-sensitive potassium channels

(C) blockade of voltage-dependent calcium channels

(D) blockade of $\beta_1$-adrenergic receptors

(E) blockade of sodium channels

**686.** Oral anticoagulants such as warfarin exert their anticoagulant effects by

(A) blocking calcium binding to clotting factors

(B) acting as a template for complexing thrombin and antithrombin III

(C) breaking down thrombin

(D) inhibiting hepatic post-translational carboxylation of clotting factors

(E) forming an active complex with plasminogen

**687.** Potassium supplementation often is necessary for patients taking

(A) spironolactone

(B) triamterene

(C) furosemide

(D) amiloride

(E) captopril

**688.** Which of the following disease entities is most likely to respond to the use of the drug ranitidine?

(A) motion sickness

(B) seasonal rhinitis

(C) urticaria

(D) duodenal ulcer

(E) conjunctivitis

**689.** Which of the following statements is correct regarding angiotensin-converting enzyme (ACE) inhibitors?

(A) chronic therapy with ACE inhibitors impairs hemodynamic response to exercise

(B) rebound hypertension after abrupt cessation of therapy is a frequent problem

(C) use of ACE inhibitors depresses renin activity

(D) therapy with ACE inhibitors appears useful in essential hypertension

(E) ACE inhibitors are of little value in therapy of congestive heart failure

**690.** Which of the following tricyclic/heterocyclic antidepressants is most selective in blocking reuptake of norepinephrine as compared with serotonin?

(A) doxepin

(B) desipramine

(C) amitriptyline

(D) fluoxetine

(E) trazodone

**691.** Renal excretion of an overdose of an organic weak acid (pKa = 5.5) can be hastened by

(A) alkalinization of urinary pH by administration of sodium bicarbonate

(B) acidification of urinary pH by administration of ammonium chloride

(C) administration of low doses of probenecid

(D) administration of phenobarbital

(E) none of the above

692. The most common problem associated with use of nonsteroidal anti-inflammatory drugs (NSAIDs) such as ibuprofen is

   (A) prolonged bleeding time
   (B) fluid retention
   (C) gastrointestinal complaints
   (D) bronchospasm
   (E) drowsiness

693. An early sign of phenytoin intoxication following oral dosing is

   (A) nystagmus
   (B) hyperexcitability
   (C) loss of seizure control
   (D) gastrointestinal complaints
   (E) tremor

694. Microcytic hypochromic anemia due to inadequate nutrition is best treated with

   (A) oral ferric chloride
   (B) oral ferrous sulfate
   (C) oral vitamin $B_{12}$
   (D) IM vitamin $B_{12}$
   (E) oral folic acid

695. Which of the following insulin preparations has the longest duration of action?

   (A) semilente insulin
   (B) lente insulin
   (C) neutral protamine Hagedorn (NPH) insulin
   (D) regular insulin
   (E) ultralente insulin

696. Which of the following items correctly associates the mechanism of action with the corresponding agent used in hyperlipidemia?

   (A) nicotinic acid—altered excretion of bile acids
   (B) clofibrate—decreased activity of lipoprotein lipase
   (C) lovastatin—inhibition of hepatic hydroxymethylglutaryl coenzyme A (HMG-CoA) reductase
   (D) cholestyramine—increased activity of lipoprotein lipase
   (E) gemfibrozil—decreased plasma concentrations of high-density lipoprotein (HDL)

697. Calcium disodium edetate is an antidote for poisoning with

   (A) mercury
   (B) atropine
   (C) Paris green
   (D) lead
   (E) phosphorus

698. Which is the following is used for the prevention of ventricular arrhythmias during acute myocardial infarction?

   (A) lidocaine
   (B) digoxin
   (C) quinidine
   (D) flecainide
   (E) propranolol

699. The current drug of choice for treatment of *Ascaris* or *Enterobius* infections is

   (A) thiabendazole
   (B) pyrantel pamoate
   (C) tetrachloroethylene
   (D) antimony potassium tartrate
   (E) diethylcarbamazine

700. Although the mechanisms underlying the antihypertensive effects of propranolol are still unclear, a plausible candidate is

   (A) α-adrenergic receptor blockade
   (B) inhibition of renin release
   (C) depletion of amines in adrenergic nerves
   (D) blockade of norepinephrine reuptake into prejunctional neurons
   (E) down-regulation of vascular β-adrenergic receptors

701. Co-administration of which of the following drugs with warfarin will put the patient at risk for an embolic episode?

(A) phenobarbital

(B) aspirin

(C) phenylbutazone

(D) cimetidine

(E) sulfinpyrazone

702. The leukotrienes (LTC$_4$, LTD$_4$, and LTE$_4$)

(A) are important mediators in the pathophysiology of asthma

(B) have their biosynthesis greatly reduced by aspirin

(C) have few cardiovascular effects

(D) are synthesized in platelet granules

(E) are potent chemotactic agents for polymorphonuclear leukocytes

703. The thrombolytic mechanism of action of streptokinase involves

(A) direct conversion of plasminogen to plasmin

(B) proteolytic breakdown of fibrin

(C) depletion of $\alpha_2$-antiplasmin

(D) formation of an active complex with plasminogen

(E) proteolytic activation of fibrinogen

704. A major mechanism underlying the ability of carbamazepine to suppress partial and generalized epileptic seizures is exerted through

(A) increased binding of gamma-aminobutyric acid (GABA) to its receptor

(B) blockade of sodium channels

(C) inhibition of the breakdown of GABA

(D) stimulation of depolarization-dependent neurotransmitter release

(E) competitive blockade of serotonin receptor

705. The mechanism of action of local anesthetics is related to

(A) ganglionic blockade

(B) inhibition of pain receptors

(C) inhibition of nerve conduction via blockade of Na$^+$ channels

(D) inhibition of nerve conduction via blockade of Ca$^{2+}$ channels

(E) hyperpolarization of neurons via enhanced Cl$^-$ influx

706. Acute poisoning with antihistamines is correctly described as

(A) treatable with histamine therapy

(B) characterized by fever and flushing in adults

(C) causing severe respiratory depression

(D) producing a state similar to atropine poisoning in children

(E) producing joint pain

707. Which of the following describes the mechanism of action for the stimulation of insulin release from pancreatic beta cells by glyburide?

(A) inhibition of Na/K (adenosine triphosphatase) ATPase

(B) activation of fast sodium channels

(C) inhibition of ATP-sensitive potassium channels

(D) activation of sodium/calcium exchanger

(E) inhibition of voltage-dependent calcium channels

708. Which of the following properties best correlates with the rate of onset of anesthesia for a series of inhalational general anesthetic agents each administered at its minimum alveolar concentration (MAC) partial pressure?

(A) MAC for anesthesia

(B) Blood : oil partition coefficient

(C) Anesthetic potency

(D) Blood : gas partition coefficient

(E) Lipid solubility

709. Which of following sets of drugs and description or mechanism of action correctly pairs the drug with its correct description or mechanism?

    (A) pralidoxime—reversible cholinesterase inhibitor

    (B) isoflurophate—used in treatment of myasthenia gravis

    (C) physostigmine—irreversible cholinesterase inhibitor

    (D) neostigmine—cholinesterase inhibitor specific for muscarinic synapses

    (E) edrophonium—short-acting cholinesterase inhibitor

710. Which of the following agents is used in thyroid storm because of its ability to inhibit both thyroid iodine organification and peripheral deiodination of $T_4$ and $T_3$?

    (A) reverse $T_3$

    (B) propylthiouracil

    (C) radioactive iodine ($^{131}$I)

    (D) propranolol

    (E) potassium perchlorate

711. Which of the following drugs is used to promote ovulation through inhibitory actions in the hypothalamus?

    (A) flutamide

    (B) ethinyl estradiol

    (C) norethindrone

    (D) clomiphene

    (E) diethylstilbestrol

712. An antihyperlipidemic agent whose actions in lowering low-density lipoprotein (LDL) cholesterol depend on the expression of functional LDL receptors in the liver is

    (A) gemfibrozil

    (B) probucol

    (C) niacin

    (D) etretinate

    (E) colestipol

713. A drug with a half-life of 12 hours is administered by continuous intravenous infusion. How long will it take for the drug to reach 94% of its final steady-state level?

    (A) 18 hr

    (B) 24 hr

    (C) 30 hr

    (D) 40 hr

    (E) 48 hr

714. Treatment of severe digitalis intoxication consists of

    (A) administration of Fab fragments (digitalis antibodies)

    (B) infusion of lidocaine

    (C) serum potassium repletion

    (D) infusion of atropine

    (E) supportive therapy only

715. Which of the following agents is useful in the acute treatment of cardiogenic shock because of its ability to increase cardiac inotropicity without producing large increases in chronotropicity?

    (A) epinephrine

    (B) dobutamine

    (C) propranolol

    (D) digoxin

    (E) atropine

716. Which of the following descriptions best fits the time course for blockade of the motor end plate by a single dose of succinylcholine?

    (A) reversible by edrophonium at all times until recovery

    (B) reversible by edrophonium—not reversed by edrophonium

    (C) not reversed by edrophonium—reversed by edrophonium

    (D) not reversed by edrophonium at all times until recovery

    (E) reversible by pralidoxime at all times

717. Which of the following agents may be used as a cardiac stimulant in the treatment of β-blocker overdose?

   (A) insulin
   (B) glucagon
   (C) atrial natriuretic peptide
   (D) human growth hormone
   (E) epinephrine

718. A drug has a $V_d$ of 30 L and a total systemic clearance rate of 20 L/hr, with 80% being eliminated by the liver and 20% eliminated by the kidney. The maintenance infusion rate for a normal patient is 20 mg/hr. Which of the following infusion rates should be used to maintain the same steady-state plasma concentration in a patient with 50% renal function?

   (A) 4 mg/hr
   (B) 10 mg/hr
   (C) 15 mg/hr
   (D) 18 mg/hr
   (E) 20 mg/hr

719. Epinephrine is found in much higher concentrations in the adrenal medulla than any other tissue site because of the exposure of adrenal medullary (chromaffin) cells to high concentrations of

   (A) acetylcholine
   (B) corticotropin
   (C) DOPA decarboxylase
   (D) cortisol
   (E) vasopressin

720. The current agent of choice for treatment of bipolar affective (manic-depressive) disorder is

   (A) chlorpromazine
   (B) haloperidol
   (C) diazepam
   (D) clozapine
   (E) lithium carbonate

721. At a blood alcohol level of 200 mg/dL (0.2%), which of the following correctly describes the systemic elimination process for ethanol?

   (A) zero order elimination via hepatic metabolism
   (B) first order elimination via pulmonary exhalation
   (C) first order elimination via renal excretion
   (D) second order elimination via biliary secretion
   (E) constant clearance via liver, kidney, and lungs

722. A patient was treated topically with eye drops and later complained that she was blinded by bright light and was unable to focus on near objects for several days. She probably had been administered

   (A) tropicamide
   (B) edrophonium
   (C) atropine
   (D) phenylephrine
   (E) isoflurophate

723. The effects of this drug include increased motor activity, loss of appetite, excitement, and, with prolonged administration, stereotyped and psychotic behavior. Frequent repeated use causes a rapid, progressive decline in the central nervous system (CNS) stimulatory activity. The drug is

   (A) amphetamine
   (B) cocaine
   (C) tetrahydrocannabinol
   (D) heroin
   (E) ethanol

**DIRECTIONS (Questions 724 through 773): Each set of matching questions in this section consists of a list of lettered options followed by several numbered items. For each numbered item, select the ONE lettered option that is most closely associated with it. Each lettered heading may be selected once, more than once, or not at all.**

**Questions 724 through 727**

Use the following graph (Fig. 6.2) for Questions 724 through 727.

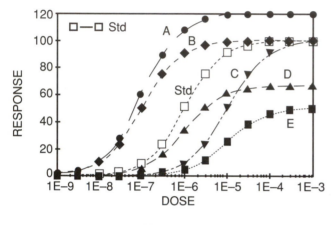

**Figure 6.2**

Consider a hypothetical synapse that uses the neurotransmitter Q, which is removed from the synaptic cleft by uptake into the presynaptic terminal. The curve above labeled Std shows the relationship between externally applied concentrations of Q (which can enter the synaptic cleft by diffusion) and the biological response. Use these data for the next four items.

724.  This curve shows the dose-response curve for external additions of Q expected in the presence of a competitive antagonist added at ten times the antagonist's $K_i$ concentration?

725.  This curve shows the dose-response curve for external additions of Q expected in the presence of a noncompetitive antagonist added at a concentration sufficient to inactivate 33% of the receptors for Q

726.  This curve shows the dose-response curve for external additions of Q expected in the pres-

ence of an inhibitor of the presynaptic uptake of Q

727.  This curve shows the dose-response curve for additions of R, which is an agonist for the Q receptor with 50% the efficacy of that for Q (assume that Q is not present)

**Questions 728 through 734**

(A)  acyclovir
(B)  amikacin
(C)  azathioprine
(D)  bleomycin
(E)  cyclosporine
(F)  cytarabine (cytosine arabinoside)
(G)  ketoconazole
(H)  methotrexate
(I)  metronidazole
(J)  primaquine
(K)  rifampin
(L)  sulfisoxazole
(M)  tetracycline
(N)  trimethoprim
(O)  vancomycin
(P)  zidovudine (AZT)

728.  Toxic levels of this immunosuppressive agent cause kidney damage but little bone marrow depression

729.  When this anti-trichomonas agent is prescribed, patients should be warned about its disulfiram-like actions

730.  Because this oral antifungal agent inhibits certain mammalian cytochrome P450 isoforms, serious arrhythmias may result from accumulation of antihistamines such as terfenadine taken concurrently

731.  Because this anti-herpesvirus agent uses the viral thymidine kinase as part of its activation pathway, resistance is associated with thymidine-kinase deficient strains of herpesvirus

**732.** Resistance to this agent that is used in *Escherichia coli* urinary tract infections can arise through bacterial expression of altered forms of dihydrofolate reductase acquired by spontaneous mutation or plasmid transfer

**733.** Because this anti-tubercular agent is an inducer of hepatic cytochrome P450, dosing regimens for oral anticoagulants must be adjusted when these drugs are administered together

**734.** Use in the central nervous system requires intrathecal or intraventricular injection of this antibacterial agent that produces nephrotoxicity and ototoxicity as adverse effects

**Questions 735 through 738**

For each patient description, choose the agent whose properties best match the patient description.

   (A) atenolol
   (B) clonidine
   (C) diltiazem
   (D) enalapril
   (E) guanethidine
   (F) hydralazine
   (G) hydrochlorothiazide
   (H) methyldopa
   (I) metoprolol
   (J) minoxidil
   (K) phenylephrine
   (L) prazosin
   (M) propranolol
   (N) sodium nitroprusside
   (O) trimethaphan

**735.** A 54-year-old male being treated for hypertension with this agent responded well initially but complained of dizziness upon standing; subsequently, when he was treated for depression with a tricyclic antidepressant, this antihypertensive agent lost its effectiveness

**736.** A 47-year-old male being treated for hypertension with this agent responded well with minimal adverse effects (dry mouth and some sedation); however, when the patient neglected to take his medication during a vacation, a severe headache and tachycardia led him to seek treatment at a hospital emergency room where he was found to be in hypertensive crisis

**737.** A 44-year-old female being treated for hypertension with this agent complained of arthralgia and myalgia along with skin rashes and fever; the lupus-like syndrome disappeared upon discontinuance of this agent

**738.** A 34-year-old male flutist was treated for hypertension with this agent; although his blood pressure was reduced, he complained that he was now unable to play his instrument because of a dry cough

**Questions 739 through 742**

Match the description with the appropriate drug.

   (A) allopurinol
   (B) BCNU (carmustine)
   (C) bleomycin
   (D) busulfan
   (E) cisplatin
   (F) cyclophosphamide
   (G) dactinomycin
   (H) daunorubicin (Adriamycin)
   (I) etoposide (VP-16)
   (J) fluorouracil
   (K) mercaptopurine
   (L) methotrexate
   (M) prednisone
   (N) tamoxifen
   (O) vincristine

**739.** Cancer chemotherapeutic agent that requires metabolism by cytochrome P450 for formation of the active species

**740.** Agent used in treating testicular cancer whose use requires hydration and diuresis to prevent nephrotoxicity associated with the agent

741.  Chemotherapeutic agent whose mechanism of action involves inhibition of thymidylate synthase and incorporation into ribonucleic acid (RNA)

742.  Chemotherapeutic agent whose mechanism of action involves inhibition of topoisomerase II, resulting in deoxyribonucleic acid (DNA) strand breakage

**Questions 743 and 744**

For each condition listed, choose the body fluid which best fits the description.

| | Body fluid | pH |
|---|---|---|
| (A) | alkalinized urine | 8.0 |
| (B) | acidified urine | 5.0 |
| (C) | breast milk | 6.4 |
| (D) | jejunum, ileum contents | 7.6 |
| (E) | stomach contents | 2.0 |

743.  When a steady state concentration of drug is present in the systemic circulation and equilibration between the systemic circulation and tissue compartments has been achieved, this fluid compartment will have the largest total fluid : blood concentration ratio for the weak acid sulfadiazine (pKa = 6.5)

744.  When a steady state concentration of drug is present in the systemic circulation and equilibration between the systemic circulation and tissue compartments has been achieved, this fluid compartment will have the largest total fluid : blood concentration ratio for the weak base pyrimethamine (pKa = 7.0) (assume equal fluid volumes)

**Questions 745 through 748**

For each laxative agent, select the group in which it is classified.

  (A)  bulk-forming
  (B)  lubricant
  (C)  stimulant
  (D)  stool softener
  (E)  osmotic

745.  Psyllium

746.  Bisacodyl

747.  Docusate

748.  Lactulose

**Questions 749 through 752**

For each agent listed, select the site or mechanism of action with which it is most closely associated.

  (A)  indirectly acting sympathomimetic agent
  (B)  $\alpha_1$-adrenergic agonist
  (C)  $\beta$-adrenergic blocker
  (D)  $\beta$-adrenergic agonist
  (E)  $\alpha_1$-adrenergic antagonist

749.  Isoproterenol

750.  Propranolol

751.  Amphetamine

752.  Methoxamine

**Questions 753 through 755**

For each agent listed, select the physiologic response with which it is most closely associated after clinically relevant doses of the agent are administered.

  (A)  tachycardia
  (B)  cholinesterase inhibition
  (C)  decreased intraocular pressure
  (D)  muscle paralysis
  (E)  sedation

753.  Pilocarpine

754.  Atropine

755.  Succinylcholine

## Questions 756 through 760

For each drug listed, choose the description which best describes its pharmacological properties.

(A) adenosine antagonist
(B) non-selective adrenergic agonist
(C) muscarinic antagonist
(D) $\beta_2$-selective adrenergic agonist
(E) $\beta$-selective adrenergic agonist

756. Theophylline

757. Isoproterenol

758. Terbutaline

759. Epinephrine

760. Ipratropium bromide

## Questions 761 through 764

For each description of mechanism of action or physiologic response, choose the drug which best fits the description.

(A) nitroglycerin (glyceryl trinitrate)
(B) diltiazem
(C) propranolol
(D) digoxin
(E) quinidine

761. Stimulates guanylyl cyclase

762. Blocks $\beta$-adrenoceptor mediated stimulation of adenylyl cyclase

763. May induce reflex tachycardia

764. Blocks calcium entry into smooth and cardiac myocytes

## Questions 765 through 768

For each description, choose the drug which best fits the description.

(A) aspirin
(B) acetaminophen
(C) indomethacin
(D) ibuprofen
(E) phenylbutazone

765. Is effective in the treatment of patent ductus arteriosus

766. Tinnitus is a symptom of toxicity

767. Has replaced colchicine as the initial treatment for acute gout

768. Inhibits platelet aggregation

## Questions 769 through 773

(A) penicillin
(B) tetracycline
(C) clindamycin
(D) sulfamethoxazole
(E) dapsone

769. Binds to the 50S subunit of bacterial ribosomes

770. Binds to the 30S subunit of bacterial ribosomes

771. Has a $\beta$-lactam structure

772. Frequently combined with trimethoprim

773. Used in the treatment of leprosy

DIRECTIONS (Questions 774 through 800): Each of the numbered items or incomplete statements in this section is followed by answers or by completions of the statement. Select the ONE lettered answer or completion that is BEST in each case.

774. All of the following statements regarding vasopressin (antidiuretic hormone, ADH) and its actions are correct EXCEPT

    (A) thiazide diuretics are useful in treating nephrogenic (vasopressin-resistant) diabetes insipidus

    (B) ethanol inhibits vasopressin secretion

    (C) intranasal desmopressin (1-deamino-8-$d$-arginine vasopressin) is useful in treating diabetes insipidus

    (D) hyperosmolality stimulates vasopressin secretion

    (E) vasopressin relaxes vascular smooth muscle

775. Opioids including morphine are useful in all of the clinical settings described EXCEPT

    (A) pain in terminal illness

    (B) acute pulmonary edema

    (C) premedication before surgery

    (D) headache associated with concussion

    (E) diarrhea

776. Aminoglycoside antibiotics are associated with all of the following adverse side effects EXCEPT

    (A) ototoxicity

    (B) neuromuscular blockade

    (C) nephrotoxicity

    (D) hepatotoxicity

    (E) optic nerve dysfunction

777. All of the following statements concerning propranolol are true EXCEPT

    (A) it competitively blocks $\beta_1$-adrenergic receptors

    (B) it can be used as a prophylaxis for migraine

    (C) it competitively blocks $\beta_2$-adrenergic receptors

    (D) it can be safely used by asthma sufferers

    (E) it can be used to treat atrial fibrillation

778. All of the following mechanisms are utilized to relieve angina EXCEPT

    (A) decreased myocardial contractile force

    (B) relaxation of coronary arteries in spasm

    (C) increased extraction of oxygen from blood

    (D) decreased heart rate

    (E) decreased venous return to the heart

779. Chronic lead poisoning is characterized by all of the following EXCEPT

    (A) gastrointestinal effects

    (B) muscle weakness

    (C) encephalopathy

    (D) impaired hemoglobin synthesis

    (E) skin rashes

780. All of the following are predictable adverse effects of treatment with phenothiazines such as chlorpromazine EXCEPT

    (A) orthostatic hypotension

    (B) Parkinson's syndrome

    (C) excessive salivation

    (D) hyperprolactinemia

    (E) constipation

781. All of the following pharmacokinetic statements are correct EXCEPT

    (A) the oral route of administration has more potential for first-pass metabolism than the IV route

    (B) inhalation has the advantage of very rapid absorption

    (C) passive diffusion typically does not involve stereochemical selectivity for drug enantiomers

    (D) for drugs highly bound to serum proteins, pharmacological activity correlates best with the total drug rather than the free drug concentration

    (E) an exceptionally large volume of distribution usually indicates that the drug is cleared by hepatic metabolism

782. Correct statements regarding multiple dosing therapeutics include all of the following EXCEPT

(A) the mean plasma level with multiple dosing depends on clearance

(B) the approach (rate) to steady-state (plateau) drug concentration depends only on the half-life of the drug

(C) there is a greater mean plasma concentration for drugs administered via continuous infusion than by multiple dosing

(D) an initial loading dose is often desirable when the time to reach steady-state is appreciable

(E) halving both the dose and dosage interval reduces fluctuations but leaves mean steady-state plasma concentration unchanged

783. All of the following are advantages to combining carbidopa with levodopa EXCEPT

(A) adverse effects of levodopa on the central nervous system are reduced

(B) allows reduction of the dosage of levodopa

(C) permits more rapid dosage titration

(D) avoids pyridoxine antagonism of levodopa

(E) causes fewer gastrointestinal side effects

784. Prostacyclin ($PGI_2$) has all of the following actions EXCEPT

(A) potent vasodilation

(B) inhibition of platelet aggregation

(C) suppression of gastric ulceration

(D) reduction of renal blood flow

(E) lowering of the threshold of nociceptors at afferent nerve endings

785. Common electrocardiographic (ECG) effects of digitalis glycosides include all of the following EXCEPT

(A) prolongation of the PR interval

(B) shortening of the QT interval

(C) widening of the QRS complex

(D) ST-segment depression

(E) T-wave inversion

786. Potential mechanisms of resistance to antineoplastic drugs include all of the following EXCEPT

(A) quantitative increase in target enzyme

(B) decreased affinity of the target enzyme for the drug

(C) reduced cellular uptake of the drug

(D) enhanced active efflux of the drug

(E) decreased tumor cell heterogeneity

787. An individual who has ingested a toxic dose of acetaminophen may experience all of the following EXCEPT

(A) nausea and vomiting

(B) hepatic enzyme elevation

(C) impaired coagulation

(D) tinnitus

(E) abdominal pain

788. Chronic abusers of barbiturates will often display cross-tolerance to all of the following EXCEPT

(A) diazepam

(B) alcohol

(C) morphine

(D) methaqualone

(E) chlordiazepoxide

789. Renal failure occurring during gentamicin therapy is characterized by all of the following EXCEPT

(A) the inability to concentrate urine

(B) the presence of protein and casts in the urine

(C) rising trough concentrations of the drug

(D) reversibility

(E) decreased plasma creatinine

790. All of the following are predictable adverse effects of tricyclic anti-depressants EXCEPT

   (A) decrease in seizure threshold
   (B) weight gain
   (C) insomnia
   (D) dry mouth
   (E) orthostatic hypotension

791. All of the following sedatives have pharmacologically active metabolites EXCEPT

   (A) prazepam
   (B) chlordiazepoxide
   (C) diazepam
   (D) lorazepam
   (E) chlorazepate

792. All of the following are important side effects of glucocorticoids when used as anti-inflammatory agents EXCEPT

   (A) suppression of pituitary–adrenal function
   (B) masculinization of female patients
   (C) increased susceptibility to infections
   (D) osteoporosis
   (E) Cushing's habitus

793. Hormonal side effects of estrogen excess related to oral contraceptive use may include all of the following EXCEPT

   (A) weight gain
   (B) headaches
   (C) amenorrhea
   (D) edema
   (E) breast tenderness

794. All of the following are factors that may increase the sensitivity of the myocardium to digoxin EXCEPT

   (A) hypercalcemia
   (B) hypoxia
   (C) hypokalemia
   (D) hyperthyroidism
   (E) hypomagnesemia

795. All of the following agents are useful in the treatment of bronchial asthma EXCEPT

   (A) aminophylline
   (B) isoproterenol
   (C) ipratropium bromide
   (D) cromolyn sodium
   (E) propranolol

796. Epinephrine increases all of the following EXCEPT

   (A) total peripheral resistance
   (B) heart rate
   (C) systolic arterial pressure
   (D) oxygen consumption
   (E) blood glucose

797. All of the following drugs are useful in treating an acute gout attack EXCEPT

   (A) allopurinol
   (B) ibuprofen
   (C) phenylbutazone
   (D) colchicine
   (E) indomethacin

798. $H_1$ receptor antagonists are used to treat all of the following EXCEPT

   (A) motion sickness
   (B) allergic rhinitis
   (C) sleep disorders
   (D) bronchial asthma
   (E) urticaria

799. All of the following are true about phenytoin EXCEPT that it

   (A) is highly bound to plasma proteins
   (B) is mainly excreted unchanged in the urine
   (C) has dose-dependent elimination kinetics
   (D) is effective in grand mal seizures
   (E) induces the metabolism of certain drugs

**800.** Cimetidine has been associated with all of the following side effects EXCEPT

(A) gynecomastia

(B) neural dysfunction

(C) reduction of sperm count

(D) relapse of ulcer symptoms on withdrawal

(E) increased hepatic drug-metabolizing capability

# Pharmacology
## Answers and Explanations

**674. (D)** The apparent volume of distribution is a function of the elimination process and is calculated from the formula, $V_d = X/C$, where $V_d$ is the volume of distribution, X is the amount of drug present in the body, and C is the plasma (or blood) concentration. We must use time zero for our calculations since this is the only time at which we know the amount in the body because the drug will immediately be subjected to elimination. The curvature seen in the early data points results from distribution of the drug from blood into tissue compartments. The linear portion of the data reflects the elimination process and must be extrapolated back to time zero to determine the plasma concentration which would have been obtained if distribution had been instantaneous. The administered amount (X) of 30 mg divided by the extrapolated plasma concentration of 1 μg/mL (or 1 mg/L) yields an apparent $V_d$ of 30 L. *(Rang, p 94)*

**675. (C)** Using the linear portion of the data (including the dashed extrapolation), the concentration at time zero is 1 μg/mL. By definition, the half-life is the time interval for 50% reduction in concentration for single-dose drug disappearance. The plasma concentration of 0.5 μg/mL is reached after 7 hrs. The half-life will predict the approach to plateau for any situation in which first-order kinetics apply. Single-dose disappearance kinetics can be thought of as the approach to a plateau of zero. *(Craig and Stitzel, p 56)*

**676. (A)** The anxiolytic agent diazepam, like most CNS active drugs, gains access to the CNS by virtue of possessing high lipid solubility. Hepatic metabolism is the elimination fate of drugs with high lipid solubility. Because the blood flow from the GI tract first passes through the liver, orally administered diazepam will undergo extensive first-pass hepatic metabolism, decreasing the amount reaching the systemic circulation and thus reducing the AUC. The other routes bypass first-pass hepatic metabolism except for the rectal route, which may have a component of first-pass metabolism. *(Katzung, p 39)*

**677. (D)** The loading dose is the amount of drug given in a single bolus that will achieve the steady-state plasma level. From the equation given in the answer to Question 674, the loading dose is equal to the steady-state plasma concentration times the apparent volume of distribution. Since the apparent volume of distribution is four times larger in the obese patient, the loading dose must be four times larger to achieve the same plasma concentration. *(Katzung, p 33)*

**678. (A)** Comparison of the clearances (calculated from the product of $V_d \times k_{elimination}$) indicates the clearances are the same in both patients. Since the target plasma concentrations are the same, the maintenance infusion rates must be the same. *(Smith and Reynard, p 45)*

**679. (D)** The relatively large volume of distribution of 50 L in the normal patient and 200 L in the obese patient indicates high lipid solubility as evidenced by distribution out of the blood and the increase in $V_d$ with obesity. Drugs with high lipid solubility (high lipophilicity) are usually cleared by hepatic metabolism. *(Rang, pp 80–81)*

680. **(C)** When the infusion rate is increased by a factor of 2 while clearance remains constant, the plasma concentration will approach the new steady state level of 400 µg/mL (2 times the original). In one half-life (6 hr), the plasma level will be at 300 µg/mL, 50% of the distance to the new steady state. In two half-lives (12 hr), the plasma level will be at 350 µg/mL or 75% of the way to the new steady state. *(Katzung, pp 38–39)*

681. **(C)** Clearance equals input rate divided by the plasma steady-state concentration. Thus, the clearance is (1 mg/min)/(4 mg/L) or 250 mL/min. *(Katzung, p 42)*

682. **(B)** Botulinum toxin has an intrinsic zinc protease activity, which enters the presynaptic motor nerve terminal and cleaves proteins involved in neurotransmitter exocytosis. This activity can be used therapeutically for severe muscle spasms. *(Ahnerthilger and Bigalke, pp 83–96)*

683. **(B)** The muscarinic agonist pilocarpine will cause contraction of the sphincter muscle of the iris, thereby producing miosis, which reduces intraocular pressure by facilitating outflow of aqueous humor through the canal of Schlemm. *(Katzung, pp 91–92, 98)*

684. **(B)** Orthostatic hypotension, manifested as dizziness upon standing and arising from $\alpha_1$-adrenergic blocking effects, is frequently observed with therapy using the phenothiazine antipsychotic agents. Chlorpromazine may cause orthostatic hypotension and reflex tachycardia because of the combination of α-adrenergic blockade and central actions of the drug. Meprobamate, benzodiazepines, or fluoxetine have little or no α-adrenergic blocking activity. *(Katzung, p 437)*

685. **(E)** Lidocaine, a class IB antiarrhythmic agent, exerts its effects through blocking both active and inactive sodium channels. By adding to depolarization-induced blockade or inactivation of sodium channels, lidocaine will selectively suppress electrical activity in depolarized arrhythmogenic tissue. *(Katzung, p 220)*

686. **(D)** Oral anticoagulants such as warfarin block the vitamin K-dependent step in the synthesis of clotting factors. Carboxylation of descarboxyprothrombin to form prothrombin requires the reduced form of vitamin K ($KH_2$), which is converted to vitamin K epoxide (KO). $KH_2$ is regenerated by an epoxide reductase requiring NADH. It is this step that is blocked by warfarin. Heparin exerts its anticoagulant actions by acting as a template for combining thrombin and antithrombin III. *(Gilman et al, pp 1317–1319)*

687. **(C)** Spironolactone is a competitive antagonist of aldosterone and, therefore, may cause hyperkalemia if administered concomitantly with potassium supplements. Likewise, the potassium-sparing diuretics triamterene and amiloride cause potassium retention. Captopril inhibits production of angiotensin II and, therefore, inhibits aldosterone production. Furosemide promotes renal potassium excretion and often requires concomitant supplemental potassium administration. *(Gilman et al, pp 721–728)*

688. **(D)** Ranitidine is a histamine$_2$ ($H_2$) receptor-blocking agent. $H_2$ receptors have been identified in numerous sites, including the stomach, uterus, ileum, and bronchial musculature. Gastric acid secretion involves activation of $H_2$ receptors; disorders of acid secretion, such as duodenal ulcer, have responded to treatment with $H_2$ receptor antagonists. The remaining choices listed in the question do respond to conventional antihistamines ($H_1$-blocking drugs) but not to $H_2$ antagonists. *(Katzung, pp 259–262)*

689. **(D)** ACE inhibitors, such as captopril and enalapril, are effective agents in the treatment of systemic hypertension and congestive heart failure. Although initially perceived as being most useful for the therapy of renovascular disease and high renin hypertension, these drugs are now used routinely in many cases of essential hypertension. By

inhibiting ACE, these drugs impair conversion of angiotensin I to angiotensin II while also prolonging the half-life of bradykinin, a vasodilator that normally is partially degraded by ACE. Accordingly, renin levels will rise as feedback inhibition via production of angiotensin II is removed. Unlike β-blockers, these drugs do not interfere with reflex sympathetic activity, and thus the response to exercise is unimpaired. Unlike centrally acting agents, such as clonidine, there is no indication of rebound hypertension. The drugs are being used routinely as adjuvant therapy in congestive heart failure where a combination of decreased afterload and increased cardiac output is of great benefit to the patient. (*Katzung, pp 163–165*)

690. **(B)** Tricyclic/heterocyclic antidepressants block reuptake of biogenic amine neurotransmitters into the presynaptic nerve terminals. Although increased synaptic concentrations of neurotransmitter should, according to the biogenic amine-deficient model of depression, result in a cure, clinical improvement seems to correlate temporally better with downregulation of receptors. These agents are relatively selective for certain neurotransmitters. Desipramine is the most selective agent for blocking uptake of norepinephrine; amitriptyline, fluoxetine, and trazodone are relatively selective for blocking reuptake of serotonin. Imipramine, nortriptyline, and doxepin are intermediate in their selectivity. (*Katzung, p 454*)

691. **(A)** Alkalinization of urine to pH 8 will cause the weak acid to be in the ionized anionic form that will not be passively reabsorbed back into the blood, thus promoting renal excretion. Urinary acidification will decrease renal clearance because the protonated form of the acid will predominate, and it is the protonated or uncharged form that undergoes passive reabsorption. Low doses of probenecid will probably decrease renal excretion, since probenecid (which is itself an organic acid) will compete for the active tubular secretion system. Phenobarbital, because it is also an organic acid, will also decrease the renal clearance of the weak organic acid by competing for the organic acid active tubular secretion system. Phenobarbital will also induce activity of hepatic cytochrome P450, which will increase hepatic clearance of substrate drugs, but this should have no effect on renal clearance of the parent drug. Induction of cytochrome P450 also takes a period of days to become evident. (*Katzung, p 6*)

692. **(C)** The most common side effect of NSAIDs is gastrointestinal complaints, including gastric upset, gastritis, and peptic ulceration. These symptoms, along with the others listed that occur less frequently, are all the result of inhibition of the prostaglandin portion of eicosanoid metabolism. (*Katzung, p 541; Craig and Stitzel, pp 486–487*)

693. **(A)** Therapeutic plasma levels for phenytoin range from 10 to 20 μg/mL. Above 20 μg/mL, dose-related cerebellar–vestibular effects occur. At concentrations of 20 μg/mL, nystagmus is initially observed. Ataxia is observed at levels of 30 μg/mL, and at 40 μg/mL, lethargy is seen. Increased frequency of seizures also has occurred at very high plasma levels. (*Gilman et al, p 443*)

694. **(B)** Oral iron preparations in the form of ferrous salts (sulfate, fumarate, gluconate) are the preferred and most inexpensive treatments for microcytic, hypochromic (iron-deficiency) anemia. The bioavailability of various oral ferrous salts is relatively similar. Ferrous sulfate is less expensive than the other forms however, and should be considered the treatment of choice. Ferric salts show poorer absorption. Macrocytic megaloblastic anemias arise from derangements in DNA metabolism and are symptoms of either vitamin $B_{12}$ or folate deficiency. Diagnosis of the underlying cause of the anemia must precede the treatment, since folate administration will apparently correct the anemia but allow undetected neurological damage associated with $B_{12}$ deficiency to progress. (*Katzung, pp 495, 500–502*)

695. **(E)** The duration of action of various insulin preparations is related to the rate of absorption from the subcutaneous injection site.

Formation of complexes with various compounds such as protamine results in slower absorption of insulin. Ultralente insulin has a particularly long duration of action (approximately 36 hours) for the latter reasons. Regular insulin and semilente insulin are fast-acting insulins, with duration of action ranging from 6 to 14 hours. Intermediate-acting preparations with duration of action of approximately 24 hours include NPH insulin and lente insulin. *(Katzung, p 643)*

696. **(C)** Lovastatin is an inhibitor of HMG-CoA reductase, the rate-limiting enzyme in cholesterol biosynthesis. It is the most efficacious agent in the treatment of heterozygous familial hypercholesterolemia. Bile acid-binding resins are somewhat less efficacious and more bothersome to take orally (gritty fluid suspensions or chewable bars). Both the HMG-CoA reductase inhibitors (lovastatin, simvastatin, prevastatin, and fluvastatin) and the bile acid-binding resins (cholestyramine, colestipol) lower LDL cholesterol levels through increased expression and activity of hepatic LDL receptors that endocytose LDL particles. By lowering intrahepatic free cholesterol levels, these two classes of hypolipidemic agents remove cholesterol (or oxycholesterol) repression of transcription of the genes for LDL receptors and HMG-CoA reductase. These agents do not work in patients who are homozygous for defective LDL receptor. Niacin (nicotinic acid), through unknown mechanisms, decreases the production of very low-density lipoprotein (VLDL) particles, which in turn lead to less conversion to LDL particles. Clofibrate (and probably the other fibric acid derivatives including gemfibrozil) reduces plasma triglyceride levels by decreasing the VLDL content of apoprotein CIII, which acts as an inhibitor of lipoprotein lipase activity. The resulting increased lipoprotein lipase activity allows more rapid catabolism of VLDL particles in skeletal muscle and adipose tissue vascular beds. Gemfibrozil causes a beneficial increase in HDL cholesterol levels through unknown mechanisms. *(Katzung, pp 522–533; Hertz et al, pp 13470–13475)*

697. **(D)** The calcium in calcium disodium edetate is readily displaced by heavy metals, such as lead, forming stable complexes (chelates), which are excreted in the urine. Calcium disodium EDTA will bind in vivo any available divalent or trivalent metal that has a greater affinity for EDTA than has calcium. Mobilization and excretion of lead indicate that the metal is accessible to EDTA. Mercury poisoning does not respond to EDTA in vivo. *(Gilman et al, pp 1607–1608)*

698. **(A)** Lidocaine is beneficial in preventing ventricular arrhythmia during myocardial infarction (MI) . Moreover, it is relatively safe for patients during the acute phase of this condition, since it lacks significant depressant effects on the cardiovascular system and has a short duration of action. During acute MI, digoxin may promote arrhythmia; quinidine and propranolol are generally not used during the acute phase of MI. Because the general use of flecainide was associated with mortality rates higher than placebo in the Cardiac Arrhythmia Suppression Trial (CAST), use of flecainide is limited to severe ventricular tachyarrhythmias. *(Katzung, pp 214–221)*

699. **(B)** Although thiabendazole has a high degree of activity against a wide variety of nematodes, including *Ascaris* and *Enterobius*, the high incidence (up to 50%) of adverse reactions including nausea, vomiting, epigastric pain, diarrhea, and neuropsychiatric symptoms precludes its routine use. Pyrantel pamoate is a broad-spectrum anthelminthic that is effective against these nematodes. Side effects, which occur only occasionally, include gastrointestinal upset, headache, or dizziness. Tetrachloroethylene is useful in the treatment of hookworm but is seldom used, since more effective and less toxic agents are available. Trivalent antimonials such as antimony potassium tartrate are also not used because of unacceptable toxicity. Diethylcarbamazine is used primarily in the treatment of filariae of the genus *Wuchereria*. *(Katzung, pp 804–820)*

**700.** **(B)** The mechanism by which propranolol relieves hypertension is most likely related to blockade of β-receptors. Blockade of brain β-receptors has been proposed but seems to be ruled out by observations that propranolol derivatives that do not enter the CNS are still active as antihypertensive agents. The release of renin from the juxtaglomerular apparatus of the kidney is mediated by $\beta_1$-adrenergic receptors, and propranolol seems to be especially effective in patients with hypertension associated with elevated plasma renin levels. Propranolol in therapeutic doses does not significantly affect α-adrenergic receptors, depletion of amines, or the reuptake of norepinephrine. Propranolol would tend to induce up-regulation of β-adrenergic receptors rather than down-regulation. *(Gilman et al, p 232; Katzung, p 157)*

**701.** **(A)** Phenobarbital is the archetypal inducer of hepatic cytochrome P450 activity. One or more of the induced P450 isoforms metabolizes the coumarin anticoagulants so that hepatic clearance of the anticoagulants is increased. This results in a reduction of anticoagulant activity. Aspirin, phenylbutazone, and sulfinpyrazone will increase the risk of hemorrhage by inhibiting platelet function and promoting gastric ulceration. Displacement of coumarin anticoagulants from serum protein-binding sites by these compounds will also contribute acutely to increased anticoagulant activity. Cimetidine will also increase anticoagulant activity by inhibiting the hepatic metabolism of the coumarins. *(Katzung, p 514)*

**702.** **(A)** Leukotrienes are thiolether-linked lipoxygenase metabolites of arachidonic acid. They appear to play a critical role in bronchospasm, edema, and mucous hypersecretion common to many forms of asthma. Among their profound cardiovascular effects is their ability to constrict coronary arteries, supporting a potential role for leukotrienes in shock and myocardial ischemia. Because most commonly used nonsteroidal antiinflammatory drugs, including aspirin, inhibit cyclo-oxygenase without affecting 5'-lipoxy-genase, arachidonic acid may be shunted to the lipoxygenase pathway. Platelets do not contain 5'-lipoxygenase (although they do contain 12'-lipoxygenase), and leukotrienes are not stored in platelet granules. The cyclo-oxygenase product of arachidonic acid, $TXA_2$, is critical in platelet physiology, and acetylation of this enzyme by aspirin accounts for the effect of this drug in inhibiting platelet function. $LTB_4$ is a potent chemotactic agent for polymorphonuclear leukocytes, but not for the other leukotrienes. *(Gilman et al, pp 605–610)*

**703.** **(D)** Streptokinase forms a complex with plasminogen. This complex gains plasmin activity and will lyse fibrin clots. Urokinase differs from streptokinase in that it directly converts plasminogen to plasmin. The endogenous activity which converts plasminogen to plasmin is tissue plasminogen activator (t-PA). Streptokinase, urokinase, and t-PA are all useful in treating clots associated with pulmonary embolism, deep vein thrombosis, and acute myocardial infarction. Streptokinase, a bacterial product, is much less expensive than the other two agents that are produced in tissue culture using recombinant DNA technology. To date, no distinct clinical advantage of any of these agents has been shown. *(Katzung, p 515)*

**704.** **(B)** In neuronal tissue culture, carbamazepine blocks sodium channels and inhibits high-frequency repetitive neuronal firing. It also presynaptically decreases synaptic transmission. The GABAergic systems are relatively unaffected by carbamazepine. Carbamazepine is an inducer of its own hepatic metabolism as well as that of other substrate drugs. *(Katzung, pp 366–367)*

**705.** **(C)** Local anesthetics inhibit sensory nerve conduction via blockade of voltage-sensitive sodium channels. As a result of this blockade, the threshold of excitability of the nerve is increased, and the ability of the nerve to propagate an action potential is decreased. Ultimately, the transmission of sensory stimuli to the CNS is suppressed. *(Katzung, pp 397–398)*

**706. (D)** In an individual severely poisoned by antihistamines, the central effects, both the depressant and stimulant actions, cause the greatest danger. There is no specific therapy for poisoning, and treatment is usually supportive. In a child, the dominant effect is excitation; and hallucinations, ataxia, incoordination, athetosis, and convulsions may occur. Symptoms such as fixed and dilated pupils, a flushed face, and fever are common and markedly resemble those of atropine poisoning. Deepening coma and cardiorespiratory collapse characterize terminal poisoning. Fever and flushing generally are not manifestations of antihistamine poisoning in adults. *(Gilman et al, pp 586–587)*

**707. (C)** Pancreatic beta cells are electrically active and exhibit a slow phase IV spontaneous depolarization rate. Depolarization causes entry of calcium and activation of insulin exocytosis. Under conditions of low glucose, the tendency to depolarize is counteracted by the activity of an ATP-sensitive hyperpolarizing potassium channel. When glucose levels are high, glucose enters beta cells via an insulin-independent transporter and is metabolized to yield ATP. The increased ATP levels inhibit the potassium channel, allowing the cell to depolarize and secrete insulin. Sulfonylureas such as glyburide bind to a cell surface protein to cause inhibition of the hyperpolarizing potassium channel, thereby allowing the beta cell to spontaneously depolarize and secrete insulin. *(Katzung, p 639)*

**708. (D)** The blood : gas partition coefficient determines the rate of onset of anesthesia. Blood provides the means of delivery to the brain. The solubility of the agent determines how rapidly the partial pressure rises in the blood. Agents with high solubility (large blood gas partition coefficients) require large amounts of the anesthetic to be put into the blood before the partial pressure in the blood will increase enough to effectively deliver the agent to the brain. The MAC value and the other properties listed are all measures of the anesthetic potency, which is independent of the rate of onset. Desirable properties for inhalation anesthetic agents include high po-

tency and low blood solubility. The halogenated hydrocarbons, such as desflurane and isoflurane, fit these criteria and are extensively used. *(Katzung, p 383)*

**709. (E)** Edrophonium, because it is short-acting, is used in the diagnosis of myasthenia gravis, an autoimmune disease characterized by deficiency in acetylcholine actions at neuromuscular junctions due to the presence of antibodies directed against nicotinic receptors. Pralidoxime is a reactivator of organophosphate-inhibited cholinesterase. Isoflurophate, an organophosphate cholinesterase inhibitor, is used in the treatment of glaucoma where long duration of action is needed. Physostigmine is a reversible cholinesterase inhibitor whose lipid solubility allows it to be used to treat the CNS anticholinergic actions of overdoses of atropine. Neostigmine is the anticholinesterase drug of choice for myasthenia gravis because of its lack of CNS effects and direct agonist actions at nicotinic sites. *(Katzung, pp 98–100)*

**710. (B)** The thioamide propylthiouracil exerts its primary antithyroid actions by inhibiting the thyroid peroxidase, which carries out iodine organification and coupling of iodotyrosines. The ability of propylthiouracil (and to a lesser extend methimazole) to block the deiodination of $T_4$ to $T_3$ adds to the treatment of thyroid storm. Propranolol is used in thyroid storm to lessen sympathetic components involved but has no direct actions on thyroid hormone status. Radioactive iodine is used to ablate thyroid tissue in hyperthyroidism (Graves' disease). Perchlorate anion will block iodine transport into the thyroid gland but is not used therapeutically because it causes aplastic anemia. *(Katzung, pp 584–585)*

**711. (D)** Clomiphene is a weak partial agonist at estrogen receptors. When clomiphene is bound, it acts as a competitive antagonist of endogenous estrogen. Clomiphene is thought to block estrogen feedback inhibition of gonadotropin-releasing hormone secretion from the hypothalamus. This allows gonadotropin-releasing hormone and the gonadotropins to increase, stimulating ovulation.

Flutamide is an antiandrogen used in the palliative treatment of prostate cancer. Ethinyl estradiol, a synthetic estrogen, and norethindrone, a synthetic progestin, are commonly used separately for replacement therapy or combined for oral contraception. The nonsteroidal synthetic compound diethylstilbestrol is used as a postcoital contraceptive. *(Katzung, p 626)*

712. **(E)** The bile acid-binding resins colestipol and cholestyramine, as well as the HMG-CoA reductase inhibitors, depend on increased activity of hepatic LDL receptors to lower LDL cholesterol. By trapping bile acids in the intestinal lumen, the intrahepatic free cholesterol levels are lowered due to decreased absorption from the gut and increased intracellular conversion of cholesterol to bile acids as a result of removal of feedback inhibition of the conversion pathway. The lowered intracellular free cholesterol levels remove repression of transcription for the LDL receptor gene. The expressed gene product must be functional, as evidenced by the relative lack of response of patients homozygous in defective LDL receptors to both bile acid-binding resins and HMG-CoA reductase inhibitors. *(Katzung, pp 530–532)*

713. **(E)** The kinetics for the approach to the steady-state concentration are controlled by the elimination half-life. If we think of the difference between the starting concentration (zero in this case) and the final steady-state concentration as a distance that must be traversed, the concentration will traverse half of the remaining distance in each half-life. In this case, after 12 hours or one half-life, the concentration will be 50% of the steady state. After 24 hours or two half-lives, the concentration will be at 75% of steady state. After 96 hours or four half-lives, the concentration will be at 93.75% of the steady-state level. Mathematically, the steady-state asymptote is only achieved after an infinite amount of time, but the normal rule of thumb is to use 4 × half-life as a measure of the time to essentially achieve the steady-state level. *(Katzung, p 38)*

714. **(A)** Severe digitalis intoxication is best treated by using digitalis antibodies to neutralize the drug. Administration of antiarrhythmic agents may cause cardiac arrest. Serum potassium will be high because of the profound inhibition of Na/K ATPase. *(Katzung, p 199)*

715. **(B)** Dobutamine is used in acute, reversible heart failure such as following cardiac surgery or cardiogenic shock because it increases force of contraction but causes less tachycardia than does a dose of epinephrine giving the same inotropic response. Less tachycardia means less of an increase in myocardial oxygen demand in the compromised heart. Propranolol through its β-blocking activity will depress contractility. Digitalis is not useful in acute situations, and its use is reserved for chronic irreversible heart failure. Atropine will increase heart rate by blocking vagal effects. *(Katzung, p 196)*

716. **(C)** Initial blocking actions of succinylcholine are attributable to the agonist activity of the drug in causing depolarization of the motor end plate. Because succinylcholine is not metabolized by synaptic acetylcholinesterase, it produces a persistent depolarization blockade until the drug diffuses away to be metabolized by plasma pseudocholinesterase. Thus, addition of the short-acting anticholinesterase edrophonium is unable to overcome the blockade. At later times, the blockade changes to a competitive-type blockade, perhaps as a result of receptor desensitization and/or metabolism of succinylcholine to the monocholine derivative, which is thought to behave like d-tubocurarine, a competitive nicotinic antagonist. *(Rang et al, p 137; Katzung, p 410)*

717. **(B)** The heart contains glucagon receptors linked to stimulation of adenylyl cyclase. Glucagon exerts inotropic and chronotropic effects in the heart. Atrial natriuretic peptide is released from the atria and stimulates sodium excretion in the urine. Epinephrine will be ineffective in the presence of profound β-receptor blockade. *(Katzung, p 909)*

**718. (D)** At steady state, the output rate equals the input rate. Since 20 mg/hr is going into the patient, 20 mg/hr is also coming out of the patient. The total systemic clearance is the sum of the clearances for the individual organs (usually liver and kidney) contributing to the drug elimination. Since the liver accounts for 80% of the loss, this means that the liver is eliminating 16 mg/hr and the kidney is eliminating 4 mg/hr. In the patient with 50% renal function, the liver will still eliminate 16 mg/hr, but the kidney will eliminate only 2 mg/hr, giving a total of 18 mg/hr at the same steady-state plasma concentration. Thus, the infusion rate should be adjusted to 18 mg/hr for this patient with impaired renal function. *(Katzung, p 34)*

**719. (D)** The expression of phenylethanolamine-N-methyltransferase (PNMT), the enzyme which converts norepinephrine to epinephrine, is regulated by cortisol. Because the adrenal chromaffin cells are bathed in cortisol released from the adrenal cortex, PNMT activity in the medulla is high, thus allowing expression of the transferase activity. *(Gilman et al, p 104)*

**720. (E)** Lithium carbonate is the current agent of choice, particularly during the manic phase. Because the onset of action is slow, concurrent use of antipsychotic agents such as chlorpromazine or haloperidol may be necessary to control mania. Concurrent use of tricyclic antidepressants may be necessary in the depressive phase. Monitoring of lithium levels is necessary because of the serious nature of the adverse effects (neurologic, renal, cardiac). *(Katzung, pp 444–445)*

**721. (A)** Ethanol is metabolized by alcohol dehydrogenase (and to a lesser extent the microsomal ethanol oxidizing system) to acetaldehyde primarily in the liver. When ethanol concentrations are very high (relative to cellular metabolites), the metabolizing system becomes rate limited at the level of oxidation of the NADH formed. As a result, zero-order kinetics are observed. A typical adult will show a constant elimination rate, which translates as a decline in blood level of 22 mg/dL/hr. As blood alcohol levels drop below about 100 mg/dL (the legal limit for intoxication in many states), elimination has characteristics intermediate between zero and first order. Only at concentrations below 1 mg/dL is the elimination first order. At the high levels of ethanol where zero-order kinetics apply, clearance is not constant, since constant clearance implies first-order elimination. *(Katzung, pp 658–659)*

**722. (C)** The description best fits the antimuscarinic agent atropine which causes pupillary dilation (mydriasis) and spasm of accommodation (cycloplegia) for several days. Tropicamide is more routinely used for ophthalmologic examinations because its actions have a shorter duration. Phenylephrine will produce mydriasis without cycloplegia. The anticholinesterases will produce pupillary constriction (miosis) and cycloplegia. *(Katzung, p 106)*

**723. (A)** The description indicates a CNS stimulant such as amphetamine or cocaine. The rapid loss of activity with frequent repeated use is indicative of amphetamine for which tolerance rapidly develops (tachyphylaxis). This may arise in part from depletion of cytoplasmic biogenic amine stores caused by amphetamine displacement. Cocaine, by virtue of its actions in inhibiting synaptic reuptake of biogenic amines, is also a stimulant. Cocaine exhibits a shorter duration of action and has a lower tendency to produce stereotyped behavior than does amphetamine. Rapidly developing tolerance to the stimulating actions is not seen with cocaine. *(Rang et al, pp 636–640)*

**724. (C)** Competitive antagonists shift the agonist dose-response curve to the right without altering the efficacy or maximum response. *(Rang et al, pp 15–19)*

**725. (D)** Noncompetitive antagonists, by inactivating receptors or interfering with postreceptor steps leading to the biological response, lower the apparent efficacy of the agonist. In the absence of space receptors, a loss of 33% of the receptors will allow a new maximum response of 67% of the original response. *(Rang et al, pp 15–19)*

726. **(B)** After Q diffuses into the synaptic cleft, uptake of Q results in a lower concentration of Q reaching the postsynaptic receptors than was applied externally. Thus, the real dose-response curve in terms of the actual synaptic concentration of Q lies to the left of that measured. When uptake is inhibited, the synaptic concentrations more closely parallel the concentrations externally applied so that the observed dose-response curve is shifted to the left. The maximum response obtainable is unchanged by the presence or absence of synaptic uptake. *(Rang et al, pp 155–156)*

727. **(E)** R is, by definition, a partial agonist with 50% of the efficacy of the standard. Curve E, which levels off at 50% of the standard response, is the only one fitting the description. *(Rang et al, pp 11–13)*

728. **(E)** The list includes two immunosuppressive agents—azathioprine and cyclosporine. Azathioprine is an imidazolyl derivative of mercaptopurine and owes its immunosuppressive activity to cleavage to the active agent mercaptopurine. Because mercaptopurine interferes with DNA metabolism, it inhibits the growth of rapidly proliferating cells, including bone marrow. The cyclic peptide cyclosporine achieves a degree of tissue specificity by forming complexes with a family of cyclosporine-binding proteins known as cyclophilins whose expression is tissue specific. In antigen-stimulated T cells, the cyclophilin–cyclosporine complex inhibits the activity of calcineurin, a protein phosphatase involved in activation of gene transcription of cytokines including IL-2, IL-3, and IFN-γ. Cyclosporine causes nephrotoxicity, hyperglycemia, and hyperlipidemia through mechanisms not yet understood. *(Katzung, p 864)*

729. **(I)** Metronidazole is the current drug of choice for treatment of urogenital trichomoniasis. It is also used for *Giardia* and *Helicobacter*. As happens with the aldehyde dehydrogenase inhibitor disulfiram (Antabuse), GI distress, vomiting, and flushing occur when alcohol is consumed by patients taking metronidazole. *(Katzung, pp 799–800)*

730. **(G)** By inhibiting cytochrome P450 3A4 in the liver, ketoconazole can cause toxic accumulation of substrate drugs, including terfenadine and cyclosporine. *(Katzung, pp 725–726)*

731. **(A)** Acyclovir is the only anti-herpetic agent in the list. The intracellular active form of the drug is acycloguanosine triphosphate. The viral thymidine kinase is more active in phosphorylating to the monophosphate than is the host cell kinase so that resistance can be associated with viral thymidine kinase deficiency. Cytarabine can inhibit DNA viruses but is relatively ineffective in vivo so that its use is limited to cancer chemotherapy. AZT works in HIV infections by inhibiting the retroviral reverse transcriptase. *(Katzung, pp 732–733)*

732. **(N)** Trimethoprim is the only antibacterial agent listed that works by binding tightly to bacterial dihydrofolate reductase, thereby inhibiting the enzymatic activity. This mechanism of action is used to advantage when trimethoprim is combined with the para-aminobenzoic acid antagonist sulfamethoxazole to synergistically inhibit sequential steps in bacterial reduced folate synthesis. Resistance to trimethoprim usually involves bacterial expression of a mutated form of dihydrofolate reductase, which does not bind trimethoprim so avidly. *(Craig and Stitzel, p 548)*

733. **(K)** Rifampin selectively inhibits bacterial DNA-dependent RNA polymerase. It is highly useful in treating mycobacterial infections, since it can penetrate cells and kill intracellular mycobacteria. It is an inducer of cytochrome P450, leading to increased hepatic clearance of substrate molecules such as the oral anticoagulants and cyclosporine. *(Katzung, p 709)*

734. **(B)** The need to introduce the antibacterial agent locally indicates that the agent must have limited ability to cross the blood–brain barrier. This indicates a highly polar mole-

cule, ruling out all but the aminoglycoside amikacin. Nephrotoxicity and ototoxicity are properties of the aminoglycosides and vancomycin. *(Katzung, p 703)*

**735.** **(E)** Orthostatic hypotension is associated more with antihypertensive agents working peripherally rather than centrally; thus, we can rule out clonidine and methyldopa. The interference by a tricyclic antidepressant points to guanethidine. This agent, which appears to work within the sympathetic nerve terminal by preventing exocytotic vesicle fusion with the plasma membrane as well as depletion of catecholamine, requires entry into the terminal via the catecholamine transporter, which is inhibited by tricyclic antidepressants. *(Katzung, p 155)*

**736.** **(B)** Minimal adverse effects associated with the antihypertensive agent suggests a centrally acting agent or ACE inhibitor. Dry mouth and sedation are common side effects of clonidine. Rebound hypertension leading to hypertensive crisis after abrupt cessation of clonidine treatment is a potential problem of which patients should be warned. *(Katzung, pp 153–154)*

**737.** **(F)** Appearance of a reversible lupus-like syndrome is associated with hydralazine use. *(Katzung, p 161)*

**738.** **(D)** Onset of a dry cough is a troublesome adverse effect seen with the use of ACE inhibitors such as enalapril. *(Katzung, p 165)*

**739.** **(F)** Cyclophosphamide, an alkylating agent used most often in combination chemotherapy, requires metabolism by cytochrome P450 to form the active species for this drug. *(Katzung, p 829)*

**740.** **(E)** Cisplatin, whose actions involve DNA-adduct formation and oxidative stress, causes little bone marrow depression but does produce kidney damage, which can be minimized by diuresis using saline hydration or osmotic diuretics. *(Katzung, pp 830–831)*

**741.** **(J)** The pyrimidine analog fluorouracil is metabolized within cells to nucleotide forms. The fluoro-deoxyUMP metabolite irreversibly inhibits thymidylate synthase, shutting down the synthesis of thymidine nucleotides and causing "thymineless death." Fluorinated metabolites are also incorporated into RNA, thereby inhibiting RNA processing and function. *(Katzung, p 834)*

**742.** **(I)** The relaxation of DNA supercoiling by topoisomerases is necessary for replication and transcription. DNA topoisomerase II forms an enzyme–DNA intermediate in breaking one DNA strand during the passing of one strand through the other. By arresting topoisomerase at this step, etoposide causes lethal DNA damage in target cells. *(Katzung, p 836)*

**743.** **(A)** Alkalinized urine has the highest pH listed. Sulfadiazine is a weak acid. The protonated form, which is membrane permeant, will equilibrate across the membranes separating blood from these fluid compartments. The unprotonated charged form will accumulate according to the pH of the compartment; its contribution to the total amount present in each compartment can be calculated using the Henderson–Hasselbalch equation. As a general rule, acids will be pH trapped in the fluid compartment with the highest pH, whereas bases will be pH trapped in acidic compartments. Sulfadiazine will accumulate to the greatest extent in alkaline urine. Alkalinization of urine is useful in hastening the renal of excretion of weak organic acids. *(Katzung, p 7)*

**744.** **(D)** The stomach has the lowest pH. Following the reasoning given for Question 743, the base pyrimethamine will be pH trapped and thus accumulate to the greatest extent in the stomach. *(Katzung, p 7)*

**745–748.** **(745-A, 746-C, 747-D, 748-E)** Proprietary laxatives are traditionally classified into bulk laxatives, lubricants, stimulants, stool softeners, and osmotic laxatives. Bulk-forming preparations, which expand and soften the stool via their ability to retain water, include such preparations as bran and psyllium. Lubricants, such as mineral oil, have no pharmacologic effect on the gut and simply lubricate the passage of stool. Bisacodyl is a stimulant-type laxative. Its effect was believed to be due to the initiation of peristalsis in the colon but may be more closely related to the intraluminal accumulation of water. Additional stimulant-type laxatives include phenolphthalein, senna, cascara, danthron, and castor oil. Docusate is an anionic detergent that softens the stool by net water accumulation in the intestine. Osmotic laxatives are believed to hold water in the lumen by an osmotic action. Lactulose is a disaccharide compound that is broken down by colonic bacteria to form osmotically active molecules. Magnesium salts (magnesium sulfate and magnesium citrate) also act as osmotic laxatives. *(Gilman et al, pp 915–924)*

**749–752.   (749-D, 750-C, 751-A, 752-B)** Effector cells stimulated by the sympathetic nervous system have alpha and beta receptors. Agents acting through these receptors and producing the biological effect are direct agonists. Methoxamine is a direct agonist at α-adrenergic receptors. Isoproterenol is a direct beta agonist. Some sympathomimetic agents act indirectly by displacing norepinephrine from presynaptic storage sites. Amphetamine acts in this way. α-Adrenergic and β-adrenergic blocking agents bind to adrenergic receptors, but the resulting drug-receptor complex is unable to produce the biological response; the blockers are thus able to interfere with the effects of endogenous norepinephrine and epinephrine and sympathomimetic agents. Propranolol is the prototype beta blocker, and phenoxybenzamine is a noncompetitive alpha blocker. *(Gilman et al, pp 187–240)*

**753–755.   (753-C, 754-A, 755-D)** The agents listed affect cholinergic transmission in different manners, and their clinical use is in large part a manifestation of their cholinergic effect. Pilocarpine is a naturally occurring alkaloid that is cholinomimetic in effect and acts predominantly at muscarinic sites. In mimicking the effect of acetylcholine, it will cause pupillary constriction, spasm of accommodation, and a transient rise in intraocular pressure that is followed by a prolonged and greater decrease in intraocular pressure. Small doses of pilocarpine are associated with bradycardia and arousal. Atropine is the prototypic antimuscarinic agent, and by competitively blocking the effect of acetylcholine at muscarinic receptors, atropine usually is associated with tachycardia. Central effects of low doses of atropine usually include excitation. Atropine causes mydriasis and cycloplegia but does little to intraocular pressure, with the exception of increasing it in patients with narrow-angle glaucoma. Succinylcholine is the typical depolarizing neuromuscular blocker that produces fasciculation of muscle followed by total paralysis. Succinylcholine may raise intraocular pressure by contracting extraocular muscles and may cause bradycardia because of stimulation of vagal ganglion. Although tachycardia is possible (via stimulation of sympathetic ganglion) after succinylcholine, it is unlikely. None of the drugs listed have appreciable effects on the activity of acetylcholinesterase, the enzyme responsible for hydrolysis of acetylcholine as well as pilocarpine and succinylcholine. Typical inhibitors of cholinesterase are physostigmine, neostigmine, edrophonium, and diisopropyl fluorophosphate. *(Gilman et al, pp 122–127)*

**756–760.   (756-A, 757-E, 758-D, 759-B, 760-C)** Bronchodilator drugs are the mainstay of therapy for patients with bronchial asthma. Bronchodilators exert their anti-bronchoconstrictor effect via different mechanisms. β-Adrenergic receptor agonists such as epinephrine, isoproterenol, and terbutaline activate the enzyme adenylyl cyclase, which increases the intracellular concentration of cyclic AMP. The result is bronchodilation. Terbutaline has the advantage of being specific for β$_2$-adrenergic receptors and therefore produces less cardiac stimulation than epinephrine or isoproterenol. Theophylline is a methylxanthine derivative that inhibits the phosphodiesterase that metabolizes cyclic adenosine monophosphate (AMP). However, current studies suggest its mechanism of action may be blockade of adenosine receptors. Ipratropium bromide inhibits cholinergic receptors, which play a role in initiating bronchoconstriction in response to irritant chemicals. *(Craig and Stitzel, pp 509–521)*

**761–764.    (761-A, 762-C, 763-A, 764-A)** Organic nitrates such as nitroglycerin, beta-blockers such as propranolol, and calcium channel blockers including diltiazem are used in the management of angina pectoris. Nitrates mimic the actions of nitric oxide in stimulating the enzyme guanylyl cyclase, which, through a series of steps, facilitates the relaxation of vascular smooth muscle. Vasodilation decreases the preload and afterload of the heart, thus decreasing oxygen demand and consequently, angina. Decreased blood pressure in response to organic nitrates, however, may also result in reflex tachycardia. Beta-blockers, such as propranolol, prevent the receptor-mediated stimulation of adenylyl cyclase, which ultimately results in a decrease in the force of contraction of the heart and hence decreased oxygen demand. Calcium is a key regulatory component for both smooth and cardiac muscle contraction. By blocking calcium entry, diltiazem can induce vasodilatation and also reduce myocardial contractility. *(Katzung, pp 172–184)*

**765–768.    (765-C, 766-A, 767-C, 768-A)** Nonsteroidal anti-inflammatory drugs (NSAIDs) have as their primary mechanism of action the inhibition of prostaglandin synthesis via inhibition of the enzyme cyclo-oxygenase. However, the particular agents differ in their potency, therapeutic effects, and toxicity. Indomethacin is one of the most potent NSAIDs. Its anti-inflammatory and analgesic properties has made it especially effective in the treatment of acute gout. Moreover, its application as an inhibitor of the prostaglandins responsible for maintaining the patency of ductus arteriosus in newborns has resulted in a significant reduction in the need for surgical repair of this lesion. Aspirin, the prototype for this class of drugs, through its ability to inhibit platelet $TXA_2$, prolongs bleeding time and is under investigation for the treatment of disorders associated with thrombi such as myocardial infarction and stroke. Aspirin toxicity is characterized by a syndrome, salicylism, which includes ringing of the ears (tinnitus) as one of its symptoms. Acetaminophen has only weak activity as a prostaglandin synthesis inhibitor and, as a consequence, has no significant anti-inflammatory action. *(Smith and Reynard, pp 148–160)*

**769–773.    (769-C, 770-B, 771-A, 772-D, 773-E)** Both clindamycin and tetracycline bind to bacterial ribosomes and inhibit protein synthesis of the bacteria. Clindamycin binds to the 50 S subunit where it inhibits a translocation step in peptide synthesis. Tetracycline binds to the 30 S subunit and prevents the addition of amino acids to peptide chains in the process of formation. Tetracycline requires an active transport mechanism to reach its site of action, and the inhibition of its transport is one mechanism of bacterial resistance to this drug. The β-lactam structure of penicillin plays a central role in the inhibition of the bacterial cell wall synthesis. Sulfamethoxazole is a competitive antagonist of para-aminobenzoic acid, a metabolic precursor of folic acid, which is required for purine synthesis. Sulfamethoxazole has increased in use since it was found to be very effective when administered in combination with another antibiotic, trimethoprim. Dapsone is a drug with a mechanism of action similar to sulfamethoxazole and is used in the treatment of leprosy. *(Gilman et al, pp 1065–1135, 1159)*

**774.    (E)** Vasopressin is a peptide hormone secreted by the posterior pituitary gland. Osmoreceptors in the hypothalamus, close to nuclei that synthesize and secrete ADH, are stimulated by an increase in plasma osmolality. Vasopressin acts through receptors in the distal tubule and collecting ducts to increase permeability to water, thus aiding in the formation of hypertonic urine. Desmopressin is used as an intranasal spray for the treatment of diabetes insipidus. This derivative is less susceptible to peptidase breakdown, and the intranasal route avoids GI tract peptidases. Other uses of vasopressin include treatment of bleeding esophageal varices, since the vasoconstrictor effects of ADH appear to be marked in splanchnic circulation. In a seemingly paradoxical manner, vasopressin-resistant diabetes insipidus can be treated with thiazide diuretics which act by decreasing plasma volume and decreasing fluid delivery to the distal tubules. *(Gilman et al, pp 732–740, Katzung, p 247)*

**775.** **(D)** Morphine or other opioids such as meperidine and fentanyl are mainstays in severe pain such as in terminal illnesses or post-surgery and as a premedication before surgery to lessen anxiety. Morphine also finds use in treating the anxiety associated with acute pulmonary edema. All opioids will control diarrhea, but synthetic opioids such as diphenoxylate with little or no CNS actions are preferred over morphine. Opioids, because they depress respiration, are contraindicated in head injuries because increased blood carbon dioxide levels will dilate cerebral vessels, causing elevated intracranial pressure. *(Katzung, p 472)*

**776.** **(D)** All the aminoglycosides produce varying degrees of ototoxicity (either hearing loss or vertigo) and nephrotoxicity. The nephrotoxicity is particularly troublesome, since it will cause aminoglycoside accumulation, which creates a cycle of damage and accumulation. In extremely high doses, aminoglycosides can cause a reversible, curare-like blockade of neuromuscular junctions. Streptomycin may affect optic nerve function, and scotomas, which present as enlargement of the blind spot, have been reported. Hepatic failure has not been associated with the administration of this class of antibiotic. *(Katzung, p 701; Gilman et al, pp 1104–1108)*

**777.** **(D)** Propranolol is a non-selective β-adrenergic antagonist blocking both $\beta_1$- and $\beta_2$-adrenergic receptor subtypes. As an antiarrhythmic drug, it is used primarily to treat arrhythmias of atrial origin such as supraventricular tachycardia, atrial fibrillation, or atrial flutter. The mechanism of this action is antagonism of adrenergic tone at the AV node, thereby increasing its refractoriness. Propranolol can also be effective in migraine prophylaxis, al-

though the mechanism for this benefit is unknown. Seventy percent of patients with migraine experience fewer or less severe attacks following daily administration of propranolol. *(Gilman et al, pp 865–866, 946)*

**778.** **(C)** A high proportion of oxygen (70%) is extracted from the coronary circulation under normal circumstances, and drugs have little effect on this component of oxygen utilization. The major benefit of anti-anginal drugs is their ability to reduce the oxygen demand of the heart by reducing cardiac work load. This is accomplished through peripheral vasodilation (organic nitrates, calcium channel blockers) which reduces venous return and decreases intracardiac volume, or decreased heart rate and force of contraction (beta-blockers, calcium channel blockers). Secondarily, angina can be alleviated through decreasing myocardial oxygen demand, which allows better perfusion of ischemic areas. In variant angina where coronary artery vasospasm is involved, nitrates may directly relax the epicardial coronary arteries. Overall, organic nitrates do not increase coronary blood flow selectively. *(Katzung, pp 172–184)*

**779.** **(E)** The six major manifestations of plumbism (chronic lead poisoning) are gastrointestinal, neuromuscular, CNS, hematologic, renal, and miscellaneous symptoms. Intestinal symptoms consist of anorexia and constipation. Lead palsy, as the neuromuscular syndrome is sometimes called, is progressive, initially resulting in muscle weakness and fatigue and eventually producing paralysis. Encephalopathic symptoms, more common in children, include loss of motor skills, vertigo, ataxia, insomnia, restlessness, and, progressively, seizures. Punctate basophilic stippling is the hematologic hallmark of chronic lead ingestion. Progressive and irreversible renal insufficiency may result as well. Miscellaneous symptoms, such as pallor, gingival lead line, and emaciation, have been observed. Skin rashes are not noted. *(Gilman et al, pp 1593–1598)*

**780.** **(C)** The anti-psychotic agent chlorpromazine is the prototype for the phenothiazines, which exert their therapeutic actions through their ability to block several receptor classes, the most prominent being dopamine receptors. Most antipsychotic agents strongly block $D_2$ receptors, especially in the mesolimbic system. Newly developed antipsychotic agents seem to block 5-$HT_2$ receptors better than $D_2$ receptors, suggesting that blockade of dopamine receptors is not the entire story for antipsychotic activity. Phenothiazines also possess antimuscarinic activity, which results in blurred vision, dry mouth, difficulty in urination, and constipation. $\alpha_1$-Blocking activity results in orthostatic hypotension. Blockade of dopamine receptors results in parkinsonism and hyperprolactinemia, which can lead to amenorrhea and infertility in females and impotence in males. *(Katzung, p 437)*

781. **(D)** For most drugs, the free drug is the form that reversibly binds to receptors and exerts the pharmacologic activity. The oral route of administration has the most potential for first-pass hepatic metabolism, since the GI tract blood flow passes into the hepatic portal system before gaining access to the systemic circulation. Although the vascular permeability of the lungs is not greatly different from other beds, the inhalational route allows a very rapid onset of action because of the blood flow (equal to cardiac output) and large surface area available. Passive diffusion of molecules depends upon the lipid solubility of the agent, the concentration gradient, and the area involved. A large volume of distribution for a compound is indicative of high lipid solubility, since the compound has a large tendency to move through lipid membranes out of the systemic circulation into tissues. High lipid solubility implies that clearance by the kidney will be low, since the kidney does not readily clear compounds with high lipid solubility. Such compounds undergo hepatic metabolism for their clearance. *(Katzung, pp 4–5)*

782. **(C)** The kinetics for the approach to a new plateau (steady state) are independent of the dose administered and are solely a function of the half-life of the drug. The actual plateau concentration depends only on clearance and the dosage administered per dosing interval. Fluctuations in concentration during given intervals are proportional to the ratio of dosage interval to half-time; halving both the dose and dosage interval will produce a smoother rise to plateau concentration, with blunted fluctuations, but the actual plateau concentration will be unchanged. The mean plateau plasma concentration of a drug is a function of the dose administered and not whether it was administered in a constant infusion or multiple doses. *(Gilman et al, pp 25–28)*

783. **(A)** The major advantage of combining a decarboxylase inhibitor (carbidopa) with levodopa is that more levodopa is available for CNS penetration. In addition, far fewer gastrointestinal effects are observed, and interference by pyridoxine is avoided. The time for titration is reduced, since the limiting gastrointestinal side effects are diminished. Adverse cardiovascular effects of levodopa are also decreased. However, CNS side effects remain and may even develop earlier in the course of treatment and be more pronounced. *(Gilman et al, p 471)*

784. **(D)** Prostacyclin is a short-lived product of arachidonic acid metabolism. Prostacyclin is a very potent vasodilator in most systemic vascular beds and therefore increases renal blood flow. It is also an inhibitor of platelet aggregation. Since vascular endothelium is capable of synthesizing $PGI_2$, it has been suggested that it plays a role in maintaining vascular patency via these two mechanisms. In addition, $PGI_2$ is cytoprotective and is capable of inhibiting gastric ulceration by inhibiting the volume of secretion, acidity, and pepsin content. This effect is useful in counteracting the gastrointestinal ulcerative effects of non-steroidal anti-inflammatory drugs. *(Gilman et al, pp 605–607)*

785. **(C)** ECG effects of digitalis glycosides include prolongation of the PR interval, T-wave inversion, ST-segment depression, and shortening of the QT interval. The QRS complex duration does not increase, even during toxicity. If this should occur, other

causes, such as conduction defects, should be sought. *(Gilman et al, p 824)*

786. **(E)** Tumors have a wide range of mechanisms by which they can resist the effects of anti-neoplastic agents. Among these are increases in target enzymes or alterations in the structure of target enzymes, which decreases the affinity of the drug for the enzyme. This mechanism is seen most frequently with anti-metabolite drugs such as methotrexate. Some tumor cells have genes that decrease the uptake or enhance the elimination of anti-cancer drugs. This form of resistance is termed pleiotropic, or multidrug resistance, and is effective against such drugs as the anthracyclines, vinca alkaloids, and dactinomycin. Tumors that are heterogeneous tend to be more resistant to drug therapy because a wide variety of cell types tends to increase the probability of cells with resistant mechanisms. *(Katzung, pp 823–826)*

787. **(D)** The course of acute acetaminophen overdose follows a fairly consistent pattern. During the initial 24 hours, nausea, vomiting, anorexia, and abdominal pain occur. Indications of hepatic damage become evident, biochemically, within 2 to 6 days of ingestion of toxic doses. Prominent increases in alkaline phosphatase are common. The hepatotoxicity may precipitate jaundice and coagulation disorders and progress to encephalopathy, coma, and death. Tinnitus, or ringing in the ears, is a feature of chronic salicylate intoxication and is not encountered in acetaminophen overdose. The mechanism of toxicity involves generation of a highly reactive alkylating species by cytochrome P450, which is detoxicated by glutathione. When glutathione becomes depleted, damage to cellular components, including protein and nucleic acid, occurs. Treatment of overdose consists of administration of acetylcysteine, which acts as a nucleophile in the same manner as does glutathione in detoxicating alkylating agents. *(Gilman et al, pp 658–659; Katzung, p 909)*

788. **(C)** Chronic abuse of sedative-hypnotics (eg, barbiturates) results in drug tolerance to other agents within this class by (1) enhanced metabolism of similar agents, and (2) cross-pharmacodynamic tolerance. Cross-tolerance by a pharmacodynamic mechanism has implications in the clinical management of withdrawal symptoms or detoxification. Patients who chronically abuse short-acting barbiturates, benzodiazepines (eg, secobarbital, diazepam), or alcohol may undergo detoxification using a longer-acting agent, such as phenobarbital. Cross-tolerance does not extend to opiates. Sedative-hypnotics may be useful in symptomatic management of symptoms associated with withdrawal from opiates. *(Khantzian and McKenna, pp 361–372)*

789. **(E)** Nephrotoxicity associated with gentamicin therapy resembles acute tubular necrosis. Manifestations include the inability to concentrate urine, proteinuria, casts in the urine, and increased plasma creatine. Rising trough concentrations appear to be an early indicator of renal damage. If gentamicin is discontinued, damage is reversible. *(Gilman et al, p 1106)*

790. **(C)** Tricyclic anti-depressants produce sedation rather than arousal. Use of tricyclics can be therapeutic for insomnias associated with depression. Other effects include antimuscarinic effects (dry mouth, blurred vision, tachycardia, urinary retention), α-adrenergic effects (orthostatic hypotension), weight gain, and a decrease in seizure threshold, which means that patients are more susceptible to having seizures. *(Katzung, p 401)*

791. **(D)** All benzodiazepines, with the exception of oxazepam and lorazepam, are converted via hepatic metabolic pathways. This usually occurs via N-alkylation or oxidation to metabolites that are pharmacologically active. This property may contribute to prolonged duration of action of the benzodiazepines. *(Katzung, p 337)*

792. **(B)** Glucocorticoids are valuable adjuvants in anti-inflammatory therapy and inhibit all phases of inflammation (vascular, cellular, and connective tissue repair). Usual therapy

involves a synthetic derivative (eg, prednisolone, triamcinolone, dexamethasone, betamethasone, beclomethasone) of the endogenous hormone, cortisol. Unfortunately, the biologic effects of glucocorticoids are myriad, and all effects aside from anti-inflammatory effects may become unwanted. Because of negative feedback from adrenal to pituitary gland, prolonged therapy with glucocorticoids can result in suppression of functions associated with this particular axis. Perhaps the most disastrous side effect is increased susceptibility to infection of all kinds secondary to effects of the drug on the immune system as well as inhibition of the inflammatory process. Decreased formation (decreased osteoblast activity) and increased resorption (secondary to elevated levels of parathyroid hormone due to decreased intestinal calcium absorption) of bone may lead to osteoporosis. Cushing's habitus, consisting of moonface, buffalo hump, enlargement of supraclavicular fat pads, central obesity, and other aspects of supraphysiologic affects of adrenal corticosteroids, also may occur. Masculinization of female patients is a common concern in androgen therapy. (Gilman et al, pp 1448–1455)

793. **(C)** Oral contraceptive agents with a high estrogen content can produce adverse effects reflective of excess estrogen. These effects include weight gain, headache, edema, and breast tenderness. Amenorrhea is associated with estrogen deficiency. (Katzung, pp 622–623)

794. **(D)** Several factors are known to sensitize the myocardium to digoxin, predisposing patients to digoxin toxicity. These factors include hypercalcemia, hypokalemia, hypomagnesemia, and hypoxia. Hypothyroidism (not hyperthyroidism) also makes patients more sensitive to the effects of digoxin. (Gilman et al, p 834)

795. **(E)** Pharmacotherapy of the complex syndrome of bronchial asthma is aimed at reversing the bronchospasm, bronchial edema, and mucosal hypersecretion that are associated with the disease. Much of this pathophysiology is the result of altered autonomic control of the airways as well as contribu-

tions of chemical mediators from resident pulmonary and inflammatory cells. Airway smooth muscle appears to have a predominance of $\beta_2$-receptors, and such agents as isoproterenol are useful in dilating constricted airways and relieving some of the symptoms. Propranolol, a non-selective $\beta$-antagonist, is contraindicated in asthma. $\beta$-Agonists with improved selectivity for $\beta_2$-receptors include terbutaline and albuterol. Theophylline, or its more soluble derivative, aminophylline, also is useful in the treatment of asthma. Although xanthine derivatives are the drug of choice for many forms of asthma, their mechanisms remain obscure and probably involve (1) phosphodiesterase inhibition, (2) adenosine antagonism, (3) inhibition of other mediator release, and (4) increased sympathetic activity. Ipratropium bromide is a quaternary isopropyl derivative of atropine, which when administered by inhalation, relaxes bronchial smooth muscle by virtue of its antimuscarinic effects. Cromolyn sodium (disodium cromoglycate) is not a bronchodilator but is effective in asthma by preventing the release of chemical mediators from various cell types, including the mast cell. Cromolyn is effective only when used prophylactically and thus is of no value for reversal of acute episodes of asthma. (Katzung, pp 305–317)

796. **(A)** In general, epinephrine decreases peripheral resistance because of the stimulation of $\beta_2$-receptors in skeletal muscle blood vessels, resulting in vasodilatation in these beds. Cardiac rate rises as a direct result of $\beta_1$ stimulation. Systolic blood pressure rises because of positive inotropic and chronotropic effects, as well as precapillary vasoconstriction. Myocardial stimulation increases oxygen consumption. Insulin secretion is inhibited as a result of $\alpha_2$ stimulation, and glucose levels rise. (Craig and Stitzel, pp 118–124, 799)

797. **(A)** Gout is a disease characterized by inflammatory processes triggered by formation of uric acid crystals in joints. The xanthine oxidase inhibitor allopurinol is used in preventing attacks by blocking metabolism of purines to uric acid. It is not useful in acute attacks. The tubulin-binding compound col-

chicine produces anti-inflammatory actions by inhibiting assembly of microtubules from tubulin, thereby inhibiting leukocyte migration and phagocytosis. The non-steroidal anti-inflammatory drugs (NSAIDs) including indomethacin, phenylbutazone and ibuprofen inhibit prostaglandin formation and uric acid crystal phagocytosis. *(Katzung, pp 552–554)*

798.  **(D)** Although histamine release is likely to be a part of the pathophysiology of asthma, antihistamines are ineffective in treating the disease. Nevertheless, their ability to block histamine binding is used in treating a variety of hypersensitivity reactions, of which urticaria is one. $H_1$ antagonists have anticholinergic properties that make them useful secondary agents in treating motion sickness. Their sedative effect is used to treat sleep disorders. *(Smith and Reynard, pp 164–172)*

799.  **(B)** Phenytoin is effective therapy for most types of epileptic seizures except absence (petit mal) seizures. It is approximately 90% bound to plasma proteins. Phenytoin is eliminated mainly through metabolism that is saturable at attainable serum concentrations. The dose-dependent (nonlinear) elimination of phenytoin often presents a clinical problem, since small changes in dosage may result in large increases in serum concentration and toxicity. Dosage adjustment in an individual patient is best accomplished through careful monitoring of serum concentrations and close observation for early signs of toxicity that include nystagmus, vertigo, ataxia, and drowsiness. *(Katzung, pp 363–365)*

800.  **(E)** The use of cimetidine has been associated with a decrease in the hepatic metabolism of various drugs, including warfarin, diazepam, and theophylline. Cimetidine has been noted to cause gynecomastia, presumably by elevating prolactin levels. Suppressed spermatogenesis also has been observed. A broad range of CNS problems, including dizziness, confusion, lethargy, and coma, has been observed, particularly in patients with pre-existing renal disease. Relapse of ulcer symptoms has prompted the use of low-dose maintenance cimetidine therapy in selected patients. *(Katzung, p 951)*

## REFERENCES

Ahnerthilger G, Bigalke H. Molecular aspects of tetanus and botulinum neurotoxin poisoning. *Prog Neurobiol.* 46:83–96; 1995

Craig CR, Stitzel RE, eds. *Modern Pharmacology.* 4th ed. Boston: Little, Brown and Co.; 1994

Gilman AG, Goodman RW, Nies AS, Taylor P, eds. *The Pharmacological Basis of Therapeutics.* 8th ed. New York: Pergamon; 1990

Hertz R, Bisharashieban J, Bartana J. Mode of action of peroxisome proliferators as hypolipidemic drugs—suppression of apolipoprotein C-III. *J Biol Chem.* 270:13470–13475; 1995

Katzung BG, ed. *Basic & Clinical Pharmacology.* 6th ed. Norwalk, CT: Appleton & Lange; 1995

Khantzian EJ, McKenna GJ. Acute toxic and withdrawal reactions associated with drug use and abuse. *Ann Intern Med.* 90:361–372; 1979

Rang HP, Dale MM, Ritter JM, Gardner P. *Pharmacology.* New York: Churchill Livingstone; 1995

Smith CM, Reynard AM, eds. *Essentials of Pharmacology.* Philadelphia: Saunders; 1995

# Subspecialty List—Pharmacology

674. General principles
675. General principles
676. General principles
677. General principles
678. General principles
679. General principles
680. General principles
681. General principles
682. Autonomic system/ Cholinergics
683. Autonomic system/ Cholinergics
684. Autonomic system/ Adrenergics
685. Cardiovascular system
686. Blood and blood-forming organs/Anticoagulants
687. Renal/Diuretics
688. Autacoids/Antihistamines
689. Cardiovascular system/ Antihypertensives
690. Autonomic system/ Adrenergics
691. General principles
692. Autacoids/Anti-inflammatory agents
693. Central nervous system/ Antiepileptics
694. Blood and blood-forming organs/Anemias
695. Endocrine/Insulin
696. Cardiovascular system/ Hyperlipidemia

697. Toxicology
698. Cardiovascular system/ Antiarrhythmics
699. Antimicrobial/ Chemotherapy/Parasites
700. Autonomic system/ Autonomics
701. Blood and blood-forming organs/Anticoagulants
702. Autacoids/Eicosanoids
703. Blood and blood-forming organs/Thrombolysis
704. Central nervous system/ Anti-epileptics
705. Central nervous system/ Local anesthetics
706. Toxicology
707. Endocrine/Hypoglycemics
708. Central nervous system/ General anesthetics
709. Autonomic system/ Cholinergics
710. Endocrine/Thyroid
711. Endocrine/Gonadal steroids
712. Cardiovascular system/ Anti-hyperlipidemics
713. General principles
714. Cardiovascular system/ Inotropic agents/Toxicology
715. Cardiovascular system/ Inotropic agents
716. Autonomic system/ Cholinergics

717. Autonomic system/Autonomics/Toxicology
718. General principles
719. Autonomic system/ Adrenergics
720. Central nervous system/ Anti-depressants
721. Central nervous system/ Alcohol
722. Autonomic system/ Cholinergics
723. Central nervous system/ Drug abuse
724. General principles
725. General principles
726. General principles
727. General principles
728. Chemotherapy/Immunosuppressants
729. Antimicrobial/Chemotherapy/Parasites
730. Antimicrobial/Chemotherapy/Antifungals
731. Antimicrobial/Chemotherapy/Antivirals
732. Antimicrobial/Chemotherapy
733. Antimicrobial/Chemotherapy/Anti-tuberculars
734. Antimicrobial/Chemotherapy
735. Autonomic system/Auto-

nomics/Antihypertensives
736. Autonomic system/Autonomics/Anti-hypertensives
737. Cardiovascular system/Antihypertensives
738. Cardiovascular system/Antihypertensives
739. Chemotherapy/Cancer
740. Chemotherapy/Cancer
741. Chemotherapy/Cancer
742. Chemotherapy/Cancer
743. General principles
744. General principles
745. Gastrointestinal system
746. Gastrointestinal system
747. Gastrointestinal system
748. Gastrointestinal system
749. Autonomic system/Autonomics
750. Autonomic system/Autonomics
751. Autonomic system/Autonomics
752. Autonomic system/Autonomics
753. Autonomic system/Cholinergics
754. Autonomic system/Cholinergics
755. Autonomic system/Cholinergics
756. Respiratory/Asthma
757. Respiratory/Asthma
758. Respiratory/Asthma
759. Respiratory/Asthma

760. Respiratory/Asthma
761. Cardiovascular system/Angina
762. Cardiovascular system/Angina
763. Cardiovascular system/Angina
764. Cardiovascular system/Angina/Antihypertensives
765. Autacoids
766. Autacoids
767. Inflammation/Gout
768. Autacoids/Anti-inflammatory agents
769. Antimicrobial/Chemotherapy
770. Antimicrobial/Chemotherapy
771. Antimicrobial/Chemotherapy
772. Antimicrobial/Chemotherapy
773. Antimicrobial/Chemotherapy
774. Renal system
775. Central nervous system/Opioids
776. Antimicrobial/Chemotherapy
777. Autonomic system/Autonomics
778. Cardiovascular system/Angina
779. Toxicology

780. Central nervous system/Anti-psychotics
781. General principles
782. General principles
783. Central nervous system/Movement disorder
784. Autacoids/Eicosanoids
785. Cardiovascular system/Inotropic agents
786. Chemotherapy/Cancer
787. Toxicology
788. Central nervous system/Drug abuse
789. Antimicrobial/Chemotherapy/Renal system
790. Central nervous system/Anti-depressants
791. Central nervous system/Anxiolytic agents
792. Endocrine/Adrenal steroids
793. Endocrine/Gonadal steroids
794. Cardiovascular/Inotropic agents
795. Respiratory/Asthma
796. Autonomic system/Adrenergics
797. Inflammation/Gout
798. Autacoids/Histamine
799. Central nervous system/Anti-epileptics
800. Autacoids/Histamine

# CHAPTER 7

# Behavioral Sciences
## Questions

*Hoyle Leigh, MD, FAPA, FACP*

**DIRECTIONS (Questions 801 through 830): Each of the numbered items or incomplete statements in this section is followed by answers or by completions of the statement. Select the ONE lettered answer or completion that is BEST in each case.**

801. A patient who had a painful bee sting is now afraid of flies and birds. This is an example of

    (A) shaping
    (B) classical conditioning
    (C) flooding
    (D) operant conditioning
    (E) stimulus generalization

802. Which of the following is a superego function?

    (A) psychological defense mechanisms
    (B) reality testing
    (C) conscience
    (D) perception
    (E) cognition

803. In a prospective randomized study comparing drug A to placebo, by the luck of the draw, 80 of the 120 patients assigned to placebo were young and had relatively minor disease severity, whereas 80 of the 120 patients in the group assigned to drug A were older and more severely diseased. The authors report that 95 placebo-treated patients and 98 patients treated with drug A are alive at the end of 5 years. They calculate chi-square and report that drug A is no better than placebo. Which of the following statements is true?

    (A) drug A is no more effective than placebo
    (B) matched pair analysis might demonstrate that drug A is better than placebo

    (C) since the patients were assigned by random allocation, it is not possible that the two groups would vary so much in baseline characteristics
    (D) stratified analysis of the data might demonstrate that drug A is more effective than the placebo
    (E) this is an example of $\beta$ error

804. The multiaxial diagnostic system in psychiatric disorders implies that

    (A) psychiatric disorders are complex
    (B) psychiatric disorders and other diseases can coexist
    (C) all psychiatric disorders are personality disorders
    (D) all medical diseases have psychiatric symptoms
    (E) all of the above

805. Which of the following statements concerning psychotherapy is correct?

    (A) psychotherapy can be performed only by professionals with special training in an accredited psychoanalytic institute
    (B) reliving childhood experience is the fundamental objective of psychotherapy
    (C) physical examination may be psychotherapeutic
    (D) giving advice is countertherapeutic
    (E) insight is always the goal in psychotherapy

806. A delusion may be distinguished from a hallucination on the basis of

  (A) consensual validation
  (B) perceptual experience
  (C) grandiosity
  (D) laboratory tests
  (E) intelligence tests

807. All of the following statements concerning the drug treatment of elderly patients is true EXCEPT

  (A) drug clearance may be delayed because of increased fat/muscle ratio
  (B) there may be increased toxicity due to decreased plasma albumin levels
  (C) excretion half-life of drugs may be increased because of decreased liver function
  (D) there may be decreased extrapyramidal side effects with neuroleptics because of decreased nigrostriatal dopamine
  (E) there may be increased sensitivity to anticholinergic drugs due to decreased central nervous system (CNS) cholinergic functioning

808. Goslings that are exposed to humans early in life may follow them as if humans were their mothers. This conduct is an example of

  (A) instrumental conditioning
  (B) imprinting
  (C) cognitive map
  (D) instinctual behavior
  (E) counterphobic behavior

809. A health maintenance organization (HMO) may be described as all of the following EXCEPT

  (A) it provides comprehensive care
  (B) it emphasizes prevention and health promotion
  (C) it is fee for service
  (D) physicians may be salaried
  (E) it is a form of managed care

810. Assuming that 98% of all people with a particular illness, such as depression, will have positive results on a hypothetical new screening test and that 90% of all people without the illness will have a negative result, which of the following statements will be true when the test is used to screen a general population?

  (A) someone having a positive result has a 98% chance of having the illness
  (B) someone having a negative result has a 2% chance of having the illness
  (C) someone having a positive result has a 90% chance of having the illness
  (D) ten percent of the people with negative results will have the illness
  (E) none of the above

811. During human development, the capacity to discriminate between different sounds can first be demonstrated

  (A) in the newborn
  (B) at 3 months
  (C) at 6 months
  (D) at 9 months
  (E) at 12 months

812. According to projections for the United States for the year 2000, as of 1992, which of the following statements is true?

  (A) there will be an overall shortage of physicians
  (B) there will be an overall shortage of surgical specialists
  (C) there will be a shortage of family practitioners
  (D) there will be a shortage of pediatricians
  (E) there will be an overall increase in primary care physicians

813. The suicide rate is highest among

  (A) boys between the ages of 11 and 14 years
  (B) girls between the ages of 15 and 19 years

(C) boys between the ages of 15 and 19 years

(D) girls between the ages of 11 and 14 years

(E) women between the ages of 20 and 25 years

814. Which of the following statements is true concerning infant mortality in the United States?

(A) infant mortality in the United States is high compared to other developed nations

(B) the leading cause of infant mortality in the United States is the acquired immune deficiency syndrome (AIDS)

(C) prenatal care, disappointingly, has not been shown to reduce infant mortality

(D) the mortality rate for white infants is greater than that of black infants

(E) very few Asian-Americans receive prenatal care as compared to African-Americans or Hispanic-Americans

815. Among children who are severely retarded, the percentage that shows some type of psychiatric disorder is

(A) 10

(B) 20

(C) 30

(D) 50

(E) 75

816. All the following terms are associated with alcohol abuse EXCEPT

(A) alpha

(B) epsilon

(C) crash

(D) blackouts

(E) gamma

817. The most significant contraindication to electroconvulsive therapy (ECT) is

(A) recent cerebrovascular accident

(B) history of fracture

(C) advanced age

(D) cachexia

(E) history of seizure disorder

818. All of the following are examples of biofeedback EXCEPT

(A) electric shock given to a person when antisocial behavior is manifested

(B) electronic display of skin temperature

(C) a physician's telling a patient that, as a result of diet, the patient's blood pressure (BP) is reduced

(D) ECT given to a depressed patient

(E) tension headache treated with electromyogram

819. Tardive dyskinesia may be caused by all of the following EXCEPT

(A) perphenazine

(B) amoxapine

(C) trifluoperazine

(D) clorazepate

(E) haloperidol

820. A 38-year-old woman tells her physician that for several months she has been experiencing palpitations, shortness of breath, and a feeling of impending doom. She also has episodes of dizziness and a feeling that she is going to drop dead. The physician's first course of action should be to

(A) provide psychotherapy

(B) treat the patient with benzodiazepines

(C) perform a physical examination

(D) refer the patient to a psychiatrist

(E) teach the patient self-hypnosis

821. A patient is convinced that an IV injection she received has made her immortal. This is an example of

(A) reality testing

(B) illusion

(C) hallucination

(D) delusion

(E) delirium

822. Drugs used in the treatment of schizophrenia have in common their ability to

    (A) block α-adrenergic receptors in the locus ceruleus
    (B) block dopamine receptors in the brain
    (C) sensitize the dopamine receptors in the locus ceruleus
    (D) increase functional levels of norepinephrine in the synapses
    (E) increase serotonin synthesis in the CNS

823. All of the following have been implicated as possible neurotransmitters EXCEPT

    (A) norepinephrine
    (B) endorphins
    (C) γ-aminobutyric acid (GABA)
    (D) serum pepsinogen
    (E) glycine

**Questions 824 through 827**

A 35-year-old man is admitted to the hospital for an elective operation. After a week's stay in the hospital, during which various examinations are performed, he receives general anesthesia for an abdominal operation. Two days after the operation, he becomes agitated, visibly tremulous, and seems to be hallucinating. He also accuses the nurses of being unsympathetic and uncaring, just like his own mother.

824. In relation to this patient's agitation and hallucination, a history of which of the following would have most immediate relevance in management plans?

    (A) schizophrenic family members
    (B) alcoholism
    (C) LSD use
    (D) depression
    (E) traumatic early childhood

825. This patient's accusatory behavior toward the nurses may be attributed to all of the following EXCEPT

    (A) transference
    (B) displacement

    (C) sublimation
    (D) regression
    (E) organic brain syndrome

826. If this patient's hallucinations are predominantly visual, the likelihood of which of the following diagnoses is increased?

    (A) organic brain syndrome
    (B) schizophrenia
    (C) depressive syndrome
    (D) anxiety neurosis
    (E) transference neurosis

827. Which of the following is LEAST likely to be essential in formulating effective management plans for this patient?

    (A) laboratory studies, eg, electrolytes, blood urea nitrogen (BUN)
    (B) chart review to determine intraoperative complications
    (C) interview with the patient's mother to determine the quality of interaction in childhood
    (D) interview with the patient to get a good description of the hallucinations
    (E) interview with the patient's girlfriend to determine drug and alcohol history

828. During the first year of life, infants manifest all of the following EXCEPT

    (A) the smiling response
    (B) sense of body image
    (C) reality testing
    (D) attachment behavior
    (E) sense of gender

829. An example of rapid-eye-movement (REM) sleep disorder may be

    (A) narcolepsy
    (B) epilepsy
    (C) catalepsy
    (D) polydipsia
    (E) cachexia

830. All of the following are examples of biologic rhythms EXCEPT

   (A) REM sleep
   (C) menstrual cycle
   (C) vernal equinox
   (D) basic rest–activity cycle
   (E) depressive mood swings

**DIRECTIONS (Questions 831 through 904): Each set of matching questions in this section consists of a list of lettered options followed by several numbered items. For each numbered item, select the ONE lettered option that is most closely associated with it. Each lettered heading may be selected once, more than once, or not at all.**

## Questions 831 through 839

For each item listed below, choose the brain wave or phenomenon with which it is usually associated.

   (A) α wave
   (B) β wave
   (C) Λ wave
   (D) REM sleep
   (E) cataplexy

831. Concentrating on mental arithmetic  B

832. Sudden loss of muscle tone  E

833. Non-REM (NREM) sleep  C

834. Sleepwalking  C

835. Irregular pulse rate and respiration  D

836. Visual dreams  C (D)

837. Narcolepsy  D (E)

838. Comatose state  C

839. Relaxed, awake state  A

## Questions 840 through 847

For each sentence listed below, choose the appropriate diagnosis, treatment, or procedure.

   (A) depression
   (B) masturbation
   (C) orgasmic dysfunction
   (D) dyspareunia
   (E) vaginismus
   (F) erectile dysfunction
   (G) stop–start technique
   (H) yohimbine
   (I) none of the above

840. A treatment method for premature ejaculation  G

841. A normal sexual activity that may be used as an auxiliary treatment technique for sexual dysfunctions  B

842. May be associated with childhood fantasy of penile damage by the vagina  E

843. Women who do not attain orgasm through vaginal intercourse but attain orgasm through other means  C

844. A woman who has enjoyed sex and was orgasmic loses sexual desire; she is also apathetic to other activities that used to be pleasurable and develops insomnia  A

845. Pain during sexual intercourse  D

846. An α₂-receptor antagonist, sometimes used to assist the treatment of some sexual dysfunctions  H

847. "Impotence" and "frigidity" are examples of this sexual dysfunction  F

## Questions 848 through 854

For each statement below, choose the most appropriate syndrome or disease.

    (A) Alzheimer's disease

    (B) multi-infarct dementia

    (C) pseudodementia

    (D) dementia praecox

    (E) Down syndrome

    (F) Creutzfeld–Jakob disease

848. Most common dementing disease of the elderly

849. Secondary to underlying vascular disease

850. All patients who have trisomy of autosome 21 who survive to adulthood develop this condition

851. Often reversible with treatment with tricyclics, such as imipramine, or serotonin reuptake inhibitors, such as fluoxetine

852. A congenital condition characterized by mental retardation

853. A slow-virus infection causing dementia

854. More common in men than in women, between the ages of 40 and 60, with a history of atherosclerosis

## Questions 855 through 861

For each description below, choose the defense mechanism with which it is most closely associated.

    (A) repression

    (B) projection

    (C) isolation

    (D) regression

    (E) identification

855. A patient described, without showing any emotion, the details of an automobile accident in which his closest friend died

856. A 6-year-old child was brought to the doctor for bedwetting; he had been successfully toilet trained previously. The mother is expecting a baby soon

857. Free association may be effective against this

858. Paranoid patients often manifest this

859. Persons who had been abused as children often become child abusers

860. This may explain why so many people think the old days were so good

861. A psychotic patient is found in bed in the fetal position

## Questions 862 through 869

For each description below, choose the neurotransmitter with which it is usually associated.

    (A) serotonin

    (B) norepinephrine

    (C) dopamine

    (D) acetylcholine

    (E) GABA

862. Much of this substance in the brain is produced by the locus ceruleus

863. This substance opens the chloride channel

864. Blockers of this substance are effective in schizophrenia

865. An indoleamine

866. Decreased in Alzheimer's disease

867. Ingestion of L-tryptophan increases the levels of this substance in the brain

868. Dryness of mouth, constipation, and blurred vision are side effects of many antidepressants caused by the blocking effects of this substance

869. A depletion of this substance in the brain often results in muscular rigidity and tremors

**Questions 870 through 873**

For each developmental phase described below, select the age at which it is most likely to occur.

    (A)  0 to 2 months
    (B)  2 to 8 months
    (C)  9 to 10 months
    (D)  10 to 17 months
    (E)  18 to 36 months

870.  Normal autisic phase

871.  Separation–individuation phase

872.  Normal symbiotic phase

873.  Object constancy

**Questions 874 through 878**

For each statement below, choose the most appropriate substance of abuse.

    (A)  cocaine
    (B)  tobacco
    (C)  cannabis
    (D)  solvents
    (E)  alcohol
    (F)  phencyclidine
    (G)  narcotics

874.  This is the most common type of drug dependency in the United States

875.  Since the Surgeon General's report in 1964, there has been a trend toward a decrease in this drug use; the decrease in its use among females, however, has not been as pronounced as in males

876.  The incidence of addiction to this drug by physicians is estimated to be 30 to 100 times greater than that of the general population

877.  The abstinence syndrome to this drug is triphasic; during the second phase, protracted dysphoria occurs with decreased activation, amotivation, and intense boredom and anhedonia

878.  One sensitive laboratory indicator of heavy use is an elevation of $\gamma$-glutamyltransferase (GGT)

**Questions 879 through 885**

For each statement below, choose the most appropriate item.

    (A)  specificity theory
    (B)  pattern theory
    (C)  gate control theory
    (D)  endorphins
    (E)  placebo
    (F)  narcotic analgesics
    (G)  C fibers
    (H)  thalamus
    (I)  locus ceruleus
    (J)  hypothalamus

879.  The activity of this is suppressed by opioids, clonidine, and GABA, and it produces most of the noradrenergic input into the brain

880.  "Burning pain sensation" is carried by this

881.  Hypothesizes "reverberating circuits"; developed to explain phantom pain

882.  This may induce the secretion of endorphins

883.  Pain sensations from various parts of the body are represented here

884.  This may explain why "counter-irritation" might reduce pain

885.  Pain receptors are a necessary component of this theory

## Questions 886 and 887

For each of the following hypothetical situations, choose the most appropriate control population.

(A) community control
(B) hospital control
(C) matched control
(D) historical control
(E) no control necessary

886. A new case-control study designed to rebut criticisms that a previous study was flawed by Berkson's bias

887. Investigation of a new treatment for a uniformly fatal disease

## Questions 888 through 896

(A) oral stage
(B) anal stage
(C) phallic stage
(D) genital stage
(E) sensorimotor stage
(F) latency

888. Problems in this stage may lead to excessive dependency

889. Problems in this stage may lead to parsimony and/or obsessive traits

890. This is NOT a developmental stage described by Sigmund Freud

891. Pleasure in this stage revolves around sucking

892. Oedipal complex occurs during this stage

893. Corresponds to Erikson's developmental stage of industry vs. guilt

894. Usually engages in play with peers of the same gender

895. Autonomy is of paramount importance

896. Love and sexual intimacy can be achieved during this stage

## Questions 897 through 904

(A) β-endorphin
(B) serotonin
(C) norepinephrine
(D) cholecystokinin
(E) morphine
(F) dopamine

897. A substance made by the human body whose effect can be blocked by naloxone

898. Antipsychotic medications block its receptors

899. An alkaloid

900. A drug used to control pain

901. This substance is secreted together with corticotropin, cleaved from a larger molecule that also contains the moiety for melatonin

902. Locus ceruleus is a major source of this substance in the brain

903. This substance contains the indole ring

904. Fluoxetine (Prozac) is a potent re-uptake blocker of this substance

**DIRECTIONS (Questions 905 through 909): Each of the numbered items or incomplete statements in this section is followed by answers or by completions of the statement. Select the ONE lettered answer or completion that is BEST in each case.**

905. Depressive symptoms are LEAST likely associated with

(A) levodopa
(B) cancer of the pancreas
(C) hypothyroidism
(D) viral infection
(E) cocaine abuse

906. A 30-year-old woman complains of episodic faintness, tingling sensation in her hands, shortness of breath, and severe anxiety. Thorough medical workup reveals no pathologic condition. During an episode of these symp-

toms, chemical analysis of the serum will probably reveal

(A) decreased chloride

(B) increased blood urea nitrogen (BUN)

(C) decreased protein

(D) increased serum amylase

(E) increased pH

## Questions 907 through 908

A 42-year-old widow complains of persistent burning pain in her right forearm. The patient has a history of recurrent depression. Her husband died of a myocardial infarction within the past year.

907. Possible diagnoses include

(A) causalgia

(B) depressive equivalent

(C) psychogenic pain

(D) myocardial infarction

(E) all of the above

908. If the patient described has difficulty falling asleep and frequently awakens from sleep because of pain, all of the following statements are true EXCEPT

(A) depression is possible

(B) causalgia is possible

(C) the pain is not likely to have an organic basis

(D) the symptoms may indicate the presence of anxiety

(E) bereavement may contribute to the symptoms

909. Values of serum normitase (a fictitious substance) have been determined on 10,000 hospitalized patients by the hospital laboratory. Fortunately, the values follow a normal distribution, with a mean normitase level of 6.3 units and a standard deviation of 2.2 units. A valid conclusion that can be reached from these data is

(A) a serum normitase level of 12.8 units is incompatible with life

(B) 95% of the serum normitase values fall between 1.9 and 10.5 units

(C) the range of normal serum normitase level is 4.1 to 8.5

(D) approximately half of the patients tested have a serum normitase level of 6.3 units

(E) all of the above

**DIRECTIONS (Questions 910 through 937): Each set of matching questions in this section consists of a list of lettered options followed by several numbered items. For each numbered item, select the ONE lettered option that is most closely associated with it. Each lettered heading may be selected once, more than once, or not at all.**

## Questions 910 through 912

(A) rooting reflex

(B) Moro reflex

(C) 0- to 1-month-old infant

(D) symbiotic stage of development

(E) passive, undifferentiated organism

(F) active, stimulus-seeking organism

(G) 2- to 3-month-old infant

(H) 4- to 5-month-old infant

910. Seen in newborn babies when the cheek is touched; aids feeding

911. The newborn baby

912. The infant begins to smile selectively and recognizes its mother

## Questions 913 through 922

(A) Harry Harlow's terrycloth mother

(B) executive monkeys

(C) ethology

(D) transitional object

(E) superego

(F) adolescence

(G) latency

(H) Oedipus complex

913. A 3-year-old boy dreams of marrying his mother

914. The stress associated with this causes bleeding ulcers

915. Imprinting is an example

916. Identity issues are important in this

917. A child will not part from a dirty, old blanket

918. School work and playing with same-sex children becomes more important

919. Abstract thinking becomes important

920. Concrete operation is predominant

921. Unsuccessful resolution of this may result in chronic symptoms

922. This represents the expectations and prohibitions of the society in the child's personality system

**Questions 923 through 932**

    (A) delirium
    (B) normal pressure hydrocephalus
    (C) subcortical dementia
    (D) Wernicke's syndrome
    (E) secondary dementia

923. Verbal and perceptuomotor abilities are largely preserved; may be seen in Parkinson's disease

924. Fluctuations in consciousness is a prominent feature

925. A severe amnestic disorder often follows this neurologic entity

926. Visual and auditory hallucinations are common, with reduced clarity of awareness of the environment

927. Intoxications often cause this

928. Vitamin deficiency associated with chronic alcoholism is often etiologic

929. A shunt operation may be indicated

930. Human immunodeficiency virus (HIV) infection may be the cause of this

931. Slowing of the electroencephalogram (EEG) activity is typical

932. Addison's disease and Cushing's disease may cause this

**Questions 933 through 937**

    (A) free association
    (B) squeeze technique
    (C) sensate focus exercise
    (D) reciprocal inhibition
    (E) positive reinforcement

933. Nondemanding, mutually pleasurable explorations of one another's bodies without sexual intercourse

934. A person has difficulty achieving sexual arousal under conditions of duress

935. Used to treat premature ejaculation

936. The primary technique of psychoanalysis

937. A spouse becomes sexually enthusiastic after a compliment from the other spouse

# Behavioral Sciences
## Answers and Explanations

801. **(E)** Stimulus generalization is a process through which a conditioned response is transferred from one stimulus to another stimulus that, in some sense, resembles the conditioned stimulus. In this case, the patient generalized the conditioned stimulus from bees to other flying objects—bees and birds. *(Kaplan and Sadock, p 166)*

802. **(C)** The superego is the collection of psychological functions having to do with conscience: moral/ethical attitudes and standards. The ego functions mediate between the personality system on one hand and the demands of the external reality and the superego on the other hand. Thus, psychological defense mechanisms, reality testing, perception, and cognition are all ego functions. *(Leigh and Reiser, p 358)*

803. **(D)** Despite randomization, the two groups described in the question differed in baseline susceptibility, and drug A may be more effective than placebo. Matching must be performed before randomization and is probably logistically impossible. Stratified analysis would allow comparison of groups stratified according to equivalent baseline susceptibility—outcome for young and relatively healthy patients in one group would be compared with outcome for young and relatively healthy patients in the other group. Similarly, outcome for older and more severely diseased patients would be compared for each treatment. β Error (or type II error), which refers to the failure to reject the null hypothesis when the experimental hypothesis is true, results from not having a large enough sample size to demonstrate a particular level or magnitude of difference. *(MacMahon and Pugh, pp 278–281)*

804. **(B)** Axis I of the multiaxial system (Diagnostic and Statistical Manual for Mental Disorders-IV, American Psychiatric Association) is for clinical psychiatric disorders such as schizophrenia and mood disorders. Axis II is for personality disorders and mental retardation. Axis III is for general medical conditions (such as myocardial infarction, etc.). Axis IV is for psychosocial and environmental problems, and axis V is for global assessment of functioning. This classificatory system clearly indicates that psychiatric disorders (axis I) and general medical disorders (axis III) often do co-exist and may influence each other. *(DSM-IV, pp 25–31)*

805. **(C)** Physical examination is a potent psychotherapeutic tool in that it can reduce the patient's anxiety and provide effective reassurance. Psychotherapy may be performed by any clinician, knowingly or not. Whereas insight is the goal of depth psychotherapy, increase in coping ability is often the goal in supportive and other types of phychotherapy. *(Leigh and Reiser, pp 421–436)*

806. **(B)** Both hallucination and delusion lack consensual validation. Delusion is a fixed idea or belief that is not based on reality. Hallucinations are perceptual experiences that are not based on stimulus from reality and that cannot be substantiated by normal observers. *(Leigh and Reiser, pp 145–178)*

807. **(D)** With increasing age, there is decreased nigrostriatal dopamine, resulting in an increase rather than decrease in extrapyramidal side effects with neuroleptics. Other age-related changes include delayed absorption because of the antacids, milk of magnesia, or anticholinergic drugs that many elderly patients take, decreased first-pass effect with age and congestive heart failure, decreased hepatic function in general, decrease in renal function causing decreased lithium clearance and delay in reaching steady-state of lithium, and increased CNS sensitivity to benzodiazepines. *(Leigh and Reiser, pp 179–209)*

808. **(B)** Imprinting refers to early learning that occurs during a critical period. It is characterized by rapidity and specificity. Instinctual behavior refers to preprogrammed, unlearned behavior. *(Kaplan and Sadock, pp 424–443)*

809. **(C)** HMO is an organized system providing comprehensive care in all specialities. Members enroll in a plan and prepay a premium (or a capitation fee paid by the employer or government) to cover all health-care services for a fixed period of time. The emphasis of an HMO is to reduce health-care costs through prevention and health promotion and reduction of unnecessary health-care costs. The physicians may contract with an HMO as a group through an individual practice association (IPA) or may be salaried. *(Kaplan and Sadock, p 213)*

810. **(E)** The percentage of people having positive (or negative) test results who have (or do not have) an illness (eg, depression) will depend on the prevalence of that illness in the population studied. For example, if the prevalence of depression is 1 in 10,000 and 1,000,000 people are studied, 100 people will have the illness, 10% of the 999,900 people without it will have positive results (99,900 false positives), and 98% of the 100 people affected will have positive results (98 true positives). In this situation, only 98 of 100,088 people with positive results will have depression (less than 1%). Alternatively, if the population consisted only of people with the illness, 100% of the people with positive results would have depression. *(Feinstein, pp 215–226)*

811. **(A)** Infants appear to be programmed to move in rhythm to the human voice. Observations have shown that they will orient with eyes, head, and body to animated sound stimuli. Within a few weeks after birth, infants are able to differentiate between sounds and make more appropriate responses. Obviously, this ability increases with maturity during the first year. *(Friedlander, p 7)*

812. **(E)** It is estimated that there will be more than 650,000 physicians in the United States by the year 2000. There will be an oversupply of physicians in surgery, ophthalmology, internal medicine, obstetrics and gynecology, and neurosurgery. It is expected that the supply will equal the demand in dermatology, family practice, otolaryngology, and pediatrics. There is a trend toward increasing primary care physicians to approximately 50% of all physicians, especially with the advent of managed care and certain legal initiatives. *(Kaplan and Sadock, p 209)*

813. **(C)** The ratio of attempted suicide increases by a factor of 10 between the ages of 15 and 19 years, compared with the rate between the ages of 10 and 14 years. At the same time, the ratio of boys to girls who commit suicide is 3:1. In 1979, suicide was the fourth cause of death among adolescents and rose to the second cause of death in 1982, surpassed only by accidents. *(Committee on Adolescence, American Academy of Pediatrics, pp 144–146)*

814. **(A)** Infant mortality in the United States is 8.9 deaths per 1,000 live births as of 1989, which ranks the United States behind 11 other developed countries. The leading causes of infant death are congenital anomalies, respiratory distress syndrome, and sudden infant death syndrome. Prenatal care does reduce infant mortality, but only 80% of Caucasian women receive prenatal care, followed by 75% of Asian-American women, 65% of African-American women, and 60% of

Native American women. AIDS is a significant cause of infant mortality for African-Americans. *(Kaplan and Sadock, p 208)*

815. **(D)** The rate of psychiatric disorders among mentally retarded children is 50%. The rate found among the general population is 37%. There is nothing particularly characteristic about the kind of psychiatric disorder found among retarded children. *(Rutter et al)*

816. **(C)** Jellinek defined the types of alcoholism as alpha through epsilon. Alpha alcoholics drink to deal with discomfort and have not yet lost control. Epsilon alcoholics are characterized by periodic or binge drinking. Gamma alcoholics conform closely to the popular notion of alcoholism, with loss of control, tolerance, physical dependence, and withdrawal symptoms. Blackouts are also common. Crash is the first phase of cocaine abstinence, characterzed by crash of mood and energy immediately following the cessation of a binge. *(Leigh and Reiser, pp 245–270)*

817. **(A)** Electroconvulsive therapy is a safe and painless procedure as it is performed with muscle relaxation and general anesthesia. The only serious contraindication is increased intracranial pressure, as in recent cerebrovascular accident, because of the danger of herniation due to transient further increase in intracranial pressure during the ECT. *(Leigh and Reiser, pp 136–137)*

818. **(D)** Although biofeedback usually involves modern electronic instrumentation, the essence of the technique is the feedback of biologic information. ECT does involve the use of an electrical instrument, but there is no feedback element in this treatment. Although no sophisticated instrumentation is involved, a physician's telling the patient that the BP has been reduced entails all aspects of biofeedback, including a reward for desirable behavior (diet). *(Kaplan and Sadock, pp 1024–1025)*

819. **(D)** Tardive dyskinesia is caused by neuroleptics that are dopamine receptor blockers (phenothiazines and butyrophenones).

Amoxapine is an antidepressant that has dopamine-blocking function and has similar side effects as neuroleptics. Clorazepate is a benzodiazepine and is a muscle relaxant anti-anxiety agent. *(Leigh and Reiser, pp 441–455)*

820. **(C)** The symptoms of the patient described in the question may result from anxiety alone, but a number of other causes must be ruled out first. These include hyperthyroidism, drug-induced states, and CNS-depressant withdrawal states. Physical examination and routine laboratory tests must be performed on all patients with anxiety symptoms before a specific course of treatment can be considered. *(Leigh and Reiser, pp 41–78)*

821. **(D)** Reality testing refers to a person's ability to determine what perceptions are real. Illusion and hallucination are examples of impaired reality testing. In illusion, a stimulus is misperceived. Hallucination is perception without stimulus. Delirium involves an alteration of the sensorium, with confusion and disorientation. Delusion is a fixed idea or belief that does not correspond to reality. *(Leigh and Resier, pp 147–148)*

822. **(B)** All antipsychotic agents except rauwolfia alkaloids block dopamine receptors in the brain. Locus ceruleus is the site of most noradrenergic neurons in the brain. The dopaminergic neurons in the brain are primarily found in three areas—the basal ganglia (nigrostriatal tract), the midbrain (mesolimbic tract), and the hypothalamus. *(Leigh and Reiser, pp 437–455)*

823. **(D)** Putative neurotransmitters include biogenic amines, such as norepinephrine, dopamine, and serotonin. Peptides duch as endorphins are also neurotransmitters. GABA is a general inhibitory neurotransmitter. Glycine and substance P are also neurotransmitters. Serum pepsinogen is an enzyme. *(Leigh and Reiser, pp 49–62)*

824. **(B)** The tremor and hallucinations experienced by the patient described in the question indicate the presence of delirium tremens. Physicians should be aware that

alcoholic patients often do drink in the hospital. Following an operation, however, the patient is often allowed nothing by mouth, which may precipitate an alcoholic withdrawal state. *(Leigh and Reiser, pp 305–324)*

825. **(C)** Transference may play a role in accusatory behavior, especially since the patient described in the question accused the nurses of being like his own mother. Regression results in the patient's feeling and thinking as though he were a child, which may in turn contribute to impulsiveness and increased transference feelings. His feelings concerning the nurses may be displacements from his mother. Organic brain syndrome, through reduction of higher cortical inhibitory functions, may increase distortion and impulsive behavior. Sublimation is the channeling of unacceptable impulses into acceptable and creative channels. *(Leigh and Reiser, pp 79–100)*

826. **(A)** Visual hallucinations are more common in patients with organic brain syndrome as opposed to schizophrenia. Visual hallucinations are particularly common in delirium tremens. Schizophrenia usually is characterized by auditory hallucinations. *(Leigh and Reiser, pp 145–178)*

827. **(C)** Intraoperative factors may be important in causing postoperative organic brain syndrome. Laboratory tests may document a metabolic derangement that may account for the organic brain syndrome. Drug and alcohol history are important in considering withdrawal states. The patient's own description of the hallucinations is important in determining the possible cause of the syndrome; patient interview also is important to document the mental status. Early developmental history is of secondary importance in the management of acute organic brain syndrome. *(Leigh and Reiser, pp 179–209, 325–340)*

828. **(E)** Sense of gender, or gender identity, is established usually during the second year of life. The smiling response develops at about 3 months of age. A sense of body boundary develops after the first three months of life,

which leads to reality testing. Attachment behavior is manifest in infancy, including smiling, clinging, and the development of stranger anxiety. *(Simons, pp 165–181)*

829. **(A)** Narcolepsy may be an REM sleep disorder. Hypnagogic hallucinations and cataplexy (sudden loss of muscle tone), often seen in patients with narcolepsy, may be caused by the dissociation of REM phenomena from sleep. Catalepsy refers to the waxy flexibility seen in patients with catatonic syndrome. *(Leigh and Reiser, pp 271–302)*

830. **(C)** Biologic rhythms include ultradian, diurnal, and circadian rhythms. REM–non-REM (NREM) cycles, hormonal cycles (eg, cortisol), and even pathologic cycles such as manic-depressive cycles are examples of biologic rhythms. Biologic rhythms are a subset of periodic phenomena, such as the vernal equinox, which is related to the earth's rotation around the sun. *(Leigh and Reiser, pp 271–302)*

831–839. **(831-B, 832-E, 833-C, 834-C, 835-D, 836-D, 837-E, 838-C, 839-A)** α Waves are associated with a relaxed, awake state in which the subject's eyes are closed. Concentration, as during mental arithmetic, is associated with faster, β waves. Δ Waves (3 or less cycles per sec) are associated with NREM sleep (stages 3 and 4). Sleepwalking and night terrors occur during Δ wave sleep. Δ Waves are also prominent in comatose patients (the EEG tracing may be flat in very deeply comatose patients). REM sleep is characterized by visual dreams, relaxation of skeletal muscles, irregular respiration and pulse, and physiologic arousal, such as erection. Cataplexy is the sudden loss of muscle tone that occurs in narcolepsy. *(Leigh and Reiser, pp 271–302)*

840. **(G)** Stop–start technique is one of two methods used to treat premature ejaculation. During manual stimulation of the penis by the partner, as soon as he feels premonitory urge to ejaculate, he signals the partner to stop. The urge then disappears, and stimulation is begun again. Ejaculation is permitted in the fourth sequence. *(Simons, p 371)*

**841. (B)** Masturbation is virtually universal among men and women of all cultures. It is common among married people as well as among the single. Many sex therapists recommend self-stimulation as an auxiliary treatment technique for a variety of sexual dysfunctions. *(Simons, p 365)*

**842. (E)** Vaginismus is a spasm of the muscles around the vagina preventing penile penetration. This is often associated with a childhood fantasy of the vagina holding on to the penis, or childhood trauma concerning sex. This is a sexual dysfunction that can be treated by therapy. *(Simons, p 340)*

**843. (I)** While 90% of women are orgasmic by some means, about 40% of those women do not attain orgasm through vaginal intercourse alone. *(Simons, p 370)*

**844. (A)** Anhedonia, including sexual desire and interest, is part of the symptomatology of depression. Depression is an important diagnosis to consider whenever a sexual complaint is the presenting problem. *(Simons, pp 363–364)*

**845. (D)** Dyspareunia is defined as pain experienced by a woman during sexual intercourse. It is a common concomitant of vaginal infections, pelvic inflammatory disease, endometriosis, or episiotomy scars. *(Simons, p 352)*

**846. (H)** Afrodex, a combination of yohimbine, testosterone, and nux vomica, has been used in erectile dysfunctions. *(Simons, p 373)*

**847. (C)** Orgasmic phase dysfunctions include anorgasmia ("frigidity"), premature ejaculation, and erectile dysfunction ("impotence"), as well as delayed ejaculation. *(Simons, pp 370–374)*

**848–854. (848-A, 849-B, 850-A, 851-C, 852-E, 853-F, 854-B)** Alzheimer's disease is the most common primary dementia in the elderly. About 50% of brains of demented patients show evidence of Alzheimer's disease. The sex ratio may be about even or slightly more in women. Multi-infarct dementia is sec-

ondary to repeated cerebrovascular accidents in patients with underlying atherosclerosis and/or hypertension. It is more common among men than women. Down syndrome is a congenital mental retardation associated with trisomy of autosome 21. All patients with Down syndrome who survive into adulthood develop the brain pathologies of Alzheimer's disease, rendering support to the notion that at least one form of Alzheimer's disease may be associated with an autosome 21 abnormality. Creutzfeldt–Jakob disease and kuru are slow-virus infections that show clinical and histological features similar to Alzheimer's disease. Pseudodementia of depression is an important differential diagnosis in evaluating patients with symptoms of cognitive deficit. In pseudodementia, the patient also exhibits symptoms and signs of the mood disorder as well as cognitive deficits. Successful treatment of the underlying depression results in reversal of the pseudodementia. *(Leigh and Reiser, pp 179–205)*

**855–861. (855-C, 856-D, 857-A, 858-B, 859-E, 860-A, 861-D)** Isolation is the process by which painful emotions are selectively detached from factual memory, which may allow for factual report of a very traumatic event, such as an accident, without an emotional outburst. Regression is a pervasive change in personality to assume the attributes of an earlier age and, in severe form, is characteristic of severely ill schizophrenic patients. In less severe form, a child may unconsciously use this mechanism for increased attention. Repression relegates memories of conflictual or painful experiences into the unconscious, thus making the past appear to be better than it was. Free association may reveal the unconscious material by decreasing the alertness of the critical or sensoring function (superego) of the mind. Projection is a distortion of perception in which a characteristic of the self is attributed to someone else. Exaggerated projection leads to feelings of persecution (projected hostility) and paranoid symptoms. Identification is a process by which a person becomes like the person who is either admired or hated ("identification with the aggressor" as in case of a child abuser.) *(Leigh and Reiser, pp 79–100)*

**862–869. (862-B, 863-E, 864-C, 865-A, 866-D, 867-A, 868-D, 869-C)** The amino acid L-tryptophan is the precursor for serotonin, which is a neurotransmitter needed for non-rapid-eye-movement (NREM) sleep as well as for mood and pain modulation. Up to 70 to 90% of brain norepinephrine is produced in the pontine nucleus, locus ceruleus. Dopamine is implicated in schizophrenia and also in an important neurotransmitter for the extrapyramidal system. Depletion of this substance, as in parkinsonism, causes muscular rigidity and tremors. Acetylcholine is the neurotransmitter associated with higher cortical functioning and is depleted in Alzheimer's disease. Acetylcholine also is an important neurotransmitter for the autonomic nervous system (parasympathetic system and the sympathetic nerves to the sweat glands). Many antidepressants have an anticholinergic action, thus dryness of mouth, constipation, and blurred vision. GABA is an important inhibitory transmitter that opens the chloride channels directly associated with the GABA receptors, hyperpolarizing the cell. *(Simons, pp 553–564; Leigh and Reiser, pp 59–61, 114–120, 157–165, 184–188)*

**870–873. (870-A, 871-C, 872-B, 873-E)** The stages listed in the question form part of the developmental line that psychoanalytic theorists describe as occurring from dependency to adult object relationships. This sequence leads from the newborn's dependence on maternal care to the adult's emotional and material independence and self-reliance. The following eight steps, or stages, are described: period of biologic unity, part-object stage, stage of object constancy, preoedipal ambivalent stage, object-centered phallic-oedipal stage, latency period, preadolescent period, and adolescent stage. *(Freud)*

**874–878. (874-B, 875-B, 876-G, 877-A, 878-E)** Tobacco addiction is the most common type of drug dependency in the United States. Nicotine is extremely addicting. Since the Surgeon

General's report in 1964 that identified the health risks of tobacco smoking, there has been an encouraging trend in the United States. Approximately 42% of the United States adult population smoked cigarettes in 1965. The rate was 37% in 1975 and 30% in 1985. The reduction rate of smoking has been more pronounced in males than in females. Because of easy availability and high stress, physicians are at a high risk for narcotic drug addiction; the incidence is estimated to be 30 to 100 times greater than the general population. The abstinence syndrome to cocaine is triphasic: Phase 1 is called "crash," phase 2 is a withdrawal phase with protracted dysphoria, and phase 3 is an "extinction" phase that follows the resolution of withdrawal anhedonia. An elevated GGT level may be the only laboratory abnormality in an alcohol abuse patient. At least 70% of persons with a high GGT (over 30 units) are persistent heavy drinkers. Heavy drinkers may also have increased mean corpuscular volume (MCV). *(DSM-IV, p 200; Leigh and Reiser, pp 245–270)*

**879–885. (879-I, 880-G, 881-B, 882-E, 883-H, 884-C, 885-A)** Pain perception historically involved (1) the specificity theory that postulates specific pain receptors transmitting specific pain signals through specific neurons to specific areas of the brain, (2) the pattern theory that postulates "reverberating circuits" to explain phantom pain, and (3) gate-control theory that postulates an interaction between pain sensation and other sensations competing for transmission at the spinal cord level. It is now believed that specific pain receptors (free nerve endings) are stimulated mainly by chemicals such as bradykinin, and that two types of pain sensations ("pricking pain" and "burning pain") are transmitted by different types of nerves. The "burning pain" sensation is transmitted by small C fibers, while the "pricking pain" sensation is transmitted by larger, myelinated A delta fibers. The pain fibers eventually terminate in the thalamus in a somatotopical fashion. The locus ceruleus, located in the pons, produces most of the noradrenergic input to the brain, and has receptors for opioids, autoreceptors for norepinephrine (alpha 2), as well as GABA. As opioid antagonists can block the analgesic effects of placebo, the latter's effect is probably mediated by the secretion of endorphins. *(Leigh and Reiser, pp 211–243)*

**886–887.** **(886-A, 887-D)** Berkson's bias, a form of selection bias, may result when the exposure factor or other characteristic of interest differentially affects the probability of admission to a hospital for those persons with the disease and those without the disease. Berkson's bias occurs when cases are hospitalized patients with the disease of interest and controls are hospitalized patients with another illness (with a different rate of admission than that for the disease of interest) and when the exposure factor affects these rates of admission. In order to avoid Berkson's bias, controls could be drawn from the community.

The situation described in Question 887 is one in which the use of historical controls may provide compelling evidence for the efficacy of a new treatment. Usually, historical controls are considered inadequate to demonstrate efficacy, since numerous factors (including the severity of the illness in the patients studied or other changes that have occurred over time in the management or treatment of patients) are not adequately controlled. If a disease has been fatal in nearly 100% of all previous cases, successful treatment of a small series of patients with the disease is extremely unlikely unless the new treatment is efficacious. The value of insulin in treating diabetic coma was demonstrated in comparison with historical controls. *(Lilienfeld and Lilienfeld, pp 199–202, 260–268)*

**888.** **(A)** The oral stage of development, during the first year of life, is characterized by gratification related to the activities of the mouth and nurturance, including dependency needs. A fixation at this stage results in dependent character traits. *(Leigh and Reiser, pp 358–361)*

**889.** **(B)** The anal stage of development occurs during the second year of life with toilet training. Control of bowel movement is an important task. Fixation in this stage may lead to parsimony, rigidity, sadistic tenden-

cies, and obsessive-compulsiveness. *(Leigh and Reiser, pp 358–361)*

**890.** **(E)** The sensorimotor stage or period is a developmental stage described by Jean Piaget. This period denotes the first 18 months to two years of life during which the infant learns through repetition—initially, from blind imitative repetition to repetition in anticipation of results and invention of new methods. Response-feedback loops called "circular reactions" from an important part of the experience. *(Leigh and Reiser, p 363)*

**891.** **(A)** During the oral stage of development, pleasure is concentrated on oral activities such as sucking and, later, biting. *(Leigh and Reiser, pp 358–361)*

**892.** **(C)** The phallic stage takes place between the ages of 3 and 6. During this stage, erotic sensation concentrates in the genital organs, and the child experiences strong love toward the parent of the opposite sex. The boy, during this stage, feels an intense desire to possess the mother and replace the father as her primary lover—the Oedipus complex. The boy gradually relinquishes this wish, due to the fear of the father's anger (castration anxiety), and, instead, identifies with the father. *(Leigh and Reiser, pp 358–361)*

**893.** **(F)** The latency period, ages 7 till adolescence, is characterized by a relative absence of intense sexual interest. Children tend to identify with the parent of the same sex. *(Leigh and Reiser, pp 358–361)*

**894.** **(F)** During the latency period, children tend to play with playmates of the same sex, perhaps due to their intense identification with the parent of the same sex and general turning away from sexuality. *(Leigh and Reiser, pp 358–361)*

**895.** **(B)** During the anal stage of development, bowel control is the major task. This stage corresponds to Erikson's stage of autonomy vs. shame and doubt, and a sense of mastery if the stage is successfully completed. *(Leigh and Reiser, pp 361, 358–361)*

896.  **(D)** According to the Freudian stages of development, the genital stage of adult sexuality is achieved when a person successfully completes adolescence and finds a partner for mature sexuality. *(Leigh and Reiser, pp 358–361)*

897.  **(A)** Endorphins including β-endorphin are endogenous peptides that have morphine-like biological effects including analgesia, respiratory depression, and potential for addiction. Their effects are blocked by opiate antagonists such as naloxone. *(Leigh and Reiser, pp 222–223)*

898.  **(F)** Most drugs that have an antipsychotic effect have the property of blocking one or more types of dopamine receptors in the brain. The dopamine-blocking effect of antipsychotics is also responsible for their extrapyramidal side effects, including rigidity and tremor. *(Leigh and Reiser, pp 160–161)*

899.  **(E)** Morphine is an alkaloid obtained from the poppy plant. Although the biologic effects are similar, endorphins and morphine have entirely different chemical structures. *(Leigh and Reiser, pp 222–223)*

900.  **(E)** Morphine is a drug used to control pain, while endorphins are endogenous substances released by the body. Endorphins are thus not drugs. *(Leigh and Reiser, pp 222–223)*

901.  **(A)** β-endorphin is a part of pro-opiomelanocortin molecule (POMC). POMC is cleaved in the anterior pituitary gland into β-endorphin, corticotropin (ACTH), and melanocyte-stimulating hormone (MSH). *(Kaplan and Sadock, pp 52–57)*

902.  **(C)** The locus ceruleus is located in the pons and provides the principal noradrenergic input into the brain. The stimulation of locus ceruleus in animals results in typical anxiety-fear behaviors, and most antianxiety drugs inhibit locus ceruleus. *(Leigh and Reiser, pp 59–61)*

903.  **(B)** Serotonin (5-hydroxytryptamine, 5-HT) is synthesized from the essential amino acid, tryptophan, with tryptophan hydroxylase serving as the initial and rate-limiting enzyme. Serotonin is degraded by monoamine oxidase (MAO) to 5-hydroxy-indole-acetic acid (5HIAA). *(Kaplan and Sadock, p 49)*

904.  **(B)** After being released from the presynaptic membrane, serotonin is normally reabsorbed into the presynaptic neuron. Fluoxetine potently blocks this reuptake, resulting in a functional increase of available serotonin at the synaptic junction. *(Leigh and Reiser, pp 444–448)*

905.  **(A)** Many cancers, especially cancer of the tail of the pancreas, all endocrine disorders, and viral infections are known to be associated with depressive symptoms. Cocaine abuse may result in severe withdrawal depression. Levodopa, on the other hand, is often associated with manic symptoms and seldom with depression. *(Leigh and Reiser, p 127)*

906.  **(E)** Anxiety, coupled with shortness of breath, tingling sensations in the hands, and faintness in the absence of an underlying physical condition, suggests hyperventilation syndrome. Hyperventilation causes respiratory alkalosis (reduced $P_{CO_2}$ and thus increased pH). The increased blood pH leads to decreased ionization of calcium, causing tingling sensations. *(Leigh and Reiser, p 64)*

907.  **(E)** The amount of information is not sufficient to rule out any of the possible etiologies for pain listed. The history of depression and recent bereavement rule in the possibility of depressive equivalent, psychogenic pain, as well as myocardial infarction, as bereavement often contributes to morbidity from any cause. *(Leigh and Reiser, pp 110–112, 211–243)*

908.  **(C)** Sleep disturbance often indicates the presence of anxiety and/or depression. Being awakened by pain is often indicative of an organic basis for pain. *(Leigh and Reiser, pp 211–243)*

909.  **(B)** In a normal distribution curve, 95% of the values fall within two standard deviations (in this example, 6.3 ± 4.4). The physio-

logic effect of normitase level cannot be determined from the data. Normal range for normitase cannot be determined because the sample was exclusively hospitalized patients, not the normal population. *(Kaplan and Sadock, pp 340–355)*

**910.** **(A)** The rooting reflex denotes the turning of the face (and mouth) toward the object that touches the infant's cheek. This reflex, as well as the Moro or startle reflex, palmar grasp reflex, and positive Babinski reflex, is seen typically in infancy, and gradually disappears. *(Simons, p 167)*

**911.** **(F)** Contrary to the old notion that a newborn baby is a relatively passive, undifferentiated organism who behaves primarily to reduce tension and stimulation, modern observations have shown that the newborn is, in fact, active, stimulus-seeking, and creative in the ways it begins to construct its world. *(Simons, p 168)*

**912.** **(G)** By the time an infant reaches 2 to 3 months of age, it will begin to smile selectively, recognizing the mother. This is sometimes called a "social smile," which is particularly pleasurable to parents. This indicates that the child is emerging from an "autistic stage" of life into one that recognizes an external world. *(Simons, pp 179–171)*

**913–922.** **(913-H, 914-B, 915-C, 916-F, 917-D, 918-G, 919-F, 920-G, 921-H, 922-E)** Childhood plays an important role in personality development. During infancy, the presence of a mothering figure and contact comfort with her (or even her substitute, as in "terrycloth mother") provides a basic sense of security. Transitional objects are "mother substitutes" to which a child may be attached and which she/he may carry around all the time, such as a blanket or a soft toy. Imprinting is an ethological term that indicates a "critical period." For example, if goslings are exposed to humans rather than geese shortly after hatching, they will follow humans rather than their mother. During the ages of approximately 3 to 5, a child develops so-called "Oedipus Complex," an intense love toward the parent of the opposite sex with a wish to have an exclusive relationship with him/her. As marrying and having a sexual relationship with a parent is socially unacceptable (the development of "superego"), the child eventually veers away from this intense love and turns his/her attention to school work and peers of the same sex, while identifying with the parent of the same sex. This period (approximately 6 years of age until adolescence) is the "latency period." During latency, the child learns to use concrete operations in problem solving. Unsuccessful resolution of the Oedipus complex may result in symptoms such as anxiety, inability to develop intimate relationships, etc. Puberty ushers in major personality development— the ability to think abstractly, and sexual maturation of the body. Erikson described the important issues related to identity during adolescence. "Executive monkeys" were monkeys who had to keep on pressing bars to avoid electric shock. Bleeding gastric ulcers ensued. *(Leigh and Reiser, pp 64–66, 357–365)*

**923–932.** **(923-C, 924-A, 925-D, 926-A, 927-A, 928-D, 929-B, 930-E, 931-A, 932-E)** Delirium is characterized by fluctuations in sensorium, with clouding of consciousness and reduced awareness of the environment. Many perceptual abnormalities accompany delirium, including visual and auditory hallucinations. Delirium is often caused by intoxications with prescribed or non-prescribed drugs, as well as any other metabolic abnormality. As delirium represents a metabolic encephalopathy, slowing of the EEG is often present. Wernicke's syndrome, caused by chronic thiamine deficiency usually due to chronic alcoholism, has prominent neurologic signs, including confusion, ataxia, and ophthalmoplegia. It may progress to Korsakoff's syndrome, a severe amnestic syndrome with prominent confabulation. Secondary dementia, or dementia due to general medical condition, is often caused by endocrinopathies such as Addison's disease and Cushing's syndrome. It may also be caused by CNS infections, including HIV and syphilis. Normal pressure hydrocephalus is characterized by progressive dementia, ataxia, and urinary incontinence. A ventricular shunt of CSF to the atrium or peritoneal space is often effective for this condition. In subcortical dementias, as in parkinsonism, there is usually a marked slowing of the thought process with memory impairment, with preservation of verbal and perceptuomotor abilities. *(Leigh and Reiser, pp 179–206; Kaplan and Sadock, pp 92, 336–373)*

**933.** **(C)** Sensate focus exercises are a key factor in most brief sex therapies. Initially, genital touching is excluded, and attention is focused on giving and receiving pleasure without performance demands. *(Simons, p 364)*

**934.** **(D)** Reciprocal inhibition denotes that the elicitation of certain emotional states will inhibit the experience of another mutually incompatible emotional state. The emotions of fear, arising under conditions of duress, may be incompatible with the emotional state of sexual arousal. This principle is often used in the treatment of anxiety, especially phobias, by inducing states of relaxation through training or hypnosis in the presence of the phobic object, thus inhibiting the development of the incompatible emotion of anxiety. *(Kaplan and Sadock, p 112)*

**935.** **(B)** In this Masters and Johnson technique to treat premature ejaculation, the woman squeezes the coronal area of the penis just before the man reaches orgasm. The erection is lost, and stimulation is begun again. This technique, together with the stop–start technique, is an effective means of controlling ejaculation. *(Simons, pp 371–373)*

**936.** **(A)** Free association, the cornerstone of psychoanalytic technique, refers to the patient's saying aloud anything that passes through his or her mind. Its functions, besides providing content for the analysis, include induction of the necessary regression and passive dependence that facilitate the development of the transference neurosis. *(Kaplan and Sadock, p 396)*

**937.** **(E)** Positive reinforcement refers to the process by which certain consequences of a behavior increase the probability that the behavior will occur again. In this case, the increased sexual enthusiasm is likely to increase the probability that the spouse will pay more compliments. *(Kaplan and Sadock, p 264)*

## REFERENCES

American Psychiatric Association. *Diagnostic and Statistical Manual of Mental Disorders, 4th Edition.* Washington, DC: American Psychiatric Association; 1994

Committee on Adolescence, American Academy of Pediatrics. Teenage Suicide. *Pediatrics.* July 1980

Feinstein AR. *Clinical Biostatistics.* St. Louis: CV Mosby Co.; 1977

Freud A. *Normality and Pathology in Childhood.* New York: International Universities Press; 1965

Friedlander BZ. Receptive language development in infancy: Issues and problems. *Merrill–Palmer Q.* January 1970

Kaplan HI, Sadock BJ, eds. *Comprehensive Textbook of Psychiatry.* 5th ed. Baltimore: Williams & Wilkins Co.; 1989

Leigh H, Reiser MF. *The Patient. Biological, Psychological, and Social Dimensions of Medical Practice.* 3rd ed. New York: Plenum Publishing Corp.; 1992

Lilienfeld A, Lilienfeld D. *Foundations of Epidemiology.* 2nd ed. New York: Oxford University Press, 1980

MacMahon B, Pugh T. *Epidemiology, Principles and Methods.* Boston: Little, Brown & Co.; 1970

Rutter M, Tizard J, Whitmore K. *Education, Health, and Behavior.* London: Longman Group, Ltd; 1970

Simons RC, ed. *Understanding Human Behavior in Health and Illness.* 3rd ed. Baltimore: Williams & Wilkins Co.; 1985

# Subspecialty List—
# Behavioral Sciences

801. Psychologic and social factors
802. Life cycle/Psychologic and social factors
803. Epidemiology
804. Psychologic and social factors
805. Doctor–patient relationship psychotherapy
806. Psychological assessment/Psychodynamics
807. Life cycle/Organic mental syndromes
808. Correlates of animal and human behavior
809. Medical ethics/Jurisprudence
810. Epidemiology
811. Life cycle/Psychodynamics
812. Medical ethics/Jurisprudence
813. Life cycle/Psychodynamics
814. Life cycle
815. Life cycle/Psychodynamics
816. Psychosocial, cultural, and environmental influences/Nervous system
817. CNS, mood disorders
818. Physiological correlates of behavior/Learning theory
819. Pharmacological correlates of behavior
820. Emotions/Anxiety disorder

821. CNS, schizophrenia, and other psychotic disorders
822. Psychological assessment/Psychodynamics
823. Nervous system and behavior
824. Biochemical correlates of behavior/Substance abuse disorder
825. Biochemical correlates of behavior/Substance abuse disorder
826. Biochemical correlates of behavior/Substance abuse disorder
827. Biochemical correlates of behavior/Substance abuse disorder
828. Life cycle
829. Sleep
830. Physiological correlates of behavior
831. Sleep/Nervous system and behavior
832. Sleep/Nervous system and behavior
833. Sleep/Nervous system and behavior
834. Sleep/Nervous system and behavior
835. Sleep/Nervous system and behavior
836. Sleep/Nervous system and behavior

837. Sleep/Nervous system and behavior
838. Sleep/Nervous system and behavior
839. Sleep/Nervous system and behavior
840. Human sexuality
841. Human sexuality
842. Human sexuality
843. Human sexuality
844. Mood disorder/Human sexuality
845. Human sexuality/Genitourinary system
846. Human sexuality
847. Human sexuality
848. CNS, dementia, mood disorder
849. CNS, dementia, mood disorder
850. CNS, dementia, mood disorder
851. CNS, dementia, mood disorder
852. CNS, dementia, mood disorder
853. CNS, dementia, mood disorder
854. CNS, dementia, mood disorder
855. Personality/Psychodynamics
856. Personality/Psychodynamics

857. Personality/Psychodynamics
858. Personality/Psychodynamics
859. Personality/Psychodynamics
860. Personality/Psychodynamics
861. Personality/Psychodynamics
862. Nervous system and behavior
863. Nervous system and behavior
864. Nervous system and behavior/Psychosis
865. Nervous system and behavior
866. Nervous system and behavior/Life cycle/Organic mental syndromes
867. Nervous system and behavior/Pharmacological correlates of behavior
868. Pharmacological correlates of behavior
869. Nervous system and behavior
870. Life cycle
871. Life cycle
872. Life cycle
873. Life cycle
874. Psychologic and social factors/CNS/Substance abuse
875. Psychologic and social factors/CNS/Substance abuse
876. Psychologic and social factors/CNS/Substance abuse
877. Psychologic and social factors/CNS/Substance abuse
878. Psychologic and social factors/CNS/Substance abuse
879. Nervous system/Pain
880. Nervous system/Pain
881. Nervous system/Pain
882. Nervous system/Pain
883. Nervous system/Pain
884. Nervous system/Pain
885. Nervous system/Pain
886. Epidemiology

887. Epidemiology
888. Personality and psychodynamics
889. Personality and psychodynamics
890. Life cycle
891. Sexual development and behavior
892. Personality and psychodynamics/Sexual development and behavior
893. Life cycle/Personality and psychodynamics
894. Life cycle/Personality and psychodynamics
895. Life cycle/Personality and psychodynamics
896. Life cycle/Sexual development and behavior
897. Biochemical correlates of behavior/Pharmacological correlates of behavior
898. Biochemical correlates of behavior/Pharmacological correlates of behavior
899. Pharmacological correlates of behavior
900. Pharmacological correlates of behavior
901. Biochemical correlates of behavior/Physiological correlates of behavior
902. Biochemical correlates of behavior/Pharmacological correlates of behavior
903. Biochemical correlates of behavior/Physiological correlates of behavior
904. Pharmacological correlates of behavior
905. Physiological correlates of behavior/Pharmacological correlates of behavior
906. Emotions, motivations, perception, cognition, and memory
907. Stress and adaptation/Psychological assessment
908. Stress and adaptation/Psychological assessment

909. Biostatistics/Social epidemiology
910. Life cycle/Child development
911. Life cycle/Child development/Child psychology
912. Life cycle/Child development/Child rearing practice
913. Life cycle/CNS/Stress
914. Life cycle/CNS/Stress
915. Life cycle/CNS/Stress
916. Life cycle/CNS/Stress
917. Life cycle/CNS/Stress
918. Life cycle/CNS/Stress
919. Life cycle/CNS/Stress
920. Life cycle/CNS/Stress
921. Life cycle/CNS/Stress
922. Life cycle/CNS/Stress
923. CNS, dementia, substance abuse
924. CNS, dementia, substance abuse
925. CNS, dementia, substance abuse
926. CNS, dementia, substance abuse
927. CNS, dementia, substance abuse
928. CNS, dementia, substance abuse
929. CNS, dementia, substance abuse
930. CNS, dementia, substance abuse
931. CNS, dementia, substance abuse
932. CNS, dementia, substance abuse
933. Sexual development and behavior
934. Learning theory/Emotions, anxiety
935. Sexual development and behavior
936. Personality and psychodynamics
937. Learning theory, including behavior modification

# CHAPTER 8

# Practice Test

**Carefully read the following instructions before taking the Practice Test.**

1. This examination consists of 311 questions that are from each of the subject areas you will encounter on the actual examination. They are integrated in an effort to simulate the examination style.
2. Remember that the examination allows approximately 50 seconds for each item.
3. The test items are explained in the Introduction to this book. We suggest you read the entire Introduction prior to taking this practice test.
4. Be sure you have an adequate number of pencils and erasers, a clock, a comfortable setting, and enough distraction-free time to complete the test.
5. Use the answer sheet on pages 333–335 when recording your answers. This simulates the actual practice you will experience when taking the USMLE Step 1.
6. Once you complete the practice test, be sure to check your answers and assess your areas of weakness against the subspecialty lists on pages 329–331.

# Practice Test
## Questions

**DIRECTIONS (Questions 1 through 143): Each of the numbered items or incomplete statements in this section is followed by answers or by completions of the statement. Select the ONE lettered answer or completion that is BEST in each case.**

1.  Based on the part of the brain it supplies, an occlusion of which of the following vessels would produce a visual field deficit?

    (A)  lenticulostriate artery
    (B)  calcarine artery
    (C)  PICA
    (D)  $A_2$
    (E)  medial striate artery

2.  Which of the following fatty acids can be the precursor of prostaglandins in humans?

    (A)  oleic
    (B)  palmitic
    (C)  stearic
    (D)  arachidonic
    (E)  palmitoleic

3.  Mutations of the p53 gene are associated with

    (A)  carcinogenesis
    (B)  micrognathia
    (C)  cystic fibrosis
    (D)  pulmonary fibrosis
    (E)  essential hypertension

4.  During the course of a neurologic exam, you notice that your patient exhibits a loss of all somatosensation on the right side of the body accompanied by obvious weakness and hyperreflexia in the arm and leg on that side. When protruded, the patient's tongue also deviates to the right. Occlusion of which of the following vessels would account for these deficits?

    (A)  anterior spinal artery on left
    (B)  lenticulostriate arteries on left
    (C)  paramedian branches of basilar bifurcation on right
    (D)  lenticulostriate arteries on right
    (E)  posterior spinal artery on right

5.  Which of the following symptoms can be attributable to the vitamin deficiency most commonly observed in chronic alcoholics?

    (A)  corneal vascularization
    (B)  weakening of the rectus muscles of the eye
    (C)  dark scaling skin lesions of the mouth
    (D)  severe eye itch and burning
    (E)  periosteal hemorrhaging

6.  Which type of cancer is the leading cause of female cancer deaths in the United States?

    (A)  lung cancer
    (B)  breast cancer
    (C)  ovarian cancer
    (D)  colon cancer
    (E)  uterine cancer

7.  Bipolar cells are located in the

    (A)  spinal cord
    (B)  retina
    (C)  dorsal root ganglion
    (D)  olfactory bulb
    (E)  semilunar ganglion

8. The second law of thermodynamics states that

(A) reactions that are spontaneous proceed as written because the products of the reaction possess a minimal energy content

(B) the natural tendency of molecules is to increase their state of disorder

(C) the total energy of a molecule is equal to the sum of all internal energies of all the bonds within that molecule

(D) the total energy of the universe cannot increase or decrease

(E) energy cannot change form

9. The occurrence of malignant mesothelioma has been correlated with industrial exposure to

(A) beryllium
(B) silica
(C) coal dust
(D) asbestos
(E) nitrogen dioxide

10. In the illustration below (Fig. 8.1), a patient receives a continuous infusion of gastrin. The production of gastric acid and pancreatic bicarbonate secretion is monitored before and after administration of peptide x (at arrow).

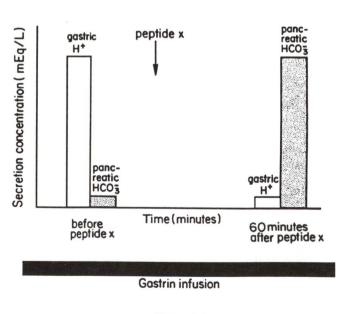

Figure 8.1

At the arrow, a peptide is administered. Which of the following is most likely to produce the changes observed?

(A) motilin
(B) angiotensin II
(C) cholecystokinin (CCK)
(D) somatostatin
(E) secretin

11. The sinoatrial (SA) node is located at the superior end of the

(A) interventricular septum
(B) septomarginal bundle
(C) conus arteriosus
(D) crista terminalis
(E) orifice of the coronary sinus

12. Temporary occlusion of both common carotid arteries is promptly accompanied by

(A) vasodilatation throughout the peripheral circulation

(B) an increase in the number of impulses from the carotid sinus nerve

(C) an increase in venous capacity

(D) an increase in arterial pressure

(E) a decrease in heart rate

13. Binding of $O_2$ to hemoglobin

(A) results in a release of the heme from the interior to the exterior of the β subunits leading to an increase in $O_2$ affinity of the α subunits

(B) causes a large shift of the surrounding secondary structures which leads to decreased affinity of the deoxy subunits for $CO_2$

(C) is cooperative, meaning that after the first $O_2$ binds, the other subunits are more readily oxygenated

(D) occurs with equal affinity at all four subunits

(E) results in a release of the heme from the interior to the exterior of the α subunits leading to an increase in $O_2$ affinity of the β subunits

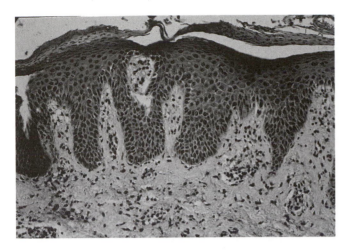

**Figure 8.2**

14. An adult male has recurrent skin lesions which first appeared over his elbows and knees as well defined pink papules covered by a micaceous silvery scale. A skin biopsy microphotograph is displayed from one of his lesions (Fig. 8.2). The diagnosis is

   (A) basal cell carcinoma
   (B) malignant melanoma
   (C) squamous cell carcinoma
   (D) pemphigus vulgaris
   (E) psoriasis

(See Color Insert following page 272.)

15. Destruction of the superior gluteal nerve may disturb the normal gait by paralyzing the

   (A) gluteus medius muscle
   (B) gluteus maximus muscle
   (C) biceps femoris muscle
   (D) adductor magnus muscle
   (E) obturator internus muscle

16. Long-term regulation of arterial blood pressure (BP) is primarily a function of

   (A) the CNS
   (B) the sympathetic nervous system
   (C) peripheral baroreceptors
   (D) urine output and fluid intake
   (E) total peripheral vascular resistance

17. The major amino acid precursor for gluconeogenesis is

   (A) alanine
   (B) aspartate
   (C) cysteine
   (D) glutamate
   (E) serine

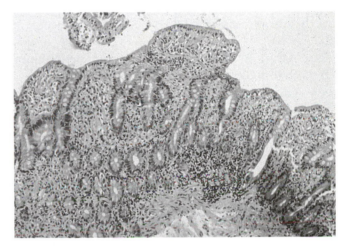

**Figure 8.3**

18. A 6-year-old child presents with diarrhea, malabsorption, and steatorrhea. A microphotograph (Fig. 8.3) from a small intestinal mucosal biopsy is displayed. An appropriate treatment would be

   (A) anti-neoplastic drugs
   (B) β-interferon therapy
   (C) a diet free of gluten
   (D) surgical resection of a segment of small bowel
   (E) a referral to hospice for supportive care

(See Color Insert following page 272.)

19. If in a medical school department it is observed that most of the junior faculty and residents dress and speak like the department's chairperson, this phenomenon may be an example of

   (A) sublimation
   (B) projection
   (C) denial
   (D) reaction formation
   (E) identification

20. The transversalis fascia forms all of the following EXCEPT

   (A) femoral sheath
   (B) deep inguinal ring
   (C) internal spermatic fascia
   (D) psoas fascia
   (E) extraperitoneal fat

21. Atrial fibrillation is a common arrhythmia that accompanies several forms of heart disease. During atrial fibrillation, the atria do not contract sequentially and thus do not contribute to ventricular filling. Which of the following statements best describes this pathophysiologic condition?

   (A) the P waves on ECG recordings usually are normal in atrial fibrillation
   (B) a drug such as quinidine, which acts in part by prolonging the effective refractory period of conducting tissue, is useful therapy
   (C) the interval between QRS complexes remains constant
   (D) atrial fibrillation is life threatening and usually requires application of strong electric current to place the entire myocardium in refractory period
   (E) since the atria contribute little to ventricular function, the pulse is usually extremely regular in spite of the abnormality

22. Hepatic pyruvate kinase is inhibited by which of the following?

   (A) PFK-2-mediated phosphorylation
   (B) PKA-mediated phosphorylation
   (C) oxaloacetate acting allosterically
   (D) citrate-mediated polymerization
   (E) proteolytic cleavage by chymotrypsin

23. Glomerular wire-loop lesions are most often found in renal biopsy specimens of patients with

   (A) diabetes mellitus
   (B) systemic lupus erythematosus
   (C) hypertension
   (D) hepatorenal syndrome
   (E) acute tubular necrosis

24. All of the following are common examples of society's sick-role expectations EXCEPT

   (A) individuals are exempt from normal responsibilities
   (B) individuals are responsible for maintenance of health
   (C) being sick is an undesirable state
   (D) a sick person cannot be expected to get well by "pulling himself together"
   (E) a sick person should seek help from a competent professional

25. An indirect inguinal hernia leaves the abdominal cavity lateral to the

   (A) anterior superior iliac spine
   (B) deep inguinal ring
   (C) inferior epigastric artery
   (D) superficial circumflex iliac vessels
   (E) crest of the ilium

26. A tetraplegic patient has a complete spinal transection between the cervical and thoracic levels. Which of the following statements apply to this patient?

    (A) the maximal inspiratory pressures are more compromised than the expiratory ones
    (B) the inspiratory reserve volume is greatly reduced (less than 10% of normal)
    (C) functional residual capacity equals residual volume
    (D) vital capacity is only slightly compromised
    (E) the ventilatory response to limb exercise is characterized by an increase in tidal volume contributed by the expiratory reserve volume

27. Which of the following amino acids is purely ketogenic?

    (A) cysteine
    (B) serine
    (C) glycine
    (D) leucine
    (E) alanine

28. The inclusion body seen in cells infected with rabies virus is called

    (A) a Negri body
    (B) a Quarnieri body
    (C) a reticulate body
    (D) an elementary body
    (E) an Ammon's body

29. A 56-year-old male is slowly losing vision in his right eye. The ophthalmologist notes that the conjunctiva, sclera, and lens are normal on examination. The intraocular pressure, however, is markedly elevated and there is pressure atrophy of the optic disk. What is the likely diagnosis?

    (A) glaucoma
    (B) cataract

    (C) retrolental fibroplasia
    (D) arcus senilis
    (E) pinguecula

30. What is the plasma clearance for a drug that is infused at a rate of 2 mg/min and achieves a steady-state plasma concentration of 4 mg/L?

    (A) 50 mL/min
    (B) 200 mL/min
    (C) 250 mL/min
    (D) 500 mL/min
    (E) 2000 mL/min

31. When a person thinks about biting into a sour apple, he/she may have increased salivation. This phenomenon is probably an example of

    (A) classical conditioning
    (B) cognitive learning
    (C) operant conditioning
    (D) shaping
    (E) imprinting

32. All of the following structures are formed from the aponeurosis of the external abdominal oblique EXCEPT the

    (A) linea alba
    (B) inguinal ligament
    (C) lacunar ligament
    (D) arcuate line
    (E) superficial inguinal ligament

33. Figure 8.4 represents filtration through the glomerular membrane and shows the locations of the Starling forces.

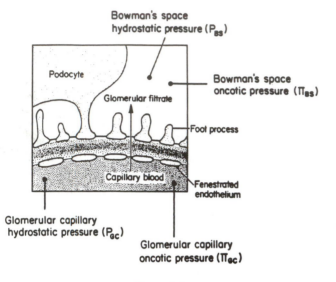

Figure 8.4

In which of the following is there a positive ultrafiltration pressure ($P_{uf} > 0$) for formation of glomerular filtrate? (Numbers in mm Hg.)

| | $P_{GC}$ | $P_{BS}$ | $\Pi_{GC}$ | $\Pi_{BS}$ |
|---|---|---|---|---|
| (A) | 40 | 20 | 30 | 10 |
| (B) | 40 | 15 | 25 | 0 |
| (C) | 40 | 10 | 20 | 0 |
| (D) | 50 | 20 | 30 | 0 |
| (E) | 55 | 25 | 40 | 5 |

34. Phosphofructokinase-2 can best be characterized as

(A) one of the enzymes whose activity is required in the TCA cycle

(B) an enzyme regulated by phosphorylation, an event that increases the rate at which the enzyme itself phosphorylates its substrate

(C) an enzyme that has F1,6BP as a substrate

(D) a bifunctional enzyme that can function as a kinase or as a phosphatase

(E) an allosteric activator of PFK-1

35. Activator of the alternate complement pathway is

(A) interleukin-1 (IL-1)

(B) β-interferon

(C) lipoproteins

(D) endotoxin

(E) complement component C1

36. Cretinism results from a lack of

(A) vitamin D

(B) lipase

(C) myeloperoxidase

(D) hexokinase

(E) thyroxine

37. In the unlikely event of imminent exposure to $^{131}$I-iodide released from a nuclear power plant accident, the rational treatment for minimizing the risk of future thyroid cancer would be

(A) reverse $T_3$

(B) levothyroxine

(C) propylthiouracil

(D) potassium iodide

(E) thyrotropin (TSH)

38. The functions of the limbic system include all of the following EXCEPT

(A) cognition

(B) emotion

(C) reproduction

(D) nutrition

(E) aggression

39. Which of the following structures is retroperitoneal?

(A) kidney

(B) transverse colon

(C) stomach

(D) spleen

(E) sigmoid colon

40. The stimulation in salivary gland acini results in a loss of intracellular and a rise in extracellular potassium ions. The efflux of potassium ions is believed to be primarily due to the action of

(A) a $Na^+$-$K^+$ exchange mechanism
(B) voltage-dependent nonspecific cation channels
(C) calcium-activated $K^+$ channels
(D) $Na^+$-$K^+$-$Cl^-$ cotransport
(E) an ouabain-sensitive pump

41. The conversion of fibrinogen to fibrin is catalyzed by

(A) prothrombin
(B) thrombin
(C) antithrombin III
(D) plasmin

42. The human immunodeficiency virus (HIV)

(A) is a double-stranded DNA virus
(B) is a member of the adenovirus group
(C) lacks reverse transcriptase
(D) destroys $T_4$ lymphocytes

43. Adrenocortical carcinoma is a rare malignant tumor that is

(A) most common among children
(B) a small occult lesion
(C) associated with Cushing's syndrome
(D) of neural crest origin
(E) usually bilateral

44. All of the following statements are true concerning tobacco use EXCEPT

(A) it is the most common type of drug dependency in the United States
(B) nicotine is associated with psychological dependence but not physical withdrawal symptoms

(C) tobacco dependence usually begins in adolescence
(D) the relapse rate of most smoking cessation programs is 60 to 70%
(E) physical complications of chronic tobacco use usually begin to appear in 20 pack-years

45. All of the following are associated with the use of benzodiazepines EXCEPT

(A) muscle relaxant effects
(B) anti-anxiety effects
(C) addictive effects
(D) impaired conditioned avoidance learning
(E) paradoxical agitation in the elderly

46. The movements occurring at the ankle (talocrural) joint are

(A) abduction and adduction
(B) inversion and eversion
(C) pronation and supination
(D) plantar flexion and dorsiflexion
(E) medial rotation and lateral rotation

47. A patient's laboratory analysis of arterial plasma showed a pH of 7.44, bicarbonate 15 mEq/L, $P_{O_2}$ = 80 mm Hg, and $P_{CO_2}$ = 25 mm Hg. This patient probably

(A) has severe chronic lung disease
(B) is a lowlander who has been vacationing at high altitude for two weeks
(C) is a subject in a clinical research experiment who has been breathing a gas mixture of 10% oxygen and 90% nitrogen for a few minutes
(D) is an emergency room patient with severely depressed respiration as a result of a heroin overdose
(E) is an adult psychiatric patient who swallowed an overdose of aspirin

48. Phosphofructokinase-1 (PFK-1) can best be characterized by which of the following statements?

   (A) the enzyme is activated as the concentration of adenosine monophosphate (AMP) rises

   (B) the enzyme is negatively regulated by F1,6-BP

   (C) the enzyme is positively regulated F1,6-BPase

   (D) the enzyme is activated when the concentration of NADH is rising

   (E) the enzyme uses AMP in a substrate level phosphorylation to yield adenosine triphosphate (ATP)

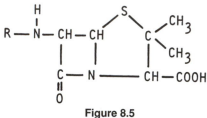

**Figure 8.5**

49. Figure 8.5 represents the antibiotic

   (A) streptomycin
   (B) cephalothin
   (C) erythromycin
   (D) penicillin
   (E) gentamicin

50. In the International Working Formulation for the classification of non-Hodgkin's lymphomas, which of the following neoplasms is identified as low grade?

   (A) follicular, predominantly small cleaved cell lymphoma

   (B) Burkitt's lymphoma

   (C) follicular, predominantly large cell lymphoma

   (D) large cell immunoblastic lymphoma

   (E) diffuse, mixed small and large cell lymphoma

51. The following statements concerning neuroleptic anti-psychotic drugs are true EXCEPT

   (A) most are dopamine receptor blockers

   (B) most are ineffective against negative symptoms of schizophrenia

   (C) most of them increase serum prolactin levels

   (D) combined use with anticholinergic agents is contraindicated

   (E) most of them have a sedative action

52. All of the following statements are true concerning aggression EXCEPT

   (A) XYY syndrome may contribute to aggression

   (B) males are more likely to commit homicide, battery, or rape than females

   (C) aggression is more common toward unfamiliar, strange persons than to familiar persons

   (D) the sex ratio for domestic violence is about equal between males and females

   (E) psychiatric in-patients have a higher rate of aggression than the general population

53. Spinal nerves contain all of the following functional components EXCEPT

   (A) special visceral efferent
   (B) general somatic afferent
   (C) general visceral afferent
   (D) general somatic efferent
   (E) general visceral efferent

54. Most blood vessels dilate under ischemic conditions. In which arterial region does hypoxia cause vasoconstriction?

   (A) coronary arteries
   (B) pulmonary arteries
   (C) renal arteries
   (D) gastrointestinal arteries
   (E) skeletal muscle arteries

55. Ethanol consumption inhibits the delivery of glucose to the blood primarily as a consequence of the activity of alcohol dehydrogenase. The effect of this reaction is to reduce the level of $NAD^+$, which in turn

   (A) activates glycolysis by increasing the rate of ATP utilization, signalling a need to oxidize more carbohydrate within hepatocytes

(B) activates the glycolytic reaction catalyzed by G3PDH, thereby inhibiting the rate of gluconeogenesis

(C) inhibits the ability of the cell to deliver gluconeogenic substrates in the form of PEP as a result of a shift in the equilibrium of the malate dehydrogenase catalyzed reaction

(D) inhibits the gluconeogenic reaction catalyzed by G3PDH which requires $NAD^+$ as a substrate

(E) signals a reduced level of hepatocyte ATP which results in an activation of PFK-1

56. The antibody residues that predominantly make up the antigen-combining site as the "contract" amino acids are located within the

(A) constant domains
(B) heavy chains
(C) hypervariable regions
(D) disulfide bonds
(E) framework regions

57. The changes seen in the kidney shown in the photograph below (Fig. 8.6) may be produced by

(A) postrenal obstruction
(B) renal infarct
(C) hypertension
(D) renal cell carcinoma
(E) abuse of analgesics

(See Color Insert following page 272.)

58. Bacterial resistance to penicillin usually occurs by

(A) thickening of the bacterial wall
(B) changes in the activity of the transpeptidase required for wall formation
(C) reduced requirement for folic acid
(D) enzymatic hydrolysis of the β-lactam ring
(E) decreased affinity of the ribosomal subunit for the drug

59. An attenuated form of anxiety that plays an important role in psychologic defense mechanisms is

(A) signal anxiety
(B) actual anxiety
(C) neurotic anxiety
(D) panic anxiety
(E) psychotic anxiety

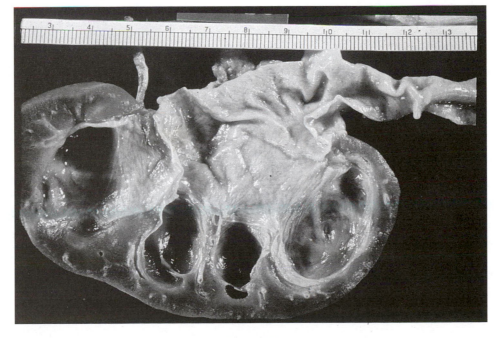

Figure 8.6

60. Herniation of the uncal region of the temporal lobe over the free edge of the tentorium and through the tentorial notch compresses the ipsilateral crus cerebri and nearby structures. Which of the following combinations of signs might be seen in such a case?

(A) contralateral hemiplegia—ipsilateral lower facial paralysis

(B) contralateral hemiplegia—ipsilateral third cranial nerve signs

(C) contralateral hemiplegia—contralateral upper facial paralysis

(D) ipsilateral hemiplegia—deviation of the tongue toward the side opposite the lesion

(E) ipsilateral hemiplegia—contralateral lower facial paralysis

61. In normal adult men, the major source of circulating estradiol is provided by

(A) secretion from the Leydig's cells in the testes

(B) secretion from the Sertoli's cells in the testes

(C) the action of aromatase on circulating androgens

(D) the action of aromatase on circulating estrone

(E) release from the inner layers of the adrenal cortex

62. Which of the following is present only in the intrinsic pathway of clotting?

(A) fibrinogen (factor I)

(B) accelerin (factor V)

(C) prothrombin (factor II)

(D) anti-hemophilic factor (factor VIII)

(E) Stuart factor (factor X)

63. If bacterial food poisoning is due to *Clostridium perfringens*, final confirmation will rest upon

(A) toxin production and neutralization by specific antiserum

(B) the presence of large gram-positive rods in food

(C) demonstration of spores in suspected food

(D) growth of large bacilli in thioglycolate broth

64. Down syndrome is characterized by the karyotype

(A) trisomy 13

(B) trisomy 18

(C) trisomy 21

(D) XO

(E) XXY

65. Intolerance to aspirin can arise from a single dose of aspirin and is manifested as

(A) infertility

(B) hepatotoxicity

(C) nephrotoxicity

(D) asthma and hypotension

(E) hemolytic anemia

66. A physician neglected to discuss with a patient potential complications of proposed surgery. When a colleague pointed this out, the physician claimed that the patient did not want to know it anyway. This may be an example of

(A) reaction formation

(B) denial

(C) organic brain syndrome

(D) rationalization

(E) sublimation

67. Irrigation of the right ear with warm water should produce

(A) slow conjugate eye movement to the right

(B) fast conjugate eye movement to the left

(C) slow conjugate eye movement to the left

(D) slow movement of right eye and fast movement of left eye

(E) no eye movements

68. Which of the following organs receives the highest specific blood flow (mL/min kg)?

    (A) kidneys
    (B) lungs
    (C) heart
    (D) skeletal muscles during rest
    (E) skeletal muscles during exercise

69. The blood protein thrombin is known to

    (A) have an enzymatic specificity similar to trypsin
    (B) form clots by complexing with fibrin
    (C) be an oligomeric protein
    (D) require vitamin K in its activated form
    (E) contain γ-carboxyglutamate residues

70. A 3-year-old child has a temperature of 38.3°C (101°F). On examination, discrete vesiculoulcerative lesions (Koplik's spots) are noted on the mucous membranes of the mouth. The most probable diagnosis is

    (A) rubella
    (B) herpangina
    (C) measles
    (D) herpetic gingivostomatitis
    (E) scarlet fever

71. In the United States the most common etiology of an abdominal aortic aneurysm is

    (A) Marfan's syndrome
    (B) atherosclerosis
    (C) syphilitic infection
    (D) bacterial infection
    (E) acute rheumatic fever

72. A 9-year-old boy with the 21-hydroxylase deficiency form of congenital adrenal hyperplasia is showing signs of precocious sexual development. The appropriate treatment is

    (A) testosterone
    (B) ethinyl estradiol
    (C) flutamide
    (D) bromocriptine
    (E) cortisol

73. Which of the following statements correctly characterizes unsuccessful attempts at suicide?

    (A) advanced age is usually a factor
    (B) females are more likely than males to attempt suicide
    (C) subsequent successful suicide attempts are unlikely
    (D) interpersonal difficulties usually are not a factor
    (E) such attempts are infrequent among Catholics

74. Which of the following statements concerning the processing of pain and temperature sensations from the face is correct?

    (A) signals from the right side of the face reach the ipsilateral chief sensory nucleus
    (B) signals from the right side of the face reach the ipsilateral spinal trigeminal nucleus
    (C) pain sensation from the upper teeth is carried in the contralateral spinal trigeminal tract
    (D) the ventral posterior medial nucleus of the thalamus receives information from the ipsilateral side of the face
    (E) the ventral trigeminothalamic tract terminates in the chief sensory trigeminal nucleus

75. Which of the following clinical situations is associated with an increase in predominantly conjugated ("direct") bilirubin?

    (A) physiological jaundice of the neonate
    (B) kernicterus following rhesus incompatibility
    (C) Gilbert's syndrome
    (D) pancreatic head tumor
    (E) colon tumor

76. The number of moles of ATP produced by complete mitochondrial oxidation of 1 mol of pyruvate to $CO_2$ and water is

    (A) 1
    (B) 6
    (C) 12
    (D) 15
    (E) 24

77. The DiGeorge syndrome is characterized by

    (A) a depletion of lymph node lymphocytes in both T- and B-dependent areas
    (B) defective development of the third and fourth pharyngeal pouches
    (C) an absence of isohemagglutinins
    (D) a defect in neutrophil chemotaxis
    (E) a depletion of B-dependent areas in lymph nodes

78. A clinically apparent accumulation of fluid in the peritoneal cavity is termed

    (A) empyema
    (B) varicosity
    (C) urticaria
    (D) acantholysis
    (E) ascites

79. In a patient on chronic oral anticoagulant therapy, an acute decrease in the prothrombin time would be expected with administration of

    (A) phenobarbital
    (B) rifampin
    (C) phenylbutazone
    (D) cholestyramine
    (E) glutethimide

80. Which of the following are considered to be pain receptors?

    (A) Meissner's corpuscles
    (B) Vater–Pacini corpuscles
    (C) basal cells
    (D) rods
    (E) free nerve endings

81. The nerve fibers terminating in the nucleus gracilis originate in the

    (A) face
    (B) lower extremities
    (C) upper extremities
    (D) neck
    (E) head

82. In the absence of hormone replacement therapy, adrenalectomy may result in death within a few days. This is most likely to be caused by the loss of the adrenal hormone

    (A) cortisol
    (B) corticosterone
    (C) aldosterone
    (D) dehydroepiandrosterone
    (E) epinephrine

83. Which of the following reflects the most accurate effects of the increased cyclic adenosine monophosphate (cAMP) that results in hepatocytes in response to glucagon?

    (A) increased activity of pyruvate kinase
    (B) increased activity of PFK-1
    (C) increase in the kinase activity of PFK-2
    (D) increase in the phosphatase activity of PFK-2
    (E) increased activity in phosphoprotein phosphatases

84. Sterilization of surgical instruments that are sensitive to heat can best be accomplished by

    (A) the autoclave
    (B) ionizing radiation
    (C) ethylene oxide
    (D) phenol
    (E) ethyl alcohol

85. The characteristic pathologic lesion of sarcoid is

    (A) fibroblastic proliferation
    (B) non-caseating granuloma
    (C) pyogenic abscess
    (D) mucoid cyst
    (E) hyaline membrane formation

86. Propranolol is beneficial in the treatment of angina because it

    (A) dilates capacitance vessels
    (B) increases coronary blood flow
    (C) increases oxygen delivery
    (D) decreases contractile force
    (E) reduces oxygen requirements

87. Lithium salts are most effective in

    (A) generalized anxiety disorder
    (B) unipolar depression
    (C) panic disorder
    (D) acute mania
    (E) schizophrenia

88. With a lesion of the lemniscal pathway, all of the following occur EXCEPT

    (A) loss of position sense
    (B) loss of two-point discrimination
    (C) loss of the ability to recognize objects by feel and palpation
    (D) loss of vibratory sense
    (E) loss of pain

89. The secretion of glucagon from alpha cells of pancreatic islets is

    (A) inhibited by elevated amino acid concentrations in plasma
    (B) inhibited by elevated AMP levels
    (C) stimulated by elevated plasma glucose
    (D) stimulated by insulin
    (E) enhanced by sympathetic stimulation

90. When lactate is used as a source of carbon atoms for gluconeogenesis, the NADH required for the glyceraldehyde-3-P dehydrogenase reaction comes from the action of which enzyme?

    (A) glyceraldehyde-3-P dehydrogenase
    (B) glycerol-3-P dehydrogenase
    (C) malate dehydrogenase
    (D) lactate dehydrogenase
    (E) PEP carboxykinase

91. In a positive viral hemagglutination inhibition test, hemagglutination is inhibited by which of the following substances in the serum?

    (A) antiviral antibody
    (B) latex agglutinins
    (C) Rh antibody
    (D) hemolysin
    (E) virus

92. A non-lethal cutaneous disorder characterized by a partial or complete loss of pigment producing melanocytes within the epidermis is

    (A) vitiligo
    (B) ichthyosis
    (C) melasma
    (D) alopecia
    (E) lentigo senilis

93. In persons suffering from severe anaphylactic shock, the drug of choice for restoring circulation and relaxing bronchial smooth muscle is

    (A) epinephrine
    (B) norepinephrine
    (C) isoproterenol
    (D) phenylephrine
    (E) dopamine

94. All of the following statements concerning suicide are true EXCEPT

    (A) most people who commit suicide give definite warnings about their intent
    (B) suicide may occur when the patient's mood seems to be lifting
    (C) people who habitually talk of suicide seldom commit suicide
    (D) most people who commit suicide see a physician before the suicidal act
    (E) suicide is more common among professional persons than individuals in lower economic groups

95. Histologic examination of a lymph node reveals the presence of lymphoid nodules but an absence of the deep cortical (paracortical) zone. This finding is consistent with a condition of

    (A) agammaglobulinemia
    (B) thymic hypoplasia
    (C) combined immunodeficiency
    (D) an acute bacterial infection
    (E) thrombocytopenia

96. The graph below (Fig. 8.7) shows a cardiac pacemaker potential (bold line = "control"). Which of the curves best represents the effect of sympathetic stimulation on the pacemaker potential?

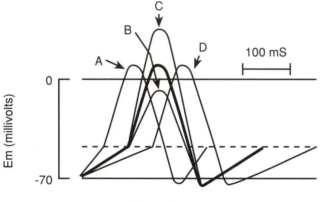

**Figure 8.7**

    (A) curve A
    (B) curve B
    (C) curve C
    (D) curve D
    (E) sympathetic stimulation does not alter the pacemaker potential

97. Symptoms of von Gierke's disease include massive enlargement of the liver, severe hypoglycemia, ketosis, hyperlipemia, and hyperuricemia. Biopsy of the tissues of an affected person would show that the liver had a specific deficiency of the enzyme

    (A) glucokinase
    (B) hexokinase
    (C) glucose-6-phosphatase
    (D) phosphofructokinase
    (E) α-1,4-glucosidase

98. In an influenza virus complement-fixation procedure, the indicator system consists of sheep RBCs plus

    (A) $^{51}$Cr-labeled sheep RBCs
    (B) antibody to influenza virus
    (C) fluorescent-tagged virus
    (D) antibody to sheep RBCs
    (E) complement

99. A 35-year-old woman has noticed a slowly growing mass in her left breast over the past four months. At surgery, the mass is found to be predominantly solid, tan-white, rubbery, well circumscribed, and measuring about 3 × 3 × 3 cm. A representative photomicrograph of the lesion is displayed in Figure 8.8. What is the diagnosis?

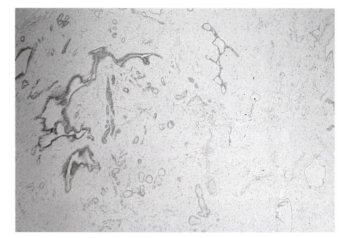

**Figure 8.8**

    (A) medullary carcinoma
    (B) fibroadenoma
    (C) Paget's disease
    (D) intraductal carcinoma
    (E) scirrhous carcinoma

(See Color Insert following page 272.)

100. Which of the following anti-epileptic agents is a branched-chain fatty acid and is associated with an idiosyncratic hepatotoxicity that is rare but has a high fatality rate?

    (A) phenobarbital
    (B) carbamazepine
    (C) felbamate

(D)  gabapentin

(E)  valproic acid

101. All of the following occur during the rapid-eye-movement (REM) sleep EXCEPT

(A)  rapid eye movements

(B)  sleepwalking

(C)  visual dreams

(D)  penile and clitoral erection

(E)  irregular heart rate

102. The linea semilunaris indicates the lateral border of the

(A)  sternum

(B)  rectus abdominis muscle

(C)  inguinal ligament

(D)  infrasternal angle

(E)  external abdominal aponeurosis

103. Damage to Wernicke's area in the cerebral cortex is associated with

(A)  impaired vocalization

(B)  impaired comprehension of speech

(C)  impaired recognition of visual forms

(D)  dyslexia

(E)  loss of short-term memory

104. The figure shown below (Fig. 8.9) demonstrates enzyme kinetics of

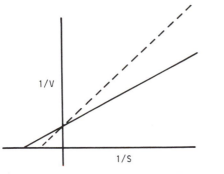

Double-reciprocal plot of enzyme kinetics.

**Figure 8.9**

(A)  a competitively inhibited enzyme

(B)  a non-competitively inhibited enzyme

(C)  an allosteric enzyme with and without effector

(D)  two enzymes, each with a different $V_{max}$

(E)  an irreversibly inhibited enzyme

105. A graft-versus-host reaction may occur

(A)  because the graft is contaminated with gram-negative microorganisms

(B)  only when tumor tissues are grafted

(C)  when immunocompetent lymphoid cells are present in the graft and the recipient is immunosuppressed

(D)  because the graft has histocompatibility antigens not found in the recipient

(E)  when a histocompatible graft is irradiated before engraftment

106. A 67-year-old man has a primary well-differentiated adenocarcinoma of the sigmoid colon that invades into but not through the muscularis propria. Eleven lymph nodes in the sigmoid resection specimen are examined pathologically and two are found to contain metastatic carcinoma. During surgery there was no evidence of distant metastases to the liver. How would you stage this cancer?

(A)  T1,N0,M0

(B)  T2,N0,M1

(C)  T2,N1,M0

(D)  T3,N0,M1

(E)  T4,N0,M1

107. The parameter which best correlates with the potency (MAC value) for a series of inhalational anesthetics is

(A)  the ability to alter blood flow to the brain

(B)  the ability to alter blood flow to adipose tissue

(C)  extent of liver metabolism

(D)  blood:gas partition coefficient

(E)  blood:oil partition coefficient

108. Insight-oriented psychotherapy is an example of which of the following models of doctor–patient relationships?

    (A)  activity–passivity
    (B)  exploitive
    (C)  guidance–cooperation
    (D)  mutual participation
    (E)  authoritarian

109. Which of the following arteries is a branch of the external iliac artery?

    (A)  inferior epigastric
    (B)  external pudendal
    (C)  superficial epigastric
    (D)  superficial circumflex iliac
    (E)  superior epigastric

110. In a young, healthy individual performing a forced expiration from total lung capacity down to residual volume, airflow over the last half of the vital capacity measurement is limited by

    (A)  the maximal force that can be generated by the expiratory muscles
    (B)  dynamic collapse of large intrathoracic airways (third to fourth generation)
    (C)  the intrapleural pressure
    (D)  collapse of extrathoracic airways
    (E)  airway collapse at the level of terminal bronchioles

111. The appearance of high levels of phenylpyruvate and phenyllactate in the urine is indicative of which disorder?

    (A)  Hartnup disease
    (B)  phenylketonuria
    (C)  ifosfamide-induced Fanconi's syndrome
    (D)  alcaptonuria
    (E)  hepatorenal tyrosinemia

112. Staphylococcal enterotoxin

    (A)  is produced by over 90% of the strains of *Staphylococcus epidermidis*
    (B)  disrupts the stratum granulosum in the epidermis

    (C)  disrupts the cytoplasmic membrane
    (D)  blocks the release of acetylcholine
    (E)  resists boiling for 10 minutes

113. A 35-year-old apparently healthy black male undergoes a medical examination in application for purchasing life insurance. He is not anemic. His hemoglobin electrophoresis is reported as Hb A, 62%; Hb S, 35%; Hb F, 1%; Hb A2, 1%; no variant C, D, G, or H bands detected. What is the likely diagnosis?

    (A)  thalassemia minor
    (B)  thalassemia major
    (C)  sickle trait
    (D)  sickle cell disease
    (E)  sickle thalassemia minor

114. A patient will be undergoing surgery requiring skeletal muscle relaxation. He has impaired hepatic and renal function and is known to have a genetic deficiency in plasma pseudocholinesterase activity. The neuromuscular blocking agent of choice for this patient is

    (A)  succinylcholine
    (B)  atracurium
    (C)  tubocurarine
    (D)  vecuronium
    (E)  gallamine

115. All of the following factors have been clearly associated with poor adherence to medical regimens EXCEPT

    (A)  field dependence
    (B)  very old age
    (C)  male sex
    (D)  socially marginal status
    (E)  severe physical illness

116. The lateral umbilical folds are formed by the elevations of peritoneum covering the

    (A)  umbilical arteries
    (B)  umbilical vein
    (C)  inferior epigastric arteries
    (D)  urachus
    (E)  deep circumflex iliac arteries

117. Left coronary blood flow is greatest

    (A) in early systole
    (B) at the peak aortic systolic
    (C) near the end of systole
    (D) in early diastole
    (E) near the end of diastole

118. Introns are correctly described as

    (A) non-coding intervening sequences splitting genes for a single protein
    (B) non-coding intervening sequences separating genes for different proteins
    (C) all non-coding sequences of DNA
    (D) untranslated regions of mature mRNA that separate different protein messages
    (E) untranslated regions of mature mRNA that intervene in the message for a single protein

119. $Rh_0$-specific immune globulin (RhoGAM) therapeutic preparations are correctly described as composed of

    (A) anti-inflammatory agents
    (B) blocking antibodies
    (C) anti-lymphocyte antibodies
    (D) anti-allergen antibodies
    (E) enhancing antibodies

120. A 22-year-old white male is found dead at home. Urine obtained at autopsy contains benzoylecgonine. What conclusion can be drawn from this result?

    (A) the decedent was taking chemotherapy for cancer
    (B) the decedent had recently used cocaine
    (C) death was due to status asthmaticus
    (D) a congenital deformity of the lower limb is likely
    (E) a chromosomal abnormality was present

121. Which of the following is a fibrinolytic agent that elicits an immune-mediated response, reducing therapeutic response and produc-

ing allergic reactions that limit extended and repeated usage?

    (A) tissue plasminogen activator (t-PA)
    (B) urokinase
    (C) streptokinase
    (D) plasmin
    (E) ε-aminocaproic acid (EACA)

122. A patient complains of pain in the chest and nausea. A thorough medical workup does not reveal any organic pathologic condition. It is learned that the patient's mother, who died recently, had exactly these symptoms. This patient's symptoms may be caused by

    (A) generalized anxiety disorder
    (B) pathologic grief reaction
    (C) post-traumatic stress disorder
    (D) major depression
    (E) none of the above

123. The pampiniform plexus of veins is associated with the

    (A) liver
    (B) heart
    (C) lung
    (D) testis
    (E) uterus

124. Average hemoglobin levels are 16 g/dL for males and 14 g/dL for females. What is the main reason for the low hemoglobin level in females?

    (A) shorter erythrocyte half-life time
    (B) decreased responsiveness of bone marrow stem cells to erythropoetin
    (C) smaller number of bone marrow stem cells
    (D) low testosterone levels in the female
    (E) blood loss during menstruation

125. Which glycosaminoglycan is a major component of mast cells lining the blood vessels?

    (A) hyaluronate
    (B) chondroitin sulfate
    (C) heparan sulfate
    (D) keratan sulfate
    (E) heparin

126. The virulence of *Streptococcus pneumoniae* is primarily associated with the presence of

    (A) cell wall teichoic acid
    (B) pneumolysin
    (C) polysaccharide capsule
    (D) M protein
    (E) peptidoglycan

127. Wound healing would likely be retarded by which of the following?

    (A) fibroblasts secreting tropocollagen
    (B) cross-linkage of collagen
    (C) the absence of foreign debris in the wound
    (D) the presence of collagenase
    (E) the hydroxylation of collagen

128. The most serious result of acute acetaminophen intoxication is

    (A) hypoglycemic coma
    (B) methemoglobinemia
    (C) respiratory depression
    (D) renal tubular necrosis
    (E) hepatic necrosis

129. The single best approach that physicians may use in dealing with a chronically angry patient is to

    (A) express their own emotions freely
    (B) let the patient use catharsis
    (C) be neutral and objective
    (D) consult a psychiatrist
    (E) use sarcasm to defuse the anger

130. An injury to the long thoracic nerve would usually result in

    (A) a loss of cutaneous innervation over the medial wall of the axilla
    (B) paralysis of the latissimus dorsi muscle
    (C) protrusion of the inferior angle and medial border of the scapula
    (D) inability to adduct the arm
    (E) paralysis of the subclavius muscle

131. With different levels of dynamic (aerobic) exercise under steady-state conditions,

    (A) cardiac output is almost linearly related to oxygen uptake
    (B) stroke volume is linearly related to oxygen uptake up to maximal oxygen consumption
    (C) arterial diastolic blood pressure decreases substantially
    (D) blood pressure in the pulmonary artery approaches that of the systemic arteries
    (E) blood perfusion of the skin decreases

132. The reaction order for $A + B \rightarrow P$ is

    (A) first order
    (B) second order
    (C) third order
    (D) pseudo first order
    (E) apparent second order

133. The microphotograph below (Fig. 8.10) displays the organism that may cause

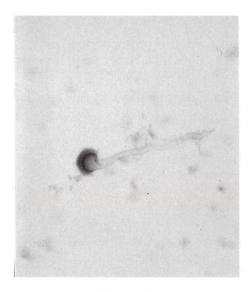

**Figure 8.10**

(A) phycomycosis

(B) tinea barbae

(C) tinea corporis

(D) tinea pedis

(E) aspergillosis

(See Color Insert following page 272.)

134. The most important component in the formation of the hemostatic plug is

(A) red blood cells

(B) fibrin

(C) lymphocytes

(D) platelets

(E) collagen

135. The phenothiazine anti-psychotic that is LEAST likely to have extrapyramidal side effects is

(A) chlorpromazine

(B) trifluoperazine

(C) thioridazine

(D) haloperidol

(E) prochlorperazine

136. All of the following are often associated with decreased sexual activity EXCEPT

(A) mania

(B) depression

(C) chronic schizophrenia

(D) diabetes mellitus

(E) multiple sclerosis

137. The tail of the epididymis is continuous with the

(A) testis

(B) prostate

(C) ductus deferens

(D) bladder

(E) seminal vesicle

138. The main route of renal H$^+$ excretion is as

(A) non-titratable acid

(B) uric acid

(C) phosphoric acid

(D) bicarbonate

(E) free protons (urine pH < 5)

139. The family of diseases termed "mucopolysaccharidoses" are the result of

(A) the inability of neuronal cells to synthesize the glycoprotein portion of their myelin sheaths

(B) the excess synthesis of glycosaminoglycans in heptatocytes

(C) the excess synthesis of proteoglycans in nerve cells

(D) the loss of lysosomal enzymes necessary for the degradation of glycosaminoglycans

(E) the loss of enzymes necessary for the synthesis of lysosomal glycosaminoglycans

140. A patient is suffering from eruptions and multiple draining sinuses with copious suppuration. The lesions are located in the cervicofacial region. Microscopic examination of material taken from the lesions reveals small sulfur granules. This patient is most likely suffering from

(A) amebiasis

(B) mucormycosis

(C) histoplasmosis

(D) candidiasis

(E) actinomycosis

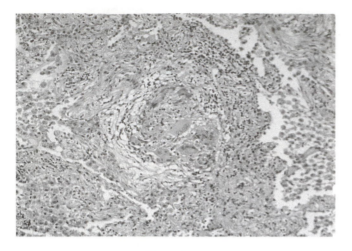

**Figure 8.11**

141. The lesion shown in Figure 8.11 is characteristic of

    (A)  an abscess
    (B)  a granuloma
    (C)  a keloid
    (D)  an infarct
    (E)  a thrombus

    (See Color Insert following page 272.)

142. Which of the following oral hypoglycemic agents has the longest duration of action and is not recommended for use in elderly patients because of its propensity to produce prolonged hypoglycemia in the elderly?

    (A)  tolazamide
    (B)  tolbutamide
    (C)  acetohexamide
    (D)  chlorpropamide
    (E)  glipazide

143. If a diagnostic test is positive in 98 of 100 patients with a particular disease and is negative in 90 of 100 controls without the disease, which of the following statements is true?

    (A)  specificity is 98% and sensitivity is 90%
    (B)  specificity is 90% and sensitivity is 98%
    (C)  positive predictive accuracy is 98%
    (D)  negative predictive accuracy is 98%
    (E)  none of the above

**DIRECTIONS (Questions 144 through 232): Each set of matching questions in this section consists of a list of lettered options followed by several numbered items. For each numbered item, select the ONE lettered option that is most closely associated with it. Each lettered heading may be selected once, more than once, or not at all.**

**Questions 144 through 147**

Match the following hormones with the proper signal transduction pathway.

    (A)  activation of tyrosine kinase
    (B)  increase in cAMP
    (C)  decrease in cAMP
    (D)  increase in cGMP
    (E)  decrease in cGMP
    (F)  increase in inositol-tris-phosphate
    (G)  regulation of gene expression

144. Endothelin

145. Insulin

146. Thyroid hormone

147. Epinephrine acting on β receptors

**Questions 148 through 150**

For each vitamin listed below, select the clinical symptoms that would most likely result from its prolonged deficiency.

    (A)  riboflavin
    (B)  vitamin C
    (C)  niacin
    (D)  vitamin A
    (E)  thiamine

148. Angular stomatitis, photophobia, seborrhea

149. Mental depression, diarrhea, dementia, dermatitis

150. Muscle fatigue, hemorrhaging, anemia, osteoporosis

**Questions 151 through 153**

    (A) benign hyperplasia

    (B) sinus histiocytosis

    (C) metastatic carcinoma

    (D) non-Hodgkin's disease

    (E) metastatic melanoma

    (F) Hodgkin's disease

    (G) sarcoidosis

    (H) angiosarcoma

    (I) lipid granuloma

    (J) tuberculosis

**151.** A 4-cm lymph node is removed from an otherwise healthy 32-year-old dentist. Microscopically, the nodal architecture is effaced by a polymorphous infiltrate of neutrophils, plasma cells, eosinophils, and Reed–Sternberg cells

**152.** Numerous enlarged inguinal lymph nodes are removed from a 45-year-old female. Microscopically, the nodal architecture is effaced by anaplastic non-cohesive cells with prominent nucleoli and cytoplasmic melanin. Two years earlier the woman had a "black" lesion removed from the ipsilateral foot

**153.** An enlarged axillary lymph node is removed from a 61-year-old female. Microscopically, the nodal architecture is effaced by anaplastic gland-forming cells. Special studies on the tissue confirm the presence of estrogen and progesterone receptor proteins

**Questions 154 through 157**

For each antihypertensive agent, select the side effect with which it is most commonly associated.

    (A) bradycardia

    (B) tachycardia

    (C) first-dose syncope

    (D) depression

    (E) sedation

**154.** Hydralazine

**155.** Propranolol

**156.** Prazosin

**157.** Methyldopa

**Questions 158 through 161**

For each age listed below, select the developmental stage, described by Erikson, with which it is most likely to be associated.

    (A) basic trust vs. mistrust

    (B) initiative vs. guilt

    (C) industry vs. inferiority

    (D) identity vs. role diffusion

    (E) autonomy vs. shame, doubt

    (F) intimacy vs. isolation

    (G) integrity vs. despair

    (H) generativity vs. stagnation

**158.** First year

**159.** Fourth year

**160.** Tenth year

**161.** Fifteenth year

**Questions 162 through 165**

    (A) systemic lupus erythematosus

    (B) primary biliary cirrhosis

    (C) amyloidosis

    (D) pemphigus

    (E) pernicious anemia

**162.** Autoantibodies against parietal cells or intrinsic factor

**163.** Autoantibodies against surface antigens in keratinocytes

**164.** Autoantibodies against mitochondria

**165.** Autoantibodies against nuclear antigens

**Questions 166 through 168**

For each phase of the cardiac cycle listed below, choose the portion of the electrocardiogram with which it is most closely associated.

   (A)  P wave
   (B)  QRS complex
   (C)  ST segment
   (D)  T wave
   (E)  QT interval

166.  Ventricular repolarization

167.  Atrial contraction

168.  Plateau phase of cardiac action potential

**Questions 169 through 171**

For each of the techniques listed below, choose the most likely enzyme utilized.

   (A)  HpaII
   (B)  Polynucleotide kinase
   (C)  Taq polymerase
   (D)  DNA polymerase "Klenow" fragment
   (E)  DNA ligase

169.  PCR

170.  RFLP analysis

171.  LCR

**Questions 172 through 174**

For each of the steps of eukaryotic translation listed, choose the most correct set of proteins, RNAs and/or factors required.

   (A)  eEF-2, GTP, eIF-1, 60S ribosome
   (B)  eIF-2, GTP, 40S ribosome
   (C)  ATP, eIF-2, eIF-3, 80S ribosome
   (D)  eRF, GTP, 80S ribosome
   (E)  GTP, 80S ribosome, eEf-2, eEF-1

172.  Initiation

173.  Elongation

174.  Termination

**Questions 175 through 178**

For each of the findings described below, choose the disease with which it is usually associated.

   (A)  Marfan's syndrome
   (B)  Pompe's disease
   (C)  Tay–Sachs disease
   (D)  Niemann–Pick disease
   (E)  Lesch–Nyhan syndrome

175.  Connective tissue disorder with skeletal, ocular, and cardiovascular abnormalities

176.  Accumulation of $GM_2$ ganglioside in the nervous system

177.  Spingomyelin buildup in reticuloendothelial cells

178.  Cardiac and neurologic glycogen storage disease

**Questions 179 through 184**

For each of the following agents, select the pharmacologic action associated with the therapeutic effect of the drug.

   (A)  blockade of muscarinic receptors
   (B)  selective blockage of $\beta_1$-adrenergic receptors
   (C)  inhibition of acetylcholinesterase
   (D)  stimulation of $\alpha_1$-adrenergic receptors
   (E)  blockade of ganglionic nicotinic receptors
   (F)  blockade of neuromuscular junction nicotinic receptors

179.  d-Tubocurarine

180.  Physostigmine

181.  Phenylephrine

182.  Trimethaphan

183.  Metoprolol

184.  Norepinephrine

**Questions 185 through 189**

For each age listed below, select the vocalization or language likely to be heard at that age.

   (A) cooing and vowel sounds
   (B) consonant sounds
   (C) conjunctions
   (D) pronouns
   (E) babbling

**185.** 3 months

**186.** 5 months

**187.** 6 months

**188.** 24 months

**189.** 36 months

**Questions 190 through 194**

For each diuretic agent, select the group in which it is classified.

   (A) carbonic anhydrase inhibitors
   (B) loop diuretics
   (C) thiazide diuretics
   (D) potassium-sparing diuretics
   (E) osmotic diuretics

**190.** Mannitol

**191.** Ethacrynic acid

**192.** Spironolactone

**193.** Triamterene

**194.** Furosemide

**Questions 195 through 197**

For each function, select the appropriate cellular location.

   (A) euchromatin
   (B) heterochromatin
   (C) nucleolus
   (D) nuclear pore

   (E) rough endoplasmic reticulum (rER)
   (F) smooth endoplasmic reticulum (sER)
   (G) Golgi complex

**195.** Microscopic manifestation of transcriptionally inactive DNA

**196.** Assembly and packaging of proteoglycans for secretion

**197.** Removal of the signal sequence by the enzyme signal peptidase

**Question 198 and 199**

Figure 8.12 represents five left ventricular pressure-volume loops, each labeled by a letter (A through E). Loop D represents the normal pressure-volume loop of a healthy adult at rest. Match each numbered description below the illustration with the appropriate letter choice.

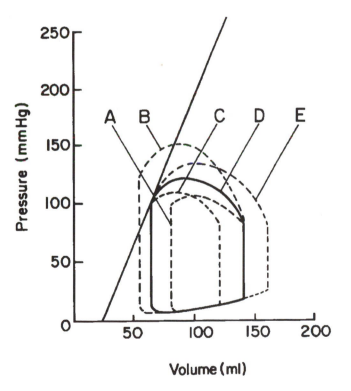

Figure 8.12

**198.** The pressure-volume loop that represents an increase in stroke volume (above normal) by an increase in contractility (positive inotropic effect)

**199.** The pressure-volume loop that represents a decrease in preload (below normal)

**Question 200 through 202**

For each characteristic of the citric acid cycle, choose the correct number.

(A) two
(B) three
(C) twelve
(D) fifteen
(E) twenty-four

**200.** NADH molecules produced in one turn of the cycle

**201.** $CO_2$ molecules released in one turn of the cycle

**202.** Moles of nucleoside triphosphate that can be generated as a result of one turn of the cycle

**Questions 203 and 204**

(A) clonidine
(B) propranolol
(C) labetalol
(D) hydralazine
(E) captopril

**203.** Blocks both α- and β-adrenergic receptors

**204.** Angiotensin-converting enzyme (ACE) inhibitor

**Questions 205 and 206**

(A) synovial chondromatosis
(B) osteoarthritis
(C) synovial sarcoma
(D) rheumatoid arthritis
(E) pigmented villonodular synovitis

**205.** A 31-year-old female complains of the gradual onset of knee pain. During arthroscopic examination, the knee joint is found to be filled by brownish fingerlike projections of synovium. Histologic examination of the resected synovium reveals a mixture of giant cells, bland mononuclear cells, and hemosiderin deposits. What is the likely diagnosis?

**206.** A 76-year-old male complains of the gradual onset of knee pain. During arthroscopic examination the articular cartilage demonstrates eburnation and osteophyte formation. The synovium appears normal. What is the likely diagnosis?

**Questions 207 through 216**

(A) first pharyngeal arch
(B) head somites
(C) third pharyngeal arch
(D) second pharyngeal arch
(E) first pharyngeal pouch
(F) second pharyngeal pouch
(G) fourth and sixth pharyngeal arches
(H) third pharyngeal pouch
(I) fourth pharyngeal pouch

**207.** This structure gives rise to the stapes

**208.** This structure gives rise to the stylopharyngeus muscle

**209.** The superior parathyroid gland is formed from this structure

**210.** The malleus and incus are formed from this structure

**211.** The thyroid, arytenoid, corniculate, and cuneiform cartilages of the larynx are formed from this structure

**212.** The auditory tube is formed from this structure

**213.** The muscles of facial expression are formed from this structure

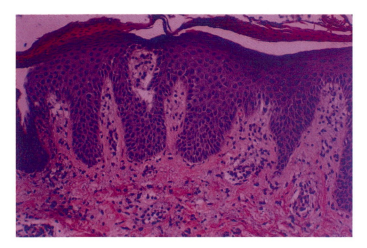

Figure 8.2 (Question 14)

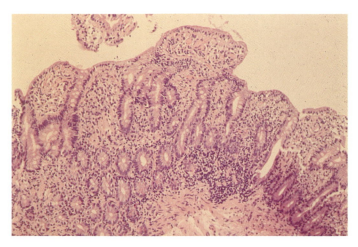

Figure 8.3 (Question 18)

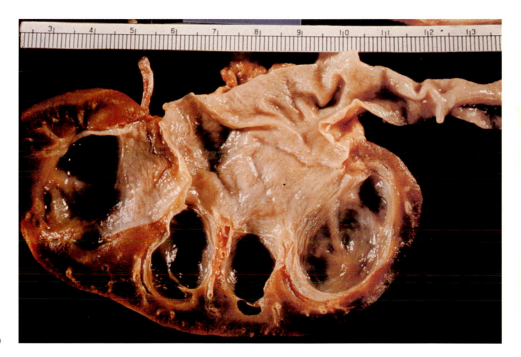

Figure 8.6 (Question 57)

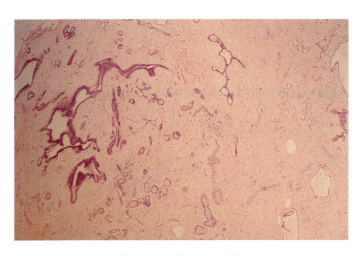

Figure 8.8 (Question 99)

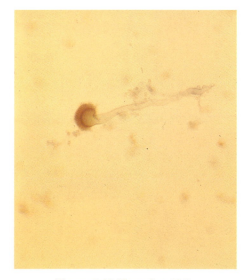

Figure 8.10 (Question 133)

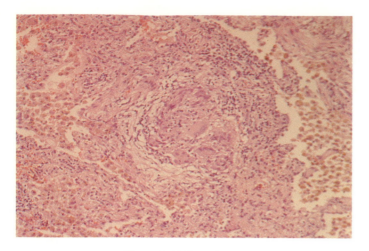

**Figure 8.11 (Question 141)**

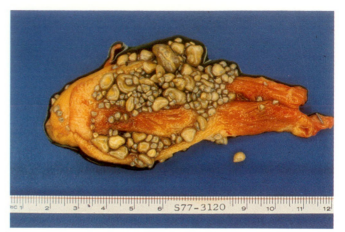

**Figure 8.14 (Question 239)**

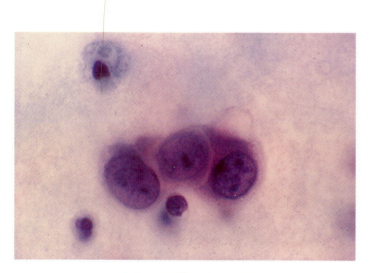

**Figure 8.15 (Question 243)**

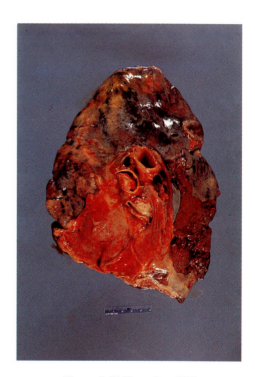

**Figure 8.17 (Question 295)**

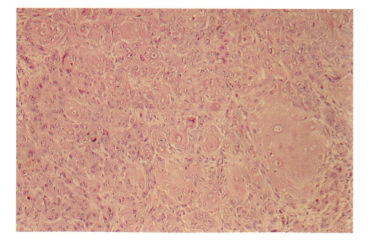

**Figure 8.19 (Question 302)**

214. The muscles of mastication are formed from this structure

215. The thymus gland is formed from this structure

216. The anterior two-thirds of the tongue is formed from this structure

**Questions 217 through 223**

    (A) operant conditioning
    (B) classical conditioning
    (C) cognitive map
    (D) stimulus generalization
    (E) shaping
    (F) reciprocal inhibition
    (G) Premack's principle
    (H) extinction

217. A child likes to play pinball and neglects eating food; the parents are told to allow the child to play pinball only after eating

218. A child who was bitten by a snake is afraid of a rope

219. A child who developed a phobia of ropes after being bitten by a snake is exposed to a rope repeatedly; he is no longer phobic of the rope

220. A bell is rung just before presenting food to a dog; eventually, the dog salivates at the sound of the bell alone

221. A patient who is phobic of spiders is put in a relaxed state by suggestion and soothing music; while in this relaxed state, a photograph of a spider is presented to the patient

222. In order to induce an animal to press a lever, food is given when the animal approaches the lever. Then, food is given when it touches the lever. Then, food is given only when the animal actually presses the lever

223. When a person thinks about biting into a sour apple, salivation occurs

**Questions 224 through 226**

The graph below (Fig. 8.13) represents a patient who has a febrile episode. Temperatures measured are rectal and in degrees C. Match each numbered statement with the appropriate letter choice from the graph (A through G). For this set of questions, letter choices may be used once, more than once, or not at all.

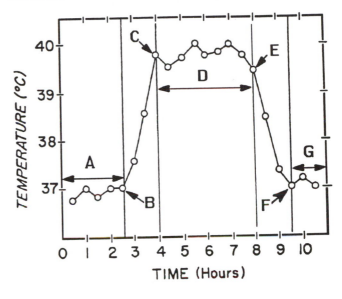

Figure 8.13

224. Period during which patient claims to be fairly comfortable (although the patient's set point is above normal)

225. Point at which patient begins to behave as if in a hot environment (sweats and complains of "burning up")

226. Point at which patient begins to behave as if in a cold environment (complains of chills and has shivering)

**Questions 227 and 228**

    (A)  translocation (8;14)

    (B)  translocation (2;13)

    (C)  translocation (11;22)

    (D)  isochromosome 17q

    (E)  translocation (9;22)

227.  Ewing's sarcoma and peripheral neuroep-
      ithelial tumor

228.  Burkitt's lymphoma

**Questions 229 through 232**

    (A)  von Recklinghausen's disease

    (B)  myelomeningocele

    (C)  syringomyelia

    (D)  von Hippel–Lindau disease

    (E)  Creutzfeldt–Jacob disease

229.  A slow-virus infection of the central nervous
      system

230.  Adult disorder caused by fluid-filled spaces
      that develop in the cervical spinal cord

231.  Neonatal disorder caused by a defect in the
      posterior spine through which there is a her-
      niation of the spinal cord

232.  Hereditary disorder with skin pigmentation
      and multiple neurofibromas

**DIRECTIONS (Questions 233 through 311): Many
of the numbered items or incomplete statements
in this section are negatively phrased, as indicated by a capitalized word such as NOT, LEAST
or EXCEPT. Select the ONE lettered answer or
completion that is BEST in each case.**

233.  All of the following are DNA viruses EX-
      CEPT

    (A)  variola virus

    (B)  herpes simplex virus

    (C)  molluscum contagiosum virus

    (D)  papova virus

    (E)  measles virus

234.  The microbicidal oxygen-dependent mecha-
      nisms of phagocytes depend on all of the fol-
      lowing EXCEPT

    (A)  superoxide radical

    (B)  singlet oxygen

    (C)  ferrous ions

    (D)  hydrogen peroxide

    (E)  hydroxyl radicals

235.  All of the following are common features of
      allosteric enzymes EXCEPT

    (A)  they are composed of multiple subunits

    (B)  they undergo conformational changes

    (C)  they exhibit sigmoidal-shaped kinetic
         curves

    (D)  their activities are controlled in part by
         allosteric effectors that closely resemble
         substrate structure

236.  All of the following are transmitted to man
      by ingestion of undercooked meat EXCEPT

    (A)  *Trichinella*

    (B)  *Leishmania*

    (C)  *Diphyllobothrium*

    (D)  *Toxoplasma*

    (E)  *Clonorchis*

237.  Synthesis of hepatic glycogen from glucose
      requires each of the following enzymes EX-
      CEPT

    (A)  glucokinase

    (B)  glycogen synthase

    (C)  phosphohexose isomerase

    (D)  phosphoglucomutase

    (E)  UDP-glucose pyrophosphorylase

238.  Antibody-mediated antiviral immunity may
      operate through which of the following
      mechanisms?

    (A)  complement-independent neutralization

    (B)  complement-dependent neutralization

    (C)  opsonization

    (D)  lysis of infected host cells

    (E)  all of the above

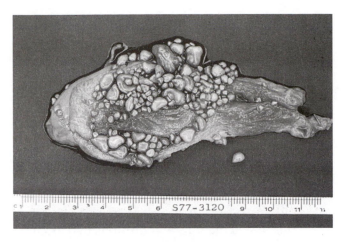

**Figure 8.14**

239. A 46-year-old female complains of abdominal pain in the right upper quadrant after eating fatty foods. A photograph of her opened gallbladder is displayed in Figure 8.14. Which of the following statements is LEAST likely to be true about this woman?

(A) she is probable very thin
(B) if left untreated, she may develop acute or chronic cholecytitis
(C) her bile has an increased amount of cholesterol present compared to acalculous individuals
(D) laparoscopic surgical removal of her gallbladder is the usual treatment
(E) obstructive jaundice may result if a stone becomes lodged in the common bile duct

(See Color Insert following page 272.)

240. The risk factors for suicide include

(A) young age
(B) female sex
(C) Catholic religion
(D) living alone
(E) absence of a medical disorder

241. The enzyme, succinyl-CoA-acetoacetate transferase (3-ketoacid CoA transferase), is found in all the following tissues EXCEPT

(A) skeletal muscle
(B) kidney

(C) brain
(D) lung
(E) liver

242. All of the following are stages of conjugation EXCEPT

(A) effective pair formation
(B) plasmid or chromosome mobilization
(C) recombination
(D) competency
(E) transfer of a unique strand of DNA

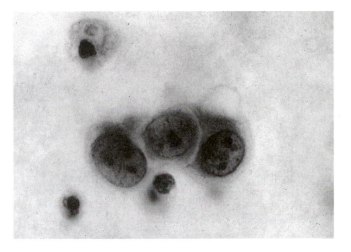

**Figure 8.15**

243. In the photomicrograph of a cytologic preparation shown in Figure 8.15, malignant cells may be characterized by all of the following features EXCEPT

(A) decreased mitotic rate
(B) elevated nuclear to cytoplasmic ratio
(C) hyperchromic nuclei
(D) cellular pleomorphism
(E) enlarged nucleoli

(See Color Insert following page 272.)

244. Which of the following is LEAST likely to cause depression?

(A) cancer of the pancreas
(B) antihypertensive drugs
(C) hyperparathyroidism
(D) acetylsalicylic acid
(E) hypothyroidism

245. All of the following apply to the normal uterus EXCEPT

    (A) it is anteflexed
    (B) it is anteverted
    (C) it has an inner mucous coat called the endometrium
    (D) it has a middle muscular coat called the perimetrium
    (E) the body of the uterus is enclosed between the layers of the broad ligament

246. All of the following are important compensatory mechanisms in hemorrhagic shock EXCEPT

    (A) tachycardia
    (B) venoconstriction
    (C) decreased peripheral vascular resistance
    (D) absorption of fluid from interstitial space
    (E) formation of angiotensin II

247. Compounds derived from the amino acid tyrosine include all of the following EXCEPT

    (A) histamine
    (B) melanin
    (C) dopamine
    (D) p-hydroxyphenylpyruvate
    (E) epinephrine

248. All of the following statements concerning influenza viruses are true EXCEPT

    (A) there are three antigenic types (A, B, and C)
    (B) they have a non-segmented genome
    (C) they are typed according to the ribonucleoprotein in the virion
    (D) they have RNA as their genetic information
    (E) they may cause respiratory diseases in susceptible individuals

249. All of the following are true statements about gestational trophoblastic disease EXCEPT

    (A) serum levels of chorionic gonadotropin are elevated
    (B) it occurs more frequently in the United States than in the Far East

    (C) partial mole has a triploid karyotype
    (D) most cases of complete mole have a normal female karyotype
    (E) choriocarcinoma can follow a normal pregnancy, an abortion, a molar pregnancy, or an ectopic pregnancy

250. The following statements concerning acute grief reaction are true EXCEPT

    (A) depressive symptoms are common
    (B) waves of somatic distress are common
    (C) hallucinations and illusions may occur
    (D) all symptoms must subside within four to eight weeks
    (E) antidepressant therapy may be indicated

251. An inability to extend the knee joint would indicate damage to the

    (A) obturator nerve
    (B) femoral nerve
    (C) sciatic nerve
    (D) tibial nerve
    (E) common peroneal nerve

252. Certain tumors produce a substance closely resembling PTH in its biologic activity. The physiologic effects of this substance would include all of the following EXCEPT

    (A) stimulation of bone resorption
    (B) decreased renal phosphate excretion
    (C) increased serum calcium
    (D) increased metabolism of vitamin D to the 1,25-OH form
    (E) increased serum calcitonin levels

253. All of the following enzymes are found in the liver, but not muscle, EXCEPT

    (A) glucose-6-phosphatase
    (B) hexokinase
    (C) pyruvate carboxylase
    (D) fructose-1,6-biphosphatase
    (E) glucokinase

254. Receptors for C3b are present in the membranes of all of the following EXCEPT

(A) macrophages
(B) B lymphocytes
(C) neutrophils
(D) T lymphocytes
(E) monocytes

255. Which of the following statements is NOT true about thymomas?

(A) anterior mediastinum is the most common location
(B) they are associated with myasthenia gravis
(C) they are associated with red cell hypoplasia
(D) most are malignant
(E) they are composed of epithelial cells and lymphocytes

256. Depressive syndrome is characterized by all of the following EXCEPT

(A) suicidal thoughts
(B) auditory hallucinations
(C) apathy
(D) anhedonia
(E) anorexia

257. All of the following muscles converge at the perineal body EXCEPT the

(A) transverse perineal
(B) ischiocavernosus
(C) bulbospongiosus
(D) levator ani
(E) external anal sphincter

258. Mixed micelles ("biliary micelles") within the intestinal lumen contain all of the following EXCEPT

(A) apolipoproteins
(B) bile salts
(C) cholesterol

(D) lecithin
(E) lipid-soluble vitamins

259. All of the following bonding reactions are important in the stabilization of the tertiary structure of proteins EXCEPT

(A) peptide bonds
(B) hydrogen bonds between peptide groups
(C) ionic bonds
(D) hydrophobic interactions
(E) hydrogen bonds between side chains of amino acids

260. A remnant of the cranial end of the mesonephric duct is known as

(A) a hydrocele of the testis
(B) a hematocele of the testis
(C) the appendix of the testis
(D) the appendix of the epididymis
(E) the processus vaginalis

261. You are able to perform a spinal tap with confidence because you know that the spinal cord ends at the level of the second lumbar vertebrae but the subarachnoid space extends downward to the level of

(A) L4
(B) L5
(C) S1
(D) S2
(E) S3

262. In obsessive–compulsive disorder, all of the following statements are true EXCEPT

(A) the patient may be disabled
(B) fixation in the anal sadistic phase causes the syndrome
(C) the superego may be rigid
(D) serotonergic antidepressant drugs may be helpful
(E) psychosurgery may be helpful

263. All of the following structures are associated with the auditory pathway EXCEPT

   (A) lateral lemniscus
   (B) mamillary bodies
   (C) inferior colliculus
   (D) medial geniculate body
   (E) cochlear nuclei

264. All of the following statements about the skeletal muscle circulation of experimental animals are true EXCEPT

   (A) it contributes significantly to the maintenance of systemic arterial blood pressure
   (B) blood flow within a given group of muscles is relatively homogeneous
   (C) an increase in carotid sinus pressure produces vasodilatation of the vascular bed of most muscles
   (D) contracting muscle can be shown to autoregulate
   (E) stimulation of a pathway from the cortex and hypothalamus may produce vasodilatation

265. Which of the following symptoms would likely NOT be observed in a patient homozygous for HbS?

   (A) cholelithiasis
   (B) increased protein concentration in the urine
   (C) mild to severe jaundice
   (D) chronic hemolytic anemia
   (E) abnormal growth

266. All of the following statements concerning bacterial spores are true EXCEPT that they

   (A) are stable to heating at 80°C for several minutes
   (B) require alanine, adenine, or other effector molecules for germination
   (C) may form when nutritional conditions become unfavorable for bacterial growth
   (D) are an important constituent of all gram-negative organisms
   (E) contain high levels of calcium dipicolinate

267. Serum sickness can be associated with all of the following EXCEPT

   (A) circulating immune complexes
   (B) complement activation
   (C) fever, arthralgias, or vasculitis
   (D) delayed hypersensitivity
   (E) glomerulonephritis

268. The onset and duration of sedative–hypnotic activity of the ultrashort-acting barbiturates such as thiopental is influenced by all of the following EXCEPT

   (A) serum elimination half-life
   (B) lipid solubility
   (C) cerebrovascular blood flow
   (D) extent of tissue binding
   (E) amount of body fat

269. Psychological defense mechanisms may be described as all of the following EXCEPT

   (A) maladaptive modes of adjustment leading to psychopathology
   (B) accentuated during hospitalization
   (C) unconsciously mobilized
   (D) reduce anxiety
   (E) may be associated with hormonal states

270. The pyramidal decussation occurs in the

   (A) diencephalon
   (B) internal capsule
   (C) pons
   (D) midbrain
   (E) medulla

271. All of the following statements regarding systemic hemodynamics are true EXCEPT that the

   (A) greatest cross-sectional area is within the capillaries rather than small veins
   (B) greatest percentage of blood volume is in the small veins and the least is in the arterioles
   (C) greatest drop in pressure occurs in the arterioles rather than the large arteries

(D) compliance of the venous circulation is less than the arterial circulation

(E) velocity of blood flow is lowest in the capillaries

**Questions 272 and 273**

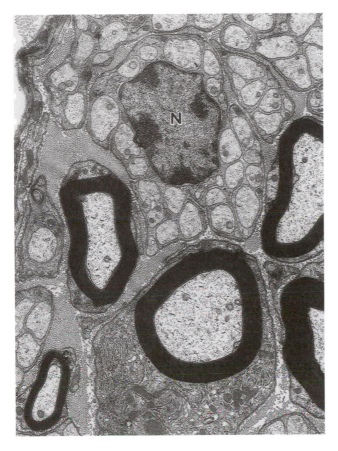

**Figure 8.16**

272. The electron micrograph (Fig. 8.16) illustrates a section of

(A) cerebral cortex
(B) red nucleus
(C) gray matter of the spinal cord
(D) nerve fiber tract in the central nervous system
(E) peripheral nerve

273. The nucleus labeled "N" belongs to

(A) a Schwann cell
(B) an oligodendroglial cell

(C) a sensory neuron
(D) a somatic motor neuron
(E) a microglial cell

274. Which item is LEAST likely to delay wound healing?

(A) diabetes mellitus
(B) excessive scar formation at wound site
(C) infection of wound
(D) closely opposed clean wound edges
(E) foreign material in wound

275. Tolerance develops to all of the following effects of opioids EXCEPT

(A) sedation
(B) nausea
(C) constipation
(D) antidiuresis
(E) respiratory depression

276. Factors that influence how a patient perceives a symptom include all of the following EXCEPT

(A) the frequency of the symptom in a given population
(B) the familiarity of the symptom
(C) the predictability of the outcome of the illness
(D) the degree of threat associated with the illness
(E) all of the above are correct statements

277. A temporary increase in the number of circulating reticulocytes will likely result if an individual

(A) has a bacterial infection
(B) receives a vaccination against measles
(C) has a viral infection
(D) moves from sea level to a high altitude
(E) experiences an allergic reaction to ragweed pollen

278. Tumors of the adrenal medulla that are actively producing catecholamines are called pheochromocytomas. Patients with these tumors experience sudden, periodic increases in catecholamine blood levels. During such an episode, all of the following physical signs are expected EXCEPT

(A) increase in blood pressure
(B) increase in heart rate
(C) increased sweat secretion
(D) decreased blood glucose
(E) cardiac ischemia

279. Each of the following statements concerning nucleosomes are true EXCEPT

(A) the "core" structure encompasses a stretch of DNA about 150 base pairs long
(B) the "core" structure contains histones H2A, H2B, H3, and H4 along with DNA
(C) DNA is wound around the histone proteins of the core
(D) histone H2B and 2A are disulfide bonded to histone H1 to stabilize the "core"
(E) histone H1 is known as the linker histone

280. Bacterial contamination is LEAST likely to occur with which of the following commercial methods of food storage?

(A) pasteurization
(B) canning
(C) refrigeration
(D) freezing
(E) drying

281. Penicillin would be LEAST effective in treating

(A) syphilis
(B) gonorrhea
(C) pneumococcal pneumonia
(D) mycoplasma pneumonia
(E) streptococcal pharyngitis

282. Hypokalemia is a likely result of therapy with all of the following drugs EXCEPT

(A) chlorothiazide
(B) furosemide
(C) spironolactone
(D) ethacrynic acid
(E) bumetanide

283. Which of the following factors will increase the likelihood of a person's seeking medical help?

(A) unpleasant experience with physicians
(B) being Hispanic
(C) high level of stress
(D) low socioeconomic class
(E) all of the above

284. All of the following statements can be correctly applied to spasticity EXCEPT

(A) spasticity is usually associated with hypertonia
(B) lesions involving upper motor neurons are typically associated with spasticity
(C) spasticity involves a decrease in the resistance to passive movement
(D) a C8 spinal cord hemisection would lead to spasticity in the ipsilateral lower extremity
(E) clinically, spasticity and rigidity are different entities and reflect injury to different brain systems

285. Which of the following is NOT associated with secondary hyperaldosteronism?

(A) Conn's syndrome
(B) heart failure
(C) pregnancy
(D) dietary salt restriction
(E) liver cirrhosis with ascites

286. The carbon atoms of fatty acids synthesized in humans can be derived from all of the following EXCEPT

(A) citrate
(B) glucose

(C) cholesterol

(D) leucine

(E) phenylalanine

287. Protective strategies for prevention of the septic shock syndrome could include all of the following EXCEPT

(A) anticachectin antibody

(B) core polysaccharide-specific antibody

(C) lipid A-specific antibody

(D) antibody to terminal polysaccharides of O antigen

(E) pharmacologic antileucotriene agents

288. True statements about acute rejection of renal transplants include all of the following EXCEPT

(A) serum creatinine levels are usually increased

(B) occurs within minutes after transplantation

(C) lymphocytes, monocytes, and neutrophils may be involved in the rejection process

(D) interstitial, peritubular, and intratubular inflammation may be present

(E) vasculitis may be present

289. All of the following are antitubercular agents that are administered orally EXCEPT

(A) isoniazid

(B) rifampin

(C) streptomycin

(D) pyrazinamide

(E) ethambutol

290. The basic elements of informed consent include all of the following EXCEPT

(A) a reasonable explanation of the procedures

(B) advising patients that they are free to withdraw consent at any time

(C) a description of potential risks and benefits

(D) a discussion of potential alternatives

(E) advising patients that they are entitled to a lawyer

291. Failure of the anterior neuropore to close is termed

(A) spina bifida occulta

(B) meningomyelocoele

(C) rachischisis

(D) anencephaly

(E) agenesis of the corpus callosum

292. The electroencephalogram (EEG) during a petit mal epileptic attack is characterized by

(A) generalized high-voltage spikes

(B) 3 per second "spikes and domes"

(C) REM onset sleep

(D) spikes in temporal lobes only

(E) no consistent EEG abnormalities

293. The cycle that is utilized by cells in the transport of acetyl-CoA from the mitochondria to the cytoplasm requires all of the following enzymes EXCEPT

(A) pyruvate carboxylase

(B) ATP-citrate lyase

(C) malic enzyme

(D) isocitrate dehydrogenase

(E) malate dehydrogenase

294. All of the following statements are true about hairy cell leukemia EXCEPT

(A) it is a malignant disorder of B lymphocytes

(B) splenic enlargement is common

(C) it is a disease of children

(D) males are afflicted more often than are females

(E) the diseased cells demonstrate acid phosphatase activity that is resistant to tartrate inhibition

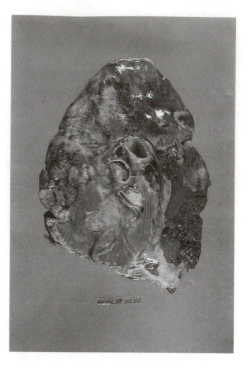

**Figure 8.17**

295. An autopsy specimen of an abnormal lung is depicted in Figure 8.17. Which item is LEAST likely to be associated with the abnormality?

(A) heparin therapy
(B) cardiovascular collapse and sudden death
(C) recently postoperative patient
(D) deep vein thrombosis
(E) pulmonary hemorrhage or infarction

(See Color Insert following page 272.)

296. All of the following are effects associated with the use of nifedipine EXCEPT

(A) relaxation of vascular smooth muscle
(B) reduction in cardiac contractility
(C) depression of skeletal muscle contraction
(D) relaxation of gastrointestinal smooth muscle
(E) relaxation of bronchiolar smooth muscle

297. All of the following statements about anxiety are true EXCEPT

(A) it usually increases sympathetic tone
(B) it may improve performance
(C) it may be a conditioned response
(D) it may be enhanced by stimulation of locus ceruleus
(E) all of the above

298. Which of the following cortical areas is associated with receptive aphasia?

(A) Broca's area
(B) Wernicke's area
(C) Brodmann area 17, 18, 19
(D) precentral gyrus
(E) postcentral gyrus

299. All of the following statements about end-plate potentials (EPPs) and miniature end-plate potentials (MEPPs) at the neuromuscular junction are correct EXCEPT

(A) MEPPs have an amplitude of about 0.4 mV, which is not sufficient to bring the postsynaptic membrane to threshold to generate an action potential
(B) MEPPs are due to spontaneous release of single quanta of ACh from the nerve terminal
(C) EPPs normally have an amplitude of about 40 mV, are non-regenerative and spread passively
(D) the ion channels which cause the EPP at the motor end-plate are non-selective cation channels
(E) normally, a single neuronal action potential at the presynaptic site of the neuromuscular junction is unable to generate an action potential in the muscle unless it summates with other action potentials arriving at the same time (temporal summation)

**300.** The graph below (Fig. 8.18) shows the response of retinal photo receptors as a function of light wave length. Which of the following is correct?

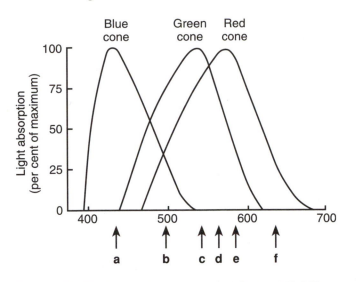

**Figure 8.18.** (*Reprinted with permission from Guyton & Hall.* Textbook of Medical Physiology. 9th ed. *W. B. Saunders Co.; 1995.*)

(A) there are 4 receptor types in the retina corresponding to the primary colors (Red–Green, Blue–Yellow)

(B) a "green" sensation is elicited by maximally stimulating the Green cone (arrow c)

(C) a "red" sensation is elicited by maximally stimulating the Red cone (arrow e)

(D) a "yellow" sensation is elicited by about equal stimulation of the Green cone and Red cone (arrow d)

(E) color is a subjective sensation and cannot be measured objectively

**301.** All of the following statements concerning stem cells are correct EXCEPT that they

(A) lack $CD_3$ molecules on their surface

(B) lack $CD_4$ molecules on their surface

(C) lack $CD_8$ molecules on their surface

(D) differentiate into B and T cells

(E) have $CD_{12}$ molecules on their surface

**302.** A 65-year-old male complains of difficulty swallowing. A mass of the lower esophagus is found on endoscopic examination and biopsied. A microphotograph of the biopsy (Fig. 8.19) is displayed. Which of the following statements concerning this esophageal mass is NOT true?

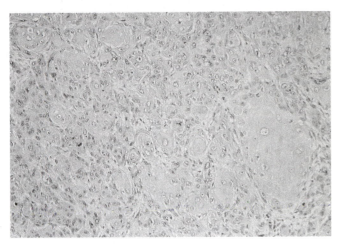

**Figure 8.19**

(A) the incidence is higher in the Far East than in the United States

(B) squamous carcinoma is the most frequent malignant cell type

(C) there is a decreased incidence with alcoholism

(D) there is an increased incidence with smoking

(E) those that are adenocarcinomas usually arise in Barrett's metaplasia

(See Color Insert following page 272.)

**303.** All of the following are treatments or agents useful in the management of parkinsonism EXCEPT

(A) dopamine

(B) bromocriptine

(C) amantadine

(D) levodopa

(E) benztropine

304. To study the psychiatric morbidity of Spielmeyer–Vogt syndrome, all patients with the syndrome being treated in the city, as identified by medical records, were interviewed by psychiatric clinicians. A demographically controlled control group was also interviewed. This is an example of

(A) prospective cohort study

(B) case control study

(C) cross-sectional prevalence survey

(D) lifetime prevalence study

(E) census survey

305. All of the following statements concerning a person who lacks $CD_8$ lymphocytes are correct EXCEPT that this person

(A) has a diminished capacity to destroy tumor cells

(B) has a reduced ability to kill allograft cells

(C) will not show suppression of delayed hypersensitivity reactions

(D) will not show suppression of immunoglobulin production by B cells

(E) will show cytotoxicity for virus infected cells

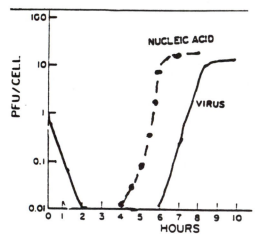

Figure 8.20

306. All of the following statements concerning Figure 8.20, depicting viral multiplication are true EXCEPT

(A) the time interval 0 to 6 hr represents the eclipse period

(B) during the time interval 0 to 6 hr, the viral nucleic acid is separated from its capsid

(C) during the time interval 0 to 6 hr, the virus loses its infectivity

(D) the period 6 to 8 hr represents the appearance of mature virus

(E) the viral multiplication curve is similar to the bacterial growth curve

307. The causative agents for the following infections are dimorphic fungi EXCEPT

(A) sporotrichosis

(B) candidiasis

(C) cryptococcosis

(D) histoplasmosis

(E) blastomycosis

308. A cardiothoracic surgeon places his finger into the transverse pericardial sinus from the right side and with his thumb clamps the vessel lying just in front of his finger. Which vessel has he occluded?

(A) superior vena cava

(B) ascending aorta

(C) arch of the aorta

(D) pulmonary trunk

(E) right pulmonary artery

309. Extensive diffuse pulmonary fibrosis is LEAST likely to occur with prolonged inhalation of

(A) silica

(B) *Thermopolyspora polyspora*

(C) asbestosis

(D) nitrogen dioxide

(E) carbon monoxide

310. All of the following are agents useful in acute or prophylactic treatment of asthma EXCEPT

(A) propranolol

(B) ipratropium bromide

(C) aminophylline

(D) cromolyn sodium

(E) albuterol

311. All of the following statements concerning human immunodeficiency virus (HIV) infection are correct EXCEPT

(A) affected individuals should not engage in vaginal or anal intercourse without a condom

(B) affected individuals should not donate blood

(C) affected individuals may manifest a sub-cortical dementia

(D) affected individuals should not engage in any kissing

(E) affected individuals may safely mastur-bate

# Practice Test
## Answers and Explanations

1.  **(B)** As its name implies, the calcarine artery courses through the calcarine sulcus to supply the primary visual cortex. Occlusion of this vessel will produce a defect in the contralateral visual field. Lesions that involve the lenticulostriate vessels typically produce upper motor neuron signs in the contralateral extremities. Occlusion of the PICA leads to a characteristic somatosensory deficit involving the loss of pain and temperature over the ipsilateral one-half of the face and the contralateral trunk and extremities. Vascular lesions involving the anterior cerebral artery or its medial striate branch do not lead to visual field defects. *(Burt, pp 184–186)*

2.  **(D)** Except for arachidonate, all of the fatty acids listed in the question are nonessential and cannot be precursors for the synthesis of essential fatty acids in humans. Prostaglandins are synthesized from arachidonic acid (*cis*-5,8,11,14-eicosatetraenoic acid) or other 20-carbon fatty acids that have at least three double bonds. Prostaglandins are 20-carbon fatty acids that contain a 5-carbon ring. They are hormonelike in their action, but unlike hormones, they often directly modulate the activities of the cells in which they are synthesized. *(Stryer, pp 624–625)*

3.  **(A)** The p53 gene is a negative regulator of cell division. When a cell's DNA is damaged, the p53 gene senses this abnormality and holds the aberrant cell in the S phase of the cell cycle to allow enzymatic repair of the damaged DNA to occur. Thus, mutations of the gene encourage replication of cells with abnormal DNA and increase the cell's propensity for malignant transformation. Mutations of the p53 gene are found in about 75% of human colon carcinomas and in a significant percentage of breast carcinomas, hepatomas, and small cell carcinomas of the lung. *(Rubin and Farber, p 182)*

4.  **(B)** Lesions involving the left lentriculostriate branches result in upper motor neuron signs in the contralateral extremities as well as in the musculature innervated by cranial nerves VII, IX, X, XI, and XII, which have been deprived of their cortical motor input. Damage to the left anterior spinal artery will produce ipsilateral lower motor neuron signs in the musculature innervated by the damaged levels of the spinal cord. Lesions involving the paramedian branches of the basilar bifurcation on the right, the right lenticulostriate vessels, and the right posterior spinal artery do not lead to upper motor neuron signs on the right side nor will they cause the protruded tongue to deviate to the right. *(Kandel, Schwartz, and Jessell, p 1046)*

5.  **(B)** Chronic alcoholics are prone to many physiological problems due to their poor dietary patterns and the effects of alcohol itself on the gastrointestinal tract leading to impaired nutrient absorption. The most common problem of chronic alcoholics are neurologic in nature, including mental confusion and depression, ataxia, and uncoordinated eye movements. The most severe symptoms are related to those seen in Wernicke–Korsakoff syndrome. Although thiamine deficiency is only one of many nutritional deficiencies seen in chronic alcoholics, adminis-

tration of thiamine has a dramatic effect on reversing the course of these severe symptoms. *(Devlin, pp 1127–1128)*

6. **(A)** Lung cancer is presently the leading type of cancer responsible for the largest fraction of American female cancer deaths. It has only recently surpassed breast cancer, which had previously been the most common site of fatal female cancers. The leading sites of female cancer deaths in the United States are in order: lung, breast, colon, and leukemia/lymphoma. *(Chandrasoma and Taylor, p 264)*

7. **(B)** The bipolar cells in the nasal mucosa, retina, and the spiral ganglia are first-order neurons. First-order sensory neurons in the dorsal root ganglia and the semilunar ganglion are pseudounipolar first-order sensory neurons. Neurons in the spinal cord are neither bipolar nor first-order sensory neurons. *(Noback et al, p 53)*

8. **(B)** The second law of thermodynamics states that in order for a reaction to proceed spontaneously, the total entropy of the system must increase. Entropy is a measure of the disorder of a system, therefore the natural thermodynamically driven tendency is for systems (and the molecules of a system) to tend toward maximum disorder. *(Murray et al, p 105)*

9. **(D)** Mesothelioma is the most common malignant tumor of the pleura. It is a highly invasive lesion and has been linked to asbestos fibers—especially in persons in the shipbuilding and insulation industries. A history of smoking also increases the risk of developing a mesothelioma. Histologically, the tumor may be either sarcomatous (composed of mesenchymal stromal cells), carcinomatous (resembling tubular or papillary structures), or a combination of these two types. These tumors are highly malignant, and most patients die within 1 year of diagnosis. *(Cotran et al, pp 730–732)*

10. **(E)** Gastrin infusion stimulates gastric acid secretion. Thus, initially, before peptide x was given, there was high gastric acid concentration. Secretin, sometimes called "nature's antacid," must have been peptide x because it is known to inhibit gastric acid secretion and to stimulate pancreatic bicarbonate production. Peptide x could not have been motilin, which has mainly to do with motility. Nor could it have been angiotensin II, which has several functions (eg, stimulation of aldosterone secretion), none of which include inhibition of gastric acid secretion or stimulation of pancreatic bicarbonate secretion. Nor could it have been CCK, which mainly stimulates pancreatic enzyme secretion and gallbladder contraction. Somatostatin has many inhibitory effects and does not stimulate pancreatic bicarbonate production. *(Johnson, pp 7–10)*

11. **(D)** The SA node is located at the superior end of the crista terminalis at the junction of the anteromedial aspect of the superior vena cava and the right auricle. The sinoatrial node is a collection of specialized cardiac muscle fibers (nodal tissue) in the wall of the right atrium, which initiates the impulses for contraction. It is the natural pacemaker of the heart. *(Moore, p 104)*

12. **(D)** Temporary occlusion of both common carotid arteries will decrease vascular pressure within the carotid sinus area. This peripheral baroreceptor responds to changes in pressure and is an important reflex in maintaining relatively constant arterial pressure on a short-term basis. A decrease in pressure will depress the number of impulses that travel from the carotid sinus nerve. Since these impulses normally inhibit the central vasoconstrictor area and excite the vagal center, a decrease in impulses will reflexively cause arterial pressure to rise and heart rate and contractility to increase. The entire circulation will be stimulated to constrict, and thus there will be a reduction in venous capacitance. *(Guyton and Hall, pp 213–215)*

13. **(C)** The deoxygenated subunits of the hemoglobin tetramer exist in the T ("tense") conformational state. As erythrocytes enter the capillaries of the lung alveoli, the partial

pressure of $O_2$ has increased sufficiently to allow binding to hemoglobin. When one mole of $O_2$ binds, it causes a shift in the overall conformation of the other subunits to a more R ("relaxed") conformational state. This change in conformation leads to higher affinity of the remaining monomers for $O_2$. Each deoxygenated monomer has a progressively increased affinity for $O_2$ as more oxygen binds. This cooperative binding is observed as a sigmoidal saturation curve when plotting the partial pressure of oxygen versus moles of $O_2$ bound. (*Devlin, pp 126–130*)

14. **(E)** The microscopic features of psoriasis usually include hyperkeratosis, parakeratosis, acanthosis, club-shaped dermal papilla, and clusters of neutrophils in the upper epidermis (Munro microabscesses). Clinically, the disease displays erythematous scaly plaques, which preferentially occur over the extensor dorsal cutaneous surfaces. Mild cases may respond to topical applications of coal or wood tar soaps. Recalcitrant cases can be treated with systemic corticosteroids, phototherapy, or methotrexate. (*Rubin and Farber, pp 1187–1190*)

15. **(A)** The gluteus medius, gluteus minimus, and tensor fasciae latae are innervated by the superior gluteal nerve. The gluteus medius and minimus are abductors of the hip, but their important function is to tilt the pelvis when one leg is off the ground, as in walking. This action aligns the center of gravity over the planted foot. Paralysis of the gluteus medius and minimus markedly affects the gait as the trunk must be swayed from side to side to prevent falling to the unsupported side. (*Hall–Craggs, pp 382–383*)

16. **(D)** Although short-term regulation of arterial BP is primarily affected by the integrated responses of peripheral baroreceptors and the central and sympathetic nervous systems, the primary determinant of regulation of BP in the long run is the relationship of urine output to fluid intake. This system is normally capable of returning BP to normal levels (infinite gain), which is different from the short-term nervous regulation. By adjusting extracellular fluid and blood volumes, renal–body fluid mechanisms alter venous return. Individual beds then adjust their resistance because of the interplay of local and neuronal factors, and thus arterial pressure is slowly readjusted to control levels. The total peripheral vascular resistance is thus altered by those mechanisms rather than being the variable that directly determines BP. (*Guyton and Hall, pp 221–224*)

17. **(A)** The primary precursors for gluconeogenesis in liver are lactate and alanine, which are produced in muscle during intense activity. Alanine is formed from pyruvate by transamination in a reaction catalyzed by alanine aminotransferase. Alanine is converted back to pyruvate in liver and employed in the synthesis of glucose. (*Stryer, pp 577–578, 630*)

18. **(C)** Celiac disease is an infrequent disorder with a familial tendency and an association with HLA-B8 and HLA-DR3 histocompatibility antigens. Children are most often afflicted and present clinically with diarrhea, malabsoption, and steatorrhea. Microscopically, there is villous atrophy of the small intestinal mucosa. The disorder is a result of a hypersensitivity reaction to gluten in the diet. Withdrawal of gluten from the diet is usually curative. (*Chandrasoma and Taylor, pp 580–581*)

19. **(E)** Identification is the psychologic defense mechanism by which an individual becomes like an admired (or otherwise psychologically important) person. Identification is an important phenomenon in personality development. (*Leigh and Reiser, pp 79–100*)

20. **(E)** The extraperitoneal fat is located between the peritoneum and the transversalis fascia. The internal spermatic fascia, the femoral sheath, deep inguinal ring, and the psoas fascia are all formed from transversalis fascia. As the processus vaginalis evaginates the transversalis fascia at the deep inguinal ring, it carries a thin layer of fascia before it that becomes the internal spermatic fascia. It constitutes the filmy, innermost covering of the spermatic cord. (*Moore, p 147*)

21. **(B)** Atrial fibrillation is a common arrhythmia that accompanies several forms of chronic heart disease. It probably represents some form of reentry phenomenon in which part of the tissue may be excited at an inappropriately early part of the cardiac cycle. Since the atria do not contract, there are no P waves. Activation of conducting tissue in the atrioventricular node becomes variable in time from cycle to cycle, and thus the QRS complex interval becomes less constant. The strength of ventricular contraction is related to the timing of filling, and thus failure of the atria to effectively contract alters ventricular filling. This produces an extremely irregular pulse. Direct current shock is an effective mechanism to return the heart to normal rhythm and reverse atrial fibrillation. However, atrial fibrillation per se is not a life-threatening event, and placing the entire myocardium into refractory period frequently is not the appropriate course of action. A number of drugs are available to prolong the effective refractory period of selective parts of the heart, and these drugs would represent an effective manner in which to revert atrial fibrillation to normal atrial contraction. *(Berne and Levy, p 393)*

22. **(B)** One non-allosteric mechanism for regulating the activity of the hepatic form of pyruvate kinase is covalent modification. Both glucagon and epinephrine signal hepatocytes to deliver glucose to the blood. Each of these hormones bind to specific receptors that are coupled to activation of adenylate cyclase which in turn produces cAMP from ATP. The increased cAMP leads to activation of cAMP-dependent protein kinase (PKA) which phosphorylates numerous substrates. One hepatic substrate is pyruvate kinase. Upon being phosphorylated the activity of pyruvate kinase is reduced. This prevents any phosphoenolpyruvate (PEP) that is formed during gluconeogenesis from being converted to pyruvate ensuring its continued entry into glucose production. It is important to distinguish the effects of epinephrine on the activity of hepatic versus muscle pyruvate kinase. In skeletal muscle, epinephrine stimulates glycolysis, not gluconeogenesis.

The muscle form of pyruvate kinase is not a substrate for PKA. *(Devlin, pp 322–324)*

23. **(B)** Wire-loop lesions in glomeruli in renal biopsy specimens, though not pathognomonic, are generally associated with renal involvement by systemic lupus erythematosus. The formation of the wire loops is caused by subendothelial electron-dense deposits that produce thickened, refractile capillary walls. Small subepithelial deposits, or spikes, may also be present and produce extension of the deposits through the basement membrane. Wire-loop lesions also may be seen in glomerular lesions of patients with cryoglobulinemia. Diabetes mellitus, hypertension, and acute tubular necrosis may be associated with histologic changes in the renal glomeruli or tubules or both. These entities are not typically associated with wire-loop lesions, however. In the hepatorenal syndrome, renal dysfunction appears to be functional rather than associated with anatomic renal changes. *(Rubin and Farber, pp 834–836)*

24. **(B)** Society's sick-role expectations, as described by Parsons, include exemption from normal social role expectations, the recognition that the individual is not responsible for being sick and that he or she cannot be expected to get well simply by wanting to get well, being sick is an undesirable state, and the individual should try to get well, and that the sick person should seek competent help to get well. The idea that an individual is responsible for the maintenance of his or her health is contrary to the second expectation described above. *(Leigh and Reiser, pp 17–24)*

25. **(C)** An indirect inguinal hernia leaves the abdominal cavity lateral to the inferior epigastric artery and veins. The herniating mass is medial to the crest of the ilium, anterior superior iliac spine, deep inguinal ring, and the superficial circumflex iliac vessels. *(Moore, pp 147–149)*

26. **(C)** Injuries affecting upper cervical segments (above C3) usually quickly cause death from loss of respiratory muscle function. However, a transection of the spinal

cord between C8 and T1 only severs neural connections between the brain stem and some of the muscles involved in respiration (eg, intercostal and abdominal muscles) while sparing connections to the diaphragm (phrenic nerves come off spinal neurons in segments C3-C5 ["C-three, four, and five keep the diaphragm alive"]). In this tetraplegic patient, there is essentially complete loss of expiratory muscle function, but only modest loss of inspiratory action (the diaphragm is the major muscle of inspiration). Normal quiet expiration is passive. However, forced expiration, as in the latter part of vital capacity measurement, requires active participation by expiratory muscles. In this patient, you might expect a vital capacity that is at best only about 50 percent of normal. By definition, functional residual (FRC) is the volume at which the respiratory system stays when all respiratory muscles are inactive. On the other hand, residual volume (RV) is the volume left after maximal expiratory effort (involves intercostal and abdominal muscles). RV is normally about one liter less than FRC. Since this patient has no expiratory muscle function, there cannot be a RV less than FRC. That is, in this patient, FRC = RV. *(Berne and Levy, pp 553–554)*

27. **(D)** Alanine, cysteine, glycine, and serine are all converted to pyruvate during amino acid degradation. Thus, each of these amino acids can give rise to glucose via conversion of pyruvate to oxaloacetate and then phosphoenolpyruvate. In addition, ketone body formation can proceed by conversion of pyruvate to acetyl-CoA. In contrast, leucine can only be converted to potential ketone body precursors. The degradation of leucine leads to the formation of acetyl-CoA and acetoacetate. *(Stryer, pp 638–646)*

28. **(A)** The Negri bodies associated with rabies are large cytoplasmic granules containing rabies viral particles. They are most abundant in the area of the hippocampus known as Ammon's horn. The Negri bodies are best detected by special stains, such as Seller's stain, which reveals the cytoplasmic granules con-

taining the rabies virus as cherry red in color with dark blue spots; immunofluorescence is another reliable method of identifying these granules. Quarnieri bodies are seen in poxvirus-infected cells. Reticulate and elimentary bodies are seen in chlamydial infections. *(Joklik et al, pp 720–721)*

29. **(A)** Glaucoma is a disorder characterized by an increased intraocular pressure with resultant pressure atrophy of the optic disk and decreased visual acuity. Primary open-angle glaucoma presents slowly, usually occuring in adults over the age of 40 years old. Medicinal treatment with pupillary constrictors can provide temporary relief. Definitive surgical correction is successful in about 80% of cases. *(Chandrasoma and Taylor, pp 489–490)*

30. **(D)** Clearance is equal to the dosing rate divided by the steady-state plasma (target) concentration. Since the infusion rate is 2 mg/min and the steady state level is 4 mg/L, the quotient is 0.5 L/min or 500 mL/min. *(Katzung, p 42)*

31. **(A)** By repeated exposure to the pairing of a stimulus (thinking of an apple) to another stimulus (sour taste) that produces a response (salivation), simply thinking of sour apple produces salivation. This type of learning is called classical (Pavlovian) conditioning. *(Leigh and Reiser, pp 45–47)*

32. **(D)** The inferior limit of the posterior wall of the rectus sheath is marred by a crescentic border called the arcuate line. The aponeurosis of the external abdominal oblique ends medially in the linea alba. Inferiorly, it folds back on itself to form the inguinal ligament. The medial part of the inguinal ligament is reflected horizontally back and is attached to the pecten pubis at the lacunar ligament. The opening in the aponeurosis is called the superficial inguinal ring. *(Moore, pp 133, 136)*

33. **(C)** Filtration pressure ($P_{uf}$) is calculated from the Starling equation involving four forces:

$$P_{uf} = (P_{GC} - P_{BS}) - (\Pi_{GC} - \Pi_{BS})$$

Normally, the filtrate in Bowman's space has such negligible amounts of protein that $\Pi_{BS}$ is considered to be zero and is often left out of the Starling equation for glomerular filtration. Choices A, B, and D all give zero $P_{uf}$ (ie, glomerular filtration equilibrium). Choice E gives a negative filtration pressure of –5 mm Hg, which would favor absorption instead of filtration. (*Vander, pp 28–29*)

34. **(D)** The bifunctional enzyme, phosphofructokinase-2 (PFK-2) contains a kinase and a phosphatase domain. The kinase domain phosphorylates fructose-6-phosphate (F-6-P) to yield fructose-2,6-bisphosphate (F-2,6-BP), whereas the phosphatase dephosphorylates F-2,6,-BP yielding F-6-P. F-2,6-BP is a potent allosteric activator of the rate limiting enzyme of glycolysis, phosphofructokinase-1 (PFK-1), as well as a potent allosteric inhibitor of the gluconeogenic enzyme, fructose-1,6-bisphosphatase. The activity of PFK-2 is regulated by cAMP-dependent protein kinase (PKA) mediated phosphorylation. When phosphorylated PFK-2 functions as a phosphatase, and as a kinase when dephosphorylated. The PKA-mediated change in activity of PFK-2 allows the level of F-2,6-BP to be regulated by circulating hormones such as glucagon and epinephrine, ultimately controlling the flux through glycolysis. (*Devlin, pp 317–323*)

35. **(D)** The classic complement pathway is usually activated by the antigen–antibody union then involving complement components C1q, C4, C2, and C3–C9. The alternate complement pathway proceeds through C3–C9, and it can be activated by aggregated immunoglobulins IgA, IgG₄, IgE, lipopolysaccharides, and endotoxins, but not IL-1. β-Interferon is an antiviral protein, and the complement component C1 binds to the antigen–antibody complex and initiates the cascade of the classic complement pathway. (*Joklik et al, pp 286–295*)

36. **(E)** Cretinism is due to a neonatal lack of thyroxine. Thyroid agenesis, iodine deficiency, ingestion of goitrogens, and hereditary enzymatic deficiencies may all result in a

relative lack of biologically active thyroxine. Clinically, the children display lethargy, jaundice, hypothermia, muscular hypotonia, delayed bone growth and mental retardation. Medicinal replacement of thyroxine is therapeutic. Unfortunately, the mental retardation is usually not reversible unless treatment was instituted promptly early in the disease. (*Chandrasoma and Taylor, pp 831–832*)

37. **(D)** The objective is to minimize both entry of radioactive iodide into the thyroid gland and isotopic dilution of the iodide that does enter the gland. High serum concentrations of non-radioactive iodide will decrease iodide uptake by the thyroid gland and formation of thyroid hormone within the gland. This autoregulation probably exists to prevent a massive release of thyroid hormone in an individual who has been nutritionally deficient in iodide for a period of time. Studies of the Chernobyl nuclear power plant radionuclide release indicate that iodide ingestion of 15 to 150 mg daily significantly reduced the incidence of childhood thyroid cancer. (*Gilman et al, p 1377; Reiners, pp 229–234*)

38. **(A)** The limbic system is concerned with basic instinctual and emotive behaviors and memory. Higher functions, such as thinking (cognition), are performed by the cerebral cortex. (*Leigh and Reiser, pp 52–59*)

39. **(A)** The disposition of the peritoneum in the adult appears meaningless and complex if its developmental changes and modifications are not considered. The primordia of the viscera are located outside this peritoneal sac in the extraperitoneal tissue. Later, as the viscera develop, they protrude into the peritoneal sac to varying degrees. The kidneys protrude only slightly and are called retroperitoneal. The transverse colon, stomach, spleen, and sigmoid colon protrude completely, and the peritoneum forms the serosa of the walls of these organs. (*Moore, pp 152–153*)

40. **(C)** The stimulation of afferent nerves to salivary gland acini results in the secretion of a solution that resembles plasma. This is ac-

companied by a loss of cellular potassium ions, which is brought about by a rise in the intracellular concentration of calcium ions. In experiments in which single ionic channels have been recorded directly, it has been demonstrated that the basolateral plasma membranes of salivary gland acinar cells contain calcium-activated potassium channels. It is believed that these account for the efflux of potassium following stimulation. $Na^+-K^+-Cl^-$ cotransport and the ouabain-sensitive $Na^+-K^+$ pump may each contribute to the reuptake of potassium ions by these cells. (Petersen and Maruyama, pp 693–696)

41. **(B)** Fibrinogen is converted to fibrin monomers by the action of thrombin, which cleaves several peptide bonds in fibrinogen to yield fibrin. The fibrin monomers, thus formed, aggregate with each other to form a clot. Thrombin itself is derived by proteolytic cleavage of its precursor, prothrombin. Antithrombin III is an inhibitor of thrombin activity. It inactivates the enzyme by forming an irreversible complex with it. This inhibition can be enhanced by the presence of heparin and is the basis of the latter's anticoagulant properties. Fibrin clots can be dissolved by the action of plasmin, a serine protease. (Murray et al, pp 680–684)

42. **(D)** The human immunodeficiency virus (HIV) is a member of the retrovirus group that contains single stranded RNA viruses and an enzyme that synthesizes DNA from RNA (reverse transcriptase). The HIV multiplies in $CD4^+$ lymphocytes and this multiplications leads to severe lymphopenia due to the lysis of $CD4^+$ lymphocytes. (Joklik et al, pp 1048–1053)

43. **(C)** Adrenocortical carcinoma is a rare malignant tumor of the adrenal cortex. It almost never affects children. These tumors are consistently large, bulky, and unilateral, with extension into the soft tissues and retroperitoneum apparent at the time of diagnosis. They often show necrosis and hemorrhage, invade vascular and lymphatic structures, and frequently metastasize. The tumor is considered to be an adenocarcinoma and

ranges in structure from well differentiated to anaplastic. About half of the tumors are functional and secrete steroids, especially cortisol. Clinically, affected patients may have symptoms of Cushing's syndrome—hypoglycemia, virilization, feminization, or a combination of these. These tumors are thought to arise from the adrenal cortical cells and are not of neural crest origin. (Rubin and Farber, pp 1136)

44. **(B)** Nicotine is an extremely addicting substance, and sudden cessation of its use results in both physical and psychological withdrawal symptoms. (Leigh and Reiser, pp 258–259)

45. **(D)** Benzodiazepines are anti-anxiety agents. They are also muscle relaxants, anticonvulsants, as well sedatives. Because of the sedative action, an elderly patient may develop paradoxic agitation due to the disinhibition of higher cortical function. Benzodiazepines, unlike neuroleptics, do not cause impaired conditioned avoidance learning. (Leigh and Reiser, pp 437–455)

46. **(D)** The ankle joint is a synovial hinge joint between the lower ends of the tibia and fibula, and the upper end of the talus. The single plane of action allows for flexion and extension, which are more commonly called plantar flexion and dorsiflexion. The other movements occurring in the foot are inversion, and eversion which take place at the subtaler joint. (Hall–Craggs, pp 420–421, 430)

47. **(B)** The blood gas data from this patient illustrate chronic respiratory alkalosis with renal compensation. Either severe chronic lung disease or an overdose of heroin would have caused respiratory acidosis due to abnormally high arterial $P_{CO_2}$ (not low $P_{CO_2}$ which this subject has). Acute aspirin overdose in adults usually presents first with a respiratory alkalosis, which includes a low $P_{CO_2}$, but not a low $P_{O_2}$. Breathing a low oxygen gas mixture is similar to being at high altitude, but if this is only for a few minutes there will be no time for renal compensation. A lowlander at high altitude for two weeks is ex-

pected to have low $P_{O_2}$ plus low $P_{CO_2}$ because of hypoxia-induced hyperventilation. Renal compensation in the form of bicarbonate excretion reduces plasma bicarbonate and returns the pH to a nearly normal value. *(Rose, 1994, pp 629–637)*

48. **(A)** Phosphofructokinase-1 (PFK-1) is the rate-limiting enzyme of glycolysis catalyzing the phosphorylation of fructose-6-phosphate, yielding fructose-1,6-bisphosphate. PFK-1 is under tight allosteric control, being maximally active when energy levels are low and inhibited when energy levels are high. When the level of AMP is rising in the cell, it signals a decrease in overall energy charge. AMP is an allosteric activator of PFK-1. In contrast to AMP, ATP is a potent allosteric inhibitor of PFK-1 by binding to a site distinct from that of the ATP substrate site. As the level of ATP declines there is less allosteric inhibition of PFK-1 and a concomitant increase in allosteric activation by AMP. This allows PFK-1 to "sense" the energy status of the cell and in turn regulate the flux through the glycolytic pathway. *(Devlin, pp 313–323)*

49. **(D)** The penicillin binucleate core structure is a cyclized dipeptide formed by condensation of L-cysteine and D-valine. Several different side chains are found at the R portion of the figure that accompanies the question. These impart important biologic characteristics to the molecule, such as acid stability, resistance to β-lactamase, broadened spectrum, and so forth. *(Joklik et al, pp 154–162)*

50. **(A)** The International Working Formulation (IWF) is an attempt to codify the classification of non-Hodgkin's lymphoma throughout the world. Based on historical clinical outcomes, the IWF separates these neoplasms into three grades: low, intermediate, and high. Low-grade lymphomas have a more favorable and less aggressive course when compared to those tumors which are classified as intermediate or high-grade. In general, low-grade neoplasms tend to recapitulate normal lymph node architecture, retaining such morphologic features as folli-

cle formation and a small cell population. *(Rubin and Farber, pp 1076–1085)*

51. **(D)** Most neuroleptic anti-psychotic agents are dopamine receptor blockers. Most, except clozapine, are ineffective against the negative symptoms of schizophrenia, such as flat affect, thought blocking, etc. Most neuroleptics have some sedative action, and serum prolactin levels increase because of the dopamine blockade in the hypothalamus. Pseudoparkinsonism is a frequent and bothersome side effect of anti-psychotic drugs, which may be effectively managed with anticholinergic agents such as benztropine (Cogentin). *(Leigh and Reiser, 441–451)*

52. **(C)** The majority of adults with and without psychiatric disorders who commit aggressive acts are more likely to commit them against familiar persons, usually family members. Some XYY syndrome persons may be more prone to engage in aggression. Other metabolic disorders predisposing to aggression include Sanfilippo syndrome, Spielmeyer–Vogt syndrome, and phenylketonuria. While males are more likely to commit homicide, battery, or rape; domestic violence is engaged in equally by both sexes. The rate of aggression among psychiatric inpatients may be as high as 10 to 15% during the year prior to hospitalization. *(Kaplan and Sadock, pp 271–282)*

53. **(A)** Each spinal nerve contains nerve fibers classified into one of four functional components, namely: (1) general somatic afferent, (2) general visceral afferent, (3) general somatic efferent, and (4) general visceral efferent. Special visceral efferent fibers supply the branchiomeric musculature. *(Noback, p 107)*

54. **(B)** Pulmonary arterioles are unique for their ability to constrict under conditions of hypoxia. This results in a local adjustment of perfusion to ventilation. For example, if a bronchiole is obstructed, the lack of $O_2$ causes contraction of the pulmonary vascular smooth muscle in the corresponding area, shunting blood away from the hypoxic re-

gion to better ventilated regions. Similarly, systemic hypoxia causes an increase in pulmonary artery resistance and increased workload for the right ventricle. *(Ganong, pp 605–606)*

55. **(C)** Under normal conditions, lactate delivered to the liver is oxidized to pyruvate with the concomitant reduction of NAD$^+$ to NADH. The pyruvate is then transported to the mitochondria for conversion to oxaloacetate (OAA) catalyzed by pyruvate carboxylase. In the presence of mitochondrial PEP carboxykinase the OAA is converted to PEP. In cells lacking mitochondrial PEP carboxykinase, OAA is transaminated to aspartate for transport to the cytoplasm. In the cytoplasm, the aspartate is converted back to OAA. Cytoplasmic OAA is then converted to PEP by the cytolpasmic PEP carboxykinase. When alcohol is consumed, cytoplasmic alcohol dehydrogenase (ADH) catalyzes the following reaction:

$$Ethanol + NAD^+ \rightarrow acetaldehyde + NADH$$

Metabolism of ethanol occurs primarily in the liver and leads to an inhibition of hepatic gluconeogenesis. The large amounts of NADH generated by ADH must be transported to the mitochondria by the malate-aspartate shuttle. The excess cytoplasmic NADH forces the lactate dehydrogenase and cytoplasmic malate dehydrogenase reactions in the direction of lactate and malate production, respectively. The direction of the lactate dehydrogenase reaction inhibit the utilization of lactate as a gluconeogenic substrate. The direction of the cytoplasmic malate dehydrogenase reaction rapidly converts any cytoplasmic OAA to malate preventing its conversion to PEP by PEP carboxykinase. The net result of the oxidation of ethanol on the direction of these two reactions is that ethanol and OAA are converted to acetaldehyde and malate, respectively. Although the increase in cytoplasmic NADH favorably drives the glyceraldehyde-3-phosphate dehydrogenase reaction in the gluconeogenic direction, the equilibrium shift in lactate dehydrogenase and malate dehydrogenase re-

duces the concentrations of pyruvate and OAA for use by the gluconeogenic enzyme pyruvate carboxylase and PEP carboxykinase, respectively. *(Devlin, pp 336–337)*

56. **(C)** The biologic activity of an antibody molecule centers on its ability to specifically bind antigen. The combining site is located on the amino-terminal end of the antibody molecule and is composed of hypervariable segments within the variable regions of both light and heavy chains. Antibody specificity is a function of both the amino acid sequence and its three-dimensional configuration. *(Joklik et al, pp 227–230)*

57. **(A)** The photograph that accompanies the question demonstrates severe hydronephrosis of the kidney. Hydronephrosis refers to dilatation of the renal pelvis and calices associated with progressive atrophy of the kidney due to obstruction of the flow of urine from the kidney. The obstruction may be located at any site along the urinary outflow tract and may be partial or total, unilateral or bilateral. Since glomerular filtration may continue for some time after the development of the obstruction, the renal pelvis and calices become dilated by the continued urine production. The resultant back pressure produces atrophy of the renal parenchyma with obliteration of the pyramids. The degree of hydronephrosis depends on the extent and rapidity of the obstructive process. *(Cotran et al, pp 982–984)*

58. **(D)** Resistant organisms produce penicillinase, a β-lactamase that hydrolyzes the β-lactam ring to form penicilloic acid, which has no antibacterial activity. β-Lactamases are elaborated by a number of clinically important organisms, including staphylococci. Resistant strains of many organisms, including streptococci, which were previously predictable in their sensitivity to penicillin are now being encountered. Such resistance arises in part through indiscriminate and profligate use of antibiotics, resulting in selection of bacterial strains expressing resistance mechanisms such as β-lactamases. For treatment of β-lactamase-producing staphy-

lococci, resistant penicillins such as oxacillin or nafcillin are used. β-Lactamase inhibitors such as clavulanic acid and sulbactam are also being used in combination with penicillins. *(Katzung, pp 681–684, 689)*

**59.** **(A)** An individual usually is not consciously aware of signal anxiety, a type of anxiety that serves as a signal of an impending danger intrapsychically. Panic anxiety, neurotic anxiety, and psychotic anxiety are severe forms of anxiety and are pathologic. *(Leigh and Reiser, pp 41–78)*

**60.** **(B)** The uncal herniation syndrome includes contralateral hemiplegia and ipsilateral oculomotor nerve signs. Paralysis of the contralateral lower portion of the facial expression muscles may also be present and the protruded tongue might deviate toward the contralateral side. Typically, ipsilateral hemiplegia is not seen although it is possible for the contralateral cerebral peduncle to be compressed against the tentorial notch and if this occurs, then paralysis might be present in the extremities ipsilateral to the herniated uncus. *(Brodal, p 90)*

**61.** **(C)** Aromatase is the enzyme that controls the conversion of testosterone to estradiol. It also catalyzes the formation of estrone from androstenedione. The major proportion of circulating estradiol in adult men is formed directly by aromatization of these circulating androgens. Lesser amounts may be secreted by both the Leydig cells and the Sertoli cells in the testes and by the adrenal cortex. *(Ganong, pp 405–406)*

**62.** **(D)** The activation of factor X is the final reaction of both the extrinsic and intrinsic pathways of clotting. Activated factor X proteolytically cleaves prothrombin to thrombin, which in turn cleaves fibrinogen to fibrin. Factor V stimulates the activation of factor X, and fibrin-stabilizing factor (factor XIII) stabilizes the clot by cross-linking fibrin. All of these factors are part of the common pathway. The defect in hemophilia is a deficiency in factor VIII, or the anti-hemophilic factor. This factor acts as the last step of the intrinsic pathway. Factor VIII acts in concert with factor IX, a proteolytic enzyme, to activate factor X. *(Murray et al, pp 678–683)*

**63.** **(A)** In bacterial food poisoning caused by *Clostridium perfringens*, final confirmation rests upon toxin production by *C. perfringens* and its neutralization by specific antiserum. Demonstration of the presence of large gram-positive rods, or spores in the suspected food is not very helpful for the identification of *C. perfringens* because of confusion with other clostridia or of large bacilli in thioglycolate broth will not allow classification of the various anaerobic large gram-positive rods. *(Ryan, pp 298–300, 769–772)*

**64.** **(C)** Down syndrome is the most common chromosome abnormality, occurring in 1 of 800 live births. It is characterized by a trisomy 21 karyotype with an extra G group chromosome (chromosome 21), making 47 total chromosomes. In the majority of cases, the parents are phenotypically and genetically normal, and Down syndrome is secondary to a meiotic error in the ovum. The risk of having a Down syndrome child is proportional to increasing maternal age. The clinical features of Down syndrome include fat facies, epicanthic folds, oblique palpebral fissures, and severe mental retardation. The majority of affected individuals die early from cardiac or infectious complications. Thirty percent have a ventricular septal defect.

Trisomy 13 is also called Patau syndrome, and affected children have microcephaly and severe mental retardation, with absence of a portion of the forebrain. These children die soon after birth. Trisomy 18, or Edwards' syndrome, is also a very severe genetic defect, and the average life span is 10 weeks. Affected children have severe mental retardation and cardiac anomalies, including a ventricular septal defect. The chromosome abnormality is an extra chromosome 18 due to a meiotic error. Patients with an XO karyotype have Turner syndrome and are phenotypically females. Only 3% of affected fetuses survive to birth. Fetuses that survive birth have severe edema of the hands, feet, and neck. They have a webbed neck, short stature, and congenital heart disease. At puberty, there is failure to develop normal secondary sex characteristics, so their genitalia remain immature. The ovaries are atrophic and infertile, with primary amenorrhea. Klinefelter syndrome, or testicular dysgenesis, is characterized by an XXY karyotype. It occurs in 1 of 600 live births. Affected individuals usually are diagnosed after puberty and have eunuchoid habitus, long legs, and small atrophic testes and penis. Secondary male characteristics fail to develop. These men are infertile and often have a low IQ. *(Cotran et al, pp 152–162)*

65. **(D)** In patients with endogenous asthma and nasal polyps, a single dose of aspirin may cause bronchoconstriction and vasomotor collapse. These effects are shared by other cyclo-oxygenase inhibitors and may reflect effects of increased leukotriene formation brought on by shunting of arachidonic acid from the cyclooxygenase pathway into the lipooxygenase pathway. Analgesic nephropathy, hepatotoxicity, and infertility are rare side effects, which occur most often during protracted or high-dose therapy. *(Gilman et al, pp 643, 652)*

66. **(D)** Rationalization is a defense mechanism in which the person gives a post hoc plausible explanation for an unacceptable action. *(Leigh and Reiser, pp 79–100)*

67. **(C)** Irrigation of the right ear with warm water produces increased output from the right vestibular sensory apparatus, and this leads to activation of the left lateral rectus and right medial rectus muscles. These two muscles then produce slow conjugate movement of the eyes to the left which is followed immediately by rapid conjugate movement to the right. *(Burt, p 280)*

68. **(A)** Blood flow to various organs can be either expressed as perfusion in percentage of cardiac output, or as specific perfusion in mL/min · kg tissue. The kidneys receive by far the highest specific perfusion, about 150 times that of skeletal muscle, eight times that of the brain, and five times that of cardiac

muscle. This renders the kidneys particularly vulnerable during conditions such as hypovolemic shock. During severe exercise, blood flow to skeletal muscles can increase up to 25-fold and, when expressed as percentage of cardiac output, will exceed all other organs including heart muscle. However, the specific perfusion to exercising skeletal muscle still remains far below that of the kidneys. *(Ganong, p 555)*

69. **(A)** The proteolytic blood enzyme thrombin has a specificity for arginine–glycine bonds similar to trypsin. Thrombin is synthesized as prothrombin, which contains γ-carboxyglutamate residues deriving from vitamin K-dependent, post-translational modification of glutamate. In order to be activated, prothrombin is proteolytically cleaved by factor $X_a$ after being anchored to platelet membranes in a calcium-γ-carboxyglutamate-dependent reaction. The γ-carboxyglutamate end of the prothrombin molecule is removed, leaving an active thrombin. Fibrinogen is converted to fibrin by the proteolytic cleavage of four arginine–glycine bonds. The A and B fibrinopeptides released spontaneously associate to form a clot of insoluble fibrin fibers. *(Murray et al, pp 678–681)*

70. **(C)** Koplik's spots on the buccal mucosa are characteristic of infection with the measles virus. Microscopic examination of these lesions would reveal giant cells containing viral nucleocapsids. Macroscopically, these lesions will appear as small, erythematous macules with white centers. Rubeola (German measles) is an acute febrile disease characterized by fever, maculopapular rash, and respiratory symptoms. A cell culture-produced attenuated vaccine is available. There is only one antigenic variety of measles virus, so the vaccine is monovalent. It should not be given until after 12 months of age to allow maternal antibody, which could interfere with the infection established by the vaccine strain, to dissipate from the infant's circulation. *(Joklik et al, pp 1011–1012)*

71. **(B)** Atherosclerosis is the most common cause of aortic abdominal aneurysms in the

United States. These aneurysms are rare before age 50 and are more common in males than in females. Hemodynamic and genetic factors may potentiate the development of the aneurysms. Small asymptomatic aneurysms may be inconsequential. Larger aneurysms, particularly those that are symptomatic, may be treated surgically. *(Cotran et al, pp 500–501)*

72. **(E)** Congenital deficiency in adrenal cortical 21-hydroxylase activity results in decreased cortisol formation and accumulation of precursors that can enter the androgen pathway, leading to virilization. If the deficiency in 21-hydroxylase is not extreme, cortisol levels may be near normal because of high corticotropin (ACTH) levels secondary to loss of hypothalamic feedback regulation. Cortisol administered in dosages adjusted to allow normal growth will decrease the corticotropin levels, thereby decreasing the formation of androgens. *(Katzung, p 897)*

73. **(B)** Persons who unsuccessfully attempt suicide tend to be young and female, unlike persons who complete suicide. Suicidal attempt often occurs at times of interpersonal difficulties and is not infrequent among Catholics. *(Leigh and Reiser, pp 101–144)*

74. **(B)** Pain and temperature sensations from the right side of the face (including the teeth) travel via the ipsilateral trigeminal nerve and spinal trigeminal tract to the ipsilateral spinal trigeminal nucleus. From here, the signals travel across the midline via the ventral trigeminothalamic tract and eventually reach the contralateral (left) ventral posteromedial thalamic nucleus. The cells of this nucleus then project ipsilaterally to the face representation in the ventrolateral portion of the postcentral gyrus. *(Burt, pp 209–212)*

75. **(D)** Of the conditions listed, only pancreatic head tumors are associated with an increase in conjugated ("direct") bilirubin ("obstructive jaundice"). Increased levels of unconjugated ("indirect") bilirubin result from hemolysis or liver defects that impair uptake or conjugation mechanisms in liver cells (Gilbert's syndrome, Crigler–Najjar's syndrome). Unconjugated bilirubin may cross the immature blood–brain barrier of the newborn and cause kernicterus. The physiological jaundice of the neonate observed during the first week of birth is usually mild and due to relatively immature liver conjugation. *(Guyton and Hall, pp 886–888, 1052)*

76. **(D)** Conversion of pyruvate to acetyl-CoA results in the production of 1 mol of NADH. Oxidation of the resultant acetyl-CoA to $CO_2$ and water via the citric acid cycle yields 3 mol of NADH, 1 mol of $FADH_2$ and 1 mol of guanosine triphosphate (GTP). Oxidation of each mol of NADH during electron transport yields 3 mol of ATP, whereas oxidation of $FADH_2$ results in the formation of 2 mol of ATP. Therefore, beginning with pyruvate, the yield is 12 mol of ATP from 4 mol of NADH, 2 mol of ATP from 1 mol of $FADH_2$, and 1 mol of ATP equivalent (GTP) from substrate level phosphorylation, giving a total of 15 mol of ATP. *(Stryer, pp 509–510, 513–514)*

77. **(B)** The DiGeorge syndrome is a form of glandular aplasia due to defective embryonic development of the third and fourth pharyngeal pouches, which give rise to the thymus, parathyroid, and thyroid glands. This anomaly results in a depletion of thymic-dependent areas in lymphoid tissues. In Bruton's hypogammaglobulinemia, B-dependent areas are depleted. Hence, antibody formation is severely restricted. In severe combined immunodeficiency disease, both B- cell and T-cell functions are absent, and the affected individual is completely without any immune capability. Job's disease, or lazy leukocyte syndrome, is characterized by a defect in the chemotactic response of neutrophils. *(Joklik et al, pp 329–332)*

78. **(E)** Ascites is a collection of excess fluid within the peritoneal cavity. At least 500 mL has to accumulate before it becomes clinically apparent. Transudative ascites is associated with portal hypertension and certain renal diseases. Exudative ascites may occur with widely metastatic ovarian carcinoma. *(Cotran et al, pp 836–837)*

79. **(C)** Phenylbutazone impairs platelet aggregation and displaces anticoagulant drugs from their binding with blood proteins. Barbiturates, glutethimide, and rifampin all induce microsomal enzyme systems in the liver that increase drug metabolism and thus reduce the response. Cholestyramine, a plasma cholesterol-lowering agent, binds anticoagulants in the intestine, reducing their absorption. *(Craig and Stitzel, p 377)*

80. **(E)** Pain receptors are considered to be free nerve endings. Meissner's and Vater–Pacini corpuscles are thought to be involved with touch and proprioception. Rods are retinal light-sensitive cells. *(Leigh and Reiser, pp 211–243)*

81. **(B)** The fibers terminating in the nucleus gracilis originate from below $T_6$, including the lower extremities, and those in the nucleus cuneatus originate from above $T_6$, including the upper extremities. The longest neuronal fibers in the body are those of the fasciculus gracilis. They extend without interruption from receptors in the foot through the spinal nerves, dorsal roots (location of their cell bodies), and fasciculus gracilis to the nucleus gracilis. *(Noback, p 146)*

82. **(C)** Aldosterone is synthesized and secreted by cells of the adrenal cortex. A primary role for mineralocorticoids, such as aldosterone, is to stimulate the renal reabsorption of sodium ions. After adrenalectomy, the excretion of sodium ions in the urine is significantly increased and plasma sodium ion concentrations fall. At the same time, plasma potassium concentrations increase. If mineralocorticoids are not administered, blood pressure and the volume of the plasma decrease and death ensues. Although the loss of glucocorticoids, such as cortisol and corticosterone, may also become lethal in certain circumstances, such as fasting, their loss in adrenalectomy is not as critical as is the loss of aldosterone. Neither the loss of the androgen dehydroepiandrosterone, secreted by the adrenal cortex, nor the loss of catecholamines, such as epinephrine, secreted by the adrenal medulla, produce similar life-threatening changes in body functions. *(Ganong, p 346)*

83. **(D)** Glucagon-stimulated increases in cAMP levels leads to increased activity of cAMP-dependent protein kinase (PKA). There are numerous hepatic substrates for PKA, including pyruvate kinase, PFK-2, and an inhibitor of protein phosphatases identified as inhibitor-1 (also called protein phosphatase inhibitor-1, PPI-1). The net result of PKA-mediated phosphorylation of these three proteins is a decrease in pyruvate kinase activity, a decrease in the level of active protein phosphatases (by their being bound to PPI-1) and an increase in the phosphatase activity of PFK-2. The phosphatase activity of PFK-2 leads to a decrease in the level of fructose-2, 6-bisphosphate which is a potent allosteric activator of PFK-1; therefore, the activity of PFK-1 will decrease in response to increased hepatic cAMP levels. *(Devlin, pp 317–323)*

84. **(C)** For sterilization of surgical instruments sensitive to heat, the method of choice is ethylene oxide. The autoclave uses high temperatures for sterilization. Both phenol and ethyl alcohol are used for disinfection, but neither can be relied on to kill spores. Ethylene oxide is effective against all types of bacteria, including the tubercle bacilli and spores. It is a gas and can be used for the sterilization of fragile and heat-labile materials and other items packaged in cloth or paper containers. Sterilization is complete in 4 to 12 hours, which must be followed by 12 to 24 hours of aeration to allow dissipation of the dissolved gas. Ionizing radiation would not penetrate many surgical instruments evenly and hence would not sterilize effectively. *(Joklik et al, pp 195–196)*

85. **(B)** Sarcoidosis is a multisystem disease of unknown cause. The characteristic histologic lesion is a poorly formed non-caseating epitheloid granuloma that contains foreign-body-type multinucleate giant cells. Schaumann bodies and intracellular crystalline inclusion bodies may also be evident microscopically. *(Cotran et al, pp 712–714)*

86. **(E)** The β-blocker propranolol is useful in treating angina because, by decreasing heart rate and contractility (especially during exercise), the myocardial oxygen consumption is decreased. Because β-blockers do not produce vasodilation, propranolol is often combined with a calcium-channel blocker to produce a therapeutic response more effective than either drug alone. (*Katzung, pp 182–184*)

87. **(D)** Lithium salts are particularly effective in treating acute mania. They also may be effective in preventing recurrences of unipolar depression, but not to the extent of their use in treatment of mania. Lithium is not particularly effective in panic disorders, anxiety disorder, or schizophrenia. (*Leigh and Reiser, pp 439–455*)

88. **(E)** A loss of pain occurs in lesions involving the lateral spinothalamic tract, which is located in the lateral funiculus. A lesion in the posterior funiculus involving the fasciculi cuneatus and gracilis may result in loss of vibratory sense, the inability to recognize a common object by feel and palpation, a loss of two-point discrimination, and a loss of position sense. (*Noback, pp 131, 156*)

89. **(E)** Activity in the sympathetic afferent nerves to the pancreas results in the enhanced secretion of glucagon from the α cells within the pancreatic islets. The stimulation of sympathetic afferents also inhibits insulin secretion from the β cells. The increase in glucagon secretion is a β-adrenergic response that uses a cyclic AMP second messenger mechanism. Thus, agents that elevate cyclic AMP promote glucagon secretion. An inhibitory α-adrenergic receptor also is present, but the β-adrenergic response usually is dominant on sympathetic stimulation. The secretion of glucagon is enhanced also by elevated amino acid concentrations in plasma and is inhibited by glucose and insulin. (*Ganong, p 321*)

90. **(D)** When lactate enters hepatocytes for conversion to glucose it is oxidized to pyruvate by lactate dehydrogenase. In this direction, lactate dehydrogenase reduces $NAD^+$ to NADH. The NADH thus generated can be used by glyceraldehyde-3-phosphate dehydrogenase in the gluconeogenic direction converting 1, 3-bisphosphoglycerate to glyceraldehyde-3-phosphate. During this reduction reaction, NADH is oxidized to $NAD^+$, completing the cycle between the two enzymes of the gluconeogenesis pathway that require the nicotinamide nucleotide as a cofactor/substrate. (*Devlin, pp 326–327*)

91. **(A)** In a positive viral hemagglutination test, the virus is the hemagglutinating particle. Antibody specific to the viral hemagglutinin will block this activity and inhibit hemagglutination. The assay is similar to a neutralization test, with the erythrocyte taking the place of a susceptible nucleated host cell. Many different viruses possess hemagglutinating activity. Hence, this assay can be used to identify serum antibodies that are reactive with numerous different viral agents. The limiting ingredient is the availability of the viruses. (*Joklik et al, p 946*)

92. **(A)** Vitiligo is a non-lethal cutaneous disorder characterized by a loss of pigment-producing melanocytes within the epidermis. The disorder is most obvious in darkly pigmented individuals. An autoimmune etiology is suspected, since many of these individuals have antibodies against melanocytes. (*Cotran et al, pp 1175–1176*)

93. **(A)** Epinephrine is the drug of choice for treating severe anaphylactic shock because it has both α and β activity. The α effects will support blood pressure and shunt blood flow to vital organs. The β effects will produce bronchodilation, overcoming the bronchoconstriction present in anaphylactic shock. Norepinephrine, dopamine, and phenylephrine would not be drugs of choice because their weak or absent $β_2$ actions will not produce bronchodilation. While the β-agonist isoproterenol will produce bronchodilation, it is devoid of α activity so that vasodilation rather than the desired vasoconstriction would be produced. (*Katzung, p 128*)

94. **(C)** Suicide and suicidal attempt occur more frequently among people who seem to think of suicide or consider it as an option. Most people who commit suicide have seen a physician or given warnings of their intent. Suicide may occur when a patient's mood seems to be lifting. At this time, these persons may either gain more energy or experience a sense of resolution as the option of suicide has been decided. *(Leigh and Reiser, pp 101–144)*

95. **(B)** Interactions among antigen-presenting cells, T lymphocytes, and B lymphocytes are necessary for immune responses, and these cellular associations are promoted by the organization of lymph nodes. The deep cortical (paracortical) zone of a lymph node is the T-lymphocyte domain, and it will not develop if the thymus fails in its function of T-lymphocyte production. The presence of lymph nodules in the outer cortex indicates that B-lymphocyte responses are underway, precluding a condition of agammaglobulinemia or combined immunodeficiency. An acute bacterial infection can lead to enlargement of all zones in lymph nodes. A deficiency in platelet numbers does not change lymph node organization. *(Junqueira at al, p 260)*

96. **(A)** Sympathetic stimulation releases the neurotransmitter norepinephrine at the nerve terminals. Norepinephrine acts by increasing membrane permeability to $Na^+$ and $Ca^{2+}$ ions, resulting in an increased slope of the diastolic depolarization. Therefore, membrane potential reaches the threshold for self-excitation (broken line) earlier, increasing the heart rate. The amplitude of the action potential is little affected by sympathetic stimulation. *(Guyton and Hall, pp 126–127)*

97. **(C)** Of the enzymes listed in the question, only glucokinase and glucose-6-phosphatase are found in the liver and not in most other tissues. A deficiency in glucokinase would lead to increased blood sugar levels, not hypoglycemia. This would occur because of the liver's decreased ability to phosphorylate free glucose for use. In contrast, a defect in glucose-6-phosphatase would cause the symptoms observed in von Gierke's disease. This endoplasmic reticulum enzyme catalyzes the dephosphorylation of glucose-6-phosphate, allowing glucose to be released into the blood when levels are low. A lesion at this point would result in massive storage of glycogen in liver. *(Stryer, pp 598–599)*

98. **(D)** Complement-fixation procedures are performed in two stages. The test system consists of antigen and antibody (one of which is unknown) plus complement. The indicator system consists of sheep erythrocytes and hemolysin (an antisheep-RBC serum), which will sensitize the cells to the lytic action of complement. If complement is fixed in the test system, it is effectively bound (or consumed) in the antigen–antibody complexes there and is not free to participate in the lysis of the sensitized erythrocytes present in the indicator system. *(Jawetz et al, pp 121–122)*

99. **(B)** The photomicrograph depicts a fibroadenoma, a benign tumor of the female breast. The microscopic features of this tumor include compressed benign ducts which are surrounded by non-atypical and normally cellular connective tissue. The usual gross appearance of a surgically removed fibroadenoma is that of a well-circumscribed, tan-white, solid rubbery mass ranging in size from 1 to 4 cm. These tumors are most frequent in women between the ages of 20 and 35 years old. *(Rubin and Farber, p 982)*

100. **(E)** Valproic acid is a branched-chain fatty acid that is very effective against absence seizures with concomitant generalized seizures. The mechanism underlying the therapeutic activity is unclear. Valproate treatment results in increased brain GABA levels, an action that could explain the anti-epileptic actions; however, clinical activity is observed at times before GABA levels are raised. Valproic acid causes an idiosyncratic hepatotoxicity most often seen in pediatric patients taking multiple medications. This valproate-induced hepatotoxicity has caused more than 50 fatalities in the United States. Monitoring

of liver function is recommended when initiating treatment with valproate since the hepatotoxicity is reversible if diagnosed early enough. Valproate use in pregnant women may be linked to spina bifida and other congenital deformities so that caution should be observed in the choice of anti-epileptic agent during pregnancy. *(Katzung, pp 372–373)*

**101.** **(B)** In REM sleep, there is autonomic activation and a suppression of skeletal muscle activity. Thus, sleepwalking does not occur during REM but rather in the slow wave phase of sleep (stages 4 and 3). *(Leigh and Reiser, pp 271–302)*

**102.** **(B)** The linea semilunaris is a curved line that extends from the ninth costal cartilage to the pubic tubercle. This semilunar line indicates the lateral border of the rectus abdominis muscle. The lines are obvious in persons with good abdominal muscular development. In such persons, three or more transverse grooves are also visible in the skin overlying the tendinous intersections of the rectus abdominis muscles. *(Moore, p 128)*

**103.** **(B)** Wernicke's area, which is located at the posterior end of the superior temporal gyrus, is believed to play an important role in the understanding of language, either written or spoken. Patients with lesions in this area have a form of fluid aphasia in which the ability to vocalize is not impaired but the subject matter of speech is not intelligible. Moreover, the ability to understand either speech or writing is impaired. This is in contrast to lesions of Broca's area, in which understanding is preserved but the ability to vocalize speech is impaired. Deficits in the processing of visual information, dyslexia, or disorders of short-term memory may each result from cerebral lesions but are not specifically associated with Wernicke's area. *(Ganong, pp 250–252)*

**104.** **(A)** The double-reciprocal Lineweaver–Burk plot that accompanies the question illustrates a competitively inhibited enzyme. In competitive inhibition, the intercept on the $y$ axis,

which is equal to $1/V_{max}$, does not change. This points out that at significantly high substrate concentration, the inhibition can be overcome. In non-competitive inhibition, the $V_{max}$, and hence the $y$-axis intercept, does change. Noncompetitive inhibition cannot be overcome by increasing the substrate concentration. Allosteric enzymes do not obey Michaelis–Menten kinetics and cannot be plotted as straight lines on double-reciprocal curves. Likewise, irreversibly inhibited enzymes cannot be treated by Michaelis–Menten kinetics. *(Stryer, pp 193–195, 197–198)*

**105.** **(C)** The graft-versus-host reaction occurs when immunocompetent lymphoid cells are transferred to a histoincompatible recipient who is unable to reject them. The donor cells then mount an immune response against the foreign histocompatibility antigens of the recipient and attempt to reject them. This usually occurs in bone marrow transplantation performed as a therapeutic modality in patients with certain leukemias or other blood diseases, such as aplastic anemia. *(Joklik et al, pp 125–126)*

**106.** **(C)** Staging of a cancer requires clinical and pathologic judgment regarding the extent of spread of the lesion. It does not depend on the tumor's microscopic appearance. T is used to grade the size and extent of the primary tumor. N indicates the presence of lymph node metastases, and M indicates distal metastases. T0 indicates a carcinoma in situ or tumor confined to the mucosa. T1 is a superficial invasive tumor without extension into the underlying muscle wall or deeper connective tissue. T2 indicates muscle wall extension, and T3 shows full-thickness involvement of the organ by tumor. A T4 lesion has local extension and spread and is larger. An N0 tumor shows no lymph node involvement, whereas N1 has positive lymph node metastases. M0 tumors show no distant metastases, and M1 indicates distant tumor. The tumor described in the question invades the muscle wall but does not extend through the wall or into adjacent organs or tissue, so it is classified as T2. The lymph nodes are involved, thus N1, but there are no other metastases, so it is M0. Thus it is regarded as a T2, N1, M0 tumor. *(Rubin and Farber, pp 156–157)*

107. **(E)** The potency or MAC value for an inhalational general anesthetic is related to the lipid solubility of the agent. The lipid solubility can be measured in several ways such as using the blood:oil, water:octanol, or gas:oil partition coefficient. Although the mechanism for general anesthetic agents is unclear, the consensus is that the effects of these agents are exerted at the membrane lipid level. Alterations in the membrane fluidity affecting ion channel and receptor activity have been suggested but not proven. Alterations in calcium channel and potassium channel activities have been observed, but it is not clear if such effects are primary or secondary. The blood:gas partition coefficient measures blood solubility of the agent and gives an indication of the rate of induction and recovery. High blood solubility is associated with slow induction and recovery. Blood flow to the brain is not grossly affected by general anesthetic agents; any alteration in blood flow should result in an alteration of rate of induction rather than potency. The extent of liver metabolism depends on the chemical structure of the anesthetic agent. Metabolism may be a determinant of toxicity. *(Gilman et al, pp 282–282; Katzung, pp 386–387)*

108. **(D)** The three basic models of the doctor–patient relationship are activity–passivity, guidance–cooperation, and mutual participation models. Activity–passivity model is the traditional model, in which the patient is a passive recipient of treatment. Guidance–cooperation model implies patient cooperation with the treatment regimen. Mutual participation implies a model of doctor–patient relationship in which the physician aids the patient in self-help. *(Simons, pp 19–32)*

109. **(A)** The main arteries of the anterior abdominal wall are the inferior epigastric and deep circumflex iliac arteries, which are branches of the external iliac artery, and the superior epigastric artery, which is a terminal branch of the internal thoracic artery. The superficial epigastric, circumflex iliac, and external pudendal are branches of the femoral artery. *(Moore, pp 132, 142)*

110. **(B)** During a forced expiration, intrapleural pressure is no longer negative, but becomes positive (above atmospheric pressure). The alveolar pressure is even more positive than this. Air moves out with ever-increasing velocity, while total airway cross-sectional area becomes smaller. As the air approaches the initial generations of the respiratory tree, air pressure in the airways diminishes. The decrease in pressure of the moving air is due to two influences: (1) loss of potential energy as pressure as airflow overcomes resistance, and (2) loss of potential energy as pressure when kinetic energy increases due to velocity increase (Bernoulli's principle). Thus, airway pressure falls with distance from the alveoli and eventually reaches a point beyond which airway pressure is less than the supra-atmospheric intrapleural pressure. Since the pressure outside the airways is higher than that within, they are compressed and increase the resistance to flow. Once airflow is maximal, any further attempts to increase expiratory effort result in additional airway collapse. A flow-limiting segment is produced that prevents additional increase in flow despite intensified expiratory efforts. That is, as expiration begins, increased effort at first results in increased flow, but eventually a maximal flow rate is reached beyond which no amount of effort can increase flow (becomes flow-independent). *(Berne and Levy, pp 572–573)*

111. **(B)** Normal catabolism of phenylalanine involves hydroxylation to tyrosine catalyzed by phenylalanine hydroxylase. Mutations in the phenylalanine hydroxylase gene lead to deficiencies in the enzyme and manifests as phenylketonuria (PKU). Patients suffering from PKU have elevated levels of phenylalanine in their blood as well as the transamination product, phenylpyruvate. Phenylpyruvate is converted to phenyllactate and phenylacetate by reduction and oxidation, respectively; all three byproducts are excreted in the urine. The standard test for PKU is to

test for elevated phenylalanine in the blood of newborns. (*Devlin, pp 506–507*)

112. **(E)** Approximately 30% of strains of *S. aureus* isolated from patients produce enterotoxins. Synthesis of enterotoxin by *S. epidermidis* is doubtful. Six antigenically distinct types of enterotoxins—A, B, C, $C_2$, D, and E—are produced by *S. aureus*. Enterotoxin A has been most frequently implicated in food intoxication in the United States. Disruption of the stratum granulosum in the epidermis is due to the action of exfoliative toxins, which are produced by some strains of *S. aureus*. The exfoliative toxins A and B are responsible for the development of the staphylococcal scalded skin syndrome. Disruption of the cytoplasmic membrane is due to the action of the various hemolysins elaborated by *S. aureus*. Botulinum toxin is responsible for the blockage of the release of acetylcholine at the neuromuscular junction. The mechanism of action of staphylococcal enterotoxins has not been well defined. The enterotoxins are considered to be quite heat resistant since after boiling crude solutions for 30 min, some toxicity remains. They are also resistant to proteolytic enzymes such as trypsin, chymotrypsin, rennin, and papain. Pepsin destroys their activity at a pH of about 2, but is ineffective at pH values higher than 2. The enterotoxins are single polypeptide chains that contain relatively large amounts of lysine, aspartic and glutamic acids, and tyrosine. (*Joklik et al, pp 407–409, 649–650*)

113. **(C)** Individuals with sickle trait are healthy and not anemic. A hemoglobin electrophoresis will demonstrate a minor proportion of hemoglobin S and a major proportion of hemoglobin A. Fetal hemoglobin (Hb F) and hemoglobin A2 are usually within the normal range. Sickle cell trait confers the benefit of protecting erythrocytes from some forms of malarial infection. About 9% of blacks in the United States have sickle trait. (*Chandrasoma and Taylor, pp 384–386*)

114. **(B)** The non-depolarizing, competitive, neuromuscular junction-blocking agent atracurium undergoes a spontaneous Hofmann

elimination reaction, which terminates its actions. It is thus not dependent on renal excretion or metabolism in the plasma or liver for elimination. Succinylcholine is successively hydrolyzed by plasma pseudocholinesterase to the monocholine derivative and then to succinic acid and choline. Gallamine is eliminated by the kidney. Tubocurarine is eliminated in urine and bile. Vecuronium is excreted in bile unchanged and as the 3-hydroxy metabolite. (*Katzung, pp 405–408*)

115. **(C)** There is controversy concerning the factors influencing adherence to medical regimens. Among the demographic factors, female sex has clearly been associated with poor adherence. Field dependence has been associated with poor adherence among individuals suffering from alcoholism. Severe physical illness, contrary to what one would suspect, also has been associated with poor adherence. (*Simons, pp 38–47*)

116. **(C)** The lateral umbilical folds, formed by elevations of peritoneum covering the inferior epigastric arteries, run superomedially on each side. The medial umbilical folds are formed by elevations of peritoneum covering the medial umbilical ligaments, the obliterated parts of the fetal umbilical arteries. The median umbilical fold is formed by an elevation of peritoneum covering the median umbilical ligament, the fibrous remnant of the urachus. (*Moore, p 142*)

117. **(D)** When cardiac muscle contracts, it squeezes blood vessels that course through it, and this extravascular compression has a significant effect on coronary blood flow. In early systole, there is an actual reversal of blood flow, and although coronary blood flow increases during systole, it is not until the ventricle relaxes that maximal left coronary artery blood flows are obtained. Since aortic pressure is maximal during systole, it is obvious that choice **C** in the question is incorrect. Peak flows are obtained in early diastole, when the ventricle is relaxed and aortic pressure has not declined to its diastolic level. (*Berne and Levy, pp 511–512*)

118. **(A)** Although in bacteria a continuous sequence of triplet codons encode for each protein, genes may be discontinuous in eukaryotic cells. Noncoding intervening sequences of DNA that split genes in eukaryotes are called introns. Mature mRNA translated from such DNA does not contain the intron message. However, newly synthesized mRNA may contain intron message. These intervening sequences in the primary transcripts are specifically excised and ligated so that the mature mRNA contains no intron message. The coding sequences of split genes are called exons. *(Stryer, pp 112–115)*

119. **(B)** Erythroblastosis fetalis can occur when an $Rh_0$-positive child is being carried by an $Rh_0$-negative mother. If the mother makes antibodies against the $Rh_0(D)$ antigen, these may cross the placenta and destroy fetal erythrocytes. The induction of this immune response can be blocked if an antibody specific for the $Rh_0$ antigen is injected into the mother at the time of her first exposure to the fetal RBCs, which usually occurs at parturition. $Rh_0$ immune globulin (RhoGAM) is a human γ-globulin preparation rich in antibodies specific for the $Rh_0$ antigen. It is used to prevent the sensitization of the mother, which will then protect a subsequent antigenically incompatible fetus from this disease. *(Joklik et al, p 123)*

120. **(B)** Benzoylecgonine is the urinary metabolite of cocaine. It is detectable within urine for about 24 hr after the last episode of cocaine usage. In forensic and clinical pathology, the examination of urine specimens for drugs of abuse is commonplace. Gas chromatography, immunofluorescent, and enzyme-linked immunoassays are all frequently employed methods to detect the recent use of illict drugs. *(Cotran et al, pp 394–395)*

121. **(C)** Streptokinase is a streptococcal protein that combines with plasminogen to form a complex that is catalytically active in cleaving plasminogen to plasmin. Because it is a bacterial protein, antibodies are produced that can limit its utility. Urokinase is a recom-binant human protein that directly cleaves plasminogen to plasmin. Plasmin itself cannot be used because of the presence in blood of antiplasmin. Streptokinase and urokinase are not inhibited by endogenous plasmin inhibitors, and the active plasmin that these agents produce is shielded from the endogenous inhibitors within the fibrin mesh. Human recombinant t-PA also activates plasminogen to plasmin in the same manner as does the endogenous t-PA. *(Katzung, p 515)*

122. **(B)** Pathologic grief reactions include distorted reactions in which there may be acquisition of symptoms belonging to a deceased loved one. Post-traumatic stress disorder involves unusual and catastrophic disasters, not simple bereavement. *(Leigh and Reiser, pp 110–112)*

123. **(D)** The veins leaving the posterior surface of the testis anastomose to form a pampiniform plexus. This large, vine-like venous plexus, forming a large part of the spermatic cord, surrounds the ductus deferens and arteries in the spermatic cord. It is located within the internal spermatic fascia and ends in the testicular vein. The pam-piniform plexus of veins sometimes becomes varicose (dilated and tortuous), producing a condition known as varicocele. *(Moore, p 145)*

124. **(D)** Production of red blood cells is under the control of differentiation inducers that promote differentiation of uncommitted pluripotent stem cells into committed stem cells ("colony-forming units") and growth inducers that promote maturation but not differentiation of the cells. Erythropoietin, the principal factor that stimulates red blood cell production, promotes both differentiation of stem cells to proerythroblasts and maturation. Several other factors, including androgens, also stimulate bone marrow cells and enhance production of erythrocytes resulting in higher hematocrit and hemoglobin values in the male. Blood loss during a menstrual period averages only 30 to 60 mL and cannot explain this difference. *(Mountcastle, pp 1130–1131; Guyton and Hall, pp 426–428)*

125. **(E)** Heparin is an important glycosaminoglycan (GAG) involved in the regulation of the blood clotting cascade. Abundant levels of heparin are found in granuoles of mast cells lining the blood vessesls. In response to injury, mast cells release the contents of their granules. Release of heparin inhibits the clotting cascade by complexing with and activating antithrombin III, which in turn inhibitsw the serine proteases of the clotting cascade. It is this function of the naturally occuring GAG, heparin that has been exploited in the use of injected synthetic heparin for anticoagulation therapies. *(Murray et al, pp 640–645)*

126. **(C)** The importance of the capsule in the virulence of the pneumococcus is apparent from the observations that only encapsulated strains are virulent, and vaccine efficacy is type specific (the organisms are divided into more than eighty types on the basis of antigenic differences in the capsular carbohydrate composition). Cell wall teichoic acids and peptidoglycan are found in rough pneumococci (and most other bacteria as well) and are not intimately involved in the pathogenesis of disease. M protein is the potent anti-phagocytic cell wall component of group A streptococci. *(Joklik et al, pp 432–442)*

127. **(D)** The rapidity with which wounds heal is primarily related to fibroblast proliferation and secretion of collagen. Collagen is the major component contributing to the tensile strength of the wound. It is produced by fibroblasts as tropocollagen. Collagen is composed of a triple helix of three α chains, which are hydroxylated and have lysine oxidations. These modifications allow crosslinkages between the chains, and these crosslinks are the most important factor contributing to the stability and strength of collagen and scar tissue. Fibroblasts also synthesize elastic fibers, which aid in the repair of wounds. Collagenase is an enzyme that cleaves collagen and digests it, retarding healing. It is rarely found in uncomplicated, healing wounds. *(Cotran et al, pp 85–90)*

128. **(E)** Dose-dependent, potentially fatal hepatic necrosis is the most serious consequence of acute acetaminophen poisoning. Renal failure and hypoglycemia also may occur. Acetaminophen-induced hepatic necrosis arises through saturation of the normal glucuronidation and sulfation pathways and generation of a highly reactive electrophilic species via cytochrome P450. When the endogenous detoxifying nucleophile glutathione becomes depleted, cellular components including enzymes, ion channels, cytoskeletal components, nucleic acids and membrane lipids become damaged, ultimately resulting in cell death. Treatment consists of administration of N-acetylcysteine which acts as a glutathione surrogate in detoxifying the reactive electrophilic species. Methemoglobinemia and respiratory depression are manifestations of phenacetin poisoning. Although acetaminophen is a metabolite of phenacetin, symptoms of their toxicities are very different. *(Gilman et al, p 658; Katzung, pp 54–55, 552)*

129. **(C)** In dealing with a chronically angry patient, physicians should be as neutral and objective as possible. It may be helpful for the physician to recognize that these patients arouse anger, but an angry reaction will only increase the patient's angry behavior. Sarcasm used by a physician in this situation tends to increase the patient's anger. *(Simons, pp 101–120)*

130. **(C)** The long thoracic nerve innervates the serratus anterior muscle and has no cutaneous component. The serratus anterior draws the scapula anteriorly and holds it to the chest wall. It also rotates the inferior angle laterally, an action important in raising the arm above the head. Paralysis results in a flaring of the medial border and inferior angle of the scapula, a condition known as "winged scapula." *(Hall–Craggs, pp 82–83)*

131. **(A)** In dynamic (isotonic) aerobic exercise, workload and body oxygen consumption are directly related (indeed it is often easier to calculate the workload from the oxygen consumption than to measure it directly). With increased workload (or increased oxygen consumption), there is an almost perfectly

linear increase in heart rate, whereas the curve for stroke volume increases at first, but then levels off (plateau) at about half maximal workload (or half maximal oxygen consumption). Thus, for severe exercise, the increased levels of cardiac output depend almost entirely on increases in heart rate (at essentially a constant stroke volume). Although mean arterial blood pressure and systolic arterial blood pressure rise with increasing levels of dynamic exercise, the diastolic blood pressure remains virtually constant. With increasing levels of exercise, blood flow to the skin decreases at first, but then as heat production from the exercising muscles begins to increase, the bood flow to skin also increases to aid in temperature regulation. Blood pressures in the pulmonary circulation are much lower than in the systemic circulation. Even if the cardiac output were to increase four-fold during exercise, there would be only about a doubling of the pulmonary arterial blood pressure (eg, from 12 to 24 mm Hg), which would be nowhere near systemic arterial pressures. *(Berne and Levy, pp 532–534)*

132. **(B)** The order of a chemical reaction refers to the number of molecules involved in forming a reaction complex that is competent to proceed to the generation of product(s). In order to determine the order of a given reaction, it is necessary to sum the exponents of each concentration term of the substrates in a reaction. The reaction in this question is composed of two substrates, each with concentration exponents of one; therefore, the sum of these exponents is two and the reaction is said to be second order. *(Devlin, pp 142–143)*

133. **(E)** The organism represented in the photo that accompanies the question is septate (note the divisions, or cross-walls) in the hypha. This observation rules out any of the phycomycetes, since these organisms are coenocytic. The position of the conidiospores in strings arising from the columnella is characteristic of the genus *Aspergillus*. The dermatophytes that are the causative agents of the tinea infections usually have single conidiospores and are characterized by their macroconidial forms. *(Jawetz et al, p 312)*

134. **(D)** The simplest form of a blood clot at a site of injury is a hemostatic plug. It is composed of an aggregation of platelets with a web of fibrin, which prevents leakage of blood into the extravascular spaces. Platelets are the most important component in the formation of this plug. When the blood vessel is injured, cells and plasma start to leak out, but platelets are immediately attracted to the site of injury. They accumulate, pile up, and stop the leakage. They also release tissue thromboplastin, which activates the intrinsic blood coagulation pathway, causing the fibrin mesh to form. The fibrin tightens the plug and traps other cells, strengthening the platelet plug and forming a more permanent plug. RBCs and lymphocytes are seen in hemostatic plugs as they are trapped from the circulating blood by the aggregation of platelets and fibrin. They act as filler material in the plug and have no other defined role in the formation of hemostatic plugs. Collagen is important in the initiation of hemostasis, as when blood vessels are damaged. The collagen fibrils in the subendothelial wall of the vessel are exposed to the circulation and are the substance that the platelets initially stick to when they form a hemostatic plug. *(Cotran et al, pp 95–105)*

135. **(C)** Extrapyramidal reactions resulting from blocking of dopamine receptors in the nigrostriatal system are most likely to occur with piperazine-type phenothiazines, including trifluoperazine and prochlorperazine, as well as the butyrophenone haloperidol. Thioridazine, a piperidine-type phenothiazine, is least likely to cause extrapyramidal reactions. Prochlorperazine is mainly used as an antiemetic. *(Gilman et al, pp 396–400)*

136. **(A)** Common causes of sexual dysfunction include many types of neuropathy and chronic illnesses. Diabetic neuropathy is probably the most common organic cause of sexual dysfunction. Depression and anxiety are common functional causes of sexual dysfunction. Chronic schizophrenia is often associated with decreased sexual functions. Mania, however, is often associated with increased sexuality. *(Simons, pp 316–401)*

**137.** **(C)** The tail of the epididymis is continuous with the ductus deferens, the duct that transports sperm from the epididymis to the ejaculatory duct for expulsion into the prostatic urethra. The superior expanded part of the epididymis, called the head, is composed of lobules of the epididymis, which are the coiled ends of the efferent ductules of the testis. These ductules transmit the sperm from the testis to the epididymis. The body of the epididymis consists of the highly convoluted duct of the epididymis. The sperm are stored in the epididymis, where they undergo the final stages of maturation. *(Moore, p 149)*

**138.** **(A)** Body metabolism produces about 80 mEq of nonvolatile (ie, not $CO_2$) acid per day. Of these, less than 0.1 mEq is excreted as free acid (ie, protons) since urine contains only up to $10^{-4.5}$ Eq/L = 0.03 mEq/L $H^+$ at pH = 4.5. The majority of $H^+$ excreted by the kidneys is bound to non-titratable acid (ie, $NH_4^+$, pK > 7.4) and various titratable acids (ie, buffers with pK < 7.4). Under normal conditions, about 50% of $H^+$ eliminated by the kidneys is in the form of $NH_4^+$. Under conditions of chronic acidosis, this amount can increase more than ten-fold, making the ammonia buffer quantitatively the most important route of renal $H^+$ excretion. *(Guyton and Hall, pp 395–397)*

**139.** **(D)** Mucopolysaccharidoses are a family of diseases collectively termed "lysosomal storage diseases." These diseases result from the inability of cells to effectively degrade complex membrane glycolipids and glycoproteins. The defects in these degradative pathways result from the loss of production of specific lysosomal enzymes. This leads to an accumulation of undegraded membrane components within lysosomes eventually leading to cell death. Of particular clinical significance is the presence of large amounts of complex glycolipids in the myelin sheaths of nerve cells. Genetic defects leading to the inability to degrade these lipids during normal membrane remodeling results in accelerated neuronal cell death, such as in Tay–Sachs disease. *(Murray et al, pp 653–644)*

**140.** **(E)** Cervicofacial actinomycosis (lumpy jaw) is an endogenous infection that is usually preceded by a tooth extraction or some other traumatic injury to the mouth. The lesion commonly drains to the cheek or submandibular area. The presence of sulfur granules is of great diagnostic importance. These are actually small (approximately 1 mm in diameter) colonies of the organism in a calcium phosphate matrix. They consist of a central filamentous mass of branching bacilli surrounded by radially oriented, club-shaped structures. *(Joklik et al, pp 530–531)*

**141.** **(B)** The lesion shown in the question is a granuloma, which is a small, circumscribed collection of inflammatory cells. These cells primarily consist of modified macrophages called epithelioid cells. There is an outer rim of lymphocytes. There are also multinucleated giant cells of the Langhans type. Other cells, such as plasma cells, eosinophils, and neutrophils, may be seen in granulomas, but the epithelioid cells are the single diagnostic feature. The center of a granuloma may be necrotic, like that pictured in the question, or it may be a solid mass of epithelioid cells. Granulomas are a form of response to chronic irritants associated with either infectious or non-infectious causes. An abscess is seen in acute inflammatory processes and is a circumscribed collection of pus secondary to liquefactive tissue necrosis. It is accompanied by a neutrophilic response. A keloid is an abnormal formation of collagenous connective tissue in a scar, forming a dense, bulging tumor. It is accompanied by minimal cell response. An infarct is an area of ischemic necrosis of tissue secondary to circulatory obstruction, producing an area with coagulation necrosis and neutrophilic cell response. A thrombus is a clot in a blood vessel formed intravascularly, causing vascular obstruction. They are composed of fibrin, platelets, RBCs, and WBCs. *(Cotran et al, pp 80–82)*

**142.** **(D)** In general, the duration of action of the oral hypoglycemic agents correlates with their half-lives. The primary adverse effect of the sulfonylurea treatment is serious hypoglycemia. Several compounds (acetohexamide, tolazamide) have active metabolites that may contribute to hypoglycemic activity. Tolbutamide, the shortest-acting agent, has a duration of action of 6 to 12 hr (half-life of 7 hr). Tolazamide produces hypoglycemic activity for 12 to 16 hr or more (half-life of 7 hr). Acetohexamide, although its half-life is 6 hr, has a duration of 12 to 18 hr or more because its metabolite is more active than the parent compound. Chlorpropamide has the longest half-life (35 hr) and longest duration of action (24 to 72 hr). Glipazide is a second-generation sulfonylurea with a half-life of 2 to 4 hr. The short half-life of glipazide reduces the risk of serious and prolonged hypoglycemia. (*Katzung, pp 647–650*)

143.  **(B)** Sensitivity is defined as the extent to which patients with a particular disease or characteristic are accurately classified as having the disease, according to the diagnostic test. In this question, 98 percent of patients with the disease are accurately classified on the basis of the test result, so the sensitivity of the test is 98 percent. Specificity is defined as the extent to which patients who do not have the disease are correctly classified. In this question, 90 percent of the patients without disease had negative results and would have been correctly classified, so that specificity of the test is 90 percent. Positive and negative predictive accuracy refers to the accuracy of positive and negative results when the test is applied to a particular population, and these values will depend on the prevalence of the disease in the population. (*MacMahon and Pugh, pp 261–263*)

144–147. **(144-F, 145-A, 146-G, 147-B)** Much progress has been made in the past 10 years elucidating signal-transduction mechanisms, and this has become a popular topic in the Medical Board exams. Endothelial cells produce both vasodilator substances, eg, nitric oxide, and potent vasoconstrictor substances, eg, endothelins. The vascular smooth muscle ET-1 receptor is coupled via a G protein to phospholipase C, catalyzing the hydrolysis of $PIP_2$ to $IP_3$ and DAG. The insulin receptor is a complex molecule consisting of an α-subunit that binds insulin and a membrane-spanning

β-subunit that phosphorylates tyrosine residues (tyrosine kinase). The thyroid hormones T3 and T4 bind directly to nuclear receptors that control the function of gene operators regulating DNA transcription. β-adrenergic receptors are coupled via a stimulatory G protein to adenylate cyclase and increase production of cAMP which then binds to the regulatory subunit of protein kinase A, activating its catalytic activity. (*Ganong, pp 36–40, 296, 311, 330, 544*)

148–150.    **(148-A, 149-C, 150-B)** Riboflavin is required for conversion to the flavin nucleotide coenzymes, which are involved in numerous redox reactions. Deficiencies in riboflavin are rare in the United States due to adequate amounts in eggs, milk, meat, and cereals and are therefore usually seen only in cases of poor diet such as the diet of chronic alcoholics. Characteristic symptoms of riboflavin deficiency include angular stomatitis and chelitis, glossitis, scaly dermatitis (seborrhea), and photophobia. Niacin is required for conversion to the nicotinamide nucleotide coenzymes required for numerous redox reactions. Symptoms seen early in diet deficient in niacin include glossitis of the tongue. Severe deficiency leads to pellegra, characterized by dermatitis, diarrhea, dementia and mental depression, digestive disorders, and weight loss. Vitamin C (ascorbate) is important as a reducing agent in numerous hydroxylation reactions. The principle reaction requiring ascorbate is the hydroxylation of proline and lysine residues in procollagen. A deficiency in vitamin C leads to scurvy, characterized by subcutaneous hemorrhaging, anemia, muscle weakness, soft swollen gums, loose teeth, poor wound healing, and loss of mineralized bone. (*Murray et al, pp 574–577, 586–587*)

151–153.    **(151-F, 152-E, 153-C)** Hodgkin's disease is a malignancy of lymphoreticular tissue. Adenopathy is a common clinical finding. The diagnostic Reed–Sternberg cell is large and binucleated with prominent multiple eosinophilic nucleoli. The surrounding cellular population is composed variably of lymphocytes, histiocytes, plasma cells, eosinophils, neutrophils, and fibrocytes. Metastatic melanoma is usually seen in lymph nodes draining a primary cutaneous melanoma. The melanoma cells are noncohesive spindle or epithelioid cells with prominent nucleoli, and usually display cytoplasmic melanin. Metastatic carcinoma may be seen in surgically removed lymph nodes. The presence of estrogen and progesterone receptors, the adenocarcinomatous architecture, and the axillary location all would suggest that the metastatic tumor is mammary in origin. *(Rubin and Farber, pp 1074–1096)*

**154–157. (154-B, 155-A, 156-C, 157-E)** The antihypertensive action of hydralazine is primarily arteriolar dilation, which results in reflex tachycardia. This tachycardia may precipitate or aggravate myocardial ischemia. Propranolol is a non-selective β-adrenergic blocking agent. Blockade of cardiac, $β_1$ receptors results in slowing of the heart rate. Prazosin dilates arterioles. This may cause inadequate blood return to the right side of the heart as well as hypotension, which can result in syncopal episodes, particularly after the first dose. This phenomenon can be minimized by administering the initial dose at bedtime. Methyldopa routinely causes sedation. This usually dissipates with continued use but uncommonly may persist enough to interfere with daily living activities, particularly mental work. *(Katzung, pp 153, 157, 159, 160)*

**158. (A)** In Eriksonian developmental cycle, basic trust and a sense of security are developed during the first two years of life. That roughly parallels the Freudian oral stage. A failure to accomplish the developmental task results in mistrust and insecurity. *(Leigh and Reiser, pp 357–367)*

**159. (B)** The phase of initiative vs. guilt parallels the Freudian oedipal stage of development. During this stage, the child is more energetic and loving, and there is a quality of planning and "attacking" a task. Also during this stage, the child develops a sense of moral responsibility and unconflicted initiative. Failure to master the tasks of this stage may re-

sult in guilt and complete repression of initiative. *(Leigh and Reiser, pp 357–367)*

**160. (C)** The phase of industry vs. inferiority parallels Freud's latency period. During this phase, the child receives recognition by learning and producing things. Problems during this period may result in a sense of inferiority and inadequacy. *(Leigh and Reiser, pp 357–367)*

**161. (D)** Erikson considers adolescence to be a crucial period in developing a sense of identity, an inner sameness and direction. Career choices are made or seriously considered during this stage. Unsuccessful outcome of this stage is "role diffusion," a sense of being undefined and without direction. *(Leigh and Reiser, pp 357–367)*

**162–165. (162-E, 163-D, 164-B, 165-A)** Pernicious anemia is due to a lack of vitamin $B_{12}$. Autoimmune destruction of gastric parietal cells or immune inactivation of intrinsic factor leads to inadequate absorption of the vitamin. Megaloblastic anemia, leukopenia, thrombocytopenia, and demyelination of the posterolateral spinal cord columns are seen in the fully developed disease. Pemphigus is a bullous skin disorder caused by autoantibodies to surface antigens on keratinocytes. Primary biliary cirrhosis is an autoimmune disorder characterized by chronic destructive cholangitis in the early stages, and micronodular cirrhosis in the late stages of the disease. Anti-mitochondrial antibodies are seen in more than 90% of affected individuals. Systemic lupus erythematosis is an autoimmune disease with high titers of anti-nuclear antibodies. Facial rash, renal insufficiency, serositis, and pneumonitis are features of the disorder. *(Rubin and Farber, pp 740–743, 1017, 1190–1193, 1204–1205)*

**166–168. (166-D, 167-A, 168-C)** The depolarization observed in the P wave signals the onset of atrial contraction, whereas the QRS complex is associated with the initiation of ventricular contraction. The sustained depolarization of the plateau phase is represented by the ST interval (which is not normally associated with any voltage deflection). Finally, the T wave is associated with the onset of ventricular repolarization. *(Guyton and Hall, p 118)*

**169–171.** **(169-C, 170-A, 171-E)** The polymerase chain reaction (PCR) is used to amplify specific sequences of DNA. In particular very low levels of a sequence of DNA. A typical PCR contains a sample of DNA (eg, a single cell), specific primers for DNA synthesis, all four deoxyribonucleotides, and a DNA polymerase. The reaction is carried out over the course of 20 to 50 cycles of DNA synthesis, which results in a several million-fold amplification of the target DNA. Since the reaction requires melting of the strands of template DNA at high temperature (eg, 95°C), it would require the addition of new enzyme for each cycle if not for the discovery of thermostable bacteria such as *Thermus aquaticus*, which contain enzymes resistant to high temperatures. The DNA polymerase isolated from *Thermus aquaticus* is identified as Taq polymerase. Subtle sequence variations within genes can be identified by altered digestion patterns with restriction endonucleases. DNA is isolated from individuals (usually from blood cells), digested with specific restriction endonucleases, and the digestion products electrophoretically separated by size in agarose gels. When the separated DNA is transferred to a solid support (eg, a nylon membrane) and analyzed with gene-specific probes, size differences in the digestion products can be observed. The differences in fragment size are termed restriction fragment length polymorphisms (RFLPs). RFLPs are inherited and segregate in typical Mendellian fasion; therefore, they are useful for disease gene diagnosis and in cases paternity dispute. Many different RFLPs have been identified in numerous genes and the restriction endonuclease HpaII would be just one enzyme used in RFLP analysis. Another useful thermostable enzyme is DNA ligase. This enzyme has been exploited in the technique identified as ligase chain reaction (LCR). LCR is an extremely sensitive diagnostic technique able to detect single point mutations in DNA isolated from as little as a single cell.

The technique utilizes a set of four specific oligonucleotides complimentary to sequences of both strands of DNA at a known site. The oligonucleotides are designed such that the site of the mutation exists at the ends of one of each of the oligonucleotide pairs. The target DNA is denatured at high temperature and the oligonucleotides allowed to anneal. A perfect match between each oligonucleotide pair on each strand will allow DNA ligase to covalently ligate the oligonucleotide pairs together. A mutation will prevent the matching of the ends of each oligonucleotide pair and prevent their ligation together by DNA ligase. To amplify the amount of ligated oligonucleotides, the reaction is carried out over numerous cycles. Since the ligase is thermostable it is resistant to denaturation by each cycle of melting the template DNA. *(Murray et al, pp 458–459, 462–463)*

**172–174.** **(172-B, 173-E, 174-D)** Initiation of translation requires numerous factors including ribosomal and non-ribosomal proteins and an initiator tRNA, as well as an mRNA containing an intitiator AUG condon. The 40S and 60S ribosomal subunits must dissociate to allow the pre-initiation complex to form on the 40S subunit. Some of these factors, eIF-2, GTP, and the 40S subunit, are required for formation of a pre-initiation complex. Translational elongation also requires numerous ribosomal and non-ribosomal proteins. Some of the factors required are eEF-1, eEF-2, GTP, and the 80S complex. The termination of translation requires a single releasing factor in eukaryotic cells, eRF, which recognizes all three termination codons. An active 80S complex is also required as is energy in the form of GTP. *(Murray et al, pp 425–429)*

**175–178.** **(175-A, 176-C, 177-D, 178-B)** Marfan's syndrome is a rare, usually autosomal-dominant disease characterized by abnormally formed connective tissue. Affected patients are very tall and have long extremities and tapering fingers and toes with hyperextensive joints. They have bilateral dislocation of the ocular lens, cystic medial necrosis of the aorta, and floppy mitral valve leaflets. The underlying connective tissue defect is still unknown. Patients usually survive to 40 years of age.

Tay–Sachs disease is an autosomal recessive disease resulting from absence of hexosaminidase A. This $GM_2$ ganglioside accumulates in neurons of the central and autonomic nervous systems, retina, heart, liver, and spleen. The buildup of the ganglioside in the neurons causes their destruction, with gliosis and lipid deposits in the brain. Affected persons are normal at birth. By age 6 months, there is progressive motor and mental deterioration, and death occurs by age 3 years.

Niemann–Pick disease is an autosomal recessive disease characterized by a deficiency in sphingomyelinase, causing a buildup of sphingomyelin and cholesterol in reticuloendothelial cells and parenchymal cells in tissues. These abnormal cells are lipid laden, foamy, and large. Affected individuals suffer neurologic deterioration and organomegaly and usually die by the age of 3 years.

Pompe's disease is glycogen storage disease type II, which is autosomal recessive. It is caused by absence of the enzyme α-glucosidase in lysosomes, which causes defective glycogenolysis resulting in abnormal buildup of glycogen. The heart and nervous system show the most severe involvement, and patients die of congestive heart failure by 2 years of age.

Lesch–Nyhan syndrome is an X-linked disorder caused by a defect of the enzyme hypoxanthine guanine phosphoribosyltransferase, which is involved in purine metabolism. Affected persons suffer from hyperuricemia, gout, pyelonephritis, and renal stones. Neurologic deficits are the most prominent abnormality and include severe mental retardation, spastic cerebral palsy, and self-mutilating behavior. (*Cotran et al, pp 132–148*)

**179–184. (179-F, 180-C, 181-D, 182-E, 183-B, 184-D)** Neurohumoral transmission may be classified into two basic types—cholinergic and adrenergic transmission. Cholinergic transmission involves the stimulation of either nicotinic or muscarinic receptors by acetylcholine. Nicotinic receptors on auto-

nomic nervous system ganglia are blocked by trimethaphan, resulting in decreased sympathetic and parasympathetic end-organ activity. Nicotinic receptors at the neuromuscular junction are different in structure and are competitively blocked by D-tubocurarine, resulting in skeletal muscle relaxation. Muscarinic receptors of postganglionic parasympathetic fibers are blocked by atropine and not by D-turbocurarine. The synaptic action of acetylcholine is rapidly terminated by acetylcholinesterase. This enzyme may be inhibited reversibly by anticholinesterases such as physostigmine. Adrenergic neurotransmission occurs through stimulation of α or β receptors. Norepinephrine is a potent stimulant of postsynaptic α and $\beta_1$ receptors. Phenylephrine selectively stimulates only postsynaptic $\alpha_1$ receptors. β Receptors may be classified as either $\beta_1$ (eg, heart) or $\beta_2$ (eg, bronchial muscle) receptors. $\beta_1$ Receptors may be selectively blocked by metoprolol. (*Gilman et al, pp 96–113*)

**185–189. (185-A, 186-B, 187-E, 188-D, 189-C)** As crying diminishes during infant development, cooing and vowel sounds (eg, "oo") increase. Words appear at about 1 year, between a range of 8 and 18 months of age. Vocabulary increases to as many as 50 words by 18 months and 200 words by age 2 years. The sequence of appearance of different classes of words is as follows: nouns, verbs, adjectives, and adverbs. Pronouns appear by age 2 years, and conjunctions after the age of 2½ years. (*Lennenberg, pp 128–130*)

**190–194. (190-E, 191-B, 192-D, 193-D, 194-B)** Mannitol is an inert hexose sugar that is filtered, but not reabsorbed, by the nephron. Thus, it increases the osmotic force of the tubule fluid, leading to enhanced diuresis. The high-ceiling loop diuretics, furosemide and ethacrynic acid, block sodium reabsorption in the thick ascending limb of the loop of Henle. Both spironolactone and triamterene inhibit sodium/potassium exchange in the distal and collecting tubules, thus limiting the loss of potassium in the urine. (*Smith and Reynard, pp 573–583*)

**195. (B)** Heterochromatin is a highly condensed form of chromatin in which the DNA is inaccessible to transcription. In light microscopy, the amount and distribution pattern of heterochromatin in the nucleus is a useful feature for cell identification. *(Alberts et al, pp 353, 435; Junqueira et al, p 31)*

**196. (G)** The Golgi complex is the site of extensive glycosylation of core proteins (from the rER) and addition of glycosaminoglycan chains to form proteoglycans. *(Alberts et al, pp 606–608)*

**197. (E)** The rough endoplasmic reticulum is the site of translation and initial post-translational modification of proteins destined for export, sequestration within vesicles such as lysosomes, or incorporation into membranes. Those mRNAs coding for such proteins contain a sequence of bases at the 5′ end that codes for a signal sequence of mostly hydrophobic amino acids. This leads to docking of the ribosome-mRNA complex on the membrane of the endoplasmic reticulum. As the newly synthesized protein is inserted into the lumen of the rER, the signal sequence is enzymatically removed by the signal peptidase. *(Junqueira et al, p 31)*

**198. (B)** Of the five pressure-volume loops illustrated, only two have stroke volumes greater than normal (loops B and E). Which of these two has increased contractility can be determined from the location of the end-systolic pressure-volume point. The end-systolic pressure-volume point for loop E is on the same line as for the normal individual (diagonal line in illustration). In contrast, loop B has an end-systolic pressure-volume point at a higher level (falls on an end-systolic pressure-volume line that begins at about the same intercept with the abscissa, but has a steeper slope than for normal contractility). Thus loop B represents a pressure-volume loop for increased contractility. *(Guyton and Hall, pp 118–127)*

**199. (C)** The actual preload on myocardial fibers is the stretch placed on them at the end of diastole just before the beginning of systole. This stretch determines the resting length of the fibers prior to contraction. For practical purposes, the end-diastolic volume is used as a convenient index of preload (the greater the end-diastolic volume, the greater the stretch). The pressure-volume loop with the lowest end-diastolic volume, and therefore the lowest preload, is loop C. *(West, pp 224–231)*

**200–202. (200-B, 201-A, 202-C)** A single turn of the citric acid cycle begins with the condensation of acetyl CoA and oxaloacetate to yield citrate. NADH is produced at three steps in the cycle: oxidative decarboxylation of isocitrate to α-ketoglutarate, oxidative decarboxylation of α-ketoglutarate to succinyl CoA, and oxidation of malate to oxaloacetate. During each turn of the cycle, two molecules of $CO_2$ are released—during the decarboxylation reactions referred to above. In sum, one turn of the cycle yields 3 molecules of NADH, one molecule of $FADH_2$, and one molecule of GTP. In conjunction with electron transport and oxidative phosphorylation, each NADH molecule can yield 3 moles of ATP and each $FADH_2$ can yield two moles of ATP. Thus, one turn of the cycle can yield 15 moles of nucleoside triphosphate. *(Stryer, pp 374–378, 420)*

**203–204. (203-C, 204-E)** The treatment of hypertension utilizes drugs with a range of mechanisms of action. Clonidine activates $\alpha_2$ receptors located in the CNS; propranolol inhibits β-adrenergic receptors in the heart and kidney. Labetalol is unique in that it inhibits both $\alpha_1$- and β-adrenergic receptors. It is, therefore, effective in treating both hypertensive emergencies as well as chronic hypertension. Captopril is an effective antihypertensive agent because of its ability to inhibit angiotensin-converting enzyme (ACE), which cleaves the 10-amino acid peptide angiotensin I to the 8-amino acid peptide angiotensin II, one of the most potent vasoconstrictors. The result is a decrease in vascular tone. *(Katzung, pp 153–165)*

**205–206. (205-E, 206-B)** Pigmented villonodular synovitis often occurs in the knee joint of young adults. It is a benign neoplasm that grossly appears as abundant irregularly thickened villiform synovium with brownish discoloration. There is a solid proliferation of bland mononuclear cells, scattered multinucleate giant cells, and foci of hemosiderin deposition. Osteoarthritis is usually a disorder of older adults characterized by degeneration of the articular cartilage of major weight-bearing joints such as the knee or hip. Grossly, there is osteophyte formation, eburnation, and cortical cysts. Analgesics, weight loss, and limitation of activity may provide temporary relief. In obstinate cases, surgical prosthetic joint replacement may be necessary. *(Rubin and Farber, pp 1326–1327, 1340)*

207. **(D)** The cartilage of the second or hyoid arch (Reichert's cartilage) gives rise to the stapes. *(Sadler, p 304)*

208. **(C)** The third pharyngeal arch gives rise to the stylopharyngeal muscle. *(Sadler, p 305)*

209. **(I)** The epithelium of the dorsal wing of the fourth pharyngeal pouch forms the superior parathyroid gland. *(Sadler, p 307)*

210. **(A)** The dorsal end of the first pharyngeal arch persist to form the incus and malleus. *(Sadler, p 302)*

211. **(G)** The cartilaginous component of the fourth and sixth pharyngeal arches fuse to form the thyroid, cricoid, arytenoid, corniculate, and cuneiform cartilages of the larynx. *(Sadler, p 305)*

212. **(E)** The first pharyngeal pouch forms a stalk-like diverticulum, the tubotympanic recess, which comes in contact with the epithelial lining of the first pharyngeal cleft, the future external auditory meatus. The distal portion of the outpocketing widens into a sac-like structure, the primitive tympanic or middle ear cavity, whereas the proximal part remains narrow, forming the auditory (eustachian) tube. *(Sadler, p 302)*

213. **(D)** The muscles of the hyoid arch are the stapedius, the stylohyoid, the posterior belly of the digastric, the auricular, and the muscles of facial expression. *(Sadler, p 304)*

214. **(A)** The musculature of the first pharyngeal arch is formed by the muscles of mastication (temporal, masseter, and pterygoids), the anterior belly of the digastric, the mylohyoid, the tensor tympani, and tensor palatini. *(Sadler, p 302)*

215. **(H)** The ventral part of the third pharyngeal pouch differentiates into the thymus. *(Sadler, p 306)*

216. **(A)** The tongue appears in embryos of approximately 4 weeks in the form of two lateral lingual swellings and one medial swelling, the tuberculum impar. These three swellings originate from the first pharyngeal arch and form the anterior two-thirds of the tongue. *(Sadler, p 310)*

217. **(G)** Premack's principle holds that a behavior engaged in at a higher frequency can be used to reinforce a lower-frequency behavior. In treating a schizophrenic patient who liked to sit down, doing nothing, a plan was devised in which the patient could sit down for five minutes only after a certain amount of rehabilitation work. *(Kaplan and Sadock, pp 262–271)*

218. **(D)** A stimulus (snake) is generalized to something else that resembles the original stimulus (rope). This type of conditioning may contribute to certain types of phobias and other anxiety conditions. *(Kaplan and Sadock, pp 262–271)*

219. **(H)** Extinction occurs when the conditioned stimulus is presented repeatedly without the unconditioned stimulus. Eventually, the conditioned response gradually weakens and then disappears. *(Kaplan and Sadock, pp 262–271)*

220. **(B)** This is the classical experiment by Pavlov, in which the unconditioned stimulus, food, is paired with the neutral stimulus, bell, until the unconditioned response to food, salivation, becomes conditioned to the sound of the bell. The sound of the bell, then, becomes the conditioned stimulus. *(Kaplan and Sadock, pp 262–271)*

221. **(F)** Reciprocal inhibition means that one state of the person inhibits the elicitation of a contradictory state at the same time. When one is relaxed, one cannot be anxious at the same time. This is one of the techniques to treat phobic symptoms. *(Kaplan and Sadock, pp 262–271)*

222. **(E)** Behavior may be shaped by rewarding intermediate steps until the desired behavior is achieved. Through shaping, complex behaviors can be operantly conditioned. *(Kaplan and Sadock, pp 262–271)*

223. **(B)** Names and images may function as conditioned stimuli. Thus, thinking about biting into a sour apple may evoke the conditioned response of salivation. This type of classical conditioning may occur naturally. *(Kaplan and Sadock, pp 262–271)*

224. **(D)** Endogenous and exogenous pyrogens, resulting from the presence of infecting pathogenic microorganisms, raise the hypothalamic set point and thereby cause a rise in body temperature (fever). Once the patient's temperature has risen to match the newer, higher set point, the patient is comfortable and his new, higher temperature is well regulated around the new set point. *(Guyton and Hall, pp 920–921)*

225. **(E)** If the factors originally responsible for the fever are gone (successfully eliminated by the body's immune system), the hypothalamic set point returns to normal. For a while, the body's core temperature is above the now normal set point. This has the same effect as if the individual were too hot. The patient begins sweating and complains of "burning up" because of his hot skin (due to vasodilation). *(Guyton and Hall, pp 920–921)*

226. **(B)** When the set point is first raised, due to pyrogens, the body temperature is temporarily below the new, higher set point, just as if the body were too cool. The hypothalamus causes the usual responses to produce additional heat (shivering) and to conserve the heat present (skin vasoconstriction, lack of sweating). The patient subjectively feels chilled and seeks to raise his body temperature until he is more comfortable (piles on blankets, sits by the fire, gets a heating pad, etc.). *(Guyton and Hall, pp 920–921)*

227–228. **(227-C, 228-A)** Chromosomal abnormalities are frequently evident in certain malignant neoplasms. Translocations, such as (11;22) and (8;14), are associated with Ewing's sarcoma/peripheral neuroepithelial tumor and Burkitt's lymphoma, respectively. The presence of these genetic abnormalities may in part offer a mechanism for malignant transformation of these tissues. Also, the presence of these consistent chromosomal abnormalities in an atypical or problematic clinical case helps to secure a more confident diagnosis. *(Cotran et al, p 459)*

229–232. **(229-E, 230-C, 231-B, 232-A)** Creutzfeldt–Jacob disease an encephalopathy caused by a slow-viral infection. Syringomyelia is an adult neurologic disorder caused by the development of fluid-filled spaces within the cervical spinal cord. Myelomeningocele is a neonatal disease in which portions of the lower spinal cord and its coverings herniate through a defect in the posterior spine. von Recklinghausen's disease is a genetic disorder characterized by neurofibromatosis and abnormal skin pigmentation. *(Chandrasoma and Taylor, pp 894–908)*

233. **(E)** There are five genera of DNA animal viruses. The HAPPPy mnemonic device (**H**erpes, **A**deno, **P**apova, **P**arvo, and **P**ox) enumerates these. All others are RNA viruses. Variola is a poxvirus, as is molluscum contagiosum; measles is caused by a paramyxovirus. *(Joklik et al, pp 769–781)*

234. **(C)** Killing of microbes by phagocytes is regulated by both oxygen-dependent and oxygen- independent mechanisms. The oxygen-dependent mechanisms involve the participation of superoxide anion, hydrogen peroxide, singlet oxygen, and hydroxyl radicals, all of which are powerful microbicidal

agents. Ferrous ions are not part of the oxygen-dependent microbicidal mechanisms of phagocytes. *(Jawetz et al, pp 113–115)*

235. **(D)** Allosteric enzymes are characterized as those enzymes that contain substrate binding sites and binding sites for ligands other than substrate. The non-substrate ligands bind to and change the activity, either positively or negatively, of the enzyme. Allosteric enzymes can be monomeric or composed of multiple subunits. Allosteric enzymes undergo changes in conformation upon binding regulatory ligands. The effect of allosteric ligands on enzyme activity can be observed graphically when plotting enzyme activity versus substrate concentration. These plots have a characteristic sigmoidal shape. *(Devlin, pp 162–167)*

236. **(B)** *Leishmania* species are 1- to 3-μm protozoa that are transmitted to humans by bites of infected sand flies of the genera *Phlebotomas* and *Lutzomyia*. Following infection, *Leishmania* circulates freely in the blood and lives inside the macrophages of liver, spleen, and bone marrow. Leishmaniasis (or kala-azar) caused by *Leishmania donovani* is characterized by spleen and liver enlargement, undulant fever, loss of weight, visible pulsation of carotid arteries, anemia, and bleeding of the nose, gums, intestine, and lips. *(Joklik et al, pp 1178–1179)*

237. **(C)** A series of four reactions is required to incorporate glucose into glycogen. In the liver, the glucose is phosphorylated to glucose-6-phosphate by gluokinase. Glucose-6-phosphate is converted to glucose-1-phosphate by phosphoglucomutase. Glucose-1-phosphate is converted to UDP-glucose by UDP-glucose pyrophosphorylase (also called glucose-1-phosphate uridylyltransferase) and then incorporated into glycogen by glycogen synthase. *(Devlin, pp 343–346)*

238. **(E)** Viruses do not possess endotoxins. Viruses can be neutralized by antibody alone if the antibody is directed against a viral component important in adsorption, penetration, or uncoating. Antibody-coated viruses in the circulation or in the tissues are phagocytized and destroyed. This opsonization by antibody is due to the fact that phagocytic cells have a membrane receptor for the Fc portion of certain immunoglobulin molecules, and this antibody-receptor complex serves to hold the viral particle close to the phagocytic cell until it can be engulfed. Complement can augment this neutralization, and it also can inactivate virions directly by covering their surfaces and, in some instances, lysing the virus even in the absence of specific antiviral antibody. If infected host cells are lysed, the site of viral replication is destroyed, and the infection can be brought under control. *(Joklik et al, pp 768, 781, 783–784)*

239. **(A)** Known risk factors for the development of gallstones include obesity, increasing age, female gender, familial disposition, certain ethnic groups, diets high in calories and cholesterol, oral contraceptive use, and multiple pregnancies. The old adage "fat, fertile, forty, and female" still typifies a majority of symptomatic cases. The bile of individuals with gallstones has a higher cholesterol content than acalculous individuals. In the United States, most symptomatic individuals are treated by laparoscopic cholecystectomy to avoid potential serious complications such as acute cholecystis or common duct obstruction. *(Rubin and Farber, pp 777–782)*

240. **(D)** Increased suicide risk is associated with older age, male sex, presence of pain, Protestant religion as opposed to Catholic religion, and living alone. Living alone may contribute to the risk of suicide through loneliness, depression, and reduction in the rescue potential. *(Leigh and Reiser, pp 101–144)*

241. **(E)** The enzyme, 3-ketoacid CoA transferase, is required to transfer CoA from succinyl-CoA to acetoacetate to form acetoacetyl-CoA, which is then cleaved by thiolysis to two molecules of acetyl-CoA. Acetoacetate is a ketone body. It is produced in the liver but cannot be used by this tissue since the liver lacks the CoA transferase. Virtually all peripheral tissues that contain mitochondria possess the transferase and can, therefore,

utilize ketone bodies as an energy source. (*Murray et al, pp 226–227*)

242. **(D)** The stages of conjugation are as follows: (1) specific pair formation, in which the donor and recipient make contact through the F pili, (2) effective pair formation with cell-to-cell contact, (3) chromosome mobilization, (4) transfer of a unique strand of DNA to the recipient cell, which leads to (5) formation of partial diploids, or merozygotes (entire recipient chromosome and partial chromosome from the donor), and (6) genetic recombination, in which the donor chromosome replaces segments of the recipient chromosome. Competency is a condition that is necessary for transformation of cells and is *not* a stage of conjugation. (*Joklik et al, pp 136–145*)

243. **(A)** Malignant cells may show a variety of anaplastic changes. They show irregularities in size and shape of the cell, with extreme variation and overall increase in cell size. The nucleus has an increased amount of DNA and is hyperchromatic. The nuclei are larger than expected for the cell size, with an elevated nucleus/cytoplasm ratio approaching 1:1 instead of the normal 1:4. The nuclei may show coarsely clumped, irregularly dispersed chromatin, and one or more prominent nucleoli. Some tumors may create tumor giant cells that are multinucleated conglomerations of malignant cells. (*Chandrasoma and Taylor, pp 290–296*)

244. **(D)** Neoplasms, particularly cancer of the tail of the pancreas, all endocrinopathies including hyper- and hypothyroidism, and hyperparathyroidism can cause clinical depression. Many drugs, particularly anti-hypertensive drugs, are often associated with depression. (*Leigh and Reiser, pp 124–140*)

245. **(D)** The wall of the uterus consists of three layers. The outer, serous coat is called the perimetrium. The middle, muscular coat is called the myometrium. The inner, mucous coat is called the endometrium. The uterus is usually bent anteriorly (anteflexed) between

the cervix and the body, and the entire uterus is normally bent or inclined anteriorly (anteverted). The body of the uterus is enclosed between the layers of the broad ligament. (*Moore, pp 284–285*)

246. **(C)** Although a drop in vascular resistance due to metabolic acidosis may occur, the initial compensatory response to hemorrhage results in a large increase in total peripheral vascular resistance. The loss of blood volume initially decreases cardiac output, but baroreceptor-mediated sympathetic drive causes vasoconstriction. Thus, vascular resistance increases, heart rate increases, and blood pressure returns toward normal. In addition, the kidneys will secrete renin, and the production of angiotensin II via converting enzyme activity ultimately ensues. Fluid shifts from the interstitial compartments to the vascular space, helping to partially restore cardiac output. Other humoral agents, including epinephrine, vasopressin, and glucocorticoids, may also be released to further compensate for the cardiovascular effects of hemorrhage. (*Guyton and Hall, pp 285–287*)

247. **(A)** The cathecolamines, dopamine, norepinephrine, and epinephrine, are all derived sequentially from levodopa. The latter is synthesized from tyrosine by a hydroxylation reaction catalyzed by tyrosine hydroxylase. Levodopa is also the precursor for synthesis of the pigment melanin. p-Hydroxylphenylpyruvate is a breakdown product of tyrosine, which is ultimately converted to acetoacetate and fumarate. Histamine is a vasodilator that is formed from histidine by decarboxylation. (*Stryer, pp 647–648, 730*)

248. **(B)** Influenza viruses have a segmented genome. Three serotypes of influenza viruses are known to occur in nature. These are divided into types A, B, and C on the basis of differences in their ribonucleoprotein antigens. Within the types, there are antigenic differences based on changes in the nature of the hemagglutinin and neuraminidase spikes that protrude from the envelope. It is changes in these subtypes that cause the

emergence of epidemics and pandemics of influenza, and these changes are also the reason that vaccine prophylaxis of the disease is so difficult. Each pandemic is caused a new antigenic subtype. Hence, there has not been sufficient time to produce the large quantities of vaccine that would be needed to protect the world's population. The vaccine is usually reserved for medical personnel and the aged (who are particularly at risk of fatal influenzal disease). It is thought that the segmented genome of the virus may play a role in the antigenic changes that the organism undergoes. *(Joklik et al, pp 642, 662, 821–823)*

249. **(B)** All forms of gestational trophoblastic disease occur more commonly in Asia than in the United States. Elevated serum levels of human chorionic gonadotropin are seen with gestational trophoblastic disease. The karyotype of partial mole is triploid (69,XXY). Most (90%) of the complete moles have a normal female karyotype (46,XX). Choriocarcinoma can occur subsequent to a normal pregnancy, an ectopic pregnancy, a molar pregnancy, or an abortion. *(Chandrasoma and Taylor, pp 802–804)*

250. **(D)** While uncomplicated grief reactions usually subside within four to eight weeks, a significant proportion continue to have symptoms up to one to two years after the death of a spouse. In one study, 17% of bereaved persons were depressed at the end of 13 months. *(Leigh and Reiser, pp 101–144)*

251. **(B)** The quadriceps femoris muscle group of the anterior compartment of the thigh is one of the largest and most powerful muscles in the body and a powerful extensor of the knee joint. It is innervated by the femoral nerve. *(Hall–Craggs, p 373)*

252. **(B)** Parathyroid hormone and PTH-like substances stimulate bone resorption and vitamin D conversion, thereby elevating serum calcium levels. Serum calcitonin would consequently be expected to rise. A PTH-like effect on the kidneys would increase calcium absorption while markedly increasing phosphate excretion. *(Guyton and Hall, pp 992–994)*

253. **(B)** All cells, except liver, phosphorylate glucose to glucose-6-phosphate with a hexokinase. By contrast, glucokinase catalyzes this reaction in liver. Liver glucokinase has a significantly higher $K_m$ for glucose than does hexokinase. As a result, peripheral tissues, but not liver, will take up glucose from blood when blood sugar levels are low. Glucose-6-phosphate, derived from gluconeogenesis or glycogenolysis, is dephosphorylated in liver by glucose-6-phosphatase so that it can cross the liver plasma membrane as free glucose. Pyruvate carboxylase and fructose 1, 6-biphosphatase are involved in gluconeogenesis. This process occurs only in liver and kidney. *(Stryer, pp 495, 569–572, 585, 774–775)*

254. **(D)** Phagocytic cells, such as macrophages and neutrophils, have receptors for C3b. B lymphocytes also react with C3b. However, T lymphocytes appear to lack a membrane receptor for this molecule. It is the presence of the C3b receptor on phagocytic cells that is responsible for the opsonization of bacteria and other foreign materials by antibody and complement. The antibody reacts with an antigen on the bacterial surface, and the complement cascade is activated. During this activation, C3b is deposited onto the surface of the organism, and it interacts with the receptor in the phagocyte membrane to bring the two cells together, thus facilitating the phagocytic process. *(Joklik et al, pp 206–207, 229, 268, 280–282, 287, 351, 373)*

255. **(D)** Thymomas are neoplasms of thymic epithelial cells. Most arise in the anterior mediastinum, and about 75% are benign. Microscopically, there are varying mixtures of epithelial cells and accompanying lymphocytes. The tumor is associated clinically with both myasthenia gravis and red cell hypoplasia. Surgery is the usual mode of therapy. *(Rubin and Farber, pp 1145–1146)*

256. **(B)** While mood-congruent hallucinations may occur during psychotic depression, hallucinations are not the norm in depressive syndrome. Suicidal thoughts, anhedonia, ap-

athy, and anorexia are quite common in depression. *(Leigh and Reiser, pp 101–144)*

257. **(B)** The ischiocavernosus arises from the surface of the ischial tuberosity and ischial rami. The perineal body is the landmark of the perineum where several muscles converge (transverse perineal, bulbospongiosus, levator ani, and some fibers of the external anal sphincter. *(Moore, pp 298, 313)*

258. **(A)** Bile salts, along with lecithin (phosphatidyl choline), form small, emulsified droplets with the products of fat digestion (mainly 2-monoglycerides). These small droplets, called mixed micelles (or biliary micelles), are about 5 nanometers in diameter and contain approximately 25 molecules. Very hydrophobic molecules, such as long chain fatty acids, cholesterol, and fat-soluble vitamins, partition themselves into the interior of the micelles. Amphiphilic molecules, with both polar (hydrophilic) and nonpolar (hydrophobic) parts, have the hydrophilic parts facing outward at the surface and the hydrophobic parts within the interior (bile salts, lecithin, and 2-monoglycerides).

Apolipoproteins are not part of mixed micelles. They function in blood partly for stabilization and transport of lipids in an aqueous medium (plasma), but mainly for the specific directing of lipid components to the appropriate tissue destinations (with specific tissue receptors for the various apolipoproteins). *(Berne and Levy, pp 711–713, 842–846)*

259. **(A)** Although peptide bonds define the primary structure (the sequence of amino acids) and, hence, supply the information necessary to specify the three-dimensional structure of a protein, they play no active role in stabilizing the tertiary structure of proteins. Four major types of weak bonds are important in tertiary structure: hydrogen bonds between R groups of the amino acids composing the protein, hydrogen bonds between the peptide groupings of a-helical and b-pleated sheet regions, ionic nonds between positively and negatively charged R groups, and hy-

drophobic interactions between non-polar R groups. Study has revealed that hydrophobic interactions are the most important forces involved in maintaining the tertiary structure of proteins. *(Mathews and van Holde, pp 190–193)*

260. **(D)** The appendix of the epididymis is the remnant of the cranial end of the mesonephric duct, which is attached to the head of the epididymis. The appendix of the testis is a vesicular remnant of the cranial end of the paramesonephric duct. It is attached to the superior pole of the testis. The presence of excess fluid or blood in the tunica vaginalis is known as a hydrocele or hematocele of the testis. *(Moore, pp 151–152)*

261. **(D)** The arachnoid membrane is coextensive with the dural sac, which extends to the level of the S2 vertebral body. Thus, the subarachnoid space continues to the level of the second sacral vertebral body. *(Hall–Craggs, p 52)*

262. **(B)** In severe obsessive–compulsive disorder, the patient may be disabled due to the compulsions and may be housebound. In severe cases, psychosurgery, including cingulotomy, have been reported helpful, and serotonergic antidepressants, such as clomipramine and fluoxetine, have been helpful. While most OCD patients have rigid superego, and may, indeed, have fixation in the anal sadistic stage, there seems to be a large biological component in the etiology of the disorder. *(Kaplan and Sadock, pp 984–999)*

263. **(B)** The mamillary bodies are part of the limbic system, the original classic Papez circuit for emotion. The auditory pathway receives input from the cochlear nerve and nuclei. The auditory pathways ascend as the lateral lemnisus and terminate in the inferior colliculus, which gives rise to the brachium of the inferior colliculus. The brachium terminates in the medial geniculate body. *(Noback, pp 198, 356)*

264. **(B)** Skeletal muscle constitutes the major mass of the body, and thus alterations in its resistance will greatly affect systemic blood

pressure (ie, product of cardiac output × resistance). For instance, when carotid sinus pressure is elevated, a reflex is elicited that inhibits activity in the vasoconstrictor regions of the brain and causes vasodilatation in the skeletal muscle. This reflex may induce vasodilatation in anticipation of exercise. In addition to these extrinsic neuronal regulatory mechanisms, local metabolic factors contribute to the regulation of muscle blood flow. This is especially true in stimulated or exercising muscle. For instance, metabolically active muscle can be shown to autoregulate, that is, increase its resistance as perfusion pressure rises to maintain constant blood flow and, conversely, decrease resistance when pressure decreases. Skeletal muscle is very heterogeneous. Within the same muscle group, blood flow is high to red muscle and relatively low to white muscle. Precapillary sphincter contraction and relaxation further confound local flow patterns via intermittent activity and perhaps by shunting of blood to non-nutrient pathways. (*Berne and Levy, pp 520–521*)

265. **(B)** Sickle cell anemia is caused by a mutation in the gene encoding the β-chain of hemoglobin. This mutation is referred to as HbS. The HbS mutation leads to polymerization of deoxygenated hemoglobin, which in turn distorts the shape of erythrocytes into the classic sickle shape. Sickled erythrocytes are fragile, leading to increased hemolysis. Due to poor oxygen transport in the capillaries of peripheral tissues, growth is impaired and tissue necrosis occurs. The increased hemolysis results in excess heme delivery to the liver and an increase in bilirubin production, leading to jaundice as a result of impaired hepatic clearance. (*Murray et al, pp 56–58*)

266. **(D)** Spores are not important constituents of gram negative organisms. Bacterial spores are formed when certain gram positive bacteria multiply in culture media that lack the necessary nutrients. Spores are stable to heating for several minutes at 80°C. Spores contain 10 to 15% calcium dipicolinic acid, which is thought to play a role in the resistance of spores to heat. Actually, heating bacterial spores at 80°C for 15 to 30 min is used to initiate spore germination. However, spore germination, in addition to heating at 80°C, requires the presence of L-alanine, or adenosine, which apparently activates an autolysin that degrades the spore cortex and allows the spore to accumulate water, release calcium dipicolinate, and germinate. (*Jawetz et al, pp 27–28*)

267. **(D)** Serum sickness is a type III hypersensitivity disease characterized by circulating immune complexes. The immune complexes are deposited in the skin (vasculitis), kidney (glomerulonephritis), and joints (arthritis). Upon deposition, they evoke an inflammatory response (fever) through complement activation. Delayed hypersensitivity (type IV hypersensitivity) is not involved in serum sickness. (*Rubin and Farber, pp 110–113*)

268. **(A)** The onset and the duration of action of the ultrashort-acting barbiturates such as thiopental are controlled by blood flow and the high lipid solubility of these agents. Thiopental is given by intravenous injection and rapidly enters the CNS through a combination of high blood flow to the brain and high lipid solubility. The onset of action takes place in less than one minute, and the maximum brain concentration is achieved in about one minute. Thereafter, thiopental redistributes out of the brain, first into lean tissues with high blood flow but low fat content and eventually into adipose tissue which has low blood flow but high fat content. The redistribution process determines the duration of action. Throughout the course of action, the blood level of thiopental does not correlate with the actions of the drug, in contrast to the situation with the vast majority of drugs. Metabolism of thiopental takes place in the liver but is much slower than the redistribution process. Thus, the serum half-life is controlled by redistribution and does not correlate with duration of action. (*Katzung, p 390*)

269. **(A)** Psychological defense mechanisms are automatic, unconscious processes that reduce anxiety. These tend to be mobilized and accentuated at times of stress, including hospi-

talization. Successful deployment of defense mechanisms may be associated with decreased stress hormone activation. While certain defense mechanisms may be accentuated in some psychiatric disorders, defense mechanisms are not necessarily maladaptive. (*Leigh and Reiser, pp 51–52, 79–100*)

270. **(E)** The pyramidal decussation occurs in the caudal portion of the medulla. The most distinguishing feature is the crossing of 85 to 90% of the corticospinal fibers as the pyramidal decussation. It is composed of interdigitating descending fibers that decussate and course in a caudal and posterior direction to the dorsal aspect of the lateral funiculus of the spinal cord. Dorsal roots are absent. (*Noback, pp 200–201*)

271. **(D)** Although the capillaries are the smallest vessels, by virtue of their large number and parallel existence, their effective cross-sectional area is very large. Since velocity is inversely related to cross-sectional area, the velocity in the capillaries is very low. This large surface area and low velocity promote exchange of substances between blood and tissue. Resistance to blood flow primarily occurs in arterioles with smooth muscle, and thus this is the site of the largest pressure drop. Blood volume is greatest in small veins by nature of their high compliance (low elasticity) and may serve as a reservoir. (*Berne and Levy, pp 361–363*)

272. **(E)** Sections of all of the structures would be expected to have myelinated and unmyelinated axons, but only in the peripheral nervous system is there an investment of unmyelinated axons by Schwann cells. Moreover, the cerebral cortex, red nucleus, and spinal cord gray matter contain neuronal cell bodies, which are not evident in this electron micrograph. (*Junqueira et al, pp 157, 170, 172, 177*)

273. **(A)** In contrast to the central nervous system, unmyelinated axons in the peripheral nervous system are ensheathed by the cytoplasm of Schwann cells. Usually, a single Schwann cell supports segments of several

unmyelinated axons, as is the case in this example. Compared to myelinated axons, unmyelinated axons are thin, generally less than 1 μm in diameter. (*Junqueira et al, pp 169–172*)

274. **(D)** Wound healing is delayed by large, gaping defects, excessive scar formation, infection in the wound site, foreign material in the wound site, and metabolic processes such as diabetes mellitus, malnutrition, and scurvy. A clean wound site with closely opposed edges would be likely to heal quickly, without complications or delay. (*Rubin and Farber, pp 90–92*)

275. **(C)** Tolerance or decrease in efficacy with repeated use is seen with many of the actions of morphine and other opioids. Tolerance develops to the sedation, nausea, antidiuresis, and respiratory depression, along with the analgesia, euphoria and cough suppression produced by opioids. The mechanisms for tolerance are not well understood but appear to involve adaptation of cells at the receptor level and of long feedback loops controlling CNS activity. Little or no tolerance develops to the miosis and constipation produced by opioids. The presence of opioid-induced miosis can be utilized as a sign of drug use. (*Katzung, pp 467–468*)

276. **(E)** Mechanic proposed that four dimensions of an illness or symptom are important in influencing how the illness is perceived. They include commonality, familiarity, predictability of outcome, and the threat and loss likely to result from the illness. For example, since the common cold is both familiar and common, a person with a cold is unlikely to seek medical help. However, coughing up blood is uncommon, unfamiliar, unpredictable, and threatening, and thus is more likely to lead to medical help-seeking behavior. (*Leigh and Reiser, pp 3–15*)

277. **(D)** Movement of an individual to a higher altitude (with decreased partial pressure of oxygen) requires greater oxygen capacity of blood and, accordingly, is a stimulus for in-

creased rate of erythrocyte production. This is reflected by an increased percentage of circulating erythrocytes that are newly developed (reticulocytes). Exposure to infectious agents, vaccines, or allergins will elicit responses involving distinct populations of leukocytes. (*Junqueira et al, pp 221–233*).

278. **(D)** Catecholamines produced by healthy adrenal medulla are epinephrine and, to a lesser extent, norepinephrine. However, many pheochromocytomas produce predominantly norepinephrine resulting in α-adrenergic effects. Systemic actions of catecholamines include increased blood pressure and heart rate and increased glucose levels through insulin suppression and enhanced gluconeogenesis. Sweat glands are innervated by sympathetic fibers utilizing acetylcholine as transmitter substance and are not directly stimulated by circulating catecholamines. However, the paroxysmal release of catecholamines precipitates a generalized activation of the sympathetic nervous system and profuse sweating is characteristic for these patients. Cardiac ischemia results from increased cardiac oxygen demand and coronary artery spasm. (*Harrison's Principles of Internal Medicine, pp 1976–1977*)

279. **(D)** Nucleosomes are composed of DNA and an octamer of histone proteins. The "core" structure of nucleosomes consists of two each of histones H2A, H2B, H3, and H4 in an octamer. The DNA of the "core" is wrapped around the outside of the octamer and encompasses approximately 150 base pairs. Nucleosomes are interconnected through the "linker" histone, H1. All of the interactions are non-covalent. (*Devlin, pp 637–641*)

280. **(B)** Commercially canned foods are less likely to be contaminated by bacteria than foods stored by the other methods listed in the question. Temperatures of 120°C (250°F) or higher have to be used in the canning process. This temperature is obtained by steam under pressure and continues for a stipulated period of time that varies inversely with the amount of heat used. The desired effect begins when the temperatures achieved

are 105°C (220°F) or higher. By this method, at least 90% of all organisms are killed. Pasteurization is also a form of heat treatment, in which lower temperatures are used for longer time periods. This method is adequate to prevent bacterial growth, but it may not be bactericidal. Refrigeration and freezing prevent bacterial multiplication, but food stored by these methods needs to be adequately cooked unless, like ice cream, it is to be eaten shortly after removal from the cold environment. Drying is a relatively safe method of storage, as pathogenic bacteria tend to die in the absence of water in foods that have been dried to 10 to 20% of their original weight. (*Joklik et al, pp 195–196*)

281. **(D)** *Mycoplasma* organisms do not have a cell wall and are therefore resistant to penicillin. Other forms of bacteria that lack a cell wall are spheroplasts and protoplasts, which are formed from gram-negative and gram-positive bacteria, respectively, through the action of penicillin or by other procedures that remove the cell wall or interfere with its formation. The other organisms listed in the question are all susceptible to the action of penicillin, although certain strains of *Gonococcus* have acquired a β-lactamase-producing plasmid. Tetracyclines, erythromycin, and the aminoglycosides are effective antibiotics for the treatment of mycoplasmal infections. (*Joklik et al, pp 730–736*)

282. **(C)** Hypokalemia is a frequent complication of therapy with loop diuretics furosemide, ethacrynic acid, and bumetanide, as well as the thiazide diuretics such as chlorothiazide. Because these agents cause a large increase in the amount of sodium delivered to distal tubule and collecting tubule, the aldosterone-regulated sodium–potassium exchange in these segments will cause potassium ion to be lost. The aldosterone antagonist spironolactone produces weak diuresis by decreasing the sodium–potassium exchange activity, thus increasing sodium excretion. Spironolactone along with triamterene and amiloride, which act by inhibiting sodium ion transport in the same regions, are classified as potassium-sparing diuretics because they

do not cause potassium ion loss. *(Katzung, pp 237–241)*

**283. (C)** A high level of stress has been associated with help-seeking behavior, with or without new onset of symptoms. Hispanics were less likely to seek medical help than English-speaking populations in one study. The upper socioeconomic class is associated with medical help-seeking behavior rather than the lower socioeconomic class. *(Leigh and Reiser, pp 3–15)*

**284. (C)** Spasticity can be defined as an increase (not a decrease) in the resistance to passive movement. Hypertonia is usually associated with spasticity, which is typically the result of damage to an upper motor neuron. A hemisection of the spinal cord at C8 would lead to spasticity in the ipsilateral lower extremity due to interruption of the corticospinal tract on that side. Spasticity is typically related to pyramidal tract lesions, whereas rigidity is associated with basal ganglia lesions. *(Brodal, pp 242–245)*

**285. (A)** Mineralocorticoid excess is either "primary," due to hormone-producing tumors of the adrenal cortex (Conn's syndrome) or "secondary" due to activation of the renin–angiotensin system. Conditions of absolute or relative hypovolemia (eg, pregnancy, heart failure, shift of vascular volume to the interstitial space as in liver cirrhosis with ascites), as well as dietary sodium restriction, activate the renin–angiotensin system and result in secondary hyperaldosteronism. *(Ganong, pp 348–349, 588–589)*

**286. (C)** The immediate source of carbon atoms for fatty acid synthesis is acetyl-CoA. Thus, any precursor of acetyl-CoA can be a source of carbon atoms for fatty acid synthesis. Glucose and other carbohydrates that are converted to glycolytic intermediates can contribute carbon atoms to acetyl-CoA. Likewise, ketogenic amino acids, such as leucine and phenylalanine, derived of protein degradation, can provide carbon atoms to acetyl-CoA. Citrate is the major carrier of mitochondrial acetyl-CoA carbons to the cytosol for fatty acid synthesis, since acetyl-CoA itself cannot move across the inner mitochondrial membrane. After diffusion into the cytosol, citrate is cleaved into acetyl-CoA and oxaloacetate by the enzyme citrate lyase. Cholesterol and other steroids cannot be degraded. They are converted to bile salts and excreted. Thus, although acetyl-CoA is a precursor of cholesterol, once incorporated, the carbon atoms of cholesterol are unavailable for biosynthesis of other compounds. *(Stryer, pp 613, 638, 696)*

**287. (D)** Multiplication of a given gram-negative bacterium within the bloodstream leads to release of its specific endotoxin that produces the septic shock syndrome. The endotoxin is composed of three regions. Region I contains the non-specific, non-toxic, O antigen. Thus, administration of antibodies to the terminal polysaccharide of the O antigen, which already are present in the bloodstream, is not likely to constitute an effective protective strategy for prevention of the septic shock syndrome. Region II of the endotoxin contains the core polysaccharide that is linked to the region III, or lipid, moiety of the endotoxin. The toxicity of the endotoxin resides mostly in the lipid A moiety. Therefore, administration of specific antibody to lipid A and its associated core-linked polysaccharide should assist in prevention of the septic shock syndrome. Cachectin plays a pivotal role in the pathophysiology of sepsis and by itself can produce the septic shock syndrome in experimental animals. Conversely, animals that have been previously immunized against cachectin will survive an otherwise lethal dose of endotoxin. A well-known effect of endotoxin is that it induces vasodilation, hypotension, and increased permeability. This action is prolonged by leukotrienes. Thus, administration of antileukotriene agents should be indicated in septic shock syndrome. *(Joklik et al, pp 86–87, 390)*

**288. (B)** There are three major patterns of rejection of a tissue transplant: hyperacute, acute, and chronic rejection. With the kidney as the example, hyperacute rejection occurs within minutes after the transplantation. Acute rejection manifests itself as sudden deterioration of renal function within days or months to years following transplantation. Two histologic types of acute renal rejection are recognized and may overlap in any given patient. Acute cellular rejection demonstrates an interstitial mononuclear cell infiltrate and edema with mild interstitial hemorrhage. Focal tubular necrosis due to mononuclear cell infiltration may occur. In the absence of an arteritis, this type of rejection responds to immunosuppressive therapy. Acute humoral rejection or rejection vasculitis produces a necrotizing arteritis with endothelial necrosis, neutrophilic infiltration, deposition of immunoglobulin, complement, and fibrin, and thrombosis. This leads to severe glomerular and cortical damage that fails to respond to immunosuppressive therapy. Chronic rejection is a progressive dysfunction of the kidney with gradual increase in serum creatinine levels during a 4- to 6-month period. (*Cotran et al, pp 190–194*)

289. **(C)** Because the aminoglycoside antibiotics, including streptomycin, are highly polar molecules, they are not absorbed from the gastrointestinal tract and must be administered parenterally. Although streptomycin was the first agent to exhibit high activity against tubercle bacilli, it is now used only in life-threatening situations because of the inconvenience of the parenteral route of administration along with the adverse effect of ototoxicity. Multiple-drug oral therapy with combinations of isoniazid (an inhibitor of mycolic acid synthesis), rifampin (an inhibitor of bacterial DNA-dependent RNA synthesis), ethambutol (mechanism unknown) and pyrazinamide (mechanism unknown), are used to prevent emergence of resistance, which is common when any of these agents is used alone. (*Katzung, pp 707–710*)

290. **(E)** An informed consent to a surgical procedure, drugs, or research involves the subject or patient knowing what the proposed procedure is, that he/she may withdraw the consent, knowing what the risks and benefits are, and what the potential alternatives are. (*Kaplan and Sadock, pp 1317–1318*)

291. **(D)** Failure of the anterior neuropore to close is called anencephaly. Spina bifida occulta involves failure of the vertebral arches of the spinal canal to close but the underlying neural structures are not damaged and the patient can be symptom free. Meningomyelocele is a similar condition but includes protrusion of meninges and spinal cord through the open spinal canal. Rachischisis is a cleft in the spine of a vertebra that may or may not be accompanied by protrusion of meningeal and brain structures. Agenesis of the corpus callosum is a complete or partial failure of this large hemispheral commissure to form. (*Burt, pp 25–27*)

292. **(B)** Absence seizures ("petit mal," "blank spells") are generalized seizures characterized by momentary loss of responsiveness during which the patients are unaware of their surroundings but do not lose muscle tone. The EEG shows a characteristic "spike and dome" pattern with a frequency of 3/sec during these "blank spells." REM-onset sleep is characteristic for narcolepsy. (*Ganong, p 183*)

293. **(D)** Acetyl-CoA is the precursor for fatty acid, cholesterol, and sterol biosynthesis, all of which occurs in the cytoplasm. However, acetyl-CoA is produced in the mitochondria by various oxidation reactions (eg, pyruvate dehydrogenase, fatty acid oxidation, amino acid oxidation). Acetyl-CoA is transported from the mitochondria to the cytoplasm as citrate. Mitochondrial citrate synthase converts oxaloacetate and acetyl-CoA to citrate, which is then transported to the cytoplasm by the tricarboxylate transporter. In the cytoplasm, citrate is cleaved to oxaloacetate and acetyl-CoA by ATP-citrate lyase (also called citrate cleavage enzyme). The oxaloacetate is converted to malate by malate dehydrogenase, the malate is decarboxylated to pyruvate by malic enzyme (which generates NADPH that can be used in lipid synthesis), and the pyruvate is transported into the mitochondria where it is carboxylated by pyruvate carboxylase yielding oxaloacetate, and the cycle can then continue. (*Devlin, pp 397–398*)

**294. (C)** Hairy cell leukemia is malignant proliferation of B-cell lymphocytes. The disease is most commonly seen in middle-aged and elderly males. Splenomegaly and pancytopenia are usually clinical findings. The hairy cell present in peripheral blood smears shows distinctive thin multiple cytoplasmic projections that resemble hairs. These malignant cells also demonstrate tartate resistant acid phosphatase activity. Hemorrhage and recurrent infections characterize the late stages of the disorder. Some prolongation of survival is achieved by interferon therapy. *(Rubin and Farber, pp 1067–1071)*

**295. (A)** The lesion shown in the question is multiple emboli in the lung, occluding arteries. Pulmonary emboli are a frequent complication of bed rest and are seen in debilitated elderly people. They originate in deep leg veins from thrombi that are disloged and sent into the peripheral circulation via the inferior vena cava, where they obstruct the pulmonary arterial circulation. They may cause pulmonary hemorrhage or infarction, depending on the amount of collateral blood supply. If they are large and obstruct major blood vessels, they may cause sudden death by interrupting cardiac output. If the emboli are multiple, over time they may lead to chronic pulmonary damage and fibrosis, with pulmonary hypertension and right-sided heart failure. *(Rubin and Farber, pp 268–270)*

**296. (C)** Nifedipine is a member of the dihydropyridine class of voltage-dependent calcium channel-blockers. L-type calcium channels conduct most of the calcium ion flux in cardiac and smooth muscle. Because smooth muscle is dependent on extracellular calcium for resting tone and stimulated contraction, use of nifedipine will produce relaxation of vascular, gastrointestinal, and bronchiolar smooth muscle. Cardiac muscle is also dependent on activity of L-type calcium channels for excitation–contraction coupling so that nifedipine produces a dose-dependent decrease in cardiac contractility. Skeletal muscle is not affected by L-type voltage-dependent calcium-channel blockers because the calcium required for contraction is supplied by the intracellular stores of the sarcoplasmic reticulum. *(Katzung, pp 179–180)*

**297. (E)** The physiological arousal associated with anxiety includes increased sympathetic tone. Stimulation of locus ceruleus, which supplies a large portion of noradrenergic neurons to the CNS, is associated with anxiety. The relationship between performance and anxiety seems to be an inverted U curve, so that optimum performance requires a certain degree of anxiety. *(Leigh and Reiser, pp 41–78)*

**298. (B)** Wernicke's (receptive) aphasia results from a lesion of Wernicke's area. Although hearing and vision are normal, individuals with this disability show an essentially total failure to comprehend either the spoken and/or the written language. Their speech is fluent but meaningless. Their conversations sound normal but are actually devoid of content and full of non-existent words. *(Noback, p 408)*

**299. (E)** Miniature end-plate potentials (MEPPs) are small, spontaneous depolarizations that occur randomly at a frequency of about 1 per second and are caused by spontaneous release of a single vesicle containing acetylcholine. Quantal release of neurotransmitter had been postulated from the uniform distribution of MEPP amplitudes. End-plate potentials (EPPs), representing the simultaneous release of several hundred ACh-containing vesicles, are due to opening of ligand gated, non-selective cation channels (nicotinic ACh receptors). EPPs themselves are non-regenerative and spread passively. Under normal conditions, a single EPP always depolarize the postsynaptic muscle membrane above threshold to elicit a regenerative action potential that is actively propagated along the muscle fiber. Therefore, spatial and temporal summation is important in the CNS ("the brain computes") but not at the neuromuscular junction ("the muscle obeys"). This fact should not be confused with muscle tetanus, which is due to summation of contractions rather than electrical summation of postsynaptic potentials. *(Berne and Levy, pp 58–61)*

300. **(D)** This question is not meant to make you memorize wavelengths of various light colors, but rather to appreciate the complex relationship between objective wavelength of light and subjective color sensation and the active role the CNS plays in our perception of the world. Based on careful observation of our visual sensations and logical deductions, Helmholtz postulated in the 1860s the existence of three light receptors ("blue," "green," and "red"). When these were indeed discovered in 1965, it was found that the light absorption maxima were at 440, 535, and 565 nm, corresponding to blue, yellow-green, and orange. Nevertheless, the old names "blue," "green," and "red" were retained for historical purposes. Further processing of color information in the CNS results in opposition of red and green, as well as yellow and blue, ie, neurons excited by green are inhibited by red, etc. Any color of the spectrum can be generated by stimulating the three light receptors in ratios characteristic for each color. For example, yellow is due to 1:1 stimulation of "red" and "green" receptors. Color perception, while subjective, can be measured in an objective way using Ishihara charts or through color mixing. When mixing yellow from green and red light, patients with protanomaly (low levels of red pigment) require more red levels than normal subjects to elicit a yellow sensation. *(Ganong, pp 147–149; Guyton and Hall, pp 643–645)*

301. **(E)** Immunological responses depend primarily upon T and B cells, which are the products of differentiation of stem cells. Differentiation of stem cells into T and B cells occurs during the passage of stem cells through the thymus. It is the T cells that have the glycoproteins known as $CD_3$, $CD_4$, and $CD_8$ on their surface. Stem cells lack $CD_3$, $CD_4$, or $CD_8$ on their surface. There is no such molecule as $CD_{12}$ on stem cells or T lymphocytes. *(Levinson and Jawetz, p 277)*

302. **(C)** The development of esophageal cancer is strongly associated with alcoholism and smoking. The disease is more frequent in the Far East than in the United States. About 75% of esophageal cancers are squamous cell carcinoma. The next largest proportion (15%) are adenocarcinomas, almost all of which have arisen from metaplastic Barrett's epithelium. *(Chandrasoma and Taylor, pp 558–560)*

303. **(A)** Parkinsonism is a movement disorder characterized by tremor, muscular rigidity, and bradykinesia. Postmortem analyses have indicated a loss of dopaminergic neurons in the substantia nigra in idiopathic parkinsonism. Blockage of dopamine receptors by anti-psychotic agents and destruction of dopaminergic nigrostriatal neurons chemically also produces a parkinsonian syndrome. Treatment of idiopathic parkinsonism consists of either replacing or enhancing the inhibitory actions of dopamine or blocking the excitatory actions of acetylcholine on motor function. Exogenously administered dopamine is not effective in therapy because it does not cross the blood–brain barrier. The dopamine precursor levodopa does gain access and is converted to dopamine in the brain. Because much of the administered dose of levodopa is normally lost to peripheral decarboxylation to dopamine, the dopa decarboxylase inhibitor carbidopa is generally used in combination with levodopa. The use of the dopamine agonist bromocriptine is gaining popularity because there appears to be a lower incidence of dyskinesias and response fluctuations than is seen with levodopa. Amantadine, an antiviral agent used in prophylaxis of influenza $A_2$ virus, was discovered serendipitously to alleviate parkinsonian symptoms. Centrally acting antimuscarinic agents such as benztropine will reduce the tremor and rigidity of parkinsonism but are accompanied by antimuscarinic actions including drowsiness, blurred vision, tachycardia, urinary retention, and increase in intraocular pressure. *(Katzung, pp 419–426)*

304. **(B)** Identified cases are studied in this technique and compared to a control group with-

out the disease or syndrome. This technique is useful for very rare disorders, or for exploratory studies of possible risk factors. *(Kaplan and Sadock, pp 308– 326)*

305. **(A)** $CD_8$ lymphocytes are considered cytotoxic for virus infected cells, allograft, or tumor cells. Therefore, a person who lacks $CD_8$ T lymphocytes will show a deficiency in cytotoxicity for virus infected cells, tumor, or allograft cells. Another property of $CD_8$ T lymphocytes is the suppression of antibody by B cells and the reduction of delayed hypersensitivity reactions. Thus, a person who lacks $CD_8$ T lymphocytes cannot be expected to display functions of $CD_8$ T lymphocytes that he does not possess. *(Levinson and Jawetz, p 279)*

306. **(A)** The time interval 0 to 6 hours is called the eclipse period. During this period of viral growth cycle, the virus is absorbed to the host cell, enters the host cell, and the viral nucleic acid is separated from its capsid. These events lead to loss of viral infectivity. The bacterial growth curve is a bell-shaped curve composed of the lag phase in which the cell population is constant, the logarithmic phase of growth in which the number of cells increase in a geometric fashion (1–2–4–8–16, etc.), the stationary phase in which the cell population remains constant, and the phase of decline in which the cells die in an exponential fashion. The time period 6 to 8 hours represents a portion of the rise period, which marks the appearance of mature virus. The late period, according to the figure, begins at the 4th hour and ends at the 6th hour. During this time period viral nucleic acids and capsid proteins (proteins surrounding and protecting the nucleic acid) are synthesized and assembled into mature virus. *(Joklik et al, pp 790–795)*

307. **(C)** A common feature of the cytology of the fungi is their ability to exist in a yeastlike form as well as filaments, or hyphae, depending on the temperature (25°C or 38°C) or environment in which they are grown. This ability to exist in either the yeastlike or hyphae form is known as dimorphism. Crypto-

coccosis is meningitis caused by *Cryptococcus neoformans*, which, when cultured on Sabouraud's agar at either 25°C or 37°C, appears as a budding yeast with a large capsule. Sporotrichosis, candidiasis, histoplasmosis, and blastomycosis are all caused by dimorphic fungi. *(Jawetz et al, pp 309–326)*

308. **(B)** The transverse pericardial sinus lies between the reflections of the serous pericardium at the inflow and outflow ends of the heart. A finger placed in the transverse pericardial sinus lies anterior to the superior vena cava, posterior to the ascending aorta on the right and pulmonary trunk on the left, and superior to the pulmonary vein and left atrium. *(Hollinshead, p 521)*

309. **(E)** Honeycomb lung, or diffuse interstitial fibrosis, is a general term for pulmonary fibrosis, which is secondary to many environmental and occupational hazards. It is characterized by diffuse obliteration of the alveolar septa with fibrosis and thickening, bronchiolar dilatation, cyst formation, and squamous metaplasia. Alveolar capillary block leads to dyspnea, tachycardia, cyanosis, and right heart failure. The causes are numerous, including environmental factors, such as silica, *T. polyspora* (farmer's lung), talc, synthetic fibers, beryllium, asbestos, coal dust (anthracosis), nitrogen dioxide (silo-filler's disease), and flax (byssinosis); conective tissue diseases, such as rheumatoid arthritis, systemic lupus erythematosus, scleroderma, and sarcoidosis; drugs, such as busulfan and bleomycin; oxygen; and idiopathic etiologies. *(Chandrasoma and Taylor, pp 529–532)*

310. **(A)** Use of the non-selective β-blocker propranolol is contraindicated in asthma because of its ability to promote asthmatic attacks by inhibiting the bronchodilating actions of epinephrine. β-Agonists including epinephrine, ephedrine, and isoproterenol are used in acute asthma as bronchodilators. Use of $β_2$-selective agents such as albuterol is preferred since there is less risk of adverse cardiac effects. The β-agonists are administered by the use of inhalers or by injec-

tion. The methylxanthine drugs including the theophylline–ethylenediamine complex aminophylline are given orally and are useful in prophylaxis of asthma. The mechanism of action is not clear but may involve inhibition of cAMP phosphodiesterase or inhibition of adenosine receptors. Ipratropium bromide, an antimuscarinic agent given by metered inhalation, produces bronchodilation and decreased secretions by antagonizing the effects of acetylcholine release from the vagus nerves. The actions of ipratropium are limited to the airways because of poor absorption into the systemic circulation. Cromolyn sodium, a powder administered by inhalation, is useful in prophylactic treatment of asthma because it inhibits antigen-induced release of histamine and leukotrienes from sensitized mast cells. *(Katzung, pp 305–316)*

**311.** **(D)** As unsafe sex and intravenous injection with a contaminated needle are the major causes of dissemination of HIV, affected individuals should always prevent blood and semen from entering another person's body. Dry, social kissing, however, is considered to be safe. HIV may cause an encephalopathy with prominent subcortical dementia. *(Kaplan, Sadock, and Grebb, pp 374–382)*

## REFERENCES

### Anatomy

Alberts B, Bray D, Lewis J, et al. *Molecular Biology of the Cell.* 3rd ed. New York: Garland; 1994

Brodal P. *The Central Nervous System, Structure and Function.* New York: Oxford University Press; 1992

Burt AM. *Textbook of Neuroanatomy.* Philadelphia: W.B. Saunders Co.; 1993

Hall–Craggs ECB. *Anatomy as a Basis for Clinical Medicine.* 3rd ed. Baltimore: Williams & Wilkins; 1995

Hollinshead W. *Textbook of Anatomy.* 4th ed. Philadelphia: Harper & Row; 1985

Junqueira LC, Carneiro J, Kelly RO. *Basic Histology.* 8th ed. Norwalk, CT: Appleton & Lange; 1995

Kandel ER, Schwartz JH, Jessell TM. *Principles of Neural Science.* 3rd ed. Norwalk, CT: Appleton & Lange; 1991

Moore KL. *Clinically Oriented Anatomy.* 3rd ed. Baltimore: Williams & Wilkins; 1992

Noback CR, Strominger NL, Demarest RJ. *The Human Nervous System.* 4th ed. Philadelphia: Lea & Febiger; 1991

Sadler TW. *Langman's Medical Embryology.* 7th ed. Baltimore: Williams & Wilkins; 1995

### Pathology

Chandrasoma P, Taylor CR. *Concise Pathology.* 2nd ed. Norwalk: Appleton & Lange; 1995

Cotran RS, Kumar V, Robbins SL. *Robbins Pathologic Basis of Disease.* 5th ed. Philadelphia: W.B. Saunders Co.; 1994

Rubin E, Farber JL, eds. *Pathology.* 2nd ed. Philadelphia: JB Lippincott Co.; 1994

### Physiology

Berne RM, Levy MN, eds. *Physiology.* 3rd ed. St. Louis: Mosby Year Book; 1993

Ganong WF. *Review of Medical Physiology.* 17th ed. Los Altos, CA: Appleton & Lange; 1995

Guyton AC, Hall JE. *Textbook of Medical Physiology.* 9th ed. Philadelphia: W.B. Saunders Co.; 1995

*Harrison's Principles of Internal Medicine.* 13th ed. New York: McGraw-Hill Inc.; 1994

Johnson LR. *Gastrointestinal Physiology.* 3rd ed. St. Louis: CV Mosby Co.; 1985

Mountcastle VB. *Medical Physiology.* 14th ed. St. Louis: CV Mosby Co.; 1980

Petersen OH, Maruyama Y. *Nature 307,* Feb. 1984

Rose DB. *Clinical Physiology of Acid-base and Electrolyte Disorders.* 4th ed. New York: McGraw-Hill Inc.; 1994

Vander AJ. *Renal Physiology.* 5th ed. New York: McGraw-Hill Inc.; 1995

West JB, ed. *Best and Taylor's Physiological Basis of Medical Practice.* 12th ed. Baltimore: Williams & Wilkins; 1991

### Biochemistry

Devlin TM. *Textbook of Biochemistry With Clinical Correlations.* 3rd ed. New York; Wiley–Liss; 1992

Murray RK, et al. *Harpers Biochemistry*. 23rd ed. Stamford, CT: Appleton & Lange; 1993

Mathews CK, van Holde KE. *Biochemistry*. 1st ed. Redwood City, CA: Benjamin/Cummings Publishing Co.; 1990

Stryer L. *Biochemistry*. 4th ed. New York: W.H. Freeman and Co.; 1990

## Microbiology

Joklik WK, Willett HP, Amos DB, Wilfert CM. *Zinsser Microbiology*. 20th ed. Norwalk, CT: Appleton & Lange; 1992

Jawetz E, Melnick JL, Adelberg EA, et al, *Review of Medical Microbiology*. 19th ed. Norwalk, CT: Appleton & Lange; 1991

Levinson WE, Jawetz E. *Medical Microbiology and Immunology*. 2nd ed. Norwalk, CT: Appleton & Lange; 1992

Ryan KJ. *Sherris Microbiology*. 3rd ed. Norwalk, CT: Appleton & Lange; 1994.

## Behavioral Sciences

Kaplan HI, Sadock BJ, eds. *Comprehensive Textbook of Psychiatry*. 5th ed. Baltimore: Williams & Wilkins Co.; 1989

Kaplan HI, Sadock BJ, Grebb JA. *Kaplan and Sadock's Synopsis of Psychiatry*. 7th ed. Baltimore: Williams & Wilkins; 1994

Leigh H, Reiser MF. *The Patient. Biological, Psychological, and Social Dimensions of Medical Practice*. 3rd ed. New York: Plenum Publishing Corp.; 1992

Lennenberg EH. *Biological Foundations of Language*. New York: John Wiley & Sons, Inc.; 1967

MacMahon B, Pugh T. *Epidemiology, Principles and Methods*. Boston: Little, Brown & Co.; 1970

Simons RC, ed. *Understanding Human Behavior in Health and Illness*. 3rd ed. Baltimore: Williams & Wilkins Co.; 1985

## Pharmacology

Craig CR, Stitzel RE, eds. *Modern Pharmacology*. 4th ed. Boston: Little, Brown and Co.; 1990

Gilman AG, Goodman RW, Nies AS, Taylor P, eds. *The Pharmacological Basis of Therapeutics*. 8th ed. New York: Pergamon; 1990

Katzung BG, ed. *Basic & Clinical Pharmacology*. 6th ed. Norwalk, CT.: Appleton & Lange; 1992

Reiners C. Prophylaxis of radiation-induced thyroid cancers in children after the reactor catastrophe of Chernobyl. *Nuklearmedizin* 33:229–234; 1994 (in German)

Smith CM, Reynard AM, eds. *Essentials of Pharmacology*. Philadelphia: W.B. Saunders Co.; 1995

# Subspecialty List—Practice Test

## ANATOMY

1. Nervous system
4. Nervous system
7. Nervous system
11. Cardiovascular system
15. Musculoskeletal system
20. Musculoskeletal system
25. Musculoskeletal system
32. Musculoskeletal system
39. Digestive system
46. Musculoskeletal system
53. Nervous system
60. Nervous system
67. Nervous system
74. Nervous system
81. Nervous system
88. Nervous system
95. Hematopoietic and lymphoreticular system
102. Musculoskeletal system
109. Cardiovascular system
116. Cardiovascular system
123. Cardiovascular system
130. Nervous system
137. Reproductive system
195. General principles: Biology of cells
196. General principles: Biology of cells
197. General principles: Biology of cells
207. Musculoskeletal system
208. Musculoskeletal system

209. Endocrine system
210. Musculoskeletal system
211. Respiratory system
212. Musculoskeletal system
213. Musculoskeletal system
214. Musculoskeletal system
215. Hematopoietic and lymphoreticular system
216. Digestive system
245. Reproductive system
251. Musculoskeletal system
257. Musculoskeletal system
260. Reproductive system
261. Nervous system
263. Nervous system
270. Nervous system
272. Nervous system
273. Nervous system
277. Hematopoietic and lymphoreticular system
284. Nervous system
291. Nervous system
298. Nervous system
308. Cardiovascular system

## PHYSIOLOGY

10. Gastrointestinal
12. Circulation
16. Circulation
21. Cardiac
26. Respiratory
33. Renal

40. Cell physiology
47. Acid/Base
54. Circulation
61. Endocrinology
68. Circulation
75. Gastrointestinal
82. Endocrinology
89. Endocrinology
96. Cardiac
103. Nervous system
110. Respiratory
117. Cardiac
124. Blood
131. Exercise physiology
138. Renal
144. Cell physiology
145. Cell physiology
146. Cell physiology
147. Cell physiology
166. Cardiac
167. Cardiac
168. Cardiac
198. Cardiac
199. Cardiac
224. Thermoregulation
225. Thermoregulation
226. Thermoregulation
246. Circulation
252. Endocrinology
258. Gastrointestinal
264. Circulation
271. Circulation
278. Endocrinology
285. Endocrinology

292. Nervous system
299. Muscle
300. Sensory system

## BIOCHEMISTRY

2. Lipids
5. Vitamins
8. Thermodynamics
13. Protein structure/Function
17. Carbohydrate metabolism
22. Carbohydrate metabolism
27. Amino acids
34. Carbohydrate metabolism
41. Blood
48. Carbohydrate metabolism
55. Carbohydrate metabolism
62. Blood
69. Blood
76. Carbohydrate metabolism
83. Carbohydrate metabolism
90. Carbohydrate metabolism
97. Carbohydrate metabolism and disease
104. Enzyme kinetics
111. Amino acids and disease
118. Molecular biology
125. Complex carbohydrates and disease
132. Enzyme kinetics
139. Complex carbohydrates and disease
148. Vitamins and disease
149. Vitamins and disease
150. Vitamins and disease
169. Molecular biology
170. Molecular biology
171. Molecular biology
172. Molecular biology
173. Molecular biology
174. Molecular biology
200. Carbohydrate metabolism
201. Carbohydrate metabolism
202. Carbohydrate metabolism
235. Enzymes
237. Carbohydrate metabolism
241. Ketogenesis
247. Amino acids
253. Carbohydrate metabolism
259. Protein

265. Proteins and disease
279. Molecular biology
286. Lipids
293. Carbohydrate metabolism

## MICROBIOLOGY

28. Virology
35. Immunology
42. Virology
49. Antibacterial agents
56. Antibody structure
63. Pathogenic bacteriology
70. Virology
77. Immune deficiency disease
84. Disinfection, sterilization
91. Virology
98. Virology
105. Immunology transplantation
112. Pathogenic bacteriology
119. Immunology
126. Pathogenic Bacteriology
133. Mycology
140. Pathogenic bacteriology
233. Virology
234. Immunology
236. Parasitology
238. Virology
242. Microbial genetics
248. Virology
254. Cellular immunology
266. Bacterial cytology
280. Disinfection, sterilization
281. Pathogenic bacteriology
287. Immunology
301. Cellular immunology
305. Cellular immunology
306. Viral growth
307. Mycology

## PATHOLOGY

3. Processes of neoplasia
6. Processes of neoplasia
9. Respiratory system
14. Cutaneous pathology
18. Alimentary system
23. Kidney and urinary system
29. Ocular pathology

36. Endocrine system
43. Endocrine system
50. Blood and lymphatic system
57. Kidney and urinary system
64. Genetic syndromes and metabolic diseases
71. Cardiovascular system
78. Inflammation
85. Non-genetic syndromes
92. Cutaneous pathology
99. Breast pathology
106. Processes of neoplasia
113. Blood and lymphatic system
120. Non-genetic syndromes
127. Cell growth, healing, and repair
134. Circulatory system
141. Inflammation
151. Processes of neoplasia
152. Processes of neoplasia
153. Processes of neoplasia
162. Immunologic diseases
163. Immunologic diseases
164. Immunologic diseases
165. Immunologic diseases
175. Genetic syndromes and metabolic diseases
176. Genetic syndromes and metabolic diseases
177. Genetic syndromes and metabolic diseases
178. Genetic syndromes and metabolic diseases
205. Orthopaedic pathology
206. Orthopaedic pathology
227. Processes of neoplasia
228. Processes of neoplasia
229. Infectious diseases
230. Nervous system
231. Nervous system
232. Genetic syndromes and metabolic diseases
239. Alimentary system
243. Processes of neoplasia
249. Genital system
255. Miscellaneous
267. Immunologic diseases
274. Cell growth, injury and repair
288. Kidney and urinary system
294. Blood and lymphatic system

295. Respiratory system
302. Alimentary system
309. Respiratory system

## PHARMACOLOGY

30. General principles
37. Endocrine system
44. General principles
51. Autonomic system: Adrenergics/Hypertension
58. Antibiotics
65. Autacoids
72. Endocrine system
79. Blood and blood-forming organs
86. Cardiovascular and respiratory systems
93. Cardiovascular and respiratory systems
100. CNS drugs: anti-epileptics
107. CNS drugs/Gas anesthetics
114. Autonomic system: Cholinergics
121. Blood and blood-forming organs: fibrinolytics
128. Autacoids/Toxicology
135. Central and peripheral nervous systems psychotherapeutic agents
142. Hormone-like drugs/Oral hypoglycemics
154. Cardiovascular and respiratory systems/Antihypertensive agents
155. Cardiovascular and respiratory systems/Antihypertensive agents
156. Cardiovascular and respiratory systems/Antihypertensive agents
157. Cardiovascular and respiratory systems/Antihypertensive agents
179. Autonomic nervous system
180. Autonomic nervous system
181. Autonomic nervous system
182. Autonomic nervous system
183. Autonomic nervous system
184. Autonomic nervous system
190. Kidneys, fluids, electrolytes
191. Kidneys, fluids, electrolytes
192. Kidneys, fluids, electrolytes
193. Kidneys, fluids, electrolytes
194. Kidneys, fluids, electrolytes
203. Cardiovascular antihypertensive agents
204. Cardiovascular antihypertensive agents
268. Central and peripheral nervous systems
275. Central and peripheral nervous systems
282. Kidneys, fluids, electrolytes
289. Antimicrobiol chemotherapy
296. Cardiovascular and respiratory systems/Antihypertensives
303. Central and peripheral nervous systems
310. Cardiovascular and respiratory systems

## BEHAVIORAL SCIENCES

19. Personality/Psychodynamics
24. Medical sociology
31. Learning theory, CNS
38. Brain/Behavior
45. CNS, psychopharmacologic agents
52. Emotions/Genetics/Social epidemiology
59. Personality/Psychodynamics
66. Personality/Psychodynamics
73. Suicide/Epidemiology
80. Pain/Neurophysiology
87. Psychopharmacology
94. Suicide/Epidemiology
101. Sleep and dreaming
108. Doctor–patient relationship
115. Medical sociology
122. Grief/Depression
129. Patient management/Individual dynamics
136. Human sexuality
143. Epidemiology
158. Life cycle
159. Life cycle, personality, and psychodynamics
160. Life cycle, personality, and psychodynamics
161. Life cycle, personality, and psychodynamics
185. Life cycle/Psychodynamics
186. Life cycle/Psychodynamics
187. Life cycle/Psychodynamics
188. Life cycle/Psychodynamics
189. Life cycle/Psychodynamics
217. Learning theory
218. Learning theory
219. Learning theory
220. Learning theory
221. Learning theory
222. Learning theory
223. Learning theory
240. Suicide/Sociology/Depression
244. CNS, mood disorder, psychopharmacological agents
250. Depression/Grief emotions
256. Depression/Emotions
262. Personality/Psychodynamics
269. Personality/Psychodynamics
276. Medical sociology
283. Medical sociology
290. Ethics, norms, values, and beliefs
297. Emotions/Anxiety disorder/Learning theory
304. Epidemiology
311. CNS, infectious disease, human sexuality

NAME _____
          Last                    First                          Middle

ADDRESS _____
          Street

_____
City                          State                    Zip

DIRECTIONS  Mark your social security number from top to bottom
in the appropriate boxes on the right.
Use No. 2 lead pencil only.
Mark one and only one answer for each item.
Make each mark black enough to obliterate the letter
within the parentheses.
Erase clearly any answer you wish to change.

1.  (A) (B) (C) (D) (E)    25. (A) (B) (C) (D) (E)    49. (A) (B) (C) (D) (E)    73. (A) (B) (C) (D) (E)

2.  (A) (B) (C) (D) (E)    26. (A) (B) (C) (D) (E)    50. (A) (B) (C) (D) (E)    74. (A) (B) (C) (D) (E)

3.  (A) (B) (C) (D) (E)    27. (A) (B) (C) (D) (E)    51. (A) (B) (C) (D) (E)    75. (A) (B) (C) (D) (E)

4.  (A) (B) (C) (D) (E)    28. (A) (B) (C) (D) (E)    52. (A) (B) (C) (D) (E)    76. (A) (B) (C) (D) (E)

5.  (A) (B) (C) (D) (E)    29. (A) (B) (C) (D) (E)    53. (A) (B) (C) (D) (E)    77. (A) (B) (C) (D) (E)

6.  (A) (B) (C) (D) (E)    30. (A) (B) (C) (D) (E)    54. (A) (B) (C) (D) (E)    78. (A) (B) (C) (D) (E)

7.  (A) (B) (C) (D) (E)    31. (A) (B) (C) (D) (E)    55. (A) (B) (C) (D) (E)    79. (A) (B) (C) (D) (E)

8.  (A) (B) (C) (D) (E)    32. (A) (B) (C) (D) (E)    56. (A) (B) (C) (D) (E)    80. (A) (B) (C) (D) (E)

9.  (A) (B) (C) (D) (E)    33. (A) (B) (C) (D) (E)    57. (A) (B) (C) (D) (E)    81. (A) (B) (C) (D) (E)

10. (A) (B) (C) (D) (E)    34. (A) (B) (C) (D) (E)    58. (A) (B) (C) (D) (E)    82. (A) (B) (C) (D) (E)

11. (A) (B) (C) (D) (E)    35. (A) (B) (C) (D) (E)    59. (A) (B) (C) (D) (E)    83. (A) (B) (C) (D) (E)

12. (A) (B) (C) (D) (E)    36. (A) (B) (C) (D) (E)    60. (A) (B) (C) (D) (E)    84. (A) (B) (C) (D) (E)

13. (A) (B) (C) (D) (E)    37. (A) (B) (C) (D) (E)    61. (A) (B) (C) (D) (E)    85. (A) (B) (C) (D) (E)

14. (A) (B) (C) (D) (E)    38. (A) (B) (C) (D) (E)    62. (A) (B) (C) (D) (E)    86. (A) (B) (C) (D) (E)

15. (A) (B) (C) (D) (E)    39. (A) (B) (C) (D) (E)    63. (A) (B) (C) (D) (E)    87. (A) (B) (C) (D) (E)

16. (A) (B) (C) (D) (E)    40. (A) (B) (C) (D) (E)    64. (A) (B) (C) (D) (E)    88. (A) (B) (C) (D) (E)

17. (A) (B) (C) (D) (E)    41. (A) (B) (C) (D) (E)    65. (A) (B) (C) (D) (E)    89. (A) (B) (C) (D) (E)

18. (A) (B) (C) (D) (E)    42. (A) (B) (C) (D) (E)    66. (A) (B) (C) (D) (E)    90. (A) (B) (C) (D) (E)

19. (A) (B) (C) (D) (E)    43. (A) (B) (C) (D) (E)    67. (A) (B) (C) (D) (E)    91. (A) (B) (C) (D) (E)

20. (A) (B) (C) (D) (E)    44. (A) (B) (C) (D) (E)    68. (A) (B) (C) (D) (E)    92. (A) (B) (C) (D) (E)

21. (A) (B) (C) (D) (E)    45. (A) (B) (C) (D) (E)    69. (A) (B) (C) (D) (E)    93. (A) (B) (C) (D) (E)

22. (A) (B) (C) (D) (E)    46. (A) (B) (C) (D) (E)    70. (A) (B) (C) (D) (E)    94. (A) (B) (C) (D) (E)

23. (A) (B) (C) (D) (E)    47. (A) (B) (C) (D) (E)    71. (A) (B) (C) (D) (E)    95. (A) (B) (C) (D) (E)

24. (A) (B) (C) (D) (E)    48. (A) (B) (C) (D) (E)    72. (A) (B) (C) (D) (E)    96. (A) (B) (C) (D) (E)

| | | | | | | | | | | | | | | | | | | | | | | |
|---|---|---|---|---|---|---|---|---|---|---|---|---|---|---|---|---|---|---|---|---|---|---|---|
| **97.** | (A) | (B) | (C) | (D) | (E) | **128.** | (A) | (B) | (C) | (D) | (E) | **159.** | (A) | (B) | (C) | (D) | (E) | **190.** | (A) | (B) | (C) | (D) | (E) |
| **98.** | (A) | (B) | (C) | (D) | (E) | **129.** | (A) | (B) | (C) | (D) | (E) | **160.** | (A) | (B) | (C) | (D) | (E) | **191.** | (A) | (B) | (C) | (D) | (E) |
| **99.** | (A) | (B) | (C) | (D) | (E) | **130.** | (A) | (B) | (C) | (D) | (E) | **161.** | (A) | (B) | (C) | (D) | (E) | **192.** | (A) | (B) | (C) | (D) | (E) |
| **100.** | (A) | (B) | (C) | (D) | (E) | **131.** | (A) | (B) | (C) | (D) | (E) | **162.** | (A) | (B) | (C) | (D) | (E) | **193.** | (A) | (B) | (C) | (D) | (E) |
| **101.** | (A) | (B) | (C) | (D) | (E) | **132.** | (A) | (B) | (C) | (D) | (E) | **163.** | (A) | (B) | (C) | (D) | (E) | **194.** | (A) | (B) | (C) | (D) | (E) |
| **102.** | (A) | (B) | (C) | (D) | (E) | **133.** | (A) | (B) | (C) | (D) | (E) | **164.** | (A) | (B) | (C) | (D) | (E) | **195.** | (A) | (B) | (C) | (D) | (E) |
| **103.** | (A) | (B) | (C) | (D) | (E) | **134.** | (A) | (B) | (C) | (D) | (E) | **165.** | (A) | (B) | (C) | (D) | (E) | **196.** | (A) | (B) | (C) | (D) | (E) |
| **104.** | (A) | (B) | (C) | (D) | | **135.** | (A) | (B) | (C) | (D) | (E) | **166.** | (A) | (B) | (C) | (D) | (E) | **197.** | (A) | (B) | (C) | (D) | (E) |
| **105.** | (A) | (B) | (C) | (D) | (E) | **136.** | (A) | (B) | (C) | (D) | | **167.** | (A) | (B) | (C) | (D) | (E) | **198.** | (A) | (B) | (C) | (D) | (E) |
| **106.** | (A) | (B) | (C) | (D) | (E) | **137.** | (A) | (B) | (C) | (D) | (E) | **168.** | (A) | (B) | (C) | (D) | (E) | **199.** | (A) | (B) | (C) | (D) | (E) |
| **107.** | (A) | (B) | (C) | (D) | (E) | **138.** | (A) | (B) | (C) | (D) | (E) | **169.** | (A) | (B) | (C) | (D) | (E) | **200.** | (A) | (B) | (C) | (D) | (E) |
| **108.** | (A) | (B) | (C) | (D) | (E) | **139.** | (A) | (B) | (C) | (D) | (E) | **170.** | (A) | (B) | (C) | (D) | (E) | **201.** | (A) | (B) | (C) | (D) | (E) |
| **109.** | (A) | (B) | (C) | (D) | (E) | **140.** | (A) | (B) | (C) | (D) | (E) | **171.** | (A) | (B) | (C) | (D) | (E) | **202.** | (A) | (B) | (C) | (D) | (E) |
| **110.** | (A) | (B) | (C) | (D) | (E) | **141.** | (A) | (B) | (C) | (D) | (E) | **172.** | (A) | (B) | (C) | (D) | (E) | **203.** | (A) | (B) | (C) | (D) | (E) |
| **111.** | (A) | (B) | (C) | (D) | (E) | **142.** | (A) | (B) | (C) | (D) | | **173.** | (A) | (B) | (C) | (D) | (E) | **204.** | (A) | (B) | (C) | (D) | (E) |
| **112.** | (A) | (B) | (C) | (D) | (E) | **143.** | (A) | (B) | (C) | (D) | (E) | **174.** | (A) | (B) | (C) | (D) | (E) | **205.** | (A) | (B) | (C) | (D) | (E) |
| **113.** | (A) | (B) | (C) | (D) | (E) | **144.** | (A) | (B) | (C) | (D) | (E) | **175.** | (A) | (B) | (C) | (D) | (E) | **206.** | (A) | (B) | (C) | (D) | (E) |
| **114.** | (A) | (B) | (C) | (D) | (E) | **145.** | (A) | (B) | (C) | (D) | (E) | **176.** | (A) | (B) | (C) | (D) | (E) | **207.** | (A) | (B) | (C) | (D) | (E) |
| **115.** | (A) | (B) | (C) | (D) | (E) | **146.** | (A) | (B) | (C) | (D) | (E) | **177.** | (A) | (B) | (C) | (D) | (E) | **208.** | (A) | (B) | (C) | (D) | (E) |
| **116.** | (A) | (B) | (C) | (D) | (E) | **147.** | (A) | (B) | (C) | (D) | (E) | **178.** | (A) | (B) | (C) | (D) | (E) | **209.** | (A) | (B) | (C) | (D) | (E) |
| **117.** | (A) | (B) | (C) | (D) | (E) | **148.** | (A) | (B) | (C) | (D) | (E) | **179.** | (A) | (B) | (C) | (D) | (E) | **210.** | (A) | (B) | (C) | (D) | (E) |
| **118.** | (A) | (B) | (C) | (D) | (E) | **149.** | (A) | (B) | (C) | (D) | (E) | **180.** | (A) | (B) | (C) | (D) | (E) | **211.** | (A) | (B) | (C) | (D) | (E) |
| **119.** | (A) | (B) | (C) | (D) | (E) | **150.** | (A) | (B) | (C) | (D) | (E) | **181.** | (A) | (B) | (C) | (D) | (E) | **212.** | (A) | (B) | (C) | (D) | (E) |
| **120.** | (A) | (B) | (C) | (D) | (E) | **151.** | (A) | (B) | (C) | (D) | (E) | **182.** | (A) | (B) | (C) | (D) | (E) | **213.** | (A) | (B) | (C) | (D) | (E) |
| **121.** | (A) | (B) | (C) | (D) | (E) | **152.** | (A) | (B) | (C) | (D) | (E) | **183.** | (A) | (B) | (C) | (D) | (E) | **214.** | (A) | (B) | (C) | (D) | (E) |
| **122.** | (A) | (B) | (C) | (D) | (E) | **153.** | (A) | (B) | (C) | (D) | (E) | **184.** | (A) | (B) | (C) | (D) | (E) | **215.** | (A) | (B) | (C) | (D) | (E) |
| **123.** | (A) | (B) | (C) | (D) | (E) | **154.** | (A) | (B) | (C) | (D) | (E) | **185.** | (A) | (B) | (C) | (D) | | **216.** | (A) | (B) | (C) | (D) | (E) |
| **124.** | (A) | (B) | (C) | (D) | (E) | **155.** | (A) | (B) | (C) | (D) | (E) | **186.** | (A) | (B) | (C) | (D) | (E) | **217.** | (A) | (B) | (C) | (D) | |
| **125.** | (A) | (B) | (C) | (D) | (E) | **156.** | (A) | (B) | (C) | (D) | (E) | **187.** | (A) | (B) | (C) | (D) | (E) | **218.** | (A) | (B) | (C) | (D) | (E) |
| **126.** | (A) | (B) | (C) | (D) | (E) | **157.** | (A) | (B) | (C) | (D) | (E) | **188.** | (A) | (B) | (C) | (D) | (E) | **219.** | (A) | (B) | (C) | (D) | (E) |
| **127.** | (A) | (B) | (C) | (D) | (E) | **158.** | (A) | (B) | (C) | (D) | (E) | **189.** | (A) | (B) | (C) | (D) | (E) | **220.** | (A) | (B) | (C) | (D) | (E) |

| | | | |
|---|---|---|---|
| 221. (A) (B) (C) (D) (E) | 244. (A) (B) (C) (D) (E) | 267. (A) (B) (C) (D) (E) | 290. (A) (B) (C) (D) (E) |
| 222. (A) (B) (C) (D) (E) | 245. (A) (B) (C) (D) (E) | 268. (A) (B) (C) (D) (E) | 291. (A) (B) (C) (D) (E) |
| 223. (A) (B) (C) (D) | 246. (A) (B) (C) (D) (E) | 269. (A) (B) (C) (D) (E) | 292. (A) (B) (C) (D) (E) |
| 224. (A) (B) (C) (D) (E) | 247. (A) (B) (C) (D) (E) | 270. (A) (B) (C) (D) (E) | 293. (A) (B) (C) (D) (E) |
| 225. (A) (B) (C) (D) (E) | 248. (A) (B) (C) (D) (E) | 271. (A) (B) (C) (D) (E) | 294. (A) (B) (C) (D) (E) |
| 226. (A) (B) (C) (D) (E) | 249. (A) (B) (C) (D) (E) | 272. (A) (B) (C) (D) (E) | 295. (A) (B) (C) (D) (E) |
| 227. (A) (B) (C) (D) (E) | 250. (A) (B) (C) (D) (E) | 273. (A) (B) (C) (D) (E) | 296. (A) (B) (C) (D) (E) |
| 228. (A) (B) (C) (D) (E) | 251. (A) (B) (C) (D) (E) | 274. (A) (B) (C) (D) (E) | 297. (A) (B) (C) (D) (E) |
| 229. (A) (B) (C) (D) (E) | 252. (A) (B) (C) (D) (E) | 275. (A) (B) (C) (D) (E) | 298. (A) (B) (C) (D) (E) |
| 230. (A) (B) (C) (D) (E) | 253. (A) (B) (C) (D) (E) | 276. (A) (B) (C) (D) (E) | 299. (A) (B) (C) (D) (E) |
| 231. (A) (B) (C) (D) (E) | 254. (A) (B) (C) (D) (E) | 277. (A) (B) (C) (D) (E) | 300. (A) (B) (C) (D) (E) |
| 232. (A) (B) (C) (D) (E) | 255. (A) (B) (C) (D) (E) | 278. (A) (B) (C) (D) (E) | 301. (A) (B) (C) (D) (E) |
| 233. (A) (B) (C) (D) (E) | 256. (A) (B) (C) (D) (E) | 279. (A) (B) (C) (D) (E) | 302. (A) (B) (C) (D) (E) |
| 234. (A) (B) (C) (D) (E) | 257. (A) (B) (C) (D) (E) | 280. (A) (B) (C) (D) (E) | 303. (A) (B) (C) (D) (E) |
| 235. (A) (B) (C) (D) (E) | 258. (A) (B) (C) (D) (E) | 281. (A) (B) (C) (D) (E) | 304. (A) (B) (C) (D) (E) |
| 236. (A) (B) (C) (D) (E) | 259. (A) (B) (C) (D) (E) | 282. (A) (B) (C) (D) (E) | 305. (A) (B) (C) (D) (E) |
| 237. (A) (B) (C) (D) (E) | 260. (A) (B) (C) (D) (E) | 283. (A) (B) (C) (D) (E) | 306. (A) (B) (C) (D) (E) |
| 238. (A) (B) (C) (D) (E) | 261. (A) (B) (C) (D) (E) | 284. (A) (B) (C) (D) (E) | 307. (A) (B) (C) (D) (E) |
| 239. (A) (B) (C) (D) (E) | 262. (A) (B) (C) (D) (E) | 285. (A) (B) (C) (D) | 308. (A) (B) (C) (D) (E) |
| 240. (A) (B) (C) (D) (E) | 263. (A) (B) (C) (D) (E) | 286. (A) (B) (C) (D) (E) | 309. (A) (B) (C) (D) (E) |
| 241. (A) (B) (C) (D) (E) | 264. (A) (B) (C) (D) (E) | 287. (A) (B) (C) (D) (E) | 310. (A) (B) (C) (D) (E) |
| 242. (A) (B) (C) (D) (E) | 265. (A) (B) (C) (D) (E) | 288. (A) (B) (C) (D) (E) | 311 (A) (B) (C) (D) (E) |
| 243. (A) (B) (C) (D) (E) | 266. (A) (B) (C) (D) (E) | 289. (A) (B) (C) (D) (E) | |

# APPLETON & LANGE REVIEW BOOKS

## COMPREHENSIVE

Go, *First Aid for the USMLE Step 2*, 150 pp., paperback, A2591-4
Goldberg, *The Instant Exam Review for the USMLE Step 2, 2/e*, 250 pp., paperback, A4328-0
Catlin, *A&L Review for the USMLE Step 2, 2/e*, 287 pp., paperback, A0266-5
Jacobs, *MEPC USMLE Step 2 Review*, 300 pp., paperback, A6270-1
Goldberg, *The Instant Exam Review for the USMLE Step 3*, 250 pp., paperback, A4334-7
Schultz, *A&L Review for the USMLE Step 3*, 252 pp., paperback, A0227-7
Chan, *MEPC Review for the USMLE Step 3*, 259 pp., paperback, A6271-9

## INTERNAL MEDICINE

Goldlist, *A&L Review of Internal Medicine*, 275 pp., paperback, A0251-7

## OBSTETRICS & GYNECOLOGY

Julian, *A&L Review of Obstetrics and Gynecology, 5/e*, 416 pp., paperback, A0231-9

## PEDIATRICS

Hansbarger, *MEPC: Pediatrics, 9/e*, 248 pp., paperback, A6223-0
Lorin, *A&L Review of Pediatrics, 5/e*, 222 pp., paperback, A0057-8

## PUBLIC HEALTH

Hart, *MEPC: Preventive Medicine and Public Health*, 350 pp., paperback, A6319-6
Penalver, *Public Health and Preventive Medicine Review, 2/e*, 120 pp., paperback, E5936-9

## SURGERY

Metzler, *MEPC: Surgery, 11/e*, 317 pp., paperback, A6195-0
Wapnick, *A&L Review of Surgery, 2/e*, 156 pp., paperback, A0220-2

## MATCH

Le, *First Aid for the Match*, 200 pp., paperback, A2596-3

## WARDS

Le, *First Aid for the Wards*, 1200 pp., paperback, A2595-5

## SPECIALTY BOARD REVIEWS

DeKornfeld, *MEPC Specialty Board Review: Anesthesiology, 9/e*, 358 pp., paperback, A0256-6
Dershwitz, *The MGH Board Review of Anesthesiology, 4/e*, 302 pp., paperback, A8611-4
Kulick, *MEPC: Hand Surgery, 4/e*, 340 pp., paperback, A3558-2
Rob, *Specialty Board Review: General Surgery, 4/e*, 203 pp., paperback, A8638-7
Yen, *Specialty Board Review: Family Practice, 5/e*, 227 pp., paperback, A8618-9
Giesser, *MEPC Specialty Board Review: Neurology, 4/e*, 250 pp., paperback, A8650-2
Willett, *MEPC Specialty Board Review: Otolaryngology, Head & Neck Surgery*, 320 pp, paperback, A7580-2